NATURE'S BEST HOMES

HOW ANIMALS' HABITATS HELP THEM LIVE,
BREED AND RAISE YOUNG

{CONTENTS}

EVOLUTION

Evolution is the process by which living things can change gradually. Over millions of years, many tiny changes add up to some big differences. Evolution is why there are so many different species living on Earth. Some species are more closely related than others. In 1859, Charles Darwin said that related species had evolved from the same ancestor in the past. He explained how evolution could do that by a process called natural selection.

Making a home takes a lot of hard work, as this busy weaverbird shows.

Animals in a species may look the same, but they all have a unique set of variations. These differences make some animals 'fitter' than others. The fitter ones are better at surviving in wild conditions than others. Darwin said that nature 'selects' these fit animals; they have many children, while the unfit ones die off. Over time, the characteristics that make an animal fit become more common, and eventually every member of the species has them – the species has evolved a tiny bit.

It is not just the way animals look that can evolve. Natural selection also changes the way they behave. The creatures in this book have evolved many unique ways of building homes. Some build complicated dens and nests, while others carry their homes around with them. Each animal uses its home in different ways. As well as providing a place to rest and stay warm, a home is also a hideout from predators, a place from which to launch ambushes or a cosy nursery for young. Let's take a look at some of Nature's Best Homes!

CLOWNFISH

The clownfish sets up home in a sea anemone, a relative of the jellyfish with hundreds of stinging tentacles that fire poisoned darts into any animal that touches it. The clownfish has a thick layer of slime on its skin that protects it from the stings. The clownfish does not stray far, and if danger appears, it dashes back to the safety of the anemone. In return for protection, the clownfish cleans the anemone's tentacles.

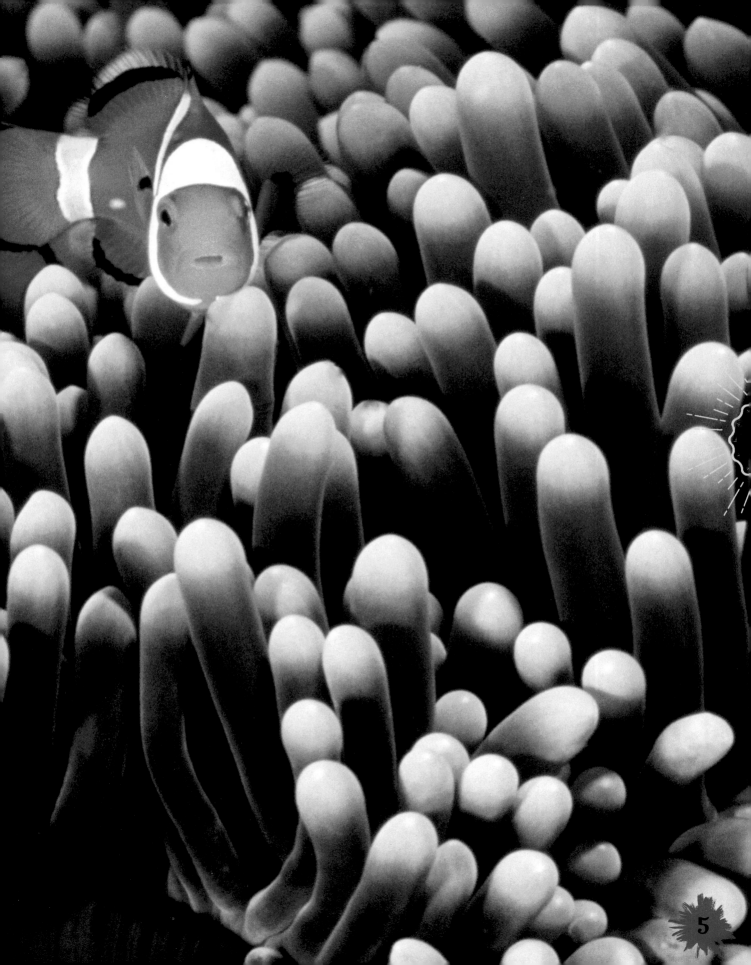

GOLDEN EAGLE

An eyrie is a messy tangle of twigs and grass. There are often scraps of fur and bones scattered around, too.

A golden eagle's home is called an 'eyrie'. This is a huge ramshackle nest of twigs built on a cliff ledge. The nest can be bigger than a bath tub and some are more than 100 years old.

Golden eagles are some of the largest birds of prey. They live in mountainous areas and hunt by swooping down from the sky to snatch prey from the ground. They will attack anything from a rabbit to a lamb, taking it back to their eyrie to eat.

Often nests are halfway up a cliff. This means the eagle can fly down with heavy food, which is easier than lifting it to reach a nest on a cliff top.

EVOLUTION SOLUTION

Golden eagles hunt animals that live on the ground, swooping down from above to grab prey. That means they are most successful in mountainous areas where they can scan the ground from high perches. As a result, natural selection favoured the birds that built their nests there, too. Any eagles that made nests low down would have spent a lot of time flying up and down, putting them at a disadvantage.

FACTS AND FIGURES

Scientific name........ Aquila chrysaetos

Location................. Northern hemisphere

Habitat................................. Mountains

Size.............................. 2m wingspan

Food.. Rodents, rabbits, birds and lambs

Lifespan...................................30 years

Young.............. Eggs laid in remote eyrie

A golden eagle's nest is on a cliff ledge where foxes and other predators cannot reach it. Each generation of eagles use the same ledges and nests as their ancestors, adding new material. As a result, some nests are very old and very large. The biggest are about 1.5m wide and may be 1m deep.

PARROTFISH

These large fish are colourful like a parrot, but they get their name from the beak-like teeth at the front of their mouth. By day, parrotfish scrape food from the rocks in coral reefs. At night they go to sleep inside a bag of snot!

Parrotfish are mostly plant eaters. They scrape away at the tiny algae that grow on the rocks, but they eat whatever else is there as well. Most fish feed during the day; when it gets dark they find shelter under a rock and go to sleep. Not every fish around the reef goes to sleep, though. Sharks patrol, sniffing out sleeping fish. To stay safe, the parrotfish's skin produces a large amount of mucus. This forms a bag around the fish, sealing in the fish's smell. The parrotfish can go to sleep safely without a shark tracking it down.

EVOLUTION SOLUTION

All fish produce mucus on their skin. This is to stop water from inside their bodies leaking out into the salty seawater, and it also makes it harder for worms and other parasites to hang on to the fish's skin. Parrotfish skin makes mucus for all these reasons but the fish has evolved another use for it – to form a smell-proof sleeping bag!

Parrotfish swallow many small chunks of rock as they feed. This does them no harm – the fish just crunch up the rock and poo it out as grains of sand.

FACTS AND FIGURES

Scientific name............ Scaridae family
Location............Indian and Pacific oceans
Habitat.................................Coral reef
Size........................... 30-130cm
Food.................................Algae
Lifespan...........................7 years
Young................Eggs float in the water

The slime bag acts like an early warning system. It wobbles if anything touches it, and that wakes up the fish inside.

WASP

For many of us a wasp is just an annoying – and a bit of a scary – stinging insect that buzzes around on summer days. However, these black and yellow minibeasts are among the animal world's best homemakers. They construct elaborate nests out of paper!

Like ants and bees, common wasps live in a colony, ruled over by a queen. A wasp colony needs a big nest and this is usually hung from a tree branch. The queen starts the nest off, building small rooms, or cells, for her young to develop inside. After about a month of hard work, the queen has enough daughters – nearly all wasps are female – to take over the work. The nest hangs from a stalk that is stuck to the branch. The stalk needs to be strengthened as the worker wasps add more cells.

A wasp's nest is made of galleries of six-sided cells.

TEMPORARY STRUCTURE
A big nest may house 1,000 wasps by the end of the summer! However, it is only built to last for one year.

FACTS AND FIGURES
Scientific name.......................... Vespula
Location..................................... Worldwide
Habitat.................. Forests, woodlands, parks and gardens
Size... 12–17mm
Food... Insects
Lifespan.......................less than 1 year
Young................. Queen lays hundreds of eggs in nest

The cells are arranged in clusters, called galleries. Eventually, the whole nest will be covered in an outer wall, with an entrance at the bottom.

The entire structure is made from paper. The wasps make this paper in the same way that humans do. They scrape fibres of wood from the surrounding trees and chew them into a pulp. The wasps then shape the wet pulp into the walls and other elements of their nests. The pulp dries out to become papery and solid. On its own, this material is very brittle, but when connected as cells and galleries it forms a surprisingly strong structure.

Worker wasps are hunters, but don't eat their insect prey. They feed it to the young back in the nest and then drink the babies' liquid poo!

EVOLUTION SOLUTION

Worker wasps have evolved to never have their own young. Instead, they spend their lives helping their mother, the queen, raise hundreds of worker sisters. This system evolved because it guarantees that the queen can produce many new queens. In autumn, dozens of young queens will leave the colony and will each try to start a new colony the following year. The job of this year's colony complete, the workers then gradually die.

A worker wasp will scrape fibres from any wooden structure – such as this fence post.

CADDISFLY

An adult caddisfly looks like a tiny moth. They flutter around streams and ponds, and only live for a short amount of time. Their young, or larvae, live underwater, and build complex homes from silk and any objects they can find.

When it is time to become an adult, the caddisfly larvae closes up the holes in its case to create a sealed cocoon. Then, it transforms in the cocoon.

As well as helping to collect food, the caddisfly's case is a well-camouflaged hiding place.

EVOLUTION SOLUTION

Some of the first insects to evolve probably looked — and lived — a lot like caddisflies. That makes the caddisfly's case an interesting evolutionary mystery. Did the insects first evolve a case for catching food? Or did the case evolve as a safe place to transform into an adult? Today, the case is used for both but no one knows which function developed first.

FACTS AND FIGURES

Scientific name.................... Trichoptera
Location.................................. Worldwide
Habitat........................ Ponds and rivers
Size.. 3–15mm
Food................ Larvae are filter feeders
Lifespan............ Adults live for 2 weeks
Young................ Lays eggs on plants and rocks under water

Caddisfly larvae are filter feeders. This means they collect tiny scraps of food by 'sifting' them out of the water around them. They build homes to help them do this. Some types of caddisfly weave a funnel-shaped net out of slimy silk produced by glands in their mouth. The silken funnel acts as a net to gather food. Other caddisflies build a house out of pebbles, shells and sticks that litter the riverbed. They glue these items together with silk to form a tube-shaped case with openings at both ends. Inside, the larva wiggles its abdomen to draw a current of water through the house, bringing any food with it.

TRAPDOOR SPIDER

The spider uses its fangs to rake the burrow walls smooth and then lines them with silk.

Trapdoor spiders do not build webs to catch prey. They spend their time inside a secret lair, where they wait just below the surface to snatch their prey.

The trapdoor fits the burrow perfectly. It is shaped by a covering of silk and has a silken hinge.

FACTS AND FIGURES

Scientific name.......... Ctenizidae family
Location.................................. Worldwide
Habitat.................................. Sandy areas
Size... 25mm
Food.. Insects
Lifespan............................... 5–20 years
Young .... Lays eggs in burow

Trapdoor spiders are small, chunky spiders with a powerful bite. They are harmless to humans, but their venom is deadly to insect prey. The spider rarely leaves its home, which is a 25cm-deep burrow. If threatened, the spider scuttles to the bottom of the burrow, but the rest of the time it is stationed by the entrance. This is covered by a trapdoor made of earth. During the day the trapdoor is shut, but at night the spider pokes out its hairy front legs. These can pick up the vibrations of an approaching insect. If one blunders too close, the spider rushes out and hauls it through the trapdoor.

EVOLUTION SOLUTION

All spiders are hunters. They have different ways of catching something to eat. Some spiders chase their prey, some snare them in webs, and some ambush their prey. The trapdoor spider is an ambush hunter. However, the spiders need to protect themselves from hunters as well. The trapdoor and burrow system evolved as a place to hide from predators and prey alike.

11

COMPASS TERMITE

If you are ever lost in the Australian Outback, termites can help you figure out which way to go. Compass termites build their tall, pointed mounds in line with Earth's magnetic field. They do this to stop their giant mud homes from getting too hot.

Individual worker termites are very weak and puny insects. However, working together in their thousands they can build some of nature's most elaborate nests.

A compass termite mound looks like a huge slab of mud. It is always higher than it is wide, and can be 4m tall and 2.5m across. However, the slab is rarely more than 1m thick, and tapers to a narrow edge. There are many thousands of termites hard at work inside a network of tunnels and chambers. The termites work together to raise the young of their mother and father – the queen and king termites.

Termites need their nest to stay at a regular temperature, and this is where its shape and direction is important. The wide sides always face east and west, with the narrow ends lined up north to south. At night, the mound loses some of its heat. In the morning, the low sun shines on the eastern

The termites make their own haystacks by drying out grass they have collected. Hay is their main food source.

All the termite mounds are facing the same way.

FACTS AND FIGURES

Scientific name........................ Amitermes
Location................................... Australia
Habitat.................................Semi-desert
Size... 5mm
Food...............................Grass and hay
Lifespan................................40 days
Young..................Queen produces up to
30,000 eggs per day

EVOLUTION SOLUTION

Mound-building termites have evolved many other ways of controlling the temperature inside their homes. Most of the termites live in tunnels beneath ground level, where the deepest chambers are dug into cool, damp soil. Warm air higher up the mound rises through chimneys. This flow pulls chilled air up from lower down.

side and warms up the mound. By the middle of the day, the sun is shining down on to the top of the mound. Only the narrow edge is in direct sunlight during the hottest time of day. As the Sun sets in the west, it warms the western side a little before nightfall. In this way, the mound gets just enough heat for the termites inside but does not get baked in the middle of the day.

MAGNET DETECTOR
{ In an experiment, termites built their mounds in the wrong direction when a powerful magnet was placed nearby. }

13

GORILLA

The gorillas are some of our nearest relatives, along with chimpanzees and orang-utans. They live in the thick jungles of Central Africa, and know how to make themselves comfortable. Every night, they settle down to sleep in a freshly made bed.

There are two main species of gorilla (some scientists believe there are more) inhabiting different parts of the African forest. However, they all live in the same way. Most of the day is spent eating leaves and fruits collected in the forest. Every day, the leader of the group, or troop, will lead his gorillas to a new feeding site nearby, where there is plenty of fresh food. As the Sun sets, the gorillas get

One of the ways scientists know the number of gorillas in an area is by counting their nests.

EVOLUTION SOLUTION

Gorillas are not the only primates to build nests — all other apes do, too. Primates evolved from small, nocturnal tree-living animals. These ancestors built nests to hide their babies at night while they went out feeding. It was safer to move to a new nest regularly, so predators did not learn where the young were. Likewise, gorillas only sleep in each nest once to avoid predators.

FACTS AND FIGURES

Scientific name	Gorilla species
Location	Central Africa
Habitat	Rainforest
Size	1.8m
Food	Leaves and fruit
Lifespan	40 years
Young	1 baby born every three years

ready to sleep by each building themselves a nest. The nest is made from piles of folded branches and leaves. Most of the time gorillas nest on the ground, but if they find a comfy tree they will build one up there. Gorillas never reuse a nest and always build a fresh one, even for an afternoon nap.

OROPENDOLA

Oropendolas are rainforest birds who build elaborate basket nests that hang from tree branches. Only the females construct these amazing homes, and they hang them all together to form a large colony.

It is normal for one tree to have a couple of dozen nests but some colonies contain 150!

There are about 10 species of oropendola and they all build the same kinds of long, dangling nests. Outside the breeding season, the males and females travel far and wide looking for insects and fruits to eat, but when it is time to mate, the females begin to construct their nests. They are made from long pieces of vine that

Oropendola males are twice the size of the females, so are too heavy for the hanging nests. They roost on branches instead.

are carefully woven together. The result is a teardrop-shaped basket that can be 2m long. There is room for one bird and a couple of eggs inside the hollowed-out bulb. The males do not help with nest building. Instead, they spend their time making noisy displays to attract a mate.

FACTS AND FIGURES

Scientific name.................... Psarocolius
Location....... Central and South America
Habitat.................................. Rainforest
Size................................. 25-35cm
Food................. Insects, seeds and fruit
Lifespan.............................15 years
Young.................... 2 eggs laid each year

EVOLUTION SOLUTION

Like oropendolas, many birds have evolved to gather as colonies during the breeding season. Forming a big group makes it less likely that the helpless chicks will be eaten. Even if a predator did get into the colony, it would soon eat its fill — and could not eat all the young!

BOWERBIRD

Many male animals show off to females to prove that they are attractive mates. However, few show off as much as the bowerbird. These songbirds from Australia and New Guinea build large tent-like nests out of twigs. They then decorate the nest with whatever brightly coloured objects they can find – petals, mushrooms, berries, even metal cans and pieces of plastic. The bird then displays in front of his palace, hoping to impress a mate.

ACACIA ANT

These tiny ants do not need to build themselves a nest. Acacia trees provide a place for them to live. The tree even supplies the ants with food. In return, the ants defend the tree from other bugs trying to eat its leaves or fruits.

The acacia's thorns do more than just prick browsing animals; they house an army of defenders!

The bullhorn acacia tree is named after the shape of its large thorns. These thorns are hollow inside; acacia ants cut tiny entrance holes to set up home inside them. The ants live in a small colony, with the queen laying her eggs inside the thorns, and workers raising the young. Soldier ants patrol the tree and sting any animal they come across — even goats. The tree's leaves have fleshy tips packed full of oils and proteins. Older worker ants harvest these food parcels to feed the colony.

EVOLUTION SOLUTION

The acacia tree and its army of ants are an example of co-evolution, where two different species have evolved to rely on each other. The acacia ants cannot live anywhere apart from on bullhorn acacias and related trees. When a tree does not house any ants, it struggles as well because other animals eat its leaves.

Each thorn has room for about 20 young.

FACTS AND FIGURES

Scientific name............ Pseudomyrmex
Location......... North and South America
Habitat........................ Acacia woodlands
Size.. 3mm
Food............ Leaf nodules and honeydew
Lifespan..................................40 days
Young........... Queen lays 20 eggs a day

STINKPOT

Turtles and tortoises are famous for carrying their homes around with them in the form of an armoured shell. Many types can pull their legs and head inside the shell for extra protection. The stinkpot, or musk turtle, defends its home in another way.

Stinkpots live in rivers and lakes. Baby stinkpots can hide inside their shells, but as they grow larger, the shell does not keep pace. It still provides a sturdy shield around the body, but there is less room to pull in the appendages. Instead, the turtle has evolved another way of staying safe. When disturbed, it squirts a foul-smelling liquid (or musk) from glands around the edge of its shell. The stench makes the turtle seem a lot less tasty to predators.

FACTS AND FIGURES

Scientific name.. Sternotherus odoratus
Location.................... North America
Habitat..................... Lake and ponds
Size................................ 5–14cm
Food..............................Shellfish, plants and insects
Lifespan..........................50 years
Young.......1–9 eggs buried in river bank

EVOLUTION SOLUTION

Turtles that spend a lot of time swimming have evolved small, streamlined shells. This sleek shell gives the legs more room to move in water; a heavy, armoured shell would make the animal sink. Although the shell gives some protection, it is not as safe as the large, rounded shells of land tortoises. That is why the stinkpot has evolved its smelly defence system.

Adult stinkpots walk along the bottom of ponds as they hunt for shellfish.

PRAIRIE DOG

Despite the name, these animals are actually a kind of large ground squirrel. They get their name from the yelping bark noises they make – and because they live on the North American prairies. Prairie dogs live burrows, and their tunnel networks are so large and well organised, they are known as 'towns'.

The mounds at the entrance to a burrow make good lookout points, and also stop floodwater from getting into the tunnels.

A prairie dog town may have 400 residents or more.

They live in a very organised society, with every prairie dog belonging to a clan, which is a family group with about 20 members. Each clan rules over a patch of grass above ground and lives in burrows below. Only members of the clan are allowed into the grassy area, and into the tunnels underneath. The burrows of neighbouring clans do join up, but the town is not one huge tunnel network. Instead, it is divided into several smaller units called wards.

Prairie dogs build tunnels because they have nowhere else to hide above ground. They dig using the claws on their front paws, flinging the soil out behind them. They then turn around and use their heads to bulldoze the earth out of the burrow, creating a mound around the entrance. Prairie dogs sleep in the deepest chambers at night. During the day they feed on the ground, and if danger threatens, they dash back to the burrow and hide in emergency shelters dug just below the surface.

EVOLUTION SOLUTION

The complicated society of prairie dogs evolved as a balance between two competing goals. Living in a big town is safer than being alone. When a predator approaches, neighbours send out a warning to each other. However, male prairie dogs do not want their females mating with anyone else, and so the clan system evolved where outsiders must stay out of other groups' territories.

PRAIRIE DOG MEGACITY
In the late 19th century, one prairie dog town in Texas, USA, was reported to be 400km long and 160km wide!

FACTS AND FIGURES

Scientific name	Cynomys
Location	North America, Europe, Asia
Habitat	Prairie
Size	30-40cm
Food	Grass
Lifespan	3-5 years
Young	4 pups born each year

Members of the same clan 'kiss' each other hello. In fact, they are giving each other a good sniff to check that they belong to the right group.

WEAVER ANT

Colonies of these ants live in trees. There may be several queens in each colony with thousands of workers. Instead of all living together, the ants construct a tent village with dozens of separate homes. The tents are made from leaves that are glued together in a very unusual way.

Weaver ant homes are chambers made from several glued leaves. It takes hundreds of ants working together to build one. First, the leaves need to be pulled into position. The ants form

New nests are needed as older ones dry out and break.

To get a larva to produce sticky silk, the worker taps it on the head.

a pyramid to reach across the gap from one leaf to another. When the ants have brought the edges of two leaves together, they need to glue them. The weaver ants do this using silk secreted by the larvae, the baby ants. The larvae are wiped along the leaves like living glue sticks!

EVOLUTION SOLUTION

Spiders are famous for using silk, but insects and other bugs use it, too. Silk is a liquid filled with proteins that forms solid strands when it meets the air. It is thought that silk evolved in various ways because insects make it very differently to spiders. For instance, adult insects cannot make silk, only the larvae. This is why weaver ants have to use their young's silk to stick their nests together.

FACTS AND FIGURES

Scientific name..................... Oecophylla
Location.........Africa. Australia and Asia
Habitat.................................... Forest
Size.. 5–6mm
Food.. Insects
Lifespan.................................. 40 days
Young............. Multiple queens lay eggs

ARCTIC FOX

Most foxes dig their own den or move into a burrow that has been abandoned by another animal. However, Arctic foxes live in a land where most of the ground is frozen solid.

Even in the Arctic, there are a few places where the ground thaws out in summer. Arctic foxes dig their dens wherever they find these sheltered spots. However, there are hardly any of them, so once a den has been established, Arctic foxes live in it for generations. A daughter inherits it from her parents and her children will live there when she has died. Some Arctic fox dens are centuries old. Around the den, the fox droppings and scraps of leftover food added to the soil make it very fertile. As a result, fox dens are often surrounded by undergrowth, whereas the rest of the habitat is pretty bare.

EVOLUTION SOLUTION

The Arctic fox evolved from a fox species that lived in warmer habitats. As a result, it hunts in the same way as other foxes and lives in the same kind of family group. However, natural selection has made the Arctic fox different in some ways. The fox has thick fur on its paws to stop it from slipping on ice. It also has small ears. Big ears would get frostbitten in the Arctic.

The Arctic fox only starts to shiver if the temperature drops below −70°C.

The Arctic fox's den is often on raised ground.

FACTS AND FIGURES

Scientific name............. Vulpes lagopus
Location... Arctic
Habitat..................................... Tundra
Size.. 60cm
Food.................. Lemmings, hares, eggs
Lifespan.................................3–6 years
Young...............5–8 kits born each year

GOLDEN ORB WEAVER SPIDER

The golden orb weaver builds a web as big as your front door. But, this web is almost impossible to see! The spider itself would cover your hand, and it gives a nasty, poisonous bite. Most of time, the spider catches flying insects, but its silken trap can even snare birds!

Only the female spiders grow large; the males are a quarter of the size. Each web may be home to several males who eat the female's leftovers.

These big spiders build the largest and most elaborate capture-webs in the world. The spider sits in the middle during the day, waiting for prey to become trapped. At night – or if disturbed – the spider scuttles over to a hideaway among the leaves on one edge of the web.

The web is built in the gaps between trees, the kind of place flying insects buzz around. It is supported by a scaffold of strands that run across the gap. These can be 3m wide, and the spider gets the first line across by feeding a strand of sticky silk into the air and letting the wind carry it across. The main part of the web is only about 1m wide and hangs from the main bridging line. As with the webs of similar spiders, prey is captured in a spiral of sticky

EVOLUTION SOLUTION

Golden orb weaver spiders build big webs to catch large flying prey, such as wasps, that are too agile or too tough to be trapped in smaller webs. Even if these insects spot the web, they cannot swoop out of danger – the web is too large. However, big webs have unwelcome visitors, too. Ants attempt to steal captured prey. To prevent this, the spider coats the web in a chemical that ants find disgusting, stopping any raids on the spider's catch.

silk, which shimmers in sunlight. However, there is also a spiral of non-sticky silk which the spider uses to clamber across the web. Most spiders produce colourless silk, but these webs are made with gold-coloured strands. No one knows why for sure but it may be that the silk reflects the green of the surrounding forest better – and that makes the web harder to see.

BARRIER THREADS
The spiders also string threads in front of the main web. Leaves blowing in the wind get stuck, which stops them from destroying the main web.

In 2012, a cape wend on display that was woven from golden orb-weaver silk. It contained more than a million threads and took eight years to produce.

This orb weaver is called the 'man's face spider' in Korea. Can you see why?

FACTS AND FIGURES

Scientific name............................ Nephila
Location.................................... Worldwide
Habitat................................Warm forests
Size................. 10–13cm (including legs)
Food.......... Flying insects, birds, lizards
Lifespan......................................1 year
Young.................... Egg sac glued to leaf

BADGER

Badgers live all over the world and most kinds live alone in a simple underground den. However, the Eurasian badger lives in groups, or clans, and builds a complex tunnel network called a sett.

Large mounds of earth are formed at each entrance as the sett is enlarged.

The largest setts have as many as 90 tunnels and are more than 10m deep.

A badger clan is made up of about 10 adults and their young. All the members build and maintain the sett and defend the territory around it. The sett is dug into banks of dry soil and is a network of tunnels with several entrances. The tunnels lead to deep chambers where the badgers sleep. The residents keep the sett clean and tidy. The sleeping areas are lined with dried grass, which the badgers carry under their chins. When it gets dirty, the bedding is thrown out. Every sett has a rubbish tip, where the badgers also go to the toilet.

EVOLUTION SOLUTION

Eurasian badgers live in cool damp habitats, such as forests and woodlands. There is plenty of food for them here, so they can live in groups without having to compete with each other over food. Badger species that live in drier areas have to spread out to find enough food, and so it is better that they live alone.

FACTS AND FIGURES

Scientific name.................. Meles meles
Location............................Europe and Asia
Habitat................................... Woodland
Size......................................68–80cm
Food............... Insects, worms, rodents
Lifespan.......................................14 years
Young................. 2 or 3 born each year

(HAZEL) DORMOUSE

Although the name may suggest it, the dormouse is not a mouse. In fact, it is more closely related to squirrels. The 'dor' part of the name comes from an old French word for sleepy, and this animal spends a lot of time snoozing in a cosy den.

FACTS AND FIGURES

Scientific name. Muscardinus avellanarius
Location.................................... Europe
Habitat..................... Bushes and hedges
Size....................................... 16–9cm
Food...............Flowers, nuts and berries
Lifespan... 4 years
Young.... 2 litters of 5 young each year

When the dormouse wakes up in spring, it gets its strength back by eating flowers.

A dormouse is a very agile climber and need not come to the ground at all until winter.

The dormouse spends the summer feeding on berries and nuts. It builds itself a nest from strips of bark that it weaves into a hollow ball. The nest is set in a bramble patch, where the thorns will prickle anything that gets close. During cold weather, the dormouse does not get up in the morning and sleeps all day – perhaps longer. As winter approaches, it prepares to hibernate by building a new nest on the ground under leaves. The dormouse sleeps inside for seven months!

EVOLUTION SOLUTION

The dormouse evolved into a hibernator as the best way to survive the winter. In winter, it is dangerously cold to be outside and there is hardly any food to be found. During hibernation, body functions, such as breathing and heart rate, slow down to save energy, so the dormouse can go without feeding for several months.

BEAVER

This big rodent is one of the animal kingdom's top construction experts. It cuts down trees, digs canals and dams rivers. It even makes its own private island – and lives inside!

Beavers live in and around forest rivers. In summer, they eat the lush grasses that grow along the bank, and they make sure they have plenty to eat by building dams to change the flow of the river. In winter, the beavers make do with a supply of rotting wood, which is stored on the riverbed.

The beaver's top teeth rub against the bottom ones, always keeping them razor sharp.

EVOLUTION SOLUTION

The way beavers make their homes has evolved to solve several problems. Damming the river creates a deep pool, and that provides plenty of room for the beaver to build a safe underwater entrance to its lodge. Only the surface of deep water will freeze in winter, and so the entrance is open all year around. This means the beaver can collect its supply of wood food from the pool even when it is iced over.

Beavers stay in their lodge for most of the winter, swimming out to collect some wood to eat from their riverbed store.

Two million years ago, giant 2-m-long beavers lived in North America.

All this is possible because beavers are powerful swimmers, and their front teeth are so sharp, they can gnaw through tree trunks!

The beaver's construction job starts in the forest, where they fell small trees and cut them into logs. Some logs are stored for winter, while the beavers pile the rest across the river to build a dam. The dam slows the flow of the water and creates a wide, shallow pool upstream. This creates more bank areas for the grass to grow. The dam also contains stones and mud, and the beaver now makes a large pile of these in the middle of the dam. Next, it dives under the water and burrows into the pile, digging out two rooms inside. The first is where the beaver dries off after swimming in through the underwater entrance. The second is a cosy, dry sleeping area. This is the beaver's lodge. Normally a male and female share the lodge with their young, or kits.

FACTS AND FIGURES

Scientific name............................ Castor
Location..... North America, Europe, Asia
Habitat......... Forest rivers and streams
Size................................. 60–90cm
Food.............................Grass, wood
Lifespan....................................25 years
Young.......... 2 or 3 kits born in winter

GLOSSARY

Arctic The region around the North Pole. The Arctic is always very cold and frequently frozen over.

canal A water channel dug into the ground.

clan An animal group where related animals and their offspring live together.

colony A large collection of animals that live in the same place and may work together to help in survival.

dam A structure that blocks the flow of a river. The result is a deep pool upstream of the dam.

evolution The process by which animals, plants and other life forms change gradually to adapt to changes in their environment.

habitat The kind of environment that an animal lives in. Each species has evolved to survive in its particular habitat.

hibernation A sleep-like state that some animals enter in winter. Body processes slow down so the animal does not use much energy to stay alive during long, cold periods.

larva A young form of an insect or other invertebrate. The larva looks different to the adult form and lives in a different way.

magnetic field A region of invisible force that surrounds a magnet. The magnetism of Earth surrounds the planet in a magnetic field.

mucus A slimy liquid used by animals to keep body parts moist or create a protective layer.

musk A strong-smelling liquid produced by animals. Musk is used to scare away predators or attract mates.

natural selection The process by which evolution works. Natural selection allows individuals that are good at surviving to increase in number, while those that are less able to compete go down in number.

nocturnal To be active at night.

parasite A life form that survives by stealing resources from another species – their host. Some parasites grow on the outside of their host, others grow inside the body.

predator An animal that hunts and kills other animals for food.

prey An animal that is hunted and killed by a predator.

primate A type of mammal that includes lemurs, monkeys, apes — and humans.

pulp A mixture of wood fibres and water to make a soft gooey material.

scaffold A framework that supports a structure.

solution Something that solves a problem.

species A group of animals that share many characteristics. The main common feature is that members of a species can breed with each other. Members of different species cannot produce young successfully.

tentacle A flexible, armlike feature seen on many different animals, mostly sea creatures.

territory An area that is controlled by an animal or group of animals. The territory is where they find food and build their homes.

FURTHER INFORMATION

BOOKS

THE WORLD IN INFOGRAPHICS: Animal Kingdom,
by Jon Richards and Ed Simkins (Wayland, 2014)

MIND WEBS: Living Things,
by Anna Claybourne (Wayland, 2014)

WHAT IS EVOLUTION?,
by Louise Spilsbury (Wayland, 2015)

WEBSITES

www.zsl.org/kids-zsl

The kids' section of the Zoological Society of London's website is packed with animal information, games and activities, as well as the latest scientific studies.

www.natgeokids.com/uk/

Animal-related facts, pictures and games from the kids' section of the National Geographic website.

www.nhm.ac.uk/

The Natural History Museum website is filled with the latest information about the world of animals.

INDEX

Published in paperback in 2018 by Wayland
Copyright © Hodder and Stoughton, 2015

All rights reserved.

Editor: Julia Adams
Designer: Rocket Design

Dewey number: 591.5'64-dc23
ISBN 978 1 5263 0763 7

Printed in China

10 9 8 7 6 5 4 3 2 1

Picture acknowledgements: Cover: © Gerard Lacz/FLPA; p.1: © Shutterstock; p. 3 © Tony Heald/naturepl.com; pp. 4–5: © David Hall/naturepl.com; p. 6: © Laurie Campbell/naturepl.com; p. 7: © Nature Production/naturepl.com; p. 8, p. 30: © Kim Taylor/naturepl.com; p. 9: © Nick Upton/2020VISION/naturepl.com; p. 10: © Jan Hamrsky/naturepl.com; p. 11: © Hans Christoph Kappel/naturepl.com; p. 12 (top and bottom): © Ingo Arndt/naturepl.com; p. 13: © Owen Newman/naturepl.com; p. 14: © Bernd Rohrschneider/FLPA; p. 15: © Patricio Robles Gil/naturepl.com; pp. 16–17: © Barrie Britton/naturepl.com; p. 18 (top and bottom): © Visuals Unlimited/naturepl.com; p. 19: © Barry Mansell/naturepl.com; p. 20, 21: © Shutterstock; p. 22: © Ann and Steve Toon/naturepl.com; p. 23:

© Paul Nicklen/National Geographic Creative/Corbis; p. 24: © Steven David Miller/naturepl.com; p. 25 (top): © John Calcalosi/naturepl.com; p. 25 (bottom): © Rick Buettner/Alamy; p. 26: © Kevin J Keatley/naturepl.com; p. 27: © Kerstin Hinze/naturepl.com; p. 28: © Vincent Munier/naturepl.com; p. 29: © Orsolya Haarberg/naturepl.com; all images used as graphic elements: Shutterstock.

The website addresses (URLs) included in this book were valid at the time of going to press. However, it is possible that contents or addresses may change following the publication of this book. No responsibility for any such changes can be accepted by either the author or the Publisher.

Every attempt has been made to clear copyright. Should there be any inadvertent omission, please apply to the publisher for rectification.

Wayland, an imprint of Hachette Children's Group
Part of Hodder & Stoughton
Carmelite House
50 Victoria Embankment
London
EC4Y 0DZ

An Hachette UK Company
www.hachette.co.uk
www.hachettechildrens.co.uk

MIX
Paper from responsible sources
FSC® C104740

CHAPTER 2

Adenocarcinoma of the Oesophagogastric Junction

The oesophagogastric junction is anatomically defined as the transition zone between the squamous epithelium of the distal oesophagus and the glandular epithelium of the cardia.

For gastroenterologists, this region has become increasingly important, and from a clinical point of view it has been proposed to separate tumours of the oesophagogastric junction from adenocarcinomas of the distal oesophagus and proximal stomach.

Epidemiological data indicate that in industrialized countries with Western-style dietary habits carcinomas at the junction increase steadily, mainly through oesophagogastric reflux which causes a chronic inflammatory reaction that ultimately results in precancerous lesions.

Adenocarcinoma of the oesophago-gastric junction

S.J. Spechler
M.F. Dixon
R. Genta

P. Hainaut
R. Lambert
R. Siewert

Definition

Adenocarcinomas that straddle the junction of the oesophagus and stomach are called tumours of the oesophagogastric (OG) junction. This definition includes many tumours formerly called cancers of the gastric cardia.

Squamous cell carcinomas that occur at the OG junction are considered carcinomas of the distal oesophagus, even if they cross the OG junction.

ICD-O code

8140/3

Definition of the oesophagogastric junction

The OG junction is the anatomical region where the tubular oesophagus joins the stomach. The squamo-columnar (SC) epithelial junction may occur at or above the OG junction. The gastric cardia has been defined conceptually as the region of the stomach that adjoins the oesophagus {1568}. The gastric cardia begins at the OG junction, but its distal extent is poorly defined.

Figure 2.01 shows endoscopically recognizable landmarks that can be used to identify structures at the OG junction. The squamocolumnar junction (SCJ or Z-line) is the visible line formed by the juxtaposition of squamous and columnar epithelia. The OG junction is the imaginary line at which the oesophagus ends and the

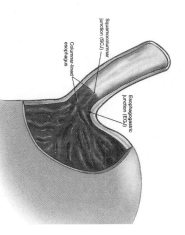

Squamocolumnar
junction (SCJ)

Columnar-lined
esophagus

Esophagogastric
junction (EGJ)

Fig. 2.01 Topography of the oesophagogastric junction and cardia {1797}.

stomach begins anatomically. The OG junction is defined endoscopically as the level of the most proximal extent of the gastric folds {1200}. In normal individuals, the proximal extent of the gastric folds generally corresponds to the point at which the tubular oesophagus flares to become the sack-shaped stomach at the distal border of the lower oesophageal sphincter. In patients with hiatus hernias, in whom there may be no clear-cut flare at the OG junction, the proximal margin of the gastric folds is determined when the distal oesophagus is minimally inflated with air because over-inflation obscures this landmark {1271}. Whenever the squamocolumnar junction is located above the OG junction, there is a columnar-lined segment of oesophagus. When the squamocolumnar junction and the OG junction coincide, the entire oesophagus is lined by squamous epithelium (i.e. there is no columnar-lined oesophagus). By definition, the gastric cardia starts at the OG junction, but there are no endoscopic landmarks that define the distal extent of the gastric cardia.

A potential source of confusion is the histological terminology used to describe the most proximal part of the stomach. Cardiac mucosa is characterized by tortuous, tubular glands that are comprised almost exclusively of mucus-secreting cells with few or no parietal (oxyntic) cells. The histological finding of cardiac mucosa does not establish that the specimen has been obtained from the cardia of the stomach, for the following reasons:

(1) Cardiac mucosa can be found in the distal oesophagus {1479, 678}.

(2) Cardiac mucosa rarely extends more than 2 to 3 mm below the SC epithelial junction in the distal oesophagus {1430, 911}. Therefore it will not line the larger anatomical area often called cardia.

(3) Recent studies have shown that the proximal stomach is lined predominantly, if not exclusively, by oxyntic epithelium {272, 1388}. Therefore, even a tumour that is unequivocally located at the cardia may not have arisen from cardiac epithe-

lium. Conversely, a tumour that clearly is located in the distal oesophagus could have arisen from oesophageal cardiac epithelium.

Some investigators actually contend that cardiac mucosa is not a normal mucosa at all, but one that is acquired as a consequence of chronic inflammation in the distal oesophagus {272, 1388}.

Diagnostic criteria

Various criteria have been used to categorize tumours in the region of the OG junction as cancers of the gastric cardia {1240, 314, 877, 1271, 638, 767, 684}. In most of these classification systems, the anatomic location of the epicenter or predominant mass of the tumour is used to determine whether the neoplasm is oesophageal or gastric in origin. Due to the use of divergent classification systems, the patient populations in studies on cancers of the gastric cardia are heterogeneous, and often include patients with gastric tumours and others with tumours of oesophageal origin. The following guidelines are based on the definition of the OG junction described above:

(1) Adenocarcinomas that cross the oesophagogastric junction are called adenocarcinomas of the OG junction, regardless of where the bulk of the tumour lies.

(2) Adenocarcinomas located entirely above the oesophagogastric junction as defined above are considered oesophageal carcinomas.

(3) Adenocarcinomas located entirely below the oesophagogastric junction are considered gastric in origin. The use of the ambiguous and often misleading term 'carcinoma of the gastric cardia' is discouraged; depending on their size, these should be called carcinoma of the proximal stomach or carcinoma of the body of the stomach.

Epidemiology

Reliable data on the incidence of tumours of the OG junction are not avaia direct role in the pathogenesis of oesophageal inflammation and metaplasia {1381, 1076, 1617, 1889, 501, 1087, 6, 1579}. Indeed, recent reports suggest that gastric infection with *H. pylori* may actually protect the oesophagus from cancer by preventing the development of reflux oesophagitis and Barrett oesophagus {2090, 998, 2094, 309, 2012, 615, 350, 504, 1948, 2213, 837, 1957}. In biopsies from the SC epithelial junction of patients with Barrett oesophagus, a peculiar hybrid cell type has been observed that has both microvilli (a feature of columnar cells) and intercellular bridges (a feature of squamous cells) on its surface {1740, 1651, 155}.

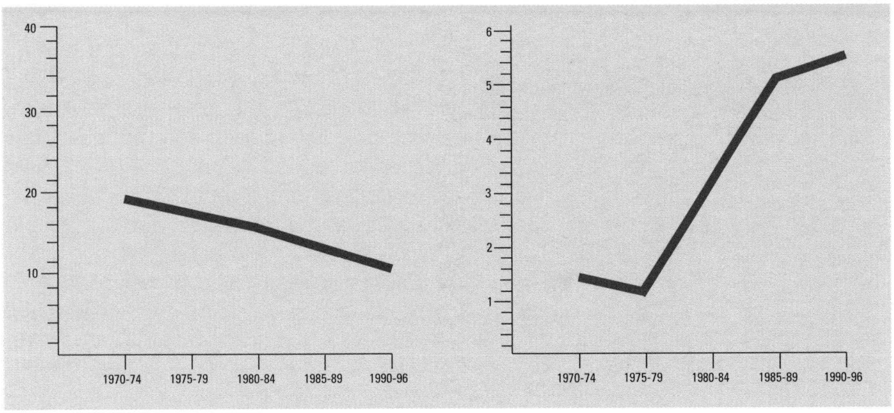

The relationship between intestinal metaplasia in the proximal stomach and in the oesophagus is disputed {1797}. Intestinal metaplasia has been found in the proximal stomach (gastric cardia) of only a minority of patients with Barrett oesophagus {1498}.

Recent studies indicate that specialized intestinal metaplasia at a normal-looking OG junction carries a much lower rate of malignancy than in Barrett oesophagus {715}. Indeed, intestinal metaplasia at the oesophagogastric junction has been found with similar frequencies in Caucasians with GERD (a high risk group for adenocarcinoma at the junction) and in African Americans without GERD (a low risk group) {269}.

Cancers of the gastric cardia resemble oesophageal adenocarcinomas in terms

oesophagus and in the stomach {1797}. However, there appear to be significant differences in the pathogenetic, morphological and histochemical characteristics, as well as in the clinical importance of intestinal metaplasia in the two organs (Fig. 2.03).

In the oesophagus, gastro-oesophageal reflux disease (GERD) is accepted as the cause of intestinal metaplasia (Barrett oesophagus); chronic reflux oesophagitis is a strong risk factor for adenocarcinoma of the oesophagus {1001}. The cancer risk for patients with intestinal metaplasia in the oesophagus appears to be substantially higher than for patients with intestinal metaplasia in the stomach {1797} In contrast to the stomach, infection with *H. pylori* does not appear to play

able at this time. Tumour registries typically distinguish only the adenocarcinoma in Barrett oesophagus and the carcinoma of the cardia.

Adenocarcinomas of the OG junction and 'cardia' share similar epidemiologic characteristics. At both sites, there is a strong predilection for middle-aged and older white males {1133, 2205, 1473}, with a marked increase in incidence in recent years. This is in contrast to the worldwide decline of adenocarcinoma of the gastric body and antrum (Fig. 2.02). Despite the increasing incidence, the cumulative rates at the OG junction and the cardia are still much lower than those observed in the 'non cardia' stomach. In the Norwegian cancer registry data for the period 1991/92 {664}, the age adjusted incidence rate for the combined adenocarcinoma of the distal third of the oesophagus and proximal stomach was 3.0 for males and 0.8 for females, while the incidence for all subsites of the stomach was 13.8 in males and 6.5 in females.

Aetiology

The most consistent association described for carcinoma at the OG junction is with gastro-oesophageal reflux. In contrast with the aetiological factors involved in 'non cardia' gastric cancer, there is no consistent association with diet (salty food in excess and lack of fruits and vitamins) nor *Helicobacter pylori* infection, while in the body and antrum of the stomach, intestinal metaplasia occurs in relation to chronic gastritis due to *H. pylori* infection {1829, 88, 343}.

Intestinal metaplasia is judged to be the precursor of adenocarcinoma both in the

Fig. 2.02 Incidence of adenocarcinoma of the stomach (left) compared to adenocarcinoma of the distal oesophagus and oesophagogastric junction (right). Rate per 10,000 hospitalisations from North America.

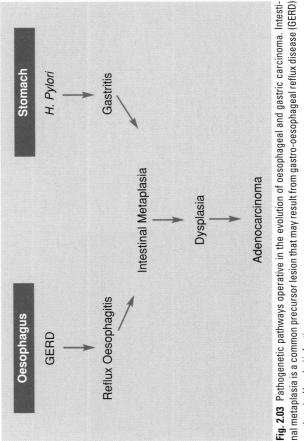

Fig. 2.03 Pathogenetic pathways operative in the evolution of oesophageal and gastric carcinoma. Intestinal metaplasia is a common precursor lesion that may result from gastro-oesophageal reflux disease (GERD) or chronic *H. pylori* infection.

Table 2.01
Features of intestinal metaplasia in the oesophagus and stomach.

	Stomach	Oesophagus
H. pylori association	Yes	No
GERD association	No	Yes
Usual type of metaplasia	Complete	Incomplete
Barrett cytokeratin pattern	No	Yes
Cancer risk	Lower	Higher

of their association with GERD {1133, 2205, 1473}.

Clinical features

Common presenting symptoms for patients with adenocarcinomas of the oesophagogastric junction include dysphagia, weight loss, and abdominal pain. Early cancers, and the metaplastic and dysplastic lesions that spawn them, usually cause no symptoms. Consequently, symptomatic patients usually have advanced, incurable disease. Oesophagogastric junction tumours are discovered at an early stage during endoscopic surveillance in patients known to have Barrett oesophagus.

Endoscopy and imaging

The diagnosis of cancer at the oesophagogastric junction is typically established by endoscopic examination with biopsy.
Endoscopy. The distal oesophagus should be examined carefully for evidence of intestinal metaplasia (Barrett oesophagus), and biopsy specimens of the metaplastic epithelium should be taken to determine whether the tumour is oesophageal in origin. The finding of intestinal metaplasia with dysplastic features above an OG junction tumour is strong evidence that the cancer began in the oesophagus. The location of the tumour in reference to the landmarks shown in Figure 2.01 should be noted. The proximal stomach is examined carefully, preferably by retroversion of the endoscope, to determine the gastric extent of the tumour. Early tumours may be polypoid, but flat lesions are more frequent. These flat lesions may appear depressed, elevated, or completely flush with the surrounding mucosa {1010}. Mucosal hyperplasia immediately distal to the squamo-columnar junction, occurs in

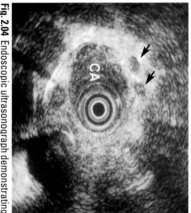

Fig. 2.04 Endoscopic ultrasonograph demonstrating adenocarcinoma at the oesophagogastric junction (CA) with deep infiltration and several lymph node metastases (arrows).

carditis and can, without biopsy sampling, be mistaken for an elevated neoplastic lesion. In advanced adenocarcinoma, the tumour is often polypoid and circumferential. Tight stenoses can be difficult to explore endoscopically and dangerous to dilate, especially when there is tortuosity.

Endoscopic ultrasonography is the modality of choice for tumour staging, and accuracy can be improved even further by using high frequency (20 or 30 MHz) miniprobes {669}. Endosonography accurately identifies the depth of tumour invasion and regional lymph node involvement in approximately 77% and 78% of cases, respectively {1301}. Endosonography is also useful in assessing the proximal extent of submucosal tumour invasion in the oesophagus. Endosonographic study of the wall of the oesophagus reveals 3 hyperechoic layers that are separated by 2 hypoechoic layers. The inner (1st) and external (3rd) hyperechoic layers correspond to the interfaces of the wall with the gut lumen and surrounding tissues, respec-

tively. The intermediate (2nd) hyperechoic layer corresponds to the submucosa. The inner (1st) and outer (2nd) hypoechoic layers represent part of the muscularis mucosae and the muscularis propria, respectively.
Computed tomography is necessary to detect distant thoracic and abdominal metastases.
Barium swallow has a limited role as a diagnostic test for cancer at the oesophagogastric junction {1058, 1180} but may be helpful in the analysis of malignant stenoses that are too narrow to be traversed by the endoscope.

Tumour spread and staging

According to TNM, in this junction area, carcinomas that are mainly on the gastric side should be classified according to the TNM for gastric tumours, while those predominantly on the oesophageal side should be staged according to the TNM for oesophageal carcinomas {698}. Adenocarcinomas at the oesophagogastric junction exhibit a great propensity for upward lymphatic spread mainly in the submucosa of the oesophagus. For this reason, intraoperative frozen-section examination of the proximal oesophageal resection margin is recommended. Upward spread can also involve lower mediastinal nodes. Lymphatic spread from the cardia frequently extends downwards to nodes in the oesophagogastric angles and around the left gastric artery, and may involve para-coeliac and para-aortic lymph nodes {26, 949}.
There are differences in the criteria for stage grouping oesophageal and gastric malignancies, and the pathological staging recommended by the AJCC {1} for lymph node involvement by gastric cancers is not easily adapted for use by endosonographers. Involvement of the coeliac lymph nodes is usually deemed regional disease for gastric cancers, whereas coeliac node involvement is considered distant metastatic disease (M1) for cancers of the thoracic oesophagus. The regional nodes of the OG junction are not well enough defined to stage OG junction cancers properly.

Histopathology
Adenocarcinoma

The vast majority of cancers arising at the cardia are adenocarcinomas {1790}. Histologically, four types are usually distinguished in the WHO classification:

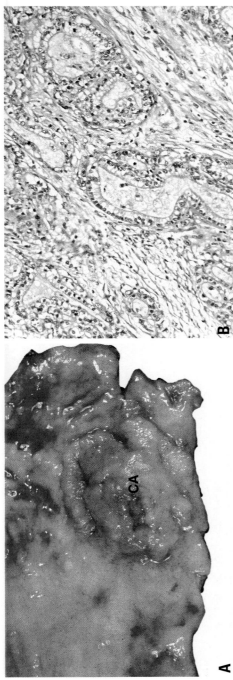

Fig. 2.05 Adenocarcinoma of the proximal stomach ('pylorocardiac type'). **A** Macroscopic appearance resembles other adenocarcinomas. **B** Glands with tall cells, pale cytoplasm, and basal or central nuclei.

papillary, tubular, mucinous, and signet-ring cell adenocarcinoma. The latter two types are uncommon. The signet-ring type is much less common in the proximal than in the distal stomach, and usually not accompanied by atrophic gastritis {2045}. Well differentiated tubular adenocarcinomas can present considerable diagnostic difficulty as the neoplastic tubules may have a deceptively regular appearance and can be readily mistaken for low-grade dysplasia or even hyperplastic glands.

Pylorocardiac carcinoma.
Mulligan and Rember {1847} termed lesions resembling normal pyloric glands as 'pylorocardiac carcinomas'. They predominate in the cardiac region and typically have tall epithelial cells with clear or pale cytoplasm and nuclei in a basal or central position. However, this pattern is difficult to distinguish reliably from other gland-forming adenocarcinomas {1847}.

Adenosquamous carcinoma
Of the less common forms of cancers in the oesophagogastric junction region, adenosquamous carcinoma is the one most likely to be encountered. The diagnosis rests on the finding of a mixture of glandular and squamous elements and not merely on the presence of small squamoid foci in an otherwise typical adenocarcinoma. The latter is a frequent finding in tumours at this site. Such composite tumours should also be distinguished from the rare *mucoepidermoid carcinoma* of the oesophagus, which arises from mucous glands and is similar to the sali-

vary gland tumour of that name. Although the term mucoepidermoid has been used synonymously for adenosquamous carcinomas {1476}, the latter are distinguished by increased nuclear pleomorphism, occasional keratin pearls, and the separation of the two components with some areas of purely glandular epithelium and mucin. While in the past there were claims that adenosquamous carcinoma represented a 'collision tumour', it is now generally accepted that this malignancy results from dual differentiation and that it

is analogous to other cancers arising at junctional sites in the body (e.g. uterine cervix and anal canal).
Small cell carcinoma can occur at this site.

Grading
Adenocarcinomas in the oesophagogastric junction region can be graded as well, moderately, or poorly differentiated. However, agreement on tumour grading is notoriously poor. Blomjous et al. {151} reported that 3.6% of gastric cardiac cancers were well differentiated, 31% moderately differentiated, and 43% poorly differentiated, but others consider a greater proportion well differentiated, particularly when early carcinomas are included {1271, 1903, 1363}.

Precursor lesions
Intraepithelial neoplasia
Interobserver agreement on the grading of intraepithelial neoplasia in the absence of invasion of the lamina propria is poor, particularly in the identification of low-grade changes, and different terms have been applied to identical appearances {1683}. Such differences in nomenclature have been reduced by the widespread acceptance of a new classification that embraces the previously discordant terminology in a unified scheme {1637}.

Intramucosal non-invasive neoplasia can be classified as flat (synonymous with dysplasia) or elevated (synonymous with adenoma); lesions can be low grade or high grade, the latter including lesions previously designated as intraglandular carcinoma.

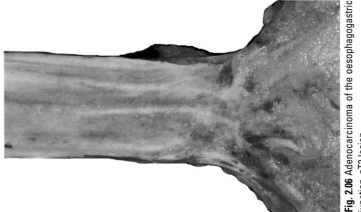

Fig. 2.06 Adenocarcinoma of the oesophagogastric junction. pT2 lesion.

Intestinal metaplasia

Putative precancerous lesions other than intraepithelial neoplasia are controversial. Intestinal metaplasia is widely regarded as carrying an increased risk of malignant change, but the frequency at which it is found in the OG junction region (5.3% to 23% of dyspeptic patients) limits its value as a criterion for surveillance {716, 1960, 1800, 2028, 1269}. Some of the variability in the reported prevalence of intestinal metaplasia can be attributed to differences in diagnostic criteria. Some authors accept the finding of columnar cells containing acidic glycoproteins ('columnar blues' in Alcian blue / PAS stained sections) as evidence for intestinal metaplasia {1398}. This staining pattern reflects immature, regenerative cells and is a common finding in biopsy specimens of the cardia in children with GERD. This finding alone is not sufficient to identify intestinal metaplasia; intestinal metaplasia should only be diagnosed if goblet cells are present.

Genetic changes

The best characterized somatic alteration found in tumours of this region are mutations of *TP53* which are present in up to 60% of carcinomas of the oesophagogastric junction. In 5 patients who had adenocarcinomas at the junction associated with Barrett oesophagus, the same mutation was detected in the tumour and in the surrounding oesophageal intestinal metaplasia, indicating an oesophageal origin. No association has been found between p53 status and tumour stage or subtype. The *TP53* alterations noted in tumours at the oesophagogastric junction show a predominance of transition mutations at CpG sites, similar to the pattern seen in adenocarcinomas in Barrett oesophagus {585}. Transitions at CpG dinucleotides in *TP53* are generally assumed to result from endogenous mutational mechanism (deamination of 5-methylcytosine) which may be enhanced by oxidative or nitrosative stress. In colon cancers that frequently exhibit CpG mutations, excess nitric oxide production resulting from nitric oxide synthase-2 expression may contribute to the transition from adenoma to carcinoma {51}.

In a study of cancers at the oesophagogastric junction that did not show evidence of associated Barrett oesophagus, the prevalence of *TP53* mutations was only 30% {1641}. Overexpression of the *MDM2* gene was found frequently in these tumours, suggesting that *TP53* may be inactivated either by mutation or by overexpression of the *MDM2* gene.

Comparative genomic hybridization has been used to compare tumours of the 'gastric cardia' and tumours in Barrett oesophagus. Gains and losses of genetic material were identified at a number of common regions in cancers from both sites {1718}. Common altered regions included chromosome 4q (loci not yet identified), 3p14 (*FHIT, RCA1*), 5q 14-21 (*APC, MCC*), 9p21 (*MTS1/CDKN2*), 14q31-32.1 (*TSHR*), 16q23, 18q21 (*DCC, p15*), and 21q21. Minimal overlapping amplified sites were seen at 5p14 (*MLV12*), 6p12-21.1 (*NRASL3*), 7p12 (*EGFR*), 8123-24.1 (*MYC*), 15q25 (*IGF1R*), 17q12-21 (*ERBB2/HER2-neu*), 19q13.1 (*TGFB1, BCL3, AKT2*), 20p12 (*PCNA*), and 20q12-13 (*MYBL2, PTPN1*). The distribution of these imbalances was similar in both groups. However, loss of 14q31-32.1 (*TSHR*) was significantly more frequent in Barrett-related adenocarcinomas than in cardiac cancers. Overall, the available genetic data suggests that within cancers of the oesophagogastric junction, a subset of tumours is genetically similar to adenocarcinomas in Barrett oesophagus, whereas another subset is genetically distinct from adenocarcinomas of both the oesophagus and distal stomach {314, 1133}.

Prognosis and predictive factors

There is a significant relationship between grade and prognosis by univariate analysis. For example, Blomjous et al. found that 31% of patients with well or moderately differentiated cardia tumours survived 5 years, whereas the survival for patients with poorly or undifferentiated tumours was only 17% {151}. When T, N, and M status were included in the analysis, however, grade was significantly related to survival only in those patients with negative lymph nodes (53% 5-year survival for well and moderate compared to 21% for poor and undifferentiated tumours).

CHAPTER 3

Tumours of the Stomach

The incidence of adenocarcinoma of the stomach is declining worldwide. In some Western countries, rates have been reduced to less than one third within just one generation. In countries with a traditionally high incidence, e.g. Japan and Korea, the reduction is also significant but it will take more time to diminish the still significant disease burden. The main reasons for these good news is a change in nutrition, in particular the avoidance of salt for meat and fish preservation, the lowering of salt intake from other sources, and the availability in many countries of fresh fruits and vegetables throughout the year. Mortality has been further decreased by significant advances in the early detection of stomach cancer.

Infection with *Helicobacter pylori* appears to play an important additional aetiological role since it leads to chronic atrophic gastritis with intestinal metaplasia as an important precursor lesion.

The stomach is the main gastrointestinal site for lymphomas and most of these are also pathogenetically linked to *H. pylori* infection. Regression of such tumours often follows *H. pylori* eradication.

WHO histological classification of gastric tumours[1]

Epithelial tumours	
Intraepithelial neoplasia – Adenoma	8140/0[2]
Carcinoma	
Adenocarcinoma	8140/3
intestinal type	8144/3
diffuse type	8145/3
Papillary adenocarcinoma	8260/3
Tubular adenocarcinoma	8211/3
Mucinous adenocarcinoma	8480/3
Signet-ring cell carcinoma	8490/3
Adenosquamous carcinoma	8560/3
Squamous cell carcinoma	8070/3
Small cell carcinoma	8041/3
Undifferentiated carcinoma	8020/3
Others	
Carcinoid (well differentiated endocrine neoplasm)	8240/3

Non-epithelial tumours	
Leiomyoma	8890/0
Schwannoma	9560/0
Granular cell tumour	9580/0
Glomus tumour	8711/0
Leiomyosarcoma	8890/3
GI stromal tumour	8936/1
benign	8936/0
uncertain malignant potential	8936/1
malignant	8936/3
Kaposi sarcoma	9140/3
Others	
Malignant lymphomas	
Marginal zone B-cell lymphoma of MALT-type	9699/3
Mantle cell lymphoma	9673/3
Diffuse large B-cell lymphoma	9680/3
Others	

Secondary tumours

[1] The classification is modified from the previous WHO histological classification of tumours {845} taking into account changes in our understanding of these lesions. In the case of endocrine neoplasms, the classification is based on the recent WHO clinicopathological classification {1784}, but has been simplified to be of more practical utility in morphological classification.

[2] Morphology code of the International Classification of Diseases for Oncology (ICD-O) {542} and the Systematized Nomenclature of Medicine (http://snomed.org). Behaviour is coded /0 for benign tumours, /3 for malignant tumours, and /1 for unspecified, borderline or uncertain behaviour. Intraepithelial neoplasia does not have a generic code in ICD-O. ICD-O codes are available only for lesions categorized as glandular intraepithelial neoplaia grade III (8148/2), and adenocarcinoma in situ (8140/2).

TNM classification of gastric tumours

TNM classification[1]

T – Primary Tumour

TX	Primary tumour cannot be assessed
T0	No evidence of primary tumour
Tis	Carcinoma in situ: intraepithelial tumour without invasion of the lamina propria
T1	Tumour invades lamina propria or submucosa
T2	Tumour invades muscularis propria or subserosa[2]
T3	Tumour penetrates serosa (visceral peritoneum) without invasion of adjacent structures[2,3,4,5]
T4	Tumour invades adjacent structures[2,3,4,5]

N – Regional Lymph Nodes

NX	Regional lymph nodes cannot be assessed
N0	No regional lymph node metastasis
N1	Metastasis in 1 to 6 regional lymph nodes
N2	Metastasis in 7 to 15 regional lymph nodes
N3	Metastasis in more than 15 regional lymph nodes

M – Distant Metastasis

MX	Distant metastasis cannot be assessed
M0	No distant metastasis
M1	Distant metastasis

Stage Grouping

Stage 0	Tis	N0	M0
Stage IA	T1	N0	M0
Stage IB	T1	N1	M0
	T2	N0	M0
Stage II	T1	N2	M0
	T2	N1	M0
	T3	N0	M0
Stage IIIA	T2	N2	M0
	T3	N1	M0
	T4	N0	M0
Stage IIIB	T3	N2	M0
Stage IV	T4	N1, N2, N3	M0
	T1, T2, T3	N3	M0
	Any T	Any N	M1

[1] {1, 66}. This classification applies only to carcinomas.

[2] A help desk for specific questions about the TNM classification is available at http://tnm.uicc.org.

[3] A tumour may penetrate muscularis propria with extension into the gastrocolic or gastrohepatic ligaments or the greater and lesser omentum without perforation of the visceral peritoneum covering these structures. In this case, the tumour is classified as T2. If there is perforation of the visceral peritoneum covering the gastric ligaments or omenta, the tumour is classified as T3.

[4] The adjacent structures of the stomach are the spleen, transverse colon, liver, diaphragm, pancreas, abdominal wall, adrenal gland, kidney, small intestine, and retroperitoneum.

[5] Intramural extension to the duodenum or oesophagus is classified by the depth of greatest invasion in any of these sites including stomach.

Gastric carcinoma

C. Fenoglio-Preiser   N. Muñoz
F. Carneiro   S.M. Powell
P. Correa   M. Rugge
P. Guilford   M. Sasako
R. Lambert   M. Stolte
F. Megraud   H. Watanabe

Definition

A malignant epithelial tumour of the stomach mucosa with glandular differentiation. Its aetiology is multifactorial; most commonly it develops after a long period of atrophic gastritis.

Tumours of the oesophagogastric junction are dealt with in the preceding chapter.

ICD-O codes

Adenocarcinoma	8140/3
Intestinal type	8144/3
Diffuse type	8145/3
Papillary adenocarcinoma	8260/3
Tubular adenocarcinoma	8211/3
Mucinous adenocarcinoma	8480/3
Signet-ring cell carcinoma	8490/3

Epidemiology

Geographical distribution

Gastric cancer was the second commonest cancer in the world in 1990, with an estimated 800,000 new cases and 650,000 deaths per year; 60% of them occurred in developing countries {1469}. The areas with the highest incidence rates (> 40/100,000 in males) are in Eastern Asia, the Andean regions of South America, and Eastern Europe. Low rates (< 15/100,000) are found in North America, Northern Europe, and most countries in Africa and in Southeastern

Asia {1471}. There is about a 20-fold difference in the incidence rates when comparing the rates in Japan with those of some white populations from the US and those of some African countries. A predominance of the intestinal type of adenocarcinoma occurs in high-risk areas, while the diffuse type is relatively more common in low-risk areas {1296}.

Time trends

A steady decline in the incidence and mortality rates of gastric carcinoma has been observed worldwide over the past several decades, but the absolute number of new cases per year is increasing mainly because of the aging of the population {1296}. Analysis of time trends by histological types indicates that the incidence decline results from a decline in the intestinal type of carcinoma {1296}.

Age and sex distribution

Gastric carcinoma is extremely rare below the age of 30; thereafter it increases rapidly and steadily to reach the highest rates in the oldest age groups, both in males and females. The intestinal type rises faster with age than the diffuse type; it is more frequent in males than in females.

Diffuse carcinoma tends to affect younger individuals, mainly females; it

frequently has hereditary characteristics, perhaps modulated by environmental influences {1738, 1633}.

Aetiology

Diet

Epidemiological studies in different populations show that the most consistent association is diet. This is especially true of intestinal type carcinomas. An adequate intake of fresh fruits and vegetables lowers the risk {1450}, due to their antioxidant effects. Ascorbic acid, carotenoids, folates and tocopherols are considered active ingredients. Salt intake strongly associates with the risk of gastric carcinoma and its precursor lesions {869}.

Other foods associated with high risk in some populations include smoked or cured meats or fish, pickled vegetables and chili peppers.

Alcohol, tobacco and occupational exposures to nitrosamines and inorganic dusts have been studied in several populations, but the results have been inconsistent.

Bile reflux

The risk of gastric carcinoma increases 5-10 years after gastric surgery, especially when the Bilroth II operation, which increases bile reflux, was performed.

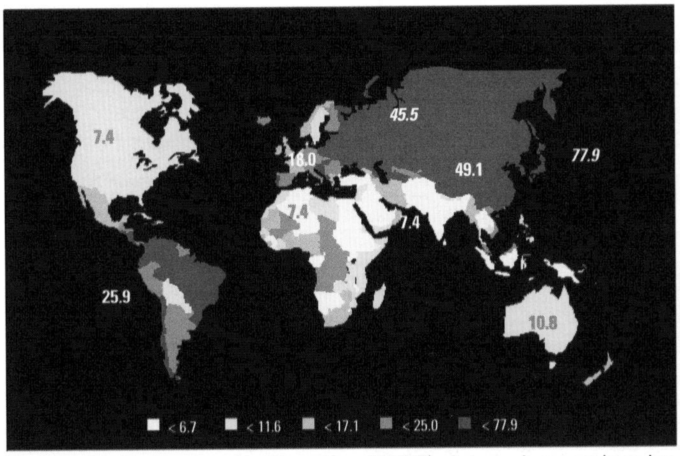

Fig. 3.01 Worldwide annual incidence (per 100,000) of stomach cancer in males. Numbers on the map indicate regional average values.

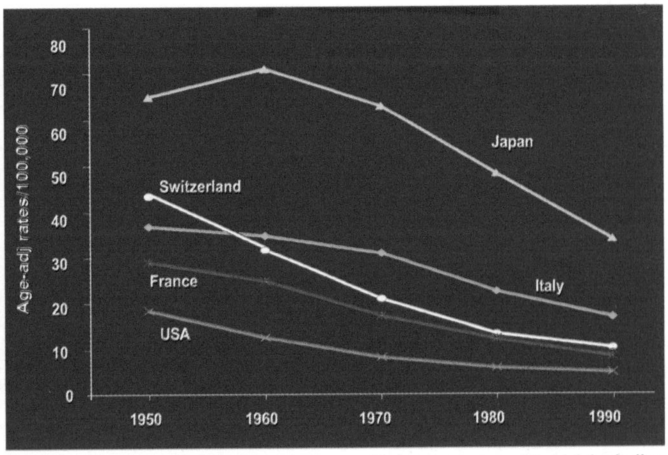

Fig. 3.02 The mortality of stomach cancer is decreasing worldwide, including countries with a high disease burden.

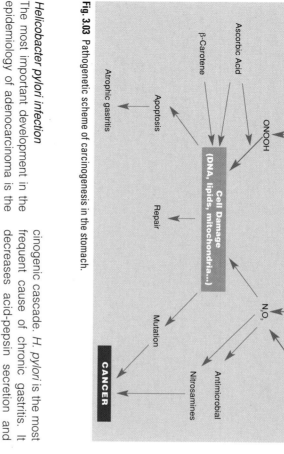

Fig. 3.03 Pathogenetic scheme of carcinogenesis in the stomach.

Helicobacter pylori infection

The most important development in the epidemiology of adenocarcinoma is the recognition of its association with *Helicobacter pylori* infection. Strong epidemiological evidence came from three independent prospective cohort studies reporting a significantly increased risk in subjects who 10 or more years before the cancer diagnosis had anti-*H. pylori* antibodies, demonstrable in stored serum samples {1371, 1473, 519}. At the pathological level, *H. pylori* has been shown to induce the phenotypic changes leading up to the development of adenocarcinoma (i.e. mucosal atrophy, intestinal metaplasia and dysplasia) in both humans and in experimental animals {1635, 350, 2069}.

A prolonged precancerous process, lasting decades, precedes most gastric cancers. It includes the following sequential steps: chronic gastritis, multifocal atrophy, intestinal metaplasia, and intraepithelial neoplasia {342}. Gastritis and atrophy alter gastric acid secretion, elevating gastric pH, changing the flora and allowing anaerobic bacteria to colonize the stomach. These bacteria produce active reductases that transform food nitrate into nitrite, an active molecule capable of reacting with amines, amides and ureas to produce carcinogenic N-nitroso compounds {2167}. *H. pylori* acts as a gastric pathogen and it is important in several steps in the car-

cinogenic cascade. *H. pylori* is the most frequent cause of chronic gastritis. It decreases acid-pepsin secretion and interferes with anti-oxidant functions by decreasing intragastric ascorbic acid (AA) concentrations. The organisms predominantly occur in the mucus layer overlying normal gastric epithelium. They are absent in areas overlying intestinal metaplasia where neoplasia originates. Thus, *H. pylori's* carcinogenic influences are exerted from a distance, via soluble bacterial products or the inflammatory response generated by the infection.

H. pylori genome. *H. pylori* is genetically heterogeneous, and all strains may not play the same role in the development of malignancy. Strains containing a group of genes named cag pathogenicity island {264} induce a greater degree of inflammation than strains lacking these genes. The mechanism involves epithelial production of interleukin 8 via a nuclear factor KappaB pathway. There is an association between an infection with a cag positive *H. pylori* strain and the development of gastric carcinoma {1549}.

The determination of the complete DNA sequence of two *H. pylori* strains has shown other similar 'islands' are also present in the *H. pylori* genome. Research is ongoing to determine whether strain-specific genes located in one of these islands named the plasticity zone, or outside on the rest of the chromo-

some, could be associated with gastric carcinogenesis. *H. pylori* can also produce a vacuolating cytotoxin named VacA. This cytotoxin, responsible for epithelial cell damage, also associates with gastric carcinogenesis {1771}. The aetiological role of *H. pylori* in gastric carcinogenesis was confirmed when inoculation of a cag and VacA positive strain was able to induce intestinal metaplasia and gastric carcinoma in Mongolian gerbils {2069}.

Excessive cell proliferation. Cell replication, a requisite of carcinogenesis, potentiates action of carcinogens targeting DNA. The higher the replication rate, the greater the chance that replication errors become fixed and expressed in subsequent cell generations. Spontaneous mutations lead to subsequent neoplastic transformation, but whether or not they cause epidemic increases in cancer rates is debatable. The latter is better explained by the presence of external or endogenous carcinogens. Proliferation is higher in *H. pylori* infected than in non-infected stomachs; it declines significantly after infection eradication {187} supporting the mitogenic influence of *H. pylori* on gastric epithelium. Ammonia, a substance stimulating cell replication, is abundantly liberated by the potent urease activity of *H. pylori* in the immediate vicinity of gastric epithelium.

Oxidative stress. Gastritis is associated with increased production of oxidants and reactive nitrogen intermediates, including nitric oxide (NO). There is an increased expression of the inducible isoform of nitric oxide synthase in gastritis {1157}. This isoform causes continuous production of large amounts of NO. NO can also be generated in the gastric lumen from non-enzymatic sources. Acidification of nitrite to NO produces the reactive nitrogen species dinitrogen trioxide (N2O3), a potent nitrosating agent that forms nitrosothiols and nitrosamines {628}. Nitrosated compounds are recognized gastric carcinogens in the experimental setting.

Interference with antioxidant functions. Ascorbic acid (AA), an antioxidant, is actively transported from blood to the gastric lumen by unknown mechanisms. Its putative anti-carcinogenic role is by preventing oxidative DNA damage. *H. pylori* infected individuals have lower AA intragastric concentrations than non-infected subjects. Following *H. pylori* treatment, intragastric AA concentrations increase to levels resembling those of non-infected individuals {1613}.

DNA damage. Free radicals, oxidants and reactive nitrogen species all cause DNA damage {344}. These usually generate point mutations, the commonest being G:C→A:T, the commonest type of transformation in cancer with a strong link to chemical carcinogenesis. Peroxynitrite forms nitro-guanine adducts that induce DNA damage, generating either DNA repair or apoptosis. The latter process removes cells containing damaged DNA from the pool of replicating cells in order to avoid introduction of mutations into the genome and an associated heightened cancer risk. NO impairs DNA repair by compromising the activity of Fpg, a DNA repair protein. Thus, NO not only causes DNA damage but it also impairs repair mechanisms designed to prevent the formation of genetic mutations.

As noted, cell proliferation increases in *H. pylori* infection. This increased replication is balanced by increased cell death. It is likely that the increased mitoses are a response to increased epithelial loss. However, the replicative rate exceeds apoptotic rates in patients infected with the virulent cagA vacA s1a *H. pylori* {1481} suggesting that cell loss also occurs via desquamation in patients infected by toxigenic *H. pylori* strains. Antitoxin derived from *H. pylori* also induces apoptosis. In patients with *H. pylori* gastritis, treatment with anti-oxidants attenuates the degree of apoptosis and peroxynitrite formation {1481}. It seems more than coincidental that dietary nitrite, nitrosamines and *H. pylori*-induced gastritis share so much chemistry and their association with cancer. As this process is chronic, the opportunity for random hits to the genome to occur at critical sites increases dramatically.

Localization

The most frequent site of sub-cardial stomach cancer is the distal stomach, i.e. the antro-pyloric region. Carcinomas in the body or the corpus of the stomach are typically located along the greater or lesser curvature.

Clinical features

Symptoms and signs

Early gastric cancer often causes no symptoms, although up to 50% of patients may have nonspecific gastrointestinal complaints such as dyspepsia. Among patients in Western countries who have endoscopic evaluations for dyspepsia, however, gastric carcinoma is found in only 1-2% of cases (mostly in men over the age of 50). Symptoms of advanced carcinoma include abdominal pain that is often persistent and unrelieved by eating. Ulcerated tumours may cause bleeding and haematemesis, and tumours that obstruct the gastric outlet may cause vomiting. Systemic symptoms such as anorexia and weight loss suggest disseminated disease.

The lack of early symptoms often delays the diagnosis of gastric cancer. Consequently, 80-90% of Western patients with gastric cancers present to the physician with advanced tumours that have poor rates of curability. In Japan, where gastric cancer is common, the government has encouraged mass screening of the adult population for this tumour. Approximately 80% of gastric malignancies detected by such screening programs are early gastric cancers. However, many individuals do not choose to participate in these screening programs, and consequently only approximately 50% of all gastric cancers in Japan are diagnosed in an early stage.

Imaging and endoscopy

Endoscopy is widely regarded as the most sensitive and specific diagnostic test for gastric cancer. With high resolution endoscopy, it is possible to detect slight changes in colour, relief, and architecture of the mucosal surface that suggest early gastric cancer. Endoscopic detection of these early lesions can be improved with chromoendoscopy (e.g. using indigo carmine solution at 0.4 %). Even with these procedures, a substantial number of early gastric cancers can be missed {745A}.

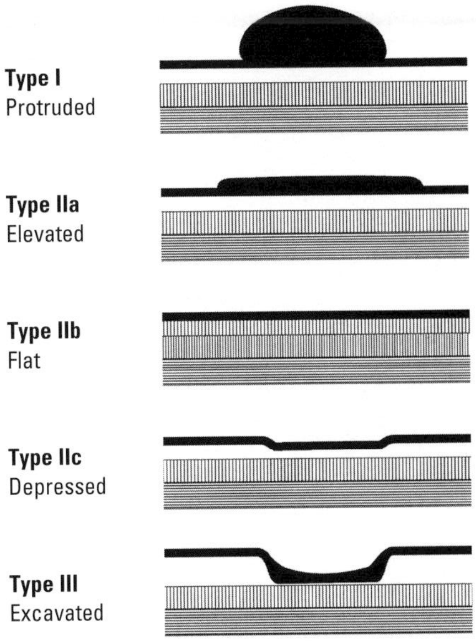

Gastric cancers can be classified endoscopically according to the growth pattern {1298, 63} The patterns I, II and III of superficial cancer (Fig. 3.03) reflect the gross morphology of the operative specimen. The risk of deep and multifocal penetration into the submucosa and the risk of lymphatic invasion is higher in type IIc, the depressed variant of type II. Infiltration of the gastric wall (linitis plastica) may not be apparent endoscopically. This lesion may be suspected if there is limited flexibility of the gastric wall. Diagnosis may require multiple, jumbo biopsies. The depth of invasion of the tumour is staged with endoscopic ultrasound. A 5-layer image is obtained at 7.5/12 MHz: in superficial (T1) cancer the second hyperechoic layer is not interrupted.

Radiology with barium meal is still used in mass screening protocols in Japan, followed by endoscopy if an abnormality has been detected. For established gas-

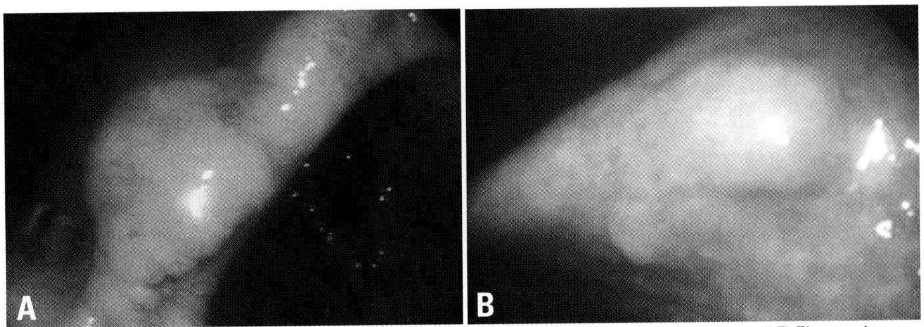

Type I Protruded

Type IIa Elevated

Type IIb Flat

Type IIc Depressed

Type III Excavated

Fig. 3.04 Growth features of early gastric carcinoma.

Fig. 3.05 Endoscopic views of early, well differentiated adenocarcinoma. **A** Polypoid type. **B** Elevated type.

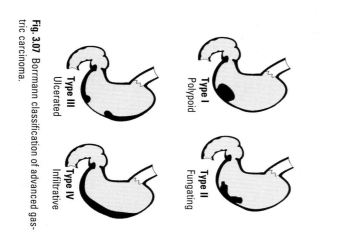

Fig. 3.07 Borrmann classification of advanced gastric carcinoma.

Type I
Polyploid

Type II
Fungating

Type III
Ulcerated

Type IV
Infiltrative

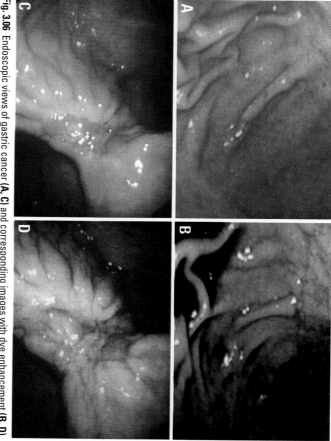

Fig. 3.06 Endoscopic views of gastric cancer (**A, C**) and corresponding images with dye enhancement (**B, D**). **A, B** Depressed early gastric cancer. **C, D** Deep ulcer scar surrounded by superficial early gastric cancer infiltrating the mucosa and submucosa.

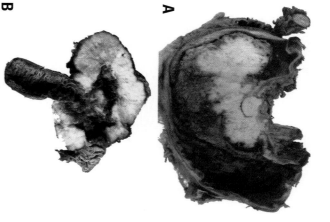

Fig. 3.08 Gastric adenocarcinoma of (**A**) polypoid and (**B**) diffusely infiltrative type.

tric cancers, radiology usually is not necessary, but may complement endoscopic findings in some cases. Tumour staging prior to treatment decision involves percutaneous ultrasound or computerized tomography to detect liver metastases and distant lymph node metastases. Laparoscopic staging may be the only way to exclude peritoneal seeding in the absence of ascites.

Macroscopy

Dysplasia may present as a flat lesion (difficult to detect on conventional endoscopy, but apparent on dye-staining endoscopy) or polypoid growth. Appearances intermediate between them include a depressed or reddish or discoloured mucosa. The macroscopic type of early gastric carcinoma is classified using critera similar to those in endoscopy (Fig. 3.03) {1298, 63}. The gross appearance of advanced carcinoma forms the basis of the Borrmann classification (Fig. 3.06) {63, 175}.

Ulcerating types II or III are common. Diffuse (infiltrative) tumours (type IV) spread superficially in the mucosa and submucosa, producing flat, plaque-like lesions, with or without shallow ulcerations. With extensive infiltration, a linitis plastica or 'leather bottle' stomach results. Mucinous adenocarcinomas appear gelatinous with a glistening cut surface.

Tumour spread and staging

Gastric carcinomas spread by direct extension, metastasis or peritoneal dissemination. Direct tumour extension involves adjacent organs. Tumours invading the duodenum are most often of the diffuse type and the frequency of serosal, lymphatic, and vascular invasion and lymph node metastases in these lesions is high. Duodenal invasion may occur

through the submucosa or subserosa or via the submucosal lymphatics. Duodenal invasion occurs more frequently than expected based on gross examination. Therefore, resection margins should be monitored by intraoperative consultation.

Intestinal carcinomas preferentially metastasize haematogenously to the liver, whereas diffuse carcinomas preferentially metastasize to peritoneal surfaces {1273, 245}. An equal incidence of lymph node metastases occurs in both types of tumours with T2 or higher lesions. Mixed tumours exhibit the metastatic patterns of both intestinal and diffuse types. When carcinoma penetrates the serosa, peritoneal implants flourish. Bilateral massive ovarian involvement (*Krukenberg tumour*) can result from transperitoneal or haematogenous spread.

The principal value of nodal dissection is the detection and removal of metastatic disease and appropriate tumour staging. The accuracy of pathological staging is proportional to the number of regional lymph nodes examined and their location. When only nodes close to the tumour are assessed, many cancers are classified incorrectly.

Histopathology

Gastric adenocarcinomas are either gland-forming malignancies composed

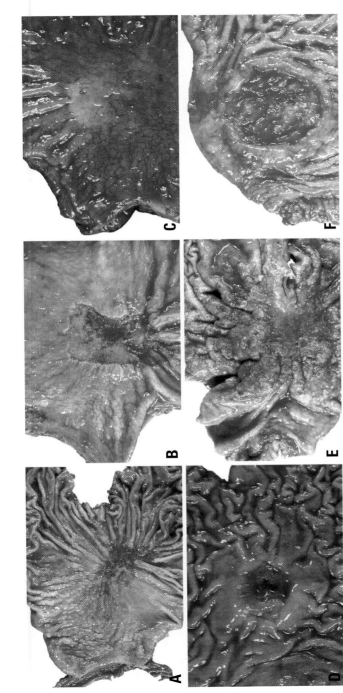

Fig. 3.09 A Depressed adenocarcinoma. **B** Depressed signet ring cell carcinoma. **C** Gastric cancer, dye sprayed (pale area). **D, E, F** Advanced gastric carcinoma with varying degrees of infiltration.

of tubular, acinar or papillary structures, or they consist of a complex mixture of discohesive, isolated cells with variable morphologies, sometimes in combination with glandular, trabecular or alveolar solid structures {243}. Several classification systems have been proposed, including Ming, Carniero, and Goseki {1623}, but the most commonly used are those of WHO and Laurén {419, 87}.

WHO classification

Despite their histological variability, usually one of four patterns predominates. The diagnosis is based on the predominant histological pattern.

Tubular adenocarcinomas

These contain prominent dilated or slit-like and branching tubules varying in their diameter; acinar structures may be

present. Individual tumour cells are columnar, cuboidal, or flattened by intra-luminal mucin. Clear cells may also be present. The degree of cytological atypia varies from low to high-grade {466, 1362}. A poorly differentiated variant is sometimes called *solid carcinoma*. Tumours with a prominent lymphoid stroma are sometimes called *medullary carcinomas or carcinomas with lymphoid stroma* {2063}. The degree of desmoplasia varies and may be conspicuous.

Papillary adenocarcinomas

These are well-differentiated exophytic carcinomas with elongated finger-like processes lined by cylindrical or cuboidal cells supported by fibrovascular connective tissue cores. The cells tend to maintain their polarity. Some tumours show tubular differentiation

(papillotubular). Rarely, a micropapillary architecture is present. The degree of cellular atypia and mitotic index vary; there may be severe nuclear atypia. The invading tumour edge is usually sharply demarcated from surrounding structures; the tumour may be infiltrated by acute and chronic inflammatory cells.

Mucinous adenocarcinomas

By definition, > 50% of the tumour contains extracellular mucinous pools. The two major growth patterns are (1) glands lined by a columnar mucous-secreting epithelium together with interstitial mucin and (2) chains or irregular cell clusters floating freely in mucinous lakes. There may also be mucin in the interglandular stroma. Scattered signet-ring cells, when present, do not dominate the histological picture. Grading mucinous adenocarci-

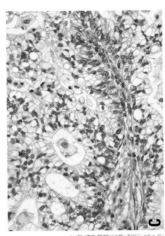

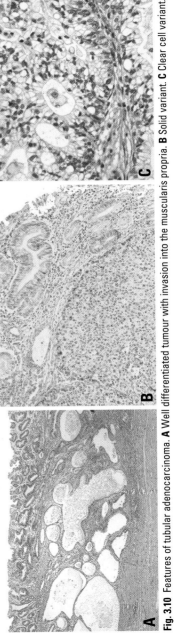

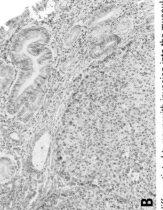

Fig. 3.10 Features of tubular adenocarcinoma. **A** Well differentiated tumour with invasion into the muscularis propria. **B** Solid variant. **C** Clear cell variant.

Fig. 3.11 A, B Tubular adenocarcinoma.

Fig. 3.12 A Papillary adenocarcinoma. **B** Well differentiated mucinous adenocarcinoma.

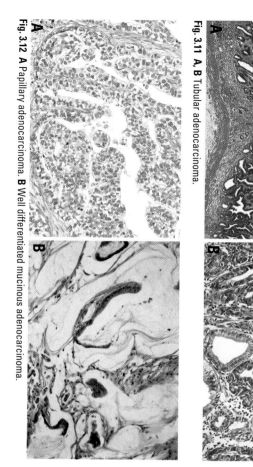

Fig. 3.13 Signet-ring cell carcinomas. **A** Overview showing infiltration of the lamina propria in the mucosa. **B** Dispersed signet-ring cells. **C** Accumulation of neoplastic signet ring cells in the mucosa. **D** Alcian green positive signet-ring cells expanding the lamina propria in this Movat stain.

nomas is unreliable in tumours containing only a few cells. The term 'mucin-producing' is not synonymous with mucinous in this context.

Signet-ring cell carcinomas

More than 50% of the tumour consists of isolated or small groups of malignant cells containing intracytoplasmic mucin.

Superficially, cells lie scattered in the lamina propria, widening the distances between the pits and glands. The tumour cells have five morphologies: (1) Nuclei push against cell membranes creating a classical signet ring cell appearance due to an expanded, globoid, optically clear cytoplasm. These contain acid mucin and stain with Alcian blue at pH 2.5; (2)

other diffuse carcinomas contain cells with central nuclei resembling histiocytes, and show little or no mitotic activity; (3) small, deeply eosinophilic cells with prominent, but minute, cytoplasmic granules containing neutral mucin; (4) small cells with little or no mucin, and (5) anaplastic cells with little or no mucin. These cell types intermingle with one another and constitute varying tumour proportions. Signet-ring cell tumours may also form lacy or delicate trabecular glandular patterns and they may display a zonal or solid arrangement.

Signet-ring cell carcinomas are infiltrative; the number of malignant cells is comparatively small and desmoplasia may be prominent. Special stains, including mucin stains (PAS, mucicarmine, or Alcian blue) or immunohistochemical staining with antibodies to cytokeratin, help detect sparsely dispersed tumour cells in the stroma. Cytokeratin immunostains detect a greater percentage of neoplastic cells than do mucin stains. Several conditions mimic signet-ring cell carcinoma including signet-ring lymphoma, lamina propria muciphages, xanthomas and detached or dying cells associated with gastritis.

Laurén classification

The Laurén classification {1021} has proven useful in evaluating the natural history of gastric carcinoma, especially with regard to its association with environmental factors, incidence trends and its precursors. Lesions are classified into one of two major types: intestinal or diffuse. Tumours that contain approximately equal quantities of intestinal and diffuse components are called *mixed carcinomas*. Carcinomas too undifferentiated to fit neatly into either category are placed in the *indeterminate* category.

Intestinal carcinomas

These form recognizable glands that range from well differentiated to moderately differentiated tumours, sometimes with poorly differentiated tumour at the advancing margin. They typically arise on a background of intestinal metaplasia. The mucinous phenotype of these cancers is intestinal, gastric and gastrointestinal.

Diffuse carcinomas

They consist of poorly cohesive cells diffusely infiltrating the gastric wall with little

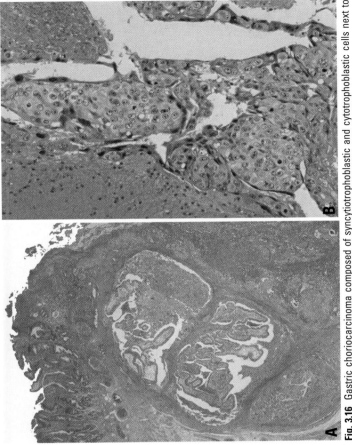

Fig. 3.16 Gastric choriocarcinoma composed of syncytiotrophoblastic and cytotrophoblastic cells next to thin-walled vascular structures. **A** Papillary carcinoma component is adjacent to the choriocarcinoma. **B** High magnification of the choriocarcinoma.

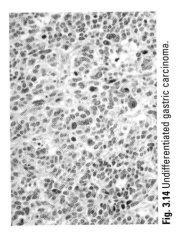

Fig. 3.14 Undifferentiated gastric carcinoma.

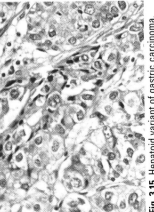

Fig. 3.15 Hepatoid variant of gastric carcinoma.

or no gland formation. The cells usually appear round and small, either arranged as single cells or clustered in abortive, lacy gland-like or reticular formations. These tumours resemble those classified as signet-ring cell tumours in the WHO classification. The mitotic rate is lower in diffuse carcinomas than in intestinal tumours. Small amounts of interstitial mucin may be present. Desmoplasia is more pronounced and associated inflammation is less evident in diffuse cancers than in the intestinal carcinomas.

Rare variants
Several other carcinomas exist that are not an integral part of the Laurén or WHO classifications.

Adenosquamous carcinoma
This lesion combines an adenocarcinoma and squamous cell carcinoma; neither quantitatively prevails. Transitions exist between both components. A tumour with a distinct boundary between the two components may represent a *collision tumour*. Tumours containing discrete foci of benign-appearing squamous metaplasia are termed adenocarcinomas with *squamous differentiation* (synonymous with adenoacanthoma).

Squamous cell carcinoma
Pure squamous cell carcinomas develop rarely in the stomach; they resemble squamous cell carcinomas arising elsewhere in the body.

Undifferentiated carcinoma
These lesions lack any differentiated features beyond an epithelial phenotype (e.g. cytokeratin expression). They fall into the indeterminate group of Laurén's scheme. Further analysis of this heterogeneous group using histochemical methods may allow their separation into other types.

Other rare tumours include mixed adenocarcinoma-carcinoid (mixed exocrine-endocrine carcinoma), small cell carcinoma, parietal cell carcinoma, choriocarcinoma, endodermal sinus tumour, embryonal carcinoma, Paneth cell rich-adenocarcinoma and hepatoid adenocarcinoma.

Early gastric cancer
Early gastric cancer (EGC) is a carcinoma limited to the mucosa or the mucosa and submucosa, regardless of nodal status. Countries in which asymptomatic patients are screened have a high incidence of EGCs ranging from 30-50% {1410, 908, 718}, contrasting with a smaller fraction of 16-24% {620, 253, 627} in Western countries. The follow-up of dysplastic lesions does appear to increase the prevalence of EGC. The cost effectiveness of such an integrated

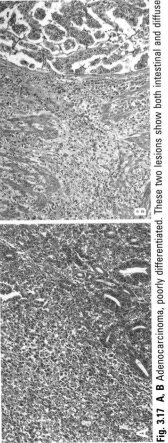

Fig. 3.17 A, B Adenocarcinoma, poorly differentiated. These two lesions show both intestinal and diffuse components (Laurén classification).

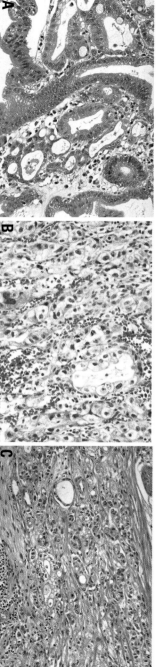

Fig. 3.18 Tubular adenocarcinoma. **A** Well differentiated; intramucosal invasion. **B** Moderately differentiated. **C** Poorly differentiated.

endoscopic/biopsy approach remains to be evaluated {1634, 1638}. Histologically, most subtypes of carcinoma occur in EGC in either pure or mixed forms. Elevated carcinomas with papillary, granular or nodular patterns and a red colour are more often well or moderately differentiated, tubular or papillary tumours with intestinal features; sometimes a pre-existing adenoma is recognizable. Flat, depressed, poorly differentiated carcinomas may contain residual or regenerative mucosal islands. Ulcerated lesions are either intestinal or diffuse cancers. Adenocarcinoma limited to the mucosal thickness has also been divided into small mucosal (< 4cm=SM) and superficial (> 4cm=SUPER) {950}. Both of them may be strictly confined at the mucosal level (small mucosal M and superficial M) or focally infiltrate the sub-mucosa (small mucosal SM and superficial SM). In the penetrating variant, (including two sub-

categories: PenA and PenB) the invasion of the submucosa is more extensive than in the two above-mentioned variants. PenA is defined by a pushing margin, and is less frequent than PenB, which penetrates muscularis mucosae at multiple sites.

The prognosis is worse in PenA carcinomas (in contrast to adenocarcinomas of the colon, where a pushing margin is associated with a better prognosis). The coexistence of more than one of the described patterns results in the mixed variant {950}.

Stromal reactions

The four common stromal responses to gastric carcinoma are marked desmoplasia, lymphocytic infiltrates, stromal eosinophilia and a granulomatous response. The granulomatous reaction is characterized by the presence of single and confluent small sarcoid-like granulomas, often accompanied by a moderately intense mononuclear cell infiltrate. The lymphoid response is associated with an improved survival.

Grading

Well differentiated: An adenocarcinoma with well-formed glands, often resembling metaplastic intestinal epithelium.
Moderately differentiated: An adenocarcinoma intermediate between well differentiated and poorly differentiated.
Poorly differentiated: An adenocarcinoma composed of highly irregular glands that are recognized with difficulty, or single cells that remain isolated or are arranged in small or large clusters with mucin secretions or acinar structures. They may also be graded as *low-grade* (well and moderately differentiated) or *high-grade* (poorly differentiated). Note that this grading system applies primarily to tubular carcinomas. Other types of gastric carcinoma are not graded.

Precursor lesions
Gastritis and intestinal metaplasia

Chronic atrophic gastritis and intestinal metaplasia commonly precede and/or accompany intestinal type adenocarcinoma, particularly in high-incidence areas {780}. *H. pylori* associated gastritis is the commonest gastric precursor lesion.

However, autoimmune gastritis also associates with an increased carcinoma risk. If gastritis persists, gastric atrophy occurs followed by intestinal metaplasia, beginning a series of changes that may result in neoplasia, especially of intestinal type cancers. In contrast, diffuse gastric cancers often arise in a stomach lacking atrophic gastritis with intestinal metaplasia.

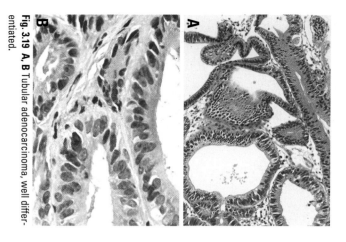

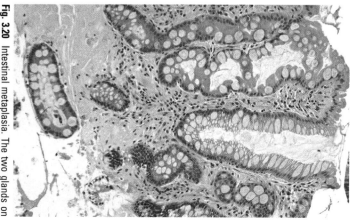

Fig. 3.19 A, B Tubular adenocarcinoma, well differentiated.

Fig. 3.20 Intestinal metaplasia. The two glands on the left exhibit complete intestinal metaplasia, others show the incomplete type.

There are two main types of intestinal metaplasia: 'complete' (also designated as 'small intestinal type' or type I), and 'incomplete' (types II and III) {843}. Different mucin expression patterns characterize the metaplasias: complete shows decreased expression of 'gastric' (MUC1, MUC5AC and MUC6) mucins and expression of MUC2, an intestinal mucin. In incomplete intestinal metaplasia, 'gastric' mucins are co-expressed with MUC2 mucin. These findings show that incomplete intestinal metaplasia has a mixed gastric and intestinal phenotype reflecting an aberrant differentiation program not reproducing any normal adult gastrointestinal epithelial phenotype {1574}.

Intraepithelial neoplasia

Intraepithelial neoplasia (dysplasia) arises in either the native gastric or of intestinalized gastric epithelia. *Pyloric gland adenoma* is a form of intraepithelial neoplasia arising in the native mucosa {2066, 1885}. In the multi-stage theory of gastric oncogenesis, intraepithelial neoplasia lies between atrophic metaplastic lesions and invasive cancer (Table 3.01).

Problems associated with diagnosing gastric intraepithelial neoplasia include the distinction from reactive or regenerative changes associated with active inflammation, and the distinction between intraepithelial and invasive carcinoma {1683, 1025}. Several proposals have been made for the terminology of the morphological spectrum of lesions that lie between non-neoplastic changes and early invasive cancer, including the recent international Padova classification {1636}.

Indefinite for intraepithelial neoplasia

Sometimes, doubts arise as to whether a lesion is neoplastic or non-neoplastic (i.e. reactive or regenerative), particularly in small biopsies. In such cases, the dilemma is usually solved by cutting deeper levels of the block, by obtaining additional biopsies, or after removing possible sources of cellular hyperproliferation. One important source of a potentially alarming lesion is the regeneration associated with NSAID-induced injury or superficial erosion/ulceration caused by gastric acid. Cases lacking all the attributes required for a definitive diagnosis of intraepithelial neoplasia may be placed into the category 'indefinite for intraepithelial neoplasia'. In native gastric mucosa, foveolar hyperproliferation may be indefinite for dysplasia, showing irregular and tortuous tubular structures with epithelial mucus depletion, a high nuclear-cytoplasmic ratio and loss of cellular polarity. Large, oval/round, hyperchromatic nuclei associate with prominent mitoses, usually located near the proliferative zone in the mucous neck region.

In intestinal metaplasia, areas indefinite for intraepithelial neoplasia exhibit a hyperproliferative metaplastic epithelium. The glands may appear closely packed, lined by cells with large, hyperchromatic, rounded or elongated, basally located nuclei. Nucleoli are an inconsistent finding. The cyto-architectural alterations tend to decrease from the base of the glands to their superficial portion.

less common than hyperplastic polyps; overall, they account for approximately 10% of gastric polyps {1843}. They tend to arise in the antrum or mid stomach in areas of intestinal metaplasia.

Morphologically, adenomas can be described as tubular (the most common), tubulovillous, or villous; the latter two have also been called papillotubular and papillary. Most have epithelium of intestinal type, but some have gastric foveolar features.

Low-grade intraepithelial neoplasia

This lesion shows a slightly modified mucosal architecture, including the presence of tubular structures with budding and branching, papillary enfolding, crypt lengthening with serration, and cystic changes. Glands are lined by enlarged columnar cells with minimal or no mucin. Homogeneously blue vesicular, rounded or ovoid nuclei are usually pseudostratified in the proliferation zone located at the superficial portion of the dysplastic tubules.

High-grade intraepithelial neoplasia

There is increasing architectural distortion with glandular crowding and prominent cellular atypia. Tubules can be irregular in shape, with frequent branching and fold-

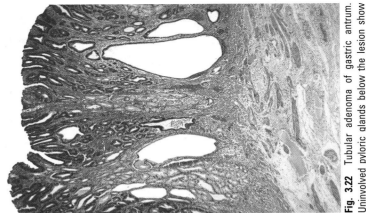

Fig. 3.22 Tubular adenoma of gastric antrum. Uninvolved pyloric glands below the lesion show cystic dilatation.

Intraepithelial neoplasia

It has flat, polypoid, or slightly depressed growth patterns; the flat pattern may lack any endoscopic changes on conventional endoscopy, but shows an irregular appearance on dye endoscopy. In Western countries, the term adenoma is applied when the proliferation produces a macroscopic, usually discrete, protruding lesion. However, in Japan, adenomas include all gross types (i.e. flat, elevated and depressed). Gastric adenomas are

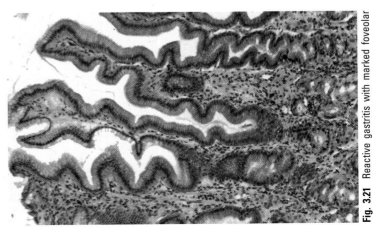

Fig. 3.21 Reactive gastritis with marked foveolar hyperplasia.

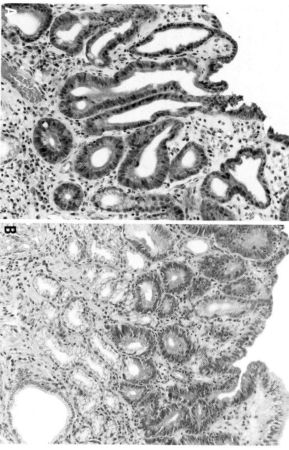

Fig. 3.23 A, B Examples of low-grade intraepithelial neoplasia of flat gastric mucosa. The atypia extends to the surface.

ing; there is no stromal invasion. Mucin secretion is absent or minimal. The pleomorphic, hyperchromatic, usually pseudostratified nuclei are cigar-shaped. Prominent amphophilic nucleoli are common. Increased proliferative activity is present throughout the epithelium.

Progression of intraepithelial neoplasia to carcinoma

Carcinoma is diagnosed when the tumour invades into the lamina propria (intramucosal carcinoma) or through the muscularis mucosae. Some gastric biopsies contain areas suggestive of true invasion (such as isolated cells, gland-like structures, or papillary projections). The term 'suspicious for invasion' is appropriate when the histological criteria for an invasive malignancy are equivocal.

Up to 80% of intraepithelial neoplasias may progress to invasion. Indeed, invasive cancer already may be present in patients found to have high-grade intraepithelial neoplasia with no obvious tumour mass. The extent of intestinal metaplasia associated with intraepithelial neoplasia, together with a sulphomucin-secreting phenotype of the intestinalized mucosa (type III intestinal metaplasia), correlate with an increased risk of carcinoma development.

Adenomas

Adenomas are circumscribed, benign lesions, composed of tubular and/or villous structures showing intraepithelial neoplasia. The frequency of malignant transformation depends on size and histological grade. It occurs in approximately 2% of lesions measuring < 2 cm and in 40-50% of lesions > 2 cm. Flat adenomas may have a greater tendency to progress to carcinoma.

Polyps

Hyperplastic polyps

Hyperplastic polyps are one of the commonest gastric polyps. They are sessile or pedunculated lesions, usually < 2.0 cm in diameter, typically arising in the antrum on a background of *H. pylori* gastritis. They contain a proliferation of surface foveolar cells lining elongated, distorted pits extending deep into the stroma. They may contain pyloric glands, chief cells and parietal cells. The surface often erodes. In a minority of cases, carcinoma develops within the polyps in areas of intestinal metaplasia and dysplasia.

Fundic gland polyps

Fundic gland polyps are the commonest gastric polyp seen in Western populations. They occur sporadically, without a relationship to *H. pylori* (who may also affect patients on long-term proton pump inhibitors or patients with familial adenomatous polyposis (FAP), who may have hundreds of fundic gland polyps {2064, 2065}.

The lesions consist of a localized hyperplasia of the deep epithelial compartment of the oxyntic mucosa, particularly of mucous neck cells, with variable degrees of cystic dilatation. Sporadic fundic gland polyps have no malignant potential. Exceptionally, patients with attenuated FAP may develop dysplasia and carcinoma in their fundic gland polyps {2214, 1204}.

Polyposis syndromes

Peutz-Jeghers polyps, juvenile polyps, and Cowden polyps generally do not occur spontaneously, but rather as part of hereditary polyposis syndromes. In the stomach, Peutz-Jeghers polyps are characterized histologically by branching bands of smooth muscle derived from

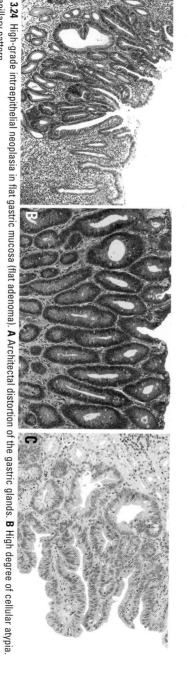

Fig. 3.24 High-grade intraepithelial neoplasia in flat gastric mucosa (flat adenoma). **A** Architectural distortion of the gastric glands. **B** High degree of cellular atypia. **C** Papillary pattern.

Table 3.01
Histological follow-up studies of gastric intraepithelial neoplasia. Proportion progressing to carcinoma and mean interval.

Reports	Low-grade dysplasia			High-grade dysplasia		
Saraga, 1987 {2355}	2%	(1/64)	4 yr.	81%	(17/21)	4 mos.
Lansdown, 1990 {2356}	0	(0/7)		85%	(11/13)	5 mos.
Rugge, 1991 {2008}	17%	(12/69)	1yr.	75%	(6/8)	4 mos.
Fertitta, 1993 {2357}	23%	(7/30)	10 mos.	81%	(25/31)	5 mos.
Di Gregorio, 1993 {2358}	7%	(6/89)	2 yr.	60%	(6/10)	11 mos.
Rugge, 1994 {2009}	14%	(13/90)	2 yr.	78%	(14/18)	9 mos.
Kokkola, 1996 {2359}	0%	(0/96)		67%	(2/3)	1.5 yr.

muscularis mucosae, and hyperplasia, elongation and cystic change of foveolar epithelium; the deeper glandular components tend to show atrophy.

Genetic susceptibility

Most gastric carcinomas occur sporadically; only about 8-10% have an inherited familial component {996}. Familial clustering occurs in 12 to 25% with a dominant inheritance pattern {597, 864}. Case-control studies also suggest a small but consistent increased risk in first-degree relatives of gastric carcinoma patients {2200}.

Gastric carcinoma occasionally develops in families with germline mutations in ATM5, TP53 (Li Fraumeni syndrome) {2001, 743, 1652}, and BRCA2 {1934}. Rare site-specific gastric carcinoma predisposition traits have been reported in several families {1147, 2130}, including that of Napoleon.

Hereditary diffuse gastric carcinoma

Germline mutations in the gene encoding the cell adhesion protein E-cadherin (CDH1) lead to an autosomal dominant predisposition to gastric carcinoma, referred to as hereditary diffuse gastric carcinoma (HDGC) {640, 568}. Predisposing germline CDH1 mutations generally resulting in truncated proteins are spread throughout the gene with no apparent hotspots {641, 640, 568, 1581}. HDGC has an age of onset ranging upwards from 14 years and a penetrance of approximately 70% {641, 568}. Histologically, HDGC tumours are diffuse, poorly differentiated infiltrative adenocarcinomas with occasional signet-ring cells {641, 640, 568}.

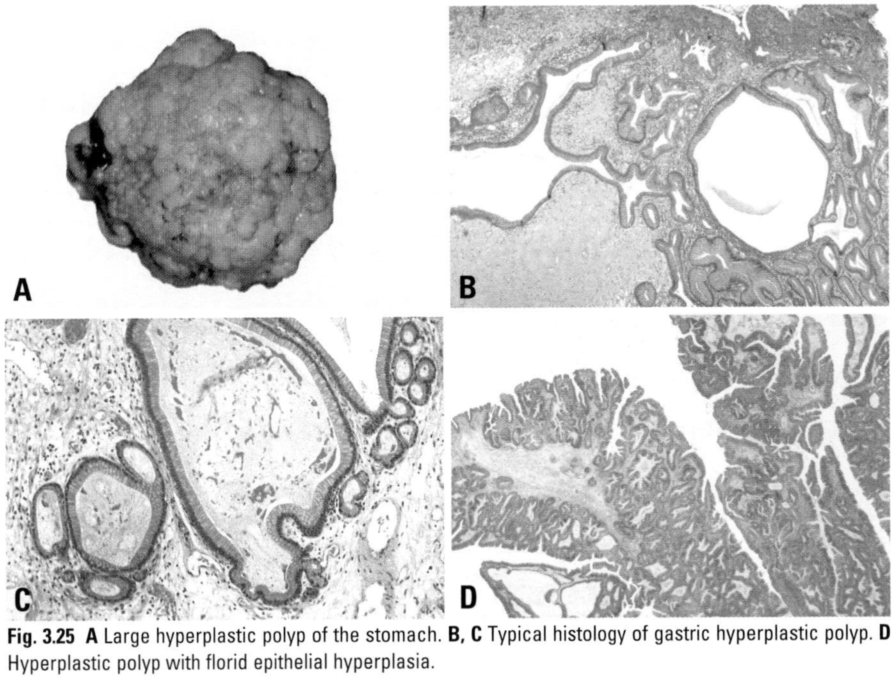

HNPCC

Gastric carcinomas can develop as part of the hereditary nonpolyposis colon cancer (HNPCC) syndrome {1130, 922}. They are intestinal type cancers, without an association with H. pylori infection; most exhibit microsatellite instability (MSI) {4} with a trend that is opposite to that found in tumours arising in young patients {1739}.

Gastrointestional polyposis syndromes

Gastric carcinomas also occur in patients with gastrointestinal polyposis syndromes including FAP and Peutz-Jeghers syndrome.
Overall, gastric carcinoma is rare in these settings, and the exact contribution of the polyposis and underlying germline alterations of APC and LKB1/STK11 to cancer development is unclear.

Blood group A

The blood group A phenotype associates with gastric carcinomas {27, 649}. H. pylori adhere to the Lewis[b] blood group antigen and the latter may be an important host factor facilitating this chronic infection {244} and subsequent cancer risk.

Molecular genetics

Loss of heterozygosity studies and comparative genomic hybridization (CGH) analyses have identified several loci with significant allelic loss, indicating possible tumour suppressor genes important in gastric carcinoma. Common target(s) of loss or gain include chromosomal regions 3p, 4, 5q, (30 to 40% at or near APC's locus) {1656, 1577}, 6q {255}, 9p, 17p (over 60 percent at TP53's locus) {1656}, 18q (over 60 percent at DCC's locus) {1981}, and 20q {1287, 449, 2192}. Similar LOH losses at 11p15 occur in proximal and distal carcinomas, suggesting common paths of develop-

Fig. 3.25 A Large hyperplastic polyp of the stomach. B, C Typical histology of gastric hyperplastic polyp. D Hyperplastic polyp with florid epithelial hyperplasia.

ment {1288}. Loss of a locus on 7q (D7S95) associates with peritoneal metastasis.

The frequency of MSI in sporadic gastric carcinoma ranges from 13% to 44% {1713}. MSI+ tumours tend to be advanced intestinal-type cancers. The degree of genome-wide instability varies with more significant instability (e.g., MSI-H: > 33% abnormal loci) occurring in only 16% of gastric carcinoma, usually of the subcardial intestinal or mixed type, with less frequent lymph node or vessel invasion, prominent lymphoid infiltration, and better prognosis {430}. Loss of either hMLH1 or hMSH2 protein expression affects all MSI-H cases {654} suggesting

inactivation of both alleles by mechanisms such as hypermethylation {1050, 510}.

Genes with simple tandem repeat sequences within their coding regions that are altered in MSI+ tumours include the TGF-β II receptor, BAX, IGFRII, hMSH3, hMSH6, and E2F-4. A study of mixed tumours displaying the MSI-H phenotype reveal that a majority contain mutated TGF-β type II receptors in a polyadenine tract {1420, 1462}. Altered TGF-β II receptor genes can also be found in MSI-lesions.

Allelic loss of TP53 occurs in > 60% of cases and mutations are identified in approximately 30-50% of cases depending on the mutational screening method and sample sizes {729, 1937}. TP53 mutations are identifiable in some intestinal metaplasias; {497} most alterations affect advanced tumours. TP53 mutations in gastric lesions resemble those seen in other cancers with a predominance of base transitions, especially at CpG dinucleotides. Immunohistochemical analyses to detect TP53 overexpression can indirectly identify TP53 mutations but do not have consistent prognostic value in gastric carcinoma patients {557, 766}. Finally, with respect to TP53, there is a polymorphism in codon 72 encoding a proline rather than an arginine that strongly associates with antral cancers {1735}.

Sporadic gastric carcinomas, especially diffuse carcinomas, exhibit reduced or abnormal E-cadherin expression {1196, 1135}, and genetic abnormalities of the E-cadherin gene and its transcripts. Reduced E-cadherin expression is associated with reduced survival {848}.

E-cadherin splice site alterations produce exon deletion and skipping. Large deletions including allelic loss and missense point mutations also occur; some tumours exhibit alterations in both alleles {135}. Somatic E-cadherin gene alterations also affect the diffuse component of mixed tumours {1136}. Alpha-catenin, which binds to the intracellular domain of E-cadherin and links it to actin-based cytoskeletal elements, shows reduced immunohistochemical expression in many tumours and correlates with infiltrative growth and poor differentiation {1189}. Beta catenin may also be abnormal in gastric carcinoma.

There is evidence of a tumour suppressor locus on chromosome 3p in gastric carcinomas {893, 1688}. This area encodes the FHIT gene. Gastric carcinomas develop abnormal transcripts, deleted exons {1411}, a somatic missense mutation in exon 6 and loss of FHIT protein expression {102}.

Somatic APC mutations, mostly missense in nature and low in frequency, affect Japanese patients with in situ and invasive neoplasia {1309}. Significant allelic loss (30%) at the APC loci suggest that there is a tumour suppressor gene important in gastric tumourigenesis nearby. Indeed, alternative loci have been mapped to commonly deleted regions in gastric carcinomas {1891}.

Amplification and overexpression of the c-met gene encoding a tyrosine kinase receptor for the hepatocyte growth factor occurs in gastric carcinoma {976}. Other growth factor and receptor signal systems that may be involved include epidermal growth factor, TGF-alpha, interleukin-1-a, cripto, amphiregulin, platelet-derived

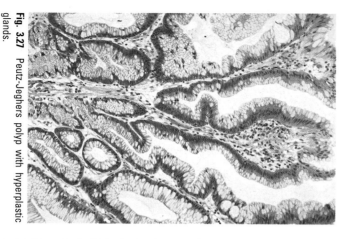

Fig. 3.27 Peutz-Jeghers polyp with hyperplastic glands.

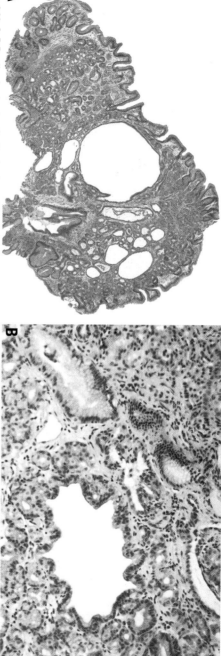

A

B

Fig. 3.26 A, B Fundic gland polyp. Cystic glands are typical.

growth factor, and K-sam {1879}. Amplification of *c-erbB-2*, a transmembrane tyrosine kinase receptor oncogene, occurs in approximately 10% of lesions and overexpression associates with a poor prognosis {375}. Telomerase activity has been detected by a PCR-based assay frequently in the late stages of gastric tumours and observed to be associated with a poor prognosis {719}.

advanced cases. Lymph node status, which is part of the TNM system, is also an important prognostic indicator. The 5th edition of the UICC TNM Classification of Malignant Tumours {66} and the AJCC Manual for the Staging of Cancer {1} published in 1997, have a number-based

classification scheme for reporting nodal involvement in gastric cancer. Roder et al recently published data supporting the value of this reporting system. These authors found that for patients who had nodal involvement in 1-6 lymph nodes (pN1), the 5-year sur-

Prognosis and predictive factors
Early gastric cancer

In early gastric cancers, small mucosal (< 4 cm), superficial (> 4 cm) and Pen B lesions have a low incidence of vessel invasion and lymph node metastasis and a good prognosis after surgery (about 90% of patients survive 10 years). In contrast, penetrating lesions of the Pen A type are characterized by a relatively high incidence of vessel invasion and lymph node metastasis and a poor prognosis after surgery (64.8% 5-year survival).

Advanced gastric cancer

Staging. The TNM staging system for gastric cancer is widely used and it provides important prognostic information. Lymphatic and vascular invasion carries a poor prognosis and is often seen in

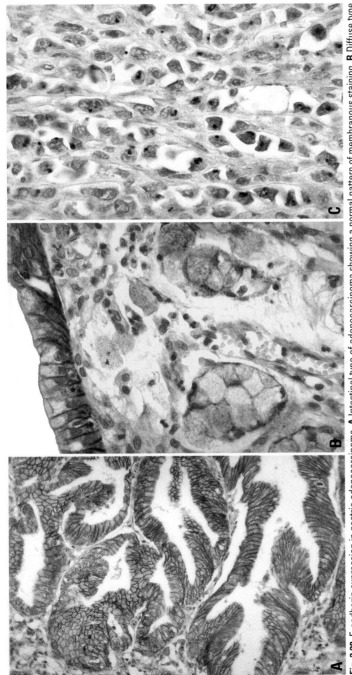

Fig. 3.28 E-cadherin expression in gastric adenocarcinoma. **A** Intestinal type of adenocarcinoma showing a normal pattern of membranous staining. **B** Diffuse type of adenocarcinoma with reduced E-cadherin expression. Normal expression can be seen in the non-neoplastic gastric epithelium overlying the tumour. **C** Undifferentiated gastric carcinoma with highly reduced membranous expression and dot-like cytoplasmic expression.

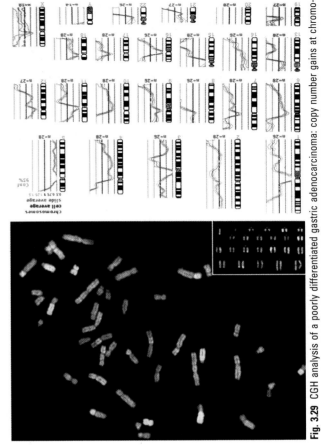

Fig. 3.29 CGH analysis of a poorly differentiated gastric adenocarcinoma: copy number gains at chromosomes 3q21, 7p15, 8q, 10p12-15, 11q13, 12q24, 13q13-14, 15q23-25, 17q24, 20 and 21q21. Copy number losses at chromosomes 4q12-28 and 5.

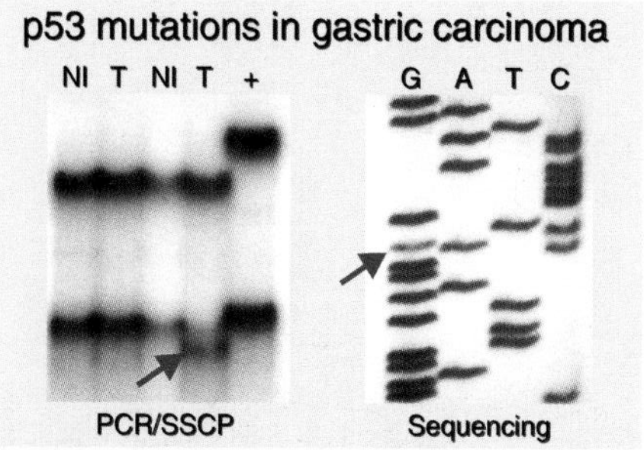

p53 mutations in gastric carcinoma

Fig. 3.30 *TP53* mutations in gastric carcinoma. The mutations are shown by both single-strand conformation polymorphisms (SSCP) as well as direct sequencing. There is a G to A substitution indicated by the right hand panel.

vival rate was 44% compared with a 30% survival rate in patients with 7-15 lymph nodes involved with tumour (pN2). Patients with more than 15 lymph nodes involved by metastatic tumour (pN3) had an even worse 5-year survival of 11% {1602}. Gastric carcinoma with obvious invasion beyond the pyloric ring, and those without evidence of duodenal invasion have 5-year survival rates of 8%, 22%, and 58%, respectively {671}. Patients with T1 cancers limited to the mucosa and submucosa have a 5-year sur-

survival of approximately 95%. Tumours that invade the muscularis propria have a 60-80% 5-year survival, whereas tumours invading the subserosa have a 50% 5-year survival {2181}. Unfortunately, most patients with advanced carcinoma already have lymph node metastases at the time of diagnosis.

Histological features. The value of the histological type of tumour in predicting tumour prognosis is more controversial. This relates in part to the classification scheme that is used to diagnose the cancers. Using the Laurén classification, some believe that diffuse lesions generally carry a worse prognosis than intestinal carcinomas. The prognosis is particularly bad in children and young adults, in whom the diagnosis is often delayed {1986, 1554} and likely fit into the category of HDGC. However, others have not found the Laurén classification to predict prognosis {1788, 1177}. One study found that only the Goseki classification {610} added additional prognostic information to the TNM stage {610}. 5-year survival of patients with mucus rich (Goseki II and IV) T3 tumours was significantly worse than that of patients with mucus poor (Goseki I and III) T3 tumours (18% vs. 53% p<0.003) {1177}. A second study

validated these findings {1788}. Another classification scheme for gastric carcinoma was proposed by Carneiro et al that may also have prognostic value {610}. The recognition of mixed carcinoma may be important since patients harbouring this type of carcinoma may also have a poor outcome {610}.

Some patients with medullary carcinomas with circumscribed, pushing growth margins and a marked stromal inflammatory reaction exhibit a better prognosis than those with other histological tumour types {430}. Some of these patients are in HNPCC kindreds who have MSI-H, a feature associated with better survival. However, not all studies agree that stromal response and pushing margins predict a better prognosis {1788, 1177}.

In summary, gastric carcinoma is a heterogeneous disease biologically and genetically, and a clear working model of gastric tumourigenesis has yet to be formulated. More tumours appear to be related to environmental than to genetic causes, although both may play a role in individual cases. Characterization of the various pathways should afford multiple opportunities to design more specific and therefore more effective therapies.

Endocrine tumours of the stomach

C. Capella
E. Solcia
L.H. Sobin
R. Arnold

Definition

Most endocrine tumours of the stomach are well differentiated, nonfunctioning enterochromaffin-like (ECL) cell carcinoids arising from oxyntic mucosa in the corpus or fundus. Three distinct types have are recognized: (1) Type I, associated with autoimmune chronic atrophic gastritis (A-CAG); (2) type II, associated with muliple endocrine neoplasia type 1 (MEN-1) and Zollinger-Ellison syndrome (ZES); type III, sporadic, i.e. not associated with hypergastrinaemia or A-CAG.

ICD-O Code

Carcinoid   8240/3
Small cell carcinoma   8041/3

Epidemiology

In the past, carcinoid tumours of the stomach have been reported to occur with an incidence of 0.002-0.1 per 100,000 population per year and to account for 2-3 % of all gastrointestinal carcinoids {587} and 0.3 percent of gastric neoplasms {1132}. More recent studies, however, based on endoscopic techniques and increased awareness of such lesions, have shown a much higher incidence of gastric carcinoids, which may now account for 11-41% of all gastrointestinal carcinoids {1588, 1764, 1782}. The incidence of gastric carcinoids is higher in Japan, where they represent 30% of all gastrointestinal carcinoids, which may be due to the high incidence of chronic atrophic gastritis in this country {1277}.

Age and sex distribution

Type I gastric ECL-cell carcinoids have been reported to represent 74% of gastric endocrine tumours and to occur most often in females (M:F ratio, 1:2.5). The mean age at biopsy is 63 years (range 15-88 years). Type II ECL-cell carcinoids represent 6% of all gastric endocrine tumours and show no gender predilection (M:F ratio, 1:1) at a mean age of 50 years (range 28-67 years) {1590}. Type III ECL-cell carcinoids constitute 13% of all gastric endocrine tumours and are

observed mainly in male patients (M:F ratio, 2.8:1) at a mean age of 55 years (range 21-38 years) {1590}. Small cell carcinoma (poorly differentiated endocrine carcinoma) accounts for 6% of gastric endocrine tumours and prevails in men (M:F ratio, 2:1) at a mean age of 63 years (range 41-61 years) {1590}. Gastrin cell tumours represent less than 1% of gastric endocrine tumours {1590} and are reported in adults (age range 55-77).

Aetiology

Gastrin has a trophic effect on ECL-cells both in humans and experimental animals {172, 652}. Hypergastrinaemic states, resulting either from unregulated hormone release by a gastrinoma or from a secondary response of antral G cells to achlorhydria, are consistently associated with ECL-cell hyperplasia {172}.

Autoimmune chronic atrophic gastritis (A-CAG)

This disease is caused by antibodies to parietal cells of the oxyntic mucosa. It leads to chronic atrophic gastritis (with or without pernicious anaemia) which leads to an increase in gastrin production.

Zollinger-Ellison syndrome

This disease results from hypergastrinaemia due to gastrin-producing neoplasms that are preferentially located in the small intestine and pancreas. ECL-cell proliferation is usually limited to hyperplastic lesions of the simple linear type {1042, 1777}.

MEN-1

This inherited tumour syndrome causes a variety of endocrine neoplasms, including gastrinomas. In patients with MEN-1 associated ZES (MEN-1/ZES), ECL-cell lesions are usually dysplastic or overtly carcinoid in nature {1779}. In the MEN-1 syndrome, the mutation or deletion of the suppressor MEN-1 oncogene in 11q13 may be involved {394} as an additional pathogenetic factor. In A-CAG, achlorhydria or associated mucosal changes may

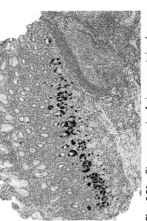

Fig. 3.31 Chromogranin A immunostain demonstrates hyperplasia of endocrine cells at the base of glandular tubules.

contribute to tumourigenesis {1785}. Several growth factors, including transforming growth factor-α (TGFα) and basic fibroblast growth factor (bFGF) seem to be involved in tumour development and progression as well as stromal and vascular proliferation of ECL-cell carcinoids {171}.

Localization

Type I, II, and III ECL-cell carcinoids are all located in the mucosa of the body-fundus of the stomach, whereas the rare G-cell tumours are located in the antro-pyloric region. Small cell carcinomas prevail in the body/fundus, but some are located in the antrum {1590}.

Clinical features

The three distinct types of ECL-cell carcinoids are well differentiated growths but with variable and poorly predictable behaviour.

Type I ECL-cell carcinoids

These are associated with A-CAG involving the corpus and fundus mucosa. Clinical signs include achlorhydria and, less frequently, pernicious anaemia. Hypergastrinaemia or evidence of antral gastrin-cell hyperplasia is observed in all cases of A-CAG. In patients with a carcinoid, ECL-cell hyperplastic changes are a constant feature and dysplastic growths are frequently observed {1590}. A-CAG associated carcinoids are typically small (usually less than 1 cm), multiple and multicentric. Of 152 cases studied by endoscopy, 57% had more than two growths {1561}.

Type II ECL-cell carcinoids

Hypertrophic, hypersecretory gastropathy and high levels of circulating gastrin are critical diagnostic findings. In all cases, ECL-cell hyperplasia and/or dysplasia were noted in the fundic peritumoural mucosa {1590}. These gastric carcinoids are usually multiple and smaller than 1.5 cm in size in the majority of cases {1590}.

Type III (sporadic) ECL-cell carcinoids

These lesions are not associated with hypergastrinaemia or A-CAG. They are generally solitary growths, and arise in the setting of gastric mucosa devoid of ECL-cell hyperplasia/dysplasia and of significant pathologic lesions except for gastritis (other than A-CAG). Rare multiple tumours have been observed {1590}. Clinically, type III tumours present (1) as a mass lesion with no evidence of endocrine symptoms (nonfunctioning carcinoid) and with clinical findings similar to those of adenocarcinoma, including gastric haemorrhage, obstruction and metastasis, or (2) with endocrine symptoms of cutaneous flushing and absence of diarrhoea, usually coupled with liver metastases and production of histamine and 5-hydroxytryptophan {1386, 1598}.

Non ECL-cell gastric carcinoids.

These uncommon tumours may present with ZES due to their gastrin production (which is more frequently found in duodenal gastrinomas) or with Cushing syndrome due to secretion of adrenocorticotrophic hormone (ACTH) {711, 1791}.

Macroscopy

Type I ECL-cell carcinoids are multiple in 57% of cases {1590}, usually appearing as small tan nodules or polyps that are circumscribed in the mucosa or, more often, to the submucosa. Most tumours (77%) are < 1 cm in maximum diameter and 97% of tumours are < 1.5 cm. The muscularis propria is involved in only a minority of cases (7%) {1590}. The stomachs with type II tumours are enlarged and show a thickened gastric wall (0.6-4.5 cm) due to severe hypertrophic-hypersecretory gastropathy and multiple mucosal-submucosal nodules

which, though larger than those of type I, are generally smaller than 1.5 cm in size in 75% of cases {1590}.

Type III ECL-cell tumours are usually single with 33% of the cases larger than 2 cm in diameter. Infiltration of the muscularis propria is found in 76%, and of the serosa in 53% of cases {1590}.

Histopathology

The histopathological categorization of endocrine tumours of the stomach described here, is a modification of the WHO classification of endocrine tumours {1784}.

Carcinoid tumour

A carcinoid is defined morphologically as a well differentiated neoplasm of the diffuse endocrine system.

ECL-cell carcinoid

The majority of type I and type II ECL-cell carcinoids are characterized by small, microlobular-trabecular aggregates formed by regularly distributed, often aligned cells (mosaic-like pattern), with regular, monomorphic nuclei, usually inapparent nucleoli, rather abundant, fairly eosinophilic cytoplasm, almost absent mitoses, and infrequent angioinvasion.

Tumours with these features (grade 1 according to Rindi et al {1589}) are generally limited to mucosa or submucosa {1589} and can be considered as tumours with benign behaviour. The ECL nature of the tumours is confirmed by strong argyrophilia by Grimelius or Sevier Munger techniques and positive immunoreactivity for chromogranin A, in the absence of reactivity for the argentaffin or diazonium tests for serotonin, and no or only occasional immunoreactivity for hormonal products {1591}. Minor cell sub-populations expressing serotonin, gastrin, somatostatin, pancreatic polypeptide (PP), or α-hCG have been detected in a minority of tumours {1591}. A few ECL-cell tumours produce histamine and 5-hydroxy-tryptophan; these lesions, when they metastasize, can produce 'atypical' carcinoid syndrome {1591}. Vesicular monoamine transporter type 2 (VMAT-2) is a suitable and specific marker for ECL-cell tumours {1592} while histamine or histidine decarboxylase immunohistochemical analysis, although specific, is less suitable for routinely processed

specimens {1865}. The ECL-cell nature of argyrophil tumours is ultimately assessed by demonstrating ECL-type granules by electron microscopy {232, 1591}.

Sporadic ECL-cell carcinoids are usually more aggressive than those associated with A-CAG or MEN-1. Histopathologically, these tumours show a prevalence of solid cellular aggregates and large trabeculae, crowding, and irregular distribution of round to spindle and polyhedral tumour cells, fairly large vesicular nuclei with prominent eosinophilic nucleoli, or smaller, hyperchromatic nuclei with irregular chromatin clumps and small nucleoli, considerable mitotic activity, sometimes with atypical mitotic figures and scarce necrosis.

Tumours with these histological features or grade 2 features {1589} show a higher mitotic rate (mean of 9 per 10 HPF), a frequent expression of p53 (60%), a higher

Fig. 3.32 Sporadic (type III) ECL-cell carcinoid of the gastric body. The surrounding mucosa is normal.

Table 3.02.
Histological classification of endocrine neoplasms of the stomach[1]

1. Carcinoid –
well differentiated endocrine neoplasm
  1.1 ECL-cell carcinoid
  1.2 EC-cell, serotonin-producing carcinoid
  1.3 G-cell, gastrin-producing tumour
  1.4 Others

2. Small cell carcinoma –
poorly differentiated endocrine neoplasm

3. Tumour-like lesions
  Hyperplasia
  Dysplasia

[1]Benign behaviour of ECL-cell carcinoid is associated with the following: tumour confined to mucosa-submucosa, nonangioinvasive, < 1 cm in size, nonfunctioning; occurring in CAG or MEN-I / ZES. Aggressive behaviour of ECL-cell carcinoid is associated with the following: tumour invades muscularis propria or beyond, > 1 cm in size, angioinvasive, functioning, and sporadic occurrence.

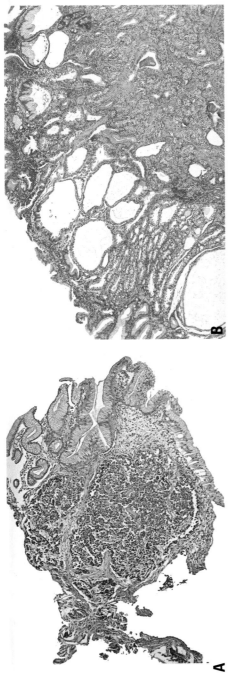

Fig. 3.33 **A** Type I ECL-cell carcinoid in a patient with pernicious anaemia. **B** Type II ECL-cell carcinoid in a patient with MEN1 and ZES.

Ki67 labelling index (above 1000 per 10 HPF) and more frequent lymphatic and vascular invasion than well differentiated ECL-cell carcinoids {1589}. In addition, deeply invasive tumours are associated with local and/or distant metastases in most cases.

EC-cell, serotonin-producing carcinoid

This is a very rare tumour in the stomach {1591}. It is formed by rounded nests of closely packed small tumour cells, often with peripheral palisading, reminiscent of the typical type A histologic pattern of the argentaffin EC-cell carcinoid of the midgut. The tumour cells are argentaffin, intensely argyrophilic and reactive with chromogranin A and anti-serotonin antibodies. Electron microscopic examination confirms the EC-cell nature by detecting characteristic pleomorphic, intensely osmiophilic granules similar to those of normal gastric EC-cells.

Gastrin-cell tumours

Most well differentiated gastrin-cell tumours are small mucosal-submucosal nodules, found incidentally at endoscopy or in a gastrectomy specimen. They may show a characteristic thin trabecular-gyriform pattern or a solid nest pattern. The cells are uniform with scanty cytoplasm and show predominant immunoreactivity for gastrin.

Small cell carcinoma (poorly differentiated endocrine neoplasm)

These are identical to small cell carcinomas of the lung. They correspond to grade 3 tumours according to Rindi et al. {1589}, and are particularly aggressive, malignant tumours {1591}.

Large cell neuroendocrine carcinoma

Large cell neuroendocrine carcinoma is a malignant neoplasm composed of large cells having organoid, nesting, trabecular, rosette-like and palisading patterns that suggest endocrine differentiation, and in which the last can be confirmed by immunohistochemistry and electron microscopy. In contrast to small cell carcinoma, cytoplasm is more abundant, nuclei are more vesicular and nucleoli are prominent {1954}. These tumours have not been well described in the gastrointestinal tract because of their apparent low frequency {1188}.

Mixed exocrine-endocrine carcinomas

These consist of neoplastic endocrine cells composing more than 30% of the whole tumour cell population. They are relatively rare in the stomach, despite the frequent occurrence of minor endocrine components inside the ordinary adenocarcinoma. They should generally be classified as adenocarcinomas.

Precursor lesions

ECL-cell carcinoids arising in hypergastrinaemic conditions (types I and II) develop through a sequence of hyperplasia-dysplasia-neoplasia that has been well documented in histopathological studies {1777}. The successive stages of hyperplasia are termed simple, linear, micronodular, and adenomatoid. Dysplasia is characterized by relatively atypical cells with features of enlarging or fusing micronodules, micro-invasion or newly formed stroma. When the nodules increase in size to > 0.5 mm or invade into the submucosa, the lesion is classified as a carcinoid. The entire spectrum of ECL-cell growth, from hyperplasia to dysplasia and neoplasia has been observed in MEN-1/ZES and autoimmune chronic atrophic gastritis (A-CAG). A similar sequence of lesions has been shown in experimental models of the disease, mostly based on hypergastrinaemia secondary to pharmacological inhibition of acid secretion in rodents {1896}.

Genetic susceptibility

ECL-cell carcinoids are integral components of the MEN-1 syndrome {1042}. In patients with familial MEN-1/ZES, type II gastric carcinoids arise in 13-30% of cases {854, 1042}. However, patients

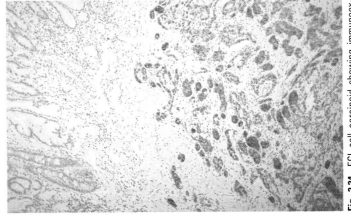

Fig. 3.34 ECL-cell carcinoid showing immunoexpression of chromogranin A.

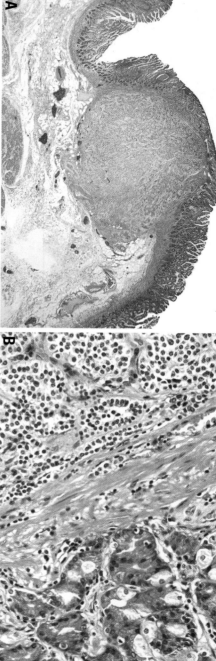

Fig. 3.35 Sporadic (type III) ECL carcinoid. **A** Tumour extends from mucosa into submucosa with well delineated inferior border. **B** The carcinoid (left) has round, regular, isomorphic nuclei.

with sporadic ZES rarely develop gastric carcinoids despite serum gastrin levels, which persist 10 fold above normal for a prolonged time.

Diagnostic criteria of MEN-1

This rare dominantly inherited disorder is characterized by the synchronous or metachronous development of multiple endocrine tumours in different endocrine organs by the third decade of life. The parathyroid glands are involved in 90-97%, endocrine pancreas in 30-82%, duodenal gastrinomas in 25%, pituitary adenomas in more than 60%, and foregut carcinoids (stomach, lung, thymus) in 5-9% of cases {394}. Other, so-called non-classical MEN-1 tumours, such as cutaneous and visceral lipomas, thyroid and adrenal adenomas, and skin angiofibromas, may occur {394, 1444}.

MEN-1 gene

MEN-1 has been mapped to chromosome 11q13 {107, 1015}. It encodes for a 610 amino acid nuclear protein, termed 'menin', whose suppressor function involves direct binding to JunD and inhibition of JunD activated transcription {271, 18}. The tumour suppressor function of the gene has been proposed based on the results of combined tumour deletion and pedigree analysis {107, 271, 394}. High rates of loss of heterozygosity (LOH) at the MEN-1 gene locus have been reported in classic tumours of the MEN-1, such as endocrine pancreatic, pituitary and parathyroid neoplasms {1553, 1923}. LOH at 11q13 of type II gastric carcinoids was found in 9 of 10 MEN-1 patients investigated {123, 173, 219, 394}.

These findings support the concept that these gastric tumours are integral components of the MEN-1 phenotype, sharing with parathyroid and islet cell tumours the highest frequency of LOH at 11q13. In multiple carcinoids from the same stomach, the deletion size in the wild-type allele differed from one tumour to another, suggesting a multiclonal origin {394}. One of the type II tumours showing LOH at 11q13 was in a patient who had neither ZES nor hypergastrinaemia {173}, suggesting that inactivation of the MEN-1 gene alone is capable of causing ECL-cell tumours without requiring the promoting effect of hypergastrinaemia.

The role of MEN-1 in non MEN-associated gastric carcinoids is more controversial. Analysing six type I gastric carcinoids, Debelenko et al. {394} found 11q13 LOH in one tumour while D'Adda et al. {363} detected 11q13 LOH in 12 out of 25 cases (48%). Large deletions in both the 11q13 and 11q14 regions were observed in two poorly differentiated endocrine carcinomas {363}.

Prognosis and predictive factors

The prognosis of carcinoids is highly variable, ranging from slowly growing benign lesions to malignant tumours with extensive metastatic spread.
Benign behaviour of ECL-cell carcinoids is associated with the following: tumour confined to mucosa-submucosa, nonangioinvasive, < 1 cm in size, nonfunctioning; occurring in CAG or MEN-1/ ZES. Type I, A-CAG associated tumours, have an excellent prognosis, as do most type II MEN-1/ZES tumours.
Aggressive behaviour of ECL-cell carcinoid is associated with the following: tumour invades muscularis propria or beyond, is > 1 cm in size, angioinvasive, functioning, with high mitotic activity and sporadic occurrence {1591, 1590, 1589}.
Metastasis: Lymph node metastases are detected in 5% of type I and 30% of type II cases, while distant (liver) metastases are found respectively in 2.5% and 10% of cases. No tumour-related or only exceptional death was observed among patients with type I carcinoid, while only 1/10 patients died of type II carcinoid. On

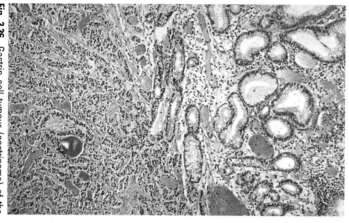

Fig. 3.36 Gastrin cell tumour (gastrinoma) of the pylorus with trabecular growth pattern.

more than on the behaviour of gastric tumours, although some aggressive ECL-cell carcinomas may be fatal {173}. In such patients, careful search for associated pancreatic, duodenal, parathyroid, or other tumours and family investigation for the MEN-1 gene mutation are needed. Type III (sporadic) ECL-cell carcinoids > 1 cm generally require surgical resection even when they are histologically well differentiated.

Therapy
Polypoid type I carcinoids < 1cm, fewer than 3-5 in number, associated with A-CAG can be endoscopically excised and have an excellent prognosis. If larger than 1 cm or more than 3-5 lesions are present, antrectomy and local excision of all accessible fundic lesions is recommended.

In type II carcinoids the clinical evolution depends on the behaviour of associated pancreatic and duodenal gastrinomas

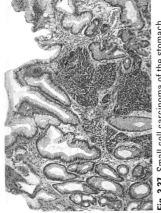

Fig. 3.37 Small cell carcinoma of the stomach.

the other hand, lymph node metastases are found in 71% and distant metastases in 69% of patients with type III tumours;

death from the tumour occurs in 27% of patients with a mean survival of 28 months {1590}.

Lymphoma of the stomach

A. Wotherspoon
A. Chott
R.D. Gascoyne
H.K. Müller-Hermelink

Definition
Primary gastric lymphomas are defined as lymphomas originating from the stomach and contiguous lymph nodes. Lymphomas at this site are considered primary if the main bulk of disease is located in the stomach. The majority of gastric lymphomas are high-grade B-cell lymphomas, some of which have developed through progression from low-grade lymphomas of mucosa associated lymphoid tissue (MALT). The low-grade lesions are almost exclusively B-cell MALT lymphomas.

Historical annotation
Classically, primary gastric lymphomas have been considered to be lymphomas that are confined to the stomach and the contiguous lymph nodes {378}. While this excludes cases of secondary involvement of the stomach by nodal-type lymphomas – which may occur in up to 25% of nodal lymphomas {508} – this definition is excessively restrictive and excludes more disseminated, higher stage lymphomas arising within the stomach as well as those with bone mar-

row involvement. Today, stomach lymphomas are considered primary if the main bulk of disease is present in the stomach. Recognition of morphological features characteristic of primary extranodal lymphomas of mucosa-associated lymphoid tissue-type helps in defining these lesions as primary to the stomach irrespective of the degree of dissemination.

Epidemiology
Approximately 40% of all non-Hodgkin lymphomas arise at extranodal sites {1438, 527}, with the gastrointestinal tract as the commonest extranodal site, accounting for about 4-18% of all non-Hodgkin lymphomas in Western countries and up to 25% of cases in the Middle East. Within the gastrointestinal tract, the stomach is the most frequent site of involvement in Western countries while the small intestine is most frequently affected in Middle Eastern countries. Lymphoma constitutes up to 10% of all gastric malignancies; its incidence appears to be increasing but this may, at least in part, be due to the recognition of

the neoplastic nature of lesions previously termed 'pseudolymphoma' {677}. Gastric lymphoma has a worldwide distribution; somewhat higher incidences have been reported for some Western communities with a high prevalence of *Helicobacter pylori* infection {420}. Primary Hodgkin disease is very rare in the gastrointestinal tract.

Age and sex distribution
Incidence rates are similar in men and women. The age range is wide but the majority of patients are over 50 years at presentation.

Aetiology
Helicobacter pylori infection
Initial studies of low-grade MALT lymphoma suggested that the tumour was associated with *H. pylori* in 92-98% of cases {447, 2135}; subsequent studies have suggested an association in 62-77% {1316, 583, 2146, 890, 178}. *H. pylori* infection is seen less frequently in high-grade lymphomas with a low-grade component (52-71%) and in pure high-grade lymphomas (25-38%) {583,

890, 178). The organism has been shown to be present in 90% of cases limited to the mucosa and submucosa, falling to 76% when deep submucosa is involved, and is present in only 48% of cases with extension beyond the submucosa {1316}. It has been shown that the infection by *H. pylori* precedes the development of lymphoma, both by sequential serological studies {1474} and by retrospective studies of archival gastric biopsy material {2211, 1314}.

There is some controversy surrounding the role of the organism's genetic features and the risk of lymphoma development. Studies of the association between MALT lymphoma and cagA bearing *H. pylori* strains have produced conflicting results, ranging from a lack of association between cagA and lymphoma {1492, 384} to a strong association {441}. One study claimed no association with low-grade lymphoma but a high frequency of cagA strains in high-grade lesions {1492}. Recently, a truncated form of an *H. pylori* associated protein, fidA, has been shown to be closely associated with gastric MALT lymphoma. All strains of *H. pylori* associated with MALT lymphoma showed a nucleotide G insertion at position 481 of the *fidA* gene, compared to 6/17 strains unassociated with lymphoma. This mutation causes a short truncation in the protein and antibodies to this truncated protein could be detected in 70% of the patients studied with MALT lymphoma, compared to 17% of control patients {274}.

Immunosuppression

Lymphomas may arise or involve the stomach in patients with both congenital and acquired immunodeficiencies. In general, the incidence, clinical features and the histology of the lesions is indistinguishable from those that develop outside the stomach. Up to 23% of gastrointestinal tract non-Hodgkin lymphomas arising in HIV infected patients occur in the stomach and the vast majority of these are large B-cell or Burkitt/Burkitt-like lymphomas, {122} although occasional low-grade MALT lymphomas are described {2132}.

Clinical features
Symptoms and signs

Patients with low-grade lymphomas often present with a long history of non-specific symptoms, including dyspepsia, nau-

sea and vomiting. High-grade lesions may appear as a palpable mass in the epigastrium and can cause severe symptoms, including weight loss.

Imaging

Low-grade MALT lymphomas present as intragastric nodularity with preferential location in the antrum {2180}. A more precise assessment is obtained with spiral CT, particularly if this is used in conjunction with distension of the stomach by water. This technique can identify up to 88% of cases, most of which have nodularity or enlarged rugal folds, and it can assess the submucosal extent of the tumour {1493}. High-grade lymphomas are usually larger and more frequently associated with the presence of a mass and with ulceration. In some cases, the radiological features may mimic diffuse adenocarcinoma {1059}. Endoscopic ultrasound is emerging as the investigation of choice in the assessment of the extent of lymphoma infiltration through the gastric wall. Local lymph node involvement can also be assessed by this technique.

Endoscopy

Some cases show enlarged gastric folds, gastritis, superficial erosions or ulceration. In these cases the surrounding normal appearing gastric mucosa may reveal lymphoma. High-grade lymphoma of the lesion requires multiple biopsies from all sites including areas appearing macroscopically normal. In a proportion of cases, endoscopic examination shows very minor changes such as hyperaemia and in a few cases random biopsies of apparently entirely normal mucosa may reveal lymphoma. High-grade lymphoma is usually associated with more florid lesions, ulcers and masses. It is often impossible to distinguish lymphoma from carcinoma endoscopically.

MALT lymphomas
Pathogenesis

The normal gastric mucosa contains scattered lymphocytes and plasma cells but is devoid of organised lymphoid tissue. The initial step in the development of primary gastric lymphoma is the acquisition of organised lymphoid tissue from within which the lymphoma can develop. In most cases, this is associated with infection by *H. pylori* {572}, although it has also been seen following infection by

Fig. 3.38 Multifocal malignant lymphoma of the stomach. The two larger lesions are centrally ulcerated.

Helicobacter heilmannii {1842} and in association with coeliac disease {227}. This organised lymphoid tissue shows all the features of MALT, including the infiltration of the epithelium by B-lymphocytes reminiscent of the lymphoepithelium seen in Peyer patches {2135}. The cellular basis of the interaction between *H. pylori* and MALT lymphoma cells has been studied in detail. When unseparated cells isolated from low-grade gastric MALT lymphomas are incubated in vitro with heat treated whole cell preparations from *H. pylori*, the tumour cells proliferate while those cultured in the absence of the organism or stimulating chemical mitogen rapidly die {768}. The proliferative response appeared to be strain specific for individual tumours but varied between tumours from different patients {768}. When T-cells were removed from the culture system the proliferative response was not seen and this could not be induced if the T-cells were replaced by supernatant from other cultures containing unseparated tumour derived cells {769}. Together these studies show that the proliferation of the MALT lymphoma is driven by the presence of the *H. pylori* but that this, rather than being a direct effect on the tumour

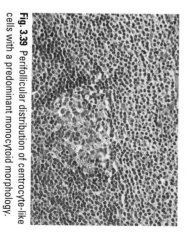

Fig. 3.39 Periollicular distribution of centrocyte-like cells with a predominant monocytoid morphology.

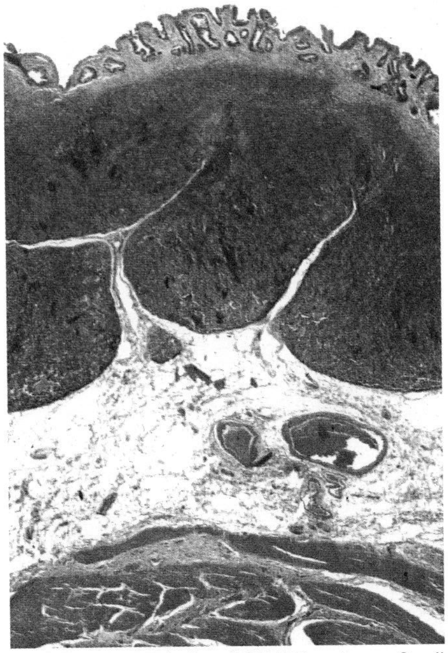

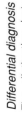

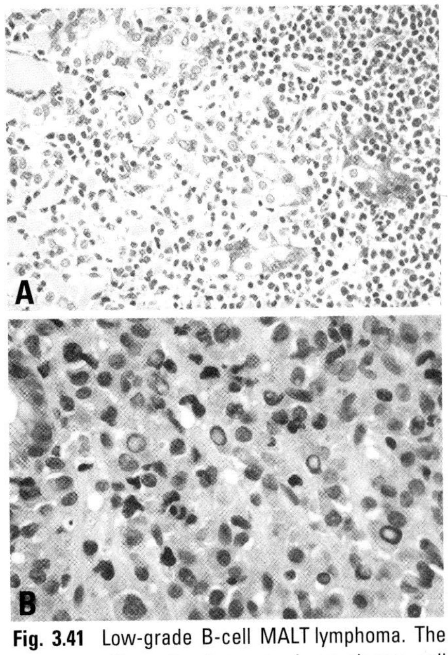

Fig. 3.41 Low-grade B-cell MALT lymphoma. The centrocyte-like cells show prominent plasma cell differentiation with **(A)** extracellular immunoglobulin deposition, and **(B)** prominent Dutcher bodies.

cells, is due to a mechanism mediated via T-cells and that this help is contact dependant. Further studies have shown that the T-cells responsible for the proliferative drive are specifically those found within the tumour and their function cannot be replaced by T-cells derived from elsewhere (e.g. the spleen) in the same patient {769}.

Histopathology

The organisation of the lymphoma mimics that of normal MALT and the cellular morphology and immunophenotype is essentially that of the marginal zone B-cell. The neoplastic cells infiltrate between pre-existing lymphoid follicles, initially loca-lised outside the follicular mantle zone in a marginal zone pattern. As the lesion progresses, the neoplastic cells erode, colonize and eventually overrun the lymphoid follicles resulting in a vague nodularity to an otherwise diffuse lymphomatous infiltrate {800}. The morphology of the neoplastic cell can be variable even within a single case. Characteristically, the cell is of intermediate size with pale cytoplasm and an irregular nucleus. The resemblance of these cells to the centrocyte of the follicle centre has led to the term 'centrocyte-like (CCL)' cell being applied to the neoplastic component of MALT lymphomas. In

Fig. 3.40 Low-grade B-cell MALT lymphoma. Small lymphoid cells form a diffuse infiltrate extending into the submucosa.

some cases, the CCL cell may be more reminiscent of a mature small B lymphocyte while in other cases, the cell may have a monocytoid appearance with more abundant, pale cytoplasm and a well defined cell border. Plasma cell differentiation is typical and may be very prominent. Dutcher bodies may be identified. The CCL cells infiltrate and destroy adjacent gastric glands to form lymphoepithelial lesions. Lympho-epithelial lesions typical for MALT lymphoma are defined as infiltration of the glandular epithelium by clusters of neoplastic lymphoid cells with associated destruction of gland architecture and morphological changes within the epithelial cells, including increased eosinophilia.

Immunohistochemistry

The immunophenotype of the CCL cell is similar to that of the marginal zone B-cell. There is expression of pan-B-cell antigens such as CD20 and CD79a and the more mature B-cell markers CD21 and CD35. The cells do not express CD10. They are usually positive for bcl-2 protein and may express CD43 but do not express CD5 or CD23. They express surface and, to a lesser extent, cytoplasmic immunoglobulin (usually IgM or IgA, rarely IgG) and show light chain restriction. Immunostaining with anti-cytokeratin antibodies is useful in demonstrating lymphoepithelial lesions. Immunostaining with antibodies that highlight follicular dendritic cells (anti-CD21, anti-CD23 or anti-CD35) help to demonstrate underlying follicular dendritic cell networks in those cases in which the lymphoid follicles have been completely overrun by the lymphoma.

Differential diagnosis

The distinction between florid gastritis and low-grade MALT lymphoma may be difficult. In such cases it is essential to have sufficient biopsy material (up to eight biopsies from endoscopically suspicious areas) with good preservation of morphology and correct orientation of the biopsy specimen. For the distinction between reactive and neoplastic infiltrates, histological evaluation remains the gold standard, but accessory studies may be helpful. In both reactive and neoplastic cases, lymphoid follicles are present and these may be associated with active inflammation, crypt abscesses and reactive epithelial changes. In gas-

tritis, the infiltrate surrounding the lymphoid follicles in the lamina propria is plasma cell predominant while in MALT lymphoma the infiltrate contains a dominant population of lymphocytes with CCL cell morphology, infiltrating through the lamina propria and around glands. Prominent lymphoepithelial lesions, Dutcher bodies and moderate cytological atypia are associated only with lymphoma. All of these features may not be present in biopsy material from a single case. In some cases it is justifiable to make the diagnosis of low-grade MALT lymphoma in the absence of one or more of these features if the overall histological appearances are those of lymphoma. Rare or questionable lymphoepithelial lesions, dense lymphoid infiltration, mild cytological atypia and muscularis mucosae invasion are features more often associated with, but not limited to, lymphoma {2212}.

In some cases it will not be possible to make a definite distinction between reactive infiltrates and lymphoma and in these cases a diagnosis of 'atypical lymphoid infiltrate of uncertain nature' is appropriate.

Effect of H. pylori eradication

The histological appearances of gastric biopsies from patients showing complete regression of lymphoma after *H. pylori* eradication are characteristic. The lamina propria appears 'empty' with gland loss. Scattered lymphocytes and plasma cells are seen within the lamina propria and there are usually focal nodular collections of small lymphocytes. These collections frequently contain a mixture of B- and T-cells and may be based on follicular dendritic cell networks.

In most cases, the appearances are insufficient for a diagnosis of residual lymphoma. The significance of these lymphoid nodules remains uncertain. In cases showing partial regression or no change following *H. pylori* eradication, the lamina propria contains an infiltrate morphologically indistinguishable from that seen at diagnosis, but in these treated cases lymphoepithelial lesions may be very scanty or absent. In some cases of partial regression and in cases with relapsed low-grade MALT lymphoma following *H. pylori* eradication, the lymphoma may be largely confined to the submucosa with only minimal involvement of the mucosa.

PCR based diagnosis

The role of genetic analyses in the diagnosis and follow up of low-grade MALT lymphoma remains controversial. Up to 10% of well characterized cases of MALT lymphoma identified as clonal through demonstration of rearrangement of the immunoglobulin heavy chain gene by Southern blot fail to show a clonal pattern when examined for immunoglobulin heavy chain gene rearrangement by PCR using fresh frozen tissue {418}. This false negative rate increases if paraffin embedded material is studied {417}. Several studies have revealed clonal B-cell populations in biopsies from patients with uncomplicated chronic gastritis and no morphological evidence of lymphoma {1677, 225, 388}. In conjunction with histological assessment, PCR studies may be useful in monitoring regression of MALT lymphomas following conservative therapy {25}. However, PCR detected clonal B-cell populations may still be detected in cases showing complete histological

regression. Some, but no all of these will eventually show molecular regression but there may be a prolonged time lag between histological and molecular regression {1677}. In the absence of histological evidence of residual lymphoma, the clinical significance of a persistent clonal population remains uncertain.

Progression to high-grade lymphoma

The emergence of clusters of large transformed 'blastic' B-cells reflects transformation to high-grade lymphoma {383}. Eventually, these areas become confluent to form sheets of cells indistinguishable from the cells of a diffuse large B-cell lymphoma. As long as a low-grade component remains, these tumours may be termed high-grade MALT lymphomas but during further progression, all traces of the pre-existing low-grade lymphoma are lost, making it impossible to distinguish the lesion from a diffuse large B-cell lymphoma of unspecified type. In cases with both low- and high-grade components, genetic studies have con-

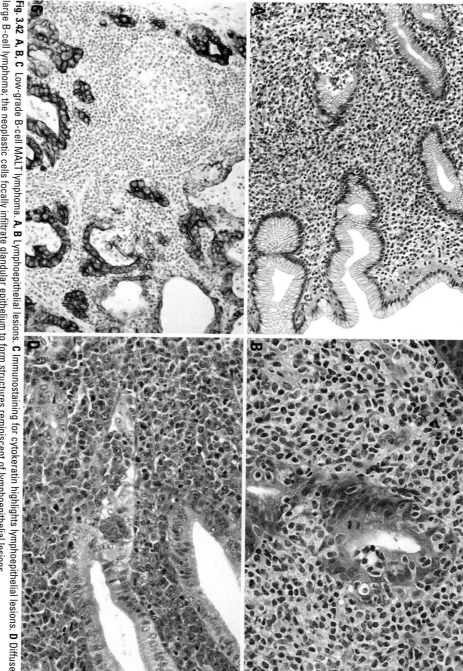

Fig. 3.42 A, B, C Low-grade B-cell MALT lymphoma. **A, B** Lymphoepithelial lesions. **C** Immunostaining for cytokeratin highlights lymphoepithelial lesions. **D** Diffuse large B-cell lymphoma; the neoplastic cells focally infiltrate glandular epithelium to form structures reminiscent of lymphoepithelial lesions.

firmed the transformation of low-grade to high-grade lymphoma in the majority of cases {1263} while in other cases both components appear clonally unrelated, suggesting the development of a second primary lymphoma {1184, 1491}.

Molecular genetics of MALT lymphomas

Early studies confirmed the presence of immunoglobulin gene rearrangement in each case {1803} and suggested that there was no involvement of the *bcl-1* or *bcl-2* oncogenes {2136}. The translocation t(11;18)(q21;q21) has been identified in a significant number of low-grade MALT lymphomas and may be the sole genetic alteration in these cases. However, this translocation appears to be less common in high-grade lesions {1435, 95}. Trisomy 3 has been detected in up to 60% of cases in some studies using both metaphase and interphase techniques {2134, 2137}, but this finding has not been confirmed by other studies {1434}. The translocation t(1;14) (p22; q32) has also been described in a small proportion of cases {2138} and this is associated with increased survival of tumour cells in unstimulated cell culture. Cloning of the breakpoint involved in this translocation has led to the discovery of a novel gene, *bcl-10*, on chromosome 1 that may be significant in determining the behaviour of MALT lymphomas {2116}.

Studies of the immunoglobulin gene of MALT lymphoma cells has shown the sequential accumulation of somatic mutations, consistent with an ongoing, antigen driven selection and proliferation {279, 434, 1546}. Study of the third complementary determining region of the immunoglobulin heavy chain gene shows a pattern of changes associated with the generation of antibody diversity and increased antigen binding affinity {131}. Transformation of low-grade MALT lymphoma to a high-grade lesion has been associated with several genetic alterations. While the t(11;18) chromosomal translocation is not seen in high-grade MALT lymphoma and may be protective against transformation, alterations in the genes coding for p53, p16, c-myc and trisomy 12 have all been identified in high-grade lesions {1489, 1490, 1341, 270, 435, 1992}. Bcl-6 protein has also been described in high-grade lymphomas while being absent from low-grade lesions {1425}. Some studies have shown a high level of *bcl-6* gene hyper-

mutations in diffuse large B-cell lymphomas independent of a rearrangement of the gene {1070}. Epstein-Barr virus is not associated with low-grade lymphomas and has only been seen in some high-grade lymphomas {1038, 1437}.

Mantle cell lymphoma

Mantle cell lymphoma of the stomach is typically a component of multiple lymphomatous polyposis of the gastrointestinal tract and infrequently encountered outside this clinical context {1380}. Morphologically and immunophenotypically, the lymphoma is indistinguishable from mantle cell lymphomas of lymph nodes, with a diffuse and monotonous infiltrate of cells with scanty cytoplasm and irregular nuclei that express B-cell markers together with CD5 and cyclinD1.

Other low-grade B-cell lymphomas

Although the lymphoid tissue in the stomach contains all the B-cell populations encountered in nodal lymphoid tissue, other low-grade B-cell lymphomas, such as follicle centre cell lymphomas, are very rare and usually indistinguishable from their nodal counterparts.

Diffuse large B-cell lymphoma

These lymphomas are morphologically indistinguishable from diffuse large B-cell lymphomas that arise within lymph nodes. There is complete destruction of the gastric glandular architecture by large cells with vesicular nuclei and prominent nucleoli. Variants of large B-cell lymphoma (e.g. plasmablastic lymphoma) may also be encountered {1541}.

Burkitt lymphoma

Although rare, classical Burkitt lymphomas may be encountered in the stomach {55}. The morphology is identical to that of Burkitt lymphoma encountered elsewhere, with diffuse sheets of medium sized cells with scanty cytoplasm and round/oval nuclei containing small nucleoli. Within the sheets there are numerous macrophages, giving a 'starry-sky' appearance. Mitoses are frequent and apoptotic debris abundant. The cells express CD10 in addition to pan-B-cell markers. Close to 100% of nuclei are immunoreactive for Ki-67.

T-cell lymphoma

Primary gastric T-cell lymphomas are rare. Most have been reported from

areas of endemic HTLV-1 infection and probably represent gastric manifestations of adult T-cell leukemia/lymphoma (ATLL). In these regions, T-cell lymphoma may represent up to 7% of gastric lymphomas {1741}. Most of the remainder are similar to peripheral T-cell lymphomas encountered in lymph nodes but occasionally, gastric NK cell lymphomas are also seen {1741}. It has recently been demonstrated that some gastric T-cell lymphomas display features of intraepithelial T lymphocyte differentiation (e.g. expression of the human mucosal lymphocyte 1 antigen, CD103), similar to those seen in intestinal T-cell lymphomas {520}.

Hodgkin disease

Hodgkin disease may involve the gastrointestinal tract but this is usually secondary to nodal disease. Primary gastric Hodgkin disease is very rare {2210}.

Prognosis and predictive factors

Studies on the regression of low-grade MALT lymphoma through *H. pylori* eradication have shown remission in 67-84% of cases {1926, 1520, 2133}, but this applies only to low-grade lesions and is most effective for lesions showing superficial involvement of the gastric wall. Although remission following *H. pylori* eradication has occasionally been seen in advanced tumours, the highest success rate of 90-100% is seen in tumours confined to the mucosa and superficial submucosa. The time taken to achieve remission in these patients varies from 4-6 weeks to 18 months. The stability of these remissions remains to be determined; one study has reported a relapse in 10% of patients after a mean follow-up period of 24 months {1338} while others have found sustained remissions for up to six years {801}.

Surgical resection is associated with prolonged survival {552} in many cases. Involvement of the resection margins and advanced stage are poor prognostic features, but not with the addition of chemotherapy {1262}. Irrespective of treatment modality, the only significant independent prognostic variables are stage and tumour-grade {260, 1653, 1262, 320, 383}.

Mesenchymal tumours of the stomach

M. Miettinen
J.Y. Blay
L.H. Sobin

Definition

Most gastrointestinal mesenchymal neoplasms are gastrointestinal stromal tumours (GIST) or smooth muscle types. They are predominantly located in the stomach. The definitions of other mesenchymal lesions follow the WHO histological classification of soft tissue tumours {2086}.

Terminology

The designation GIST was originally introduced as a neutral term for tumours that were neither leiomyomas nor schwannomas. The term GIST is now used for a specific group of tumours comprising the majority of all gastrointestinal mesenchymal tumours. These tumours encompass most gastric and intestinal mesenchymal tumours earlier designated as leiomyoma, cellular leiomyoma, leiomyoblastoma and leiomyosarcoma {80, 76, 78, 79, 1227}. Currently, the terms leiomyoma and leiomyosarcoma are reserved for those tumours that show smooth muscle differentiation, histologically or by immunohistochemistry, e.g. with strong and diffuse actin and desmin positivity. Most tumours historically called leiomyosarcoma {31, 1559, 1750} are now classified as GISTs; hence the old literature on gastric (and intestinal) leiomyosarcomas largely reflects GISTs.

Epidemiology

GIST accounts for 2.2% of malignant gastric tumours in SEER data. There is no gender preference (M:F, 1.1:1), in contrast to carcinomas which have a M:F of 2:1 {1928}. Adults between the 6th and 8th decade are primarily affected. The ratio of the age-adjusted incidence rates for Blacks and Whites is greater for sarcomas (3 to 1) than for carcinomas (2 to 1). Black women are affected six times more frequently than white women (0.6 versus 0.1 per 100,000 per year, analogous to the ratio for uterine leiomyosarcomas) {1584}.

Localization

GISTs occur at every level of the tubular gastrointestinal tract and additionally

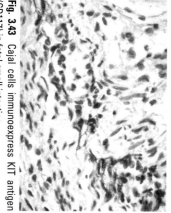

Fig. 3.43 Cajal cells immunoexpress KIT antigen (CD117) in fetal small intestine.

may be primary in the omentum and mesentery. They are most common in the stomach (60-70%), followed by small intestine (20-30%), colorectum and oesophagus (together < 10%) {1227}.

Clinical features

GISTs present a spectrum from clinically benign, small to medium-sized tumours, to frank sarcomas. According to our estimate, approximately 30% of GISTs are clinically malignant, and a substantial number of patients with apparent radical surgery will relapse {1344, 462}. Typical of the malignant GISTs at all locations is intra-abdominal spread as multiple tumour nodules, and distant metastases most commonly to liver followed by lung and bone in decreasing frequency {478A, 1984, 1855}. Vague abdominal discomfort is the usual complaint in symptomatic tumours. Both benign and sarcomatous GISTs that project into the lumen may ulcerate and be a source of bleeding {80, 78, 79}.

Macroscopy

Small gastric GISTs appear as serosal, submucosal or intramural nodules that are usually incidental findings during abdominal surgery or endoscopy. Some tumours may ulcerate, especially the epithelioid stromal tumours. The larger tumours protrude intraluminally or to the serosal side, and may have a massive extragastric component that masks the gastric origin. Intraluminal tumours are often lined by intact mucosa, but ulcera-

tion occurs in 20-30% of cases. Infiltration by direct extension to the pancreas or liver occurs. On sectioning GISTs vary from slightly firm to soft, tan, often with foci of haemorrhage. Larger tumours may undergo massive haemorrhagic necrosis and cyst formation leaving only a narrow rim of peripheral viable tissue; malignant tumours may form complex cystic masses. Multinodular peritoneal seeding is typical of malignant GISTs.

Histopathology

Typically GISTs are immunohistochemically positive for KIT tyrosine kinase receptor (stem cell factor receptor), which is perhaps their single best defining feature {920, 713, 1665, 1762}. The c-kit positivity of GISTs parallels that seen in the interstitial cells of Cajal, the pacemaker cells regulating autonomic motor activity {1139, 1654}. Based on this, and on the expression of an embryonic form of smooth muscle myosin heavy chain in GISTs and Cajal cells {1648} the origin from Cajal cells has been proposed {920, 1762}. However, considering the origin of Cajal cells and smooth muscle from a common precursor cell {1035, 2186}, the hybrid Cajal cell and smooth muscle differentiation seen in many GISTs, and the occurrence of GISTs in the omentum and mesentery {1225}, their origin from such a precursor cell pool with differentiation towards a Cajal cell phenotype is more likely. Electron microscopic observations showing hybrid autonomic nerve and smooth muscle features in many GISTs are also consistent with origin from a multipotential precursor cell {474, 1227}.

Morphology

GISTs may resemble smooth muscle tumours histologically as well as grossly. The majority of gastric GISTs are spindle cell tumours that show a variety of histological patterns {1866}. Some, including many of the smaller ones, are collagen-rich and paucicellular. A perinuclear vacuolization pattern is common. Tumours with moderate cellularity and focal nuclear palisading can resemble nerve sheath tumours. Peri-

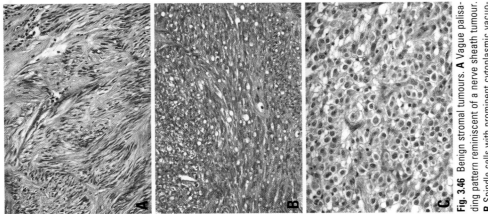

Fig. 3.44 Radiograph demonstrating mass defect in stomach due to a stromal tumour.

vascular hyalinization can accompany myxoid change. The epithelioid pattern occurs in approximately one-third of gastric GISTs and corresponds to tumours previously designated as leio-myoblastoma or epithelioid leiomyosarcoma. Some of the epithelioid tumours show mild pleomorphism. Marked pleomorphism is rare.

Immunohistochemistry. Most GISTs are positive for KIT (CD117), which may show membrane, diffuse cytoplasmic or a perinuclear accentuation pattern. Approximately 70-80% of GISTs are positive for CD34 (typically membrane pattern). 30-40% are focally or diffusely positive for α-smooth muscle actin, very few show reactivity for desmin (< 5%), and very few for S100-protein (< 5%, usually weak reactivity) {526, 1229, 1260, 1991, 1227, 1232}.

Assessment of malignancy and grading. Histological assessment of malignancy is essentially based on mitotic counts and size of the lesion. Tumours less than 5 cm are usually benign. Different limits have been applied for low-grade malignant tumours. This designation has been used for tumours showing mitotic counts

greater than 5 per 50 HPF, or tumours showing as many as 5 mitoses per 10 HPF. Tumours over 5 cm, but with fewer than 5 mitoses per 50hpf, are often assigned to the category of 'uncertain malignant potential'. However, large tumours (especially over 10 cm) with no detected mitotic activity may develop late recurrences and even metastases. DNA-aneuploidy, high proliferative index (over > 10%) by proliferation markers (especially Ki67 analogs, such as MIB1) may reflect higher malignant potential {338, 362, 929, 525, 1048, 1632, 461, 462}.

Histological grading follows the systems commonly used for soft tissue sarcomas. Mitotic activity is the main criterion, namely those tumours with over 10 mitoses per 10 hpf are considered high-grade. Lower mitotic activity (over 1-5 mitoses/10 HPH) is considered low-grade.

Genetics

Both benign and malignant GISTs commonly show losses in chromosomes 14 and 22 in cytogenetic studies and by comparative genomic hybridization. Losses in 1p and chromosome 15 have been shown less frequently. Gains and high level amplifications occur in malignant GISTs in 3q, 8q, 5p and Xp {450, 451}. A proportion of GISTs, more commonly the malignant examples, show mutations in the regulatory juxtamembrane domain (exon 11) of the *c-kit* gene. A family with germline KIT mutations and GISTs has also been described. These *c-kit* mutations have been shown to represent gain-of-function mutations leading to ligand-and-independent activation (autophos-

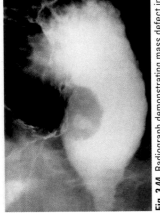

Fig. 3.46 Benign stromal tumours. **A** Vague palisading pattern reminiscent of a nerve sheath tumour. **B** Spindle cells with prominent cytoplasmic vacuolation. **C** An epithelioid pattern corresponding to the previous designation of leiomyoblastoma.

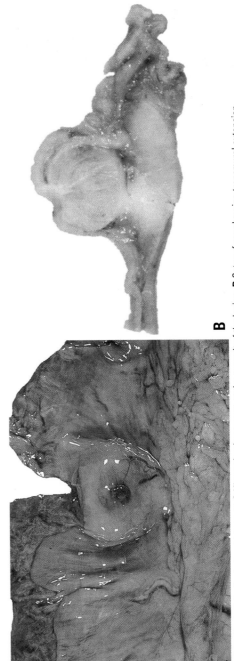

Fig. 3.45 Gastrointestinal stromal tumour. **A** Ulceration is present at the summit of the lesion. **B** Cut surface showing transmural extension.

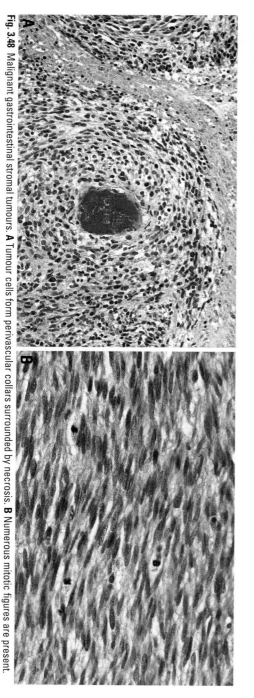

Fig. 3.48 Malignant gastrointestinal stromal tumours. **A** Tumour cells form perivascular collars surrounded by necrosis. **B** Numerous mitotic figures are present.

A

| C-kit germline Location | codon # | 508 | | | | | | | | | | | | | | | | | | | | |

Fig. 3.47 Examples of mutations of the exon 11 of the *c-kit* gene in gastrointestinal stromal tumours. **A** Nucleotide sequence of the *c-kit* gene. **B** Predicted amino acid sequences of the mutant KIT. The top line in each figure represents the germline 1 and the wild type KIT protein, respectively. Each line below them re-presents one case. The codons are indicated by numbers. The shaded areas correspond to deletions (black) or point mutations (gray). Courtesy of Dr. J. Lasota, Washington D.C.

phorylation) of the tyrosine kinase and further the phosphorylation cascade that leads into mitogenic activation {928, 713, 1310, 1356}. The most common mutations appear to be in-frame deletions of 3-21 base pairs, followed by point mutations and occasionally described insertions {475, 713, 1018, 1289}. Association of neurofibromatosis type I has been described in rare cases; these tumours represent phenotypical GISTs, but molecular genetic studies are not available {1681A}. The rare combination of

pulmonary chondroma, gastric epithelloid GIST and paraganglioma in the Carney triad has probably a common yet unknown genetic link {246}.

Prognosis and predictive factors

The prognosis of GISTs is largely dependent on the mitotic rate, size, depth of invasion, and presence or absence of metastasis {462}. Although race and gender did not play a role in survival rates in the SEER data for gastric carcinomas, the 5-year survival rates for

sarcomas varied considerably, e.g. 49% 5-year survival for males versus 74% for females; 37% for Blacks versus 66% for Whites {1928}.

Other mesenchymal tumours

Gastrointestinal autonomic nerve tumour (GANT)

Gastrointestinal autonomic nerve tumour (GANT), or the previous designation plexosarcoma, has been applied to mesenchymal tumours that have shown ultrastructural features of autonomic neurons:

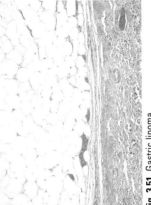

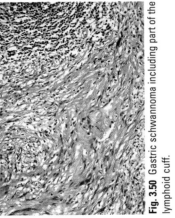

Fig. 3.50 Gastric schwannoma including part of the lymphoid cuff.

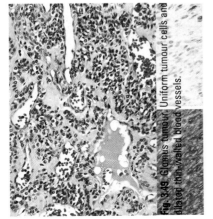

Fig. 3.49 Glomus tumour. Uniform tumour cells and dilated thin-walled blood vessels.

cell processes with neurosecretory type dense core granules and arrays of microtubules {702, 701, 1023, 2038}. Histologically, such tumours have shown a variety of spindle cell and epithelioid patterns similar to those seen in GISTs; at least some of these tumours are positive for KIT. It therefore appears that GANT and GIST groups overlap, and may even merge. Because electron microscopy is currently applied less widely for tumour diagnosis than before, GAN-type differentiation in gastrointestinal tumours is probably underestimated. Correlative light microscopic, ultrastructural, immunohistochemical and molecular genetic studies are needed to resolve the question of the relationship of GANT and GIST.

Leiomyoma and leiomyosarcoma

Well-documented true gastric leiomyomas and leiomyosarcomas are so infrequent that there is no significant data on demographic, clinical or gross features. Leiomyomas are composed of bland spindle cells showing low or moderate cellularity and slight if any mitotic activity. There may be focal nuclear atypia. The cells have eosinophilic, fibrillary, often clumped cytoplasm. Leiomyosarcomas are tumours that show histologically and immunohistochemically evident smooth muscle differentiation. They usually present in older age and are typically of high-grade malignancy. As defined here, leiomyomas and leiomyosarcomas are typically globally positive for desmin and smooth muscle actin, and are negative for CD34 and CD117 (KIT). Tumours with mitotic counts exceeding 10 mitoses per 10 high power fields are classed as high-grade.

Glomus tumours

Lesions similar to glomus tumours of peripheral soft tissue occur predominant-

ly in the gastric antrum as small intramural masses (1-4 cm in diameter, average 2 cm). They occur in older adults (mean 6th decade) with equal sex incidence {77}. One-third manifests as ulcer, one-third as bleeding, and one-third is asymptomatic. The lesions are often surrounded by hyperplastic smooth muscle and have sheets of rounded or epithelioid cells with sharp cell borders outlined by well-defined basement membranes demonstrable by PAS-stain or immunostaining for basement membrane proteins such as laminin and collagen type IV. The tumour cells have small, uniform nuclei and mitotic activity is virtually absent. The tumour cells are positive for smooth muscle actin and negative for keratins. Multiple glomus tumours with apparent intravascular spread have been described {666}.

Schwannomas

These lesions are rare in the gastrointestinal tract, but the stomach is their most common site within the digestive system. They are not associated with neurofibromatosis types I or II and occur predominantly in older adults (average 58 years in the largest series). They grossly and clinically resemble GISTs. Schwannomas are usually covered by intact mucosa and principally involve the muscularis propria. The tumours vary from 0.5-7 cm (mean 3 cm) in diameter, and are spherical or ovoid, occasionally showing a plexiform multinodular pattern. Histologically, gastrointestinal schwannomas usually show a spindle cell pattern with vague cellular schwannoma with vague nuclear palisading. The tumours often have sprinkled lymphocytes and a nodular lymphoid cuff {366, 1666}. The distinction between schwannoma and GIST is important because the former is benign even when large and mitotically

active. Schwannomas are positive for S100-protein and negative for desmin, actin and KIT.

Lipoma

Lipomas composed of mature adipose tissue may be observed in the stomach. They typically protrude into the lumen.

Granular cell tumour

Lesions similar to those in peripheral soft tissues are occasionally encountered in the stomach, where they principally occur as small submucous nodules and less commonly as intramural or subserous masses. These lesions occur predominantly in middle age, and show a strong predilection for Blacks. Associated gastric ulcer symptoms are common. See chapter on mesenchymal tumours of the oesophagus for pathological features {862}.

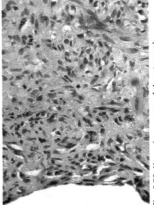

Fig. 3.51 Gastric lipoma.

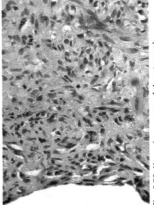

Fig. 3.52 Kaposi sarcoma of the stomach.

Kaposi sarcoma

Kaposi sarcoma may occur in the stomach as a mucosal lesion or, less commonly, as a mural mass, usually in HIV-positive patients.

Secondary tumours of the stomach

C. Niederau
L.H. Sobin

Definition

Tumours of the stomach that originate from an extra-gastric neoplasm or which are discontinuous with a primary tumour elsewhere in the stomach.

Incidence

Metastatic disease involving the stomach is unusual. An autopsy study from the USA found 17 metastases to the stomach in 1010 autopsies of cancer patients, giving a frequency of 1.7% {1220}. In a large series of autopsies from Malmö (Table 3.02), 92 gastric metastases were found in 7165 patients (1.28%) who had cancer at the time of death {130}.

Clinical features

Gastrointestinal symptoms may occur in up to 50% of patients with gastric metastases. Bleeding and abdominal pain are the most common clinical features, followed by vomiting and anorexia. Intestinal and gastric metastases were found after a median interval of 6 years (range, 0.12-12.5 years) following the diagnosis of primary breast cancer {1700}. Gastric metastasis from a breast cancer has occurred up to 30 years after diagnosis of the primary neoplasm {1148}. Occasionally, metastatic breast cancer in the stomach is detected before the primary tumour is diagnosed.

Imaging and endoscopy

An upper gastrointestinal endoscopy study identified 14 metastatic tumours in the upper gastrointestinal tract, 13 of which were in the stomach {873}. Many

metastases are described as volcano-like ulcers {618; 1108}. On endoscopy, pigmentation may not be evident in some studies have shown lung, breast, other melanomas {1069}. In patients with metastatic lobular breast carcinoma the endoscopic appearance may be that of linitis plastica. In such cases, conventional biopsies may be too superficial to include diagnostic tissue in the submucosa. Endosonography may help direct attention to the deeper infiltrate {1097}. Gastric melanomas often appear as polypoid or target lesions on barium X-ray studies {1718} and, less commonly, as a submucosal mass {1148}.

Origin

In a large Swedish autopsy series {130}, most gastric metastases were from primary breast cancer, followed by melanoma and lung cancer (Table 3.02). There were gastric metastases in 25 of 695 (3.6%) patients with breast cancer, whereas gastric metastases were found

in 10 of 747 (1.3%) of patients with lung cancer (see Table 4.01) {1220}. Several studies have shown lung, breast, other gastrointestinal carcinomas, and melanoma to be the most frequent primary lesions {1220, 158, 873, 618}. Less frequently, cancers of the ovary, testis, liver, colon, and parotid metastasize to the stomach {1220; 618; 1148; 1872}. Of all the primary cancers that can lead to gastric metastasis, breast cancer does so most frequently. Some reports show that between 50% and 75% of patients with breast cancer develop gastric metastases {1148; 455}. However, in a Dutch study covering a 15-year-period, there were only 27 patients with gastric metastases from primary breast cancer {1872}.

There is no preferential localization of metastases to subsites in the stomach. Cancers at any site can produce gastric metastases through haematogeneous spread. Lesions of the pancreas, oeso-

Fig. 3.53 Multiple gastric metastases from rhabdomyosarcoma of the spermatic cord in a 15-year old boy.

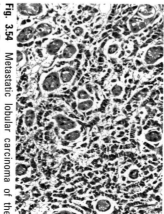

Fig. 3.54 Metastatic lobular carcinoma of the breast. Typical single file growth pattern.

Table 3.02
Metastases to the stomach, small intestine, colon and appendix. Data are from 16,294 autopsies {130}.

Site of metastasis	No. of cases with metastasis	% of all autopsies	Most frequent primary cancer	Next most frequent primary cancer
Stomach	92	0.58%	Breast (25 cases)	Melanoma (19)
Small intestine	125	0.78%	Lung (33 cases)	Melanoma (33)
Colon	62	0.39%	Lung (14 cases)	Breast (10)
Appendix	7	0.04%	Breast (2 cases)	Various (1)

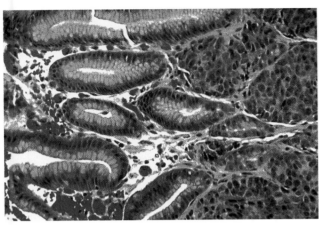

Fig. 3.55 Metastatic prostate carcinoma. The lesion resembles carcinoid. Tumour cells were positive for prostate specific antigen, negative for chromogranin.

phagus and gallbladder can extend into the stomach by direct spread or, in some cases, by lymphatic spread. Ovarian adenocarcinoma usually spreads via the peritoneum and lymphatic channels; however, gastric metastases from ovarian cancer could also be of haematogenous origin {1148}.

Macroscopy

Gastric metastases may appear as ulcers, as linitis plastica, or as polyps. The submucosal infiltration and extent of metastasis may be much more extensive than seen by endoscopy or radiography. Melanomas may or may not be pigmented.

Histopathology

The histopathology of gastric metastases is similar to that of the primary cancer and to other haematogenous metastases of that cancer. Immunohistochemical and molecular markers may help to differentiate a signet-ring cell carcinoma of the stomach from metastatic mammary disease {2174}. Gastric metastasis from primary breast cancer is usually of lobular rather than ductal type {1872; 1097; 517}.

Prognosis and predictive factors

Gastric metastases usually represent a late, disseminating stage of the disease in which other haematogenous metastases are also frequently found. The prognosis is therefore poor. In one series, the mean survival was 11 months, with a range of 3 months to 5 years {158} but the gastric metastases led to death in only 4 of 67 cases {618}.

CHAPTER 4

Tumours of the Small Intestine

The small intestine has a remarkably low incidence of primary carcinomas, especially considering their size. Those that do occur are often related to genetic syndromes, especially familial adenomatous polyposis.

Lymphomas and endocrine tumours are as frequent as carcinomas and have important associations with precursor conditions such as coeliac sprue, multiple endocrine neoplasia and Von Recklinghausen Syndrome.

The small intestine is the main site for metastatic tumours in the gastrointestinal tract.

WHO histological classification of tumours of the small intestine[1]

Epithelial tumours		
Adenoma		8140/0[2]
Tubular		8211/0
Villous		8261/0
Tubulovillous		8263/0
Intraepithelial neoplasia[2] (dysplasia) associated with chronic inflammatory diseases		
Low-grade glandular intraepithelial neoplasia		
High-grade glandular intraepithelial neoplasia		
Carcinoma		
Adenocarcinoma		8140/3
Mucinous adenocarcinoma		8480/3
Signet-ring cell carcinoma		8490/3
Small cell carcinoma		8041/3
Squamous cell carcinoma		8070/3
Adenosquamous carcinoma		8560/3
Medullary carcinoma		8510/3
Undifferentiated carcinoma		8020/3
Carcinoid (well differentiated endocrine neoplasm)		
Gastrin cell tumour, functioning (gastrinoma) or non-functioning		8153/1
Somatostatin cell tumour		8156/1
EC-cell, serotonin-producing neoplasm		8241/3
L-cell, glucagon-like peptide and PP/PYY producing tumour		
Mixed carcinoid-adenocarcinoma		8244/3
Gangliocytic paraganglioma		8683/0
Others		

Non-epithelial tumours	
Lipoma	8850/0
Leiomyoma	8890/0
Gastrointestinal stromal tumour	8936/1
Leiomyosarcoma	8890/3
Angiosarcoma	9120/3
Kaposi sarcoma	9140/3
Others	
Malignant lymphomas	
Immunoproliferative small intestinal disease (includes α-heavy chain disease)	9764/3
Western type B-cell lymphoma of MALT	9699/3
Mantle cell lymphoma	9673/3
Diffuse large B-cell lymphoma	9680/3
Burkitt lymphoma	9687/3
Burkitt-like /atypical Burkitt-lymphoma	9687/3
T-cell lymphoma	9702/3
enteropathy associated	9717/3
unspecified	9702/3
Others	
Secondary tumours	
Polyps	
Hyperplastic (metaplastic)	
Peutz-Jeghers	
Juvenile	

[1] This classification is modified from the previous WHO histological classification of tumours {845} taking into account changes in our understanding of these lesions. In the case of endocrine neoplasms, it is based on the recent WHO classification {1784} but has been simplified to be of more practical utility in morphological classification.
[2] Morphology code of the International Classification of Diseases for Oncology (ICD-O) {542} and the Systematized Nomenclature of Medicine (http://snomed.org). Behaviour is coded /0 for benign tumours, /3 for malignant tumours, /2 for in situ carcinomas and grade III intraepithelial neoplasia, and /1 for unspecified, borderline or uncertain behaviour. Intraepithelial neoplasia does not have a generic code in ICD-O. ICD-O codes are available only for lesions categorized as glandular intraepithelial neoplasia grade III (8148/2), and adenocarcinoma in situ (8140/2).

TNM classification of tumours of the small intestine

TNM classification[1] [2]

T – Primary Tumour

TX	Primary tumour cannot be assessed
T0	No evidence of primary tumour
Tis	Carcinoma in situ
T1	Tumour invades lamina propria or submucosa
T2	Tumour invades muscularis propria
T3	Tumour invades through muscularis propria into subserosa or into non-peritonealized perimuscular tissue (mesentery or retroperitoneum[3]) with extension 2 cm or less
T4	Tumour perforates visceral peritoneum or directly invades other organs or structures (includes other loops of small intestine, mesentery, or retroperitoneum more than 2 cm and abdominal wall by way of serosa; for duodenum only, invasion of pancreas)

N – Regional Lymph Nodes

NX	Regional lymph nodes cannot be assessed
N0	No regional lymph node metastasis
N1	Regional lymph node metastasis

M – Distant Metastasis

MX	Distant metastasis cannot be assessed
M0	No distant metastasis
M1	Distant metastasis

Stage Grouping

Stage 0	Tis	N0	M0
Stage I	T1	N0	M0
	T2	N0	M0
Stage II	T3	N0	M0
	T4	N0	M0
Stage III	Any T	N1	M0
Stage IV	Any T	Any N	M1

[1] {66, 361}. This classification applies only to carcinomas.
[2] A help desk for specific questions about the TNM classification is available at http://tnm.uicc.org.
[3] The non-peritonealized perimuscular tissue is, for jejunum and ileum, part of the mesentery and, for duodenum in areas where serosa is lacking, part of the retroperitoneum.

Carcinoma of the small intestine

N.H. Wright
J.R. Howe
F.P. Rossini
N.A. Shepherd

M. Pennazio
L.H. Sobin
N.J. Carr
I. Talbot

Definition

A malignant epithelial tumour of the small intestine. Neoplasms of the periampullary region include those of the duodenal mucosa, ampulla of Vater, common bile duct and pancreatic ducts.

ICD-O codes

Adenocarcinoma	8140/3
Mucinous adenocarcinoma	8480/3
Signet-ring cell carcinoma	8490/3

Epidemiology

Relative to the length and surface area of the small intestine, adenocarcinomas of the duodenum, jejunum and ileum are remarkably rare. Data from the United States SEER program {1928} for 1973 to 1987 show an age-adjusted incidence rate for adenocarcinoma of the small intestine of 0.4 per 100,000 per year. Although some reports suggest an increasing incidence of adenocarcinoma of the small intestine {1339, 1715}, this is not reflected in the SEER data base. The median age at manifestation is approximately 67 years for non-mucinous adenocarcinoma, mucinous carcinoma and carcinoids.

Aetiology

A major factor in the development of small bowel adenocarcinoma is chronic inflammation. In particular, long-standing Crohn's disease with multiple strictures is associated with small bowel carcinoma {1016, 1223, 582, 1578}. One study showed that individuals with Crohn's disease have an 86-fold increased risk of adenocarcinoma of the small intestine {623}. Coeliac disease is another well recognized aetiological factor for small bowel carcinoma {116, 1354, 2141}. There is some epidemiological evidence that cigarette use and alcohol consumption are also risk factors {1339}.

Carcinoma can develop in ileostomies in patients with ulcerative colitis or familial adenomatous polyposis (FAP) subsequent to colonic metaplasia and intraepithelial neoplasia in the ileostomy mucosa {1599, 558}. Carcinoma can also arise in ileal conduits {1965} and in ileal reservoirs, both continent abdominal (Kock) {347} and pelvic {2013, 1730}. The occurrence of adenocarcinomas in Meckel's diverticulum {985} and in small bowel duplications {496} has been reported.

Localization

The duodenum is the main site, containing more adenocarcinomas than the jejunum and ileum combined {1928}. In the duodenum, carcinomas are most common around the ampulla of Vater {1657, 2123}, possibly due to biliary or pancreatic effluents.

Clinical features
Symptoms and signs

The symptoms of small bowel adenocarcinoma are related to the size and location of the tumour.

In the *jejunum and ileum*, early symptoms are often non-specific, with vague periumbilical abdominal pain and rumbling. Later, cramp-like pain is present in up to 80% of cases, and this may be accompanied by nausea, vomiting, weight loss, asthenia, and intermittent obstructive episodes. Massive bleeding is rare (8%), but an important clinical finding is chronic bleeding with secondary iron-deficiency anaemia, which may be found in the early stages of development of the tumour. Other clinical signs are bloating of the loops of the bowel, meteorism, and the presence of a palpable mass {20}. Perforation is a possible complication of small intestinal carcinomas {681}.

Duodenal carcinomas present in a different manner, because of the larger circumference of the duodenum compared with the more distal parts of the small intestine, and because of the relative accessibility of the duodenum to endoscopy {498, 1657}. Unlike jejunal and ileal carcinomas, carcinomas of the duodenum, especially those of the proximal duodenum, do not present with bowel obstruction. Biliary obstruction, frank or occult blood loss and abdominal pain are the commonest presentations {2123}. Some tumours are largely asymptomatic and may be discovered by endoscopy {1809}.

Imaging

The radiological methods that have the highest diagnostic accuracy are spiral CT scan with contrast medium and enteroclysis; the two methods can be complementary. With enteroclysis, a filling defect, an irregular and circumscribed thickening of the folds with wall rigidity, slowed motility, eccentric passage of the contrast medium, or a clear stenosis may be observed {199}. Small bowel adenocarcinoma may appear on CT scan as an annular lesion, a discrete nodular mass, or an ulcerative lesion. CT scan, with global vision of the abdomen, can contribute to staging the tumour {1145}.

With push enteroscopy, it is possible to visualize endoscopically the entire jejunum. Expansion or infiltrative growth of the tumour causes at a relatively early phase, an alteration of the endoluminal surface; via push enteroscopy it is thus possible to identify small lesions and to take biopsies. Push enteroscopy is also a good diagnostic method to diagnose tumours causing occult bleeding {1495, 1619}.

Exploration of the ampulla of Vater requires a lateral viewing fibroscope, adapted to tissue sampling and endoscopic sphincterotomy. The terminal ileum may be visualized through retrograde ileoscopy during colonoscopy. Sonde enteroscopy can identify tumours throughout the small bowel, but it is hampered by the inability to take biopsies {1064}.

Macroscopy

The macroscopic pathology of small bowel carcinomas is determined by a number of factors, of which stage and site are the most significant. Many carcinomas of the jejunum and ileum are detected at an advanced stage {498, 189}. A further determinant of the macroscopic features is the presence or absence of predispos-

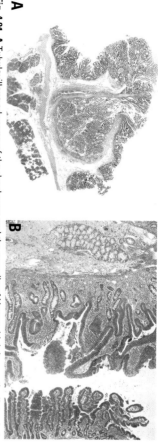

A

Fig. 4.01 A Tubulovillous adenoma of the duodenum and the ampulla of Vater which is greatly distended. **B** Villous adenoma of duodenum adjacent to normal mucosa.

B

Fig. 4.02 Adenocarcinoma of small intestine.

ing factors, namely, an associated adenoma, coeliac disease, Crohn's disease, radiotherapy, previous surgery (notably pouch surgery and ileostomy), polyposis syndromes, Meckel's diverticulum, and intestinal duplication.

Carcinomas may be polypoid, infiltrating or stenosing. Jejunal and ileal carcinomas are usually relatively large, annular, constricting tumours with circumferential involvement of the wall of the intestine {189}. Most have fully penetrated the muscularis propria and there is often involvement of the serosal surface {16}. Adenocarcinoma of the ileum may mimic Crohn's disease clinically, radiologically, endoscopically, and at macroscopic pathological assessment {745}. Although circumferential involvement can occur, duodenal carcinomas are usually more circumscribed, with a macroscopically demonstrable adenomatous component in 80% of cases {966, 496}. Thus, they are often protuberant or polypoid, and the central carcinomatous component may show ulceration {1267}. Carcinomas arising at the ampulla of Vater tend to cause obstructive jaundice before they have reached a large size; they are usually circumscribed nodules measuring not more than 2-3 cm in diameter. They may be within the wall of the duodenum or project into the lumen as a nodule.

Unusual macroscopic features, e.g., the lack of ulceration, the predominance of an extramural component and the presence of multicentricity, should alert the pathologist to the possibility that the tumour is a metastasis.

Microscopy

Histologically, small bowel carcinomas resemble their more common counterparts in the colon, but with a higher proportion of poorly differentiated tumours {496, 1006}. Some are adenosquamous carcinomas {624, 1345, 1525}. Carcinomas with prominent neoplastic endocrine cells {821} and with tripartite differentiation, i.e. with glandular, squamous, and neuroendocrine components {111, 207}, have also been reported. Small cell carcinomas (poorly differentiated endocrine carcinomas) are rare {2196} (see next chapter).

In metastatic carcinoma of the small intestine, evidence of a pre-existing adenomatous component can be mimicked by the ability of the intestinal mucosa to cause differentiation of the metastatic tumour {1732}; this phenomenon can give the erroneous impression of a primary carcinoma of the small intestine.

Tumour spread and staging

Spread of small bowel carcinomas is similar to that of the large bowel. Direct spread may cause adherence to adjacent structures in the peritoneal cavity, usually a loop of small intestine, although the stomach, colon or greater omentum may also be involved. Lymphatic spread to regional lymph nodes is common. Haematogenous and transcoelomic spread also occur. Diffuse involvement of the ovaries, Krukenberg tumour, has been reported {1089}. Staging of carcinomas of the small intestine is by the TNM classification {1, 66}. For tumours of the ampulla of Vater, because of the complicated anatomy at this site, a separate TNM classification is used. Alternative staging systems have been proposed {1888}.

Grading

Grading of small intestinal carcinomas is identical to that used in the large bowel, namely, well, moderately and poorly differentiated, or high- and low-grade.

Precursor and associated lesions

Adenomas

There is good evidence for an adenoma-carcinoma sequence in the small intestine as in the colon {1506, 1709}. Residual adenomatous tissue at the margins is seen in 80% of duodenal adenocarcinomas {966}. Perzin and Bridge {1505} described 51 patients with adenomas of the small intestine – 65% had coexisting carcinoma. In patients with familial adenomatous polyposis (FAP), 38/45 (84%) of duodenal carcinomas harboured adenomatous tissue {1709}; whereas 30% of 185 sporadic adenomas showed carcinoma {1706}. The age at diagnosis of adenomas without carcinoma is lower than for adenomas with carcinoma or for carcinomas, and there is a nearly identical spatial distribution of these three types of tumour in the small intestine {1706}.

Since the advent of endoscopic techniques, the earliest stages of malignant changes can be followed in adenomas of the duodenum and peri-ampullary region {147}, where often the size of the lesion may warrant extensive sampling. In a study of post-colectomy patients with FAP, random biopsy specimens of ileal mucosa showed foci of abnormal, dysplastic crypts resembling dysplastic aberrant crypt foci of the colon in some patients, supporting the concept that, at least in patients with FAP, oligocryptal adenomas are a step in the development of epithelial neoplasms of the small intestine {132}.

Although adenomas can occur throughout the small intestine {399}, the commonest site is the ampullary and peri-ampullary region {1366}. Adenomas can be multiple, even in patients without a history of FAP {958, 1317, 685}.

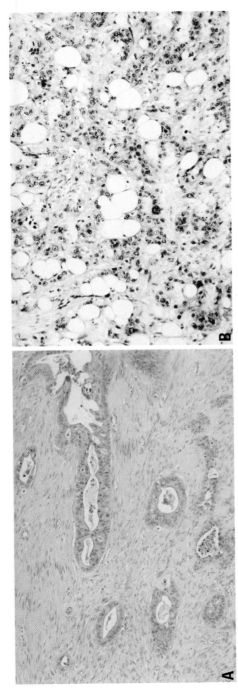

Fig. 4.03 Adenocarcinoma. **A** Well differentiated, invasive. **B** Poorly differentiated, infiltrating fat.

Histologically, adenomas in the small intestine are similar to those in the colon, but with a propensity to be more villous or tubulovillous in architecture {2127A, 1342}. The adenomatous cells resemble those of colonic adenomas, with varying degrees of dysplasia, but the columnar cells are unequivocally enterocytic in nature; goblet cells are frequent and some lesions have Paneth and endocrine cells {500, 1237}.

Other associated conditions

Juvenile polyposis and Peutz-Jeghers syndrome have a recognized association with small intestinal carcinoma {1830, 1604, 1506}.

Genetic susceptibility

These include: familial adenomatous polyposis (FAP), hereditary non-polyposis colorectal cancer (HNPCC), Crohn's disease, coeliac disease, ileostomies, ileal conduits and pouches (especially after colectomy for FAP), Peutz-Jeghers syndrome and juvenile polyposis. The highest risk is in FAP. Duodenal adenomas develop in a high proportion of FAP patients {228}, and the relative risk of duodenal carcinoma is over 300 times that of the normal population {1397}; these carcinomas represent a major cause of death in FAP patients after total colectomy.

In FAP, carcinomas are usually associated with a macroscopically definable adenomatous component and are usually accompanied by many other adenomas in the second and third parts of the duodenum {1808, 204}. Adenomas do occur elsewhere in the small bowel in FAP, including the ileum and the pelvic ileal reservoir {1376}, but carcinomas are distinctly unusual.

It has been proposed that patients with carcinoma of the small intestine have an increased incidence of multicentric carcinomas of the gastrointestinal tract, with an increased incidence of gastric and colonic carcinomas in first-degree relatives {1830}. Primary small bowel carcinoma can be the presenting neoplasm in hereditary non-polyposis colorectal cancer (HNPCC), occurring at an earlier age than sporadic cases and carrying a better prognosis {1604, 125}.

Genetics

Patients with HNPCC and germline mutations of *hMSH2* or *hMLH1* have an approximately 4% lifetime risk of small bowel cancer, which exceeds the risk of the normal population 100 fold {2005}. In Peutz-Jeghers syndrome, the most common site of polyps is in the small intestine, and 2-3% of patients are at risk for developing intestinal carcinoma {431, 721}. In juvenile polyposis, small intestinal polyps occur with less frequency, but duodenal carcinoma has been reported {749}. Genes mutated in the germline of patients with inherited syndromes that

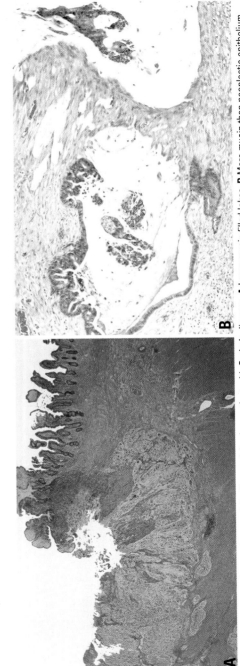

Fig. 4.04 Mucinous adenocarcinoma of the ileum arising in a patient with Crohn's disease. **A** Large mucin filled lakes. **B** More mucin than neoplastic epithelium.

predispose to small bowel neoplasia (*APC*, *hMSH2*, *hMLH1*, *LKB1*, and *Smad4*) may therefore play a role in the genesis of these tumours.

Studying the genetics of small bowel adenocarcinomas has been difficult due to the rarity of these tumours {1715}. There is evidence supporting a multistep pathway of carcinogenesis similar to that described for colorectal carcinomas {2018}. The incidence of *KRAS* mutation is 14-52% {83, 2185, 14}, p53 overexpression 40-67%, 17p loss 38-67%, and 18q loss 18-30% {14, 1562}. One report found no 5q loss {1562} while another found the frequency to be 60% {14}. 15-45% of small bowel tumours have high levels of microsatellite instability {14, 1562, 705}, and mutations in the TGF beta-RII gene have been identified

in some of these tumours {14}. In one study of Crohn-associated small bowel cancers, 43% had *KRAS* mutations, 57% had 5q overexpression, 33% had 17p loss, 17% had 5q loss, none had 18q loss, 1 had microsatellite instability, and none had TGF beta-RII mutations {1562}. These findings were similar to those seen in sporadic small bowel carcinoma, and indicate that the transformation from intraepithelial neoplasia to carcinoma may occur in a similar fashion.

Prognosis and predictive factors

In SEER data, the overall 5-year survival for adenocarcinoma of the small bowel was 28%, and for mucinous adenocarcinoma 22% {1928}. 5-year survival for localized adenocarcinomas (63%) was higher than for gastric adenocarcinoma

(56%) and lower than for colon (87%) and rectum (79%). This relation is reflected in survival figures for all stages. Another recent population-based study from Sweden showed 5- and 10-year survival rates for small intestinal adenocarcinoma of 39% and 37% for duodenal tumours and 46-41% for jejuno-ileal tumours {2201}. The survival of patients undergoing curative resection is 63% when regional lymph nodes are not involved, and 52% when there are nodal metastases {2011}. Long-term survival is associated with well differentiated tumours and local invasion only {1888, 1336}.

One study found a significant inverse association between immunoreactivity for c-neu and survival in duodenal adenocarcinoma {2208}.

Peutz-Jeghers syndrome

L.A. Aaltonen
H. Järvinen
S.B. Gruber

M. Billaud
J.R. Jass

Definition

Peutz-Jeghers syndrome (PJS) is an inherited cancer syndrome with autosomal dominant trait, characterized by mucocutaneous melanin pigmentation and hamartomatous intestinal polyposis, preferentially affecting the small intestine. Associated extra-intestinal neoplasms are less common and include tumours of the ovary, uterine cervix, testis, pancreas and breast.

MIM No.

175200

Synonyms and historical annotation

The syndrome was first described by Peutz {1512} and Jeghers {850}. Several designations have been used synonymously, including Peutz-Jeghers polyposis, periorificial lentiginosis, and polyps-and-spots syndrome.

Incidence

As the condition is rare, well documented data on the incidence are not available. Based on numbers of families registered in the Finnish Polyposis Registry, the incidence of PJS is roughly one tenth of that of familial adenomatous polyposis.

Diagnostic criteria

The following criteria are recommended: (1) three or more histologically confirmed Peutz-Jeghers polyps, or (2) any number of Peutz-Jeghers polyps with a family history of PJS, or (3) characteristic, prominent, mucocutaneous pigmentation with a family history of PJS, or (4) any number of Peutz-Jeghers polyps and characteristic, prominent, mucocutaneous pigmentation.

Some melanin pigmentation is often present in unaffected individuals, hence

the emphasis on the prominence of the pigmentation.

Intestinal neoplasms

Penetrance appears to be high, and both sexes are equally affected {691}. Polyps are most common in the small intestine,

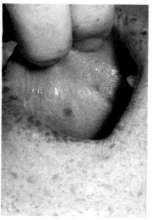

Fig. 4.05 Peutz-Jeghers syndrome. Pigmentation of lips, peri-oral skin, tongue and fingers.

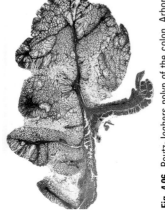

Fig. 4.06 Peutz-Jeghers polyp of the colon. Arborizing smooth muscle separating colonic glands into lobules (Masson trichrome stain).

Fig. 4.07 **A** A lobulated pedunculated Peutz-Jeghers polyp of the small intestine. **B** This small intestinal Peutz-Jeghers polyp exhibits haemorraghic infarction due to intussusception.

but may occur anywhere in the gastrointestinal tract.

Signs and symptoms

These include abdominal pain, intestinal bleeding, anaemia, and intussusception. Typical age at clinical manifestation is from two to twenty years. Characteristic pigmentation allows diagnosis of asymptomatic patients in familial cases.

Imaging

The presence of polyps may be demonstrated by upper gastrointestinal and small bowel contrast radiography, and by air contrast barium enema. Periodic small bowel X-ray examination at two to five-year intervals is advisable in the follow-up of the affected patients. Endoscopy is superior to radiological imaging in that it enables polypectomy for diagnostic and therapeutic purposes. Upper gastrointestinal tract endoscopy and colonoscopy every two years with snare excision of all polyps detected is presently recommended. Small bowel polyps may be reached by an enteroscope but rarely for the full bowel length; thus, imaging remains an integral component of clinical management.

Macroscopy

Peutz-Jeghers polyps occur within the stomach, small and large intestines, and rarely within oesophagus, nasopharynx and urinary tract. The small intestine is the site of predilection. The polyps are lobulated with a darkened head and closely resemble adenomas. The stalk is short and broad or absent. Size is typically 5 to 50 mm.

Histopathology

A typical Peutz-Jeghers polyp has a diagnostically useful central core of smooth muscle that shows tree-like branching. This is covered by the mucosa native to the region, heaped into folds producing a villous pattern. Diagnostic difficulty occurs when there is secondary ischaemic necrosis. This complication arises when a polyp has caused intussusception, a common form of presentation. Some polyps may lack diagnostic features.

Epithelial misplacement involving all layers of the bowel wall (pseudoinvasion) has been described in up to 10% of small intestinal Peutz-Jeghers polyps {1728}. Mechanical forces associated with intussusception or raised intraluminal pressure due to episodic intestinal obstruction are the likely explanation for this observation. Epithelial misplacement may be florid and extend into the serosa, thereby mimicking a well differentiated adenocarcinoma. Useful diagnostic features are the lack of cytological atypia, presence of all the normal cell types, mucinous cysts and haemosiderin deposition {1728}.

Dysplasia and cancer in Peutz-Jeghers polyps

While the Peutz-Jeghers syndrome is associated with a 10 to 18-fold excess of gastrointestinal and non-gastrointestinal cancers {579, 154}, the question of whether or not the Peutz-Jeghers polyp is itself precancerous has proved difficult to resolve. Epithelial misplacement has apparently been overdiagnosed as cancer in the past {1728}, but it is likely that the increased risk of malignancy in the stomach, small bowel and colon {154, 1807} is due to malignant progression from hamartoma to adenocarcinoma. The evidence is threefold: (1) intraepithelial neoplasia (dysplasia), though uncommon, has been described in Peutz-Jeghers polyps {1506, 2017}; (2) carcinomas may occur in contiguity with Peutz-Jeghers polyps {317, 1506}; (3) the responsible gene *LKB1 (STK11)* is located on chromosome 19p, and loss of heterozygosity at this locus has been demonstrated in the majority of Peutz-Jeghers polyps and associated intestinal cancers {633, 691, 2052}.

Extraintestinal manifestations

Predisposition to cancer of multiple organ systems is an important feature of the syndrome {579, 154}. The most well documented extra-intestinal neoplasms include sex cord tumours with annular tubules (SCTAT) of the ovary {2188}, adenoma malignum of the uterine cervix {2188}, Sertoli cell tumours of the testis

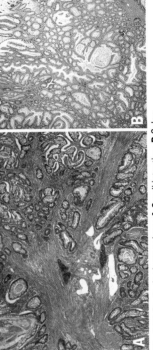

Fig. 4.08 Peutz-Jeghers polyps. **A** Small intestine. **B** Colon.

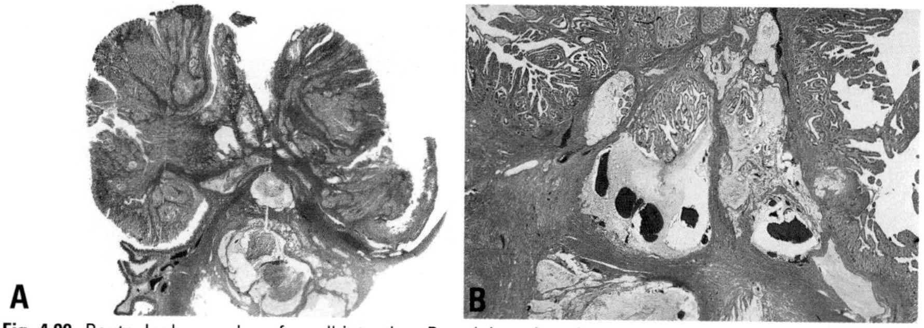

Fig. 4.09 Peutz-Jeghers polyp of small intestine. Pseudoinvasion characterized by benign mucinous cysts extending through bowel wall into mesentery. Patient was well ten years after removal.

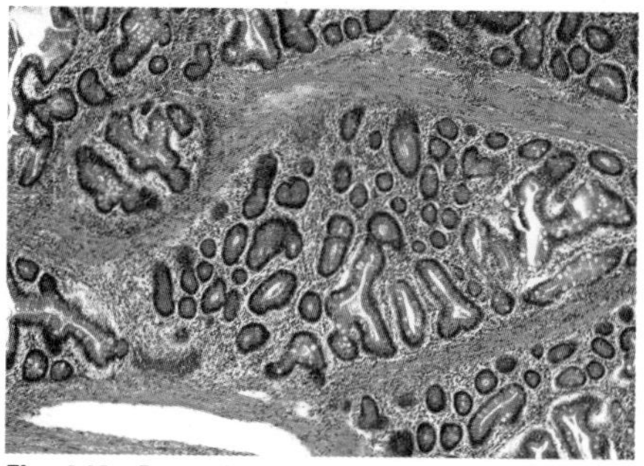

Fig. 4.10 Peutz-Jeghers polyp of small intestine. Pseudoinvasion. Islands of mucosa are separated by smooth muscle.

[231, 2118], carcinoma of the pancreas [579], and carcinoma of the breast {1587, 1952}.

The cutaneous melanin pigmentation occurs typically around the mouth as freckle-like spots. Other sites commonly affected are digits, palms and feet, buccal mucosa, and anal region. While dramatic pigmentation is a helpful sign, it may fade with time, and some affected individuals never display pigmentation.

Genetics

Chromosomal location and mode of inheritance

PJS is an autosomal dominant trait with nearly complete penetrance. The PJS gene, *LKB1* (*STK11*), maps to 19p13.3, and there is some evidence suggestive of locus heterogeneity {1210}.

Gene structure

LKB1 consists of 9 coding exons. The open reading frame consists of 1302 base pairs, corresponding to 433 amino acids. Codons 50 to 337 encode the catalytic kinase domain of the gene.

Gene product

The human *LKB1* gene is ubiquitously expressed in adults {853, 690}. It encodes a protein of 433 amino acids which possesses a serine/threonine kinase domain framed by a short N-terminus sequence (48 residues) and a more extended C-terminus region of 122 amino acids {853, 690}. *LKB1* shares a significant sequence similarity with the Saccharomyces cerevisiae SNF1 kinase which phosphorylates transcriptional repressor and regulates glucose-repressible genes. Homologs of *LKB1* have been identified in several species including mouse, *Xenopus*, and *Caenorhabditis elegans* {1852, 1768,

2072}. Sequence alignments revealed that these proteins are most conserved within the kinase domain, with 96% of identity between human and mouse and 42% identity between human and the nematode. Human *LKB1* contains a nuclear localization signal (NLS) flanking the N-terminus part of the catalytic domain {1343, 1768} and a putative prenylation motif within the C-terminus {325}. The *LKB1* gene product is located both in the nucleus and in the cytoplasm {1343}. *LKB1* displays an autocatalytic activity in vitro, and is the substrate of the

cAMP-dependent protein kinase (PKA) {325}. Although the function of *LKB1* remains to be determined, it is worth noting that *PAR-4*, the *C.elegans* orthologue of *LKB1*, is required for establishing polarity during the first cell cycles of the embryo {2072}. *PAR-4* expression is also essential for embryonic viability and for intestinal organogenesis. Since the cardinal clinical feature of PJS is the presence of intestinal hamartomatous polyps, it appears plausible that the function of *LKB1* has been conserved across evolution as it exerts a key regulatory role during intestinal development.

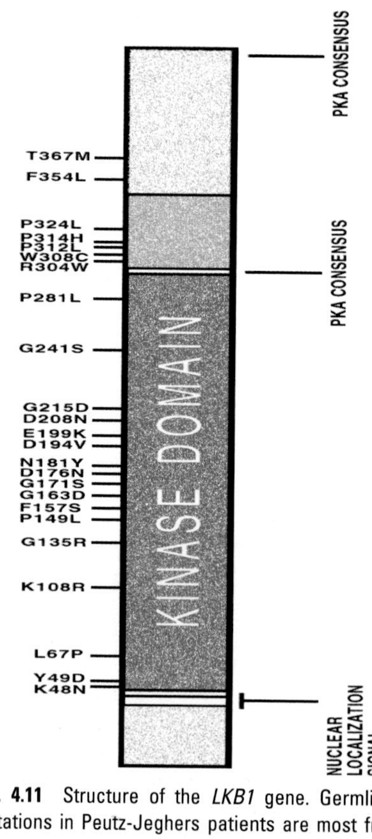

Gene mutations and their relationship to clinical manifestations

Germline mutations are usually truncating, but missense type mutations have also been described {853, 690}. Wild type *LKB1* is capable of autophosphorylation {1210, 2176}, and the effect of missense mutations occurring in the kinase domain can be evaluated observing this property in autophosphorylation assays. Somatic mutations of *LKB1* in tumours have been reported but are rare.

Prognosis

While intussusception has been a major source of mortality in PJS kindreds {2093} surgery constitutes an effective treatment. Thus, prognosis of the affected individuals is mainly related to the risk of malignancy in PJS {579, 154}. Due to the rarity of the syndrome, there is little information on prognosis, but one report suggests that PJS-associated cancers are particularly aggressive {1807}.

Fig. 4.11 Structure of the *LKB1* gene. Germline mutations in Peutz-Jeghers patients are most frequent in the kinase domain.

Endocrine tumours of the small intestine

C. Capella
E. Solcia
L.H. Sobin
R. Arnold

Definition

Endocrine tumours of the small intestine exhibit site-related differences, depending on their location in the duodenum and proximal jejunum or in the distal jejunum and ileum. They include *carcinoid tumours* (well differentiated neoplasms of the diffuse endocrine system), *small cell carcinomas* (poorly differentiated endocrine neoplasms) identical to small cell carcinomas of the lung and malignant *large cell neuroendocrine carcinomas*. The classification used here is adapted from the WHO histological classification of endocrine tumours {1784}.

ICD-O Codes

Carcinoid	8240/3
Gastrin cell tumour	8153/1
Somatostatin cell tumour	8156/1
EC-cell, serotonin-producing neoplasm	8241/3
L-cell, glucagon-like peptide and PP/PYY producing tumour	
Gangliocytic paraganglioma	8683/0
Small cell carcinoma	8041/3

Epidemiology
Incidence and time trends

Endocrine tumours of the duodenum were rare in some older series, accounting for 1.8-2.9% of gastrointestinal endocrine tumours {587, 2016}. However, in recent histopathology series, duodenal tumours amount to 22% of all gastrointestinal endocrine neoplasms {1780}. Jejunal tumours account for about 1% {587, 1780} of all gut endocrine tumours. Gastrin-cell (G-cell) tumours represent the largest group (62%) in reported series of endocrine tumours arising in the upper small intestine, followed by somatostatin-cell tumours (21%), gangliocytic paragangliomas (9%), undefined tumours (5.6%) and PP-cell tumours (1.8%) {1780}.

An extensive review of all cases recorded in the Zollinger-Ellison Syndrome (ZES) registry showed 13% of patients to have duodenal wall gastrinomas, while the majority of patients had a pancreatic tumour {726}. More recent studies have shown a higher proportion of duodenal tumours (38-50%), possibly related to improved diagnostic tools {429, 2076}.

Age and sex distribution

In a series of 99 cases of endocrine tumours of the duodenum, males were more frequently affected (M/F ratio: 1.5:1), with a mean age at manifestation of 59 years (range, 33 to 90 years) {208}. G-cell tumours associated with overt ZES (gastrinomas) differ from their apparently nonfunctioning counterpart in arising earlier in life (mean age at diagnosis is 39 years, as opposed to 66 years) {1780}. Somatostatin-cell tumours affect females slightly more frequently than males (1.2:1) and become clinically manifest at a mean age of 45 years (range 29 to 83 years) {1780}. Gangliocytic paragangliomas are slightly more common in males than in females and affect patients ranging in age from 23 to 83 years, with an average of 54 years {210}. The few cases of small cell carcinoma recorded in the literature were in males ranging in age from 51 to 76 years.

Aetiology

Apart from genetic susceptibility (see below), there is little knowledge about possible aetiological factors involved in the pathogenesis of duodenal and proximal jejunal endocrine tumours. An isolated report demonstrates that a sporadic gastrin-cell tumour of the duodenum originated from hyperplastic and differentiated G-cells located in the mucosal crypts {1114}. A case of a small multifocal somatostatin-cell tumour of the proximal duodenum has been reported in a patient with celiac sprue, showing somatostatin-cell hyperplasia in the mucosa, suggesting a relationship between D-cell growth

and a long standing chronic inflammatory process {233}.

Localization

In a series of duodenal endocrine tumours {208}, 43 lesions were located in the first part, 41 in the second part, 2 in the third part, and 2 in the fourth part. Nonfunctioning G-cell tumours are located in the duodenal bulb, while the site of about 1/3 gastrinomas associated with overt ZES is in the first, second or third part of the duodenum or in the upper jejunum {1780}. The preferential location of somatostatin-cell tumours, gangliocytic paragangliomas and small cell carcinomas is at, or very close to, the ampulla of Vater {206, 210, 233, 1149, 1780, 1870, 2196}.

Clinical features

Endocrine tumours of the duodenum produce symptoms either by virtue of local infiltration causing obstructive jaundice, pancreatitis, haemorrhage, and intestinal obstruction (nonfunctioning tumours) or, less frequently, by secreted peptide hormones (functioning tumours). The prevalent position of somatostatin-cell tumours, gangliocytic paragangliomas, and small cell carcinomas in the ampullary region explains their frequent association with obstructive biliary disease. About 20% of the tumours, especially those located in the duodenal bulb, are asymptomatic and often incidentally discovered, e.g. by imaging analysis, endoscopy or pathological examination of gastrectomy and duodenopancreatectomy specimens removed for gastric and pancreatic cancers.

Zollinger-Ellison Syndrome (ZES) with hypergastrinaemia, gastrin hypersecretion, and refractory peptic ulcer disease, is the only syndrome of endocrine hyperfunction consistently observed in association with endocrine tumours of the duodenum and upper jejunum {208, 429, 726, 1780, 2076}. The association with ZES is found in about 15% of duodenal

Endocrine tumours of the duodenum and proximal jejunum

gastrin-cell tumours {1780}. Tumours associated with overt ZES differ from their apparently nonfunctioning counterpart in arising earlier in life and having a higher incidence of metastatic and non-bulbar cases {1780}.

Argentaffin, serotonin-producing, carcinoids are unusual in the upper small intestine. It follows that duodenal carcinoids only exceptionally give rise to a clinical carcinoid syndrome, associated with liver metastases of the tumour {233, 1816}. In none of the cases of somatostatin-cell tumours, so far reported, did the patients develop the full 'somatostatinoma' syndrome (diabetes mellitus, diarrhoea, steatorrhoea, hypo- or achlorhydria, anaemia and gallstones) that has been described in association with some pancreatic somatostatin-cell tumours {1780}.

Macroscopy

Endocrine tumours of the duodenum and upper jejunum usually form small (< 2 cm in diameter) grey, polypoid lesions within the submucosa with an intact or focally ulcerated overlying mucosa. However, some examples appear as infiltrative intramural nodules of rather large size (up to 5 cm in diameter). The tumours are multiple in about 13% of cases {208}. In a large series of 96 cases, the mean size was 1.8 cm (range, 0.2 to 5.0 cm) {208}. The mean size was 0.8 cm for gastrin-cell tumours {233}, 2.3 cm for somatostatin-cell

tumours {1816} and 1.7 cm for gangliocytic paragangliomas {233}. Small cell carcinomas typically measure 2-3 cm, and present as focally ulcerated, or protuberant lesions {1870, 2196}.

Microscopy

Gastrin cell tumours. These tumours are formed by uniform cells with scanty cytoplasm, arranged in broad gyriform trabeculae and vascular pseudo-rosettes and show predominant immunoreactivity for gastrin. Other peptides detected in tumour cell sub-populations are cholecystokinin, pancreatic polypeptide (PP), neurotensin, somatostatin, insulin, and the α-chain of human chorionic gonadotrophin {233}. Interestingly, somatostatin, which is known to inhibit gastrin release from gastrinomas, is detected more frequently in nonfunctioning G-cell tumours than in tumours associated with ZES {233}. Ultrastructurally, typical G-cells with vesicular granules are found {233}.

Somatostatin cell tumours. These neoplasms usually exhibit a mixed architectural pattern with a predominant tubuloglandular component admixed with a variable proportion of insular and trabecular areas. Concentrically laminated psammoma bodies are detected mostly within glandular spaces. The glandular pattern and psammoma bodies may be so prominent that these tumours have been misdiagnosed as well differentiated ampullary adenocarcinomas. Unlike

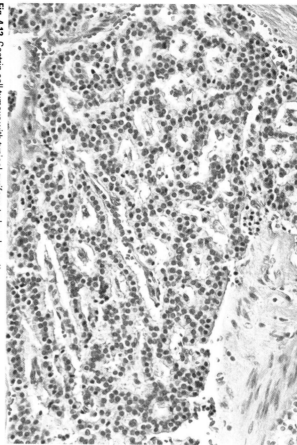

Fig. 4.12 Gastrin cell tumour with typical gyriform trabecular pattern.

adenocarcinomas, however, the somatostatin cell tumours are composed of uniform cells with rather bland nuclei and few mitotic figures. Grimelius silver stain and chromogranin A are not very useful to diagnosis this tumour, because they are negative in about 50% of cases. The presence of somatostatin in tumour cells can be demonstrated by immunohistochemistry. In addition to the somatostatin cells, some tumours have minor populations positive for calcitonin, pancreatic polypeptide and ACTH {233, 381}. In addition, the apical cytoplasm of glandular structures binds WGA and PNA lectins and expresses epithelial membrane antigen {233, 1780}. Ultrastructural examination shows large, moderately electron dense secretory granules, similar to those found in normal D-cells of the intestinal mucosa {233}.

EC-cell, serotonin-producing carcinoid. The classic argentaffin 'midgut' EC-cell carcinoid, with its characteristic pattern of solid nests of regular cells with brightly eosinophilic serotonin-containing granules and other morphological characteristics of ileal argentaffin EC-cell carcinoid, is very rare both in the duodenum and upper jejunum.

Gangliocytic paraganglioma This tumour appears as an infiltrative lesion composed of an admixture of three cell types: spindle cells, epithelial cells, and ganglion cells. The spindle cells, which usually represent the major component, are neural in nature. They form small fascicles or envelop nerve cells and axons and show intense immunoreactivity for S-100 protein. The epithelial cells are larger cells with eosinophilic or amphophilic cytoplasm and uniform ovoid nuclei that are arranged in ribbons, solid nests, or pseudo-glandular structures. These are non-argentaffin and frequently non-argyrophil endocrine cells, often containing somatostatin {233, 1816}. In addition, PP cells and rare glucagon or insulin cells have been detected in gangliocytic paragangliomas, suggesting that they may be a hamartoma of pancreatic anlage {655, 1502}. The ganglion cells may be scattered singly or aggregated into clusters. The three components of the gangliocytic paraganglioma also intermingle with the normal smooth muscle and small pancreatic ducts at the ampulla to produce a very complex lesion. Ultrastructurally, the epithelial cells have

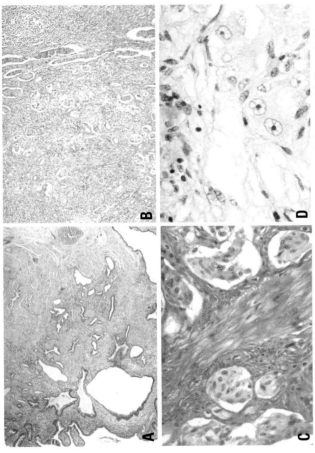

Fig. 4.13 Gangliocytic paraganglioma. **A** Distortion of duodenal glands by stromal infiltrate. **B** Masson trichrome stain highlights islands of epithelial cells (red). **C** Spindle cells and epithelial cells. **D** Ganglion cells with pale nuclei and prominent nucleoli.

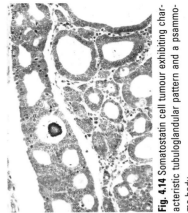

Fig. 4.14 Somatostatin cell tumour exhibiting characteristic tubuloglandular pattern and a psammoma body.

abundant cytoplasm packed with dense-core secretory granules, while the ganglion cells are larger and contain a small number of neuroendocrine granules of small size and more numerous secondary lysosomes. The spindle cells are packed with intermediate filaments and resemble either sustentacular cells or Schwann cells {1502}.

Genetic susceptibility

MEN-1. This inherited tumour syndrome is significantly associated with gastrin-cell tumours, but not with other types of endocrine tumours of the duodenum and upper jejunum. The prevalence of MEN-1 in all gastrin cell tumours of the duodenum-upper jejunum has been reported to be 5.3% {1780}. Among duodenal-upper jejunal cases with an overt ZES, the association with MEN-1 syndrome is found in 7 to 21% of cases {1780, 2076}. Loss of heterozygosity (LOH) at MEN-1 gene locus has been found in 4/19 (21%) duodenal MEN-1 gastrin cell tumours {1105}, while a slightly higher 11q13 LOH rate for MEN-1 gastrinomas (41%; 14 of 34 tumours) was reported in an extended study of MEN-1 and sporadic gastrinomas {395}. A low incidence of LOH on 11q13 in MEN-1-associated gastrinomas suggests that these tumours could arise due to inactivation of the wild-type allele via point mutations or small deletions rather than via a loss of a large segment of chromosome 11 {1105}.

Neurofibromatosis type I. Patients with von Recklinghausen disease are at significant risk for development of periampullary neoplasms {210, 233, 933, 1780}. The majority of these lesions are somatostatin cell tumours, gastrointestinal stromal tumours or gastrointestinal autonomic nerve tumours, but other neoplasms of neural crest and non-neural crest origin are known to occur. Somatostatin cell tumours were the most common periampullary neoplasms identified in one review {933}, whereas carcinoids account for only 2-3% of periampullary tumours in the general population {1149}.

Some patients with neurofibromatosis and ampullary somatostatin cell tumour also have a phaeochromocytoma involving one or both adrenal glands, a clinical situation that can have considerable implications for complicated patient management {210}. Association of gan-

gliocytic paraganglioma with neurofibromatosis type I {906} and somatostatin cell tumour has been reported {1832}.

Genetics

Point mutations of *KRAS* at codon 12, which are detected in small bowel adenocarcinomas, are absent in endocrine tumours of the small intestine, including the duodenal ones {2185}. Incidental gastrin cell tumours do not overexpress either basic fibroblast growth factor (bFGF), acidic fibroblast growth factor (aFGF), transforming growth factor-α (TGFα), or their respective receptors FGFR4 and EGFR {995}. On the contrary, these tumours overexpress the βA-subunit of activin, which may be involved in the regulation of proliferation of tumour cells {994}.

Prognosis and predictive factors

Aggressive endocrine tumours include gastrin cell, somatostatin cell, and EC-cell tumours that invade beyond the submucosa or show lymph node or distant (liver) metastases. Aggressive tumours have been reported to be 10% of all gastrin cell duodenal-upper jejunal tumours {233}; 58% of sporadic ZES cases {429} and 45% of ZES-MEN-1 cases {429}. In the case of somatostatin cell tumours, about two-thirds were aggressive in one study {381}.

Gastrin cell tumours associated with an overt ZES are prognostically less favourable than their nonfunctioning counterparts, having a higher incidence of metastases (3 of 14 cases as against 0 of 14, and being deeply infiltrative (7 of 14 as against 3 of 19) {1780}. These findings suggest a different natural history of gastrin cell tumours in the two conditions. Nonfunctioning tumours represent a generally benign condition, while ZES tumours have a low-grade malignancy, especially when arising in sites where gastrin cells are not normally present, such as in the jejunum or pancreas {233}. Metastases in regional lymph nodes have been reported in 4 of 8 cases of duodenal gastrinomas with ZES-MEN-1 syndrome {1521}, in 2 of 3 cases of jejunal gastrinomas {233} and in 25% of 103 cases of duodenal tumours with ZES, 24% of which also had MEN-1 syndrome {724}. Local lymph node metastases seem to have little influence on survival of patients with ZES {398, 2076}. In a study focusing on metastatic rate and survival in patients with ZES, no difference was found in the frequency of metastases to lymph nodes {429}, when comparing primary pancreatic (48%) and duodenal (49%) tumours. In contrast, the same study found a significantly higher frequency of metastases to the liver in patients with pancreatic gastrinomas than in patients with duodenal gastrinomas (52% vs. 5%). The 10-year survival rate of patients with duodenal gastrinomas (59%) is significantly better than for patients with pancreatic gastrinomas (9%) {2076}. The more favourable prognosis of duodenal tumours is mainly linked to their smaller size and less frequent association with liver metastases.

Somatostatin cell tumours are often malignant, despite their rather bland histological appearance {1780, 210, 381}. Malignant somatostatin cell tumours are ≥ 2 cm in diameter {381}, invade the duodenal muscularis propria, the sphincter of Oddi, and/or the head of the pancreas, and can metastasise to paraduodenal lymph nodes and liver.

Gangliocytic paragangliomas are usually benign, in contrast to gastrin and somatostatin cell tumours that arise in the same area. However, occasional large tumours (size > 2 cm) may spread to local lymph nodes, mainly attributable to the endocrine component of the lesion {197, 783}.

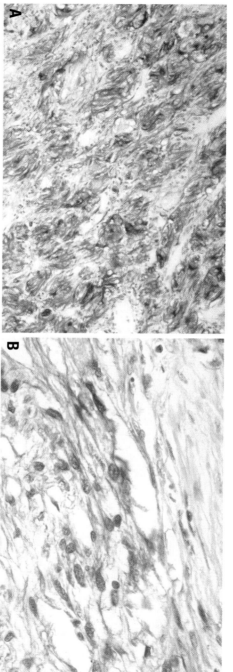

Fig. 4.15 Gangliocytic paraganglioma. **A** Immunoreactivity for cytokeratin (CAM 5.2) in epithelial cells. **B** Immunoreactivity for S100 in spindle cells.

Small cell carcinomas show histological signs of high-grade malignancy (high mitotic rate, tumour necrosis, deep mural invasion, angioinvasion, and neuroinvasion). Metastases are present in all cases {2196} and patients die usually within 7-17 months of diagnosis.

Endocrine tumours of the distal jejunum and ileum

Endocrine tumours of this segment of the small intestine are mainly EC-cell, serotonin-producing carcinoids, and, less frequently, L-cell, glucagon-like peptide and PP/PYY-producing tumours.

Epidemiology
Incidence and time trends
Endocrine tumours of the lower jejunum and ileum have an incidence of 0.28-0.89 per 100,000 population per year {60, 587}. Jejuno-ileal lesions account for 23-28% of all gastrointestinal endocrine tumours, making this site the second most frequent location for endocrine tumours, following the appendix {587, 2016}. A recent SEER analysis of 5468 cases found an increase in the proportion of ileal and jejunal carcinoids and decrease in the proportion of appendiceal carcinoids {60}.

Age and sex distribution
Endocrine tumours of lower jejunum and ileum are distributed more or less equally between males and females. Patients range in age from the third to the tenth decade, with a peak in the 6th and 7th decades {211, 587, 1253, 1780}.

Aetiology
At present, there is little knowledge about the aetiology of jejuno-ileal EC-cell carcinoids. Although endocrine tumours of lower jejunum and ileum are not generally associated with preneoplastic lesions, there have been reports of focal microproliferations of EC-cells in cases of multiple ileal tumours {1736} and of intraepithelial endocrine cell hyperplasia in the mucosa adjacent to jejuno-ileal carcinoids {1291}.

Approximately 15% of carcinoid tumours of the small intestine are associated with non-carcinoid neoplasms, most frequently adenocarcinomas of the gastrointestinal tract {1251, 1253}, supporting the hypothesis that secretion of growth factors is involved in their aetiopathogenesis {1251}.

Localization
In the AFIP series of 167 jejuno-ileal endocrine tumours {211}, 70% were located in the ileum, 11% in the jejunum, 3% in Meckel diverticulum. These data suggest that small bowel endocrine tumours occur 6.5 times more frequently in the ileum than in the jejunum. The majority of the tumours are located in the distal ileum near the ileocaecal valve.

Clinical features
Patients with jejuno-ileal endocrine tumours present most commonly with intermittent crampy abdominal pain, suggestive of intermittent intestinal obstruction {1253}. Patients frequently have vague abdominal symptoms for several years before diagnosis, reflecting the slow growth rate of these neoplasms {1253}. Preoperative diagnosis is difficult

since standard imaging techniques rarely identify the primary tumour. Scintigraphic imaging with radiolabeled somatostatin (octreotide) is widely used to localise previously undetected primary or metastatic lesions {991}.

The 'carcinoid syndrome' is found in 5-7% of patients with EC-cell carcinoid tumours {587, 1253} that typically arise in the ileum, all of which metastasise, mostly to the liver. Symptoms include cutaneous flushing, diarrhoea, and fibrous thickening of the endocardium and valves of the right heart.

Macroscopy

Jejuno-ileal endocrine tumours are multiple (ranging from 2 to 100 tumours) in about 25-30% of cases {211, 1253, 1845}. The size of the tumours is < 1 cm in 13% and ≥ 2 cm in 47% of cases {211}. They usually appear as deep mucosal-submucosal nodules with apparently intact or slightly eroded overlying mucosa. Deep infiltration of the muscular wall and peritoneum is frequent. Extensive involvement of the mesentery stimulates considerable fibroblastic or desmoplastic reaction, with consequent angulation, kinking of the bowel and obstruction of the lumen. Infarction of the involved loop of the small intestine may occur as a consequence of fibrous adhesions, volvulus, or occlusion of the mesenteric blood vessels.

Microscopy

EC-cell, serotonin-producing carcinoids are formed by characteristic rounded nests of closely packed tumour cells, often with peripheral palisading (Type A) {1775}. Often, within the solid nests, rosette type, glandular-like structures are detected. This variant of the fundamental structure designated as mixed insular + glandular (A + C) structure seems prognostically more favourable than the pure

type A structure {1780}. In areas of deep invasion with abundant desmoplastic reaction, the cell nests may be oriented into cords and files. Mesenteric arteries and veins located near the tumour, or away from it, may be thickened and their lumen narrowed or even occluded by a peculiar elastic sclerosis, which may lead to ischaemic lesions in the intestine {72}. Most tumour cells are intensely argyrophilic and reactive with chromogranin A and B antibodies. In about 30% of cases, a variable number of cells is also reactive for prostatic acid phosphatase {211}.

The identification of tumour cells as EC-cells can be accomplished using histochemical methods for serotonin, including argentaffin, diazonium, and immunohistochemical tests. Because serotonin occurs in some non EC-cell and related

tumours {655}, electron microscopic examination of serotonin-immunoreactive tumours (particularly those failing to react with histochemical tests) can confirm their EC-cell nature by detecting characteristic pleomorphic, intensely osmiophilic granules {1778}.

Substance P and other tachykinins, such as neurokinin A, are reliable markers of a fraction of jejuno-ileal EC-cell tumours {144, 1173}; foregut (gastric, pancreatic and duodenal) EC-cell tumours remain mostly unreactive {1780}. Minor populations of enkephalin, somatostatin, gastrin, ACTH, motilin, neurotensin, glucagon/glicentin, and PP/PYY immunoreactive cells, unassociated with pertinent hyperfunctional signs, have been reported in some ileal and jejunal tumours mostly composed of EC-cells {1173, 2168}. Dopamine and norepinephrine have also

Fig. 4.16 Multiple carcinoids of the ileum with mesenteric lymph node metastases.

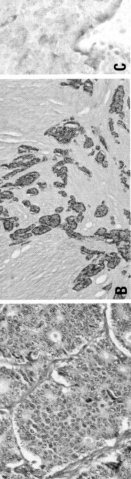
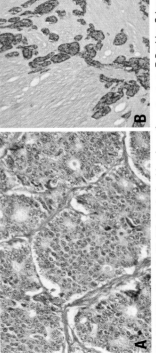

Fig. 4.17 EC-cell carcinoid. **A** Typical mixed insular-acinar structure. **B** Positive Grimelius silver reaction. **C** Immunoexpression of TGFα.

been detected in addition to serotonin in a type A (insular) argentaffin carcinoid of the ileum {588}. In many cases of jejuno-ileal EC-cell tumours, however, no other hormones apart from serotonin and substance P or related tachykinins are detected {1173}.

The main criteria for considering a jejuno-ileal carcinoid to have an aggressive potential are deep invasion of the wall (muscularis propria or beyond) and/or presence of metastases. According to these criteria, in the large AFIP series {211}, 141 of 159 cases (89%) of jejuno-ileal carcinoids were considered aggressive.

Genetic susceptibility

Unlike gastric ECL-cell tumours and duodenal gastrin cell tumours, jejuno-ileal carcinoids are only occasionally associated with MEN-1 {1444}. Rare examples of familial occurrence of ileal EC-cell carcinoids have been reported {1252A}.

Genetics

A recent study {829} reported frequent (78%) LOH on chromosome 11q13 in sporadic carcinoids of both foregut (lung and thymic) and midgut/hindgut (intestinal, including EC-cell tumours, and rectosigmoidal) origin. Other studies, however, have shown retention of heterozygosity on 11q13 in sporadic carcinoids of midgut and hindgut origin {394, 1938}, suggesting that LOH of the MEN-1 gene, unlike gastric and duodenal endocrine tumours, is not involved in the pathogenesis of EC-cell tumours.

Accumulation of p53 has not been detected in EC-cell tumours examined immunohistochemically, suggesting that

this tumour suppressor gene is not implicated in the pathogenesis of these tumours {1780, 2044, 2077}.

Several growth factors and related receptors have been localised in tumour cells of EC-cell carcinoids, including transforming growth factor-α (TGFα) and epidermal growth factor (EGF)-receptor, insulin-like growth factor-1 (IGF-1), and IGF-1 receptors, platelet-derived growth factor (PDGF), transforming growth factor-β (TGFβ), basic fibroblast growth factor (bFGF), acidic fibroblast growth factor (aFGF), and fibroblast growth factor receptor-4 (FGFR4) {22, 284, 993, 995, 1291}.

Some of these growth factors, such as TGFα, exert a proliferative effect reflected by an increased mitotic index and significantly increased DNA levels in primary cell cultures of midgut carcinoids. These findings suggest the involvement of an autocrine loop {22}. A similar growth promoting role in midgut carcinoid tumour cells is assigned to IGF-1 {22}. PDGF, TGFα, bFGF, and aFGF seem to be mainly involved in tumour stromal reaction, including stromal desmoplasia {22, 993, 995}, by acting on receptors expressed on fibroblasts or stimulating the promotion of new vasculature and tumour progression {22, 993, 995}.

Neural adhesion molecule (NCAM), a member of the immunoglobulin superfamily of cell adhesion molecules, is highly expressed in midgut carcinoid tumours {22}.

Because NCAM has not been shown in normal gut endocrine cells, the novel expression of this adhesion molecule in carcinoids may be of importance for growth and metastases.

Prognosis and predictive factors

A recent report revealed a 21% mortality rate for jejuno-ileal carcinoids, compared with 4% for duodenal, 6% for gastric, and 3% for rectal carcinoids {211}. In two studies, the overall 5-year survival rate of patients with jejuno-ileal endocrine tumours was about 60% and the 10-year survival rate was 43% {211, 1845}. In patients with no liver metastases, the 5- and 10-year survival rates were 72% and 60%, respectively, as opposed to 35% and 15% for patients with liver metastases {1845}, demonstrating the relatively slow rate of growth of some EC-cell tumours. Metastases are generally confined to regional lymph nodes and liver. Extra-abdominal metastases were found in only 0.5% of the cases reported by Moertel et al. {1253}. In one study, univariate analysis showed that survival was negatively correlated with distant metastases at the time of surgery, mitotic rate, tumour multiplicity, the presence of carcinoid syndrome, depth of intestinal wall invasion, and female gender; by multivariate analysis, survival was negatively associated with distant metastases, carcinoid syndrome, and female gender {211}.

In summary, jejuno-ileal carcinoid tumours that are clinically nonfunctioning, 1 cm or less in diameter, confined to the mucosa/submucosa and non-angioinvasive, are generally cured by complete local excision. Invasion beyond submucosa or metastatic spread indicates that the lesion is aggressive. If the lesion, although confined to the mucosa/submucosa, shows angioinvasion, or is over 1 cm in size, it is of uncertain malignant potential.

B-cell lymphoma of the small intestine

R.D. Gascoyne
H.K. Müller-Hermelink
A. Chott
A. Wotherspoon

Definition

Primary small intestinal lymphoma is defined as an extranodal lymphoma arising in the small bowel with the bulk of disease localized to this site. Contiguous lymph node involvement and distal spread may be seen, but the primary clinical presentation is the small intestine, with therapy directed to this site.

ICD-O codes

MALT lymphoma	9699/3
IPSID	9764/3
Mantle cell lymphoma	9673/3
Burkitt lymphoma	9687/3
Diffuse large B-cell lymphoma	9680/3

Epidemiology

In contrast to lymphomas involving the stomach, primary small intestinal lymphomas are uncommon in Western countries {792}. However, since epithelial and mesenchymal tumours are uncommon in the small bowel, lymphomas constitute a significant proportion (30-50%) of all malignant tumours at this site. Lymphomas of mucosa-associated lymphoid tissue (MALT) type are the most frequent lymphomas of both the small intestine and the colorectum, although controversy surrounds the histogenesis of de novo diffuse large B-cell lymphoma arising along the gastrointestinal tract. A unique form of intestinal MALT lymphoma occurs predominantly in the Middle East and Mediterranean areas, and is referred to as *immunoproliferative small intestinal disease (IPSID)* {1649}. This entity represents part of a spectrum of small intestinal lymphoproliferations, including alpha heavy chain disease (αHCD) and may represent different manifestations or phases of the same disease. αHCD and IPSID occur predominantly in the Mediterranean area, but may be seen outside this region. They typically affect young adults, whereas small intestinal lymphomas in the Western world increase in frequency with age with a peak incidence in the 7th decade. Most studies have shown a slight male predominance {424}.

Aetiology

In contrast to the well-established relationship between *Helicobacter pylori* and gastric MALT lymphoma, no infectious organism has been clearly implicated in the pathogenesis of small intestinal MALT lymphoma. IPSID appears to be related to bacterial infection, as antibiotic responsiveness is typical of the early phases of the disease. However, no specific organism has been identified. Lymphomas involving the small intestine or colorectum may occur in distinct clinical settings. Chronic inflammatory bowel disease, including Crohn disease and ulcerative colitis, are recognized risk factors for non-Hodgkin lymphoma at this site. Importantly, the risk is much less than that associated with gluten-sensitive enteropathy and primary T-cell lymphomas of the small bowel (see T-cell lymphoma section). Crohn disease is more often implicated in the development of lymphoma in the small intestine, while ulcerative colitis is associated with lymphomas of the colorectum {1733}. An increased incidence of lymphoma has been associated with both acquired and congenital immunodeficiency states, including congenital immune deficiency, iatrogenic immunodeficiency associated with solid organ transplantation, and acquired immunodeficiency syndrome (AIDS) {357}. In general, lymphomas associated with immunodeficiency show a predilection for extranodal sites, particularly the gastrointestinal tract, irrespective of the cause of the immunodeficiency {1057, 787}.

Clinical features

Symptoms produced by small intestinal lymphomas depend upon the specific histological type. Indolent lymphomas of B-cell lineage typically present with abdominal pain, weight loss and bowel obstruction {424}. Occasional cases present with nausea and vomiting, while rare cases are discovered incidentally. More aggressive tumours, such as those of T-cell lineage (described separately) or Burkitt lymphoma, may present as a large intra-abdominal mass or acutely with intestinal perforation. IPSID often manifests as abdominal pain, chronic severe intermittent diarrhoea and weight loss {1649}. The diarrhoea is mainly the result of steatorrhoea, and a protein-losing enteropathy can be seen. Peripheral oedema, tetany and clubbing are observed in as many as 50% of patients. Rectal bleeding is uncommon in small bowel lymphoma, but a common presenting sign in primary colonic lymphoma. Burkitt lymphoma is most frequently seen in the terminal ileum or ileocaecal region, and may cause intussusception.

Imaging and endoscopy

Radiological studies are useful adjuncts to the diagnosis of small intestinal lymphomas, including barium studies and computerized tomography scans. T-cell lymphomas are typically localized in the jejunum, presenting as thickened plaques, ulcers, or strictures. Most B-cell lymphomas manifest as exophytic or annular tumour masses in the ileum {792}. B-cell lymphomas of both low- and intermediate-grade may produce nodules or polyps that can be seen both endoscopically and by imaging. Most small intestinal lymphomas are localized to one anatomic site, but multifocal tumours are detected in approximately 8% of cases. *Multiple lymphomatous polyposis* consists of numerous polypoid lesions throughout the gastrointestinal tract {791}. Most often, the jejunum and terminal ileum are involved, but lesions can appear in the stomach, duodenum, colon, and rectum. This entity produces a characteristic radiological picture that is virtually diagnostic. As discussed below, the majority of such cases is caused by mantle cell lymphoma, but other subtypes of lymphoma may produce a similar radiological pattern {1034}.

IPSID. The macroscopic appearance of IPSID depends on the stage of disease. Early on, the bowel may appear endoscopically normal, with infiltration apparent only on intestinal biopsy. The disease may then progress to thickening of the upper jejunum together with enlargement of the mesenteric lymph nodes and the development of lymphomatous masses. Typically, the spleen is not involved and may even be small and fibrotic, as described in coeliac disease. Distal spread beyond the abdomen is uncommon {1649, 798}.

Histopathology
MALT lymphoma

The majority of intestinal lymphomas involving the small bowel are B-cell lymphomas of MALT type, including both low-grade and aggressive types {792, 793, 796}. These so-called 'Western' types are distinct from IPSID and αHCD. The histological features of Western type small intestinal lymphoma are similar to gastric MALT lymphoma, except that lymphoepithelial lesions are less prominent {792}.

In contrast to gastric MALT lymphomas, diffuse large B-cell lymphomas arising in the small bowel are much commoner than low-grade B-cell lymphomas of MALT-type {796}. Some of these lymphomas may have a low-grade MALT component, providing evidence that their histogenesis is related to the mucosal immune system. Precise criteria for defining a MALT lymphoma of large cell type are lacking, as are the criteria for distinguishing transformation within a low-grade MALT lymphoma {383}. When both histologies are evident, the lesion is best described as composite. When small foci of large transformed cells or early sheeting-out of large cells are detected within a background of low-grade intestinal MALT lymphoma, their prognostic impact of these findings and their effect on treatment are undetermined. Diffuse large B-cell lymphomas arising in the small bowel that lack a background of low-grade MALT lymphoma are currently best classified as extranodal diffuse large B-cell lymphoma, not otherwise specified {670}.

IPSID / αHCD

Immunoproliferative small intestinal disease and α heavy chain disease are part of a spectrum of lymphoproliferative diseases prevailing in the Middle East and Mediterranean countries {792}. They are subtypes of small intestinal MALT lym-

phoma characterized by the synthesis of α heavy chain. The histology is characteristic of MALT lymphoma with marked plasma cell differentiation.

Three stages of IPSID are recognized. In stage A, the lymphoplasmacytic infiltrate is confined to the mucosa and mesenteric lymph nodes, and cytological atypia is not present. Although the infiltrate may obliterate the villous architecture, marked cytological atypia is usually found, including Reed-Sternberg-like cells. Mitotic activity is increased. Mesenteric lymph node involvement occurs early in the course of disease, with both plasma cell infiltration of nodal sinuses and marginal-zone areas distended by small atypical lymphoma cells with moderate amounts of pale, clear cytoplasm.

Immunohistochemical studies demonstrate the production of α heavy chain without light chain synthesis {798}. IgA is almost always of the IgA1 type, with intact carboxy-terminal regions and

characteristic features of MALT lymphoma are now evident, and follicular colonization may be so marked as to mimic follicular lymphoma. Stage C is characterized by the presence of large masses and transformation to frank large cell lymphoma. Numerous centroblasts and immunoblasts are present. Plasmacytic differentiation is still evident, but marked cytological atypia is usually found, including Reed-Sternberg-like cells. Mitotic activity is increased. Resection specimens reveal normal endoscopic examination appears normal. Resection specimens reveal reactive lymphoid follicles, lymphoepithelial lesions and small clusters of parafollicular clear cells. This phase of the disease is typically responsive to antibiotic therapy. In stage B, nodular mucosal infiltrates develop and there is extension below the muscularis mucosae. A minimal degree of cytological atypia is apparent. This stage appears to represent a transitional phase, can be seen macroscopically as thickening of mucosal folds, and is typically not reversible with antibiotics. The

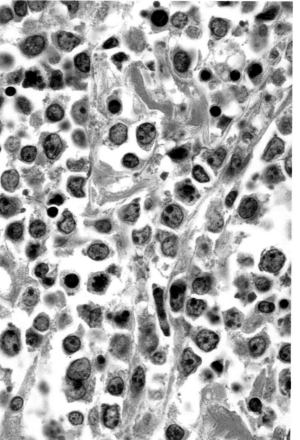

Fig. 4.18 High-grade B-cell lymphoma of the small intestine.

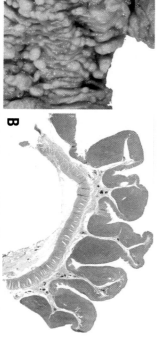

Fig. 4.19 Malignant lymphomatous polyposis. **A** Typical polypoid mucosa. **B** Polypoid mantle cell lymphoma.

deletion of most of the V and all of the CH1 domains. The molecular characterization of individual cases is variable. The small lymphoma cells express CD19 and CD20, but fail to express CD5, CD10 and CD23.

Mantle cell lymphoma

Mantle cell lymphoma (MCL) typically involves both spleen and intestines and may present as an isolated mass or as multiple polyps throughout the gastrointestinal tract where it is referred to as *multiple lymphomatous polyposis* {424, 791, 1292}. Importantly, other histological subtypes of non-Hodgkin lymphoma can also produce this clinico-pathological entity.

The polyps range in size from 0.5 cm to 2 cm with much larger polyps found in the ileocaecal region. The histology of MCL involving the small bowel is identical to MCL at nodal sites {110}. The architecture is most frequently diffuse, but a nodular pattern and a less common true mantle-zone pattern are also observed. Reactive germinal centers may be found and are usually compressed by the surrounding lymphoma cells, thereby appearing as replacing the normal mantle zones. Intestinal glands may be destroyed by the lymphoma, but typical lymphoepithelial lesions are not seen. The low power appearance is monotonous with frequent epithelioid histiocytes, mitotic figures and fine sclerosis surrounding small blood vessels. The lymphoma cells are small to medium sized with irregular nuclear outlines, indistinct nucleoli and scant amounts of cytoplasm. Large transformed cells are typically not present. The lymphoma cells are mature B-cells and express both CD19 and CD20. Characteristically the cells co-express CD5 and CD43. Surface immunoglobulin is found including both IgM and IgD. Light chain restriction is present in most cases, with some studies demonstrating a predominance of lambda. CD10 and CD11c are virtually always negative. Bcl-1 (cyclin D1) is found in virtually all cases and can be demonstrated within the nuclei of the neoplastic lymphocytes in paraffin sections.

MCL is an aggressive lymphoma, which typically presents in advanced stage with involvement of mesenteric lymph nodes and spread beyond the abdomen, including peripheral lymph nodes,

spleen, bone marrow and peripheral blood involvement {84}.

Burkitt lymphoma

Burkitt lymphoma occurs in two major forms, defined as endemic and sporadic. Endemic Burkitt is found primarily in Africa and typically presents in the jaw, orbit or paraspinal region, and is strongly associated with Epstein-Barr virus (EBV).

In other endemic regions however, it is relatively common for Burkitt lymphoma to present in the small intestine, usually involving the ileum, with preferential localization to the ileocaecal region {792}. In parts of the Middle East, primary gastrointestinal Burkitt lymphoma is a common disease of children. Sporadic or non-endemic Burkitt lymphoma is a rare disease, not associated with EBV infection, that frequently presents as primary intestinal lymphoma. Burkitt lymphoma is also seen in the setting of HIV infection when it often involves the gastrointestinal tract {236}.

The histology in all cases is identical and is characterized by a diffuse infiltrate of medium-sized cells with round to oval nuclear outlines, 2-5 small but distinct nucleoli and a small amount of intensely basophilic cytoplasm. Numerous mitotic figures and apoptotic cells are present. The prominent starry-sky appearance is caused by benign phagocytic histiocytes engulfing the nuclear debris resulting from apoptosis. Thin sections often show

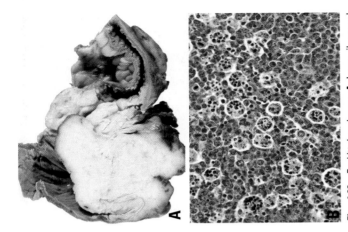

Fig. 4.20 Burkitt lymphoma. **A** Large ileocecal mass. **B** Starry-sky effect due to phagocytic histiocytes.

an unusual finding for lymphomas, whereby the cytoplasmic borders of individual cells 'square-off' against each other.

Burkitt lymphoma may rarely demonstrate a true follicular architecture, consistent with the proposed germinal center histogenesis of this neoplasm. It is a mature B-cell lymphoma and the neoplastic cells express pan-B-cell antigens

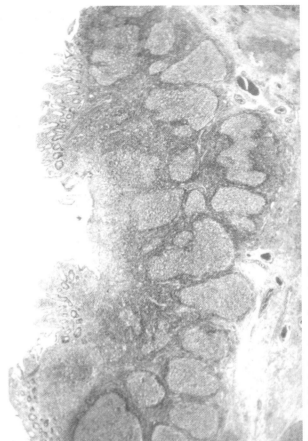

Fig. 4.21 Follicular lymphoma of terminal ileum.

CD19, CD20, CD22, and CD79a. In approximately 60-80% of cases, the neoplastic cells co-express CD10, but fail to express CD5 or CD23. Surface immunoglobulin expression is moderately intense and is nearly always IgM with either kappa or lambda light chain restriction. The growth fraction, as assessed by Ki-67 or the paraffin equivalent MIB-1, is typically in excess of 90% of tumour cells. Burkitt lymphoma cells uniformly fail to express bcl-2.

Burkitt-like lymphoma

This group of *atypical Burkitt lymphoma* appears to represent a morphological overlap between Burkitt lymphoma and diffuse large B-cell lymphoma. The overall cell size is similar to Burkitt, but with greater pleomorphism {827}. These cases lack the typical monomorphic appearance of Burkitt lymphoma and demonstrate slight variation in both cell size and shape. The cells may have multiple nucleoli as in Burkitt lymphoma or a single distinct nucleolus. A starry-sky pattern may be evident and the mitotic rate is usually significantly increased. These lymphomas have a predilection for the gastrointestinal tract of adults, and also occur in the setting of HIV infection.

Other B-cell lymphomas

Any subtype of B-cell lymphoma can present as a primary small intestinal lymphoma, including those thought to arise from peripheral lymph node equivalents. *De novo* diffuse large B-cell lymphomas are the commonest lymphomas in the small bowel, and may develop from low-grade MALT lymphomas.

Indolent lymphomas such as small lymphocytic lymphoma, lymphoplasmacytic lymphoma and follicular lymphoma (centroblastic/centrocytic) can present as primary small intestinal disease. The latter subtype can occasionally produce the clinico-pathological entity of multiple lymphomatous polyposis, but can usually be distinguished from MCL by immunophenotypic and molecular genetic analysis {1034}.

Lymphoblastic lymphoma may underlie small intestinal lymphoma and frequently produces a mass in the ileocaecal region. Characteristic nuclear features and the expression of terminal nucleotidyl transferase may aid in establishing the diagnosis.

Genetics

MALT lymphoma

Cytogenetic and molecular features of intestinal MALT lymphomas are incompletely understood; the presence of either t(1;14)(q22;q32) or t(11;18)(q21;q21) and the corresponding molecular abnormalities, rearrangement of bcl-10 or AP12-MLT, have not been described at this site; thus their relationship to gastric MALT lymphomas is unclear {2116, 412}. Trisomy 3 is common in gastric MALT lymphomas, but the frequency of this cytogenetic abnormality in primary intestinal lymphomas is unknown {413}.

IPSID

Although cytogenetic abnormalities have been detected in IPSID, no consistent changes have been described. Southern blot analysis reveals clonal immunoglobulin heavy-chain (IgH) gene rearrangements, but consensus IgH polymerase chain reaction (PCR) strategies may yield false negative results.

Mantle cell lymphoma

MCL is cytogenetically characterized by a t(11;14)(q13;q32) translocation which deregulates expression of the bcl-1 oncogene on chromosome 11. Rearrangement can be detected using Southern blot analysis, PCR or fluorescent *in situ* hybridization (FISH).

Burkitt lymphoma

Burkitt lymphoma demonstrates a consistent cytogenetic abnormality in all cases, with rearrangement of the *c-myc* oncogene on chromosome 8. The characteristic translocation, t(8;14)(q24;q32), is seen in most cases; the remainder shows variant translocations including the immunoglobulin light chain loci, t(2;8)(p12;q24) or t(8;22)(q24;q11), involving kappa and lambda light chain genes, respectively. In the classical t(8;14), the *c-myc* oncogene is translocated from chromosome 8 to the heavy chain locus on chromosome 14. In the variant translocations, a part of the light chain constant region is translocated to chromosome 8, distal to the *c-myc* gene. Thus, in the variant translocations, *c-myc* remains on chromosome 8 and is deregulated by virtue of its juxtaposition to the immunoglobulin light chain genes. The molecular characteristics of the *c-myc* translocation also differ between endemic and sporadic cases. In endemic Burkitt lymphoma, the chromosome 8 breakpoints are usually far 5' of the *c-myc* gene, while their chromosome 14 breakpoints most often occur in the location of the IgH gene joining segments. The variable chromosome 8 breakpoints and their location far from the *c-myc* coding sequences make it impossible in most cases to demonstrate *c-myc* rearrangements by Southern blot analysis. In contrast, sporadic cases frequently have *c-myc* breakpoints within non-coding introns and exons of the gene itself, typically in the first exon or intron, or in the 5' flanking regions of the gene. In most of these cases, *c-myc* rearrangements can be demonstrated using Southern analysis {670}.

Burkitt-like lymphoma/ Atypical Burkitt lymphoma

This category is cytogenetically heterogeneous and may contain three or more biological groups {1387}. Importantly, the frequency of variant *c-myc* translocations precludes the accurate recognition of cases using molecular techniques alone.

Prognostic factors

The main determinants of clinical outcome in small intestinal lymphomas are histological grade, stage, and resectability {424}. Advanced age at diagnosis, an acute presentation with perforation, and the presence of multifocal tumours have an adverse impact on survival. The behaviour of diffuse large B-cell lymphoma is not affected by the presence of a low-grade MALT component {424}. The expression of bcl-2 protein and the presence of TP53 mutations may adversely affect outcome in this group, but a systematic study of small intestinal lymphomas is lacking {567, 770}.

MCL is an aggressive neoplasm. A blastoid cytology, increased mitotic index and peripheral blood involvement are recognized as adverse factors {84}. Mutations in the p53 gene and homozygous deletions of p16 have recently been shown to be associated with poor prognosis {1099, 700}. Burkitt-like lymphomas with 'dual translocation' of both bcl-2 and c-myc oncogenes have a markedly shortened overall survival {1137}.

Intestinal T-cell lymphoma

R.D. Gascoyne
H.K. Müller-Hermelink
A. Chott
A. Wotherspoon

Definition

A peripheral T-cell lymphoma arising in the intestine, usually as a complication of coeliac disease (gluten sensitive enteropathy), histologically characterised by differentiation towards the intestinal intraepithelial T-cell phenotype.

ICD-O codes

T-cell lymphoma   9702/3
Enteropathy associated   9717/3

Epidemiology and aetiology

Intestinal T-cell lymphoma (ITL) is rare, accounting for only about 5% of all gastrointestinal lymphomas, and is normally associated with coeliac disease {305}. There is marked geographic variation in the incidence of ITL, with a high incidence in Northern Europe, reflecting the same notion that ITL arises against the same genetic background as that predisposing to coeliac disease {753}.

There is no clear sex predominance and in Europe, the median age at diagnosis is around 60 years {305, 424, 374}. In contrast, a small series of Mexican patients had a median age of 24 years and there was circumstantial evidence for a possible aetiological role of the Epstein Barr virus {1552, 795}. Congenital or acquired immunodeficiency disorders are not known to be associated with ITL.

Localization

The proximal jejunum is the most frequent site of disease, although it may occur elsewhere in the small intestine and, rarely, in the stomach and colon {305}.

Clinical features

The most frequent symptoms are abdominal pain and weight loss {303}. About 40% of patients present as acute abdominal emergencies due to intestinal perforation and/or obstruction {305, 424}. Patients may have a short history of malabsorption, sometimes diagnosed as adult coeliac disease which is usually gluten-insensitive or, less frequently, a long history of coeliac disease lasting for years or even decades {796}.

Signs and symptoms of the disease may mimic inflammatory bowel disease (IBD), particularly Crohn disease. Radiographic studies may be helpful, but they are often interpreted as consistent with a segmental or diffuse inflammatory process. Except for leukocytosis, laboratory data are usually unremarkable, including normal levels of lactate dehydrogenase {303}.

Refractory coeliac disease and ulcerative jejunitis are two conditions that frequently have a history of coeliac disease for years, become resistant to gluten-free diet and may, but not necessarily, progress to ITL {1385, 92}. In ulcerative jejunitis, patients develop non-specific inflammatory ulcers without overt histological evidence of lymphoma.

Macroscopy

The affected bowel segment is often dilated and oedematous, and usually shows multiple circumferential ulcers, ulcerated plaques and strictures, without the formation of large tumour masses {424}. The intact mucosa between the lesions may contain thickened folds or appear completely normal. Loops of bowel may adhere to each other or additionally to the left or right colon, causing palpable conglomerate tumours.

Tumour spread and staging

About 70% of the patients present with localized intestinal disease with or without contiguous lymph node involvement {305}. Disseminated disease involves liver, spleen, lung, testes, and skin, but rarely the bone marrow {303, 794}.

Histopathology

The histological appearances of ITL are variable both between cases and between different tumour sites in the same patient. The most frequently encountered type is composed of highly pleomorphic, medium to large cells, followed by a lymphoma type that shows a morphology most consistent with anaplastic large cell lymphoma. The border between these two histologies is not sharp and transition from one to the other may occur, even within the same tumour {307}.

About 20% of ITL are characterized by the monotonous appearance of densely packed small to medium-sized cells almost without any recognizable stroma components. Most of the rather monomorphic cells contain only slightly

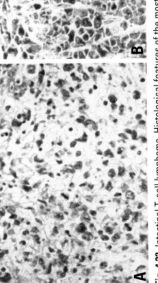

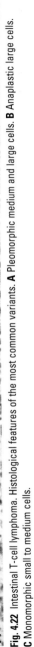

Fig. 4.22 Intestinal T-cell lymphoma. Histological features of the most common variants. **A** Pleomorphic medium and large cells. **B** Anaplastic large cells. **C** Monomorphic small to medium cells.

irregular nuclei with small nucleoli and moderately wide, pale or sometimes clear cytoplasm {307}. Rare variants of ITL are composed predominantly of pleomorphic small cells or immunoblasts. Irrespective of morphology, the lymphoma cells often invade and destroy the overlying epithelium. Most frequently, the enterocytes of the upper and intermediate villous regions, or in cases of severe villous atrophy, the epithelium of the upper parts of the elongated crypts are the preferential targets of lymphoma cell attack. These features are best appreciated at the borders of ulcerated tumours. However, they may also be present as band-like or patchy microscopic lesions entirely confined to the mucosa {303}. Fibrosis and admixed inflammatory cells are constant features of the pleomorphic medium and large cell and the anaplastic large cell ITL types; in the former, an abundance of eosinophils may mask the neoplastic infiltrate {1731}. In contrast, the monomorphic small to medium-sized variant characteristically lacks fibrotic changes and inflammatory background {307}.

Histopathology of the enteropathic mucosa

In the vast majority of cases, the macroscopically normal intestinal mucosa shows features of coeliac disease, i.e. increase in normal appearing intraepithelial lymphocytes (IEL), villous atrophy, and crypt hyperplasia {794}, which has prompted O'Farrelly and co-workers to coin the term 'enteropathy associated T-cell lymphoma' {1383}. An increase in normal appearing IEL (duodenum / jejunum, ≥ 40/100 enterocytes; ileum, ≥ 20/100 enterocytes) represents the single most important feature suggestive of coeliac disease {1172}. The severity of these enteropathic changes is highly variable and similar to coeliac disease; they are most pronounced proximally and improve distally so that the lower jejunum and ileum may appear normal. Furthermore, enteropathy may be minimal or absent if the patient is on a gluten free diet, or if enteropathic sites are missed because of their patchy distribution. Occasionally, the non-neoplastic mucosa in ITL shows a strikingly intense or florid intraepithelial lymphocytosis {2142}.

Immunological phenotyping

Similarities of the immunophenotypes in normal or activated (reactive) intraepithelial lymphocytes (IEL) and the tumour cells in ITL provide an important part of evidence that ITL cells are the neoplastic counterpart of IEL. The expression of the HML-1 defined $\alpha^E\beta_7$ (CD103) on non-neoplastic IEL and in > 50% of ITL, but not in resting peripheral blood T-cells, strongly supports this view {1802}. The vast majority of normal IEL are resting cytotoxic CD3+CD8+CD4-CD2+CD7+ CD5low TIA-1+ T-cells using the $\alpha\beta$ T-cell receptor, but minor subsets such as CD4-CD8- or CD56+ are present as well as predominantly CD4-CD8- $\gamma\delta$ T-cells {2142}; a t(4;16)(q26;p13) translocation was present in a mesenteric

Genetics

Very few data on chromosomal abnormalities in ITL exist. Deletion of the Y chromosome and chromosome 9 abnormalities were found among a phenotypically aberrant intraepithelial T-cell population {2142}; a t(4;16)(q26;p13) translocation was present in a mesenteric

CD3+CD4-CD8-CD7+CD5- and co-express the cytotoxic granule-associated protein TIA-1, often together with the activation-dependent cytotoxic molecule granzyme B {305, 382}. Some correlations between ITL morphology and phenotype exist; pleomorphic medium and large cell lymphomas and lymphomas of anaplastic large cell histology are often CD4-CD8-, the latter express CD30+ but are always ALK1 negative; the monomorphic small to medium-sized variant is frequently associated with a CD56+CD8+ phenotype {307}.

Cytologically normal IEL abundantly present in the intact enteropathic mucosa in ITL, in ulcerative jejunitis, and in refractory coeliac disease share an identical aberrant phenotype with ITL and are monoclonal, as demonstrated by PCR {103}. They therefore are considered a neoplastic population which, in the absence of concurrent overt ITL, may represent the first step in ITL lymphomagenesis ('intraepithelial lymphoma') and may have already persisted for years {238}.

ITL diagnosis of endoscopic biopsies

Most cases of ITL are diagnosed on surgical resection specimens. In a minority, however, endoscopic biopsies, usually taken from the stomach, duodenum, or colon, are available. These patients frequently have a longer than 6 months history of abdominal pain and weight loss. Some of them are clinically suspected to have inflammatory bowel disease, and occasionally patients had already been biopsied with the diagnosis of IBD or an unclear inflammatory process, thus emphasizing the challenging task of ITL diagnosis in endoscopic biopsies. The immunohistochemical demonstration of an aberrant phenotype is essential in diagnosing ITL, especially in cases which lack overt cytological atypia and/or invasiveness. Furthermore, the neoplastic infiltrate may be subtle or superficial and therefore easily overlooked in routinely stained sections.

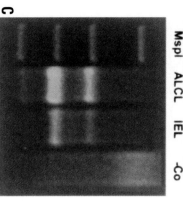
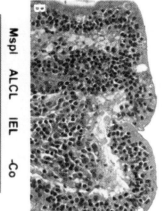

C

MspI   ALCL   IEL   -Co

Fig. 4.23 Coeliac disease. The non-neoplastic mucosa distant from an anaplastic large cell intestinal T-cell lymphoma displays villous atrophy, crypt hyperplasia (A) and an increase in cytologically unremarkable intraepithelial lymphocytes (B) without evidence of lymphoma. Both the lymphoma (ALCL) and the intraepithelial lymphocytes (IEL) share the same dominant T-cell clone (C) and the same aberrant immunological phenotype.

lymph node associated with extensive ITL {239}. In two cases of anaplastic large cell ITL very complex abnormalities were detected in ascitic fluid and lymph node, respectively {1436}.

Southern blotting and PCR studies demonstrated monoclonal rearrangements of the T-cell receptor (β-chain) in ITL, consistent with the derivation from αβ T-cells {799}. ITL using the γδ T-cell receptor are rare {86}, but nevertheless seem to outnumber the few well documented cases of true intestinal natural killer (NK) cell lymphomas {1176}. The latter finding is not surprising as NK cells are not present among IEL.

Prognosis and predictive factors

The clinical course is very unfavorable due to complications from peritonitis and malnutrition and later from progressive disease typically characterized by intestinal recurrences. The malabsorption due to underlying coeliac disease is detrimental to these patients, particularly when recovering from surgery or receiving multiagent chemotherapy {444}. Consequently, only one half of the patients is amenable to chemotherapy

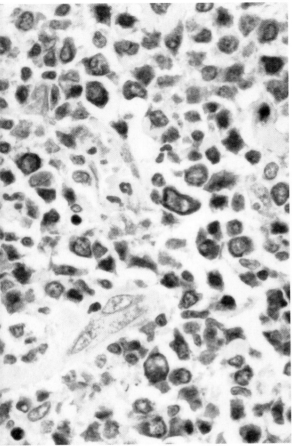

Fig. 4.24 CD3 immunoexpression in a T-cell lymphoma of the small intestine.

and only a proportion of these is able to finish the complete course. The overall median survival in the largest published series is only 3 months, and 5-year survival in this and other series ranges from 8-25% {305, 424, 444}. The small group of long-term survivors usually received chemotherapy and, interestingly, none had a previous diagnosis of coeliac disease {305, 444}.

Mesenchymal tumours of the small intestine

M. Miettinen
J.Y. Blay
L.H. Sobin

Definition

A variety of benign and malignant mesenchymal tumours can arise in the small intestine, but the neoplasms that occur in any appreciable numbers are gastrointestinal stromal tumours (GISTs).

Epidemiology

Sarcomas account for approximately 14% of malignant small intestinal tumours {1928}. Males are affected somewhat more than females (M:F 1.2:1). The peak incidence is in the 6th to 8th decade. Age of onset for sarcomas was lower than for carcinomas, with black females showing the lowest median age, 50 years. In the U.S. SEER database, the incidence rate for sarcoma was 0.2 per 100,000 per year compared to 0.3 for lymphomas, 0.4 for adenocarcinomas and 0.4 for carcinoids, {1928}. GISTs have been specifically identified in duodenum, jejunum, and ileum {183, 594, 1980}.

Localization

Sarcomas show a much more even distribution throughout the small bowel compared to adenocarcinomas and carcinoids {1928}. GISTs have been specifically identified in duodenum, jejunum, cally identified in duodenum, jejunum, than those in the stomach.

Clinical features

Vague abdominal discomfort is the usual complaint. Mesenchymal neoplasms of small bowel are more difficult to diagnose by endoscopy or imaging studies than those in the stomach.

Macroscopy

Small bowel sarcomas generally appear macroscopically as those in the stomach. Some small intestinal tumours may cause aneurysmal bowel dilatation, while others have a diverticulum-like appearance.

Histopathology

Gastrointestinal stromal tumours

Small bowel GISTs resemble those of the stomach histologically, although epithelioid lesions are uncommon. Globoid extracellular collagen accumulations (so-called skeinoid fibers) are frequently

observed, especially in benign small intestinal GISTs {1235}. Factors that correlate with malignancy are tumour size > 5 cm, mitotic count > 5 per 50 HPF, dense cellularity, and mucosal invasion (rarely observed). Even with low or absent mitotic activity, tumours larger than 5 cm are considered to have malignant potential. Small intestinal GISTs are positive for KIT (CD117) and usually for CD34, and a subset (30-50%) are positive for α-smooth muscle actin; most tumours are negative for desmin and almost all are negative for S100-protein.

Leiomyomas and *leiomyosarcomas* are rare in the small intestine, and can be identified immunohistochemically by their smooth muscle actin and desmin expression and lack of KIT.

Angiosarcomas are recognized by an anastomosing proliferation of atypical endothelial cells. Immunohistochemical demonstration of CD31, less consistently von Willebrand factor, is diagnostically useful {1904}.

Kaposi sarcomas may involve small intestine, either the mucosa alone or more extensively. Histologically typical are elongated spindle cells with vascular slits. Cytoplasmic PAS-positive hyaline globules are present in some tumour cells. Immunohistochemically, the lesional cells are positive for CD31 and CD34. Human herpesvirus 8 can be demonstrated by PCR.

Lipomas exhibit the same morphological features as their colonic counterparts.

Genetics

Small intestinal GISTs show similar *c-kit* mutations in exon 11 as observed in gastric GISTs, and most mutations occur in the malignant cases. Comparative genomic hybridization shows common losses in chromosomes 14 and 22 similar to those seen in gastric GISTs.

Prognosis

The prognosis of small bowel sarcomas is largely dependent on the mitotic count, size, depth of invasion, and presence or absence of metastasis. In the SEER database, 5-year survival for localized tumours was 45% for sarcomas, compared to 92% for carcinoids and 63% for carcinomas {1928}. In a study of over one thousand stromal/smooth muscle sarcomas, the 5-year survival rate was 55% for sarcomas of small bowel, 60% for colorectum, 70% for stomach and 75% for oesophagus {462}.

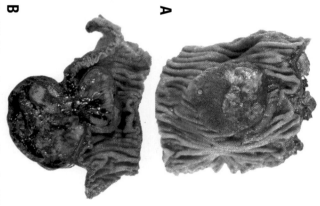

A

B

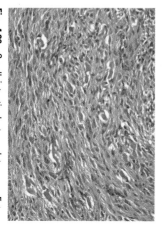

Fig. 4.26 Small intestinal stromal tumour. Extracellular accumulation of skeinoid fibres produces eosinophilic globules.

Secondary tumours of the small and large intestines

C. Niederau
L.H. Sobin

Definition

Tumours of the intestines that originate from an extra-intestinal neoplasm or which are discontinuous with a primary tumour elsewhere in the gastrointestinal tract.

Epidemiology

Metastatic spread to the small intestine is more frequent than to any other site in the gastrointestinal tract (see Table 3.02). Secondary carcinomas of the small bowel are as common as primary carcinomas at this site {1234}.

Origin

For small intestine, melanoma, lung, breast, colon and kidney are the most frequent primary sites (see Table 3.02) {130, 1022, 1378, 1209, 1457, 458}. Metastatic spread from primary lung cancer to the small intestine is more frequent than to stomach and colon (Table 4.01). Virtually all primary cancers can occasionally lead to metastases in the small intestine and, because of the low frequency of primary small bowel cancer, a high proportion of small intestinal malignancies are metastatic.

The pathogenesis of intestinal metastasis usually involves haematogenous spread of tumour cells. Invasion from neighbouring primary tumours also occurs, e.g. pancreatic carcinoma to duodenum and prostate carcinoma to rectum.

Primary melanomas of the intestine are very rare. Although most melanomas found in the small bowel have no history

Table 4.01
Frequency of metastasis from breast (695 cases) and lung (747 cases) to gastrointestinal tract {130}.

Primary site	Stomach	Small intestine	Colon
Breast	3.6%	1.7%	1.4%
Lung	1.3%	4.4%	1.9%

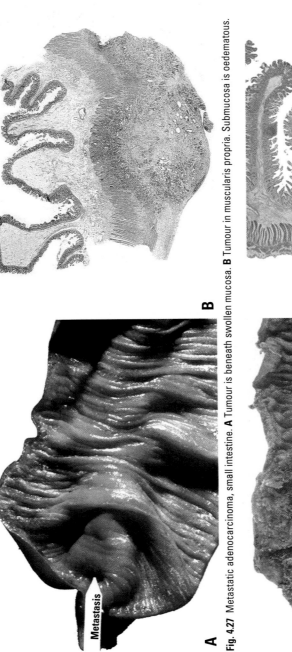

Fig. 4.27 Metastatic adenocarcinoma, small intestine. **A** Tumour is beneath swollen mucosa. **B** Tumour in muscularis propria. Submucosa is oedematous.

Fig. 4.28 A, B Metastatic malignant melanoma, small intestine.

of a primary tumour, the general consensus is that they are virtually all secondary, usually from misdiagnosed or regressed primary melanomas {458}.

Clinical features

Small intestinal metastases can cause bleeding and obstruction as well as non-specific symptoms such as abdominal discomfort, gas distension, and diarrhoea {1378, 580}.

Imaging

The identification of a small bowel tumour always raises the question of whether the tumour is primary or secondary. Contrast radiography shows narrowing and abnormalities of the small intestinal wall. Advanced cases result in stenosis with distension due to obstruction.

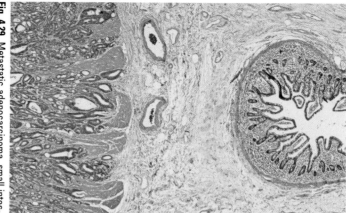

Fig. 4.29 Metastatic adenocarcinoma, small intestine. Muscularis propria contains tumour. Mucosa is free of neoplasia.

Macroscopy

Typical features of intestinal metastases include intestinal wall thickening, submucosal spread, and ulcers. Melanomas may not be pigmented and may appear as nodules or polyps.

Histopathology

Metastases are typically submucosal or subserosal making the distinction between primary and secondary tumours relatively easy. Cytokeratin immunohistochemistry may help to differentiate between primary colon cancer (positive for cytokeratin 20), metastases from ovary and breast (usually positive for cytokeratin 7) and those from liver, kidney and prostate (usually negative for both cytokeratins 7 and 20) {2047, 129}. On the other hand, the distinction between

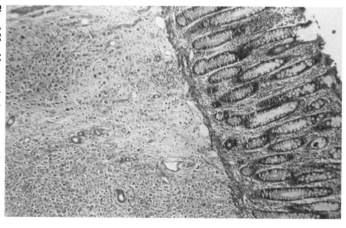

Fig. 4.30 Metastatic breast carcinoma, colon. Tumour cells expand submucosa.

multiple primary small bowel carcinoids and their metastases may not be possible. This also applies to leiomyosarcomas/stromal tumours of the small intestine.

Prognosis

Intestinal metastases usually represent a late stage of disease in which other haematogenous metastases are also frequently found. Therefore, the prognosis is poor. Exceptions are melanoma and renal cancer in which metastases confined to the bowel may be associated with prolonged survival after resection.

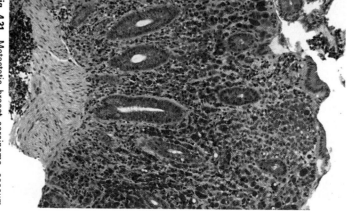

Fig. 4.31 Metastatic breast carcinoma, caecum, diastase-PAS stain. Many tumour cells are mucin positive.

CHAPTER 5

Tumours of the Appendix

The appendix is the most frequent site of carcinoids, i.e. tumours with endocrine differentiation, that span a wide range of morphological variety.

Adenocarcinomas of the appendix also show interesting morphological variations, from those that resemble the usual colorectal carcinoma to those that arise from a carcinoid and to mucinous tumours that may appear well differentiated and indistinguishable from adenoma and yet spread widely through the peritoneal cavity.

WHO histological classification of tumours of the appendix[1]

Epithelial tumours			Non-epithelial tumours		
Adenoma			Neuroma		9570/0
	Tubular	8211/0	Lipoma		8850/0
	Villous	8261/0	Leiomyoma		8890/0
	Tubulovillous	8263/0	Gastrointestinal stromal tumour		8936/1
	Serrated	8213/0	Leiomyosarcoma		8890/3
			Kaposi sarcoma		9140/3
Carcinoma			Others		
	Adenocarcinoma	8140/3			
	Mucinous adenocarcinoma	8480/3	**Malignant lymphoma**		
	Signet-ring cell carcinoma	8490/3			
	Small cell carcinoma	8041/3	**Secondary tumours**		
	Undifferentiated carcinoma	8020/3			
			Hyperplastic (metaplastic) polyp		
Carcinoid (well differentiated endocrine neoplasm)		8240/3			
	EC-cell, serotonin-producing neoplasm	8241/3			
	L-cell, glucagon-like peptide				
	and PP/PYY producing tumour				
	Others				
Tubular carcinoid		8245/1			
Goblet cell carcinoid (mucinous carcinoid)		8243/3			
Mixed carcinoid-adenocarcinoma		8244/3			
Others					

[1] This classification is modified from the previous WHO histological classification of tumours {845} taking into account changes in our understanding of these lesions. In the case of endocrine neoplasms, it is based on the recent WHO classification {1784} but has been simplified to be of more practical utility in morphological classification.
[2] Morphology code of the International Classification of Diseases for Oncology (ICD-O) {542} and the Systematized Nomenclature of Medicine (http://snomed.org). Behaviour is coded /0 for benign tumours, /3 for malignant tumours, and /1 for unspecified, borderline or uncertain behaviour.

TNM classification of tumours of the appendix

TNM classification[1,2]

T – Primary Tumour

TX	Primary tumour cannot be assessed
T0	No evidence of primary tumour
Tis	Carcinoma in situ: intraepithelial or invasion of lamina propria[3]
T1	Tumour invades submucosa
T2	Tumour invades muscularis propria
T3	Tumour invades through muscularis propria into subserosa or into non-peritonealized periappendiceal tissue
T4	Tumour directly invades other organs or structures and/or perforates visceral peritoneum

N – Regional Lymph Nodes

NX	Regional lymph nodes cannot be assessed
N0	No regional lymph node metastasis
N1	Metastasis in 1 to 3 regional lymph nodes
N2	Metastasis in 4 or more regional lymph nodes

M – Distant Metastasis

MX	Distant metastasis cannot be assessed
M0	No distant metastasis
M1	Distant metastasis

Stage Grouping

Stage 0	Tis	N0	M0
Stage I	T1	N0	M0
	T2	N0	M0
Stage II	T3	N0	M0
	T4	N0	M0
Stage III	Any T	N1	M0
	Any T	N2	M0
Stage IV	Any T	Any N	M1

[1] {1, 66}. The classification applies only to carcinomas.
[2] A help desk for specific questions about the TNM classification is available at http://tnm.uicc.org.
[3] This includes cancer cells confined within the glandular basement membrane (intraepithelial) or lamina propria (intramucosal) with no extension through muscularis mucosae into submucosa.

Adenocarcinoma of the appendix

N.J. Carr
M.J. Arends
G.T. Deans
L.H. Sobin

Definition

A malignant epithelial neoplasm of the appendix with invasion beyond the muscularis mucosae.

ICD-O codes

Adenocarcinoma	8140/3
Mucinous adenocarcinoma	8480/3
Signet-ring cell carcinoma	8490/3

Epidemiology

Adenocarcinoma of the appendix occurs in 0.1% of appendicectomies, corresponding to an estimated incidence of 0.2/100,000 per annum {393, 1928}. Adenocarcinomas accounted for 58% of malignant appendiceal tumours in the SEER database, the remainder being mostly carcinoids. The rates for the carcinomas stayed constant during the period 1973-1987 {1928}. The median age of patients with mucinous and non-mucinous adenocarcinoma was about 65 years in SEER data; other studies suggest a peak age at manifestation in the sixth decade {250, 393}. Males appear to be more commonly affected than females {393}.

Aetiology

Patients with chronic ulcerative colitis (UC) have an increased susceptibility to formation of epithelial dysplasia and malignancy in affected segments of bowel; inflammatory involvement of the appendix is seen in approximately half of UC cases with pancolitis.
Both adenoma and adenocarcinoma of the appendix have been described in patients affected by long-standing ulcerative colitis {1394}.

Clinical features

Signs and symptoms

Many patients with appendiceal adenocarcinoma have clinical features indistinguishable from acute appendicitis. Most of the remaining cases present as an abdominal mass {250, 393}. Spread to the peritoneal cavity may produce large volumes of mucus, causing pseudomyxoma peritonei. Such cases may present with abdominal distension. Rarely, external fistulation occurs {251, 393, 707}.

Imaging

Ultrasound, computerised tomography (CT) scan or barium enema are of limited benefit in the pre-operative diagnosis of cases presenting as acute appendicitis. Ultrasound and CT scan are the preferred imaging procedures in cases presenting with abdominal mass or pseudomyxoma peritonei {393, 707}. Serial CT scanning and CEA measurements can assess the extent of peritoneal involvement and the subsequent course of the disease. Intraepithelial neoplasia of the appendix may occur concurrently with a carcinoma elsewhere in the large intestine {393}.

Macroscopy

In cases of primary adenocarcinoma, the appendix may be enlarged, deformed or completely destroyed {250, 251, 1612}. Well differentiated lesions are often cystic and may be called cystadenocarcinomas. A grossly appreciated swelling of the appendix due to the accumulation of mucus within the lumen can be termed mucocoele, but this is descriptive not a pathological diagnosis {250, 251}.

Tumour spread and staging

Although the TNM classification currently uses the same criteria as for colorectal tumours, appendiceal cases should be separately classified. This is particularly important because of the special nature of pseudomyxoma peritonei, where malignant cells may be scarce and acellular mucin may seem to have spread further than the malignant cells {250}. Well differentiated mucinous appendiceal adenocarcinomas generally grow slowly, and typically produce the clinical picture of pseudomyxoma peritonei. Lymph node metastases tend to occur late. Rarely, tumour growth in the retroperitoneum may produce 'pseudomyxoma retroperitonei' {1194}. The behaviour of non-mucinous carcinomas resembles that of their colonic counterparts.

Pseudomyxoma peritonei

Pseudomyxoma peritonei is the presence of mucinous material on peritoneal surfaces. It is not a complete histological

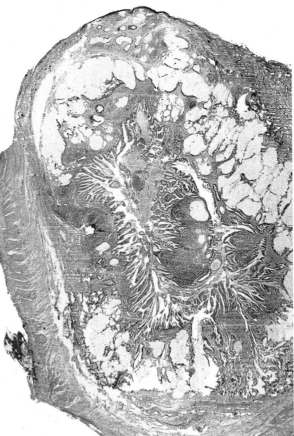

Fig. 5.01 Mucinous adenocarcinoma arising in a villous adenoma. The lumen is lined by a villous adenoma.

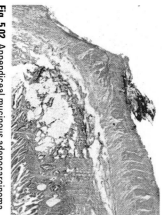

Fig. 5.02 Appendiceal mucinous adenocarcinoma.

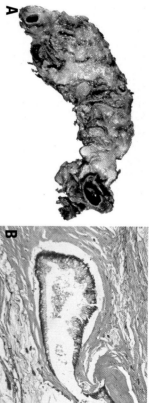

Fig. 5.03 Pseudomyxoma peritonei. **A** Several loops of bowel are encased in a multilocular mucinous mass. **B** Well differentiated mucus producing epithelium embedded in a fibrous matrix; mucus is present within the lumen and is extravasated into the stroma.

diagnosis in itself; the prognosis will depend on the nature of the causative lesion. Nevertheless, pseudomyxoma peritonei is often applied to a distinctive clinical picture produced by well differentiated mucinous adenocarcinomas in which the growth of malignant cells within the peritoneal cavity causes a slow but relentless accumulation of mucin. Cells may be very scanty within this mucinous material.

A distinctive feature of well differentiated mucinous carcinomatosis is its distribution in the abdomen. There is a tendency to spare the peritoneal surfaces of the bowel, whereas large-volume disease is found in the greater omentum, beneath the right hemidiaphragm, in the right retrohepatic space, at the ligament of Treitz, in the left abdominal gutter and in the pelvis {1854}. In these cases, tumour growth tends to remain confined to the abdomen for many years. Mucinous cysts within the spleen occur occasionally {433}.

It has been suggested that appendiceal adenomas can cause widespread pseudomyxoma peritonei with an ultimately fatal outcome, and some authors use the term 'adenomucinosis' for the spread of such lesions through the abdomen {1611, 1612}. It is considered more likely that

such cases are examples of well differentiated adenocarcinoma.

Although most cases of pseudomyxoma peritonei are due to spread from a primary carcinoma of the appendix, cases have been reported in association with mucinous carcinomas of other sites, including gallbladder, stomach, colorectum, pancreas, fallopian tube, urachus, lung, and breast {346, 612, 707, 981, 1199, 2199}.

Although the ovary has been thought of as a common primary site {104, 1705}, there is an accumulating body of evidence based on immunohistochemistry and molecular genetics suggesting that this is not the case, and that in most mucinous tumours of the ovary and appendix with pseudomyxoma peritonei the lesions are probably metastatic from an appendiceal primary {1536, 1611, 1612, 1871, 2187}.

Histopathology

The majority of appendiceal adenocarcinomas are well differentiated and mucinous {250, 706}. If signet-ring cells account for more than 50% of the neoplasm, the term signet-ring cell carcinoma is appropriate.

The term mucinous cystadenocarcinoma may be used for well differentiated mucinous tumours with cystic structures. However, this designation is descriptive and does not constitute a separate disease entity {251, 2115}.

Diagnostic criteria

The fundamental criterion for making the diagnosis of adenocarcinoma is the presence of invasive neoplasm beyond the muscularis mucosae; this is the same criterion that is applied throughout the large intestine (see Table 5.01). However, in practice it is not always easy to deter-

mine the extent of invasion, because well differentiated carcinomas of the appendix can mimic adenomas by invading on a broad front rather than showing infiltrative or single-cell invasion. Conversely, in some adenomas, acellular mucin dissects through the wall, mimicking invasion; this feature may be especially prominent if there is inflammation. If there is acellular mucin in the appendiceal wall, the diagnosis of adenoma should only be made if the muscularis mucosae is intact since this term implies that the lesion is curable by complete excision.

It is appropriate to use the term *mucinous tumour of uncertain malignant potential* for neoplasms in which the histological features do not allow distinction between a lesion that is benign (an adenoma) from one that has the potential to cause metastases (an adenocarcinoma). The term *low-grade mucinous cystic tumour* has also been used for lesions that are histologically not frankly malignant {2187A}.

Grading

Grading is the same as in the large intestine. Some adenocarcinomas of the appendix are so well differentiated that their neoplastic features may be very subtle {250}.

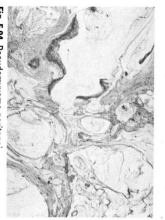

Fig. 5.04 Pseudomyxoma peritonei.

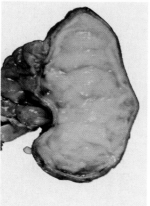

Fig. 5.05 Mucocoele of appendix.

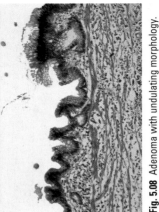

Fig. 5.06 Serrated adenoma of appendix.

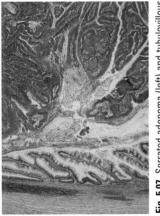

Fig. 5.07 Serrated adenoma (left) and tubulovillous adenoma (right).

Fig. 5.08 Adenoma with undulating morphology.

Precursor lesions and benign tumours

By analogy with the rest of the large intestine, an adenoma-carcinoma sequence is assumed to occur in the appendix; the finding of a residual adenoma in some cases of adenocarcinoma supports this contention {1548}. However, some adenocarcinomas appear to arise from goblet cell carcinoid tumours {209, 250}. Compared to adenomas of the colon, adenomas of the appendix are more likely to be villous or serrated {250, 706, 1548, 2115, 2110}.

Many appendiceal serrated and villous adenomas display minimal cytological abnormalities; such lesions need to be distinguished from hyperplastic polyps or mucosal hyperplasia. Pedunculated hyperplastic polyps of the type seen in the colon are unusual in the appendix, but diffuse hyperplasia is relatively common {2184}. The diagnosis of hyperplastic polyp/diffuse hyperplasia should not be made if there are cytological abnormalities in the epithelial cells; if any are present, then the diagnosis of adenoma should be considered. The presence of villous structures is also a pointer towards adenoma.

As they grow, adenomas of the appendix typically become cystic, and the lining epithelium becomes undulating rather than villous. Such lesions may produce a mucocoele and be given the descriptive appellation of cystadenoma.

Genetic susceptibility
Familial adenomatous polyposis coli (FAP)
A review of 71 000 appendix specimens revealed 33 benign and 6 malignant appendiceal tumours in patients with familial polyposis coli {324}. Several cases of adenocarcinoma of the appendix have been reported in FAP patients, including a patient with appendiceal

adenocarcinoma as the presenting feature {1464}.

Hereditary non-polyposis colorectal cancer (HNPCC)
This familial cancer syndrome confers increased susceptibility to proximal colon cancer {1936}, but it is not yet clear whether there is also an increased risk of appendiceal neoplasms.

Other polyposis syndromes
It is difficult to establish accurately the risk of genetic susceptibility to tumours of the appendix in Peutz-Jeghers and juvenile polyposis syndrome on account of the rarity of these conditions. Intussusception with an 'inside-out' appendix in Peutz-Jeghers syndrome has been reported, caused by a hamartomatous polyp of the appendix or an appendiceal

Genetics
Limited data are available on molecular genetic alterations in appendiceal tumours, and these data indicate similarities to those in colorectal tumours. *KRAS* mutations have been identified in approximately 70% of appendiceal mucinous adenomas, mostly in codon 12 and a few in codon 13 {1871}. In addition, *KRAS* mutation has been identified in an appendix cystadenoma associated with a long history of ulcerative colitis {1123}. Tumour suppressor gene allelic imbalances have been found in about half of appendiceal mucinous adenomas with loss of heterozygosity (LOH) at several chromosomal loci, including 5q22, 6q, 17p13, and 18q21. LOH was most fre-

polyp with villous adenomatous changes and focal carcinoma in situ {1243}.

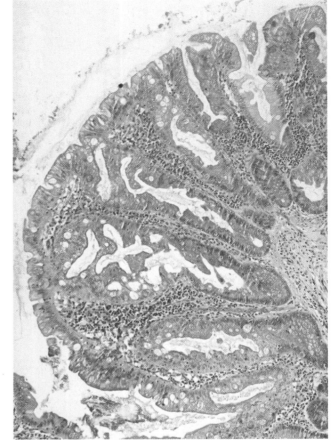

Fig. 5.09 Hyperplastic polyp of appendix. Cytological abnormalities of intraepithelial neoplasia are absent.

quent at the 5q locus linked to the APC tumour suppressor gene which in the colorectum is strongly associated with transition to adenoma {1871}. In cases of pseudomyxoma peritonei (well differentiated mucinous adenocarcinoma), LOH at one or two polymorphic microsatellite loci was seen in approximately half of the cases and was considered an indication of monoclonality.

Prognosis and predictive factors

SEER data showed the 5-year survival rates for localized adenocarcinoma to be 95%, compared with a 5-year survival of 80% for mucinous or cystadenocarcinoma. When distant metastases were present, the 5-year survival rates were 0% and 51% respectively {1928}. This reflects the low aggressive potential of mucinous tumours that spread to the peritoneum {1769}.
Features that have been associated with a poor prognosis in appendiceal adenocarcinoma include advanced stage,

high-grade, and nonmucinous histology {345, 1365, 1769}. The spread of mucus beyond the right lower quadrant of the abdomen (whether or not cells are identified within it) is an independent prognostic variable, as is the presence of neoplastic cells outside the visceral peritoneum of the appendix {250}. When pseudomyxoma peritonei is present, abdominal distension, weight loss, high histological grade, and morphological evidence of invasion of underlying structures have been found to be poor prognostic factors, whereas complete excision of tumour is associated with prolonged disease-free survival {346, 1612, 612}.
Cytological examination of aspirated mucus and DNA flow cytometry are unhelpful in predicting prognosis {612, 707}.

Table 5.01
Terminology of epithelial neoplasms of the appendix.

Diagnosis	Criteria	Significance
Adenoma (Cystadenoma)	Tumour confined to appendiceal mucosa *and* No histological evidence of invasion	Does not have the capacity to metastasize and can be cured by complete local excision.
Adenocarcinoma (Cystadenocarcinoma)	Histological evidence of mural invasion *or* Presence of metastases, including spread to peritoneal cavity	Can spread beyond the appendix with peritoneal, lymph node or distant metastases.

Endocrine tumours of the appendix

C. Capella
E. Solcia
L.H. Sobin
R. Arnold

Definition

Tumours with endocrine differentiation arising in the appendix.

Epidemiology

Incidence and time trends

Carcinoids account for 50-77% of all appendiceal neoplasms {1252, 1131}. Their incidence rate is 0.075 new cases per 100,000 population per year and appears to have been decreasing in the time period 1950-1991 {1251}. Approximately 19% of all carcinoids are located in the appendix.

Age and sex distribution

The mean age at presentation is 32-43 years (range, 6 to 80 years) {1251, 1252, 1607}. Tubular carcinoids occur at a significantly younger age than goblet cell carcinoids (average, 29 versus 53 years) {209}.

Appendiceal carcinoids occur more frequently in females than in males {1251}. This could reflect the greater number of incidental appendicectomies performed in women {1252} but in the SEER database, the frequency of non-carcinoid appendiceal tumours is similar among males and females, suggesting that the higher rate of appendiceal carcinoids in women may not be due solely to higher rates of appendicectomy {1251}. Furthermore, the prevalence of girls among children with appendiceal carcinoids can not be explained by differences in appendicectomy rates {866A, 1255}.

Clinical features

The majority of appendiceal endocrine tumours are found incidentally in appendicectomy specimens; the majority of these are asymptomatic and located in the distal end of the appendix. In a small number of cases, carcinoids involving the remaining portions of the appendix may obstruct the lumen and produce appendicitis {2059, 209}.

Carcinoid syndrome caused by an appendiceal carcinoid is extremely rare and almost always related to widespread

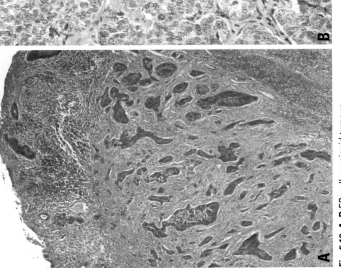

Fig. 5.10 A, B EC-cell carcinoid tumour.

metastases, usually to the liver and retroperitoneum {1252, 1927}.

Macroscopy

Appendiceal EC-cell carcinoids are firm, greyish-white (yellow after fixation), and fairly well circumscribed, but not encapsulated, and measure usually less than 1 cm in diameter {1252}. Tumours > 2 cm are rare; most are located at the tip of the appendix {1254}. Goblet-cell carcinoids and mixed endocrine-exocrine carcino-

mas of the appendix may be found in any portion of the appendix and appear as an area of whitish, sometimes mucoid induration without dilatation of the lumen. They range in size from 0.5 to 2.5 cm {442}.

Because of their diffusely infiltrative nature, goblet cell carcinoids tend not to form distinct tumours and their size generally cannot be assessed accurately. In a series of 33 cases {209} only two were suspected grossly; 11 involved the tip and 22 were circumferential.

Histopathology

Carcinoid (well differentiated endocrine neoplasm)

Most endocrine tumours of the appendix are serotonin-producing enterochromaffin (EC)-cell carcinoids, while only a minority are glucagon-like peptide and PP/PYY-producing L-cell carcinoids and mixed endocrine-exocrine carcinomas. They are classified according to the WHO histological classification of endocrine tumours {1784}.

Fig. 5.11 Carcinoid tumour of appendix with typical yellow colouration.

Fig. 5.12 Carcinoid tumour infiltrating mesoappendix.

EC-cell, serotonin-producing carcinoid

Argentaffin EC-cells, producing both serotonin and substance P, are arranged in rounded solid nests with some peripheral palisading (type A structure according to Soga and Tazawa {1775}). Occasionally, there may also be glandular formations (type C structures), forming a mixed (A+C) pattern. Most tumours display muscular and lymphatic invasion or perineural involvement; two thirds of the cases invade the peritoneum, possibly through endolymphatic spread {1252}. Despite these signs of apparent aggressiveness appendiceal carcinoids infrequently produce lymph node or distant metastases, in contrast to ileal carcinoids.

No relevant histologic, cytological, or cytochemical differences have been detected between ileal and appendiceal carcinoids, despite their very different clinical behaviour, with the exception of the presence of S100-positive sustentacular cells surrounding tumour nests in appendiceal lesions. In this respect, EC-cell appendiceal carcinoids resemble subepithelial neuroendocrine complexes rather than intraepithelial endocrine cells

{1115, 586, 1182}. In contrast, sustentacular cells are lacking in ileal and colonic EC-cell tumours, which develop from EC-cells of the mucosal crypts {1115, 1291}.

L-cell, glucagon-like peptide and PP/PYY-producing carcinoid

These are much less common. L-cell tumours are non-argentaffin, producing glucagon-like peptides (GLP-1, GLP-2, and the enteroglucagons glicentin and oxyntomodulin) and PP/PYY. They feature a characteristic tubular or trabecular pattern (type B pattern according to Soga and Tazawa {1775, 820, 1724, 1783}). These tumours generally measure only 2 to 3 mm and are the appendiceal counterpart of L-cell tumours that are most frequent in the rectum.

Mixed endocrine-exocrine neoplasms

This term is used for certain tumours of the appendix that show features of both glandular and endocrine differentiation, i.e. goblet cell carcinoid, tubular carcinoid and mixed carcinoid-adenocarcinomas {2059, 1254}.

Goblet-cell carcinoid. This tumour is characterized by a predominant submucosal growth. It typically invades through the appendiceal wall in a concentric manner that does not produce a well-defined tumour {209}. The mucosa is characteristically spared, with the exception of areas of connection of tumour nests with the base of the crypts. The tumour is composed of small, rounded nests of signet-ring-like cells resembling normal intestinal goblet cells, except for nuclear compression. Lumens are infrequently observed. Lysozyme-positive Paneth cells as well as foci resembling

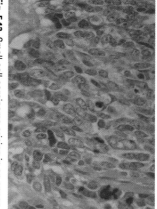

Fig. 5.13 Small cell carcinoma arising in an appendiceal tubulovillous adenoma.

Brunner glands may be present {2059, 790}. Mucin stains are intensely positive within goblet cells and extracellular mucin pools {790}. Argentaffin and argyrophil cells, sparse or forming small nests, are identified in 50% and 88% of cases, respectively {2059}.

Immunohistochemically, the endocrine cell component is positive for chromogranin A, serotonin, enteroglucagon, somatostatin, and/or PP {790, 725}. The goblet cells express CEA. On ultrastructural examination, both dense core endocrine granules and mucin droplets are found {442, 725}. Both elements are occasionally present within the cytoplasm of the same cell {442, 790}.

Tubular carcinoid. This tumour is often misinterpreted as a metastatic adenocarcinoma, because it does not resemble the typical carcinoid and shows little contact with the mucosa. It is composed of small, discrete tubules, some with inspissated mucin in their lumen. Short trabecular structures are frequent, but solid nests are generally absent. In sparse cells or in small groups of tumour cells, the argentaffin reaction is positive in 75%

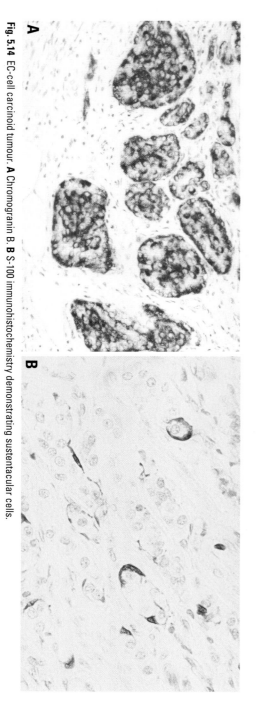

A

B

Fig. 5.14 EC-cell carcinoid tumour. **A** Chromogranin B. **B** S-100 immunohistochemistry demonstrating sustentacular cells.

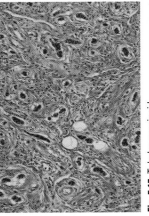

Fig. 5.15 L-cell tumour showing trabecular pattern and glicentin immunoexpression.

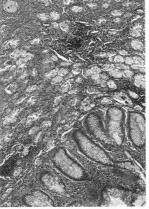

Fig. 5.16 Clear cell carcinoid.

Fig. 5.17 Tubular carcinoid.

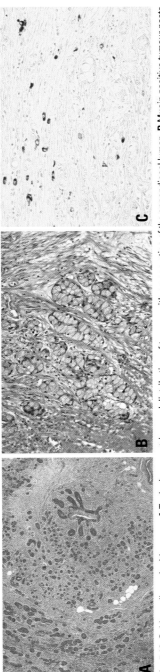

Fig. 5.18 Goblet cell carcinoid tumour. **A** Typical concentric mural distribution of tumour with preservation of the appendiceal lumen. **B** Mucin positive tumour nests (green) are seen in this Movat stain. Lumen is compressed, but intact. **C** Typical clusters of goblet cells.

and the argyrophil reaction in 89% of cases {2059}. Useful criteria for diagnosing this tumour are origin from the base of the crypts, integrity of the luminal mucosa, orderly arrangements, and absence of cytological abnormalities and mitoses. Immunohistochemically, tumour cells are often positive for chromogranin A, glucagon, serotonin, and IgA, while they are unreactive for S100 protein {586, 209}.

Mixed carcinoid-adenocarcinoma. This term has been proposed to designate carcinomas of the appendix that arise by progression from a pre-existing goblet-cell carcinoid. These carcinomas occur in the apparent absence of neoplastic change in the mucosal epithelium {209}.

Genetics

Loss of heterozygosity at *MEN-1* gene locus in sporadic appendiceal carcinoids was reported {829}, but has not been confirmed in more recent studies {394, 1938}.

Unlike colonic adenocarcinomas, *KRAS* mutations have not been detected either in typical or in goblet-cell carcinoid of the appendix {1556}, while in the same study, *TP53* mutations (mainly G:C to A:T transitions) were detected in 25% of goblet-cell carcinoids.

Prognosis and predictive factors

The majority of patients with endocrine tumours of the appendix have a favourable prognosis. Clinically non-functioning, non-angioinvasive lesions confined to the appendiceal wall, and > 2 cm in diameter are generally cured by complete local excision, whereas invasion of the mesoappendix or beyond or metastatic spread indicates that the lesion is aggressive. The most important risk factors appear to be tumour size > 2 cm and invasion of the mesoappendix {1134}. Lesions confined to the appendiceal wall that show angioinvasion or are > 2 cm in size, carry an uncertain malignant potential.

Location of tumours at the base of the appendix with involvement of the surgical margin or of the caecum is prognostically unfavourable, requiring at least a partial caecectomy to avoid residual tumour or subsequent recurrence {1931}. The reported frequency of metastases from appendiceal carcinoids ranged from 1.4% and 8.8% in older series {1252, 1927, 1254, 1780}, while in a more recent study the frequency of regional metastases was 27%, and that of distant metastases 8.5% {1251}.

The 5-year survival of patients with appendiceal carcinoid is 94% for localized disease, 85% for regional disease, and 34% for distant metastases {1251}. Goblet-cell carcinoids are more aggressive than conventional carcinoids, but not as malignant as adenocarcinomas of the appendix. In one study the percentage of patients dead of goblet cell carcinoids was 12.5% {442}. Tubular carcinoids, in contrast, are clinically benign {209}.

Miscellaneous tumours of the appendix

N.J. Carr
L.H. Sobin
C. Niederau

Neuromas are common in the appendix. The most frequent manifestation is the axial neuroma, which causes fibrous obliteration of the appendiceal lumen. Occasionally, neuromas may be found in the mucosa or submucosa without luminal obliteration {1423, 251, 1818}. Appendiceal neuromas may be reactive lesions. Histologically, they consist of a myxoid and collagenous background within which a variety of cells is present, including nerve fibres, spindle cells that immunoexpress S-100 protein, endocrine cells, mast cells and eosinophils. In this context, the presence of endocrine cells should not be mistaken for carcinoid tumour. However, it has been suggested that some carcinoids of the appendix might develop in the same setting as appendiceal neuroma. {251}.

Stromal tumours may affect the appendix on rare occasions; they have generally been described in the literature as being of smooth muscle type {324, 865}.

Kaposi sarcoma may be found in the appendix as part of the acquired immunodeficiency syndrome {406}. Rarely, it occurs in individuals without evidence of HIV infection {295}.

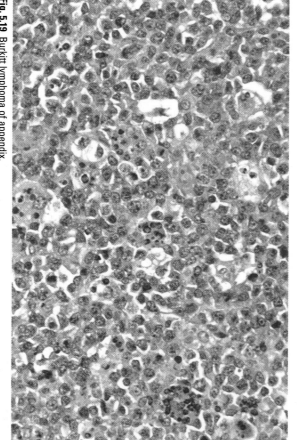

Fig. 5.19 Burkitt lymphoma of appendix.

Malignant lymphomas involve the appendix usually as part of more general intestinal spread. Lymphomas presenting as primary disease of the appendix are rare; some are of Burkitt type {1295, 1761}.

Secondary tumours are unusual in the appendix. Primary sites include carcinomas of the gastrointestinal and urogenital tract, breast, lung, and gallbladder. Metastatic thymoma and melanoma have also been reported {130, 98, 570, 607, 1051, 1407, 1615, 1822, 2129}. A common pattern is serosal involvement, presumably due to transcoelomic spread.

CHAPTER 6

Tumours of the Colon and Rectum

Colorectal carcinomas vary considerably throughout the world, being one of the leading cancer sites in the developed countries. Both environmental (diet) and genetic factors play key roles in its aetiology. Genetic susceptibility ranges from well-defined inherited syndromes, e.g. familial adenomatous polyposis, to ill-defined familial aggregations. Molecular genetic mechanisms are diverse, and recent data suggest two main pathways: a mutational pathway, which involves inactivation of tumour suppressor genes such as APC, and microsatellite instability which occurs in hereditary nonpolyposis colon cancer (HNPCC) and a proportion of sporadic carcinomas.

The main precursor lesion is the adenoma, which is readily detected and treated by endoscopic techniques. Non-neoplastic polyps are not considered precancerous unless they occur in polyposis syndromes. Inflammatory bowel diseases, such as chronic ulcerative colitis, bear resemblance to Barrett oesophagus as a precursor lesion with a potential for control by endoscopic surveillance. Cure is strongly related to anatomic extent, which makes accurate staging very important.

Lymphomas, endocrine tumours, and mesenchymal tumours are quite uncommon at this site.

WHO histological classification of tumours of the colon and rectum[1]

Epithelial tumours		
Adenoma		8140/0
	Tubular	8211/0
	Villous	8261/0
	Tubulovillous	8263/0
	Serrated	8213/0
Intraepithelial neoplasia[2] (dysplasia) associated with chronic inflammatory diseases		
	Low-grade glandular intraepithelial neoplasia	
	High-grade glandular intraepithelial neoplasia	
Carcinoma		
	Adenocarcinoma	8140/3
	Mucinous adenocarcinoma	8480/3
	Signet-ring cell carcinoma	8490/3
	Small cell carcinoma	8041/3
	Squamous cell carcinoma	8070/3
	Adenosquamous carcinoma	8560/3
	Medullary carcinoma	8510/3
	Undifferentiated carcinoma	8020/3
Carcinoid (well differentiated endocrine neoplasm)		8240/3
	EC-cell, serotonin-producing neoplasm	8241/3
	L-cell, glucagon-like peptide and PP/PYY producing tumour	
	Others	
Mixed carcinoid-adenocarcinoma		8244/3
Others		

Non-epithelial tumours	
Lipoma	8850/0
Leiomyoma	8890/0
Gastrointestinal stromal tumour	8936/1
Leiomyosarcoma	8890/3
Angiosarcoma	9120/3
Kaposi sarcoma	9140/3
Malignant melanoma	8720/3
Others	
Malignant lymphomas	
Marginal zone B-cell lymphoma of MALT Type	9699/3
Mantle cell lymphoma	9673/3
Diffuse large B-cell lymphoma	9680/3
Burkitt lymphoma	9687/3
Burkitt-like /atypical Burkitt-lymphoma	9687/3
Others	
Secondary tumours	
Polyps	
Hyperplastic (metaplastic)	
Peutz-Jeghers	
Juvenile	

[1] This classification is modified from the previous WHO histological classification of tumours {845} taking into account changes in our understanding of these lesions. In the case of endocrine neoplasms, it is based on the recent WHO classification {1784} but has been simplified to be of more practical utility in morphological classification.
[2] Morphology code of the International Classification of Diseases for Oncology (ICD-O) {542} and the Systematized Nomenclature of Medicine (http://snomed.org). Behaviour is coded /0 for benign tumours, /3 for malignant tumours, /2 for in situ carcinomas and grade III intraepithelial neoplasia, and /1 for unspecified, borderline or uncertain behaviour. Intraepithelial neoplasia does not have a generic code in ICD-O. ICD-O codes are available only for lesions categorized as glandular intraepithelial neoplasia grade III (8148/2), and adenocarcinoma in situ (8140/2).

TNM classification of tumours of the colon and rectum

TNM classification[1,2]

T – Primary Tumour		
TX	Primary tumour cannot be assessed	
T0	No evidence of primary tumour	
Tis	Carcinoma in situ: intraepithelial or invasion of lamina propria[3]	
T1	Tumour invades submucosa	
T2	Tumour invades muscularis propria	
T3	Tumour invades through muscularis propria into subserosa or into non-peritonealized pericolic or perirectal tissues	
T4	Tumour directly invades other organs or structures[4] and/or perforates visceral peritoneum	

N – Regional Lymph Nodes	
NX	Regional lymph nodes cannot be assessed
N0	No regional lymph node metastasis
N1	Metastasis in 1 to 3 regional lymph nodes
N2	Metastasis in 4 or more regional lymph nodes

M – Distant Metastasis	
MX	Distant metastasis cannot be assessed
M0	No distant metastasis
M1	Distant metastasis

Stage Grouping

Stage 0	Tis	N0	M0
Stage I	T1	N0	M0
	T2	N0	M0
Stage II	T3	N0	M0
	T4	N0	M0
Stage III	Any T	N1	M0
	Any T	N2	M0
Stage IV	Any T	Any N	M1

[1] {66, 301}. This classification applies only to carcinomas.
[2] A help desk for specific questions about the TNM classification is available at http://tnm.uicc.org.
[3] This includes cancer cells confined within the glandular basement membrane (intraepithelial) or lamina propria (intramucosal) with no extension through muscularis mucosae into submucosa.
[4] Direct invasion in T4 includes invasion of other segments of the colorectum by way of the serosa, e.g. invasion of sigmoid colon by a carcinoma of the cecum.

Carcinoma of the colon and rectum

S.R. Hamilton
B. Vogelstein
S. Kudo
E. Riboli
S. Nakamura
P. Hainaut

C.A. Rubio
L.H. Sobin
F. Fogt
S.J. Winawer
D.E. Goldgar
J.R. Jass

Definition

A malignant epithelial tumour of the colon or rectum. Only tumours that have penetrated through muscularis mucosae into submucosa are considered malignant at this site. The presence of scattered Paneth cells, neuroendocrine cells or small foci of squamous cell differentiation is compatible with the diagnosis of adenocarcinoma.

ICD-O codes

Adenocarcinoma	8140/3
Mucinous adenocarcinoma	8480/3
Signet-ring cell carcinoma	8490/3
Small cell carcinoma	8041/3
Squamous cell carcinoma	8070/3
Adenosquamous carcinoma	8560/3
Medullary carcinoma	8510/3
Undifferentiated carcinoma	8020/3

Epidemiology

An estimated 875,000 cases of colorectal cancer occurred worldwide in 1996, representing about 8.5% of all new cancers {1531}. The age-standardized incidence (cases/100,000 population) varies greatly around the world, with up to 20-fold differences between the high rates in developed countries of Europe, North and South America, Australia/New Zealand, and Asia and the still lower rates in some recently developed coun-

tries (Malaysia, Korea) and in developing countries of Africa, Asia and Polynesia. Significant differences also exist within continents, e.g. with higher incidences in western and northern Europe than in central and southern Europe {336}. Among immigrants and their descendants, incidence rates rapidly reach those of the adopted country, indicating that environmental factors are important.

According to the U.S. SEER database, the incidence rate for adenocarcinoma of the colon is 33.7/100,000 and increased by 18% during the period from 1973 through 1987 while the incidence of rectal adenocarcinoma (12.8/100,000) and mucinous adenocarcinoma in the colon and rectum (0.3 and 0.8, respectively) remained relatively constant {1928}. During the last decade of the 20th century, incidence and mortality have decreased {566}. By contrast, the incidence in Japan, Korea and Singapore is rising rapidly {737}, probably due to the acquisition of a Western lifestyle. Incidence increases with age {2121}; carcinomas are rare before the age of 40 years except in individuals with genetic predisposition or predisposing conditions such as chronic inflammatory bowel disease.

Incidence rates in the 1973-87 SEER data for colonic and rectal adenocarci-

noma for males were higher than those for females; whites had higher rates than blacks for rectal adenocarcinoma, but blacks had higher rates for colonic adenocarcinoma {1928}. During 1975-94, a decrease in incidence in whites was evident, while the incidence of proximal colon cancers in blacks still increased {1958}.

Aetiology

Diet and lifestyle

A high incidence of colorectal carcinomas is consistently observed in populations with a Western type diet, i.e. highly caloric food rich in animal fat combined

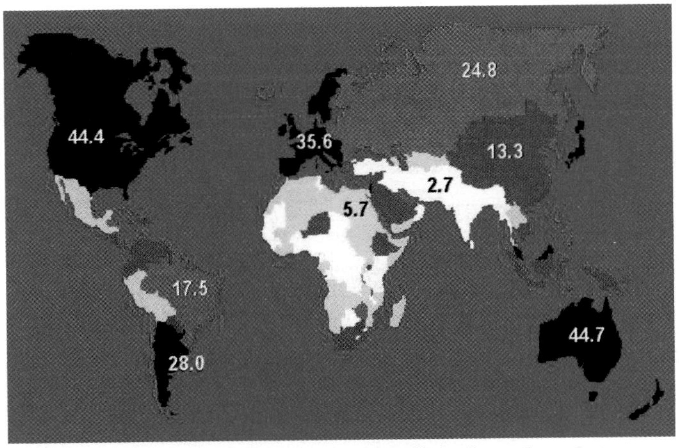

Fig. 6.03 Double contrast barium enema showing adenocarcinoma of colon. Between the proximal (top) and distal (bottom) segment of the colon the lumen is narrowed with an irregular surface, due to tumour infiltration.

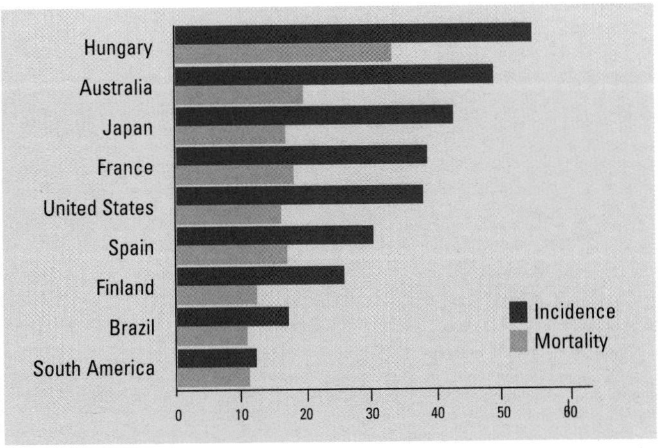

Fig. 6.02 Male incidence (blue) and mortality (orange) of colorectal cancer in some selected countries.
From: Globocan, IARC Press, Lyon.

Fig. 6.01 Worldwide annual incidence (per 100,000) of colon and rectum cancer in males. Numbers on the map indicate regional average values.
From: Globocan, IARC Press, Lyon.

with a sedentary lifestyle. Epidemiological studies have indicate that meat consumption, smoking and alcohol consumption are risk factors. Inverse associations include vegetable consumption, prolonged use of non-steroidal anti-inflammatory drugs, oestrogen replacement therapy, and physical activity {1531, 2121}. Fibre may have a protective role, but this has been questioned recently. The molecular pathways underlying these epidemiological associations are poorly understood, but production of heterocyclic amines during cooking of meat, stimulation of higher levels of fecal bile acids and production of reactive oxygen species have been implicated as possible mechanisms {416, 1439}.

Vegetable anticarcinogens such as folate, antioxidants and inducers of detoxifying enzymes, binding of luminal carcinogens, fibre fermentation to produce protective volatile fatty acids, and reduced contact time with colorectal epithelium due to faster transit may explain some of the inverse associations.

Chronic inflammation

Chronic inflammatory bowel diseases are significant aetiological factors in the development of colorectal adenocarcinomas {1582}. The risk increases after 8-10 years and is highest in patients with early-onset and widespread manifestation (pancolitis).

Ulcerative colitis. This chronic disorder of unknown aetiology affects children and adults, with a peak incidence in the early third decade. It is considered a premalignant disorder, with duration and extent of disease being the major risk factors. Population-based studies show a 4.4-fold increase in mortality from col-

orectal carcinoma {1504, 448, 1835, 1214}. In clinical studies, the increase in incidence is usually higher, up to 20-fold {647, 990}. Involvement of greater than one half of the colon is associated with a risk to develop carcinoma of approximately 15%, whereas left sided disease may bear a malignancy risk of 5% {1727, 1045}. Ulcerative proctitis is not associated with an increased carcinoma risk.

Crohn disease. Development of carcinoma is seen both in the small intestine and the large intestine. The risk of colorectal malignancy appears to be 3 fold above normal {581}. Long duration and early onset of disease are risk factors for carcinoma.

Modifying factors. Non-steroidal anti-inflammatory drugs and some naturally occurring compounds block the biochemical abnormalities in prostaglandin homeostasis in colorectal neoplasms. Some of these agents cause a dramatic involution of adenomas but their role in

proportion of more proximal carcinomas

the chemoprevention of adenocarcinoma is less clear. Polymorphisms in key enzymes can alter other metabolic pathways that modify protective or injurious compounds, e.g. methylenetetrahydrofolate reductase, N-acetyltransferases, glutathione-S-transferases, aldehyde dehydrogenase and cytochrome P-450 {1766, 686, 1300}. These polymorphisms may explain individual susceptibility or predisposition among populations with similar exposures {1555}.

Irradiation.
A rare but well recognized aetiological factor in colorectal neoplasia is therapeutic pelvic irradiation {1974}.

Localization

Most colorectal carcinomas are located in the sigmoid colon and rectum, but there is evidence of changing distribution in recent years, with an increasing

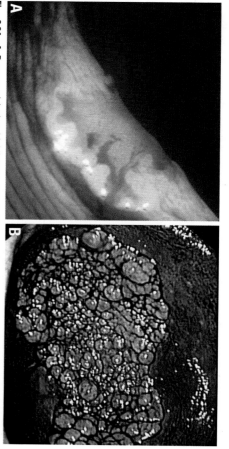

Fig. 6.04 A Depressed lesion highlighted with indigo-carmine dye spray corresponding to high-grade intraepithelial neoplasia. **B** Flat, elevated adenoma with high-grade intraepithelial neoplasia after indigo-carmine dye spray.

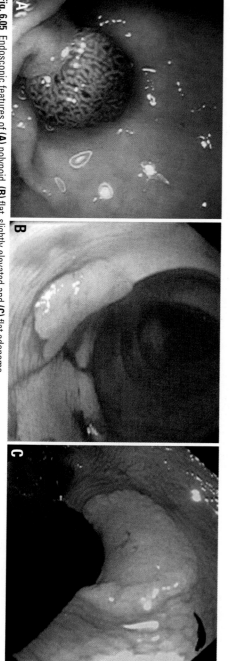

Fig. 6.05 Endoscopic features of (**A**) polypoid, (**B**) flat, slightly elevated and (**C**) flat adenoma.

[1928]. Molecular pathology has also shown site differences: tumours with high levels of microsatellite instability (MSI-H) or *ras* proto-oncogene mutations are more frequently located in the caecum, ascending colon and transverse colon. [842, 1563, 1897].

Clinical features

Signs and symptoms

Some patients are asymptomatic, especially when their neoplasm is identified by screening or surveillance. Haematochezia and anaemia are common presenting features due to bleeding from the tumour. Many patients experience change in bowel habit; in the right colon, the fluid faeces can pass exophytic masses, whereas in the left colon the solid faeces are more often halted by annular tumours so that constipation is more common. There may be associated abdominal distension. Rectosigmoid lesions can produce tenesmus. Other symptoms include fever, malaise, weight loss, and abdominal pain. Some patients present with the complications of obstruction or perforation.

Imaging

Modern imaging techniques permit non-invasive detection and clinical staging. Conventional barium enema detects large tumours, while air-contrast radiography improves the visualization of less advanced lesions. Cross-sectional imaging by CT, MRI imaging and transrectal ultra-sonography permit some assessment of the depth of local tumour invasion and the

presence of regional and distant metastases [2202]. Scintigraphy and positron emission tomography are also used.

Endoscopy

The development of endoscopy has had a major impact on diagnosis and treatment. Colonoscopy allows observation of the mucosal surface of the entire large bowel with biopsy of identified lesions. Chromoendoscopy employing dyes to improve visualization of non-protruding lesions and magnification, have been developed. The flat neoplastic lesions

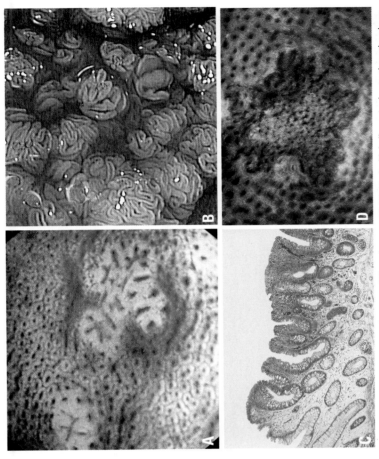

Fig. 6.06 A Endoscopic view of two small flat adenomas highlighted with indigo-carmine to show the abnormal tubular pit pattern. **B** Magnifying video endoscopy of a tubulovillous adenoma highlighted with indigo-carmine to show cribriform pattern. **C** Histological section of a flat elevated tubular adenoma showing low-grade intraepithelial neoplasia. **D** Stereomicroscopic view with indigo-carmine dye spray of a depressed adenoma with high-grade intraepithelial neoplasia containing very small round pits.

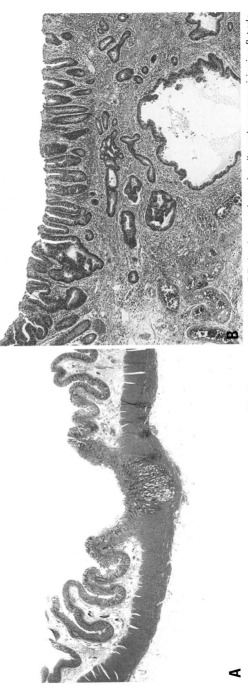

Fig. 6.07 A Small adenocarcinoma invading muscularis propria, arising in a depressed adenoma. **B** Early adenocarcinoma invading submucosa, arising in a flat adenoma.

Fig. 6.08 Advanced colorectal carcinomas. **A** Small depressed invasive carcinoma (arrow) with a nearby protruding adenoma. **B** Advanced colorectal carcinoma, depressed type. **C** Cross section of adenocarcinoma with extension into the submucosa (pT1).

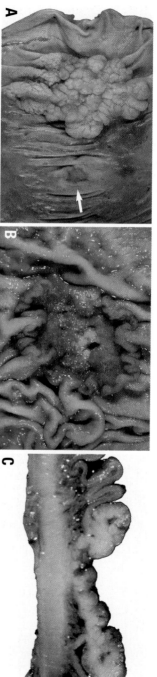

have been designated by Japanese gastroenterologists as 'type II', with three subtypes: IIa, 'en plateau' elevated; IIb, completely flat; and IIc, 'en plateau' depressed. The depressed lesions have, despite a smaller diameter, a poor prognosis with prompt penetration in the submucosa. The pit pattern of the surface at magnification 100 allows a reliable prediction of histology. Therapeutic endoscopy, including snare polypectomy and endoscopic mucosectomy, can be used to remove colorectal neoplasms, especially adenomas, and carcinomas with minimal submucosal invasion. Protruded neoplasms can usually be resected by snare polypectomy. Superficial lesions (flat and depressed) and some protruded

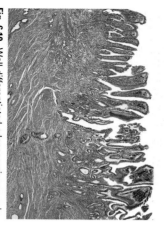

Fig. 6.09 Small ulcerating adenocarcinoma of colon producing a depressed lesion.

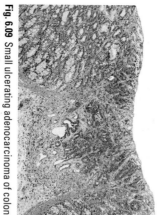

Fig. 6.10 Well differentiated adenocarcinoma arising in Crohn disease, invading wall beneath intra-epithelial neoplasia.

lesions may be removed by endoscopic mucosal resection {2121, 2122, 1164}.

Macroscopy

The macroscopic features are influenced by the phase in the natural history of discovery. Carcinomas may be exophytic/fungating with predominantly intraluminal growth, endophytic/ulcerative with predominantly intramural growth, diffusely infiltrative/linitis plastica with subtle endophytic growth, and annular with circumferential involvement of the colorectal wall and constriction of the lumen. Overlap among these types is common. Pedunculated exophytic lesions have a mural attachment narrower than the head of the tumour, with the stalk consisting of uninvolved mucosa and submucosa, while sessile exophytic tumours have broad attachment to the wall.

Carcinomas of the proximal colon tend to grow as exophytic masses while those in the transverse and descending colon are more often endophytic and annular. On cut section, most colorectal carcinomas have a relatively homogeneous appearance although areas of necrosis can be seen. Adenocarcinomas of the mucinous (colloid) type often have areas with grossly visible mucus. Carcinomas with high levels of microsatellite instability (MSI-H) are usually circumscribed and about 20% are mucinous {842}.

Tumour spread and staging

Following transmural extension through the muscularis propria into pericolic or perirectal soft tissue, the tumour may involve contiguous structures. The consequences of direct extension depend on the anatomic site. An advanced rectal carcinoma may extend into pelvic structures such as the vagina and urinary bladder, but cannot gain direct access to

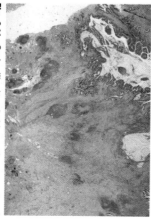

Fig. 6.11 Crohn-like lymphoid reaction associated with a colonic adenocarcinoma.

occur unless the muscularis mucosae is breached and the submucosa is invaded. This biological behaviour stands in sharp contrast to carcinomas of the stomach where metastasis occurs occa-

the peritoneal cavity when it is located distal to the peritoneal reflection. By contrast, colonic tumours can extend directly to the serosal surface. Perforation can be associated with transcoelomic spread to the peritoneal cavity (peritoneal carcinomatosis). Involvement of the peritoneal surface should only be diagnosed if the peritoneum is ulcerated or if tumour cells have clearly penetrated the mesothelium. Since the peritoneal surface infiltrated by tumour cells may become adherent to adjacent structures, direct extension into adjoining organs can also occur in colonic carcinomas that have invaded the peritoneal portion of the wall {62}. Implantation due to surgical manipulation occurs only occasionally, but has been reported after laparoscopic colectomy for cancer {1106}.

Spread via lymphatic or blood vessels can occur early in the natural history and lead to systemic disease. Despite the presence of lymphatics in the colorectal mucosa, lymphogenic spread does not

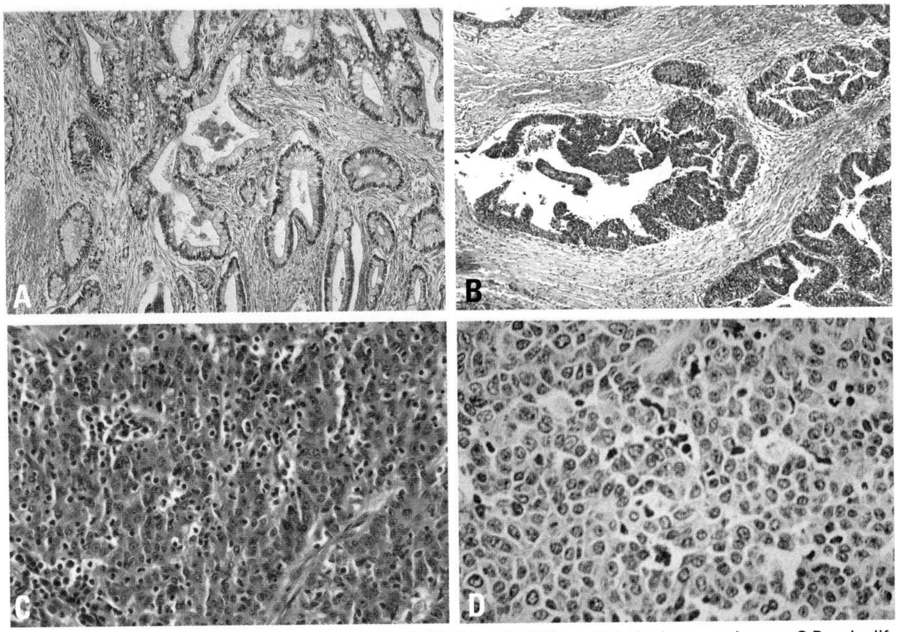

Most colorectal adenocarcinomas are gland-forming, with variability in the size and configuration of the glandular structures. In well and moderately differentiated adenocarcinomas, the epithelial cells are usually large and tall, and the gland lumina often contain cellular debris.

Mucinous adenocarcinoma

This designation is used if > 50% of the lesion is composed of mucin. This variant is characterized by pools of extracellular mucin that contain malignant epithelium as acinar structures, strips of cells or single cells. Many high-frequency micro-satellite instability (MSI-H) carcinomas are of this histopathological type.

Signet-ring cell carcinoma

This variant of adenocarcinoma is defined by the presence of > 50% of tumour cells with prominent intracytoplasmic mucin {1672}.

The typical signet-ring cell has a large mucin vacuole that fills the cytoplasm and displaces the nucleus. Signet-ring cells can occur in the mucin pools of mucinous adenocarcinoma or in a diffusely infiltrative process with minimal extracellular mucin. Some MSI-H carcinomas are of this type.

Adenosquamous carcinoma

These unusual tumours show features of both squamous carcinoma and adenocarcinoma, either as separate areas within the tumour or admixed. For a lesion to be classified as adenosquamous, there should be more than just occasional small foci of squamous differentiation. Pure *squamous cell carcinoma* is very rare in the large bowel.

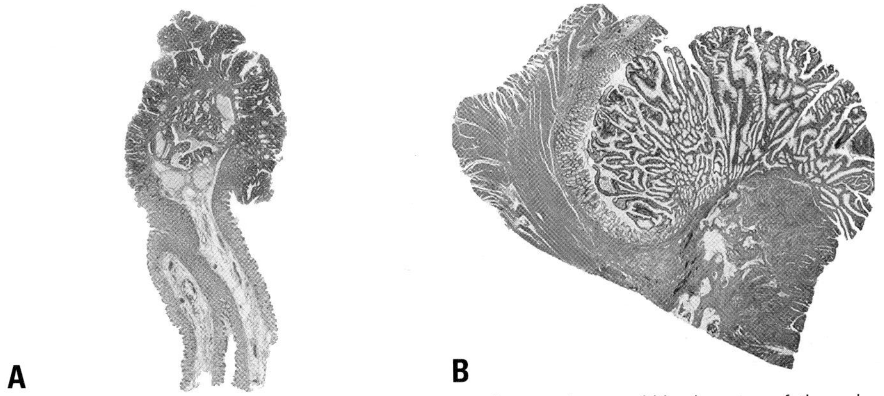

Fig. 6.12 A Well differentiated adenocarcinoma. **B** Moderately differentiated adenocarcinoma; this lesion was MSI-H and shows numerous intraepithelial lymphocytes. **C** Poorly differentiated adenocarcinoma. **D** Undifferentiated carcinoma.

sionally from purely intramucosal carcinomas. Invasion of portal vein tributaries in the colon and vena cava tributaries in the rectum can lead to haematogenous dissemination.

Staging

The classification proposed by C. Dukes in 1929-35 for rectal cancer serves as the template for many staging systems currently in use. This family of classifications takes into account two histopathological features: depth of penetration into the wall and the presence or absence of metastasis in regional lymph nodes. The TNM classification {66} is replacing the Dukes classification.

Histopathology

The defining feature of colorectal adenocarcinoma is invasion through the muscularis mucosae into the submucosa. Lesions with the morphological characteristics of adenocarcinoma that are confined to the epithelium or invade the lamina propria alone and lack invasion through the muscularis mucosae into the submucosa have virtually no risk of metastasis. Therefore, 'high-grade intra-epithelial neoplasia' is a more appropriate term than 'adenocarcinoma in-situ', and 'intramucosal neoplasia' is more appropriate than 'intramucosal adenocarcinoma'. Use of these proposed terms helps to avoid overtreatment.

Fig. 6.13 A Tubulovillous adenoma showing invasive adenocarcinoma within the core of the polyp. **B** Adenocarcinoma arising in a villous adenoma.

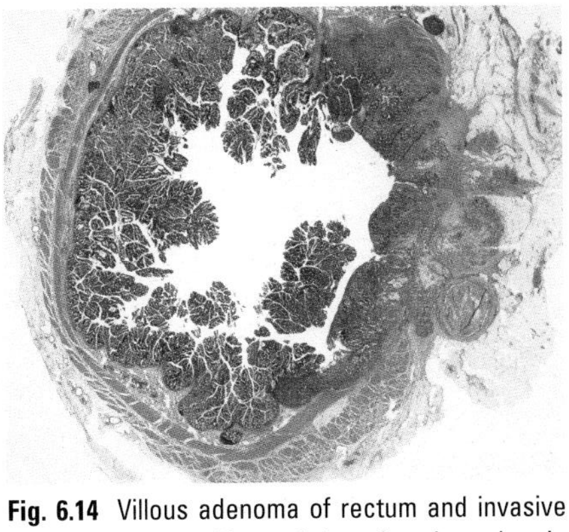

Fig. 6.14 Villous adenoma of rectum and invasive adenocarcinoma. Two of four lymph nodes in perirectal tissue have metastasis.

tiated and undifferentiated colorectal carcinomas.

Undifferentiated carcinoma

These rare tumours lack morphological evidence of differentiation beyond that of an epithelial tumour and have variable histological features {1946}. Despite their undifferentiated appearances, these tumours are genetically distinct and typically associated with MSI-H.

Other variants

Carcinomas that include a spindle cell component are best termed *spindle cell carcinoma* or *sarcomatoid carcinoma*. The spindle cells are, at least focally, immunoreactive for cytokeratin. The term *carcinosarcoma* applies to malignant tumours containing both carcinomatous and heterologous mesenchymal elements. Other rare histopathological variants of colorectal carcinoma include pleomorphic (giant cell), choriocarcinoma, pigmented, clear cell, stem cell, and Paneth cell-rich (crypt cell carcinoma). Mixtures of histopathological types can be seen.

Carcinosarcoma

Carcinomas that include a spindle cell component are best termed sarcomatoid carcinoma or spindle cell carcinoma. The spindle cells are, at least focally, immuno-reactive for cytokeratin. The term carcinosarcoma applies to malignant tumours containing both carcinomatous and heterologous mesenchymal elements.

Grading

Adenocarcinomas are graded predominantly on the basis of the extent of glandular appearances, and should be divided into well, moderately and poorly differentiated, or into low-grade (encompassing well and moderately differentiated adenocarcinomas) and high-grade (including poorly differentiated adenocarcinomas and undifferentiated carcinomas). Poorly differentiated adenocarcinomas should show at least some gland formation or mucus production; tubules are typically irregularly folded and distorted.

When a carcinoma has heterogeneity in differentiation, grading should be based on the least differentiated component, not including the leading front of invasion. Small foci of apparent poor differentiation are common at the advancing edge of tumours, but this feature is insufficient to classify the tumour as poorly differentiated {1543}.

The percentage of the tumour showing formation of gland-like structures can be used to define the grade. Well differentiated (grade 1) lesions exhibit glandular structures in > 95% of the tumour; moderately differentiated (grade 2) adenocarci-

Medullary carcinoma

This rare variant is characterized by sheets of malignant cells with vesicular nuclei, prominent nucleoli and abundant pink cytoplasm exhibiting prominent infiltration by intraepithelial lymphocytes {856}. It is invariably associated with MSI-H and has a favourable prognosis when compared to other poorly differen-

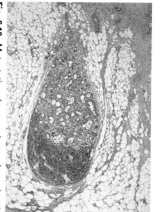

Fig. 6.15 Adenocarcinoma within lymphatic vessel.

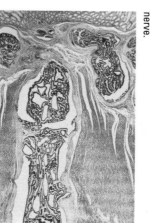

Fig 6.16 Metastatic adenocarcinoma in regional lymph node.

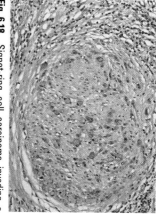

Fig 6.18 Signet-ring cell carcinoma invading a nerve.

Fig. 6.19 Adenocarcinoma with venous invasion.

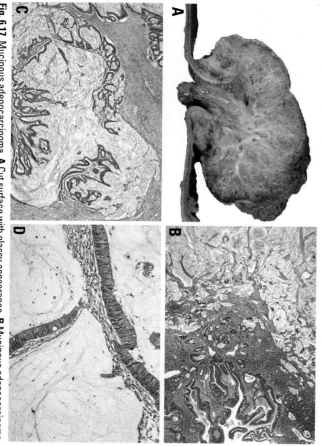

A

B

C

D

Fig. 6.17 Mucinous adenocarcinoma. **A** Cut surface with glassy appearance. **B** Mucinous adenocarcinoma beneath high-grade intraepithelial neoplasia in ulcerative colitis. **C** Well-differentiated tumour with large mucin lakes. **D** Multilocular mucin deposits with well-differentiated adenocarcinoma.

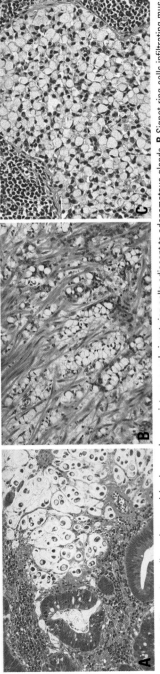

Fig. 6.20 **A** Signet-ring cell carcinoma arising in an adenoma; intramucosal signet-ring cells adjacent to adenomatous glands. **B** Signet-ring cells infiltrating muscularis propria. **C** Lymph node metastasis of a signet-ring cell carcinoma.

noma has 50-95% glands; poorly differentiated (grade 3) adenocarcinoma has 5-50%; and undifferentiated (grade 4) carcinoma has < 5%. Mucinous adenocarcinoma and signet-ring cell carcinoma by convention are considered poorly differentiated (grade 3). Medullary carcinoma with MSI-H appears undifferentiated. Additional studies of the biological behaviour of MSI-H cancers are needed to relate the morphological grade and molecular subtypes of mucinous, signet-ring cell and medullary carcinoma to outcome since MSI-H carcinomas have an improved stage-specific survival {788, 924, 1098}.

Precursor lesions

During the past decade the natural history of colorectal carcinomas has been extensively studied in correlation with the underlying accumulation of genetic alterations.

Aberrant crypt foci (ACF)

The earliest morphological precursor of epithelial neoplasia is the aberrant crypt focus (ACF). Microscopic examination of mucosal sheets dissected from the bowel wall and stained with methylene blue, or mucosal examination with a magnifying endoscope, reveal ACFs to have crypts of enlarged calibre and thickened epithelium with reduced mucin content. Microscopy shows two main types: *ACFs with features of hyperplastic polyps* and a high frequency of *ras* protooncogene mutations, and *dysplastic ACFs (micro-adenomas)* associated with a mutation of the *APC* gene {1375}. Progression from ACF through adenoma to carcinoma characterizes carcinogenesis in the large intestine {1326}.

Adenomas

These precursor lesions are defined by the presence of intraepithelial neoplasia, histologically characterized by hypercellularity with enlarged, hyperchromatic nuclei, varying degrees of nuclear stratification, and loss of polarity. Nuclei may be spindle-shaped, or enlarged and ovoid. Inactivation of the APC/beta-catenin pathway commonly initiates the process and results in extension of epithelial proliferation in dysplastic

epithelium from the base of the crypts, where it normally occurs, toward or onto the luminal surface {851, 1528}. Polyps appear to grow as a consequence of accelerated crypt fission resulting from *APC* gene mutation {564}. Intraepithelial neoplasia can be low-grade or high-grade, depending on the degree of glandular or villous complexity, extent of nuclear stratification, and severity of abnormal nuclear morphology. Paneth cells, neuroendocrine cells and squamous cell aggregates may be seen in adenomas and may become a dominant constituent of the epithelium.

Macroscopy. Colorectal adenomas can be classified into three groups: *elevated, flat,* and *depressed* {973}. Elevated adenomas range from pedunculated polyps with a long stalk of non-neoplastic mucosa to those that are sessile. Flat or non-protruding adenomas and depressed adenomas are recognized macroscopically by mucosal reddening, subtle changes in texture, or highlighting by dye techniques. The term adenoma is applied even though the lesions are not polypoid because intraepithelial neopla-

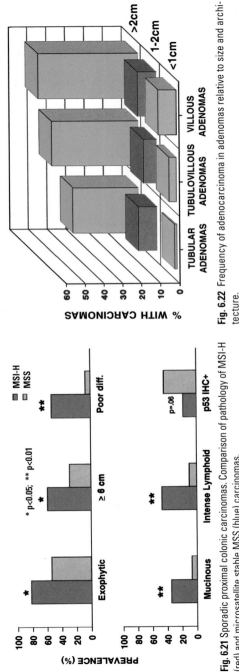

Fig. 6.21 Sporadic proximal colonic carcinomas. Comparison of pathology of MSI-H (red) and microsatellite stable MSS (blue) carcinomas.

Fig. 6.22 Frequency of adenocarcinoma in adenomas relative to size and architecture.

Fig. 6.23 Clear cell carcinoma of colon.

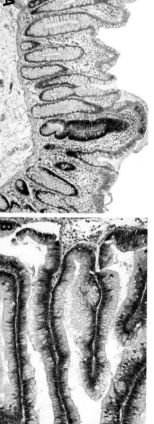

Fig. 6.26 A, B Single crypt adenomas in a patient with FAP.

sia (dysplasia) is the hallmark of these lesions. Depressed adenomas are usually smaller than flat or protruding ones and tend to give rise to adenocarcinoma while still relatively small (mean diameter, 11 mm) due to a greater tendency to progress {1628}. These adenomas have a lower frequency of *ras* mutation than polypoid adenomas {974}.

Histopathology.

Tubular adenomas are usually protruding, spherical and pedunculated, or non-protruding (flat). Microscopically, dysplastic glandular structures occupy at least 80% of the luminal surface. *Villous adenomas* are typically sessile with a hairy-appearing surface. Microscopically, leaf-like projections lined by dysplastic glandular epithelium comprise more than 80% of the luminal surface. Distinction of villous structures from elongated separated tubules is sometimes problematical. Villous architecture is defined arbitrarily by the length of the glands exceeding twice the thickness of normal colorectal mucosa. *Tubulovillous adenomas* have a mixture of tubular and villous structures with a ratio between 80%/20% and 20%/80%. Serrated adenomas are characterized by the saw-tooth configuration of a hyperplastic (metaplastic) polyp on low power microscopy, but the epithelium lining the upper portion of the crypts and luminal surface is dysplastic. Serrated adenomas can also have a tubular or villous component, but low-levels of microsatellite instability (MSI-L) and altered mucin are characteristic of these serrated lesions {840}. By contrast, *mixed hyperplastic polyp/adenoma* contains separate identifiable areas of each histopathological type {1092}. Occasionally, some villous adenomas show in the slopes of the villi closely packed small glands; those adenomas have been referred to as *villo-microglandular adenomas* {972}.

Although tiny flat or depressed adenocarcinomas are well-described, it is difficult to determine if *de novo* adenocarcinomas without a benign histopathological precursor lesion ever occur in the large bowel, because adenocarcinoma can overgrow the precursor lesion. The prolonged time interval usually required for progression of intraepithelial to invasive neoplasia offers opportunities for prevention or interruption of the process to reduce mortality due to colorectal carcinoma.

Intraepithelial neoplasia can also occur in the absence of an adenoma, in a preexisting lesion of another type (such as a hamartomatous polyp in juvenile polyposis syndrome and Peutz-Jeghers syndrome), and in chronic inflammatory diseases.

Hyperplastic (metaplastic) polyps

The definition is a mucosal excrescence characterized by elongated, serrated crypts lined by proliferative epithelium in the bases with infolded epithelial tufts and enlarged goblet cells in the upper crypts and on the luminal surface, imparting a saw-tooth outline. In the appendix, diffuse hyperplasia may occur as a sessile mucosal proliferation. The epithelial nuclei in the serrated region are small, regular, round and located at

Fig. 6.24 Tubulovillous adenoma. Pedunculated with long stalk of non-neoplastic mucosa.

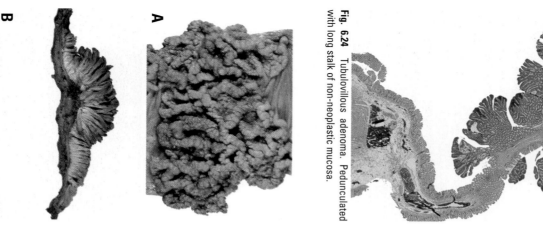

A

B

Fig. 6.25 A Sessile villous adenoma. **B** Section through a villous adenoma.

Fig. 6.27 Tubular adenoma of colon.

the base of the cells adjoining the basement membrane, which is often thickened beneath the surface epithelial cells. The cytoplasm contains prominent mucin vacuoles, which are usually larger than normal goblet cells. The proliferative zone often shows increased cellularity and mitotic activity, which can be mistaken for adenoma. Hyperplastic polyps are traditionally considered non-neoplastic, but *ras* mutation is common, clonality has been demonstrated, and biochemical abnormalities and epidemiological associations that occur in colorectal adenomas and carcinomas have been found {851, 663, 1178}. These lines of evidence suggest that hyperplastic polyps may be neoplastic but have a molecular pathogenesis that differs from the adenoma-adenocarcinoma sequence due to absence of inactivation of the APC/beta-catenin pathway.

Juvenile polyps

Sporadic juvenile polyps are typically spherical, lobulated and pedunculated and considered hamartomatous. They most commonly occur in children. The surface is often eroded and friable, and the cut surface typically shows mucin-containing cysts. On histology, the abundant stroma is composed of inflamed,

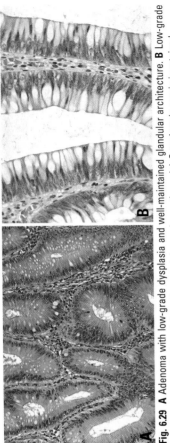

Fig. 6.28 Tubulovillous adenoma, partly sessile, partly pedunculated.

often oedematous granulation tissue that surrounds cystically dilated glands containing mucin. The glands are lined by cuboidal to columnar epithelial cells with reactive changes. The juvenile polyps in patients with juvenile polyposis syndrome may have the macroscopic and microscopic appearances of sporadic juvenile polyps, but they often have a frond-like growth pattern with less stroma, fewer dilated glands and more proliferated small glands (microtubular pattern) than their sporadic counterparts. Intraepithelial neoplasia (dysplasia) is rare in sporadic juvenile polyps. Intraepithelial neoplasia in this setting results from inactivation of the APC/beta-catenin pathway analogous to the genetic basis of adenoma formation {2145}.

Peutz-Jeghers polyps

These are discussed in the small intestine section.

Reactive lesions

Inflammatory polyps. These non-neoplastic polyps are composed of varying proportions of reactive epithelium, inflamed granulation tissue and fibrous tissue, often with morphological similarity to juvenile polyps; inflammatory polyps are seen in a variety of chronic inflammatory diseases including chronic inflammatory bowel disease and diverticulitis.

Lymphoid polyps. These result from aggregates of reactive mucosa-associated lymphoid tissue with conspicuous germinal centres located in the mucosa and/or submucosa.

Mucosal prolapse. On occasion, mucosal prolapse can produce morphological features that mimic neoplasia, including polyps, masses and ulcers characterized histologically by elongated, distorted, regenerative glands surrounded by a proliferation of smooth muscle fibres from the muscularis mucosae, together with superficial erosions, inflamed granulation tissue and fibrosis {159}. Widening of gland lumina at the surface is common. Examples of this phenomenon include inflammatory cloacogenic polyp {1083}, solitary rectal ulcer and cap polyp. The process can extend into the bowel wall, producing colitis cystica profunda.

Neoplasia in chronic inflammatory bowel disease

There is evidence that the natural history of colorectal carcinomas associated with chronic colitis differs from that of ordinary adenomas both morphologically and with respect to the type and sequence of genetic alterations.

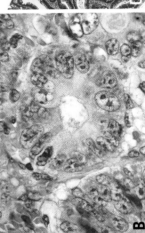

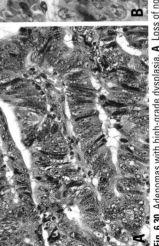

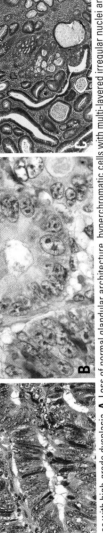

Fig. 6.29 A Adenoma with low-grade dysplasia and well-maintained glandular architecture. **B** Low-grade dysplasia with regular but slightly elongated, hyperchromatic nuclei. Cytoplasmic mucin is retained.

Fig. 6.30 Adenomas with high-grade dysplasia. **A** Loss of normal glandular architecture, hyperchromatic cells with multi-layered irregular nuclei and loss of mucin, high nuclear/cytoplasmic ratio. **B** Marked nuclear atypia with prominent nucleoli. **C** Adenoma with focal cribriform pattern .

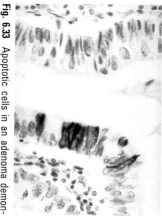

Fig. 6.33 Apoptotic cells in an adenoma demonstrated by M30 immunohistochemistry.

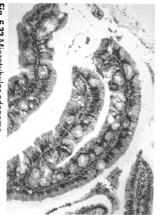

Fig. 6.32 Microtubular adenoma.

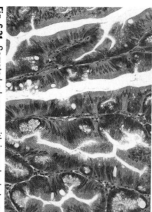

Fig. 6.31 Serrated adenoma with irregular indentation of the neoplastic epithelium.

Ulcerative colitis (UC)

Development of carcinoma is apparently metachronous to the development of intraepithelial neoplasia (classified as low-grade and high-grade) complicating chronic colitis. Because invasion can be associated with intraepithelial neoplasia exhibiting relatively mild morphological changes, high-grade intraepithelial neoplasia is diagnosed in colitis on the basis of abnormalities that are less severe than neoplasia in adenomas. It may be flat or present as a 'dysplasia associated lesion or mass' (DALM); the latter is often associated with a synchronous carcinoma arising beneath the dysplastic surface. DALMs are considered high-grade lesions through their architecture alone, and both DALM of any grade of dyspla-

sia and high-grade flat dysplasia are associated with invasive carcinoma in about 40% of cases. The diagnosis of DALM and high-grade flat dysplasia usually leads to total colectomy {1687}. It may be difficult to distinguish a DALM from an incidental adenoma in a patient with UC.

Attempts have been made to identify early dysplastic lesions in UC with cell cycle proliferation markers. Topoisomerase II alpha and Ki-67 have been shown to increase significantly over baseline expression in UC related dysplasias. Ki-67 positive cells are found both at the surface and the base of the crypts, indicating a fundamental deregulation of the proliferative cell pool {1368}. Mutations of $TP53$ appear to be an early event and are already present in intraepithelial neoplasia associated with UC, in contrast to the adenoma-carcinoma sequence in sporadic colorectal carcinomas. Some $TP53$ mutations have even been observed in non-dysplastic mucosa of chronic inflammation {516, 1463, 2175}.

Alterations of p16 have also been identified in early UC but only very infrequently in adenomas. Both tumour tissue and multiple colorectal cancer cell lines studied showed absence of LOH in 9p 1

Microsatellite instability and gene alterations in p16 and p53 may represent early events during the development of dysplasia and carcinoma, and these changes may lead to susceptibility for allelic loss of other genes such as APC and DCC. It has been shown that LOH of genetic areas close to the VHL locus on 3p is frequently present in DALM lesions and, less frequently, in flat dysplastic lesions. These changes are not usually seen in sporadic adenomas {515}. This may indicate that dysplasia in UC and sporadic adenomas may follow different genetic pathways.

Crohn disease

Intraepithelial neoplasia, classified as low-grade or high-grade, is associated with a high proportion of Crohn carcinomas, either adjacent to the invasive lesion or at a distance from it {1757}. Similar to UC, polypoid dysplastic lesions are diagnosed as DALM in Crohn's disease.

Mucinous adenocarcinomas are seen in Crohn disease more frequently than in

sporadic colorectal carcinomas {656}. There is an increased frequency of adenocarcinomas within perianal fistulas, and of squamous cell carcinomas of the anal mucosa {992}.

Similar to UC, $TP53$ and c-KRAS mutations are observed earlier in Crohn-associated intraepithelial neoplasia than in the adenoma-carcinoma sequence of sporadic colorectal cancer {1562}.

Genetic susceptibility

The spectrum of genetic susceptibility is broad, ranging from well-defined autosomal dominantly inherited syndromes with known germline genetic mutations to ill-defined familial aggregation {1531, 1928, 642}. The diseases are traditionally divided into polyposis syndromes characterized by large numbers of polyps, e.g. familial adenomatosis coli (FAP), and non-polyposis syndromes with a small number of or absence of polyps, e.g. hereditary nonpolyposis colorectal cancer (HNPCC). They are described in the following chapters.

A non-truncating polymorphism of the APC gene that induces an unstable polyadenin repeat sequence, occurs in approximately 5% of Ashkenazi Jews

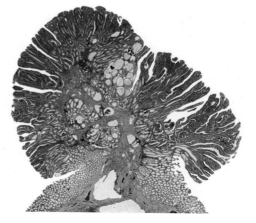

Fig. 6.34 Tubulovillous adenoma with pseudoinvasion. Small clusters of adenomatous cells produce multilocular, large mucin deposits that expand the adenoma's stalk. This growth pattern resembles mucinous carcinoma but is not malignant.

and carries a modestly elevated risk of colorectal cancer. Only small numbers of adenomas occur in patients with this form of germline APC alteration {1004}.

Li-Fraumeni syndrome

MIM No: *Li-Fraumeni syndrome* 151623; *TP53 mutations* 191170

Li-Fraumeni syndrome is an autosomal dominant disorder characterized by multiple primary neoplasms in children and young adults, with a predominance of soft tissue sarcomas, osteosarcomas and breast cancer, and an increased incidence of brain tumours, leukaemia and adrenocortical carcinomas {1403}. Criteria for proband identification are: (1) occurrence of sarcoma before age 45, (2) at least one first-degree relative with any tumour before age 45, and (3) at least one first- or second-degree relative with cancer before age 45 or with sarcoma at any age {717, 141, 1066}.

In about 70% of Li-Fraumeni kindreds, affected family members carry a germline mutation in *TP53* {1151}. From 1990 to 1999, a total of 144 families with a *TP53* germline mutation were identified. A database of these mutations is available at http://www.iarc.fr/p53/Germ. htm {699}. As with somatic mutations, germline mutations cluster in conserved regions of exons 4 to 9, with major hotspots at codons 175, 248 and 273. It has been suggested that cancer phenotype correlates with the position of the mutation within the coding sequence, with lower age of clinical manifestation in probands with mutations falling in the DNA-binding domain of the p53 protein {142}. The most frequent type of germline mutation is transition (GC to AT) at CpG dinucleotides 556. The molecular basis of tumour predispositions in families within *TP53* germline mutations is not known. Recent studies have excluded tumour suppressor genes such as *PTEN* and *CDKN2* {214}.

Gastrointestinal manifestations

Neoplasms of the digestive tract represent 7% of the tumours observed in Li-Fraumeni families. Most of these tumours are colorectal carcinoma, with a minority of stomach carcinomas. The male:female ratio is 1.5 and the mean age at clinical manifestation is 45, which correspond to a relatively long latency period as compared to other types of cancers occurring in Li-Fraumeni families {1403}. Preferential familial occurrence of stomach cancer

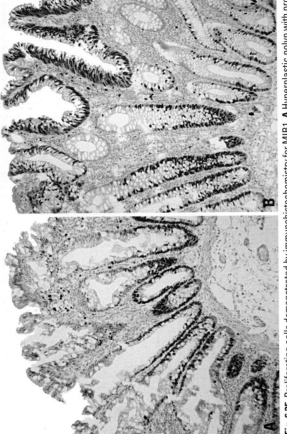

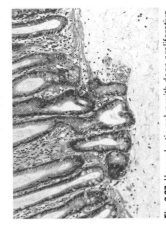

Fig. 6.35 Proliferating cells demonstrated by immunohistochemistry for MIB1. **A** Hyperplastic polyp with proliferative cells restricted to the basal parts of the crypts. **B** Tubular adenoma with proliferating adenomatous epithelium also at the luminal surface.

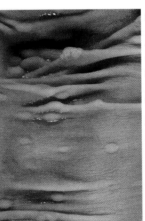

Fig. 6.36 Hyperplastic polyps. Typical sessile appearance.

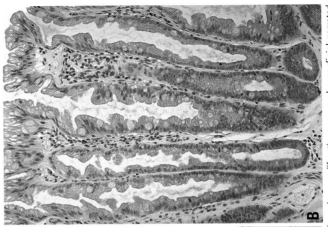

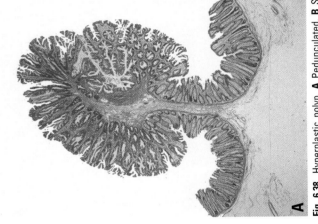

Fig. 6.37 Hyperplastic polyp with deep proliferative, non-serrated zone protruding into submucosa.

Fig. 6.38 Hyperplastic polyp. **A** Pedunculated. **B** Short deep proliferative zone and superficial serrated mature zone.

Fig. 6.41 Reactive epithelial changes in ulcerative colitis.

Fig. 6.42 Low-grade intraepithelial neoplasia in ulcerative colitis. **A** Patchy hyperbasophilic regular glands, with dysplasia extending to the luminal surface. **B** Haphazardly arranged dysplastic glands.

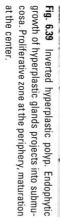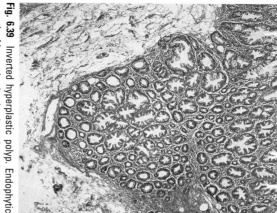

Fig. 6.39 Inverted hyperplastic polyp. Endophytic growth of hyperplastic glands projects into submucosa. Proliferative zone at the periphery, maturation at the center.

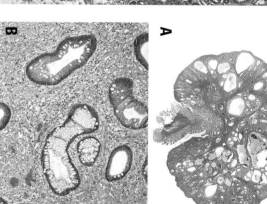

Fig. 6.40 Juvenile polyp. **A** Smooth eroded surface with numerous mucous retention cysts, typical of sporadic juvenile polyps. **B** Expanded inflamed stroma with distorted glands showing reactive atypia.

(familial clustering) has been observed only in Japan, a country at high incidence for that type of tumour. Cancers of the liver and of the upper gastrointestinal tract are exceedingly rare (less than 0.5% of all Li-Fraumeni neoplasms). In these neoplasms, sporadic cases often carry somatic TP53 mutations. The low frequency of these tumours in families with germline TP53 mutations suggests that the pre-existence of a TP53 mutation is not sufficient to increase the likelihood of cancer development.

BRCA 1 and BRCA 2

In a retrospective analysis of 33 large, high-risk breast and breast/ovarian cancer families linked to the BRCA1 locus, a significantly elevated risk of colon cancer was found, with an estimated relative risk of 4.11 (95% CI 2.36 - 7.15) {518}. This corresponds to a risk of colon cancer by age 70 of about 6%. In this study, there did not seem to be any increased relative risk at younger ages, although power to detect either sex or age effects was somewhat low in this set of data. In a similar study of BRCA2 carriers {69}, no increased risk of colorectal cancer was observed. However, there was a significantly elevated risk for both stomach and gallbladder tumours among known or likely mutation carriers with estimated relative risks associated with BRCA2 of 2.6 (95% CI 1.46 - 4.61) and 5.0 (1.50 - 16.5), respectively.

Molecular genetics

The development of most colorectal carcinomas is believed to begin in a colorectal epithelial cell with a mutational inactivation of the APC (adenomatous polyposis coli) suppressor gene {922, 636, 186}. This inactivation has multiple consequences, including interference with E-cadherin homeostasis and dysregulation of transcription of genes. Clonal accumulation of additional genetic alterations then occurs, including activation of proto-oncogenes such as c-myc {680} and ras, and inactivation of additional suppressor genes. The genes commonly inactivated during progression include genes on chromosome 18 {1583, 614} and the TP53 gene on the short arm of chromosome 17 {1056, 415}. The mutated TP53 gene product, in turn, fails to regulate normally a variety of genes regulated by wild-type p53, including p21WAF1/CIP1 cyclin-dependent kinase inhibitor which complexes with proliferating cell nuclear antigen {349}, and genes leading to apoptosis, including BAX {278}. For many suppressor genes, inactivation of one allele is often caused by loss of all or part of the chromosome where the gene resides. Various other chromosomal loci have high frequencies of loss in colorectal cancer due to chromosomal instability {1044}, but the target genes are not yet known.

Microsatellite instability (MSI)

Some colorectal cancers are distinguished by extensive nucleotide insertions or deletions in numerous, intrinsically unstable repeated sequences in tumour DNA, termed microsatellite instability (MSI), also termed ubiquitous somatic mutations, DNA replication errors (RER), or nucleotide instability {1540, 860}.

MSI is defined as a change of any length due to either insertion or deletion of repeating units, in a microsatellite within a

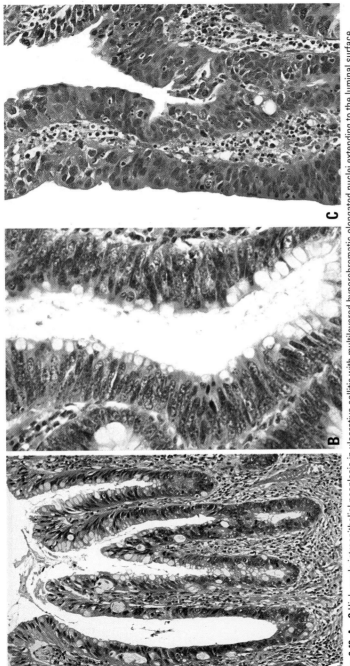

Fig. 6.43 A – C High-grade intraepithelial neoplasia in ulcerative colitis with multilayered hyperchromatic elongated nuclei extending to the luminal surface.

tumour when compared to normal tissue. It has been recommended that a panel of five microsatellites should be used as a reference standard (BAT25, BAT26, D5S346, D2S123, D17S250) for carcinomas of the large intestine {164}. If two or more of these markers show MSI, the lesion is classified as high-frequency microsatellite instability (MSI-H); if only one marker shows MSI, it is classified as low-frequency microsatellite instability (MSI-L); if no markers show MSI it is classified as microsatellite stable (MSS). If more than five markers are used, the criteria should be modified to reflect the percentage of markers demonstrating MSI. Thus, MSI-H lesions would exhibit MSI in more than 30-40% of markers tested.

MSI-H carcinomas are characteristic of hereditary nonpolyposis colorectal cancer syndrome (HNPCC) due to germline mutation of one of a group of DNA mismatch repair genes followed by somatic inactivation of the other allele. Sporadic MSI-H tumours comprise about 15% of colorectal carcinomas. They usually follow transcriptional silencing of both alleles of the hMLH1 mismatch repair gene due to aberrant methylation of cytosine residues in the cytosine and guanine-rich promoter region {886, 696}. The alterations that accumulate during progression of both hereditary and sporadic neoplasms characterized by MSI-H include mutations in microsatellites within the coding region of some genes, such as the type II receptor for TGF-beta1 and BAX {548}. In contrast to microsatellite-stable cancers, MSI-H cancers display nucleotide rather than chromosomal instability; allelic deletions are rare {1044}.

Recent studies indicate a functional link between defective DNA mismatch repair and the Wnt-signalling pathway. Approximately 25% of sporadic colorectal carcinomas with defective mismatch repair (MSI-H) were shown to contain frameshift mutations in the AXIN2 gene, which leads to a stabilization of β-catenin and activation of β-catenin/T-cell factor (TCF). This was associated with an accumulation in tumour cell nuclei which was absent in colorectal cancer without mismatch repair deficiency and in the absence of APC mutations. AXIN2 mutant protein appears to be more stable than the wild-type gene product, suggesting a dominant-negative effect {1079A}.

Prognosis and predictive factors

Morphology. Macroscopic and microscopic features reportedly related to prognosis are summarized in Table 6.01 {2348}.

Poor prognosis has been associated with both large and small tumour size, with sessile and ulcerated configuration as contrasted with polypoid cancer, with extensive involvement of the bowel circumference, with the presence of complete bowel obstruction, with perforation, and with serosal deposits.

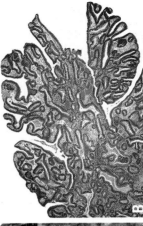

Fig. 6.44 Dysplasia associated lesion or mass (DALM). A Polypoid lesion. B Raised lesion simulating an adenoma.

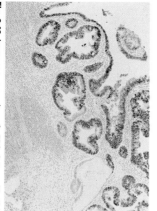

Fig. 6.45 Rectal carcinoma arising in ulcerative colitis. Surface dysplasia overlies invasive carcinoma in this DALM.

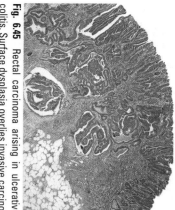

Fig. 6.47 Solitary rectal ulcer. **A, B** Two deep ulcers macroscopically simulating carcinoma.

Histopathological features related to poor prognosis include deep infiltration of the layers of the wall, extensive involvement of a particular layer, an infiltrative pattern of the invasive edge of the tumour as contrasted to an expansile pattern, and poor differentiation, including signet-ring cell and mucinous adenocarcinoma, adenosquamous carcinoma, small cell carcinoma and anaplastic carcinoma {1672, 1946, 220, 916, 266}. Mucinous adenocarcinomas of the rectum often present at a later stage and have the poorest overall prognosis {1928}, but the MSI status influences the aggressiveness of this histopathological subtype {1221}. Other studies have shown no significant difference in prognosis between mucinous and non-mucinous varieties of adenocarcinoma {1543}.

Lymph node metastasis. Metastasis to numerous nodes, those close to the mesenteric margin, at great distance from the primary tumour, or in retrograde lymph nodes, have been associated with poor prognosis while the prognostic value of identification of micrometastasis in lymph nodes by immunohistochemical or molecular techniques is still controversial {1564, 1387, 221}.

Extent of resection. A short longitudinal surgical resection margin (2-5 cm), reflecting the surgical technique employed, has been associated with poor outcome. In rectal cancer, clearance from the circumferential margin is important. The circumferential margin represents the adventitial soft tissue margin closest to the deepest penetration of the tumour. For all segments of the large intestine that are incompletely enveloped by peritoneum or not enveloped, the circumferential margin is created by blunt or sharp dissection at operation. The mesocolic margin in resection specimens of colon cancer is usually well distant from the primary tumour, but the status of the circumferential margin is particularly important in rectal carcinoma due to the anatomic proximity of pelvic structures {15}.

Genetic predictive markers. Some of the genetic alterations identified in colorectal cancers are markers for prognosis {313, 1206}. Allelic loss of chromosome 18q was found to be an adverse prognostic indicator. Other studies reported that loss of chromosomes 17p, 1p, 5q, 8p or 18q, decreased DCC gene expression, p53

Angiogenesis. Neovascularization of tumour stroma is crucial in supporting tumour growth, and high levels of microvessel density have been interpreted as an adverse prognostic feature {2010}.

Inflammatory response. The presence of an intense inflammatory infiltrate with polymorphonuclear leukocytes (particularly eosinophils), lymphocytes, plasma cells, mast cells and histiocytes, as well as prominent desmoplasia have been associated with improved prognosis {1352}. In the regional lymph nodes, hyperplasia of the paracortical T-lymphocyte areas and the B-cell germinal centers have also been reported as favourable, as has sinus histiocytosis.

Other features of colorectal carcinomas that have been shown to be of prognostic value in some studies include *angiolymphatic invasion, perineural space involvement, extramural venous involvement, peritumoural lymphocytic response, and tumour-infiltrating lymphocytes*. Some of these features are evaluated in a classification proposed by Jass {389}. A microacinar pattern of growth, defined as discrete, small, relatively regular tubules, is associated with reduced survival {559, 2100}.

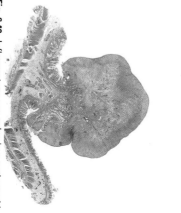

Fig. 6.46 Immunoexpression of p53 in intraepithelial neoplasia in ulcerative colitis.

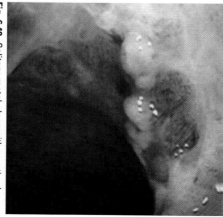

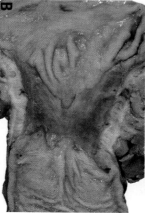

Fig. 6.48 Solitary rectal ulcer with reactive hyperplastic polyp due to prolapse. This lesion should not be confused with a neoplasm.

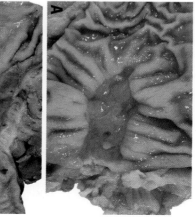

Fig. 6.49 Inflammatory cap polyp in a patient with ulcerative colitis.

overexpression, reduced p27^Kip1 expression, high expression of cyclin A, *ras* gene mutation, expression of enzymes involved in matrix degradation and their inhibitors (cathepsin-L, urokinase, tissue-type plasminogen activator, tissue inhibitors of metalloproteinases), expression of genes involved in apoptosis (*bcl2, bax, survivin*), expression of cell surface molecules (CD44 and its variants, ICAM1, galectin 3) and metabolic enzymes (GLUT1 glucose transporter, manganese-superoxide dismutase, thymidylate synthetase, ornithine decarboxylase, cyclooxygenase 2) have prognostic value. In addition, colorectal cancers manifesting MSI-H have been reported to have a lower frequency of metastasis and improved prognosis when compared to microsatellite-stable tumours.

Response to therapy. No pathological features have been reported as predictive of therapeutic response, but some molecular alterations have potential as predictive markers. Studies in cell lines of colonic and other carcinomas have shown that in vitro, the status of *TP53* is crucial {1382}. The *TP53* pathway is closely linked to regulation of the cell cycle and of apoptosis. The presence of wild-type p53 in cell lines is associated with in vitro growth inhibition in response to many chemotherapeutic agents, and with radiation-induced upregulation of p21^WAF1/CIP1 and cell cycle arrest. Tumours

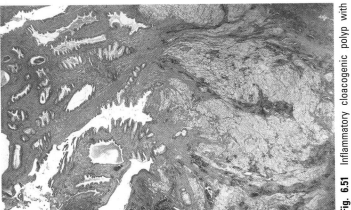

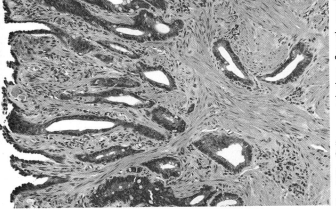

Fig. 6.50 Solitary rectal ulcer. Smooth muscle increased between glands, distorting and displacing them.

Fig. 6.51 Inflammatory cloacogenic polyp with mucous extravasation.

manifesting MSI-H may respond to 5-FU-based chemotherapy {1109}, while p53 protein accumulation was associated with lack of response to postoperative adjuvant chemotherapy with 5-FU and levamisole {24}. Chromosome 18q loss was associated with an unfavourable survival rate in this setting.

Major problems exist in the interpretation of various pathological features as prognostic and predictive markers. Many of these features are interrelated but have been treated for statistical purposes as independent variables in studies. At present, anatomic staging is the mainstay of clinical decision-making.

Table 6.01
Prognostic factors in colorectal carcinoma.

Features of the primary tumour	Evidence of vessel invasion	Evidence of host response	Consequences of surgical technique
Anatomic extent of disease (TNM)	Extramural venous involvement	Angiogenesis	Distance between resection margin
Extent of circumferential involvement	Lymphatic vessel or	Local inflammatory and desmo-	and tumour
Bowel obstruction	perineural space involvement	plastic response to infiltrating	Presence of residual tumour
Perforation	tumour	tumour	
Pattern of invasion	Reactive changes in regional		
Grade of differentiation	lymph nodes		

Familial adenomatous polyposis

I.C. Talbot
R. Burt
H. Järvinen
G. Thomas

Definition

Familial adenomatous polyposis (FAP) is an autosomal dominant disorder characterized by numerous adenomatous colorectal polyps that have an intrinsic tendency to progress to adenocarcinoma. It is caused by a germline mutation in the Adenomatous Polyposis Coli (*APC*) gene which is located on the long arm of chromosome 5 (5q21-22). Gardner syndrome is a variant of FAP that includes epidermoid cysts, osteomas, dental anomalies and desmoid tumours, in addition to colorectal adenomas. Turcot syndrome is a variant that is associated with a brain tumour (medulloblastoma). An attenuated FAP form has been distinguished from classic FAP, where the number of adenomas is less than 100 in the colon.

Synonyms

Adenomatous polyposis coli, familial polyposis coli, Bussey-Gardner polypo-

sis, Gardner syndrome, familial multiple polyposis, multiple adenomatosis, familial polyposis of the colon and rectum, familial polyposis of the gastrointestinal tract, familial adenomatous polyposis coli, etc.

MIM No.:

FAP, including Gardner syndrome, 175100; *Turcot syndrome*, 276300

Incidence

Estimates of the incidence of FAP vary between 1 per 7000 and 1 per 30,000 newborns. The mean annual incidence rate has been constantly from 1 to 2 per 1,000,000 in Denmark and Finland while the prevalence has increased to more than 25 per 1,000,000 since the creation of preventive polyposis registries {205; 836}. In general, FAP underlies less than 1% of all new colorectal cancer cases. Between 30 and 50% of new FAP patients are solitary cases, probably representing new mutations of the *APC* gene.

Diagnostic criteria

Classical FAP is defined clinically by the finding of at least 100 colorectal adenomatous polyps {216}. Endoscopic visual-

ization of diminutive polyps may require an autosomal dye spray assisted endoscopy. Histological confirmation requires examination of several polyps. In the context of endoscopic screening on the basis of definite family history the detection of fewer adenomas is sufficient at an early age. The same applies on the attenuated disease form (AAPC). Final diagnosis may be achieved by demonstration of a mutated APC, but the detection rate of mutations has only been between 60 and 80% of all FAP families. In patients where the clinical criteria remain doubtful and genetic diagnosis is not achieved the finding of extracolonic features of FAP (epidermoid cysts, osteomas, desmoid tumour, gastric fundic gland polyps, etc.) may give additional diagnostic support.
The following diagnostic criteria have been established: (1) 100 or more colorectal adenomas or (2) germline mutation of the APC gene or (3) family history of FAP and at least one of the following: epidermoid cysts; osteomas; desmoid tumour.

Colorectal polyps

The colorectal polyps are adenomas, most often tubular, and resemble their sporadic counterparts.

Localization

Colorectal adenomas in FAP occur throughout the colon but follow the general distribution of sporadic adenomas, with greatest density in the rectum and sigmoid colon. The distribution of cancers follows that of the adenomas.

Clinical features

Age at clinical manifestation

Colorectal adenomas become detectable at endoscopic examination (sigmoidoscopy) between the age of 10 and 20 years, increasing in number and size with age. The most important clinical feature of FAP is the almost invariable progression of one or more colorectal adenomas to cancer. The mean age of development of colorectal cancer is about 40 years, but the cancer risk is 1 to 6% already at

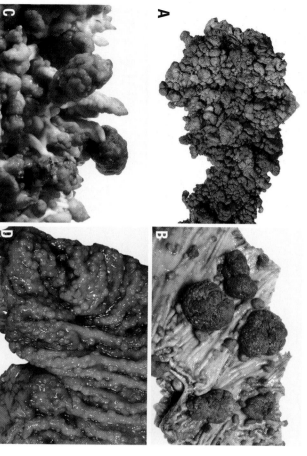

Fig. 6.52 Colectomy specimens from patients with familial adenomatous polyposis. **A** Hundreds of polyps of different size cover the entire mucosal surface. **B** Multiple adenomas in different stages of development. **C** Lateral view of polyps. **D** Numerous small early (sessile) adenomas.

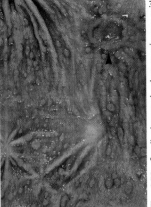

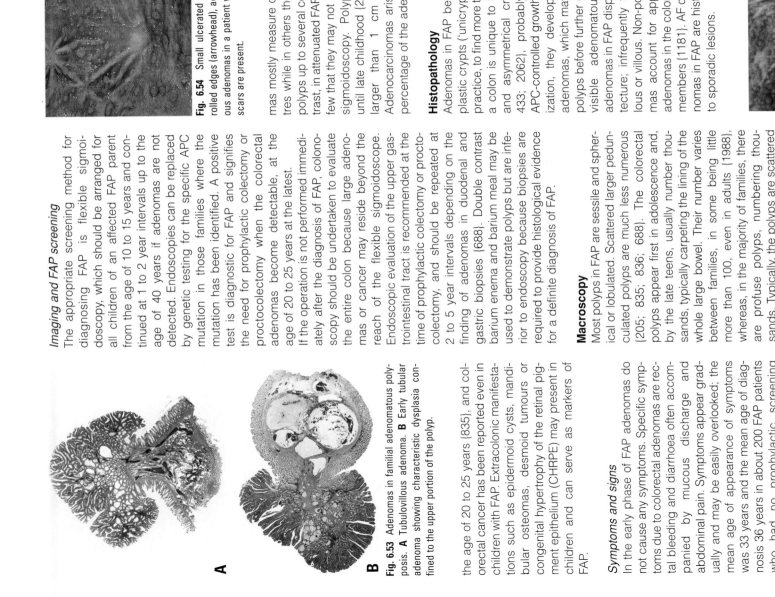

Fig. 6.53 Adenomas in familial adenomatous polyposis. **A** Tubulovillous adenoma. **B** Early tubular adenoma showing characteristic dysplasia confined to the upper portion of the polyp.

the age of 20 to 25 years {835}, and colorectal cancer has been reported even in children with FAP. Extracolonic manifestations such as epidermoid cysts, mandibular osteomas, desmoid tumours or congenital hypertrophy of the retinal pigment epithelium (CHRPE) may present in children and can serve as markers of FAP.

Symptoms and signs

In the early phase of FAP adenomas do not cause any symptoms. Specific symptoms due to colorectal adenomas are recognized by mucous discharge and abdominal pain. Symptoms appear gradually and may be easily overlooked; the mean age of appearance of symptoms was 33 years and the mean age of diagnosis 36 years in about 200 FAP patients who had no prophylactic screening arranged {216}.

Two thirds of patients diagnosed to have FAP on the basis of symptoms (propositi) already have colorectal cancer whereas in asymptomatic members of known FAP families cancer is very rare at the time of the detection of FAP provided that prophylactic endoscopic screening was arranged in good time, i.e. before the age of 20 years {836}.

Imaging and FAP screening

The appropriate screening method for diagnosing FAP is flexible sigmoidoscopy, which should be arranged for all children of an affected FAP parent from the age of 10 to 15 years and continued at 1 to 2 year intervals up to the age of 40 years if adenomas are not detected. Endoscopies can be replaced by genetic testing for the specific APC mutation in those families where the mutation has been identified. A positive test is diagnostic for FAP and signifies the need for prophylactic colectomy or proctocolectomy when the colorectal adenomas become detectable, at the age of 20 to 25 years at the latest.

If the operation is not performed immediately after the diagnosis of FAP, colonoscopy should be undertaken to evaluate the entire colon because large adenomas or cancer may reside beyond the reach of the flexible sigmoidoscope. Endoscopic evaluation of the upper gastrointestinal tract is recommended at the time of prophylactic colectomy or proctocolectomy, and should be repeated at 2 to 5 year intervals depending on the finding of adenomas in duodenal and gastric biopsies {688}. Double contrast barium enema and barium meal may be used to demonstrate polyps but are inferior to endoscopy because biopsies are required to provide histological evidence for a definite diagnosis of FAP.

Macroscopy

Most polyps in FAP are sessile and spherical or lobulated. Scattered larger pedunculated polyps are much less numerous {205; 835; 836; 688}. The colorectal polyps appear first in adolescence and, by the late teens, usually number thousands, typically carpeting the lining of the whole large bowel. Their number varies between families, in some being little more than 100, even in adults {1988}, whereas, in the majority of families, there are profuse polyps, numbering thousands. Typically, the polyps are scattered evenly along the whole large bowel but, in over one third of cases, their density is greatest in the proximal colon. Adult patients with rectal sparing have been described, even when adenocarcinoma was present in the right colon {1503}.

In any one patient the polyps range from barely visible mucosal nodules to pedunculated polyps of up to 1 cm or more. In some patients and families the adeno-

Fig. 6.54 Small ulcerated adenocarcinoma with rolled edges (arrowhead), accompanied by numerous adenomas in a patient with FAP. Polypectomy scars are present.

mas mostly measure only a few millimetres while in others they are larger, with polyps up to several centimetres. In contrast, in attenuated FAP, the polyps are so few that they may not be noticed at rigid sigmoidoscopy. Polyps rarely appear until late childhood {216} and are rarely larger than 1 cm until adulthood. Adenocarcinomas arise in only a small percentage of the adenomas.

Histopathology

Adenomas in FAP begin as single dysplastic crypts ('unicryptal' adenomas). In practice, to find more than one of these in a colon is unique to FAP. By excessive and asymmetrical crypt fission {1086; 433; 2062}, probably due to loss of APC-controlled growth and tissue organization, they develop into oligocryptal adenomas, which may not be visible as polyps before further growth into grossly visible adenomatous polyps. Most adenomas in FAP display a tubular architecture; infrequently they are tubulovillous or villous. Non-polypoid, flat adenomas account for approximately 5% of adenomas in the colon of affected family members {1181}. AF denomas and carcinomas in FAP are histologically identical to sporadic lesions.

Fig. 6.55 Adenocarcinoma and innumerable adenomas in a case of FAP.

Proliferation

The histologically normal intestinal mucosa in FAP shows no increase in the rate of epithelial cell proliferation {2062}. Mitotic activity is not increased {1315} except in the adenomatous epithelium, in which cell proliferation is identical with that in sporadic adenomas.

Small intestinal polyps

Small bowel polyps, particularly duodenal polyps, are also adenomas. They develop preferentially in the periampullary region of the duodenum, probably due to a co-carcinogenic effect of bile {1679; 1805}. They become evident ten years later than the colorectal polyps. Using side-viewing endoscopy, adenomas have been found in 92% of patients with FAP at routine screening {1809}. They increase in size and number with time and carry a lifetime risk of duodenal or periampullary cancer of about 4% {688}. Ampullary and periampullary adenocarcinoma is one of the principal causes of death in patients who have undergone prophylactic proctocolectomy {1809}.

Extra-intestinal manifestations

Several other organs are involved in FAP but extra-intestinal manifestations rarely determine the clinical course of the disease.

Stomach

Gastric adenomas do occur with increased frequency {425} but the most common abnormality is the fundic gland polyp. This is a non-neoplastic mucus retention type of polyp, grossly visible as a smooth dome-shaped nodule in the gastric body and fundus, usually multiple. Histologically, the lesion is characteristically undramatic, consisting of gastric body mucosa that is often normal apart from cystic dilatation of glands There is evidence of increased cell proliferation and dysplasia developing in these polyps {2144} but progression to adenocarcinoma is only a rare occurrence {2214}.

Liver and biliary tract

There is an increased incidence of hepatoblastoma in the male infants of families with FAP {563; 578}. Dysplasia has been demonstrated in the bile duct and gall-bladder epithelium in patients with FAP {1377} and these patients are at risk of developing adenocarcinoma of the biliary tree {1806}.

Extra-gastrointestinal manifestations

Soft tissues

Tissues derived from all three germ layers are affected in FAP. As well as the endodermal lesions so far described, mesodermal lesions in the form of a fibromatosis unique to FAP, usually referred to as desmoid tumour, develop in a substantial minority of patients {315}. Desmoid tumours arise in either the retroperitoneal tissues or in the abdominal wall, often after trauma or previous surgery involving that site.

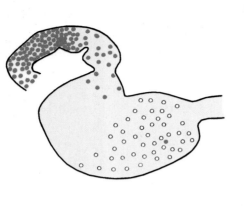

Fig. 6.56 Diagram of stomach and duodenum showing the distribution of fundic gland polyps (open circles) and adenomas (solid circles) in FAP {425}. Adenomas are concentrated in the second part of the duodenum.

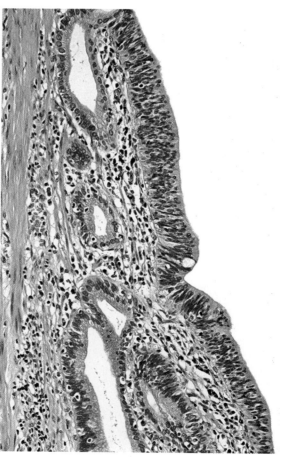

Fig. 6.57 Intraepithelial neoplasia (dysplasia) of the common bile duct from a patient with FAP.

A desmoid is a mass of firm pale tissue, characteristically growing by expansion, usually rounded in shape. Desmoids begin as small scar-like foci of fibrosis in the retroperitoneal fat and, when large, typically extend around and between other structures such as the small or large bowel, ureters and major blood vessels. Histologically, these lesions are composed of sheets of elongated myofibroblasts, arranged in fascicles and whorls. The lesions have a dense, tough consistency and there is a variable amount of collagen. They are well vascularized and contain numerous small blood vessels that bleed profusely when incised.

Bones

Bone lesions include exostoses and endostoses. Endostoses of the mandible are found in the majority of patients {203}. They are almost always small and symptomless. Exostoses may be solitary or multiple and tend to arise in the long bones.

Teeth

Dental abnormalities have been described in 11 to 80% of individuals with FAP {241}. The abnormalities may be impaction, supernumerary or absent teeth, fused roots of first and second molars or unusually long and tapered roots of posterior teeth.

Eye

In 75-80% of patients, ophthalmoscopy reveals multiple patches of congenital

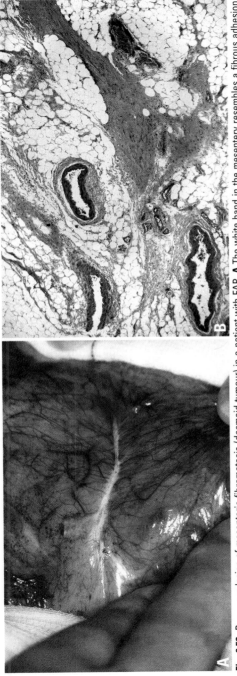

Fig. 6.58 Precursor lesion of mesenteric fibromatosis (desmoid tumour) in a patient with FAP. **A** The white band in the mesentery resembles a fibrous adhesion. **B** Histology shows a band of fibromatosis in the mesenteric fat.

hypertrophy of retinal pigment epithelium (CHRPE) {280}. Ultrastructurally, they are freckle-like plaques of enlarged melanin-containing retinal epithelial cells {1466}. Their value for diagnosis is limited by inconsistency and variation between families.

Skin

Epidermal cysts, usually of the face and often multiple, were first described in FAP by Gardner {565}.

Fig. 6.59 Epidermoid cyst on the dorsal surface of the hand of an FAP patient.

Endocrine system

There is a definite but relatively slight increase in the incidence of endocrine tumours in FAP, including neoplasia of pituitary, pancreatic islets and adrenal cortex {1160}, as well as multiple endocrine neoplasia syndrome, type 2b {1500} but these are of insufficient frequency or gravity to form part of a routine screening protocol. The best documented endocrine association is papillary carcinoma of thyroid {268}, largely restricted to women {202}.

Nervous system

The concurrent presence of a brain tumour and multiple colorectal polyps constitutes Turcot syndrome. Some individuals affected in this way are victims of FAP, with a germline defect of *APC*. These are infants or young children who present with medulloblastoma and colorectal polyps {658}.

Other individuals present later in life with a glioma, usually an astrocytoma or glioblastoma multiforme and are usually associated with hereditary non-polyposis colon cancer (HNPCC) rather than FAP {262}.

Genetics

FAP is an autosomal dominant disease with almost complete penetrance by 40 years of age. *APC* germline mutations are the only known cause of FAP.

Gene structure and expression

The *APC* gene was localized to chromosome 5q21-22 by Bodmer et al. {156} and Leppert et al. {1047}. It was isolated by the group of White {868; 629} and by the laboratories of Nakamura and Vogelstein {920; 1364}. It spans over a region of 120 Kb and is composed of at least 21 exons, 7 of which are alternatively expressed {1658}. 16 *APC* transcripts that differ in their 5'-most regions and arise by the alternative inclusion of 6 of these exons have been identified.

The *APC* gene is ubiquitously expressed in normal tissues, with highest levels in the central nervous system. Tissue-specific differences were observed in the expression of *APC* transcripts without

exon 1, a coding region for a heptad repeat that supports homodimerization of the APC protein.

Gene product and function

The APC protein is a 2,843-amino acid polypeptide that is a negative regulator in the Wnt signaling pathway. The protein contains several functional domains that act as binding and degradation sites for β-catenin and control the β-catenin intracellular concentration. A protein-binding domain near the carboxy-terminal of *APC* mediates phosphorylation by glycogen synthase kinase 3 β (GSK3b) and stabilizes the formation of a complex between the two proteins {1627}. In an unstimulated cell, GSK3b promotes phosphorylation of the protein conductin/axin which is added to the APC GSK3b complex {2107; 124}. Phosphorylated axin recruits β-catenin, which is in turn phosphorylated and targeted for degradation through an APC-dependent ubiquitin-proteasome pathway {11}. Normal Wnt signalling inhibits GSK3b activity and dephosphorylates axin. As a result, β-catenin is released from the complex {2107}.

In the cytoplasm, β-catenin is involved in cytoskeletal organization with binding to microtubules. It also interacts with E-cadherin, a membrane protein involved in cell adhesion. Free β-catenin shuttles to the nucleus where it binds to the transcription factors of the TCF/LEF family. The resulting complexes activate *c-MYC* {680} and cyclin D1 transcription {1753; 1922}. Lack of functional APC causes unregulated intracellular accumulation of β-catenin and thereby constitutive expression of *c-MYC* and of the cyclin D1 gene (CDD1).

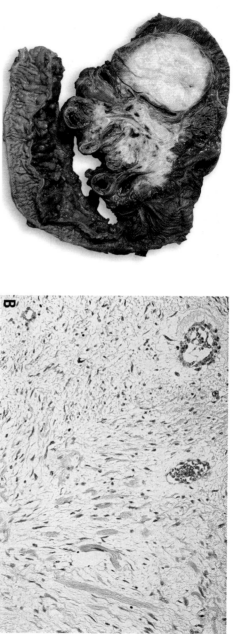

Fig. 6.60 Mesenteric fibromatosis (desmoid tumour) in a patient with FAP. **A** The lesion entraps loops of small intestine. **B** Collagen bands and small vessels.

Gene mutations

The germline mutation rate leading to a new deleterious APC allele is estimated to be 5 to 9 per million gametes. As a result, most families exhibit unique mutations, and individuals with no previous family history of FAP are not uncommon. They may represent up to one fourth of propositi {143}.

A deleterious APC mutation may be found in about 95% of FAP patients. The vast majority of the mutant alleles lead to the synthesis of a truncated protein. About 10% of the mutations are large interstitial deletions that may involve the entire gene. Rare missense mutations, most with uncertain functional consequences, have been described. Mutations at codons 1061 and 1309 account for 20% of all identified germline mutations in the APC gene. In up to 5% of families, the genetic defect causing FAP is not yet known {1003}.

Genetics of FAP associated tumours

Consistent with the 2-hit model of carcinogenesis by tumour suppressor genes, the wild type APC allele is lost or mutated in the vast majority of FAP associated tumours, including colorectal adenomatous polyps and carcinoma. Each colorectal adenomatous polyp is a premalignant lesion that may progress to carcinoma in an unpredictable fashion. In addition to APC mutations, colon carcinomas in FAP patients contain somatic mutations that are similar to those found in the most fre-

quent type of sporadic colon cancers not associated with replication errors. TP53 mutation and 17p allele loss have been observed in 40% of invasive carcinomas {910}. However, in some families TP53 may not be involved {30}. Loss of alleles on chromosome 18 and 22 were observed in 46% and 33% respectively. The KRAS mutation frequency increases from 11% immoderately to 36% in severely dysplastic adenomas {30}. KRAS mutations may potentiate cyclin D1 transcription {680}. Interestingly, the type of APC germline mutation may influence the mode of inactivation of the second APC allele {30}.

Animal model

Heterozygous mutant mice for a defective Apc allele develop multiple intestinal neoplasia {1245}. The homozygous mutant embryos die prior to gastrulation {1811}. Expression of the secretory phos-

pholipase Pla2g2a is associated with a decreased number and size of adenoma in heterozygous mutant Apc mice {1283}. Implication of PLA2G2A polymorphism in FAP expressivity has not been demonstrated in humans.

Genotype / phenotype relationships

There are well documented relationships between the location of the mutation on the APC gene and the FAP phenotype. APC mutations in the first or last third of the gene are associated with attenuated colorectal polyposis (AAPC) characterized by the occurrence of less than 100 polyps and a late onset {1284}. Fundic gland polyposis is prevalent in the attenuated form of FAP but desmoids may be present only if the AAPC causing mutation lies in the 3' end of the APC gene. Indeed, mutations after codon 1444 are associated with an increased susceptibility to desmoid tumours {340}. CHRPE

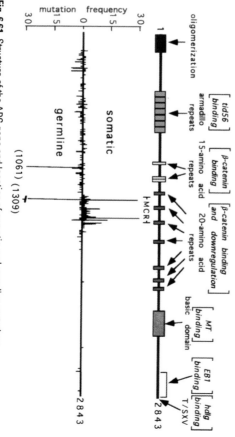

Fig. 6.61 Structure of the APC gene and location of somatic and germline mutations. From: P. Polakis, Biochim Biophys Acta 1332: F127-F147 (1997)

lesions are a consistent feature, except if the APC mutation is located before exon 9 and after codon 1387 {1810; 340}. Mutations in the central region of the gene, including the mutational hotspot at codon 1309, correlate with a severe phenotype characterized by development of thousands of polyps at a young age {258}. In contrast to mutant APC proteins truncated at codon 386 or 1465, which interfered only weakly with wild-type APC activity in an in vitro system, a mutant APC protein truncated at codon 1309 was shown to be a strong inhibitor and may thus have dominant negative properties {1422}. These observations point to a possible mechanism that could contribute to the genotype/phenotype relationships observed in FAP. There may also be a correlation between slow acetylation genotypes and extracolonic manifestations of the disease {1308}.

Application of genetic testing in the clinical setting

In the absence of systematic, family based screening programs, the presenting features are usually those of malignancy, such as weight loss and inanition, bowel obstruction, or bloody diarrhoea. In such cases, patient evaluation will frequently find a colorectal carcinoma. Occasionally, the extracolonic features of the condition may lead to presentation and diagnosis. Cases of new mutation still present in these ways, but in areas with well organized registers, gene carriers among relatives of affected patients are identified prior to symptoms either by DNA-based genetic tests or by bowel examination.

The most commonly used commercially available genetic testing for FAP involves identification of the mutant APC allele by in vitro detection of truncated APC protein {414}. This approach is referred to as in vitro protein synthesis (IVPS) testing. IVPS testing is able to detect mutation carriers in about 80% of families. Once evidence of a disease-causing mutation is found in an index case by this method, testing is near 100% predictive in other family members. It is imperative that genetic counselling be undertaken throughout the process of genetic testing. Without this, genetic testing and the use of the results are poorly applied in the clinical setting {1703}.

Screening in gene carriers is similar to that in families where genetic testing is not applied or does not work and usually involves sigmoidoscopy every 1 to 2 years, beginning between age 10 and 12 years. If a genetic diagnosis is made after that age, full colonoscopy should probably be done in view of the risk of lesions higher in the colon. Preventive total colectomy is proposed to gene carriers when polyposis becomes conspicuous. Genotype/phenotype correlations may be used to adapt clinical management to individual FAP patients.

A family member who has a negative DNA based genetic test can forgo screening if (1) the mutation found in other affected family members is obviously deleterious and (2) if the individual with a negative test has been unambiguously shown to be a non-gene carrier by DNA testing. Such individuals need no further screening as their risk to develop colon cancer is similar to that of the general population.

Hereditary nonpolyposis colorectal cancer

P. Peltomäki
H. Vasen
J.R. Jass

Definition

Hereditary nonpolyposis colorectal cancer (HNPCC, Lynch syndrome) is an autosomal dominant disorder, characterized by the development of colorectal carcinoma, endometrial carcinoma, and cancer of the small intestine, ureter, or renal pelvis.

MIM No.   120435-6

Diagnostic criteria

In 1990, the International Collaborative Group on HNPCC (ICG-HNPCC) proposed a set of selection criteria to provide a basis for uniformity in collaborative studies {2003}. These criteria, referred to as Amsterdam Criteria I (ACI), have been widely used since then. Recently, the criteria have been revised to include the extracolonic cancers that are part of the syndrome. The new set of diagnostic criteria (ACII), is shown in Table 6.02 {2004}. They identify families that are very likely to represent HNPCC. On the other hand, they are not intended to serve as a guide to exclude suspected families from genetic counselling and mutation analysis.

Clinical features

Predisposed individuals from HNPCC families have a high lifetime risk of devel-

oping colorectal carcinoma (70-85%), endometrial carcinoma (50%), as well as certain other cancers (below 15%) {5, 2071, 2005}. Colorectal lesions are often diagnosed at an early age (mean, 45 years), and are located in the proximal part of the colon in about two-thirds of the patients. Synchronous or metachronous colorectal carcinoma is present in 35% of patients. In over 90% of the cases, it shows microsatellite instability (MSI) (Table 6.04) {839, 1166, 1129}. The adenomas that occur in HNPCC tend to develop at an early age, to have villous components and to be more dysplastic than adenomas detected in the general population. Although multiple adenomas may be observed in HNPCC, florid polyposis is not a feature.

Extracolonic lesions include cancer of the endometrium, renal pelvis/ureter, stomach, small bowel, ovary, brain, hepatobiliary tract, and also sebaceous tumours. Among these tumours, carcinoma of the endometrium, ureter, renal pelvis, and small bowel have the highest relative risk, and are therefore the most specific for HNPCC (Table 6.03).

The occurrence of sebaceous gland tumours together with HNPCC type internal malignancy is referred to as the Muir-Torre syndrome {322}. The association of primary brain tumours (usually glioblas-

tomas) with multiple colorectal adenomas is referred to as the Turcot syndrome {1979}. The latter has a shared genetic basis with HNPCC on the one hand and FAP on the other hand {658}.

Pathology

The pathology of HNPCC tumours is similar to that of sporadic colorectal carcinoma showing high levels of instability at short tandem repeat sequences, microsatellites (MSI-H). Many studies make no distinction between familial and non-familial MSI-H carcinomas. The following descriptions apply to all MSI-H carcinomas, but highlight subtle differences between HNPCC cancers and their sporadic counterparts where these are known.

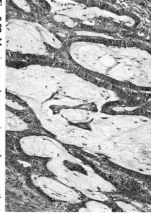

Fig. 6.62 Mucinous adenocarcinoma from a patient with HNPCC.

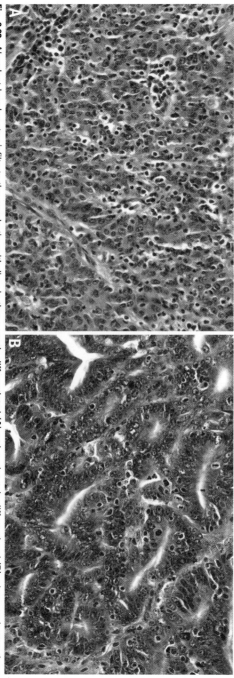

Fig. 6.63 Abundant lymphocytes infiltrate the neoplastic epithelium in these poorly differentiated **(A)** and moderately differentiated **(B)** adenocarcinomas from patients with HNPCC.

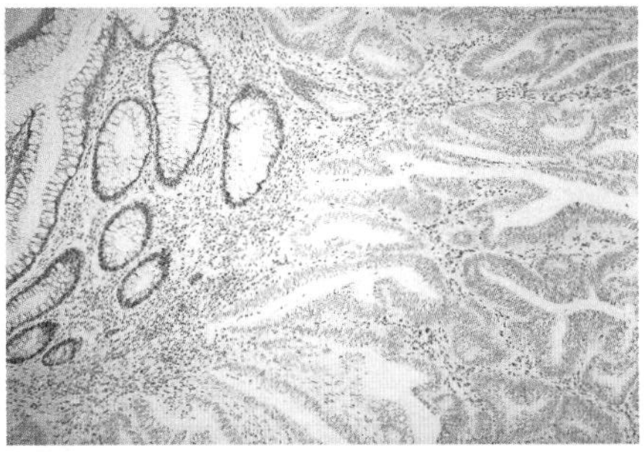

Fig. 6.64 Immunohistochemistry for the MLH1 gene product in a patient with HNPCC. Normal expression is seen in the non-neoplastic epithelium (left). Expression is lost in the adenocarcinoma (right).

Macroscopy

HNPCC cancers show a predilection for the proximal colon including caecum, ascending colon, hepatic flexure and transverse colon {1130}. At least 60% occur in the proximal colon. The gross appearances have not been studied in detail. However, since HNPCC and MSI-H colorectal carcinomas show a consistent trend towards good circumscription {842, 1723}, they are more likely to present as polypoid growths, plaques, ulcers or bulky masses and less likely to present as diffuse growths or tight strictures.

Adenomas are not numerous but are likely to be more frequent in HNPCC subjects than age-matched controls {846}. Colonoscopic studies indicate that the distribution of adenomas in HNPCC may not mirror the proximal colonic predilection of carcinoma {846}. This could be due to the occurrence of sporadic distal adenomas in older HNPCC subjects or because proximal adenomas are more likely to progress to cancer.

Histopathology

No individual microscopic feature is specific to HNPCC, but particular groups of features are diagnostically useful {1723}. Identical features are found in the 10 to 15% of sporadic colorectal cancers that show high levels of DNA microsatellite instability (MSI-H) {842}. However, sporadic MSI-H cancers present in older subjects lacking a family history of bowel cancer. HNPCC and sporadic MSI-H colorectal cancers fall into three groups based on site and microscopic criteria:

Proximally located mucinous adenocarcinomas. These are usually well circumscribed and well or moderately differentiated. Lymphocytic infiltration is not prominent but tumour infiltrating (intraepithelial) lymphocytes (TIL) may be evident in non-mucinous areas. Tubulo-villous or villous adenomatous remnants adjacent to the cancer may be present. Mucin production may be more common in subjects with an *MSH2* germline mutation {1723}.

Proximally located, poorly differentiated adenocarcinomas. Poor differentiation indicates a failure of gland formation, the malignant epithelium being arranged in small clusters, irregular trabeculae or large aggregates. Tumours are well circumscribed and lack an abundant desmoplastic stroma. Some are peppered with TIL. A Crohn-like lymphocytic reaction may be present. This subtype has been described as medullary or 'undifferentiated', though the majority contains subclones in which glandular differentiation is evident. This subtype may be more common in subjects with an *MSH2* mutation {1723}. In general, colorectal cancers showing TIL and/or a Crohn-like lymphocytic reaction appear to be more common in subjects with an *MLH1* germline mutation {1723}.

Adenomas in HNPCC. These are more likely to show features indicative of increased cancer risk including villosity and high-grade intraepithelial neoplasia {846}. Immunohistochemical staining to demonstrate loss of expression of MLH1 or MSH2 may assist in pinpointing the underlying germline mutation. However, antigenicity may be retained in the case of MLH1, even if genetic changes have resulted in a non-functioning protein {1924A; 1924B}. Virtually all sporadic MSI-H carcinomas lose MLH1 through methylation.

Immunohistochemical staining of MSI-H colorectal cancers confirms that the majority of TIL are CD3 positive T-cells and most, in turn, are cytotoxic (CD8 positive) {423}. In H&E sections, lymphocytes are difficult to discern when the percentage of CD3 positive lymphocytes (out of all epithelial nuclei) is less than about 5%. CD3 counts in excess of 5% occur in around 70% of MSI-H cancers. CD3 counts in excess of 10% are highly specific for MSI-H cancers. The nodular arrangements of lymphocytes occurring peri-tumourally or within the serosa (Crohn-like reaction) are B-lymphocytes surrounded by T-lymphocytes.

Genetics

Acquired genetic changes in HNPCC cancers

The demonstration of DNA microsatellite instability serves as an important biomarker for HNPCC cancers. Bandshifts in BAT26 are highly sensitive for both familial and sporadic MSI-H cancers {3}, though some cases may be missed {548}.

Table 6.02
Revised diagnostic criteria for HNPCC (Amsterdam criteria II)

There should be at least three relatives with an HNPCC-associated cancer: colorectal cancer (CRC), or cancer of the endometrium, small bowel, ureter or renal pelvis.

- One patient should be a first degree relative of the other two
- At least two successive generations should be affected.
- At least one tumour should be diagnosed before age 50.
- Familial adenomatous polyposis should be excluded in the CRC case(s) if any.
- Tumours should be verified by histopathological examination.

Table 6.03
Summary of clinical, pathological and genetic features of HNPCC (Lynch syndrome)

- Familial clustering of colorectal and/or endometrial cancer
- Excess risk of cancer of the ovary, ureter/renal pelvis, small bowel, stomach, brain, hepatobiliary tract, and skin (sebaceous tumours)
- Development of multiple cancers at an early age
- Features of colorectal adenoma include: (1) variable numbers from one to a few; (2) increased proportion of adenomas with a villous growth pattern (3) a high degree of dysplasia; (4) rapid progression from adenoma to carcinoma and (5) high frequency of microsatellite instability (MSI-H)
- Features of colorectal cancer include: (1) predilection for proximal colon; (2) improved survival; (3) multiple colorectal cancers (4) increased proportion of mucinous tumours, poorly differentiated tumours, and tumours with marked host-lymphocytic infiltration and lymphoid aggregation at the tumour margin.

Fig. 6.65 Tubular adenoma from a patient with HNPCC immunostained for **(A)** MLH and **(B)** MSH2. The neoplastic epithelium shows loss of MSH2 expression (upper portion of B)

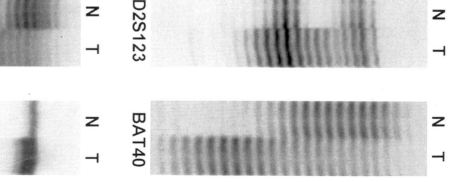

A panel of five markers (BAT25, BAT26, D2S123, D5S346 and D17S250) has been recommended for screening purposes {164}. Bandshifts at two or more microsatellite loci are indicative of MSI-H. Around 60% of HNPCC adenomas are MSI-H {2}.

Most MSI-H cancers are diploid or near diploid and the frequency of loss of heterozygosity (LOH) is low for the traditional loci 5q, 17p and 18q {962, 841}. The frequency of APC, KRAS and TP53 mutation is reduced {962, 841}. Conversely, mutations are encountered in TGFRII, IGF2R, BAX, E2F-4, MSH3, MSH6 and caspase 5 {548, 1165, 1699, 1793, 2156, 1558}. In general, the driving force for colorectal cancer development and progression may be DNA instability (mutator pathway) or chromosomal instability (suppressor pathway). HNPCC cancers and sporadic MSI-H cancers share the mutator pathway.

Mode of inheritance, chromosomal location, and structure

HNPCC is transmitted as an autosomal dominant trait. It is associated with germline mutations in five genes with verified or putative DNA mismatch repair function, namely MSH2 (MutS homologue 2), MLH1 (MutL homologue 1), PMS2 (Postmeiotic segregation 1), PMS2

(Postmeiotic segregation 2), and MSH6 (MutS homologue 6). Structural characteristics of these genes are given in Table 6.04. Homozygous MLH1 mutations confer to a neurofibromatosis 1 like phenotype {2048, 1580}.

Gene product

HNPCC genes are ubiquitously expressed in adult human tissues, and therefore, the expression pattern does not seem to explain the selective organ involvement in this syndrome. Expression is particularly prominent in the epithelium of the digestive tract as well as in testis and ovary {505, 1030, 2120}. In the intestine, expression is confined to the replicating compartment, i.e. the bottom half of the crypts. Immunohistochemical staining against these proteins is nuclear.

Function

The protein products of HNPCC genes are key players in the correction of mismatches that arise during DNA replication {957}. Two different MutS-related heterodimeric complexes are responsible for mismatch recognition: MSH2-MSH3 and MSH2-MSH6. While the presence of MSH2 in the complex is mandatory, MSH3 can replace MSH6 in the correction of insertion-deletion mismatches, but not single-base mispairs. Following mis-

match binding, a heterodimeric complex of MutL-related proteins, MLH1-PMS2 (and possibly another alternative complex formed by MLH1-MLH3) is recruited, and this larger complex, together with numerous other proteins, accomplishes mismatch repair. The observed functional redundancy in the DNA mismatch repair protein family may help explain why mutations in MSH2 and MLH1 are prevalent in HNPCC families, while mutations in PMS1, PMS2, and MSH6 are much less frequent, and no germline mutations in MSH3 or MLH3 have been reported, so far (see below). Mismatch repair deficiency gives rise to microsatellite instability, and as such may aid in the diagnosis of this syndrome {3}.

Fig. 6.66 Microsatellite instability in HNPCC. Shifts of allele size are evident in dinucleotide and mononucleotide markers. N = normal tissue, T = tumour.

Table 6.04
Characteristics of HNPCC-associated human DNA mismatch repair genes.

Gene	Chromosomal location	Length of cDNA (kb)	Number of exons	Genomic size (kb)	References
MSH2	2p21	2.8	16	73	{509, 956, 1029, 1079, 1686, 1486}
MLH1	3p31-p23	2.3	19	58-100	{193, 660, 955, 1077, 1075, 1453}
PMS1	2q31-q33	2.8	not known	not known	{1350}
PMS2	7p22	2.6	15	16	{1347, 1350}
MSH6	2p21	4.2	10	20	{13, 1686, 1451, 1349}

However, microsatellite instability is not specific to HNPCC, occurring in 10 to 15% of apparently sporadic colorectal and other tumours as well {164}.
Correction of biosynthetic errors in the newly synthesized DNA is not the only function of the DNA mismatch repair system. In particular, it is also able to recognize lesions caused by exogenous mutagens, and has been shown to participate in transcription-coupled repair {134, 1215}.

Gene mutations

The International Collaborative Group on HNPCC maintains a database for HNPCC-associated mutations and polymorphisms (http://www.nfdht.nl). The great majority is found in *MLH1* and *MSH2*, with a few mutations in *MSH6*, *PMS1* and *PMS2*. These mutations occur in over 400 HNPCC families from different parts of the world {485}.
Most *MSH2* and *MLH1* mutations are truncating {1488}. However, one-third of *MLH1* mutations is of missense type, which constitutes a diagnostic problem concerning their pathogenicity. Commonly used theoretical criteria in support of pathogenicity include the following: the

mutation leads to a nonconservative amino acid change, the involved codon is evolutionarily conserved, the change is absent in the normal population, and it segregates with the disease phenotype. A subset of such mutations was directly assessed for pathogenicity using a yeast-based functional assay, and there was a good correlation {1745}. As a rule, the mutations are scattered throughout the genes, but exon 12 in *MSH2* and exon 16 in *MLH1* constitute particular hot spots {1488}.
Mutations in the five DNA mismatch repair genes account for two-thirds of all classical HNPCC families meeting the Amsterdam criteria and showing MSI in tumours {1078}. Occurrence of these mutations is clearly lower (< 30%) in HNPCC kindreds not meeting the Amsterdam criteria {1379, 2103}. Moreover, clinically indistinguishable phenotype (non-polypotic colon cancer plus variable extracolonic cancers) may be associated with germline mutations in genes that are not involved in DNA mismatch repair, such as TGFβ-RII {1103} and E-Cadherin {1581}. As expected, tumours from such families do not characteristically show MSI.

Prognosis and predictive factors

HNPCC mutations generally have a high penetrance. There is no clear-cut correlation between the involved gene, mutation site within the gene, or mutation type vs. clinical features. *MSH2* mutations may confer higher risk for extracolonic cancer as compared to *MLH1* mutations {2005}. *MSH6* mutations may be associated with atypical clinical features, including common occurrence of endometrial cancer {2102} and late age of onset {29}. Finally, capability of the mutant protein to block the normal homologue by a dominant negative fashion may lead to a severe phenotype, in which even normal cells may manifest mismatch repair deficiency {1475, 1348}. Conversely, inability to do so may be associated with a milder phenotype and lack of extracolonic cancers {828}. Kindreds with the Muir-Torre phenotype {971} as well as a subset of those with Turcot syndrome {658} show mutations similar to those observed in classical HNPCC.

Juvenile polyposis

L.A. Aaltonen
J.R. Jass
J.R. Howe

Definition

Juvenile polyposis (JP) is a familial cancer syndrome with autosomal dominant trait, characterized by multiple juvenile polyps of the gastrointestinal tract, involving predominantly the colorectum, but also the stomach and the small intestine. In addition to colorectal cancer, JP patients carry an increased risk for the development of tumours in the stomach, duodenum, biliary tree and pancreas.

MIM No.

174900, 175050

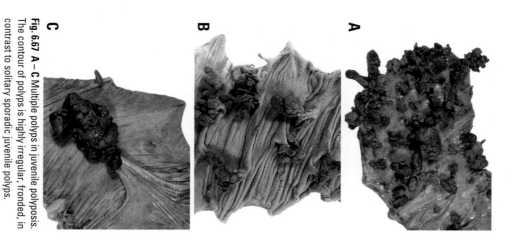

Fig. 6.67 A – C Multiple polyps in juvenile polyposis. The contour of polyps is highly irregular, fronded, in contrast to solitary sporadic juvenile polyps.

Synonyms

Generalized juvenile polyposis; juvenile polyposis coli; juvenile polyposis of infancy; juvenile polyposis of the stomach; familial juvenile polyposis; hamartomatous gastrointestinal polyposis.

Diagnostic criteria

Following the initial report by Stemper in 1975 {1831}, the following diagnostic criteria have been established: (1) more than 5 juvenile polyps of the colorectum, or (2) juvenile polyps throughout the gastrointestinal tract, or (3) any number of juvenile polyps with a family history of JP {847}. Other syndromes that display hamartomatous gastrointestinal polyps should be ruled out clinically or by pathological examination.

Epidemiology

Incidence

JP is ten-fold less common than familial adenomatous polyposis {838}, with an incidence of from 0.6 to 1 case per 100,000 in Western nations {297, 215}. JP may be the most common gastrointestinal polyposis syndrome in developing countries {1576, 2109}, and approximately half of cases arise in patients with no family history {316}.

Age and sex distribution

Two-thirds of patients with juvenile polyposis present within the first 2 decades of life, with a mean age at diagnosis of 18.5 years {316}. Some present in infancy, and others not until their seventh decade {749}. Though extensive epidemiological data do not exist, incomplete penetrance and approximately equal distribution between the sexes can be presumed.

Localization

Polyps occur with equal frequency throughout the colon and may range in number from one to more than a hundred. Some patients develop upper gastrointestinal tract polyps, most often in the stomach, but also in the small intestine. Generalized juvenile gastrointestinal polyposis is defined by the presence of

polyps in the stomach, small intestine and colon {1643}.

Clinical features

Signs and symptoms

Patients with juvenile polyposis usually present with gastrointestinal bleeding, manifesting as haematochezia. Melaena, prolapsed rectal polyps, passage of tissue per rectum, intussusception, abdominal pain, and anaemia are also common.

Imaging

Air contrast barium enema and upper gastrointestinal series may demonstrate filling defects, but are non-diagnostic for juvenile polyps.

Endoscopy

Biopsy or excision of polyps by colonoscopy can be both diagnostic and therapeutic. Small juvenile polyps may resemble hyperplastic polyps, while larger polyps generally have a well-defined stalk with a bright red, rounded head, which may be eroded. In the stomach, polyps are less often pedunculated and are more commonly diffuse.

Macroscopy

Most subjects with juvenile polyposis have between 50-200 polyps throughout the colorectum. The rare and often lethal form occurring in infancy may be associated with a diffuse gastrointestinal polyposis {1643}. In cases presenting in later childhood to adulthood, completely unaffected mucosa separates the lesions. This is unlike the dense mucosal carpeting that is characteristic of familial adenomatous polyposis. The polyps are usually pedunculated, but can be sessile in the stomach. Smaller examples have the spherical head of a typical solitary juvenile polyp. They may grow up to 5 cm in diameter, with a multilobated head. The individual lobes are relatively smooth and separated by deep, well-defined clefts. The multilobated polyp therefore appears like a cluster of smaller juvenile polyps attached to a common stalk. Such multilobated or atypical juvenile polyps account for about 20% of the total number of polyps {847}.

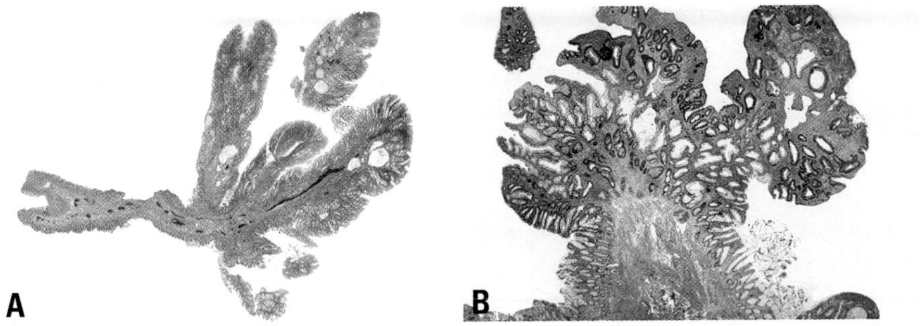

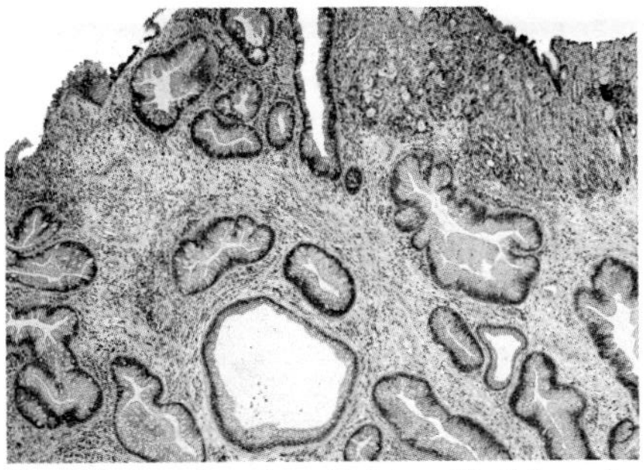

Fig. 6.69 Juvenile polyp with intraepithelial neoplasia and early adenocarcinoma.

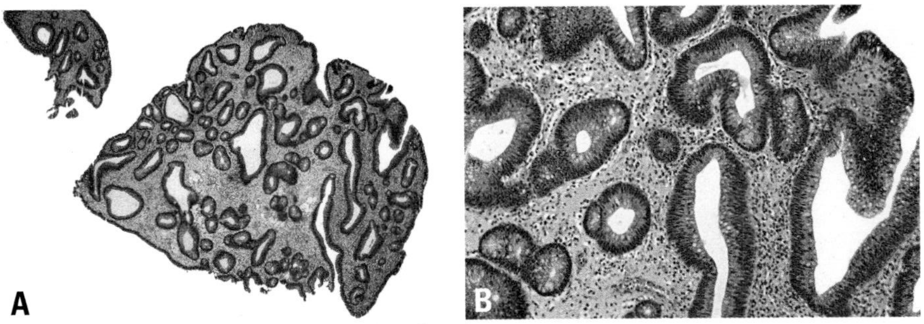

Fig. 6.68 A, B Juvenile polyposis. The bizarre architecture differs from the round, uniform structure of sporadic juvenile polyps.

Fig. 6.70 A, B Intraepithelial neoplasia in a juvenile polyp.

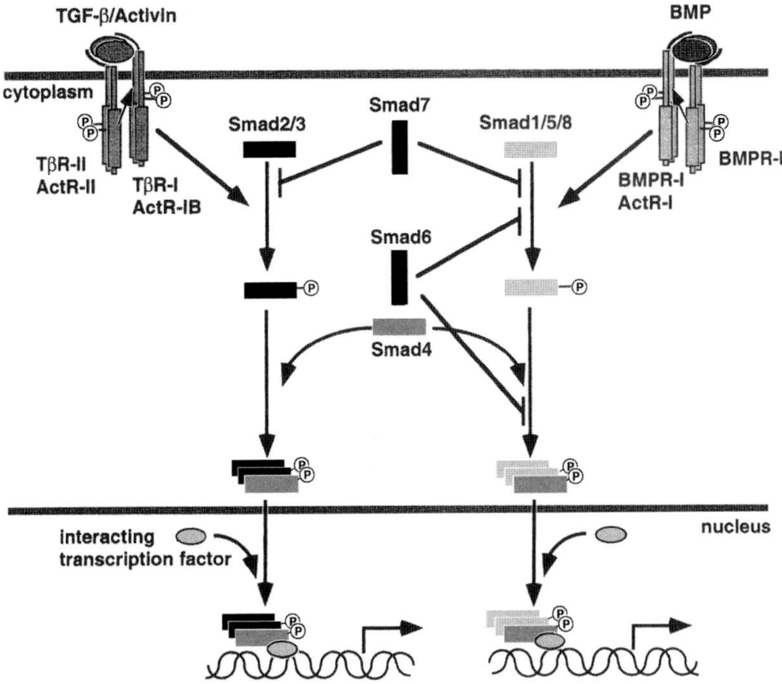

Fig. 6.71 TGF-β superfamily signaling through signal-transducing SMAD (1,2,3,4,5 and 8) and inhibitory SMAD (6 and 7) proteins. SMAD4, the protein defective in juvenile polyposis, plays a key role in the network. After type I receptor activation, SMADs 1,2,3,5 and 8 become phosphorylated, form homomeric complexes with each other, and assemble into heteromeric complexes with SMAD4. The complexes translocate into the nucleus, where they regulate transcription of target genes. Inhibitory Smads act opposite from R-Smads by competing with them for interaction with activated type I receptors or by directly competing with SMADs 1,2,3,5 and 8 for heteromeric complex formation with SMAD4. From: E. Piek et al. *FASEB J* 13: 2105 (1999).

Histopathology

Smaller polyps are indistinguishable from their sporadic counterparts. In the multilobated or atypical variety the lobes may be either rounded or finger-like. There is a relative increase in the amount of epithelium versus stroma. Glands show more budding and branching but less cystic change than the classical solitary polyp {847}.

Cancer in juvenile polyposis

There are two histogenetic explanations for the well documented association between colorectal cancer and juvenile polyposis. Cancers could arise in co-existing adenomas. Alternatively, they may develop through dysplastic change within a juvenile polyp. While both mechanisms may apply, pure adenomas are uncommon in juvenile polyposis. By contrast, foci of low-grade dysplasia may be demonstrated in 50% of atypical or multilobated juvenile polyps. The dysplastic areas may increase in size, generating a mixed juvenile polyp/adenoma. The adenomatous component may be tubular, tubulovillous or villous. Carcinomas are more likely to be poorly differentiated and/or mucinous {847}.

Extraintestinal manifestations

Congenital anomalies have been reported in 11 to 15% of JP patients {316, 727}, with the majority occurring in sporadic cases {217}. These anomalies most commonly involve the heart, central nervous system, soft tissues, gastrointestinal tract and genitourinary system {316, 1202}. Several patients have been reported with ganglioneuromatous proliferation within juvenile polyps {428, 1218, 1513, 2081}, and others with pulmonary arteriovenous malformations and hypertrophic osteoarthropathy {348, 1760, 101, 333}.

Genetics

JP is autosomal dominant. Germline mutations in *SMAD4/DPC4* tumour suppressor gene account for some of the cases {748, 751}. *SMAD4* maps to chromosome 18q21.1 {651}; i.e. a region that is often deleted in colorectal carcinomas.

Gene structure and product

SMAD4 has 11 exons, encoding 552 amino acids. It is expressed ubiquitously in different human organ systems, as well as during murine embryogenesis. The gene product is an important cellular mediator of TGF-β signals relevant for development and control of cell growth and an obligate partner for SMAD2 and SMAD3 proteins in the signalling pathway from the TGF-β receptor complex to the nucleus {2099}.

Gene mutations

While relatively few germline mutations have been described thus far, three studies have confirmed, in different white populations, the frequent occurrence of a four base pair deletion in *SMAD4* exon 9 {531, 751, 1622}. Haplotype analyses indicate that this is due to a mutation hotspot, rather than an ancient founder mutation {531, 751}. The families segregating this particular mutation tend to be large, perhaps indicating high penetrance. It seems likely that *SMAD4* is not the only gene underlying JP since only a subset of the families have *SMAD4* germline mutations {531, 748, 751, 1622}, and many families are not compatible with 18q linkage {748, 751, 1622}. The *PTEN* gene has also been proposed as underlying JP {1421}, but this report has not been confirmed by other studies and the present notion is that individuals with *PTEN* mutations should be considered as having Cowden syndrome, with a risk of breast and thyroid cancer {469}.

Prognostic factors

The most severe form of juvenile polyposis presents in infancy, with diarrhoea, anemia, and hypoalbuminemia; these patients rarely survive past 2 years of age. Although polyps in juvenile polyposis patients have classically been described as hamartomas, they do have malignant potential. The risk of colorectal carcinoma is approximately 30-40% and that of upper gastrointestinal carcinoma is 10-15% {749}. Typical age of colon carcinoma diagnosis is between 34 and 43 years (range 15-68 years), and upper gastrointestinal carcinoma 58 years (range 21-73 years) {749, 847, 834}. Most cases occur in patients who have not been screened radiologically or endoscopically, suggesting that cancers may be preventable through close surveillance.

Cowden syndrome

C. Eng
I.C. Talbot
R. Burt

Definition

Cowden syndrome (CS) is an autosomal dominant disorder characterized by multiple hamartomas involving organs derived from all three germ cell layers. The classical hamartoma associated with CS is the trichilemmoma. Affected family members have a high risk of developing breast and non-medullary thyroid carcinomas. Clinical manifestations further include mucocutaneous lesions, thyroid abnormalities, fibrocystic disease of the breast, gastrointestinal hamartomas, early-onset uterine leiomyomas, macrocephaly, mental retardation and dysplastic gangliocytoma of the cerebellum (Lhermitte-Duclos). The syndrome is caused by germline mutations of the *PTEN/MMAC1* gene.

MIM No.   158350

Synonyms

Cowden disease; multiple hamartoma syndrome.

Diagnostic criteria

Because of the variable and broad expression of CS and the lack of uniform diagnostic criteria prior to 1996, the International Cowden Consortium {1334} compiled operational diagnostic criteria for CS (Table 6.05), based on the published literature and their own clinical experience {467}. Trichilemmomas and papillomatous papules are particularly important to recognize. CS usually presents by the late 20s. It has variable expression and an age-related penetrance although the exact penetrance is unknown. By the third decade, 99% of affected individuals have developed the mucocutaneous stigmata although any of the other features could be present already (see Table 6.05). Because the clinical literature on CS consists mostly of reports of the most florid and unusual families or case reports by subspecialists interested in their respective organ systems, the spectrum of component signs is unknown. Despite this, the most commonly reported manifestations are mucocutaneous lesions, thyroid abnormalities, fibrocystic disease and carcinoma of the breast, gastrointestinal hamartomas, multiple, early-onset uterine leiomyoma, macrocephaly (specifically, megencephaly) and mental retardation {1819, 665, 1152, 1096}.

Epidemiology

The single most comprehensive clinical epidemiological study estimated the prevalence to be 1 per million population {1819, 1334}. Once the gene was identified {1071}, a molecular-based estimate of prevalence in the same population was 1:200 000 {1333}. Because of the difficulty in recognizing this syndrome, prevalence figures are likely underestimates.

Intestinal neoplasms

Hamartomatous polyps. In a small but systematic study comprising 9 well documented CS individuals, 7 of whom had a

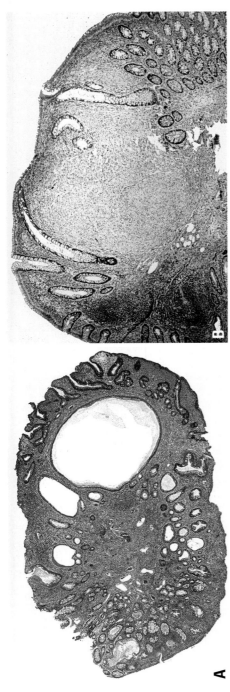

A

B

Fig. 6.72 A, B Colonic polyps in Cowden syndrome. Distorted glands and fibrous proliferation in lamina propria.

germline *PTEN* mutation, all 9 had hamartomatous polyps {2075}. Several varieties of hamartomatous polyps are seen in this syndrome, including lipomatous and ganglioneuromatous lesions {2075}. Presumably, these polyps can occur anywhere in the gastrointestinal tract. Those in the colon and rectum usually measure from 3 to 10 millimetres in diameter. Some of the polyps are no more than tags of mucosa but others have a more definite structure. Most are composed of a mixture of connective tissues normally present in the mucosa, principally smooth muscle in continuity with the muscularis mucosae {1017}. Examples containing adipose tissue have been described. The mucosal glands within the lesion are normal or elongated and irregularly formed but the epithelium is normal and includes goblet cells and columnar cells {242}. Lesions in which autonomic nerves are predominant, giving a ganglioneuroma-like appearance, have been described but seem to be exceptional {1017}. The vast majority of CS hamartomatous polyps are asymptomatic. In a study of 9 CS individuals, *glycogenic acanthosis of the oesophagus* was found in 6 of the 7 with *PTEN* mutation {2075}.

Gastrointestinal malignancies are generally not increased in CS {1819, 468} although rare individual CS families appear to have an increased prevalence of colon cancer (Eng, unpublished observations).

Extraintestinal manifestations

Breast cancer. The two most commonly recognized cancers in CS are carcinoma of the breast and thyroid {1819}. In the general population, lifetime risks for breast and thyroid cancers are approximately 11% (in women), and 1%, respectively. Breast cancer has been rarely observed in men with CS {1167}. In women with CS, lifetime risk estimates for the development of breast cancer range from 25 to 50% {1819, 665, 1096, 467}. The mean age at diagnosis is likely 10 years earlier than breast cancer occurring in the general population {1819, 1096}. Although Rachel Cowden died of breast cancer at the age of 31 {196, 1081} and the earliest recorded age at diagnosis of breast cancer is 14 {1819}, the great majority of breast cancers are diagnosed after the age of 30-35 (range 14 – 65) {1096}. The predominant histology is ductal adenocarcinoma. Most CS breast carcinomas occur in the context of DCIS, atypical ductal hyperplasia, adenosis and sclerosis {1691}.

Thyroid cancer. The lifetime risk for thyroid cancer can be as high as 10% in males and females with CS. Because of small numbers, it is unclear if the age of onset is truly earlier than that of the general population. Histologically, the thyroid cancer is predominantly follicular carcinoma although papillary histology has also been rarely observed {1819, 665, 1152} (Eng, unpublished observations). Medullary thyroid carcinoma has not been observed in patients with CS.

Benign tumours. The most important benign tumours are trichilemmomas and papillomatous papules of the skin. Apart from those of the skin, benign tumours or disorders of breast and thyroid are the most frequently noted and probably represent true component features of this syndrome (Table 6.05). Fibroadenomas

and fibrocystic disease of the breast are common signs in CS, as are follicular adenomas and multinodular goitre of the thyroid. An unusual central nervous system tumour, cerebellar dysplastic gangliocytoma or Lhermitte-Duclos disease, has recently been associated with CS {1445, 468, 932}.

Other malignancies and benign tumours have been reported in patients or families with CS. Some authors believe that endometrial carcinoma could be a component tumour of CS as well. It remains to be shown whether other tumours (sarcomas, lymphomas, leukaemia, meningiomas) are true components of CS.

Genetics

Chromosomal location and mode of transmission

CS is an autosomal dominant disorder, with age related penetrance and variable expression {468}. The CS susceptibility gene, *PTEN*, resides on 10q23.3 {1071, 1334, 1068}.

Gene structure

PTEN/MMAC1/TEP1 consists of 9 exons spanning 120-150 kb of genomic distance {1167, 1820, 1068}. It is believed that intron 1 occupies much of this (approximately 100 kb). *PTEN* is predicted to encode a 403-amino acid phosphatase. Similar to other phosphatase genes, *PTEN* exon 5 specifically encodes a phosphatase core motif. Exons 1 through 6 encode amino acid sequence that is homologous to tensin and auxilin {1065, 1820, 1068}.

Gene product

PTEN is virtually ubiquitously expressed {1820}. Detailed expression studies in development have not been performed. However, early embryonic death in pten -/- mice would imply a crucial role for PTEN in early development {1526, 1868, 407}.

PTEN is a tumour suppressor and is a dual specificity phosphatase {1304}. It is a lipid phosphatase whose major substrate is phosphatidylinositol-3,4,5-triphosphate (PIP3) which lies in the PI3 kinase pathway {553, 1814, 1142, 364, 1067}. When PTEN is ample, PIP3 is converted to 4,5-PIP2, which results in hypophosphorylated Akt/PKB, a known cell survival factor. Hypophosphorylated Akt is apoptotic. Transient transfection studies have shown that ectopic expression of PTEN results in apoptosis in breast cancer lines mediated by Akt {1067} and G1 arrest in glioma lines {553, 554}. The G1 arrest is not fully explained by the PTEN-PI3K-Akt pathway. It is also believed that PTEN can dephosphorylate FAK and inhibit integrin and MAP kinase signalling {637, 1892}.

Gene mutations

Approximately 70-80% of CS cases, as strictly defined by the Consortium criteria, have a germline PTEN mutation {1167, 1071}. If the diagnostic criteria are relaxed, then mutation frequencies drop to 10-50% {1335, 1964, 1124}. A formal study which ascertained 64 unrelated CS-like cases revealed a mutation frequency of 2% if the criteria are not met, even if the diagnosis is made short of one criterion {1168}.

A single research centre study involving 37 unrelated CS families, ascertained according to the strict diagnostic criteria of the Consortium, revealed a mutation frequency of 80% {1167}. Exploratory genotype-phenotype analyses revealed that the presence of a germline mutation was associated with a familial risk of developing malignant breast disease {1167}. Further, missense mutations and/or mutations 5' of the phosphatase core motif seem to be associated with a surrogate for disease severity (multi-organ involvement). A small study comprising 13 families with 8 PTEN mutation-positive members could not find any genotype-phenotype associations {1333} but this may be due to the small sample size.

Bannayan-Riley-Ruvalcaba syndrome (BRR). Previously thought to be clinically distinct, BRR (MIM 153480), characterized by macrocephaly, lipomatosis, haemangiomatosis and speckled penis, is likely allelic to CS {1169}. Approximately 60% of BRR families and isolated cases combined carry a germline PTEN mutation {1170}. There were 11 cases classified as true CS-BRR overlap families in this cohort, and 10 of these had a PTEN mutation. The overlapping mutation spectrum, the existence of true overlap families and the genotype-phenotype associations which suggest that the presence of germline PTEN mutation is associated with cancer strongly suggest that CS and BRR are allelic and part of a single spectrum at the molecular level. The aggregate term of PTEN hamartoma tumour syndrome (PHTS) has been suggested {1170}.

The identification of a germline PTEN mutation in a patient previously thought to have juvenile polyposis {1421} excludes that diagnosis, and points to the correct designation as CS or BRR {469, 751, 983, 750, 1171}.

Prognosis

There have been no systematic studies to indicate if CS patients who have cancer have a prognosis different from that of their sporadic counterparts.

Table 6.05
International Cowden Consortium diagnostic criteria for CS.

Diagnostic criteria	Operational diagnosis in an individual	Operational diagnosis in a family where one individual is diagnostic for Cowden
Pathognomonic Criteria Mucocutaneous lesions: Trichilemmomas, facial Acral Keratoses Papillomatous papules Mucosal lesions	1. Mucocutaneous lesions alone if: a) there are 6 or more facial papules, of which 3 or more must be trichilemmoma, or b) cutaneous facial papules and oral mucosal papillomatosis, or c) oral mucosal papillomatosis and acral keratoses, or d) palmoplantar keratoses, 6 or more	1. At least one pathognomonic criterion
Major Criteria Breast CA Thyroid CA, esp. follicular carcinoma Macrocephaly (Megencephaly) (≥ 97%ile) Lhermitte-Duclos disease (LDD)	2. Two major criteria but one must include macrocephaly or LDD	2. Any one major criterion with or without minor criteria
Minor Criteria Other thyroid lesions (e.g. adenoma or multinodular goiter) Mental retardation (IQ ≤75) Gastro-intestinal hamartomas Fibrocystic disease of the breast Lipomas Fibromas Genitourinary tumours (e.g. uterine fibroids) or malformation	3. One major and three minor criteria 4. Four minor criteria	3. Two minor criteria

Hyperplastic polyposis

R. Burt
J.R. Jass

Definition

Multiple or large hyperplastic (metaplastic) polyps of the large intestine, typically located proximally, and often exhibiting familial clustering.

Synonyms and historical annotation

The term metaplastic polyposis has been used synonymously. Early descriptions emphasized a multiplicity of hyperplastic polyps throughout the colorectum and caused diagnostic confusion with familial adenomatous polyposis (FAP) {2114}. The condition was also reported to occur in young male subjects. These descriptions (predating the colonoscopic era) were biased towards cases mimicking FAP or showing unusual aspects such as young age of onset. In the colonoscopic era, the features of large polyp size and/or distribution throughout the colorectum serve to distinguish hyperplastic polyposis from the far more common occurrence of small hyperplastic polyps in the distal colon and rectum. Hyperplastic polyposis should be distinguished from sporadic hyperplastic polyps in view of its association with colorectal neoplasia {1198, 126} and reports of familial clustering {849}.

Diagnostic criteria

In the absence of generally accepted guidelines on what would constitute the minimum number of polyps or polyp size to warrant a diagnosis of hyperplastic polyposis, the following criteria are recommended: (1) At least five histological-

ly diagnosed hyperplastic polyps proximal to the sigmoid colon of which two are greater than 10 mm in diameter, or (2) any number of hyperplastic polyps occurring proximal to the sigmoid colon in an individual who has a first degree relative with hyperplastic polyposis, or (3) more than 30 hyperplastic polyps of any size, but distributed throughout the colon.

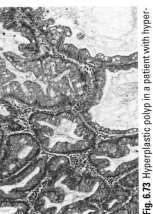

Fig. 6.73 Hyperplastic polyp in a patient with hyperplastic polyposis.

Clinical features

Unless there is associated malignancy, hyperplastic polyposis is generally asymptomatic. Larger hyperplastic polyps may occasionally present with rectal bleeding. The condition may be diagnosed in adults of all ages. Although considered as rare, the condition is probably under-reported.

Firm management guidelines have not been developed. The rather frequently observed association with adenomatous polyps and colon carcinomas suggests that some surveillance of patients is required, with generous biopsy sampling and polypectomy as appropriate, particularly of larger polyps, to determine if neoplasia is present. Subtotal colectomy is occasionally necessary in patients with multiple adenomatous polyps if there are numerous and rapidly growing hyperplastic polyps that make it nearly impossible to selectively eliminate neoplastic lesions.

Imaging

Small polyps may be indistinguishable from diminutive adenomas. High resolution videoendoscopy, combined with dye spraying, will demonstrate the diagnostic star-shaped crypt opening {1191}. Larger hyperplastic polyps may either present as pale flat lesions on the crest of a mucosal fold or may become protuberant. The head may darken and become lobulated, simulating an adenoma. The colonoscopic phenotype in some patients simulates FAP with scores to hundreds of 1mm to 5mm in diameter polyps, while others exhibit a smaller number of centimeter sized darker ses-

sile lesions that grossly may be confused with multiple villous adenomas. With either phenotype, one or several adenomas may be found in addition to the hyperplastic polyps. High resolution videoendoscopy suggests that a mixed hyperplastic and cerebriform pattern may be indicative of serrated adenoma {1191}.

Histopathology

Most hyperplastic polyps are indistinguishable from their common counterparts, apart from their large size. As in the sporadic hyperplastic polyp, the proliferative zone is increased but remains confined to the lower crypt. There is abnormal retention of cells in the upper maturation zone associated with the characteristic appearance of serration. A small proportion contains foci of intraepithelial neoplasia (dysplasia) that may

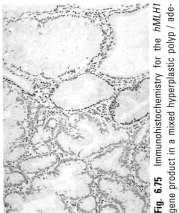

Fig. 6.74 Colectomy specimen, hyperplastic polyposis.

Fig. 6.75 Immunohistochemistry for the *hMLH1* gene product in a mixed hyperplastic polyp / adenoma in a case of hyperplastic polyposis. Normal expression (right) is lost in the glands with intraepithelial neoplasia (left).

either resemble a tubular, tubulovillous, or villous adenoma, or retain a serrated architecture supporting a diagnosis of serrated adenoma {1987, 1092, 337}. Hyperplastic polyps and serrated adenomas show a similar mucinous phenotype exemplified by upregulation of the goblet cell mucin MUC2, reduction of the intestinal mucin MUC4 and neo-expression of the gastric mucin MUC5AC. This suggests that hyperplastic polyps and serrated adenomas represent a histogenetic continuum {139}.

Unusual growth patterns, including inversion and pseudoinvasion, with associated disorganization of the muscularis mucosae, are more characteristic of large polyps {1729, 1773} and will there-

fore be over-represented in hyperplastic polyposis.

It has been suggested that hyperplastic polyposis be distinguished from 'serrated adenomatous polyposis' {1944}. However, the histological distinction between a large hyperplastic polyp and a serrated adenoma is not straightforward and there is probably no sharp division between hyperplastic polyposis and 'serrated adenomatous polyposis'.

Genetics

Despite being regarded as non-neoplastic, hyperplastic polyps may show clonal genetic changes, including chromosomal rearrangements at 1p, KRAS mutation and low levels of DNA microsatellite insta-

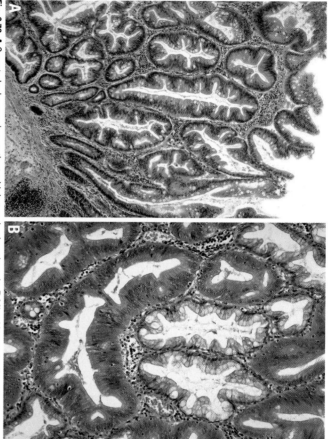

Fig. 6.76 A Serrated adenoma in a patient with hyperplastic polyposis. **B** Mixed hyperplastic polyp / adenoma in a patient with hyperplastic polyposis.

Prognosis

Sporadic hyperplastic polyps are generally believed not to be associated with an increased cancer risk. Evidence for hyperplastic polyposis being a precancerous lesion includes the observation of mixed hyperplastic/adenomatous polyps in this condition and the synchronicity of hyperplastic polyposis and colorectal cancer {1198, 126}. The genetic changes noted above offer further evidence for a direct relationship between hyperplastic polyposis and colorectal carcinoma, and support the concept of a hyperplastic polyp-adenoma-carcinoma sequence {775}.

bility {775}. Mutations of TP53 and increased immunoexpression of p53 are limited to areas of high-grade intraepithelial neoplasia in serrated adenomas {720}. In hyperplastic polyposis, microsatellite instability is seen in areas of intraepithelial neoplasia. High levels of microsatellite instability (MSI-H) are associated with loss of expression of the DNA mismatch repair protein hMLH1 in these lesions {844}. This observation fits with the suggestion that DNA microsatellite instability may be caused by the silencing of DNA mismatch repair genes by methylation of the promoter region {361}. A mutation affecting a gene that controls methylation might account for familial and non-familial cases of hyperplastic polyposis, placing this condition within the spectrum of colorectal lesions showing mismatch repair deficiency {1950}. An epigenetic mechanism involving disordered methylation would explain polyp multiplicity and the tendency for hyperplastic polyps to regress spontaneously {986}.

Endocrine tumours of the colon and rectum

C. Capella
E. Solcia
L.H. Sobin
R. Arnold

Definition
Endocrine tumours of the large intestine are defined as in the small intestine.

Epidemiology
Incidence and time trends
Endocrine tumours of the colon have an incidence of 0.07-0.11 up to 0.21 cases per 100,000 population per year {1251}. In a recent series, carcinoids from caecum to transverse colon (midgut) represented about 8% and descending colon and rectosigmoid (hindgut) carcinoids about 20% of 5973 gastrointestinal carcinoids {1251}. Rectal carcinoids had a reported incidence of 0.14-0.76 cases per 100,000 population per year. In the 40-year time period (from 1950 to 1991) the percentage of caecal carcinoids, among carcinoids of all sites, nearly doubled, as did the percentage of rectosigmoid lesions {1251}.

Age and sex distribution
The reported average age at diagnosis is 58 years, for rectal, and 66 years, for colonic carcinoids, and the M/F ratio is 1.06, for rectal, and 0.66, for colonic carcinoids {1251}.

Aetiology
Some colorectal carcinoids have been reported in the large bowel of patients with ulcerative colitis {584, 622} or Crohn disease {722, 622}. In association with these conditions, the tumours tend to be multiple {1208}. However, there appears to be no evidence to substantiate a direct association between inflammatory bowel

disease and carcinoid tumours, because almost all cases were found incidentally after surgery for inflammatory bowel disease {622}.

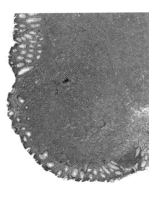

Fig. 6.77 Endoscopically resected carcinoid tumour of rectum.

Localization
Endocrine tumours are more common in the rectum (54% of the cases), followed by the caecum (20%), sigmoid colon (7.5%), rectosigmoid colon (5.5%) and ascending colon (5%) {1251, 1784}.

Clinical features
Patients with colonic carcinoid tumours most commonly present in the seventh decade with symptoms of abdominal pain and weight loss, though some present late with liver metastases {1616}. Less than 5% of patients present with the carcinoid syndrome {1616, 128}. Carcinoids of the colon are associated with metachronous or synchronous non-carcinoid neoplasms in 13% of cases {1251}. Half of rectal endocrine tumours are asymptomatic and are discovered at rou-

tine rectal examination or endoscopy, while the other half give rise to symptoms, typically rectal bleeding, pain or constipation {857, 1836}. Rectal carcinoids are practically never associated with the carcinoid syndrome {857, 1836, 212}.

Small cell carcinomas are aggressive neoplasms and can present with symptoms due to local disease or to widespread metastases.

Macroscopy
The majority of colonic carcinoids are detected in the right colon {1616, 128} and are larger than carcinoids of the small intestine, appendix, and rectum. The average size was 4.9 cm in cases reviewed by Berardi {128}.

Rectal carcinoids appear as submucosal nodules, sometimes polypoid, often with apparently intact overlying epithelium {968}. Larger lesions tend to be somewhat fixed to the rectal wall. In the great majority of cases the tumour is found 4 to 13 cm above the dentate line and on the anterior or lateral rectal walls {222}. The majority of rectal endocrine tumours are solitary and measure less than 1 cm in diameter {222}. Reviewing 356 cases reported in the literature, Caldarola et al. {222} found that only 13% of rectal carcinoids measured more than 2 cm in diameter.

Histopathology
Carcinoid – well differentiated endocrine neoplasm
Colonic *serotonin-producing EC-cell tumours* show histological, cytological, cytochemical, and ultrastructural features that are identical to those of jejunoileal EC-cell tumours, including the absence of S100 protein positive sustentacular cells {1784}.

L-cell, glucagon-like peptide and PP/PYY-producing tumours are characterized histologically by a predominance of a type B {1775} ribbon pattern, often admixed with type C (tubuloacini or broad, irregular trabeculae with rosettes) and only occasionally with areas of type A solid nest structures. These patterns are different from

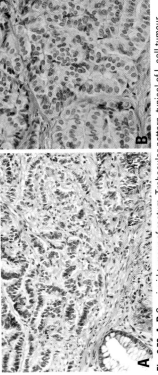

Fig. 6.78 A, B Carcinoid tumour of rectum. Trabecular pattern, typical of L-cell tumour.

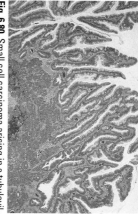

Fig. 6.80 Small cell carcinoma arising in a tubulovillous adenoma of the sigmoid colon.

Fig. 6.79 Rectal carcinoid showing prostatic acid phosphatase immunoreactive cells.

Fig. 6.81 Small cell carcinoma. **A** Typical oval or moulded nuclei with diffuse chromatin, scant cytoplasm and little stroma. **B** Neuroendocrine granules in electronmicrograph.

those of EC-cell tumours, in which type A structures prevail. The argentaffin reaction is usually negative {146}, while consistently positive results are obtained with Grimelius stain {488}. Immunohistochemically, they stain for panendocrine markers (neuron-specific enolase, synaptophysin, chromogranins) and for a variety of peptide hormones {488}. Among 62 rectal carcinoids derived from surgical pathology files, about 80% displayed more or less abundant glucagon-like peptide (GLP-1, GLP-2, glicentin) and/or PP/PYY immunoreactivities typical of intestinal L-cells, whereas only 30% showed serotonin immunoreactivity and 20% somatostatin immunoreactivity, usually in only few cells {1780, 507}. Although there is a prevalence of L-cells in these tumours, minority populations of substance P, insulin, enkephalin, beta-endorphin, neurotensin, and motilin immunoreactive cells have also been identified {1780, 488, 212}. The vast majority (82%) of colorectal carcinoids tested in one series of 84 cases showed immunoreactivity for prostatic acid phos-

phatase, a finding that is unusual in other gut carcinoids and possibly is related to the common origin of the rectum and prostate from cloacal hindgut {488}. Ultrastructurally, rectal L-cells show round to slightly angular secretory granules similar to those of L-cells of the normal human intestine {506}.

Small (≤ 2 cm) benign L-cell rectal carcinoids show an immunohistochemical Ki-67 index ≤ 1%, while large (> 2 cm) L-cell carcinomas show a Ki-67 index ≥ 5% (La Rosa S, Capella C, Solcia E, unpublished observations, 1999).

Small cell carcinoma (poorly differentiated neuroendocrine neoplasm)

These are morphologically identical to small cell carcinomas of the lung, and correspond to grade 3 tumours according to Rindi et al. {1589}. They are usually found in the right colon, and are frequently associated with an overlying adenoma or adjacent adenocarcinoma {2085}, but are not associated with carcinoid tumours. Small cell carcinomas typically express neuroendocrine markers (e.g. chromogranin, synaptophysin) by immunohistochemistry. Patients usually have liver metastases at the time of original surgery, and the prognosis is poor {207}.

Large cell neuroendocrine carcinoma is a malignant neoplasm composed of large cells having organoid, nesting, trabecular, rosette-like and palisading patterns that suggest endocrine differentiation, which can be confirmed by immunohistochemistry and electron microscopy. In contrast to small cell carcinoma, cyto-

plasm is more abundant, nuclei are more vesicular and nucleoli are prominent {1954}. These tumours have not been well described in the gastrointestinal tract because of their apparent low frequency.

Genetics

Loss of heterozygosity at MEN-1 locus has been reported in two sporadic colonic and two sporadic rectosigmoidal carcinoids {829}. However, this finding has not been confirmed by more recent studies {394, 1938}. Colorectal carcinoids do not represent an integral part of MEN-1 {1444}. A case of rectal carcinoid tumour associated with Peutz-Jeghers syndrome has been reported {2032}.

Prognosis

Colonic EC-cell carcinoids are frequently malignant, local spread of the tumours was found in 36-44% of patients and distant metastases in 38% {1251, 1616}. The reported 5-year survival rate was 25-42% and the 10-year survival rate was 10% {1251, 1616}. Modlin found malignant (non-localized) tumours represented 71% of the cases among colonic carcinoids, and 14% of cases among rectal carcinoids {1251}. The alleged poor prognosis of colonic carcinoids has been questioned as possibly being the result of a proportion actually being poorly differentiated adenocarcinomas with carcinoid-like growth patterns {1928}.

For rectal carcinoids, an overall malignancy rate of 11% to 14% has been calculated in some studies {1251, 488}. Recognised malignancy criteria include: a size of the tumour greater than 2 cm {857, 1328, 930}, invasion of the muscularis propria {857, 212, 1328}, atypical histology {964}, presence of more than 2 mitoses per 10 high power (X 400) micro-

scopic fields, and DNA aneuploidy {1963}. Patients with rectal carcinoids generally have a good prognosis, showing a 5-year survival rate of 72%-89% {1251, 1931}, which is better than the 5-year survival rate of 60% for patients with jejuno-ileal carcinoids {211}. The prognosis is excellent if the tumour diameter is 1 cm or less {294}.

B-cell lymphoma of the colon and rectum

H.K. Müller-Hermelink
A. Chott
R.D. Gascoyne
A. Wotherspoon

Definition

Primary lymphoma of the colorectum is defined as an extranodal lymphoma arising in either the colon or rectum with the bulk of disease localized to this site {796}. Contiguous lymph node involvement and distal spread may be seen, but the primary clinical presentation is the colon and/or rectum.

Epidemiology

Primary lymphomas arising in the large intestine are less frequent than either gastric or small bowel lymphomas {792}. Primary colorectal lymphomas account for about 0.2% of all neoplasms at this site. The lymphoma subtypes that present in the colorectum are similar to those that involve the small intestine, with the exception of immunoproliferative small intestinal disease (IPSID). Mucosa-associated lymphoid tissue (MALT) lymphomas of both small and large cell type account for the majority of lymphomas of the colorectum {1733}. Mantle cell lymphoma (MCL), often in the form of multiple lymphomatous polyposis, is less frequent but accounts for a larger propor-

tion of primary lymphomas in the colorectum than in the small bowel {1733}.

Most colorectal lymphomas occur in older patients without a clear sex predominance. Amongst aquired immunodeficiency syndrome (AIDS) patients, the median age is lower and the majority of cases occur in homosexual men. Involvement of the colorectum by Burkitt lymphoma is distinctly uncommon in immunocompetent individuals.

Aetiology

The factors involved in the aetiology of colorectal lymphomas are similar to those in the small intestine. Inflammatory bowel disease, particularly ulcerative colitis, is a recognized predisposing factor {1733}. Diverticular disease does not appear to be a risk factor for the development of lymphoma.
Immunodeficiency disorders giving rise to lymphoma have a predilection for the gastrointestinal tract. The frequency of colorectal lymphomas has significantly increased, partly due to the AIDS epidemic.

Localization

Most colorectal lymphomas involve the distal large bowel, rectum and anus. There is a preference for rectal lymphoma in patients infected with the human immunodeficiency virus (HIV) {787, 1057}. Multifocal involvement is uncommon with the exception of *multiple lymphomatous polyposis* {1733}.

Clinical features

The presenting features are very similar to epithelial neoplasms at this site. Rectal bleeding is the most common symptom, followed by diarrhoea, abdominal pain, passage of mucus per rectum, constipation, abdominal mass, weight loss, irregular bowel habit, anal pain and worsening of ulcerative colitis symptoms. Occasional cases are found incidentally, while an acute presentation with rupture of the colon is distinctly uncommon {1733, 611}.
Similar to gastric lymphomas, colorectal lymphomas can be diagnosed using endoscopy and biopsy. Computerized tomography and barium enema have a role in diagnosis and determining the

Macroscopy

Most low-grade lymphomas present as well defined protuberant growths that deeply invade the bowel wall. Diffuse large B-cell lymphoma (DLBCL) and Burkitt lymphoma tend to form larger masses with stricture and ulcer formation involving long segments of the colorectum. Low-grade and aggressive MALT lymphomas typically remain localized for prolonged periods, but may spread to involve loco-regional lymph nodes. Mantle cell lymphoma (MCL) may present as an isolated mass or as multiple polyps producing the clinical picture of multiple lymphomatous polyposis {2084}. In most cases, the colon is more significantly involved than the small bowel. Importantly, other histological subtypes of lymphoma can produce this clinicopathological entity (see below). The polyps range in size from 0.5 cm to 2 cm with much larger polyps found in the ileocaecal region {791, 1292}. MCL frequently spreads to involve the spleen, extra-abdominal lymph nodes, bone marrow and peripheral blood.

Histopathology
MALT lymphoma

The majority of intestinal lymphomas involving the large bowel are B-cell lymphomas of MALT type, including both low-grade and aggressive histologies {796}. The histological and immunophenotypic features are discussed in detail in the section describing lymphomas of the stomach. Colorectal low-grade MALT

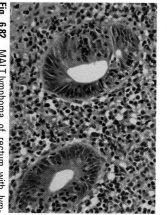

Fig. 6.82 MALT lymphoma of rectum with lymphoepithelial lesions.

lymphomas resemble those of the small intestine in that lymphoepithelial lesions are less prominent than in the stomach. Precise criteria for defining a MALT lymphoma of large cell type are lacking, as are the criteria for distinguishing transformation within a low-grade MALT lymphoma. When both histologies are evident, the neoplasm is best described as composite. When small foci of large transformed cells or early sheeting-out of large cells are detected within a background of low-grade intestinal MALT lymphoma, their presence should be noted {383}. Currently, the prognostic impact of these findings and their effect on treatment are undetermined. DLBCLs arising in the large bowel that lack a background of low-grade MALT lymphoma are best classified as extranodal diffuse large B-cell lymphoma, not otherwise specified, until such time as confirmatory tests can be established to clearly determine the histogenesis of these neoplasms from the mucosal immune system.

Mantle cell lymphoma

The morphology of MCL involving the large bowel is identical to MCL at nodal sites {110}. The architecture is most frequently diffuse, but a nodular pattern and a less common true mantle-zone pattern are also seen. Reactive germinal centers may be found and are usually

Fig. 6.83 Malignant lymphoma of rectum.

compressed by the surrounding lymphoma cells, imparting the appearance of replacing the normal mantle zones. Intestinal glands may be destroyed by the lymphoma, but typical lymphoepithelial lesions are not seen. The low power appearance is monotonous with frequent epithelioid histiocytes, mitotic figures and fine sclerosis surrounding small blood vessels. The lymphoma cells are small to medium sized with irregular nuclear outlines, indistinct nucleoli and scant amounts of cytoplasm. Large transformed cells are typically not present.

The lymphoma cells are mature B-cells and express both CD19 and CD20. Characteristically the cells co-express CD5 and CD43. Surface immunoglobulin is found including both IgM and IgD. Light chain restriction is present in most cases, with some studies demonstrating a predominance of lambda. CD10 and CD11c are virtually always negative. Bcl-1 (cyclin D1) is found in virtually all cases and can be demonstrated within the nuclei of the neoplastic lymphocytes in paraffin sections.

Burkitt lymphoma

The details of the histology, immunophenotype, cytogenetics and molecular genetics are described in detail in the small intestinal lymphoma section (Chapter 4).

Burkitt-like lymphoma

The histological and cytogenetic features have been previously described in the small intestinal lymphoma section. AIDS patients have a preponderance of cases with this histology. Many are of small non-cleaved cell type with the typical molecular and cytogenetic changes associated with classical Burkitt lymphoma, and

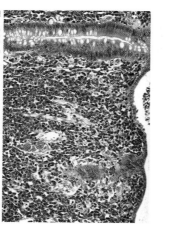

Fig. 6.84 Burkitt lymphoma of colon. The malignant cells infiltrate the lamina propria and produce lymphoepithelial lesions.

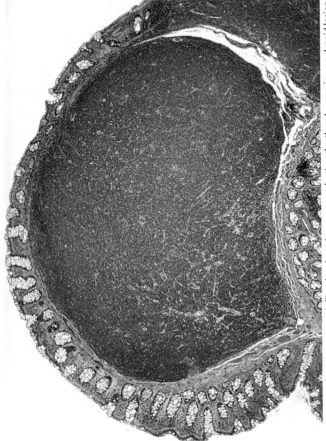

Fig. 6.85 Mantle cell lymphoma infiltrating the submucosa predominantly, thereby causing a polypoid lesion.

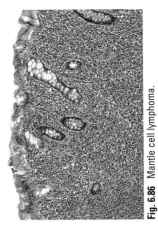

Fig. 6.86 Mantle cell lymphoma.

are best considered to be part of the same biological entity {236}. However, patients with AIDS have also been recognized to have another lymphoma, with features intermediate between small non-cleaved cell lymphoma with plasmablastic differentiation and immunoblastic lymphoma, plasmacytoid type. This latter lymphoma subtype is strongly associated with EBV infection and *TP53* mutations {236}.

Other B-cell lymphomas

Any subtype of B-cell lymphoma can arise in a colorectal site, including those thought to arise from peripheral lymph node equivalents. *De novo* DLBCLs are equal in frequency to low-grade MALT lymphomas in the colorectum {1733}, and are particularly common in the setting of HIV infection. Rectal involvement in AIDS patients typically demonstrates DLBCL with either centroblastic or immunoblastic cytomorphology. These lymphoma subtypes can be distinguished using phenotypic markers including Bcl-6, CD138 (syndecan-1) and EBV-related protein, latent membrane protein (LMP-1). Small non-cleaved and centroblastic lymphomas express Bcl-6, but fail to express CD138 or LMP-1 in the majority of cases. Immunoblastic lymphomas in the HIV setting do not express Bcl-6, but are positive for both CD138 and LMP-1, in keeping with a non-germinal center histogenesis {237}.

Genetics

MALT lymphoma

Cytogenetic and molecular features of intestinal low-grade MALT lymphomas are incompletely understood. The presence of either t(1;14)(p22;q32) or t(11;18)(q21;q21) and the corresponding molecular abnormalities, rearrangement of *bcl-10* or *AP12-MLT*, have not been described at this site, thus the relationship of these lesions to gastric MALT lymphomas is unclear {2116, 412}.

Furthermore, trisomy 3 is common in gastric MALT lymphomas, but the frequency of this cytogenetic abnormality in primary intestinal lymphoma is unknown. Some of these DLBCLs may have a low-grade MALT component evident, providing compelling evidence that their histogenesis is related to the mucosal immune system.

Mantle cell lymphoma

MCL is characterized by a recurrent cytogenetic abnormality, the t(11;14) (q13;q32). This translocation deregulates expression of the *bcl-1* oncogene on chromosome 11. Rearrangement can be detected using Southern blot analysis, PCR or fluorescent in situ hybridization (FISH).

Prognosis

The relevant prognostic factors in colorectal lymphomas are similar to those for the small intestine, and have been described in detail in that section. MCL is

an aggressive lymphoma, which typically presents in advanced stage; there is often involvement of mesenteric and peripheral lymph nodes, spleen, bone marrow and peripheral blood {670}.

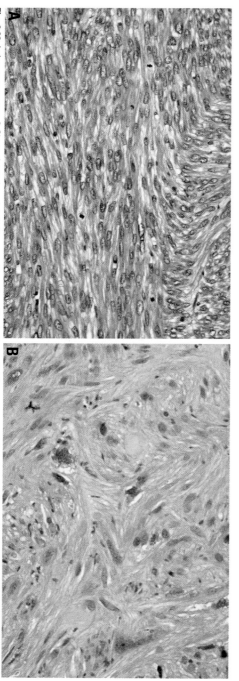

Fig. 6.88 Leiomyosarcoma. **A** Cigar-shaped nuclei. **B** Pleomorphic cells with atypical mitosis.

Mesenchymal tumours of the colon and rectum

M. Miettinen
J.Y. Blay
L.G. Kindblom
L.H. Sobin

Definition

A variety of benign and malignant mesenchymal tumours that arise in the large intestine as a primary site.

Classification

The morphological definitions of these lesions follow the WHO histological classification of soft tissue tumours {2086}. Stromal tumours are described in detail in the chapter on gastric mesenchymal tumours.

Epidemiology

Sarcomas accounted for 0.1% of malignant large intestinal tumours in SEER data {1928}. Males were affected slightly less than females. Adults between the 6th and 8th decades were primarily affected.

Aetiology

Aetiological factors are poorly understood for most colorectal mesenchymal tumours. *Kaposi sarcoma* usually occurs in association with AIDS, but it has also been described in connection with inflammatory bowel disease, in one case following immunosuppressive therapy {1930, 1584}. Human herpesvirus 8 is usually demonstrable by PCR in Kaposi sarcoma cells. An angiosarcoma has been reported in the colon, related to a persistent foreign body {149}.

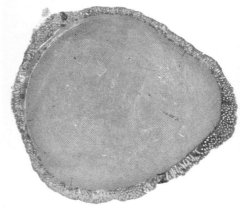

Fig. 6.87 Leiomyoma of rectum.

Pathological features

Lipomas are composed of mature adipose tissue and are surrounded by a fibrotic capsule. They usually arise in the submucosal layer of the caecum or the sigmoid colon. When ulcerated, the lipocytes may become irregular and hyperchromatic. Lipomas should be distinguished from lipohyperplasia of the ileocaecal valve {1726}. *Neurofibromas and schwannomas* occur in the colorectum. Most patients with the former have neurofibromatosis, and in

these cases plexiform neurofibromas are common. *Ganglioneuromas* occur rarely in the mucosa.

Vascular tumours are classified into benign (such as haemangiomas, lymphangiomas and angiomatosis) and malignant (such as haemangioendotheliomas and angiosarcomas). *Kaposi sarcoma* is mostly asymptomatic; a few present with GI-bleeding {319}. Intestinal lesions may be observed without cutaneous disease {114}. The tumours are often multiple mucosal or submucosal nodules. Histologically typical are sheets of spindle cells interspersed by clusters of extravasated erythrocytes. Cytoplasmic hyaline PAS-positive globules are usually seen. The spindle cells are generally positive for CD31 and CD34 and are negative for actin, desmin and c-kit.

Leiomyomas usually are detected in the rectum and colon as small polyps arising from the muscularis mucosae, and consist of well-differentiated smooth muscle cells with a similar immunohistochemical profile as observed in oesophageal leiomyomas {1227}. Leiomyomatosis has been described in the colon with a circumferential semiconstrictive growth in a 35 cm long segment {529}. It is not known whether colorectal leiomyomas and leiomyomatosis have the same colla-

gen type IV deletions as the oesophageal leiomyomas.

Gastrointestinal stromal tumours (GISTs)
of the colorectum are similar to those in
the stomach and small intestine and are
discussed in the section on gastric mesenchymal neoplasms. Most reports ante-
date the separation of GISTs and
leiomyosarcoma. GISTs occur mainly
between the 6th and 8th decades, and
most are malignant {89}. Many tumours
grow beyond the rectal wall making radical surgery difficult and recurrences
common. Histologically, the examples
reviewed by us have all been of the spindle cell variety, all have been c-kit positive, and most of them CD34-positive.
Actin-positivity occurs, but the tumours
are desmin-negative. *C-kit* mutations
have been shown in rectal GISTs {1018}.
The survival from large bowel stromal/
smooth muscle sarcomas appears to be
slightly higher than that of the small
bowel and lower than that of the stomach
and oesophagus {461}.

Fig. 6.89 Colonic lipoma.

Fig. 6.90 Malignant stromal tumour.

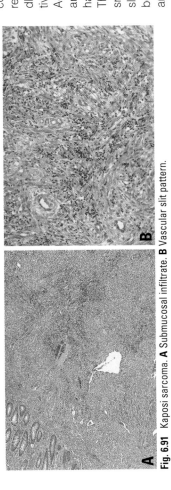

Fig. 6.91 Kaposi sarcoma. **A** Submucosal infiltrate. **B** Vascular slit pattern.

CHAPTER 7

Tumours of the Anal Canal

Although incidence rates are still low, there has been a significant increase in squamous cell carcinoma over the last 50 years. HIV infected homosexual men appear particularly at risk. HPV DNA is detectable in most anal squamous cell carcinomas.

Despite its short length, the anal canal produces a variety of tumour types reflecting its complex anatomic and histological structure. Squamous, glandular, transitional, and melanocytic components occur at this site, either alone, or in combination.

WHO histological classification of tumours of the anal canal

Epithelial tumours		
Intraepithelial neoplasia (dysplasia)		
Squamous or transitional epithelium		
Glandular		
Paget disease	8542/3[2]	
Carcinoma		
Squamous cell carcinoma	8070/3	
Adenocarcinoma	8140/3	
Mucinous adenocarcinoma	8480/3	
Small cell carcinoma	8041/3	
Malignant melanoma		8720/3
Non-epithelial tumours		
Secondary tumours		
Carcinoid tumour	8240/3	
Undifferentiated carcinoma	8020/3	
Others		

[1] Behaviour is coded /0 for benign tumours, /3 for malignant tumours, /2 for in situ carcinomas and grade III intraepithelial neoplasia, and /1 for unspecified, borderline or uncertain behaviour. Intraepithelial neoplasia does not have a generic code in ICD-O. ICD-O codes are available only for lesions categorized as squamous intraepithelial neoplasia, grade III (8077/2), squamous cell carcinoma in situ (8070/2), transitional cell carcinoma in situ (8120/2), glandular intraepithelial neoplasia, grade III (8148/2), and adenocarcinoma in situ (8140/2).

[2] Morphology code of the International Classification of Diseases for Oncology (ICD-O) {542} and the Systematized Nomenclature of Medicine (http://snomed.org).

TNM classification of tumours of the anal canal

TNM classification[1,2]

T – Primary Tumour

TX Primary tumour cannot be assessed
T0 No evidence of primary tumour
Tis Carcinoma in situ
T1 Tumour 2 cm or less in greatest dimension
T2 Tumour more than 2 cm but not more than 5 cm in greatest dimension
T3 Tumour more than 5 cm in greatest dimension
T4 Tumour of any size invades adjacent organ(s), e.g., vagina, urethra, bladder (involvement of sphincter muscle(s) alone is not classified as T4)

N – Regional Lymph Nodes

NX Regional lymph nodes cannot be assessed
N0 No regional lymph node metastasis
N1 Metastasis in perirectal lymph node(s)
N2 Metastasis in unilateral internal iliac and/or inguinal lymph node(s)
N3 Metastasis in perirectal and inguinal lymph nodes and/or bilateral internal iliac and/or inguinal lymph nodes

M – Distant Metastasis

MX Distant metastasis cannot be assessed
M0 No distant metastasis
M1 Distant metastasis

Stage Grouping

Stage 0	Tis	N0	M0
Stage I	T1	N0	M0
Stage II	T2	N0	M0
	T3	N0	M0
Stage IIIA	T1	N1	M0
	T2	N1	M0
	T3	N1	M0
	T4	N0	M0
Stage IIIB	T4	N1	M0
	Any T	N2, N3	M0
Stage IV	Any T	Any N	M1

[1] {66, 361}. This classification applies only to carcinomas.
[2] A help desk for specific questions about the TNM classification is available at http://tnm.uicc.org.
[3] This includes cancer cells confined within the glandular basement membrane (intraepithelial) or lamina propria (intramucosal) with no extension through muscularis mucosae into submucosa.

C. Fenger
M. Frisch
M.C. Marti
R. Parc

Tumours of the anal canal

Definition

Tumours that arise from or are predominantly located in the anal canal. The most frequent neoplams of this region are human papilloma virus (HPV)-associated squamous cell carcinomas and adenocarcinomas.

Topographic definition of anal canal and anal margin

The anal canal is defined as the terminal part of the large intestine, beginning at the upper surface of the anorectal ring and passing through the pelvic floor to end at the anus {68}. The most important macroscopic landmark in the mucosa is the dentate (pectinate) line composed of the anal valves and the bases of the anal columns. Histologically, the mucosa can be divided into three zones. The upper part is covered with colorectal type mucosa. The middle part is the anal transitional zone (ATZ), which is covered by a specialized epithelium with varying appearances; it extends from the dentate line and on average 0.5-1.0 cm upwards {490, 1929}. The lower part extends from the dentate line and downwards to the anal verge and has formerly been called the pecten. It is covered by squamous epithelium, which may be partly keratinized, particularly in case of mucosal prolapse.
The perianal skin (the anal margin) is defined by the appearance of skin appendages. There exists no generally accepted definition of its outer limit {62, 66, 845}. The term anus refers to the distal external aperture of the alimentary tract. Anal margin tumours are classified according to the WHO histological typing of skin tumours {682}.

Squamous cell carcinoma

Definition

Squamous cell carcinoma (SCC) of the anal canal is a malignant epithelial neoplasm that is frequently associated with chronic HPV infection.

ICD-O code   8070/3

Epidemiology

SCC of the anal canal and anal margin typically occurs among patients in their 6th or 7th decade of life {540}. However, anal SCCs may occur in young adults, particularly in patients with cellular immune incompetence {1212}. Unselected, population-based studies show an approximate 2:1 female predominance among patients with anal SCC {540, 600, 1213}.
There are few published, histologically verified incidence rates of anal cancer {540, 600, 1213}. Data from most population-based cancer registries worldwide show age standardized incidence rates of anal SCC of between 0.5 and 1.0 per 100,000 in women and between 0.3 and 0.8 per 100,000 in men {1471}. Still a relatively rare disease, anal SCC has shown a remarkable increase in incidence during the past half century {540, 600, 1213}. From being similar in the two sexes until approximately 1960 at 0.2 per 100,000, annual age-adjusted incidence rates in Denmark rose 2.5-fold in men and 5-fold in women during the period 1943-1994.
For both men and women, urban populations are at higher risk than rural populations {540, 600, 1213}, and there are considerable racial differences in incidence. In the United States, blacks tend to have higher incidence rates than whites {1213}, while Asians and Pacific Islanders appear to be at very low risk {70}.
Homosexual men appear to constitute a group at particular risk {368, 538, 140, 96, 369, 540, 1213, 1690, 730}. In the United States, the incidence of anal SCC in homosexual men has been estimated to be 11 to 34 times higher than in the general male population and approximately as high as the incidence of cervical cancer before the introduction of cervical cytology screening {369, 1447}. HIV infected homosexual men appear to be at particularly risk {1212, 1449, 598}. Other sexual factors strongly associated with anal SCC include number of sexual partner, receptive anal intercourse, and co-existence of sexually transmitted diseases {368, 538, 730, 733}.

Aetiology

Sexually transmittable human papillomaviruses (HPVs) are detected by PCR in the majority of anal SCC {355, 367, 538, 704, 732, 1448}. One large study showed that SCCs involving the anal canal are more often high-risk HPV positive (92%) than lesions confined to the perianal skin (64%) {536}, suggesting that HPV-unrelated pathways may apply particularly to cancers of the perianal skin. A strong association with tobacco smoking has been established in women, but the role of smoking in men is less clear {367, 539, 730, 733}. States of cellular immunosuppression are associated

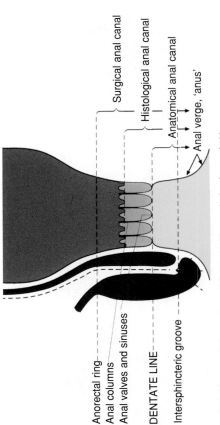

Fig. 7.01 Anatomy of the anal canal. Printed with permission from ref **490**.

Anorectal ring
Anal columns
Anal valves and sinuses
DENTATE LINE
Intersphincteric groove

Surgical anal canal
Histological anal canal
Anatomical anal canal
Anal verge, 'anus'

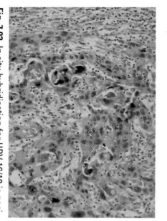

Fig. 7.03 In situ hybridisation for HPV 16/18 is positive in this anal carcinoma.

Fig. 7.02 Normal histology of the anal transition zone.

with increased risk of anal squamous cell carcinoma. This has been observed for renal transplant recipients {150, 1494} and for patients with HIV infection and AIDS {1212}.

Haemorrhoids and fissures, fistulae and abscesses in the anal region were long considered predisposing factors {192, 198, 1618}. However, three case-control studies {368, 537, 733} and two cohort studies {541, 1074} failed to support the association. Crohn's disease of long duration, which has been implicated in the aetiology of anal SCC based on case reports {992, 1765}, was not associated with risk in the only controlled study addressing the issue {537}.

Oestrogen and androgen receptors have been found in the anal mucosa and its supportive tissue {1396}, suggesting a physiological role of sex hormones in their maintenance. Women who reach menarche late and women with short fertile periods may be at elevated risk of anal SCC {539}.

Clinical features

Symptoms and signs

Anal intraepithelial neoplasia is often an unexpected finding in minor surgical specimens. Clinical manifestations of anal cancer are often late and non-specific and are mainly related to tumour size and extent of infiltration. They include anal pruritus, discomfort in sitting position, sensation of a pelvic mass, pain, change in bowel habit, incontinence due to sphincter infiltration, discharge, bleeding, fissure, or fistula. The initial non-specificity of clinical features explains why diagnosis can be delayed {855, 1621, 1719, 1835}.

The clinical diagnosis of an anal tumour should always be confirmed by histological examination. A forceps or needle biopsy is usually sufficient to establish the diagnosis. The biopsy should be accompanied by an exact description of location and appearance of the biopsy site. An excisional biopsy is inadvisable, because wound healing delay would postpone optimal chemo-radiotherapy treatment. Enlarged lymph nodes may be excised or biopsied with needle aspiration under radiological control.

Imaging

Computerised tomography (CT) scan, magnetic resonance imaging (MRI), and needle aspiration are used to detect inguinal and pararectal node involvement. Endoanal ultrasonography (EUS) enables assessment of spread in terms of proximal and circumferential extension and infiltration of deep layers. Furthermore, EUS enables the follow-up of irradiated carcinomas {703}. CT scan and MRI allow detection of involved lymph nodes and distant metastases {1835}.

Exfoliative cytology

In patients with increased risk such as individuals with HIV or women with genital tract SCC, the use of anal smears taken with a cytology brush from the area below the dentate line is recommended {1689}.

Macroscopy

The tumour may present as a small ulceration or fissure with slightly exophytic and indurated margins, and irregular thickening of the anoderm and anal margin with chronic dermatitis. The lesion may have a different colour from the surrounding tissue.

If ulceration and infiltration develop, the lesion becomes fixed to the underlying structures and may bleed. In advanced stages, the sphincteric muscles are deeply infiltrated although there may be little mucosal ulceration.

Fig. 7.04 Ulcerating nodular squamous cell carcinoma of anus.

Tumour spread and staging

Anal SCC should be staged according to the TNM system {66}. Treatment for anal SCC has now changed from surgery alone to sphincter preserving procedures including radiation and chemotherapy, sometimes in combination with local excision. Large surgical specimens are therefore rare. The examination should include resection lines in all directions and a careful search for lymph nodes. Clinical results of the combined treatment regimes are comparable or even better than those for surgery alone, but detection of residual disease can be more difficult by imaging techniques due to local fibrosis. In such cases a transanal full thickness tru-cut needle biopsy may be helpful {785}. Identification of residual

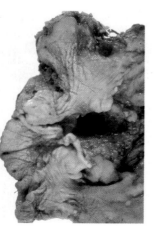

Fig. 7.05 Squamous cell carcinoma arising at dentate line.

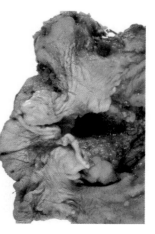

tumour cells may be facilitated by immunostaining for high molecular weight cytokeratins (CKs).

In 15-20% of cases, the lesion may infiltrate the lower rectum and the neighbouring organs including the rectovaginal septum, bladder, prostate and posterior urethra, sometimes with suppuration and fistulas. The vulva is usually spared.

Lymphatic spread occurs in up to 40 percent of cases {165, 1174, 1621, 1719, 2033}. Tumours proximal to the pectinate line drain into the pelvis along the middle rectal vessels to the pelvic side walls and internal iliac chains and superiorly via the superior rectal vessels to the periaortic nodes. Tumours distal to the dentate line drain along cutaneous pathways to the inguinal and the femoral nodal chains. Inguinal nodes are involved in about 10-20% of cases {230, 575, 1174, 1650, 1692}. Inguinal lymph nodes can be involved bilaterally in a small number of cases at time of presentation. Retrograde lymphatic drainage occurs in advanced cases when the lymphatics are obstructed by malignant spread {1621, 1719}.

Histopathology

Squamous cell carcinoma of anal canal

Anal SCC may show a single predominant line of differentiation, but most exhibit a mixture of areas with different histological features. One pattern is that of large, pale eosinophilic cells and keratinization of either lamellar or single cell type. Another is that of small cells with palisading of the nuclei in the periphery of tumour cell islands. The latter often contain necrotic eosinophilic centres. Intermediate stages between these two extremes are often present. Differentiation into tubular or spindle cell configuration may be found. The invasive margin can vary from well circumscribed to irreg-

ular, and a lymphocytic infiltrate may be pronounced or absent. None of these features have been shown to have any prognostic significance, but poor keratinization, prominent basaloid features and small tumour cell size are related to infection with 'high risk' HPV {536}. The keratin profile of anal SCC is complex and variable {2112, 2113}. The usual immunoexpression pattern is shown in Table 7.01. The second edition of the WHO classification of SCC in the anal canal included the large-cell keratinizing subtype, the large-cell non-keratinizing subtype, and the basaloid subtype {845}. The value of this classification of anal SCC has been questioned in recent years. Many tumours show more than one subtype. Thus in a study of 100 cases of anal carcinomas, 99 showed some features of squamous differentiation (keratinisation, stratification and prickles), 65 showed basaloid features (small cell change, palisading, retraction artefact and central eosinophilic necrosis) and 26 showed focal evidence of ductal proliferation and occasionally positive staining for PAS after diastase digestion {2111}. Furthermore, the diagnostic reproducibility of these subtypes is low {492}. This is probably the reason that the proportion of basaloid carcinoma in larger series has varied from 10 to almost 70 %, and that no significant correlation between histological subtype and prognosis has been established. In addition, the histological diagnosis is nowadays nearly always performed on small biopsies, that may not be representative for the whole tumour {492}. Therefore, it is recommended that the generic term 'squamous carcinoma' be used for these tumours, accompanied by a comment describing those histopathological features that may possibly affect the prognosis or reflect different aetiolo-

gies, i.e. size of predominant neoplastic cell, basaloid features, degree of keratinisation, adjacent squamous intraepithelial neoplasia, or presence of mucinous microcysts.

Apart from the verrucous carcinoma mentioned below, only two rare histological subtypes seem to have a different biological course, both having a less favourable prognosis {1734}. One is characterized by areas with well formed acinar or cystic spaces containing mucin that reacts with Alcian dyes or PAS after diastase digestion. This is termed *squamous cell carcinoma with mucinous microcysts*. The other is characterized by a rather uniform pattern of small tumour cells with nuclear moulding, high mitotic rate, extensive apoptosis and diffuse infiltration in the surrounding stroma. This has been called *small cell (anaplastic) carcinoma*, but should not be confused with small cell carcinoma (poorly differentiated neuroendocrine carcinoma).

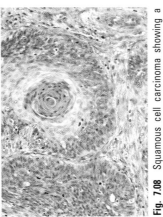

Fig. 7.08 Squamous cell carcinoma showing a combination of basaloid and squamous features.

Squamous cell carcinoma of anal margin

The distinction between anal canal and anal margin SCC may be difficult, as tumours often involve both areas at the time of diagnosis. This may account for the varying data on prognosis, but this is generally better for anal margin SCC than for anal canal SCC, in particular if local resection is possible {392, 530, 1484}. Anal margin SCC is often of the large cell variant {536, 1484}.

Verrucous carcinoma

In the anogenital area, this tumour is also called giant (malignant) condyloma or Buschke-Lowenstein tumour. It has a cauliflower-like appearance, is larger than the usual condyloma with a diameter up to 12 cm, and fails to respond to

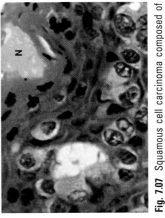

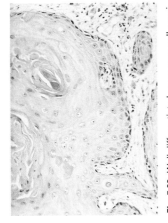

Fig. 7.07 Squamous cell carcinoma composed of basaloid cells. Central necrosis (N) of tumour nests is typical.

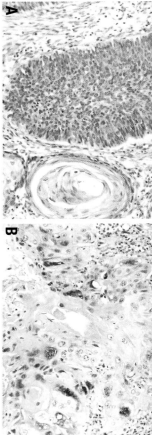

Fig. 7.09 Squamous cell carcinoma of anus. **A** Combination of basaloid features and keratinization. **B** Large cells, poorly differentiated.

conservative treatment. In contrast to an ordinary condyloma, it is characterized by a combination of exophytic and endophytic growth. Histologically, it shows acanthosis and papillomatosis with orderly arrangement of the epithelial layers and an intact but often irregular base with blunt downward projections and keratin-filled cysts. The endophytic growth is accompanied by destruction of the underlying tissues. Cytologically, the epithelial cells appear benign. Large nuclei with prominent nucleoli may be present, but dysplasia is usually minimal and mitoses are restricted to the basal layers {162}.

Some verrucous carcinomas contain HPV, the most common types being 6 and 11. They are regarded as an intermediate state between the ordinary condyloma and SCC, and the clinical course is typically that of local destructive invasion without metastases. Among 33 published anorectal cases, 42 per cent have shown malignant transformation {133}. The presence of severe cytological changes, unequivocal invasion or metastases should lead to the diagnosis of SCC and to the appropriate therapy.

Grading

Poor prognosis has been related to poor differentiation {165}, especially if this was defined only by the degree of dissociation of tumour cells {599}. However, such differences may be related to tumour stage in multivariate analysis {1734}. Grading on biopsies is not recommended, as these may not be representative for the tumour as a whole.

Precursor lesions and benign tumours

Chronic HPV infection

Warts in the perianal skin and lower anal canal (condyloma acuminatum) show the same histology as their genital counterparts. Flat koilocytic lesions also occur. They should always be totally embedded and examined histologically for possible presence of intraepithelial neoplasia.

Intraepithelial neoplasia

Precancerous anal intraepithelial neoplasia (AIN) in the anal transition zone (ATZ) and the squamous zone, has also been termed dysplasia, carcinoma in-situ and anal squamous intraepithelial lesion (ASIL) {494, 1449}. The corresponding lesions in the perianal skin are commonly referred to as Bowen disease. This terminology is complicated by the fact that the precancerous changes are not always restricted to one area. Leukoplakia is a clinical term and should not be used as a histological diagnosis.

Anal intraepithelial neoplasia (squamous cell dysplasia in the anal canal). Most cases of AIN are incidental findings in minor surgical specimens for benign conditions. When macroscopically detected, AIN may present as an eczematoid or papillomatous area, or as papules or plaques. The latter may be irregular, raised, scaly, white, pigmented or erythematous and occasionally fissured. Induration or ulceration may indicate invasion. Histologically, AIN is characterized by varying degrees of loss of stratification and nuclear polarity, nuclear pleomorphism and hyperchromatism, and increased mitotic activity with presence of mitoses high in the epithelium. The surface may or may not be keratinized, and koilocytic changes may be present. AIN has been graded into I, II or III, or into mild, moderate and severe dysplasia {494}. Reproducibility studies have shown considerable observer variation {254}. A two grade system (low- and high-grade) may be more appropriate.

Squamous dysplasia at the anal margin - Bowen disease. Clinically, this presents as a white or red area in the perianal skin that may be in continuity with dysplastic lesions in the anal canal. HPV DNA is sometimes identified, including types 16 and 18, among others. Histologically it shows full thickness dysplasia of the squamous and sometimes the pilosebaceous epithelium, with disorderly maturation, mitoses at all levels and dyskeratosis. Occasionally, atypical keratinocytes may resemble Paget cells, but are negative for low molecular weight CKs and for mucin. In pigmented Bowen disease the neoplastic cells are invariably negative

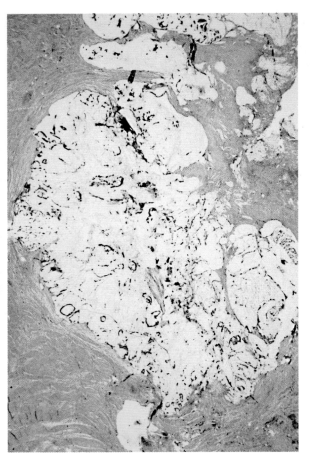

Fig. 7.10 Mucinous carcinoma of anus. Tumour extends to anal sphincter.

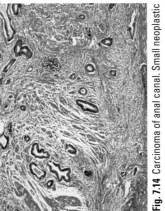

Fig. 7.11 Giant condyloma.

for S-100 protein and HMB-45.
Bowen disease has a strong tendency to recurrence after local treatment but only a few percent will progress to SCC. It is often associated with genital neoplasia but not with internal malignancies {1161, 1668}.

Bowenoid papulosis. This condition presents as multiple 2-10 mm reddish brown papules or plaques, most commonly in sexually active young adults. Aetiologically it is related to HPV infection, usually HPV 16. Bowenoid papulosis is similar histologically to Bowen disease, and the distinction is made on a combination of clinical and pathological observations. Bowenoid papulosis tends to resolve spontaneously, but can recur {635}. It does not progress to carcinoma.

Genetic susceptibility
Human leukocyte antigens (HLAs) are involved in the presentation of viral antigens to the immune system. Since the aetiology of most anal SCCs involves HPV infection {536}, susceptibility to cancer development might be HLA type dependent. However, no study has addressed the association between specific HLA class I or II alleles and the risk, and attempts to identify other genetic susceptibility markers for anal SCC have so far been unsuccessful {286, 287}.

Genetics
HPV DNA is detectable in most anal SCCs; in a large population-based series of anal SCCs in Denmark and Sweden, 84% contained HPV DNA, with higher proportions of HPV-DNA positive cancers among women and homosexual men than among non-homosexual men {536}.
Loss of functional tumour suppressor protein p53 appears to be centrally involved in the development of anal and

anogenital SCCs {355, 356, 704, 1040}. Inactivation of p53 may occur at the gene level through point mutations leading to the production of inactive p53 or, less frequently, by means of deletions in the relevant area of chromosome 17p {704}. More typically, p53 inactivation occurs at the protein level through formation of a complex between the viral protein E6 (expressed by 'high-risk' HPV types) and a cellular protein, the E6-associated protein, which when bound to p53 leads to rapid proteolytic degradation of p53 {2092}. The level of p53 expression does not correlate with HPV status {704}. The E7 protein of 'high risk' HPV types binds to the retinoblastoma protein, pRb {440}, disrupting signals that normally restrict proliferation to the basal epithelial layer. The resulting increased proliferation increases the risk of malignant transformation on exposure to DNA damaging stimuli. The combination of increased cell proliferation (pRb inactivation) and impaired ability to induce cell cycle arrest or apoptosis following DNA damage (p53 inactivation) are two central mechanisms through which 'high risk' types of HPV increase the risk of anogenital cancer.
Additional gene alterations appear to be involved in malignant progression and invasion. In one study, the *c-myc* gene

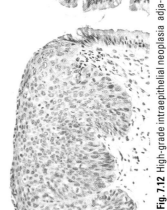

Fig. 7.12 High-grade intraepithelial neoplasia adjacent to normal rectal epithelium.

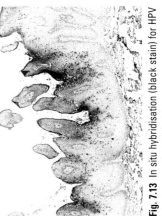

Fig. 7.13 In situ hybridisation (black stain) for HPV 6/11 in an anal condyloma.

was found to be amplified in 30% of anal SCCs {355}, while other cellular oncogenes, including *ras* and *cyclin D*, do not seem to be centrally involved {708, 1737}. Several chromosomal aberrations have been observed in anal SCCs {704, 1294}. Using comparative genomic hybridization, one study identified consistent gains in chromosomes 3q, 17, and 19 as well as losses in chromosomes 4p, 11q, 13q, and 18q {704}.

Prognosis and predictive factors
The most important prognostic factors in recent larger series of anal canal SCC are tumour stage and nodal status {530, 1483, 1734}. SCC of the anal margin has a slightly better prognosis, which depends only on inguinal node involvement {1484}. DNA ploidy status has only been shown to be of independent prognostic significance in one of three larger series {599, 1702, 1734}. Expression of p53, cathepsin D, c-erb B2 and retinoblastoma gene protein are not predictive factors {169, 731, 784, 1901}.

Adenocarcinoma

Definition
Anal canal adenocarcinoma is an adenocarcinoma arising in the anal canal epithelium, including the mucosal surface, the anal glands and the lining of fistulous tracts.

ICD-O code   8140/3

Clinical features
The clinical features of anal adenocarcinoma of colorectal type do not differ from those of anal SCC. Perianal adenocarcinomas may present as submucosal tumours, sometimes in combination with fistulas. Occasionally, there may be

Fig. 7.14 Carcinoma of anal canal. Small neoplastic glands simulate anal glands.

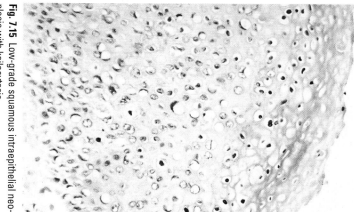

Fig. 7.15 Low-grade squamous intraepithelial neoplasia with koilocytosis.

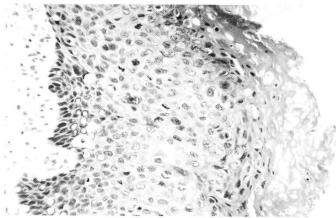

Fig. 7.16 High-grade squamous intraepithelial neoplasia with hyperkeratosis.

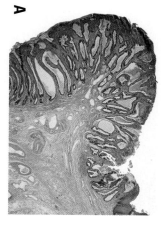

Fig. 7.17 A, B Inflammatory cloacogenic polyp. Dilated elongated hyperplastic glands showing regenerative atypia. Surface erosion is a constant feature.

Fig. 7.18 Adenocarcinoma arising in a fistula.

associated Paget disease of the anus (see below). Tumour spread and staging largely correspond to anal SCC.

Histopathology

Adenocarcinoma arising in anal mucosa

Most adenocarcinomas found in the anal canal represent downward spread from an adenocarcinoma in the rectum or arise in colorectal type mucosa above the dentate line. Macroscopically and histologically, they are indistinguishable from ordinary colorectal type adenocarcinoma, and do not seem to represent a special entity except for their low location. Adenocarcinoma in the anal transitional zone (ATZ) may develop after restorative proctocolectomy for ulcerative colitis {1711}.

Extramucosal (perianal) adenocarcinoma

Approximately two hundred cases of extramucosal adenocarcinoma have been reported, the largest series unfortunately with insufficient histological data {9}. A minimum criterion for the diagnosis is an overlying non-neoplastic mucosa, which may be ulcerated. Recent reports indicate that about two thirds of these tumours manifest in men with a mean age about 60 years. Reliable data for the prognosis for such patients have not been identified. Difficulties in establishing the correct diagnosis may delay proper treatment.

Extramucosal adenocarcinoma seem to fall into two groups, based on their association with either fistulae or remnants of anal glands. At present, no laboratory methods can distinguish between these two.

The epithelium of persistent anal fistulae is most often of the same type as found in the anal glands and ATZ {1117}, and the epithelium in these two locations show the same profile with regard to mucin composition {491} and keratin expression {2113}.

Adenocarcinoma within anorectal fistula.

These tumours develop in pre-existing anal sinuses or in fistulae {74}. Some are associated with Crohn disease {992}. Others may contain epithelioid granulomas, often related to foci of inflammation or extravasated mucin but without other signs of inflammatory bowel disease {863}.

Rarely, the tumours may be related to fistulae lined by normal rectal mucosa including muscularis mucosae, most likely representing adenocarcinomas arising in congenital duplications {863}. Histologically, carcinomas arising in fistulae usually are of the mucinous type, but tubular adenocarcinomas and squamous neoplasia can also be found {992, 2173}.

Adenocarcinoma of anal glands.

Only a few cases have been reported in which convincing evidence for origin in an anal gland has been demonstrated by continuity between anal gland epithelium and tumour {118, 650, 1472, 2087, 2131}. With a single exception {650}, these patients have had no history of previous or concomitant fistula. The tumours were all characterized by a combination of ductular and mucinous areas. Pagetoid spread was present in at least one case {2131}.

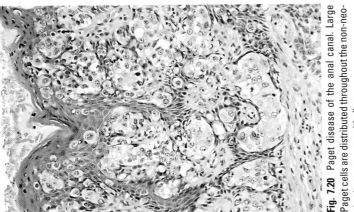

Grading

Anal adenocarcinomas are graded as colorectal adenocarcinomas.

Precursor lesions

Anal adenocarcinomas are thought to arise from glandular intraepithelial neoplasia, which can be graded as in the colorectum.

Prognosis and predictive factors

The prognosis for anal adenocarcinoma seems to be related only to the stage at diagnosis and is poorer than that for SCC {118, 930, 1305}.

Basal cell carcinoma of the anal margin

Basal cell carcinoma, the most common skin cancer, is primarily found on sun-exposed areas, and only a few more than a hundred cases have been reported in the anal area. {1353}. The aetiology is unknown and there is no evidence of HPV infection {1332}. The tumour commonly presents as an indurated area with raised edges and central ulceration, located in the perianal skin but occasionally involving the squamous zone below the dentate line. Histologically, it can show the same variability in morphology as basal cell carcinoma elsewhere, most reported cases having had a solid or adenoid pattern.

Basal cell carcinoma is sufficiently treated by local excision and metastases are extremely rare. It is therefore important to distinguish it from squamous carcinoma, and this may be particularly difficult on small biopsies. Both tumours can be found in the squamous zone, and both can show a combination of basaloid, squamous and adenoid features and an inflammatory infiltrate in the stroma {50}. Numerous and even atypical mitoses may be present in basal cell carcinomas {1538}. However, basaloid areas in squa-

mous carcinoma usually show less conspicuous peripheral palisading, more cellular pleomorphism, and often large, eosinophilic necrotic areas. Immunohistochemistry may be helpful in establishing the diagnosis. Basal cell carcinoma is positive for Ber-EP4 and negative for CKs 13, 19 and 22, and for CEA, EMA, AE 1 and UEA 1, while basaloid variants of squamous cell carcinoma usually show the opposite pattern {50, 1061}.

Paget Disease

Extramammary Paget disease usually affects sites with a high density of apocrine glands, such as the anogenital region, where it presents as a slowly spreading, erythematous eczematoid plaque that may extend up to the dentate line {1667}. Histologically, the basal part or whole thickness of the squamous epithelium is infiltrated by large cells with abundant pale cytoplasm and large nuclei. Occasional cells have the appearance of signet-rings. Paget cells invariably react positively for mucin stains and nearly always for CK 7, but Merkel cells and Toker cells may also be positive for the latter {120, 1112}.

Paget disease of the anus appears to represent two entities. About half of the cases are associated with a synchronous or metachronous malignancy, most often a colorectal adenocarcinoma. Such cases can be regarded as a pagetoid extension of the tumour. They usually react positively for CK 20 and negatively for gross cystic disease fluid protein-15, a marker for apocrine cells. This is in contrast to the other half, which are not associated with internal malignancies, but have a high local recurrence rate and may become invasive {1162}. Only this latter entity can be regarded as a true epidermotrophic apocrine neoplasm {85, 120, 595, 1374}.

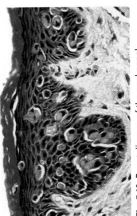

Fig. 7.19 Paget disease of the anal canal.

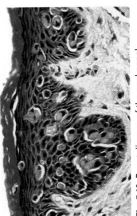

Fig. 7.20 Paget disease of the anal canal. Large Paget cells are distributed throughout the non-neoplastic squamous epithelium.

Papillary hidradenoma

This rare tumour arises in the perianal apocrine glands, typically in middle aged women and only exceedingly rarely in men {1082}. It presents as a circumscribed nodule approximately 1 cm in diameter and may resemble a haemorrhoid.

Histologically, it consists of a papillary mass with a cyst-like capsule. The papillae are lined by a double layer of epithelial cells, the outer layer being composed of cells containing mucin. The tumour does not express the eccrine marker IKH-4, but it must be remembered that adenocarcinoma metastases also are negative {811}. Convincing examples of anal apocrine adenocarcinoma have not been published.

Keratoacanthoma

There are a few reports on keratoacanthoma arising in the perianal skin {454}.

Neuroendocrine tumours

Neuroendocrine tumours may arise in the anus {493, 744}. They are, however, conventionally classified as rectal. An immunohistochemical study of 17 rectal neuroendocrine tumours showed that most were of L-cell type {294}. For details, see in chapter 5 the section on endocrine tumours of the colon and rectum.

Other lesions

Squamous cell papilloma of the anal canal

Rarely, papillomatous processes covered by normal, more or less keratinized squamous epithelium can be found in the anus. Such lesions should be tested for the presence of HPV. Negative cases are commonly regarded as 'burned-out' condylomas.

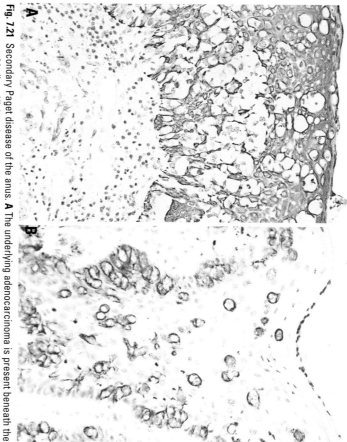

Fig. 7.21 Secondary Paget disease of the anus. **A** The underlying adenocarcinoma is present beneath the squamous epithelium. High molecular weight keratin immunostain is largely restricted to normal squamous epithelium. **B** Low molecular weight keratins 8 and 13 immunostaining of tumour cells.

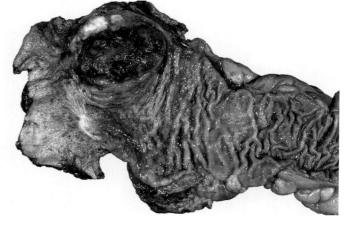

Fig. 7.22 Malignant melanoma of anus with typical polypoid appearance.

Fig. 7.23 Malignant melanoma of anus. **A** Polypoid growth is frequent. **B** Scattered tumour cells contain melanin. **C** Epithelioid melanoma cells with prominent nucleoli.

Malignant melanoma

Anal melanoma is rare. It is a disease of adults with a wide age range; most patients are white {339, 182}. Presentation is usually with mass and rectal bleeding, but tenesmus, pain and change in bowel habit also occur {339}.

Macroscopy. Lesions may be sessile or polypoid. Pigmentation of the lesion is often appreciated. Satellite nodules may occur.

Histopathology. The features resemble those of cutaneous melanomas. The majority shows a junctional component adjacent to the invasive tumour, and this finding is evidence that the lesion is primary rather than metastatic. The tumour cells express S-100 and HMB-45. Anal melanomas spread by lymphatics to regional nodes, and haematogenously to the liver and thence to other organs. Metastases are frequent at time of presentation, and the prognosis is poor; the 5-year survival is less than 10% {339, 157}. The chances of long-term survival are increased if the lesion is small.

Mesenchymal and neurogenic tumours

These are all rare and the exact point of origin may be difficult to establish. Recent reports on tumours in the anorectal and perianal area include haemangioma, lymphangioma {372}, haemangiopericytoma {478}, leiomyoma, malignant fibrous histiocytoma and leiomyosarcoma {1110}, rhabdomyoma in a newborn {1014}, and rhabdomyosarcoma in childhood {1560} and adulthood {902}, fibrosarcoma, neurilemmoma and neurofibroma {571}, granular cell tumour (myoblastoma) {862}, spindle cell lipoma and aggressive angiomyxoma {503} and extraspinal ependymoma in a newborn {2074}. HIV infected persons may, in addition to the increased risk of squamous neoplasia, develop Kaposi sarcoma in the perianal area {113}.

Malignant lymphoma

Primary lymphomas of the anorectal region are rare in the general population, but much more common in patients with AIDS, particularly homosexual men. All are of B-cell type, the most common types being large cell immunoblastic or pleomorphic {687, 786}. Langerhans cell histiocytosis has been described in children {617, 874} and an adult {329}.

Table 7.01
Anal tumours, immunoreactivity profile (exceptions occur, especially among CK and mucin)[1]

	CK 8+18	CK 7/20	CK 5+14	Mucin	CEA	Vim	Special
Colorectal adenocarcinoma	+	-/+	-	+	+	-	CK 13/19
Squamous cell variants	-	-/-	+	-	-	-	Ber EP4
Basal cell carcinoma	-	-/-	+	-	-	-	Chrom/Synap
Neuroendocrine tumour	+	-/-	-	-	-	-	S-100, HMB-45
Malignant melanoma	-	-/-	-	-	-	+	
Bowen (also pigmented)	-	-/-	+	-	-	-	
Paget cells local Paget	+	+/-	-	+	+	-	GCDFP-15
Paget cells, from CRC	+	+/+	-	+	+	-	
Prostatic carcinoma	+	-/-	-	-	-	-	PSA, PSAP
Malignant lymphoma	-	-/-	-	-	-	+	LCA and others

[1]
Chrom	=	Chromogranin A	
CK	=	Cytokeratin	
CRC	=	Colorectal carcinoma	
GCDFP	=	Gross cystic disease fluid protein	

PSA	=	Prostate specific antigen
PSAP	=	Prostate specific acid phosphatase
Synap	=	Synaptophysin
Vim	=	Vimentin

Secondary tumours

Metastases to the anal canal and perianal skin are rare. Most primaries are found in the rectum or colon, but occasionally also in the respiratory tract, breast and pancreas {157, 182, 379, 888, 1767, 489}. There are few reports of metastatic squamous cell carcinoma {574}. Malignant lymphoma, leukaemia and myeloma may infiltrate the anal canal, and eosinophilic granuloma has also been described {489}.

Clinically, anal metastases cause similar symptoms to primary tumours at this site, including pain, bleeding and incontinence.

Neoplasia-like lesions
Fibroepithelial polyp

Also called fibrous polyp or anal tag, this is one of the most frequent anal lesions. It may be found in the squamous zone or the perianal skin in up to half of all individuals {2101}. Grossly, the polyp is spherical or elongated with a greater diameter ranging from a few mm up to 4 cm. The surface is white or grey and may show superficial ulceration. Histologically, it consists of a fibrous stroma covered by squamous epithelium, which usually is slightly hyperplastic and may be keratinized. The stroma may be more or less dense and often contains fibroblastic cells with two or more nuclei and a considerable number of mast cells {630}. Neuronal hyperplasia is a common feature {495}.

Fibroepithelial polyps may be associated with local inflammation such as fissure or fistula {1084}.

Granulomas can be found in about one third of skin tags in cases of Crohn's disease {1905}. Others may represent the end stage of a thrombosed haemorrhoid, but remnants of haemorrhoidal vessels or signs of previous bleeding are rarely found. Most are probably of idiopathic nature as the incidence is rather similar in patients with or without anal diseases {2101}.

Inflammatory cloacogenic polyp

This polyp was first described in 1981 {1083}. It arises in the ATZ and forms a rounded or irregular mass measuring from 1 to 5 cm in diameter. Histologically, it consists of hyperplastic rectal mucosa, partly covered with ATZ type or squamous epithelium. The surface is typically eroded and the stroma shows oedema, vascular ectasia, inflammatory cells and granulation tissue. Vertically oriented smooth muscle fibres are found between the elongated and tortuous crypts. The inflammatory cloacogenic polyp is commonly associated with mucosal prolapse, sometimes in company with haemorrhoids {296, 1052}.

Malacoplakia

Cutaneous malacoplakia may arise in immunocompromised patients and present as perianal nodules {1102}.

CHAPTER 8

Tumours of the Liver and Intrahepatic Bile Ducts

The most frequent and important hepatic neoplasm is the primary hepatocellular carcinoma (HCC). In many parts of the world, in particular Africa and Asia, it poses a significant disease burden. In these high incidence regions, chronic infection with hepatitis B virus (HBV) is the principal underlying cause, with the exception of Japan which has a high prevalence of hepatitis C infection. HBV vaccination has become a powerful tool in reducing cirrhosis and HCC, but implementation is still suboptimal in several high risk regions. In Western countries, chronic alcohol abuse is a major aetiological factor.

Hepatic cholangiocarcinoma has a different geographical distribution, with peak incidences in Northern Thailand. Here, it is caused by chronic infection with the liver fluke, *Opisthorchis Viverrini*, which is ingested through infected raw fish.

WHO histological classification of tumours of the liver and intrahepatic bile ducts

Epithelial tumours

Benign

Hepatocellular adenoma (liver cell adenoma)	8170/0[1]
Focal nodular hyperplasia	
Intrahepatic bile duct adenoma	8160/0
Intrahepatic bile duct cystadenoma	8161/0
Biliary papillomatosis	8264/0

Malignant

Hepatocellular carcinoma (liver cell carcinoma)	8170/3
Intrahepatic cholangiocarcinoma (peripheral bile duct carcinoma)	8160/3
Bile duct cystadenocarcinoma	8161/3
Combined hepatocellular and cholangiocarcinoma	8180/3
Hepatoblastoma	8970/3
Undifferentiated carcinoma	8020/3

Non-epithelial tumours

Benign

Angiomyolipoma	8860/0
Lymphangioma and lymphangiomatosis	9170/0
Haemangioma	9120/0
Infantile haemangioendothelioma	9130/0

Malignant

Epithelioid haemangioendothelioma	9133/1
Angiosarcoma	9120/3
Embryonal sarcoma (undifferentiated sarcoma)	8991/3
Rhabdomyosarcoma	8900/3
Others	

Miscellaneous Tumours

Solitary fibrous tumour	8815/0
Teratoma	9080/1
Yolk sac tumour (endodermal sinus tumour)	9071/3
Carcinosarcoma	8980/3
Kaposi sarcoma	9140/3
Rhabdoid tumour	8963/3
Others	

Haemopoietic and lymphoid tumours

Secondary tumours

Epithelial abnormalities

- Liver cell dysplasia (liver cell change)
  - Large cell type (large cell change)
  - Small cell type (small cell change)
- Dysplastic nodules (adenomatous hyperplasia)
  - Low-grade
  - High-grade (atypical adenomatous hyperplasia)
- Bile duct abnormalities
  - Hyperplasia (bile duct epithelium and peribiliary glands)
  - Dysplasia (bile duct epithelium and peribiliary glands)
  - Intraepithelial carcinoma (carcinoma in situ) 8500/211

Miscellaneous lesions

- Mesenchymal hamartoma
- Nodular transformation (nodular regenerative hyperplasia)
- Inflammatory pseudotumour

[1] Morphology code of the International Classification of Diseases for Oncology (ICD-O) (542) and the Systematized Nomenclature of Medicine (http://snomed.org). Behaviour is coded /0 for benign tumours, /1 for unspecified, borderline or uncertain behaviour, /2 for in situ carcinomas and grade III intraepithelial neoplasia and /3 for malignant tumours.

TNM classification of tumours of the liver and intrahepatic bile ducts

TNM classification[1,2,3]

T

T	Primary Tumour
TX	Primary tumour cannot be assessed
T0	No evidence of primary tumour
T1	Solitary tumour 2 cm or less in greatest dimension without vascular invasion
T2	Solitary tumour 2 cm or less in greatest dimension with vascular invasion; or multiple tumours limited to one lobe, none more than 2 cm in greatest dimension without vascular invasion; or solitary tumour more than 2 cm in greatest dimension without vascular invasion.
T3	Solitary tumour more than 2 cm in greatest dimension with vascular invasion; or multiple tumours limited to one lobe, none more than 2 cm in greatest dimension with vascular invasion; or multiple tumours limited to one lobe, any more than 2 cm in greatest dimension with or without vascular invasion.
T4	Multiple tumours in more than one lobe; or tumour(s) involve(s) a major branch of the portal or hepatic vein(s); or tumour(s) with direct invasion of adjacent organs other than gallbladder; or tumour(s) with perforation of visceral peritoneum.

N – Regional Lymph Nodes

NX	Regional lymph nodes cannot be assessed
N0	No regional lymph node metastasis
N1	Regional lymph node metastasis

M – Distant Metastasis

MX	Distant metastasis cannot be assessed
M0	No distant metastasis
M1	Distant metastasis

Stage Grouping

Stage I	T1	N0	M0
Stage II	T2	N0	M0
Stage IIIA	T3	N0	M0
Stage IIIB	T1	N1	M0
	T2	N1	M0
	T3	N1	M0
Stage IVA	T4	Any N	M0
Stage IVB	Any T	Any N	M1

[1] (66, 361). This classification applies only to primary hepatocellular and cholangio-(intrahepatic bile duct) carcinomas of the liver.

[2] A help desk for specific questions about the TNM classification is available at http://tnm.uicc.org.

[3] For classification, the plane projecting between the bed of the gallbladder and the inferior vena cava divides the liver in two lobes.

Hepatocellular carcinoma

S. Hirohashi   H.E. Blum
K.G. Ishak   Y. Deugnier
M. Kojiro   P. Laurent Puig
I.R. Wanless   H.P. Fischer
N.D. Theise   M. Sakamoto
H. Tsukuma

Definition

A malignant tumour derived from hepatocytes. Most common aetiological factors are viral infections (HBV, HCV), dietary aflatoxin B₁ ingestion and chronic alcohol abuse.

Epidemiology

Primary liver cancer (PLC) is a major public health problem worldwide. In 1990, the global number of new cases was estimated at 316,300 for males and 121,100 for females, accounting for 7.4% (males) and 3.2% (females) of all malignancies, excluding skin cancer {1469}. Hepatocellular carcinoma (HCC) is the most common histological type of PLC. Population-based cancer registries show that HCC as a percentage of histologically specified PLCs varies considerably {1471} but in over half of the registries, the fraction is above 70%.

Regions with percentages less than 40% are exceptional, e.g., Khon Kaen (Thailand), where intrahepatic cholangiocarcinoma is predominant, due to endemic infection with liver flukes (*Opisthorchis viverrini*) {1470}. Owing to the limited availability of histological data, the following epidemiological survey is based on PLC but it can be assumed that it largely reflects HCC incidence and mortality.

Geographical distribution

The estimated PLC incidence in 1990 for 23 areas of the world is shown in Figure 8.01 {1469}. High-risk areas with an age-standardized incidence rate (ASIR, standardized to world population) of more than 20.1 per 100,000 for males are Sub-Saharan and South Africa, East Asia, and Melanesia. Low-risk areas with an ASR < 3.2 are North and South America, South-Central Asia, Northern Europe, Australia and New Zealand. Thus, developing countries carry the greatest disease burden, with more than 80% of accounted global cases. The geographical distribution of PLC is similar for males and females, although males have a considerably higher risk of developing PLC. Geographical variations in PLC risk are present even in relatively homogeneous populations and environments {1471, 176}.

Geographical variations in HCC incidence and mortality can be ascribed to different levels of exposure to HCC risk factors: chronic infections with hepatitis B virus (HBV) and aflatoxin exposure in developing countries, and smoking and alcohol abuse in developed countries {1545, 1482, 1417}. In Japan, local differences in the age-standardized mortality rate (ASMR, standardized to

world population) reflect the sero-prevalence of anti-hepatitis C virus (anti-HCV) antibodies among blood donors {1973, 1893, 1471, 67}.

Time trends

In most countries, the incidence rates stayed largely constant or have decreased over the past two decades. However, they have increased in Japan and Italy, especially for males {982, 1522}. A changing prevalence of risk factors among populations as well as changes in diagnostic techniques and in classification of the disease and appreciably affected the disease incidence.

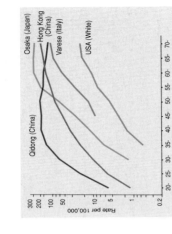

Fig. 8.03 Age-specific incidence rates of liver cancer in males for selected populations 1992. From: M. Parkin et al. {1471}.

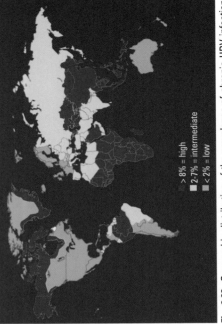

Fig. 8.02 Geographic distribution of the prevalence of chronic HBV infection, based on HBs Ag serology.

> 8% = high
2-7% = intermediate
< 2% = low

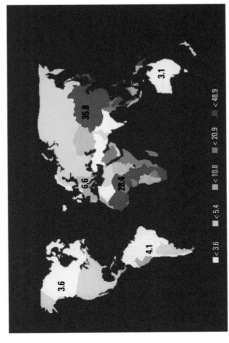

Fig. 8.01 Worldwide annual incidence (per 100,000) of liver tumours in males (1995). Numbers on the map indicate regional average values.

< 3.6   < 5.4   < 10.8   < 20.9   < 48.9
< 3.6   < 5.4   < 10.8   < 20.9   < 48.9

Age and sex distribution

Regional age-specific incidence rates differ significantly (Fig. 8.03). Qidong and Hong Kong (China) are high-risk populations for HBV-related HCC. Characteristics of their curves are a steep increase in the ages 20-34 years; in Qidong the curve levels off already at the age of 40. Osaka (Japan) is a high-risk area, but Varese (Italy) is a low to intermediate risk area; approximately 70% of HCC in these populations is related to chronic HCV infection {1417}. Their rates increase at older ages and show relatively high rates over age 55-59. The curve for whites in the USA (SEER data) is representative of both low-risk populations. Males are always more frequently affected than females but high male to female ratios of > 3 in the age-specific rates occur particularly in populations with a high incidence of HCC {1534, 402, 1906, 391, 452}.

Aetiology

Chronic infection with HBV, HCV or both is the most common cause of HCC worldwide {889}. Among Western populations, alcohol-induced liver injury is a leading cause of liver cirrhosis and constitutes the most important HCC risk {426}. In Southern China and sub-Saharan Africa, dietary ingestion of high levels of aflatoxin may present a special environmental hazard, particularly in individuals chronically infected with HBV. Other exogenous factors have also been incriminated, including iron overload {1155}, long-term use of oral contraceptives {1158, 2034}, and high-dose anabolic steroids. The development of liver cirrhosis, particularly in association with inherited genetic diseases such as alpha-1-antitrypsin deficiency or haemochromatosis, place the individual at a greatly increased risk of HCC development.

HCC risk is increased if aetiological risk factors exist in combination, e.g., HCV infection and alcohol use {341} or HBV infection and exposure to aflatoxin {1864}.

Liver cirrhosis

The major clinical HCC risk factor is liver cirrhosis, largely independent of its aetiology (Fig. 8.04). Approximately 70-90% of HCCs develop in patients with macronodular cirrhosis which is characterised by the presence of large nodules

of varying size (up to several centimeters in diameter), containing portal fields and efferent veins, separated by broad, irregularly shaped connective tissue septae and scars. Macronodular and mixed macro-micro-nodular cirrhosis are typically caused by or associated with viral hepatitis, metabolic disorders, and toxic liver injury. Micronodular cirrhosis is characterised by uniform nodules of approximately 3 mm that lack the typical role for HBV in the development of liver architecture and do not contain a central vein. They are typically observed as a consequence of alcoholic liver disease, haemochromatosis, and biliary cirrhosis.

Hepatitis B virus (HBV)

HBV is a small DNA virus belonging to the group of hepatotropic DNA viruses known as hepadnaviruses. HBV consists of an outer envelope, composed mainly of hepatitis B surface antigen (HBsAg), and an internal core (nucleocapsid), which contains hepatitis B core antigen (HBcAg), a DNA polymerase/reverse transcriptase, and the viral genome. The genome consists of a partly double-stranded circular DNA molecule of about 3200 base pairs with known sequence and genetic organisation. In recent years, HBV variants with mutations in viral genes and in some regulatory genetic elements have been detected in patients with HBV infection; these mutations can have biological consequences. Epidemiological studies have convincingly shown that HCC development is closely associated with chronic HBV infection. The incidence of HCC in chron-

ically HBV-infected individuals is approximately 100 times higher than in the uninfected population, and the lifetime risk of males infected at birth approaches 50%. In the absence of a common molecular mechanism for HBV-induced hepatocarcinogenesis, definitive proof for a direct oncogenic role of HBV is still lacking. Nevertheless, at least three lines of evidence support a direct oncogenic role for HBV in the development of HCC: (1) integration of HBV DNA into the chromosomal DNA of HCCs, (2) the role of the HBV X gene in the pathogenesis of HBV-associated HCCs, in particular its binding to and inactivation of p53, and (3) HCC development in animal models of chronic hepadnavirus infection. In addition, the declining HCC incidence following HBV vaccination clearly supports the aetiological contribution {275}. Chronic hepatitis D virus (HDV) infection does not increase the risk of HCC development over that of HBV infection alone, but the latency period between HDV infection and HCC development is 30-40

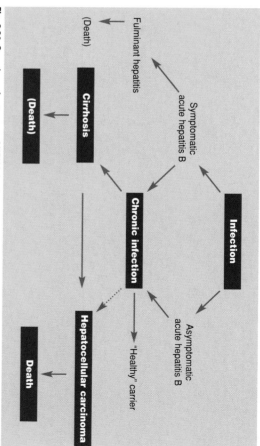

Fig. 8.04 Overview of outcome of HBV infection.

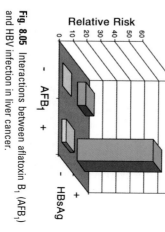

Fig. 8.05 Interactions between aflatoxin B₁ (AFB₁) and HBV infection in liver cancer.

years, compared with 30-60 years for HBV infection alone.

Hepatitis C virus (HCV)

HCV has a single-stranded RNA genome of positive polarity, around 10 kb in length, that codes for a single polyprotein consisting of 3010-3033 amino acids. Post-translational processing in the 5'-3' direction yields the structural protein C (RNA-binding nucleocapsid protein) and the E1 and E2 envelope proteins, and the non-structural proteins NS1-NS5, including RNA-dependent RNA polymerase {321}.

As soon as the HCV genome was cloned, it became evident that viruses isolated from various geographic regions have marked genetic heterogeneity. Sequence comparison shows at least 6 different HCV genotypes. Although mutations have been identified in all regions of the HCV genome, the genes for the envelope proteins E1 and E2 appear to be particularly variable. A mutation rate of 1 or 2 nucleotides per 1000 bases per infection-year appears to be characteristic of chronic HCV infection. This mutation rate is about 10 times higher than that of HBV. Some HCV genotypes may be more frequently associated with HCC development than others {321}.

Anti-HCV antibodies are found in 15-80% of HCC patients, depending on the patient population studied. HCV appears to be a major cause of HCC in Japan, Italy, and Spain, but it seems to play a less important role in South Africa and Taiwan {321}. HCV-associated HCCs typically develop after 20-30 years of infection and are generally preceded by liver cirrhosis. Thus far, there is no evidence to suggest that HCV integrates into the cellular genome or has another direct role in the molecular pathogenesis of HCC. Rather, HCC develops via HCV-induced chronic liver injury, progressing to fibrosis and cirrhosis.

alcohol and have coexisting liver disease from other causes (such as chronic HCV infection) have the highest risk for HCC development {341, 1432, 1508, 2106}.

Aflatoxin B_1 (AFB_1)

AFB_1 is a potent liver carcinogen in several animal species as well as in humans {2128}. It is produced by the moulds *Aspergillus parasiticus* and *Aspergillus flavus* which under hot and humid conditions in tropical countries typically contaminate grain, particularly ground nuts (peanuts). Dietary ingestion of high levels of aflatoxins presents a significant environmental hazard, particularly in the context of coexisting chronic HBV infection {1864, 1265} which leads to a more than 50-fold increase in the risk of developing HCC (Fig. 8.05).

AFB_1 is metabolized by cytochrome P450 enzymes to its reactive form, AFB_1-5,9-oxide, which covalently binds to cellular macromolecules. Reaction with DNA at the N7 position of guanine preferentially causes a G:C > T:A muta-

Alcohol

Among Western populations, alcohol-induced liver injury is the leading cause of chronic liver disease and liver cirrhosis and constitutes the most important HCC risk factor {426}. Regular daily consumption of > 50g ethanol in females or > 80g in males is generally considered sufficient to induce liver cirrhosis, although individual susceptibility can vary considerably. Patients who abuse

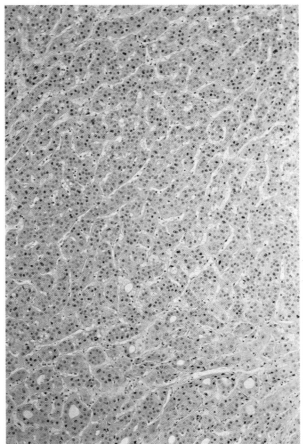

Fig. 8.06 Hepatocellular carcinoma. **A** Nodular type. **B** Massive type. **C** Diffuse type. **D** Multifocal type.

Fig. 8.07 Hepatocellular carcinoma, trabecular.

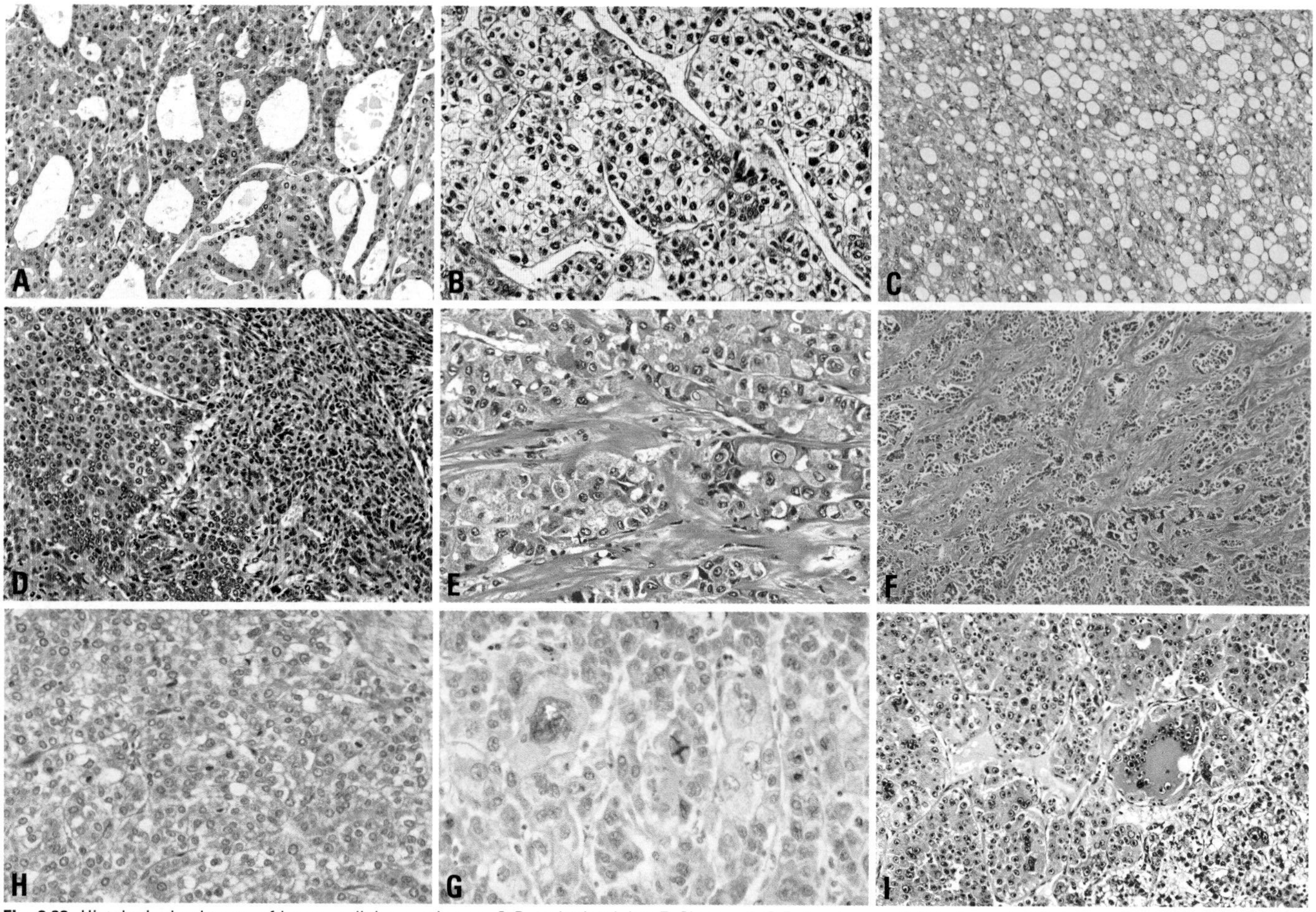

tion in codon 249 of the TP53 tumour suppressor gene, leading to an amino acid substitution of arginine to serine {188}. In Southern China and Subsaharan Africa, the two world regions with the highest levels of food contamination with AFB$_1$, this mutation is present in > 40% of HCC {1265} and can be detected in serum DNA of patients with preneoplastic lesions and HCC {924}. In regions where AFB$_1$ levels in food are very low or undetectable, codon 249 transversion mutations are either very rare or absent.

Clinical features

Symptoms and signs

Most HCC patients have a past or current history of chronic liver disease from different causes {1681}. The major clinical risk factor for HCC development is liver cirrhosis; 70-90% of HCCs develop in a macronodular cirrhosis {452}. The presenting symptoms in patients with HCC include abdominal pain, gen-eral malaise, anorexia or weight loss, and nausea or vomiting. The symptoms are caused by the underlying chronic liver disease or cirrhosis and its clinical complications, or by the HCC itself. The most common clinical signs in HCC patients are hepatomegaly, ascites, fever, jaundice, and splenomegaly.

The laboratory findings are in part determined by the underlying liver disease, which results in elevations of various liver enzymes, such as aspartate amino transferase (AST), alanine aminotransferase (ALT), alkaline phosphatase (AP), gamma-glutamyl-transpeptidase (GGT), and bilirubin. These laboratory parameters are not HCC-specific, however. A significantly raised level of alpha-fetoprotein (AFP) of > 500 ng/ml, or continuously rising values even if less than 100 ng/ml, strongly suggest HCC. However, not all cases of HCC are associated with AFP elevation, and raised AFP may also be found in liver disease without HCC. Furthermore, in the early stages of HCC development, AFP levels do not closely correlate with clinical HCC stage. AFP levels, therefore, have to be interpreted individually in the context of other clinical symptoms and signs as well as imaging studies. Another HCC-specific marker is des-gamma-carboxyprothrombin (DCP), which is roughly equivalent to AFP. Occasionally, HCC patients develop a paraneoplastic syndrome, with erythrocytosis, hypoglycaemia or hypercalcaemia.

Imaging

Imaging studies are important in patient management for the identification and localization of HCC. Useful techniques include ultrasonography of the liver and the abdomen, colour Doppler ultrasonography, computed tomography (CT), lipiodol CT, magnetic resonance imaging, angiography, and possibly positron emission tomography. The standard imaging techniques are ultrasonography and CT. In most cases, these allow HCC detection and staging. In patients

Fig. 8.08 Histological subtypes of hepatocellular carcinoma. A Pseudoglandular. B Clear cell. C Fatty change. D Spindle cell. E Scirrhous type. F Scirrhous type, Masson trichrome stain. G Poorly differentiated, with numerous mitotic figures. H Pleomorphic. I Multinucleated giant cell.

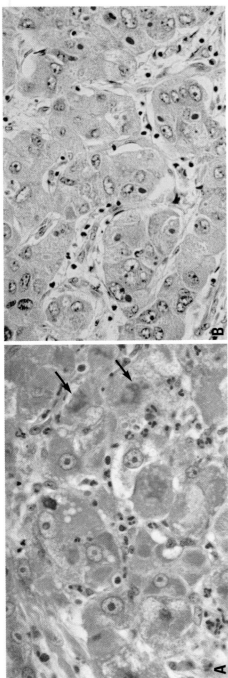

Fig. 8.09 **A** Numerous Mallory bodies in a hepatocellular carcinoma (two examples indicated by arrows). **B** Hyaline inclusions in a hepatocellular carcinoma.

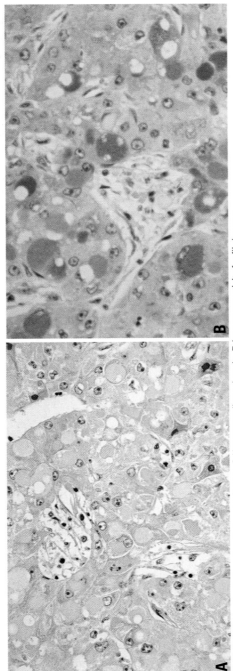

Fig. 8.10 Pale bodies in hepatocellular carcinoma. **A** Haematoxylin and eosin. **B** Immunoreactivity for fibrinogen.

with suspected HCC metastases, a chest X-ray, bone scan, or other imaging modalities may be indicated.

Liver biopsy

The definitive diagnosis of HCC depends on the histological examination of the lesion, especially in AFP-negative patients. Ultrasound- or CT-guided percutaneous biopsy with a 22-gauge needle usually provides sufficient tissue for diagnosis with minimum risk of bleeding or seeding of tumour cells along the needle tract. However, in patients with significantly elevated AFP levels who are potentially eligible for HCC resection or liver transplantation, liver biopsy is not recommended to eliminate the residual risk of tumour cells spreading before surgery.

Macroscopy

Macroscopic features of HCCs vary depending on the size of the tumour and the presence or absence of liver cirrhosis. In general, most HCCs associated

with liver cirrhosis tend to present as an expansile tumour with a fibrous capsule and intratumoural septa, while those without cirrhosis tend to be massive and non-encapsulated. Varying degrees of infiltrative growth, tumour thrombi in the portal veins, and intrahepatic metastases, which are common in advanced tumours, modify the gross appearance. Occasionally, numerous minute tumour

nodules are distributed throughout the liver and may be difficult to be distinguished from regenerative nodules in liver cirrhosis.

Hepatocellular carcinomas are occasionally pedunculated. Patients are usually females and the tumours are thought to arise in accessory lobes of the liver. Following surgical resection, the prognosis is is excellent.

Table 8.01
Immunohistochemistry of HCC.

Antigen	Result
Hepatocyte (Dako)	Positive (most useful in diagnosis)
Polyclonal carcinoembryonic antigen	Positive (canalicular pattern)
Alpha fetoprotein	Positive or negative
Fibrinogen	Positive or negative
Cytokeratins 8 and 18	Usually positive
Cytokeratins 7 and 19	Usually negative
Cytokeratin 20	Usually negative
Epithelial membrane antigen	Negative
BER EP4	Negative

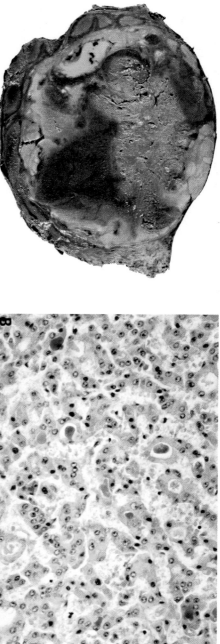

A

Fig. 8.11 Hepatocellular carcinoma in a 17-year old patient with Fanconi anaemia. **A** Green bile staining and extensive necrosis and haemorrhage. **B** Trabecular and pseudoglandular pattern with bile plugs.

B

Tumour spread

Invasion into the blood vessels, in particular into the portal vein, is a characteristic of HCC. Tumour thrombi in the portal veins are present in more than 70% of autopsies of advanced HCCs. Intrahepatic metastases is caused mostly by tumour spread through the portal vein branches. Tumour invasion into the major bile ducts is infrequent clinically, but found in about 6% of autopsy cases. Extrahepatic metastasis is mostly haematogenous, the lungs being the most common target. Regional lymphatic metastasis is frequent though distant lymph nodes are rarely involved.

Histopathology

HCCs consist of tumour cells that resemble hepatocytes. The stroma is composed of sinusoid-like blood spaces lined by a single layer of endothelial cells. Unlike the sinusoidal endothelial cells in normal liver tissue, those of HCC are immunohistochemically positive for CD34 and factor-VIII-related antigen. Ultrastructural observation shows a basement-membrane-like structure between the endothelial cells and tumour cell trabeculae, and basement-membrane-like materials are immunohistochemically positive with antibodies for laminin and type IV collagen. Thus, the sinusoid-like blood spaces resemble capillary vessels. This phenotypic change of sinusoids is called 'capillarization' {472, 919, 917}. In the sinusoidal blood spaces, varying numbers of macrophages, which show immunohistochemical positivity with anti-lysozyme and CD68, are also present and resemble Kupffer cells in well differ-

entiated tumours {1894}. HCCs vary architecturally and cytologically. The different architectural patterns and cytological variants frequently occur in combination. Immunohistochemical features of HCC are summarized in Table 8.01.

Architectural patterns

Trabecular (plate-like). This pattern is the most common in well and moderately differentiated HCCs. Tumour cells grow in cords of variable thickness that are separated by sinusoid-like blood spaces. Well-differentiated tumours have a thin trabecular pattern and trabeculae become thicker with de-differentiation. Sinusoid-like blood spaces often show varying degrees of dilatation, and peliosis hepatis-like change are occasionally observed in advanced HCCs.

Pseudoglandular and acinar. HCC frequently has a glandular pattern, usually admixed with the trabecular pattern. The glandular structure is formed mostly by a single layer of tumour cells, and some glandular or acinar structures are formed by dilatation of the bile canaliculus-like structure between cancer cells. Pseudoglands frequently contain proteinaceous fluids, which often stain with PAS but do not stain with mucicarmine or Alcian blue. Bile may be present. Cystic dilatation of the pseudoglands sometimes occurs, such dilated glands are occasionally formed by degeneration of thick trabeculae. Generally, the glandular structure is smaller in well differentiated tumours than in moderately differentiated tumours.

Compact. Sinusoid-like blood spaces are inconspicuous and slit-like, giving the tumour a solid appearance.

Scirrhous. This uncommon type is characterised by marked fibrosis along the sinusoid-like blood spaces with varying degrees of atrophy of tumour trabeculae. It is observed even in small tumours. The scirrhous type should not be confused with cholangiocarcinoma or fibrolamellar carcinoma. Similar fibrotic changes occur following chemotherapy, radiation, and transchemo arterial embolization. Such post-therapeutic fibrosis should be distinguished from the scirrhous variant. The term 'sclerosing hepatic carcinoma'

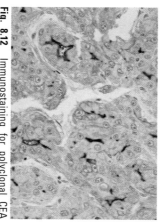

Fig. 8.12 Immunostaining for polyclonal CEA demonstrates canaliculi in a hepatocellular carcinoma.

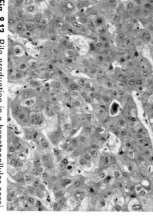

Fig. 8.13 Bile production in a hepatocellular carcinoma.

{1424}, which has been used to designate a variety of tumours arising in non-cirrhotic livers and associated with hypercalcemia, does not constitute a distinct histopathological entity {806}, some of these tumours appear to be hepatocellular, but others are intrahepatic (peripheral) cholangiocarcinomas.

Cytological variants

Pleomorphic cell. Tumour cells show marked variation in cellular and nuclear size, shape, and staining. Bizarre multinucleated or mononuclear giant cells are often present, and osteoclast-like giant cells may be seen rarely. Generally, pleomorphic tumour cells lack cohesiveness and do not show a distinct trabecular pattern. Pleomorphic cells are common in poorly differentiated tumours.

Clear cell. The tumour consists predominantly of cells with clear cytoplasm due to the presence of abundant glycogen. This type is sometimes difficult to distinguish from metastatic renal cell carcinoma of clear cell type.

Sarcomatous change. HCC occasionally appears sarcomatous, characterised by the proliferation of spindle cells or bizarre giant cells. When the tumour consists solely of sarcomatous cells, it is difficult to distinguish from sarcomas such as fibrosarcoma and myogenic sarcoma. When sarcomatous features are predominant, the tumour is called sarcomatoid HCC or sarcomatous HCC. In many cases, however, the sarcomatous change is present in a part of the tumour, and transitional features between trabecular HCC and sarcomatous components are frequent. Sarcomatous change is more frequent in cases with repeated chemo-therapy or transchemo arterial embolization {953}; but it is also seen in small tumours. Most sarcomatous cells are positive for vimentin or desmin but negative for albumin and

alpha-fetoprotein. Some are also positive for cytokeratin.

Fatty change. Diffuse fatty change is most frequent in small, early-stage tumours less than 2 cm in diameter. Its frequency declines as tumour size increases, and fatty changes are rather infrequent in advanced tumours. Metabolic disorders related to hepatocarcinogenesis and insufficient blood supply in the early neoplastic stage have been suggested as a possible mechanism for the development of fatty change in small tumours, but a definite mechanism has not yet been determined.

Bile production. Bile is occasionally observed, usually as plugs in dilated canaliculi or pseudoglands. When bile production is prominent, the tumour is yellowish in color and turns green after formalin fixation.

Mallory hyaline bodies are intracytoplasmic, irregular in shape, eosinophilic and PAS-negative. They consist of aggregated intermediate filaments and show immunohistochemical positivity with anti-ubiquitin antibodies.

Globular hyaline bodies are small, round, homogeneous, and strongly acidophilic intracytoplasmic bodies. They are PAS-positive and stain orange to red with Masson trichrome stain. Immunohistochemically, they are often positive for alpha-1-antitrypsin.

Pale bodies are intracytoplasmic, round to ovoid, amorphous and lightly eosinophilic. They represent an accumulation of amorphous materials in cystically dilated endoplasmic reticulum, and show distinct immunohistochemical positivity with anti-fibrinogen {1846}. They are commonly seen in the fibrolamellar variant of HCC but are also found in the common types of HCC, especially in the scirrhous HCC.

Ground glass inclusions are rarely observed in tumours of HBsAg-positive

patients. They stain with modified orcein, Victoria blue, or aldehyde fuchsin, and show immunohistochemical positivity with anti-HBsAg antibody. They are not seen in tumour casts in the portal vein or in extrahepatic metastases, and most are thought to be HBsAg-positive hepatocytes entrapped in a tumour.

Fibrolamellar HCC

This variant usually arises in non-cirrhotic livers of adolescents or young adults {353}. It is rare in Asian and African countries but not so rare in Western countries. The tumour cells grow in sheets or small trabeculae that are separated by hyalinized collagen bundles with a characteristic lamellar pattern. They are large and polygonal and have a deeply eosinophilic and coarsely granular cytoplasm and distinct nucleoli. The eosinophilic granularity is due to the presence of a large number of mitochondria. Pale bodies are frequently present, and stainable copper, usually in association with bile, can occasionally be shown.

Undifferentiated carcinoma

Undifferentiated carcinoma is rare, accounting for less than 2% of epithelial liver tumours. There is male preponderance but data on geographical distribution are not available. Localization, clinical features, symptoms and signs, and diagnostic procedures display no difference as compared to hepatocellular carcinoma. Undifferentiated carcinomas are postulated to have a worse prognosis (compared to HCC), although greater case numbers to support this are not available {351, 806}.

Grading

According to histological grade, HCC is classified into well differentiated, moderately differentiated, poorly differentiated, and undifferentiated types.

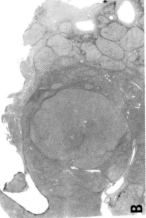

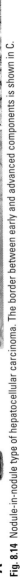

Fig. 8.14 Nodule-in-nodule type of hepatocellular carcinoma. The border between early and advanced components is shown in C.

Tumours of the liver and intrahepatic bile ducts

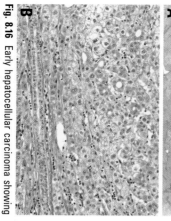

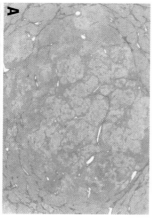

Fig. 8.15 A, B Fibrolamellar type of hepatocellular carcinoma.

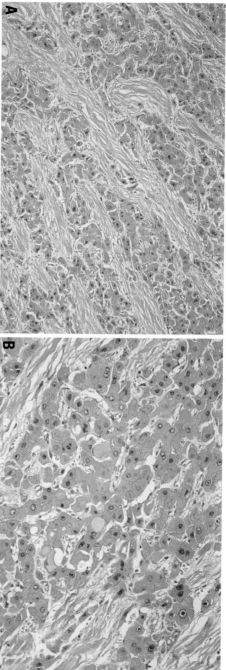

Fig. 8.15 A, B Fibrolamellar type of hepatocellular carcinoma.

Well differentiated HCC. This is most commonly seen in small, early-stage tumours less than 2 cm in diameter and is rare in advanced tumours. The lesions are composed of cells with minimal atypia and increased nuclear/cytoplasmic ratio in a thin trabecular pattern, with frequent pseudoglandular or acinar structures and frequent fatty change. In most tumours larger than 3 cm in diameter, well-differentiated carcinoma is observed only in the periphery if at all.

Moderately differentiated HCC. The moderately differentiated type is the commonest in tumours larger than 3 cm in diameter and is characterized by tumour cells arranged in trabeculae of three or more cells in thickness. Tumour cells have abundant eosinophilic cytoplasm and round nuclei with distinct nucleoli. A pseudoglandular pattern is also frequent, and pseudoglands frequently contain bile or proteinaceous fluid.

Poorly differentiated HCC. This proliferates in a solid pattern without distinct sinusoid-like blood spaces, and only slitlike blood vessels are observed in large tumour nests. Neoplastic cells show an increased nuclear/cytoplasmic ratio and frequent cellular pleomorphism, including bizarre giant cells. Poorly differentiated HCC is extremely rare in small early-stage tumours.

Malignant progression of HCC. HCC is known to vary histologically even within a single nodule. From the viewpoint of histological grade, most cancer nodules less than 1 cm in diameter have a uniform distribution of well differentiated cancerous tissues, whereas approximately 40% of cancer nodules 1.0-3.0 cm in diameter consist of more than 2 types of tissue of different histological grades {900}. Less differentiated tissues are always located inside, surrounded by well differentiated tumour on the outside. The area of well differentiated neoplasm diminishes as the tumour size increases, and they are completely replaced by less-well-differentiated cancerous tissues when the tumour size reaches a diameter of around 3 cm. When less-well-differentiated areas within a well differentiated tumour nodule are growing expansively, the nodule often has a 'nodule-in-nodule' appearance {1275}.

Multicentric development of HCC

HCCs frequently occur as multiple intrahepatic nodules. Genetic analysis of HBV integration pattern, chromosomal allele loss, and mutational inactivation of tumour suppressor genes has indicated multicentric independent development of these nodules {1647, 1392}. These studies have shown that nodules apparently growing from portal vein tumour thrombi or satellite nodules surrounding a large main tumour represent intrahepatic metastases, whereas other nodules can be considered multicentric HCCs if they satisfy any of the following three criteria: (1) multiple, small early-stage HCCs or concurrent small early-stage HCCs and classical HCCs; (2) presence of peripheral areas of well differentiated HCC in both lesions or in the smaller ones; and (3) multiple HCCs of obviously different histology.

Multicentric HCCs are associated with a high rate of tumour recurrence, even after curative resection, making treatment difficult and the prognosis poor. The presence of hyperplastic foci, small-cell dysplasia, an increase in the proliferative activity of non-tumourous liver tissue, or the progression of background liver disease are risk factors for multicentric HCC development {1902, 1859}.

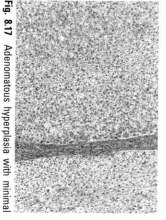

Fig. 8.16 Early hepatocellular carcinoma showing well differentiated histological features.

Fig. 8.17 Adenomatous hyperplasia with minimal nuclear atypia and without features of malignancy.

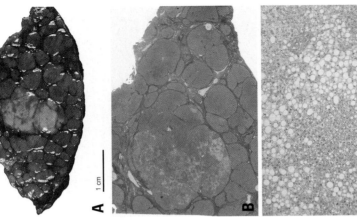

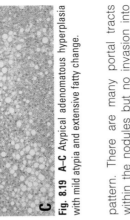

Fig. 8.19 A–C Atypical adenomatous hyperplasia with mild atypia and extensive fatty change.

Precursor and benign lesions
Early stage HCC and precancerous lesions

Because of remarkable advances in imaging techniques and their widespread availability, increased numbers of small HCCs are detected clinically. Liver transplantation has become common treatment for liver cirrhosis and HCC in highly selected cases. Studies of resected and explant livers have revealed new information about the morphological characteristics of small early-stage HCC and equivocal nodular lesions. The most striking information is that HCC associated with cirrhosis probably evolves from precancerous lesions, and well differentiated HCC further progresses to a less differentiated form {952, 1646, 1882, 1645, 81}.

Histological features of small early-stage HCC

Although some small HCCs show features of classical HCCs, most less than 1.5 cm in diameter are vaguely nodular with indistinct margins macroscopically and have a uniform distribution of well differentiated cancerous tissues. They are characterized by increased cell density with increased nuclear/cytoplasmic ratio, increased staining intensity (eosinophilic or basophilic), irregular thin trabecular pattern with a frequent acinar or pseudoglandular pattern, and fatty change {959, 1324}. Diffuse fatty change of tumour cells is present in approximately 40% of tumours less than 2 cm in diameter. Many portal tracts are present within the tumour nodule, and tumour cell invasion into some portal tracts can be seen. At the tumour boundary, neoplastic cells proliferate as though they are replacing normal hepatocytes ('replacing growth'), and there is no capsule formation. These small tumours may correspond to 'carcinoma in-situ' or 'microinvasive carcinoma' of the liver. They tend to preserve the underlying liver structures, including portal tracts, receive portal blood supply, and do not show tumour blushing in angiographic examinations. In contrast, classical HCCs, even if small and well differentiated, show tumour blushing without portal flow {1883}. Invasion into the stromal tissue can be sometimes identified, but vascular invasion and intrahepatic metastases are exceptional {1942}. Moreover, these lesions are locally curable, have a favorable long-term outcome, and can be defined clinically as 'early HCC'.

Adenomatous hyperplasia (dysplastic nodules)

This lesion is characterized by marked enlargement of individual cirrhotic nodules that show thick liver cell plates. Small nodular lesions, most of which are below 1.5 cm in size, have been noticed in the livers of patients with HCCs that have been resected surgically and in explant cirrhotic livers. The nodules show variable atypia but lack features of definite malignancy. Macroscopically, most lesions are vaguely nodular and are not much different from small, well differentiated HCC with indistinct margins; it is almost impossible to distinguish them from cancer on the one hand or from large regenerative nodules on the other hand. Microscopically, they are characterized by a moderate increase in cell density with a slightly irregular trabecular pattern. There are many portal tracts within the nodules but no invasion into the portal tracts. These nodules sometimes contain distinct, well differentiated cancer foci. Many of them gave rise to distinct HCC in clinical follow-up studies {1882, 1645} and are, therefore, considered precancerous lesions. Some of

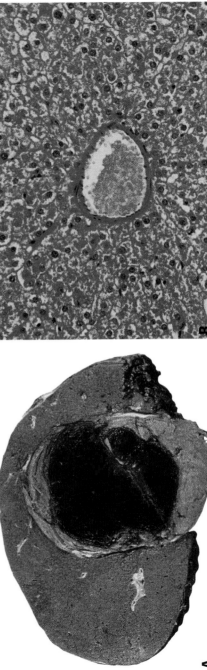

Fig. 8.18 Adenoma. **A** Extensive central haemorrhage. **B** Benign appearing hepatocytes arranged in plates, one or two cells thick.

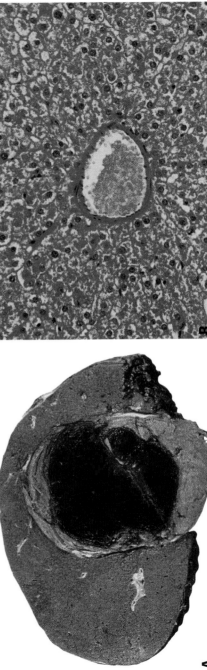

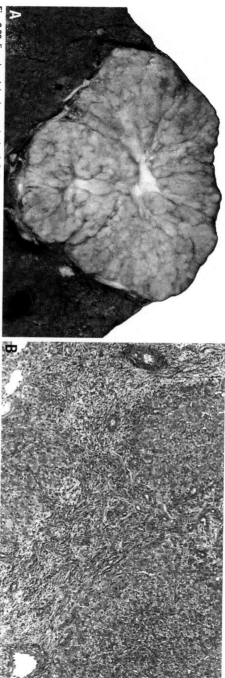

Fig. 8.20 Focal nodular hyperplasia. **A** Solitary lobulated nodule with typical central stellate scar. **B** Masson trichrome stain shows extensive blue connective tissue component.

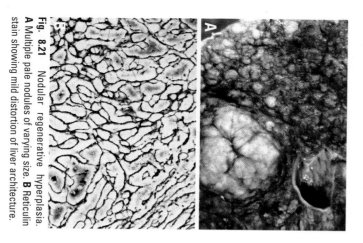

Fig. 8.21 Nodular regenerative hyperplasia. **A** Multiple pale nodules of varying size. **B** Reticulin stain showing mild distortion of liver architecture.

these nodules contain areas with a marked increase in cell density, a more irregular trabecular pattern, and frequent fatty change, characteristic of well differentiated HCC but insufficient in extent to warrant such a diagnosis.

These foci have been designated adenomatous hyperplasia {1080, 806} or dysplastic nodule {64}. Additional terms used for these lesions include macroregenerative nodule, hyperplastic nodule and borderline lesions.

Morphological criteria for the differential diagnosis of adenomatous hyperplasia (dysplastic nodule, low grade), atypical adenomatous hyperplasia (dysplastic

nodule, high grade) and early-stage HCC are still under discussion, mainly due to the lack of objective phenotypic or genotypic markers {1080, 64, 805}.

Focal liver cell dysplasia (LCD)

Large cell dysplasia. The term liver cell dysplasia (LCD) was first coined by Anthony et al. {73} to describe a change characterized by cellular enlargement, nuclear pleomorphism and multinucleation of liver cells occurring in groups or occupying whole cirrhotic nodules. The change was found in only 1% of patients with normal livers, in 7% of patients with cirrhosis and in 65% of patients with cirrhosis and HCC. There was a strong relationship between LCD and HBsAg seropositivity {73}. They concluded that the presence of LCD identified a group of patients at high risk for development of HCC, and that such patients should be followed by serial alpha-fetoprotein determinations.

Small cell dysplasia. Watanabe et al. {2068} have expanded the original definition of LCD to include a 'small cell' variant. The nuclear/cytoplasmic ratio is increased in small cell dysplasia, the ratio being between that of large cell and normal hepatocytes. This is in contrast to large cell dysplasia that has normal nuclear/cytoplasmic ratio. Also, multinucleation and large nucleoli are characteristic of large cell dysplasia but not small cell dysplasia. The small dysplastic cells have more of a tendency to form small round foci than large dysplastic cells. On the basis of their morphological and morphometric studies, Watanabe et al. {2068} proposed the

hypothesis that small cell dysplasia, rather than large cell dysplasia, is the precancerous lesion in man.

Hepatocellular adenoma

A benign tumour composed of cells closely resembling normal hepatocytes, which are arranged in plates separated by sinusoids. On gross examination, adenomas are soft, rounded, yellow or tan masses, often with areas of necrosis, haemorrhage, and fibrosis. A fibrous capsule is uncommon. Lesions are solitary in two-thirds of cases {511}. When more than 10 lesions are encountered, a diagnosis of 'adenomatosis' has been recommended {511}.

Adenoma is histologically composed of benign-appearing hepatocytes arranged in plates one or two cells in thickness {64, 803, 351, 71}. Portal tracts are absent; the lesion is supplied by arteries and veins. In most cases, the tumour cells are uniform in size and shape, but occasionally, mild to moderate cytological variation may be seen. Mitotic activity is almost never found. Lipofuscin, fat and clear cell change (due to water or glycogen accumulation) are often present in the cytoplasm. Haemorrhage, infarction, fibrosis, and peliosis hepatis may be seen.

The differential diagnosis may be difficult with small biopsies. Features suggesting hepatocellular carcinoma include mitoses, high nuclear/cytoplasmic ratio, and plates more than 2 cells in thickness. Loss of a normal reticulin pattern is common in HCC whereas it is preserved in hepatocellular adenoma. HCC typically also shows diffuse capillarization using

CD34 immunostain in comparison with hepatocellular adenoma, which is either negative or shows only focal staining. Any evidence of ductular differentiation suggests a regenerative lesion such as focal nodular hyperplasia (FNH). Portal tracts within the peripheral portion of an adenoma may cause confusion.

The clinical setting is an important consideration in differential diagnosis. Most patients have a known risk factor, especially the use of contraceptive or anabolic steroids. Glycogen storage disease has also been associated. A diagnosis of adenoma should be made with caution in the absence of a known cause or in the presence of cirrhosis, where dysplastic nodules, carcinoma, and large regenerative nodules are far more frequent.

Focal nodular hyperplasia (FNH)

A lesion composed of hyperplastic hepatic parenchyma, subdivided into nodules by fibrous septa which may form stellate scars. The majority of FNH lesions are asymptomatic. Infarction may lead to abdominal pain but rupture is rare. When more than one FNH lesion is present the patient often has other features suggesting a systemic abnormality of angiogenesis, including hepatic haemangioma, intra-cranial lesions (vascular malformations, meningeoma, astrocytoma), and dysplasia of large muscular arteries {2054, 2055}.

Most FNH lesions are solitary, firm, and lobulated nodules (Fig. 8.20). Lesions on the surface of the liver may protrude above the capsule. On cut section, they are circumscribed but not encapsulated, and paler than the surrounding liver. They typically consist of a central stellate scar surrounded by parenchymal nodules. Although most lesions are paler than the surrounding liver, a less common telangiectatic type has prominent blood-filled vascular spaces {64, 2055}.

Histologically, FNH has a regular hierarchical structure defined by the arterial supply, which is usually a single artery with several orders of branching. Each terminal branch is located in the center of a 1 mm nodule. The large arteries often have degenerative changes in the media and eccentric intimal fibrosis. The arteries are found in a fibrous stroma without portal veins and usually without ducts. Proliferating ductules are usually present and may be prominent, com- monly with visible features of chronic cholestasis (cholate stasis, copper accumulation) and neutrophil infiltration. Nascent FNH is a small region of hyperplasia or dilated sinusoids, recognised in the context of more definite FNH lesions. The rare telangiectatic type of FNH has a similar arterial supply but with markedly dilated sinusoids comprising at least a quarter of the lesion.

The histological differential diagnosis of FNH includes cirrhosis, in which septa contain portal areas, and hepatocellular adenoma. If the ductular component is not sampled, an unequivocal diagnosis may not be possible.

Nodular regenerative hyperplasia (NRH)

This condition is characterized by small regenerative nodules dispersed throughout the liver, associated with acinar atrophy with occlusive portal vascular lesions.

The liver has a normal weight and shape with a fine granularity of the capsular surface. The cut surface demonstrates a diffuse nodularity with most nodules measuring 1-2 mm. Occasionally, there are clusters of nodules up to several cm in diameter {64, 2056, 2053}. The nodules are paler than the atrophic hepatic parenchyma which surrounds them. Microscopically, the normal architecture is mildly distorted by widespread atrophy admixed with numerous monoacinar regenerative nodules. The nodules are composed of normal-appearing hepatocytes in plates 1-2 cells wide centered on portal tracts. The atrophic regions have small hepatocytes in thin trabeculae with dilated sinusoids. No significant paren-chymal fibrosis is present but numerous small portal veins are obliterated.

Histological diagnosis of NRH depends on the recognition of a nodular architecture in the absence of parenchymal fibrosis. Nodularity may be suspected when there are two adjacent populations of hepatocytes that are normal and atrophic, respectively. This pattern is best appreciated on a reticulin stain. Macro-nodular, incomplete septal, or regressed cirrhosis commonly have regions with this configuration, especially in livers with healed portal vein thrombosis {1742}. These forms of cirrhosis are difficult to exclude in a small biopsy.

Genetic susceptibility

Several rare inherited disorders of metabolism are associated with an increased risk of developing HCC.

Carbohydrate metabolism disorders

In glycogen storage disease (GSD), especially type 1 {323}, HCC can develop within preexisting adenomatous lesions {137}. Distinction between benign and malignant tumours is difficult, since GSD-associated HCCs are well differentiated, and atypical lesions ('nodule within nodule' pattern and Mallory bodies) are found commonly in GSD-related adenomas {137, 1527}. Cirrhosis is never present.

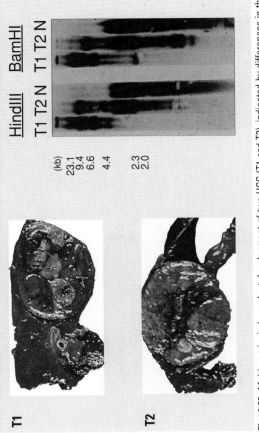

Fig. 8.22 Multicentric, independent development of two HCC (T1 and T2), indicated by differences in their HBV DNA integration pattern. (N, normal tissue)

Protein metabolism disorders

In alpha-1-antitrypsin deficiency (A1ATD) {1501}, only male A1ATD homozygotes are at high risk for HCC, even in the absence of cirrhosis {473}. Further-more, cholangiocarcinomas and combined hepatocellular and cholangiocarcinomas in non-cirrhotic livers of adult patients with heterozygous A1ATD of PiZ type are well documented {2207}. HCC occurs in 18%-35% of patients with hereditary tyrosinaemia {2082, 1996}. The non-tumourous liver is cirrhotic and often dys-plastic {808}. HCC has further been reported in 14% of adult-onset cases of hypercitrullinaemia in the absence of cir-rhosis {1324A}.

Disorders of porphyrin metabolism.

The prevalence of HCC in porphyria cutanea tarda (PCT) ranges from 7% to 47% {1755, 1073}. Almost all HCCs occur in male patients older than 50 years with preexisting cirrhosis and a long-standing history of symptomatic PCT. The involve-ment of additional risk factors is likely {396}. Rarely, PCT evolves as a para-neoplastic syndrome associated with HCC {1389}. Other hepatic porphyrias

are occasionally associated with HCC {1073, 53}.

Chronic cholestatic syndromes.

HCC may complicate paucity of intra-hepatic bile ducts {1028, 99, 898}, biliary atresia {2082}, congenital hepatic fibrosis {2082}, and Byler syndrome {1550}.

Metal-storage diseases.

The relative risk for the development of primary liver cancer in inherited haemochromatosis has been calculated as being greater than 200 {181, 1351, 487}. HCC develops usually in patients with cirrhosis {403, 951}, even after iron depletion {403}. Iron-free foci (defined as clear-cut, sublobular, hepatocytic nod-ules free of iron or having significantly less iron than the surrounding parenchy-ma) may represent an early step of HCC in genetic haemochromatosis {403}. In Wilson's disease, HCC is present only exceptionally {293}.

Hepatic vascular anomalies.

Cases of HCC have been occasionally reported in hereditary haemorrhagic

telangiectasia {831} and ataxia-telang-iectasia {2083}.

Extrahepatic inherited conditions.

Several cases of HCC have been report-ed in familial adenomatous polyposis of the colon {1000}. Occasional cases have also been described in neurofibromato-sis, Soto syndrome, and situs inversus {2082}. Cases of hepatocellular adeno-mas and HCC in young patients with Fanconi anaemia have been also described {1033}.

Genetics

Clonal expansion and subclonal progres-sion during multistage carcinogenesis

Most HCCs are associated with HBV or HCV infection. Clonal expansion of hepa-tocytes is initiated during regeneration in damaged livers; a clonal integration pat-tern of HBV was identified in cirrhotic nodules {2170}. Advanced HCCs often emerge as 'nodule-in-nodule' HCCs; the early and advanced HCC components of a 'nodule-in-nodule' type HCC showed identical integration patterns of HBV {1968, 1647}. Ordinary HCCs with in-creased cell proliferation and neovascu-larization are subsequently formed.

TP53 mutations

Point and frameshift mutations of the TP53 tumour suppressor gene are fre-quent in areas with low exposure to afla-toxin B₁ {1393}. TP53 mutations were most frequent and were clustered in domains IV and V in poorly differentiated HCCs, but were less frequent and equal-ly distributed in domains II to V in well or moderately differentiated HCCs in one study {1393}. Analysis of 'nodule-in-nod-ule' type HCC shows that TP53 mutation is associated with the progression of HCC from an early to a more advanced stage {1392, 1391}. In areas with high exposure to AFB₁, mutation of the third nucleotide in codon 249 of TP53 is frequent {758, 188}, sug-gesting that some TP53 mutations can be fingerprints of past exposure to a given carcinogen (see 'Aetiology', above).

HBV X

The HBV X open reading frame is fre-quently integrated and expressed. HBV X [MLS1] can bind to the C terminus of p53, inhibits its sequence-specific DNA binding and transcriptional activation and suppresses p53-induced apoptosis

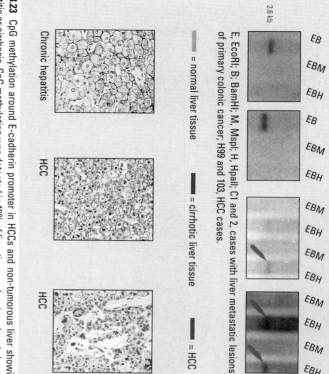

Fig. 8.23 CpG methylation around E-cadherin promoter in HCCs and non-tumorous liver showing chronic hepatitis or cirrhosis. CpG methylation was detected in 46% of liver tissues showing chronic hepatitis or cir-rhosis and 67% of HCCs. Heterogenous E-cadherin expression was detected in hepatocytes in 7 (41%) of the 17 liver tissues showing chronic hepatitis or cirrhosis; small focal areas of hepatocytes showed only slight E-cadherin immunoreactivity. Reduced E-cadherin expression was observed in 10 (59%), in which over 50% of the HCC cells in each patient lacked or showed only slight E-cadherin immunoreactivity, of the 17 HCCs.

E, EcoRI; B; BamHI; M, MspI; H, HpaII, C1 and 2, cases with liver metastatic lesions of primary colonic cancer; H99 and 103, HCC cases.

= normal liver tissue   = cirrhotic liver tissue

= HCC

{2050, 2051, 457}; HBV X may affect a wide range of p53 functions and thereby contribute to the molecular pathogenesis of HCCs. HBV X further inhibits nucleotide excision repair {858}.

Oncogenes

Mutational activation of known oncogenes is rare. Point mutations of the *c-KRAS* gene and coamplification of the cyclin D1 gene were detected in only 3% {1967} and 11% {1355} of HCCs, respectively.

Recent findings, obtained by comparative genomic hybridization of amplified sequences mapped to 11q12, 12p11, and 14q12, may lead to the characterization of new genes involved in hepatocarcinogenesis {1163}.

Wnt pathway and beta-catenin

In the wingless/Wnt pathway, mutations of the β-catenin gene were detected in 26–41% of HCCs {386, 760}. Nuclear accumulation of β-catenin was observed by immunohistochemistry in all HCCs with β-catenin mutations {760}. No mutation was detected in mutation cluster region of the *APC* gene in any of 22 HCCs analysed {760}. Deletions on chromosomes 1p, 4q, and 16p were significantly associated with the absence of β-catenin mutation, which suggests that a β-catenin-activating mutation is involved in cases without chromosomal instability {1041}.

Genetic instability and allelic loss

Frequent allelic losses have been found at loci on 1p, 4q, 5q, 8p, 11p, 13q, 16p, 16q, and 17p by restriction fragment length polymorphism analysis {2046, 200, 1970, 2203, 546, 1759, 459, 460}. Loss of heterozygosity (LOH) on chromosome 16 was detected in 52% of informative cases {1970}. The common deleted region lay between *HP* (16q22.1) and *CTRB* (16q22.3-q23.3) loci {1970}. These losses occurred more frequently in HCCs with poor differentiation, of large size, and with metastasis, and were not detected in early-stage HCCs {1970}. LOH on chromosome 16 may be involved in enhancement of tumour aggressiveness. Recent development of microsatellite markers allows an extensive allelotypic analysis {2171, 163, 1307, 1515, 659, 108}. Detailed deletion mapping revealed that allelic loss at a 1-cM-interval flanked by D4S2921 and

D4S2930 loci on 4q35 was frequent in HCCs with poor differentiation and of large size {108}. Inactivation of unidentified tumour suppressor genes within this region may contribute to progression of HCCs.

Microsatellite instability is another pathway for genetic instability other than chromosomal instability. Only 11% of HCCs had replication errors in one study, and the incidence of replication errors correlated significantly with poor differentiation and portal vein involvement of HCCs {961}.

Cell cycle regulators

The gene product of *p16*^INK4 binds to cyclin-dependent kinase (CDK) 4 and prevents CDK4 from forming an active complex with cyclin D. p16 protein loss may contribute to both early- and late-stage hepatocarcinogenesis, because it

was observed in 22% of early-stage HCCs and occurred approximately twice as often in advanced HCCs as in early-stage HCCs {763}. Neither p16 homozygous deletion/mutation nor loss of p16 mRNA expression was observed in HCCs lacking p16 protein {763}, suggesting post-transcriptional inactivation. DNA methylation around the promoter region of the p16 gene has been observed in HCC {1187}.

Expression of *p21WAF1/CIP1* mRNA, a universal CDK inhibitor, was reduced markedly in 38% of HCCs {762}. p21 mRNA expression of HCCs with *TP53* mutations was significantly lower than that of HCCs with wild-type *TP53* {762}. p21 expression is regulated predominantly by dependence on *TP53* in HCCs. mRNA expression of *p27*^Kip1, another universal CDK inhibitor, was reduced in 52% of HCCs {764}.

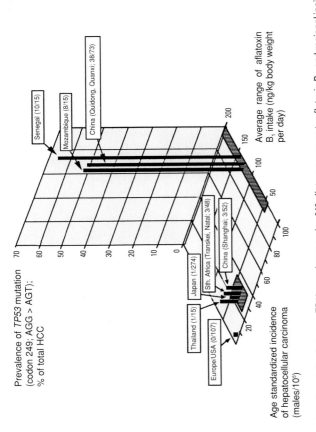

Fig. 8.24 Correlation between *TP53* mutation at codon 249, dietary exposure to aflatoxin B₁, and regional incidence of hepatocellular carcinoma (HCC).

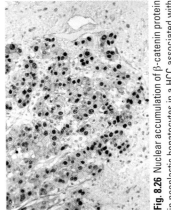

Fig. 8.26 Nuclear accumulation of β-catenin protein in neoplastic hepatocytes in a HCC associated with HCV infection {760}.

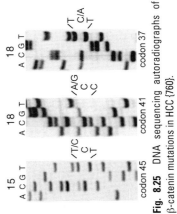

Fig. 8.25 DNA sequencing autoradiographs of β-catenin mutations in HCC {760}.

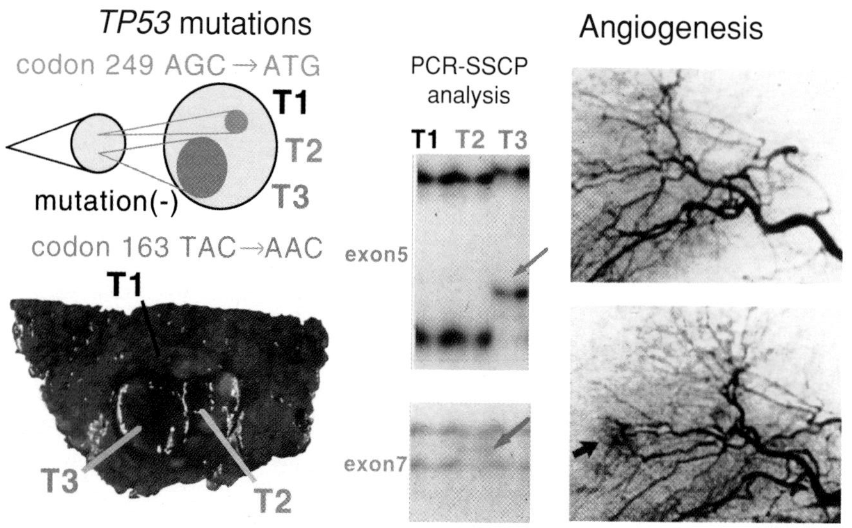

TP53 mutations

codon 249 AGC → ATG

mutation(-)

codon 163 TAC → AAC

Fig. 8.27 Malignant progression in a HCC (T1) with new tumour clones (T2, T3). Only T3 shows a mutation in *TP53*. Macroscopy shows typical 'nodule-in-nodule' pattern. Neo-angiogenesis (arrow) is restricted to one of the nodules.

Angiogenesis

Growth factors

Transforming growth factor-beta (TGF-β) was expressed at a high level in 82% of HCCs and was associated with HBV infection {756}. TGF-β expression could be part of a chain of events by which HBV contributes to the development of HCCs. TGF-β1, TGF-β2, and TGF-β3 showed marked mRNA overexpression in HCCs {818, 12}. TGF-β was expressed in both tumour and stroma cells; this suggests that TGF-β may play a role in hepatocarcinogenesis through both autocrine and paracrine pathways {12}. The mannose-6-phosphate / insulin-like growth factor-II receptor (M6P/IGF2R) regulates cell proliferation through interactions with TGF-β and IGF II. A study from the U.S.A. reported LOH at the M6P/IGF2R locus and mutations of the remaining allele were identified in 61% and 55% of HCCs, respectively {2149}, while no M6P/IGF2R mutations were detected in HCCs from Japanese patients {2031}.

Angiogenic growth factors. mRNA expression of basic fibroblast growth factor (bFGF) was high in HCCs {1746}. Strong immunoreactivity for bFGF was

localised in the progressed HCC component but not in the early-stage component of a nodule-in-nodule HCC {712}. Acquisition by cancer cells of the capacity to produce bFGF could be an important event in the stepwise progression of HCC. Greater mRNA expression of vascular endothelial growth factor (VEGF) was found in 60% of HCCs and was significantly correlated with the intensity of tumour staining in angio-grams. This suggests that VEGF contributes significantly to angiogenesis during hepatocarcinogenesis {1239, 1869}.

DNA methylation

DNA methyltransferase (*DNMT1*) mRNA expression was significantly higher in chronic hepatitis and cirrhotic nodules than in normal livers, and was even higher in HCCs {1863}. Indeed, DNA hypermethylation at D16S32, TAT, and D16S7 loci on chromosome 16 is frequently present even in chronic hepatitis and cirrhotic nodules {885}. The incidence and degree of aberrant DNA methylation increased in HCCs compared with chronic hepatitis and cirrhotic nodules

{885}. Aberrant DNA methylation may participate even in the early developmental stages of HCCs by predisposing some loci to allelic loss or silencing specific genes {885}.

DNA methylation around the promoter region of the E-cadherin tumour suppressor gene, which is located on 16q22.1, was detected in 46% of chronic hepatitis and cirrhotic nodules and in 67% of HCCs {884}. DNA hypermethylation around the promoter region correlated significantly with reduced E-cadherin expression in HCCs {884}. The HIC-1 (hypermethylated-in-cancer) tumour suppressor gene was identified at the D17S5 locus. DNA hypermethylation at the D17S5 locus was detected in 44% of chronic hepatitis and cirrhotic nodules and in 90% of HCCs {883}. LOH at this locus, which was preceded by DNA hypermethylation, was detected in 54% of HCCs {883}. The HIC-1 mRNA expression level of chronic hepatitis and cirrhotic nodules was significantly lower than that of normal livers, and that of HCCs was even lower {883}. Thus, silencing of tumour suppressor genes by aberrant DNA methylation is a significant event during hepatocarcinogenesis.

Prognosis and predictive factors

The prognosis of patients with HCC is generally very poor, particularly in cases with AFP levels greater than 100 ng/ml at the time of diagnosis, partial or complete portal vein thrombosis, and presence of a *TP53* mutation {45, 1861}. Spontaneous regression has been reported rarely. Most studies report a five-year survival rate of less than 5% in symptomatic HCC patients. HCCs are largely resistant to radio- and chemotherapy. Long-term survival is likely only in patients with small, asymptomatic HCC that can be treated by surgical resection, including liver transplantation, or non-surgical methods, including percutaneous ethanol or acetic acid injection and percutaneous radiofrequency thermal ablation.

Intrahepatic cholangiocarcinoma

Y. Nakanuma
B. Sripa
V. Vatanasapt

A.S.-Y Leong
T. Ponchon
K.G. Ishak

Definition

An intrahepatic malignant tumour composed of cells resembling those of bile ducts. Intrahepatic (or peripheral) cholangiocarcinoma (ICC) arises from any portion of the intrahepatic bile duct epithelium, i.e. from intrahepatic large bile ducts (the segmental and area ducts and their finer branches) or intrahepatic small bile ducts. Cholangiocarcinoma arising from the right and left hepatic ducts at or near their junction is called hilar cholangiocarcinoma (HCC) in most clinical series {1419}.

Epidemiology

Incidence and geographical distribution

ICC is a relatively rare tumour in most populations but second among all primary malignant liver tumours; about 15% of liver cancers are estimated to be ICC {61, 2162, 1467}. The frequency of ICC among all liver cancers ranges from 5% in males and 12% in females in Osaka, Japan, to 90% in males and 94% in females in Khon Kaen, Thailand {1467, 1471} (Fig. 8.29).

The highest incidence of ICC is found in areas of Laos and North and Northeast Thailand suffering from endemic infection with the liver fluke, *Opisthorchis viverrini*. In 1997, the age standardized incidence of ICC in Khon Kaen (Thailand) was 88 per 100,000 in males and 37/10⁵ in females {1467, 1471}. About 90% of the histologically confirmed cases of liver cancer in Khon Kaen are ICC, and almost all the ICC cases were found to be related to chronic *O. viverrini* infection {2006, 2007}. In the *Clonorchis sinensis* endemic area in Korea, there is also a high incidence of liver cancer with truncate incidence rates (35-64 years group) of 75 per 100,000 in males and 16 per 100,000 in females {23}. About 20% of liver cancers in Pusan, Korea, are ICC {871}.

Time trends

In both endemic and non-endemic areas, there have been no significant changes in the incidence of ICC in recent years {61}. It is less than 10 years since *O. viverrini* drug therapy was initiated; since it probably takes 30 years for ICC to complicate opisthorchiasis, the trends of ICC are probably not likely to change in the next decade {2007, 2009}.

Age and sex distribution

Patients with ICC are elderly, with no clear sex differences. ICC occurs at rather older ages than hepatocellular carcinoma (HCC) in most clinical series {1419}.

Aetiology

Although many aetiological factors have been characterized, the cause of ICC remains speculative in many cases.

Parasites

Clonorchis sinensis parasitizes the bile ducts of millions of individuals in the Far East, particularly China and Korea {1467}. Early reports from Hong Kong have shown that 65% of patients with ICC were infected by *C. sinensis* {747}. However, the incidence of *C. sinensis* infection in the general population was also similarly high at that time {308}. ICC from this cause appears to less frequent in recent years.

By contrast, infection of *O. viverrini* is continuing in Northeast Thailand, and

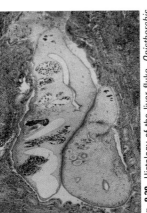

Fig. 8.28 Histology of the liver fluke, *Opisthorchis viverrini*, in a hepatic bile duct.

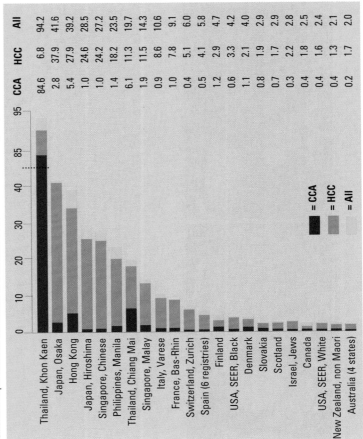

Fig. 8.29 Age-standardized incidence of liver cancer, per 100,000, in males, 1992 . Rates for cholangiocarcinoma and hepatocellular carcinoma are estimates. From: M. Parkin et al. {1468}

	CCA	HCC	All
Thailand, Khon Kaen	84.6	6.8	94.2
Japan, Osaka	2.8	37.9	41.6
Hong Kong	5.4	27.9	39.2
Japan, Hiroshima	1.0	24.6	28.5
Singapore, Chinese	1.0	24.2	27.2
Philippines, Manila	1.4	18.2	23.5
Thailand, Chiang Mai	6.1	11.3	19.7
Singapore, Malay	1.9	11.5	14.3
Italy, Varese	0.9	8.6	10.6
France, Bas-Rhin	1.0	7.8	9.1
Switzerland, Zurich	0.4	5.1	6.0
Spain (6 registries)	0.5	4.1	5.8
Finland	1.2	2.9	4.7
USA, SEER, Black	0.6	3.3	4.2
Denmark	1.1	2.1	4.0
Slovakia	0.8	1.9	2.9
Scotland	0.7	1.7	2.9
Israel, Jews	0.3	2.2	2.8
Canada	0.4	1.8	2.5
USA, SEER, White	0.4	1.6	2.4
New Zealand, non Maori	0.4	1.3	2.1
Australia (4 states)	0.2	1.7	2.0

= CCA
= HCC
= All

the evidence for the role of opisthorchiasis in the induction of ICC is compelling {2009, 2008}. Carcinogenesis is probably related to the length and severity of infection, the host's immune response, and other variables such as ingestion of dietary carcinogens, for example nitrosamines. In northeast Thailand, several carcinogenic N-nitroso compounds and their precursors exist at low levels in the daily diet {1230}. In addition, endogenous nitrosamine formation by liver fluke infection has been reported {1673}. Both exogenous and in situ nitrosamine formation may lead to DNA alkylation and deamination {1346}. It seems that the presence of parasites induces DNA damage and mutations as a consequence of the formation of carcinogens/free radicals and of cellular proliferation of the intrahepatic bile duct epithelium.

Hepatolithiasis

Hepatolithiasis (recurrent pyogenic cholangitis), which is not uncommon in the Far East, is also associated with ICC {1857, 1321}. It is frequently observed in clonorchiasis {746} but not in opisthorchiasis. Most of these cases are associated with calcium bilirubinate stones; a few cases with cholesterol stones have also been reported. Patients with intrahepatic stones and ICC have a significantly longer duration of symptoms and a higher frequency of previous biliary surgery.

Inflammatory bowel disease and primary sclerosing cholangitis

Patients with primary sclerosing cholangitis (PSC) and ulcerative colitis (UC) have a predisposition to develop colorectal neoplasia and also bile duct carcinoma, including ICC {672, 1993, 194, 2078}.

Deposition of Thorotrast

Thorotrast is a radioactive α-particle emitter that was widely used as a radio-opaque intra-arterial contrast medium between 1930 and 1955. ICC has been recorded in many patients with prior exposure to Thorotrast. The data suggest that the chronic alpha-irradiation may be the causative factor, with latent periods ranging from 25 to 48 years.

Biliary malformations and other lesions

ICC may arise rarely in solitary unilocular or multiple liver cysts, congenital segmental or multiple dilatation of the bile ducts (Caroli disease), congenital hepatic fibrosis, and von Meyenburg complexes {736, 2165}.

Clinical features

The site of the tumour, its growth pattern and the presence or absence of stricture

Epstein-Barr virus (EBV) infection

Rare examples of ICC have a lymphoepitheliomatous, undifferentiated pattern. Clonal EBV has been found in such cases {757, 2025}.

Non-biliary cirrhosis

There are several reports of ICC arising in non-biliary cirrhosis, particularly hepatitis virus-related liver cirrhosis {2159, 1940}. HCV is frequent in such cases and ICC is usually of a smaller, mass-forming type. Such ICC and combined hepatocellular-cholangiocarcinomas share apomucin profiles {1669}, suggesting that these two tumours have a similar or common histogenesis, or that ICC associated with cirrhosis might be the result of exclusive proliferation of the cholangiocellular component of the combined type. Genotypes of hepatitis B and C viruses have been shown in cholangiocarcinoma cells {2049, 1787}.

Symptoms and signs

General malaise, mild abdominal pain and weight loss are frequent clinical symptoms. When the carcinoma infiltrates the hilar region, jaundice and cholangitis become manifest. ICCs, particularly those arising from the small bile ducts, may go unnoticed until they have attained a large size. The liver is enlarged to a lesser extent, ascites is less common, and signs of portal hypertension are absent or minimal. Patients with unrelieved obstruction of the intrahepatic large bile ducts may die from complications, e.g. liver failure or sepsis.

Imaging

Advanced cases of ICC show mixed growth and spreading patterns with growth and spreading patterns with intrahepatic metastases. Computerized tomography (CT) images of ICC usually show a lobulated or fused hypodense space-occupying lesion with peripheral enhancement, probably due to central hypocellular dense fibrosis. Secondary dilated ducts around the tumour are detectable by CT and ultrasonography. A focal area of carcinoma involving the bile duct wall is identifiable by spiral CT. Endoscopic retrograde, transhepatic or magnetic resonance cholangiography is a useful adjunct for the identification of the level of biliary obstruction and secondary bile duct dilatation.

ICCs at relatively early and surgically resectable stages are classifiable into three representative types of growth patterns {1080}, and these patterns, which are evaluable by imaging studies, can be useful for the preoperative staging of

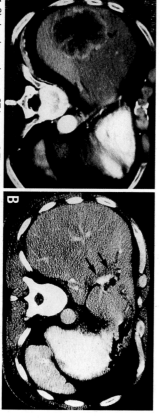

Fig. 8.31 Cholangiocarcinoma, CT images. **A** The right lobe contains a mass and shows peripheral bile duct dilation. **B** Arrows indicate a peribiliary spreading type.

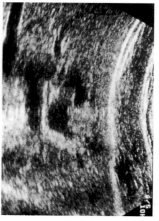

Fig. 8.30 Ultrasonography of an intrahepatic cholangiocarcinoma. **A** A hyperechoic mass is present in a dilated bile duct.

or obstruction of the biliary tree are responsible for the variable clinical features of ICC.

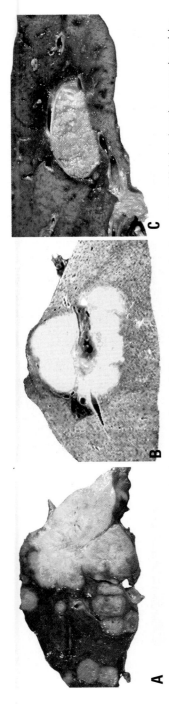

Fig. 8.32 Macroscopic features of intrahepatic cholangiocarcinoma. **A** Cut surface shows massive tumour and multiple intrahepatic metastatic nodules. Surrounding liver is non-cirrhotic. **B** White, scar-like mass in a normal liver (mass forming types) together with dilated peripheral bile ducts. **C** Intraductal growth type of intrahepatic cholangiocarcinoma.

tumour extent and for designing the surgical procedure. The mass forming type is an expansile nodule and is the most common. The tumour borders between the cancerous and noncancerous portions are relatively clear. The contrast enhanced CT scan shows a low-density tumour with peripheral ring-like increased density. The periductal-infiltrating type, which is usually associated with biliary stricture, is relatively common. The tumour exhibits diffuse infiltration along the portal pedicle. This type resembles hilar or extrahepatic bile duct carcinoma. The contrast enhanced CT demonstrates a small cancerous enlargement of the portal pedicle, or a mass central to the dilated peripheral ducts. The anatomical location of the involved ducts can be evaluated by caliber changes or the rigidity of the bile duct on high-quality cholangiographic images. The intraductal growth type (intraductal papillary cholangiocarcinoma) is less common {351}. These tumours are confined within the dilated part of an intrahepatic large bile duct, with no or mild extension

beyond the bile duct walls. Some tumours of this type of ICC might have arisen from biliary papillomatosis after malignant transformation. Marked localized dilatation of the affected duct is detectable by ultrasound or CT. Cholangiography shows filling defects in the biliary tract, due to polypoid tumours and mucin.

Macroscopy

ICC can arise from any portion of the intrahepatic bile duct epithelium {61, 1418}. Lesions are gray to gray-white, firm and solid, although some tumours show intraductal growth, sometimes with polyp formation. Typical tumours consist of variably sized nodules, usually coalescent. Portal tract infiltration is also seen. Central necrosis or scarring are common, and mucin may be visible on the cut surfaces. ICC cases involving the hepatic hilum are hardly distinguishable from hilar cholangiocarcinoma, and such cases show cholestasis, biliary fibrosis, and cholangitis with abscess formation. ICC is not often noted in a non-cirrhotic liver.

ICC in endemic areas of liver fluke infection is similar to that described in non-endemic regions; liver flukes are rarely seen nowadays due to mass treatment. In hepatolithiasis-associated ICC, the tumour tends to proliferate and spread along the stone-containing ducts. The liver lobe or segments containing stones involved by ICC are atrophic in some cases.

Tumour spread

ICC shows direct spread into the surrounding hepatic parenchyma, portal pedicle and bile duct. Intrahepatic metastases develop in nearly all cases at a relatively advanced stage. Vascular invasion is a frequent histological finding relatively early, suggesting the development of early metastasis. The incidence of metastases in regional lymph nodes is higher than in HCC. Blood-borne spread occurs later, to the lungs in particular; other sites include bone, adrenals, kidneys, spleen, and pancreas.

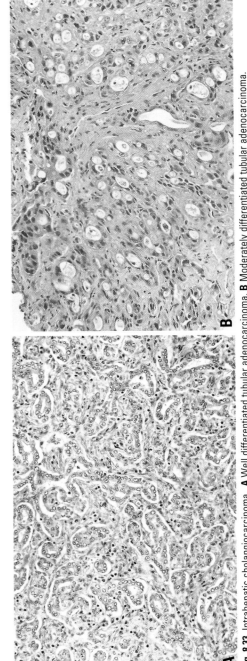

Fig. 8.33 Intrahepatic cholangiocarcinoma. **A** Well differentiated tubular adenocarcinoma. **B** Moderately differentiated tubular adenocarcinoma.

Intrahepatic cholangiocarcinoma 175

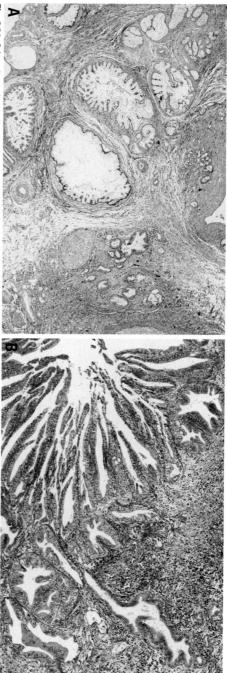

Fig. 8.34 **A** Intrahepatic cholangiocarcinoma showing papillary growth pattern involving the peribiliary glands . The bile duct lumen (top and center) is free of carcinoma. **B** Papillary cholangiocarcinoma invading the bile duct wall.

On rare occasions, the tumour shows extensive intraluminal spread of bile ducts throughout the liver. The tumour cells can also infiltrate into the peribiliary glands of the intrahepatic large bile ducts and their conduits. It may be difficult to distinguish this lesion from reactive proliferated peribiliary glands histologically.

Histopathology

Most ICCs are adenocarcinomas showing tubular and/or papillary structures with a variable fibrous stroma {326}. There is no dominant histological type of ICC in cases associated with liver flukes or hepatolithiasis when compared to those in non-endemic areas.

Adenocarcinoma

This common type of ICC growing in the hepatic parenchyma and portal pedicle reveals a significant heterogeneity of histological features and degree of differentiation. At an early stage, a tubular pattern with a relatively uniform histological picture is frequent. Cord-like or micropapillary patterns are also seen. The cells are small or large, cuboidal or columnar, and can be pleomorphic. The nucleus is small and the nucleolus is usually less prominent than that of HCC. The majority of cells have a pale, eosinophilic or vacuolated cytoplasm; sometimes, the cells have a clear and abundant cytoplasm or resemble goblet cells.

ICC arising from the large intrahepatic bile ducts shows intraductal micropapillary carcinoma and in situ like spread along the biliary lumen. Once there is invasion through the periductal tissue, the lesion may be well, moderately, or poorly differentiated adenocarcinoma, with considerable desmoplasia and stenosis or obliteration of the bile duct lumen.

Infrequently, a papillary tumour growing in the duct lumen is supported by fine fibrovascular cores. Cholangio-carcinoma arising from the intrahepatic peribiliary glands {1914} mainly involves these glands, sparing the lining epithelial cells at an early stage.

An abundant fibrous stroma is an important characteristic of ICC. Activated perisinusoidal cells (myofibroblasts) are incorporated into the tumour, producing extracellular matrix proteins that lead to fibrosis {1913}. Usually, the central parts of the tumour are more sclerotic and hypocellular, while the peripheral parts show more actively proliferating carcinoma cells. On rare occasions, the tumour cells are lost in a massive hyaline stroma, which may be focally calcified.

The secretion of mucus in one form or another can be demonstrated in the majority of tumours by mucicarmine, diastase-PAS and Alcian blue staining. Mucus core (MUC) proteins 1, 2, and 3 are detectable in the carcinoma cells {1264, 1670}. ICC cells can immunoexpress cytokeratins 7 and 19, CEA, epithelial membrane antigen, and blood group antigens. Bile may be present occasionally in ICC as a result of destruction of bile ducts or entrapment of non-neoplas-

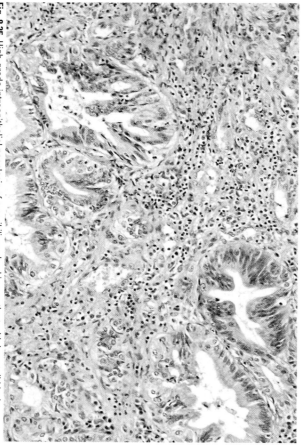

Fig. 8.35 High-grade intraepithelial neoplasia of a peribiliary gland in a patient with hepatolithiasis.

tic hepatocytes or bile ductules containing bile. It is always seen at the periphery of the tumour. Bile production by tumour cells is never found.

Carcinoma cell nests with small tubular or cord-like patterns extend by compressing the hepatocytes or infiltrating along the sinusoids. Occasionally, carcinoma cells abut directly on to hepatocytes. As a result, the portal tracts are incorporated within the tumour and appear as tracts of elastic fibre-rich connective tissue. Fibrous encapsulation is not seen.

ICC frequently infiltrates portal tracts, and invades portal vessels (lymphatics, portal venules); there is also perineural invasion, particularly in the large portal tracts. Infiltrating, well-differentiated tubular carcinoma must be differentiated from the non-neoplastic pre-existing small bile ducts. The carcinoma cells infiltrate around nerve fibres and have variably-sized cancerous lumens.

Adenosquamous and squamous carcinoma. The former is an adenocarcinoma containing significant amounts of unequivocal squamous carcinomatous elements, i.e. keratin and/or intercellular bridges. The latter is entirely composed of squamous cell carcinoma. They are occasionally seen at advanced stages of ICC.

Cholangiolocellular carcinoma. The carcinoma cells are arranged as small, regular, narrow tubular structures resembling ductules or canals of Hering {1828}. The cells are larger than the usual ICC.

Mucinous carcinoma. A predominant component of extracellular mucus (mucus lakes), usually visible to the naked eye, is present in the stroma. Carcinoma cells distended with mucus are seen floating in the mucus lakes. The histology is similar to that seen in other organs. These tumours show rapid progression clinically {1671}.

Signet-ring cell carcinoma. A malignant tumour in which there is a predominance of discrete cells distended with mucus. ICC composed only of signet ring cells is extremely rare.

Sarcomatous ICC. A cholangiocarcinoma with spindle cell areas resembling spindle cell sarcoma or fibrosarcoma or with features of malignant fibrous histiocytoma. This variant may have a more aggressive behaviour. Carcinomatous foci, including squamous cell carcinoma, are scattered focally.

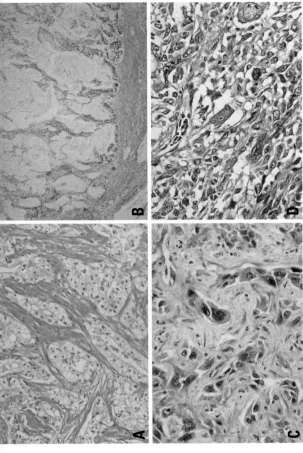

Fig. 8.36 Intrahepatic cholangiocarcinoma. **A** Clear cell type. **B** Mucinous type. **C** Pleomorphic type. **D** Spindle cell type.

Lymphoepithelioma-like carcinoma. Two cases of undifferentiated lymphoepitheliomatous lesions with adenocarcinoma have been reported {757, 2025}. In these cases, EBV-coded nuclear RNAs were demonstrable.

Clear cell variant. This lesion is characterized by distinct overgrowth of clear cells in an acinar or tubular pattern. The carcinoma cells are PAS reactive and diastase resistant, indicating the presence of mucin.

Mucoepidermoid carcinoma. This variant resembles the tumour arising in salivary glands.

Differential diagnosis

Hepatocellular carcinoma. Some ICCs grow in a cord-like pattern reminiscent of the trabeculae of HCC. The cords are always separated by a connective tissue stroma rather than by sinusoids; canaliculi and bile are also absent. Almost all

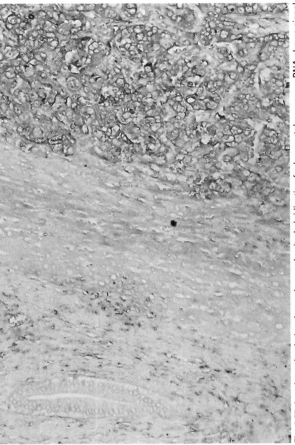

Fig. 8.37 Intrahepatic cholangiocarcinoma. In situ hybridisation for human telomerase mRNA shows signal in carcinoma cells (left). Non-neoplastic bile duct is negative (right).

Fig. 8.38 Intrahepatic cholangiocarcinoma, in a patient with heterozygous alpha-1 antitrypsin deficiency of the Piz type. A Tubular adenocarcinoma. B Cytokeratin 7 immunohistochemistry demonstrates tumour cells spreading along bile ducts and infiltrating liver tissue.

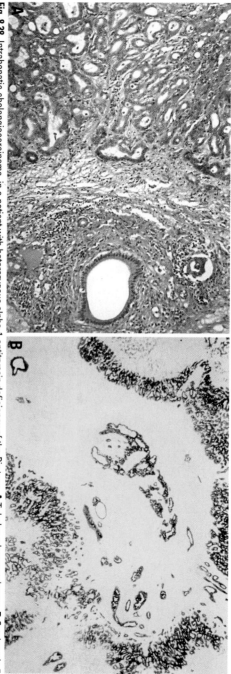

ICCs are diffusely positive for cytokeratin 7 and 19, whereas only a few cases of HCC are positive. The hepatocyte antigen (Dako) is expressed by HCC but not by ICC.

Metastatic carcinoma. ICC cannot be distinguished histologically from metastatic adenocarcinoma of biliary tract or pancreatic origin. Occasionally, dysplastic changes in neighbouring bile ducts suggest intrahepatic origin. In addition, diffuse expression of cytokeratin 20 favours metastatic adenocarcinoma, particularly from colon {1141}. While cytokeratin 7 is common in ICC, it is not so common in metastatic carcinoma.

Sclerosing cholangitis. Periductal spread of ICC may be difficult to distinguish from sclerosing cholangitis, particularly when only biopsy material is available. The most important criteria for the diagnosis of malignancy are severe cytological atypia, random and diffuse infiltration of the duct wall by the neoplastic cells, and perineural invasion.

Grading

ICCs can be graded into well, moderately, and poorly differentiated adenocarcinoma according to their morphology. In the case of the common type of adenocarcinoma, well-differentiated lesions form relatively uniform tubular or papillary structures, moderately differentiated tumours show moderately distorted tubular patterns with cribriform formations and/or a cord-like pattern, while the poorly differentiated show severely distorted tubular structures with marked cellular pleomorphism.

Precursor and benign lesions

Biliary intraepithelial neoplasia (dysplasia)
This is characterized by abnormal epithelial cells with multilayering of nuclei and micropapillary projections into the duct lumen {2078, 1322}. The abnormal cells have an increased nuclear/cytoplasmic ratio, a partial loss of nuclear polarity, and nuclear hyperchromasia. They are divisible into low-grade and high-grade lesions. Some peribiliary glands may also be dysplastic. Cell kinetic studies have disclosed proliferative activity of intraepithelial neoplasia between that of hyperplasia and ICC, and telomerase activity is demonstrable in both intraepithelial and invasive carcinoma {1915, 1440}. Carcinoembryonic antigen (CEA) is focally detectable in biliary intraepithelial neoplasia and more so in carcinoma {1322}. These findings support the concept of a hyperplasia-dysplasia-carcinoma sequence in the biliary tree {1989}.

In liver fluke infestations, the bile ducts first show desquamation of the epithelial lining with subsequent hyperplasia, periductal fibrosis, inflammation and goblet cell metaplasia {2008, 913}. The neoplastic transformation from hyperplasia in bile ducts to ICC through dysplastic changes is demonstrable in opisthorchiasis. In hepatolithiasis, the findings are those of cholangitis, with proliferation of the biliary epithelial lining and periductal biliary glandular cells, and multiple foci of biliary intraepithelial neoplasia {1323}. Hyperplasia and intraepithelial neoplasia of the duct epithelium in livers with Thorotrast-deposition and congenital biliary anomalies may be also related to the development of ICC {1626, 2165}.

It has been reported in patients with PSC that biliary intraepithelial neoplasia could evolve from papillary hyperplasia {2078, 1107}. However, recent experience at orthotopic liver transplantation of PSC has detected hardly any in situ or invasive neoplastic foci.

Biliary papillomatosis
Dilated intrahepatic and extrahepatic bile ducts are filled with papillary or villous excrescences, which microscopically are papillary or villous adenomas with delicate fibrovascular stalks covered with a columnar or glandular epithelium {806, 351}. They are soft and white, red or tan. In some cases, there are variable degrees of cellular atypia and multilayering of nuclei. Occasionally, foci of in situ or invasive carcinoma are encountered {1340}.

Von Meyenburg complex (biliary microhamartoma)
The lesions are small, up to several mm in diameter. They are usually multiple and

Fig. 8.39 Immunoexpression of at211 demonstrates alpha-1 antitrypsin deficiency of piz type.

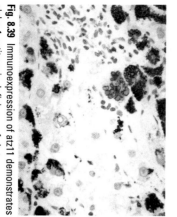

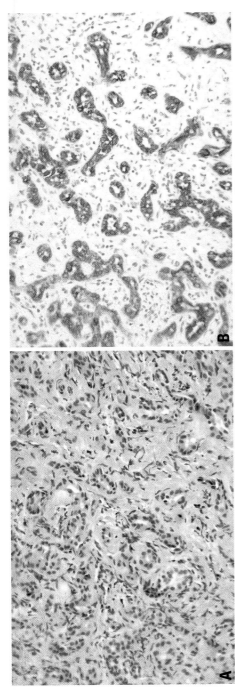

Fig. 8.40 Bile duct adenoma. **A** Frozen section. **B** Cytokeratin immunostain showing characteristic branching pattern of bile ducts.

are adjacent to a portal area. Within a fibrous or hyalinized stroma, they present as irregular or round ductal structures that appear somewhat dilated and have a flattened or cuboidal epithelium. The lumina contain proteinaceous or bile-stained secretion. These lesions carry little or no malignant potential {736, 673}.

Bile duct adenoma (BDA)

BDA is usually single and subcapsular, and is white and well circumscribed but non-encapsulated. BDA is usually less than 1 cm in size, and is composed of a proliferation of small, normal appearing ducts with cuboidal cells that have regular nuclei and lack dysplasia {44}. These ducts have no or little lumen and can elaborate mucin. Their fibrous stroma shows varying degrees of chronic inflammation and collagenization. Enclosed in the lesion are normally spaced portal tracts. They are considered to be a focal reaction to injury.

BDA and peribiliary glands share common antigens, suggesting a common line of differentiation {136}. Occasionally, BDA contains periductular endocrine cell clusters {1384}.

In addition, there are several atypical BDA with a neoplastic nature. Biliary adenofibroma is characterized by a complex tubulocystic biliary epithelium without mucin production, together with abundant fibroblastic stromal components {1972}. Its expansive growth, and foci of epithelial tufting, cellular atypia and mitoses favor a neoplastic process.

Intrahepatic peribiliary cysts

In chronic advanced liver disease and

biliary anomalies, and also in normal livers, multiple cysts may be seen around the intrahepatic large bile ducts {1319, 1320}. They are visible by ultrasound or CT. These cysts are derived from peribiliary glands and should be differentiated from ICC clinically and histologically.

Diffuse and multifocal hyperplasia of peribiliary glands

Diffuse, severe, macroscopically recognizable dilatation and hyperplasia of the peribiliary glands of intrahepatic and extrahepatic bile ducts is a rare condition {1319, 437}. Some ducts may be cystically dilated. Lack of familiarity with this lesion could lead to an erroneous diag-

nosis of a well-differentiated cholangiocarcinoma. It occurs in apparently normal livers and also in acquired liver diseases.

Molecular genetics and genetic susceptibility

Mutations of the *RAS* and *TP53* genes are the most common genetic abnormalities identified in ICC. The incidence of *KRAS* mutations ranges from 100% and 60% among British {1054} and Japanese patients respectively {1878, 1402}, to 4% among Thai patients {1510}. Taiwanese and Korean patients show an intermediate frequency {1037, 887}. The most frequently mutated position in the *KRAS*

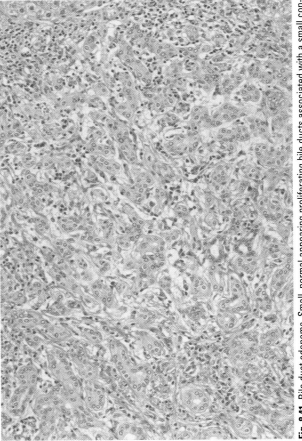

Fig. 8.41 Bile duct adenoma. Small, normal appearing proliferating bile ducts associated with a small connective tissue component and lymphocytic infiltration.

gene is codon 12 involving GGT (glycine) to GAT (aspartic acid). Less frequent mutations have been identified in codon 13, involving GGT (glycine) to GAT (aspartic acid) and codon 61, involving CAA (glutamine) to CAC (histidine) {1402, 1969, 1511}.

TP53 mutations occur between exons 5 to 8, the most common change being G to A transitions {887, 1511, 907, 1848}. The mutations are random with no specific hot spot, being mostly missense mutations and less frequently nonsense mutations {887}. p53 protein is immunohistochemically detectable in carcinoma cells in more that 70% of ICC cases. KRAS and TP53 mutations correlate with the gross morphology of ICC {1969, 1401}; a higher prevalence of KRAS gene alterations is found in the periductal and spicular forming infiltrating subtype compared to the slower growing, non-invasive mass-forming type. TP53 mutations are prominent in the mass-forming type of ICC.

The variable incidence of KRAS mutations in different populations of ICC may reflect different aetiologies. O. viverrini infection and increased consumption of nitrates and nitrites are contributing factors in Thailand where the incidence of KRAS abnormalities is low {2025, 1446}. Overexpression of c-erbB-2 occurs in one fourth to about two thirds of carcinoma of the biliary tract, and may be used as a phenotypic marker for neoplastic transformation {1912}. Membranous expression of E-cadherin, alpha-catenin, and beta-catenin is reduced in a majority of ICC and this down-regulation correlates with ICC at high-grade {91}.

Overexpression of MET, the receptor for hepatocytes growth factor, occurs in ICC and correlates with tumour differentiation, being poorly expressed in poorly differentiated tumours {1912}. It also correlates with the markedly increased proliferation indices seen in precancerous glands and cholangiocarcinoma. Biliary epithelial cells are continuously exposed to genotoxic insults such as chronic inflammation and hydrophobic bile acids, predisposing to oncogenic mutations. Progression to malignancy may be due, in part, to failure in activating apoptosis and deleting cells with genetic damages {263}. The anti-apoptotic protein bcl-2, is overexpressed in ICC {281} and telomerase activity is detectable in carcinoma cells of almost all ICC cases.

Prognosis and predictive factors

Early detection of ICC is difficult, and the overall prognosis after resection is poor compared with that of HCC. Lymph node spread, vascular invasion, positive margins and bilobar distribution are associated with a high recurrence rate and a poor prognosis. One study found the 5-year survival rate was 39% in patients with mass-forming tumours and 69% for intraductal tumours while no patients with mass-forming plus periductal-infiltrating tumours survived > 5 years {2161}.

Histologically, squamous cell or sarcomatous elements and mucinous variants confer a poor prognosis {1312, 1313}. Patients with well differentiated ICC seem to survive longer than those with moderately or poorly differentiated ICC seem to survive longer than those with moderately or poorly differentiated ones. A few cases of well differentiated ICC with bland features resembling bile duct adenoma show a good prognosis {522}. MUC 2 protein expression is relatively frequent in well differentiated ICC, suggesting a somewhat more favourable prognosis {1915}.

Lymph node metastasis is a significant prognostic factor {2160}. The 5-year survival rate in patients with lymph node metastases is significantly lower than that in patients without lymph node metastasis (51%).

In liver fluke-associated ICC, survival after right hepatectomy is better than after left hepatectomy, and is not associated with tumour size {1990}. In addition, multiple tumour masses have a poor prognosis. Concomitant hepatolithiasis prevents precise diagnosis preoperatively, and precipitates biliary sepsis. Long-term post-surgical survival of patients with stone-containing ICC compared to ICC alone is controversial {291, 1849}. ICC found in non-biliary cirrhosis is usually detectable as a small nodule during follow-up of hepatitis virus-related cirrhosis, and is treatable with hepatectomy {2159}.

C. Wittekind
H.P. Fischer
T. Ponchon

Combined hepatocellular and cholangiocarcinoma

Definition

A rare tumour containing unequivocal elements of both hepatocellular and cholangiocarcinoma that are intimately admixed.

This tumour should be distinguished from separate hepatocellular carcinoma and cholangiocarcinoma arising in the same liver {605}. Such tumours may be widely separated or close to each other ('collision tumour').

Epidemiology

This tumour type comprises less than 1% of all liver carcinomas. There are similar geographical distribution differences as for hepatocellular carcinoma and a similar age and sex distribution.

Tumour spread and staging

Some studies have found a higher frequency of lymph node metastasis compared with HCC.

Macroscopy

Gross inspection does not show significantly different morphology compared to hepatocellular carcinoma. In tumours with a major cholangiocarcinomatous component with fibrous stroma, the cut surface is firm.

Histopathology

Combined hepatocellular and cholangiocarcinoma is the term preferred for a tumour containing both hepatocellular and distinct or separate cholangiocarcinoma. The presence of both bile and mucus should be sought in the combined tumour. This category should not be used for tumours in which either form of growth is insufficiently differentiated for positive identification.

Hepatocytes preferentially express cytokeratins 8 and 18 and, like duct epithelial cells, cytokeratins 7 and 19. However, the different patterns of expression are not as clear-cut in these tumours. For practical purposes, demonstration of bile canaliculi by polyclonal CEA (mixed biliary glycoproteins) combined with Hep Par immu-

noexpression is sufficient for the diagnosis of a hepatocellular carcinomatous component, and that of neutral epithelial mucin by the PAS-diastase reaction for the diagnosis of a cholangiocarcinomatous component {1046, 1456, 667}.

Prognostic factors

Some authors have reported patients with combined hepatocellular and cholangiocarcinoma having a worse prognosis as compared with patients with HCC.

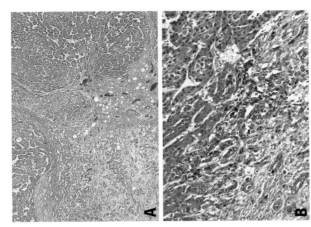

Fig. 8.43 Combined hepatocellular and cholangiocellular carcinoma. **A** Microtrabecular HCC and cholangiocarcinoma with desmoplastic response. **B** Border zone between HCC and cholangiocarcinoma.

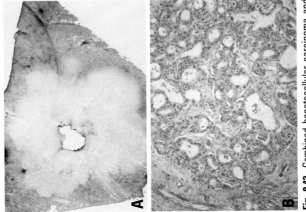

Fig. 8.42 Combined hepatocellular carcinoma and cholangiocarcinoma arising in non-cirrhotic liver tissue in a patient with heterozygous Piz type alpha-1 antitrypsin deficiency. **A** Pale, homogeneous cut surface. **B** Microscopic, showing glandular areas.

Bile duct cystadenoma and cystadenocarcinoma

C. Wittekind
H.P. Fischer
T. Ponchon

Definition

A cystic tumour either benign (cystadenoma) or malignant (cystadenocarcinoma), lined by epithelium with papillary infoldings that may be mucus-secreting or, less frequently, serous. Lesions arise from ducts proximal to the hilum of the liver. They differ from tumours that arise in cystic congenital malformation and in parasitic infections and hepatolithiasis.

Epidemiology

Bile duct cystadenoma and cystadenocarcinoma are rare {809}. Cystadenoma is seen almost exclusively in females, with cystadenocarcinoma appearing equally in males and females. The average age of patients is 50-60 years.

Clinical features

Patients often present with abdominal pain and mass. A few patients have jaundice. Elevated serum levels of tumour marker CA 19-9 may occur. Imaging techniques show multilocular cystic tumour(s), occasionally with tiny papillary folds in the cystic wall.

Macroscopy

The cysts are usually multilocular and typically range from 5 to 15 cm diameter {809}. In cystadenocarcinoma, a large papillary mass may occur as well as

solid areas of grey-white tumour in a thickened wall.

Tumour spread and staging

Cystadenocarcinomas show intrahepatic spread and metastasis to regional lymph nodes in the hepatoduodenal ligament. Distant metastases occur most frequent in the lungs, the pleura and the peritoneum. Staging is performed according to the TNM Classification of liver tumours {66}.

Histopathology

Cystadenomas are usually multilocular and are well defined by a fibrous capsule, which may contain smooth muscle fibres. The contents of the locules are either thin, opalescent or glairy fluid, or mucinous semisolid material.

Two histological variants are recognized. The *mucinous type* is more common and is lined by columnar, cuboidal, or flattened mucus-secreting epithelial cells resting on a basement membrane; polypoid or papillary projections may be present. About 5% of the tumours reveal neuroendocrine differentiation, as identified by expression of chromogranin and synaptophysin. Subjacent to the basement membrane is a cellular, compacted mesenchymal stroma, which in turn is surrounded by looser fibrous tissue. This mesenchymal component is seen only in

females and has been likened to ovarian stroma. The stromal cells express vimentin, and there are many cells that express smooth muscle actin. A xan-

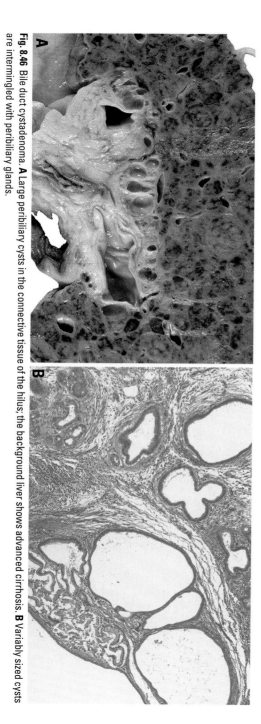

Fig. 8.46 Bile duct cystadenoma. **A** Large peribiliary cysts in the connective tissue of the hilus; the background liver shows advanced cirrhosis. **B** Variably sized cysts are intermingled with peribiliary glands.

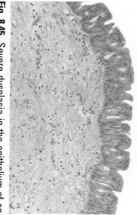

Fig. 8.45 Severe dysplasia in the epithelium of an intrahepatic large bile duct in a case of hepatolithiasis.

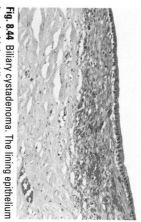

Fig. 8.44 Biliary cystadenoma. The lining epithelium is cuboidal and lies on ovarian-like stroma, beneath which is a band of dense tissue.

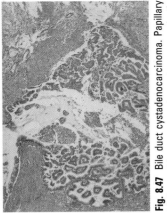

Fig. 8.47 Bile duct cystadenocarcinoma. Papillary folding with serous and mucinous neoplastic epithelium.

thogranulomatous reaction, with foam cells, cholesterol clefts and pigmented lipofuscin-containing macrophages, may be present in the cyst wall. The *serous type* consists of multiple, small locules lined by a single layer of cuboidal cells with clear cytoplasm containing glycogen. The cells rest on a basement membrane but are not surrounded by the mesenchymal stroma typical of the mucinous variety. Squamous metaplasia may also occur.

Cystadenocarcinomas are usually multilocular and contain mucoid fluid. Malignant change may not involve all of the epithelium lining the cyst; it is usually multifocal. The tumours are so well defined that complete removal can usually be

achieved with good prognosis. Differentiation from intrahepatic bile duct cystadenoma depends on the demonstration of cytological (particularly nuclear) atypia, mitosis, and invasion of the underlying stroma.

Some bile duct cystadenocarcinomas may be misdiagnosed as bile duct cystadenomas because insufficient sampling results in tumour morphology showing no cytological features of malignancy or invasion of the underlying stroma {351, 809, 1268, 2096}.

Prognostic factors

The prognosis of patients with biliary duct cystadenocarcinomas is good if a curative resection is possible. The

course of patients with unresectable tumours seems to be better than of patients with cholangiocarcinoma {71}.

Hepatoblastoma

Definition

A malignant embryonal tumour with divergent patterns of differentiation, ranging from cells resembling fetal epithelial hepatocytes, to embryonal cells, and differentiated tissues including osteoid-like material, fibrous connective tissue and striated muscle fibers.

Epidemiology

Hepatoblastoma is the most frequent liver tumour in children. Four percent of hepatoblastomas are present at birth, 68% in the first two years of life and 90% by five years of age. Only 3% are seen in patients over 15 years of age. A recent increase in the incidence of tumours in infants with birth weights below 1500 grams has been reported {776, 777, 1899}. There is a male predominance of 1.5:1 to 2:1, but no racial predilection.

Localization

Hepatoblastomas occur as a single mass in 80% of cases, involving the right lobe in 57%, the left lobe in 15% and both lobes in 27% of patients {1838}. Multiple masses, seen in the other 20% of cases, may occur in either or both lobes.

Clinical features

Hepatoblastomas are often noted by a parent or physician as an enlarging abdomen in the infant that may be accompanied by weight loss or anorexia. Less frequently nausea, vomiting, and abdominal pain are present. Jaundice is seen in 5% of cases. Rarely, tumour cells may produce human chorionic gonadotrophin, leading to precocious puberty with pubic hair, genital enlargement and deepening voice, noted most prominently in young boys.

Hepatoblastoma is accompanied by anemia in 70% of cases and by thrombocytosis in 50%, with platelet counts exceeding 800 x 10⁹/L in nearly 30% of cases {1717}. Alpha fetoprotein (AFP) is elevated in about 90% of patients at the time of diagnosis. The levels of AFP parallel the course of the disease, falling to normal levels after complete removal of the tumour and rising with recurrence of the lesion. AFP levels may be normal or only slightly elevated with small cell undifferentiated hepatoblastoma. Caution must be taken in evaluating the levels of AFP in younger infants since the 'adult' level of AFP (< 25ng/mL) is not reached until approximately six months of age.

Other laboratory abnormalities can include elevated levels of serum cholesterol, bilirubin, alkaline phosphatase, and aspartate aminotransferase {10}.

Imaging

Computed tomography (CT) shows single or multiple masses within the liver, which in 50% of cases display calcifica-

tion {1233}. Magnetic resonance imaging (MRI) along with CT can help differentiate hepatoblastoma from infantile haemangioendothelioma, mesenchymal hamartoma, and hepatocellular carcinoma by demonstrating cystic or vascular features peculiar to each lesion {1999}. MRI may also be used to characterize epithelial and mesenchymal components of hepatoblastoma {1533}.

Macroscopy

Hepatoblastomas vary in size from 5 to 22 cm in diameter and from 150 to 1,400 g in weight. Single and multiple lesions may be well circumscribed, the edge of the lesion being separated from the normal liver by an irregular pseudocapsule. Pure fetal hepatoblastomas have the tan-brown colour of normal liver, while mixed hepatoblastomas display a variety of colours from brown to green to white. The lesions are often nodular and bulge from the cut surface. Areas of necrosis and haemorrhage are usually present and may appear as soft or gelatinous, brown to red tissue {1837}.

Tumour spread

At clinical manifestation, 40-60% of hepatoblastomas are either very large or involve both lobes to the extent that they are considered unresectable {1839}. Preoperative chemotherapy, however, reduces the size of the lesion in nearly 85% of these patients to a size that renders it resectable. Tumour spread includes local extension into the hepatic

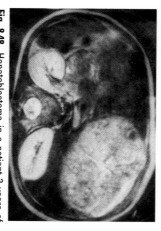

Fig. 8.48 Hepatoblastoma in a patient 3 years of age. The T2 weighted MRI shows a liver mass that histologically corresponds to fetal epithelial hepatoblastoma.

Table 8.02

Age distribution of hepatic tumours in young patients. Data are from the Armed Forces Institute of Pathology (AFIP), Washington, DC (U.S.A.)

Type of Tumour	Birth to 2 years (%) (285 cases)	Birth to 20 years (%) (716 cases)
Hepatoblastoma	43.5	27.6
Infantile haemangioendothelioma	36.1	16.5
Mesenchymal hamartoma	13.3	8.0
Hepatocellular carcinoma	1.4	18.9
Focal nodular hyperplasia	1.1	10.1
Undifferentiated "embryonal" sarcoma	1.1	7.2
Nodular regenerative hyperplasia	2.1	4.5
Hepatocellular adenoma	0.0	3.8
Angiosarcoma	1.4	2.4
Embryonal rhabdomyosarcoma	0.0	1.0

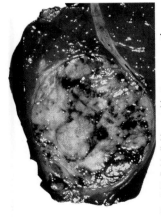

Fig. 8.49 Epithelial hepatoblastoma presenting as a large, well demarcated lesion with central haemorrhage.

Histopathology

Hepatoblastomas display a distinct variety of histological patterns that may be present in varying proportions. Some tumours are composed entirely of uniform fetal epithelial cells or small undifferentiated cells, while others contain a variety of tissue types including hepatic fetal epithelial and embryonal cells, fibrous connective tissue, osteoid-like material, skeletal muscle fibers, nests of squamous epithelial cells, and cells with melanin pigment.

Pure fetal epithelial differentiation

Accounting for nearly one third of cases, the fetal epithelial pattern is composed of thin trabeculae of small cuboidal cells resembling the hepatocytes of the developing fetal liver. These cells contain a small round nucleus with fine nuclear chromatin and an indistinct nucleolus. The cytoplasm varies from finely granular to clear, reflecting variable amounts of glycogen and lipid which can impart a 'light and dark' pattern to the lesion when viewed at lower magnifications. Canaliculi may be seen between hepatocytes of the 2-3 cell layer trabeculae, but only rarely is bile stasis present. In biopsies taken before preoperative chemotherapy, foci of extramedullary haematopoiesis (EMH) composed of clusters of erythroid and myeloid precursors may be present in the sinusoids {2023}. Sinusoids are lined by endothelial and Kupffer cells which show a more diffuse staining with UEA-1 and anti-CD34 than the focal staining of the sinusoidal endothelial cells of normal liver {1630}. The fetal phenotype has been significantly associated with both diploid DNA nuclear content and low proliferative activity assessed by flow cytometry and PCNA labeling index {1640}.

Combined fetal and embryonal epithelial

Approximately 20% of cases display a pattern combining fetal epithelial cells and sheets or clusters of small, ovoid to angulated cells with scant amounts of dark granular cytoplasm surrounding a nucleus with increased nuclear chromatin. The cells display little cohesiveness but may cluster into pseudorosette, glandular or acinar structures. These small, round, blue cells resemble the blastemal cells seen in nephroblastomas, neuroblastomas and other 'embryonal' tumours in children. While often intermixed with the fetal epithelial cells, the foci of embryonal cells, which are devoid of glycogen and lipid, can be identified by their absence of staining with PAS or oil red-O stains. Mitotic activity is more pronounced in the embryonal areas, and associated with a low TGF-alpha expression. EMH, in the absence of preoperative chemotherapy, may also be noted {925}.

Macrotrabecular

In about 3% of cases of fetal and embryonal epithelial hepatoblastomas, areas containing broad trabeculae (6-12 or more cells in thickness) are present. These macrotrabeculae are composed of fetal and embryonal epithelial cells and a third, larger cell type characterized

by more abundant cytoplasm and larger nuclei. Although the trabeculae resemble those seen in the pseudoglandular type of hepatocellular carcinoma, the cells display only mild hyperchromasia and anisocytosis, and mitotic activity is low. The term 'macrotrabecular' is applied to only those cases in which macrotrabeculae are a prominent feature of the lesion. If only an isolated focus is present, the

veins and inferior vena cava. The lung is the most frequent site of metastases; approximately 10-20% of patients have pulmonary metastases when first diagnosed. Hepatoblastomas also spread to bone, brain, ovaries, and the eye {179, 1600, 619, 463}.

Table 8.03
Staging of Hepatoblastoma according to the Children's Cancer Study Group (CCSG) classification.

Stage I	Complete resection
Stage II	Microscopic residual Negative nodal involvement No spilled tumour
Stage III	Gross residual or Nodal involvement or Spilled tumour
Stage IV	Metastatic disease

Table 8.04
Clinical syndromes, congenital malformations and other conditions that have been associated with hepatoblastoma.

Absence of left adrenal gland
Acardia syndrome
Alcohol embryopathy
Beckwith-Wiedemann syndrome
Beckwith-Wiedemann syndrome with opso-clonus, myoclonus
Bilateral talipes
Budd-Chiari syndrome
Cleft palate, macroglossia, dysplasia of ear lobes
Cystothioninuria
Down syndrome, malrotation of colon, Meckel diverticulum, pectum excavatum, intrathoracic kidney, single coronary artery
Duplicated ureters
Fetal hydrops
Gardner syndrome
Goldenhar syndrome – oculoauriculovertebral dysplasia, absence of portal vein
Hemihypertrophy
Heterotopic lung tissue
Heterozygous α1-antitrypsin deficiency
HIV or HBV infection
Horseshoe kidney
Hypoglycemia
Inguinal hernia
Isosexual precocity
Maternal clomiphene citrate and Pergonal
Meckel diverticulum
Oral contraceptive, mother
Oral contraceptive, patient
Osteoporosis
Persistent ductus arteriosus
Polyposis coli families
Prader-Willi syndrome
Renal dysplasia
Right-sided diaphragmatic hernia
Schinzel-Geidion syndrome
Synchronous Wilms tumour
Trisomy 18
Type 1a glycogen storage disease
Umbilical hernia
Very low birth weight

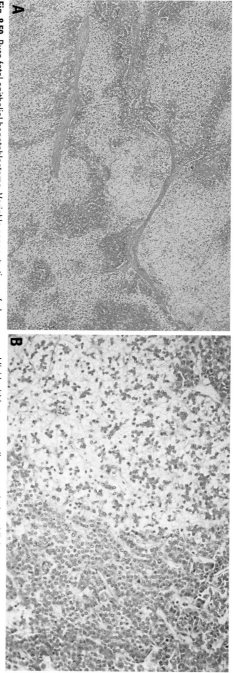

Fig. 8.50 Pure fetal epithelial hepatoblastoma. Variable concentrations of glycogen and lipid within tumour cells create dark and light areas.

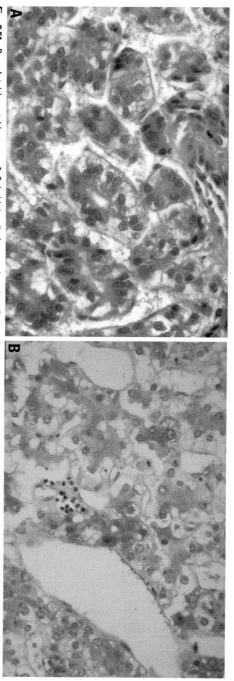

Fig. 8.51 Pure fetal hepatoblastoma. **A** Cuboidal cells form trabeculae. **B** Immunoreactivity for alpha-fetoprotein is present in most tumour cells. A cluster of hematopoietic cells is present at lower center.

classification is based on the epithelial or mixed epithelial/mesenchymal components present.

Small cell undifferentiated

Hepatoblastomas composed entirely of noncohesive sheets of small cells resembling the small blue cells of neuroblastoma, Ewing sarcoma, lymphoma, and rhabdomyosarcoma are called small cell undifferentiated hepatoblastomas and amount to about 3% of the tumours. This type is believed to represent the least differentiated form of hepatoblastoma {602}.

While often difficult to identify as hepatic in origin, the presence of small amounts of glycogen, lipid and bile pigment, along with cytoplasmic cytokeratin, helps separate this lesion from metastatic small cell tumours. The cells are arranged as solid masses with areas of cellular pyknosis and necrosis and high mitotic activity. Sinusoids are present but decreased in amount compared to the fetal epithelial pattern, and there is pronounced intracellular expression of extracellular matrix proteins and large numbers of fibers immunoreactive for collagen type III {1629}.

Mixed epithelial and mesenchymal

The largest number of hepatoblastomas (44%) display a pattern combining fetal and embryonal epithelial elements with primitive mesenchyme and mesenchymally derived tissues. Of these mixed tumours, 80% have only immature and

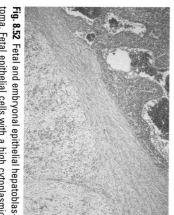

Fig. 8.52 Fetal and embryonal epithelial hepatoblastoma. Fetal epithelial cells with a high cytoplasmic lipid concentration are separated by a band of fibrous connective tissue from a vascular mass of embryonal cells.

Fig. 8.53 Fetal and embryonal hepatoblastoma. Embryonal epithelial cells occur singly and in gland-like structures.

mature fibrous tissue, osteoid-like tissue and cartilaginous tissue, in addition to the epithelial cells. The other 20% contain additional elements.

The mesenchymal elements of the 'simple' mixed tumour are interspersed with the fetal and embryonal epithelial elements. The primitive mesenchymal tissue consists of a light myxomatous stroma containing large numbers of spindle-shaped cells with elongate nuclei. The cells may display a parallel orientation with collagen fibers and cells resembling young fibroblasts. More mature fibrous septa with well differentiated fibroblasts and collagen may also be seen.

Islands of osteoid-like tissue composed of a smooth eosinophilic matrix containing lacunae filled with one or more cells are the hallmark of the mixed lesion. Rarely, they are the only 'mesenchymal' component noted in a predominantly fetal epithelial hepatoblastoma. In fact, the 'osteoid' material is positive for alpha 1-antitrypsin, alpha 1-antichymotrypsin, alpha fetoprotein, carcinoembryonic antigen, chromogranin A, epithelial membrane antigen, vimentin and S-100 protein, suggesting an origin from epithelial cells {10, 2058, 1629}. The cells within the lacunae, while 'osteoblast-like' with angulated borders, abundant eosino-philic cytoplasm and one or more round or oval nuclei, may in some areas blend with adjacent areas of embryonal epithelial cells, further supporting their epithelial origin. Cartilaginous material may also be present.

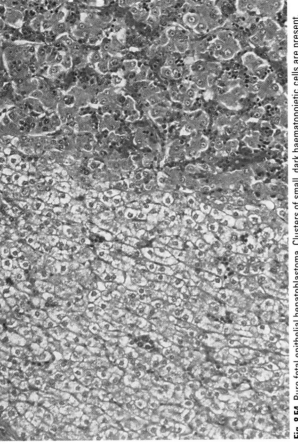

Fig. 8.54 Pure fetal epithelial hepatoblastoma. Clusters of small, dark haematopoietic cells are present.

Cancer Study Group (CCSG) classification is widely used. While 40-60% of patients are considered inoperable at the time they are first seen and 10-20% have pulmonary metastases, preoperative chemotherapy and transplantation for the more extensive lesions have resulted in resectability for nearly 90% of cases.

Precursor lesions and benign tumours

Precursor lesions of hepatoblastoma have not been identified, but hepatoblastoma must be differentiated from other liver tumours and pseudotumours that occur in the same age period. Infantile haemangioendothelioma, the most commonly occurring benign tumour of the liver, is seen almost exclusively in the first year of life and presents as an asymptomatic mass or, less frequently, as congestive heart failure due to rapid shunting of blood through the liver {1708}. MRI and arteriography are helpful in establishing the diagnosis.

Mesenchymal hamartoma, another benign lesion, occurs during the first 2-3

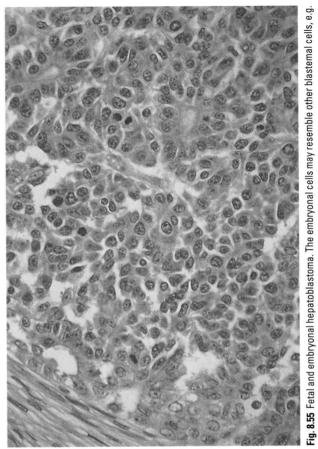

Fig. 8.55 Fetal and embryonal hepatoblastoma. The embryonal cells may resemble other blastemal cells, e.g. those encountered in nephroblastoma or neuroblastoma.

Mixed with teratoid features

In addition to the features noted in the 'simple' mixed epithelial/mesenchymal hepatoblastoma, about 20% of lesions will display additional features, including striated muscle, bone, mucinous epithelium, stratified squamous epithelium, and melanin pigment {1839}. These tissues may occur separately or be admixed with others. It is important to differentiate these teratoid features from a true teratoma, which does not contain fetal and embryonal epithelial hepatoblastoma areas. There is, however, a single case report of a discrete cystic teratoma contiguous to a hepatoblastoma {331}.

Staging

These is no official TNM classification for hepatoblastoma but a TNM-type system has been proposed {332}. The Children's

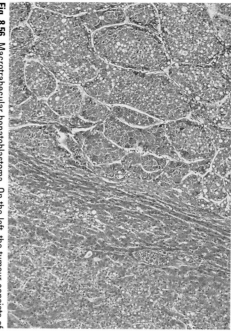

Fig. 8.56 Macrotrabecular hepatoblastoma. On the left, the tumour consists of macrotrabeculae. The one to two-cell thick trabeculae of fetal epithelial hepatoblastoma pattern are seen on the right.

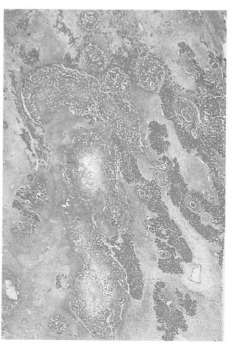

Fig. 8.57 Mixed epithelial and mesenchymal hepatoblastoma. Areas showing mesenchymal tissue and foci of osteoid-like material are present, together with areas of epithelial hepatoblastoma.

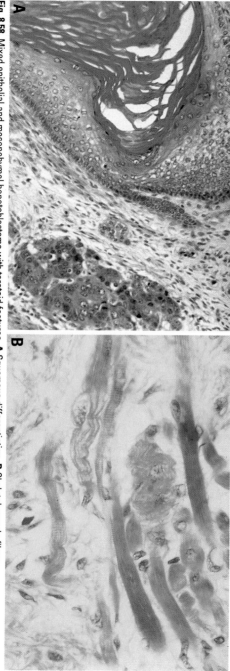

Fig. 8.58 Mixed epithelial and mesenchymal hepatoblastoma with teratoid features. **A** Squamous differentiation. **B** Skeletal muscle fibres.

years of life and presents as a rapidly enlarging mass due to accumulation of fluid within cysts formed in the mesenchymal portion of the lesion {1841}. CT and MRI are useful in defining the cystic nature of the lesion. Focal nodular hyperplasia and nodular regenerative hyperplasia may be seen in the first few years of life but are more common in older children {1839}. Hepatocellular adenoma is rarely seen in the first 5-10 years of life, but may be difficult to differentiate from a pure fetal epithelial hepatoblastoma.

Genetic susceptibility

Congenital anomalies are noted in approximately 5% of patients (Table 8.04) and include renal malformations such as horseshoe kidney, renal dysplasia and duplicated ureters, gastrointestinal malformations such as Meckel diverticulum, inguinal hernia and diaphragmatic her-

nia, and other disparate malformations such as absent adrenal gland and heterotopic lung tissue. Other syndromes with an increased incidence of hepatoblastoma include Beckwith-Wiedemann syndrome, trisomy 18, trisomy 21, Acardia syndrome, Goldenhar syndrome, Prader-Willi syndrome, and type 1a glycogen storage disease {1585}.

Hepatoblastoma and familial adenomatous polyposis (FAP) are associated due to germline mutation of the adenomatous polyposis coli (*APC*) gene. FAP kindreds include patients with hepatoblastoma who have an *APC* gene mutation at the 5' end of the gene {267, 578}. Alterations in *APC* have also been noted in cases of hepatoblastoma in non-familial adenomatous polyposis patients {1390}.

Molecular genetics

Cytogenetic abnormalities include tri-

somy for all or parts of chromosome 2, trisomy for chromosome 20 and loss of heterozygosity (LOH) for the telomeric portion of 11p (11p15.5). The material lost on 11p is always of maternal origin {43}. LOH has also been observed on the short and long arms of chromosome 1 with a random distribution of parental origin for chromosome arm 1p and a paternal origin for chromosome arm 1q {970}. *TP53* overexpression has been described in several cases, but *TP53* mutations in exons 5 to 9 are infrequent {1406}. Increased copy numbers of *c-met* and *K-sam* proto-oncogenes and cyclin *D1* genes have been described in a case of hepatoblastoma in an adult patient {977}.

The presence of oval cell antigen has been demonstrated in hepatoblastomas, which supports the stem cell origin of these tumours {1631}.

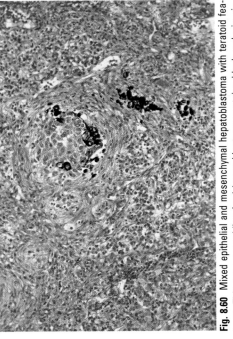

Fig. 8.59 Mixed epithelial and mesenchymal hepatoblastoma. Fetal epithelial cells upper left and embryonal epithelial cells upper right lie adjacent to a focus of osteoid-like material.

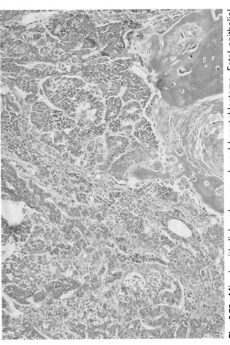

Fig. 8.60 Mixed epithelial and mesenchymal hepatoblastoma with teratoid features. This area resembling fetal hepatoblastoma contains black melanin pigment.

Prognosis and predictive factors

Prognosis is directly affected by the ability to resect the lesion entirely, i.e. to attain Stage I or II following the initial surgery {332, 446, 648, 2024}. Chemotherapy and transplantation have allowed resectability in 90% of cases, increasing the overall survival to 65-70%.

Survival in Stage I is nearly 100% and Stage II survival approaches 80%. AFP levels are useful in predicting outcome by observing their response to surgery and chemotherapy {1997}. AFP levels of 100 to 1,000,000 ng/mL at initial diagnosis are associated with a better prognosis than if they are < 100 or

> 1,000,000ng/mL. Other factors positively influencing prognosis include tumour confined to one lobe, fetal epithelial growth pattern, and multifocal dissemination (rather than unifocal growth pattern in the liver with distant metastases and vascular invasion) {2022}.

Lymphoma of the liver

A. Wotherspoon

Definition

Primary lymphoma of the liver is defined as an extranodal lymphoma arising in the liver with the bulk of the disease localized to this site. Contiguous lymph node involvement and distant spread may be seen but the primary clinical presentation is in the liver, with therapy directed to this site.

Epidemiology

Primary lymphoma of the liver is rare {796}. It is mainly a disease of white middle aged males {1043, 1217} although an occasional case has been reported in childhood {1557}. Most are B-cell lymphomas. Primary hepatosplenic T-cell lymphomas have a different distribution. Patients are almost always male (M:F approximately 5:1) but are usually younger with a mean age of 20 years (range 8-68 years) {334}.

In contrast to primary lymphoma, secondary liver infiltration is a frequent occurrence, being present in 80-100% of cases of chronic leukaemia, 50-60% of cases of non-Hodgkin lymphoma and approximately 30% of cases of multiple myeloma {2042, 261}.

Aetiology

A proportion of cases are associated with hepatitis C virus infection with and without mixed cryoglobulinaemia {390, 56, 1257, 90, 371, 1625, 311}. Other lymphomas have been reported arising within a background of hepatitis B virus infection {1441, 1183}, HIV infection {1680, 1516} and primary biliary cirrhosis {1535}.

Clinical features

The most frequent presenting symptoms are right upper abdominal/epigastric pain or discomfort, weight loss and fever {1043, 1217}. Most cases are solitary or multiple masses within the liver which may be misdiagnosed as a primary liver tumour or metastatic cancer {1043, 1217}. Some cases have been reported with diffuse infiltration of the liver associated with hepatomegaly but without a discrete mass, simulating hepatic inflammation {668}.

Hepatosplenic T-cell lymphomas present with hepatosplenomegaly, usually without peripheral lymphadenopathy and without lymphocytosis. There is almost always thrombocytopenia and most patients are anaemic. Liver function tests are usually abnormal with moderate elevation of levels of transaminases and alkaline phosphatase. Serum lactate dehydrogenase level may be very high {334}.

Histopathology

B-cell lymphoma

The majority of primary hepatic lymphomas are of diffuse large B-cell type with sheets of large cells with large nuclei and prominent nucleoli. Phenotypically these characteristically express the pan B-cell markers CD20 and CD79a.

Occasional cases of Burkitt lymphoma have been described {759} in which the morphology is typical of Burkitt lymphoma encountered elsewhere in the digestive tract. Immunophenotypically the cells express CD20, CD79a and CD10. They are generally negative with antibodies to bcl-2 protein.

Low-grade B-cell lymphomas of MALT type have also been described. These are characterized by a dense lymphoid infiltrate within the portal tracts. The atypical lymphoid cells have centrocyte-like cell morphology and surround reactive germinal centres. Lymphoepithelial lesions are formed by the centrocyte-like cells and the bile duct epithelium, and these may be highlighted by staining with anti-cytokeratin antibodies. Nodules of normal liver may be entrapped within the tumour. The cells express pan-B-cell markers CD20 and CD79a and are negative for CD5, CD10 and CD23. There is no expression of cyclinD1 {797, 1143, 923}. Secondary involvement of the liver by chronic lymphocytic leukaemia and B-cell non-Hodgkin lymphoma tends to show a distribution involving the portal triads although nodular infiltration may also be seen with non-Hodgkin lymphoma and multiple myeloma {2042}.

Hepatosplenic T-cell lymphoma

This is characterized by infiltration of the sinusoids by a monomorphic population of medium sized cells with a moderate amount of eosinophilic cytoplasm. The nuclei are round or slightly indented with moderately dispersed chromatin and contain small, usually basophilic, nucleoli. There may be mild sinusoidal dilation and there are occasional pseudo-peliotic lesions. Perisinusoidal fibrosis may be present. Portal infiltration is variable. A similar sinusoidal pattern of infiltration is seen in the spleen and bone marrow both of which are usually involved by the lymphoma at diagnosis {486, 334}.

The cells are usually immunoreactive for CD2, CD3, CD7 and the cytotoxic granule related protein TIA-1. There is usually no expression of CD5. The majority of cases are CD4-/CD8- although some are CD4-/CD8+ {486, 334}. A CD4+ variant has been described very infrequently {771}. There is variable expression of CD16 and CD56. All cases are negative for βF1 and positive with antibodies for the T-cell receptor δ.

Genetics

Hepatosplenic T-cell lymphoma exhibits rearrangement of the T-cell receptor γ gene. EBV sequences have not been detected {334}. Cytogenetic studies have shown isochromosome 7q in a number of cases and in some this has been present as the sole cytogenetic abnormality {524, 48}.

Prognosis

The prognosis of primary hepatic lymphoma is generally poor. Chemotherapy or radiotherapy alone has been reported to be ineffective but combination modalities, including surgery in resectable cases, can give relatively good results {1043, 1217}. Hepatosplenic T-cell lymphomas are very aggressive, with a mean survival of 1 year {334} although the CD4+ subtype may be associated with a slightly longer survival {771}.

Mesenchymal tumours of the liver

K.G. Ishak
P.P. Anthony
C. Niederau
Y. Nakanuma

Definition

Benign and malignant tumours arising in the liver, with vascular, fibrous, adipose and other mesenchymal tissue differentiation.

ICD-O codes

ICD-O codes, terminology, and definitions largely follow the WHO 'Histological Typing of Soft Tissue Tumours' {2086}.

Imaging

Imaging studies establish the presence of a space-occupying lesion or lesions in the liver, and may provide a diagnosis or differential diagnosis {1565}. Biopsy of a mass is, however, needed for a definitive diagnosis {806}.

Mesenchymal hamartoma

Mesenchymal hamartoma is a 'tumour malformation' that develops *in utero*. It accounts for 8% of all liver tumours and pseudotumours from birth to 21 years of age, but during the first two years of life it represents 12% of all hepatic tumours and pseudotumours, and for 22% of the benign neoplasms {1839}. It usually manifests in the first two years of life and there is a slight male predominance. Lesions involve the right lobe in 75% of cases, the left lobe in 22% and both lobes in 3%.

Presentation is typically with abdominal swelling, but rapid accumulation of fluid in the tumour can cause sudden enlargement of the abdomen {1841}. Macroscopically, it is usually a single mass that can attain a large size (up to 30 cm or more). Mesenchymal hamartoma has an excellent prognosis after resection. The fate of untreated lesions is not known but there is no convincing evidence of malignant transformation.

Histopathology. This tumour-like lesion is composed of loose connective tissue and epithelial ductal elements in varying proportions. Grossly, the cut surfaces exhibit solid, pink-tan areas and cysts containing a clear fluid. Histologically, the connective tissue is typically loose and oedematous with a matrix of acid mucopoly-

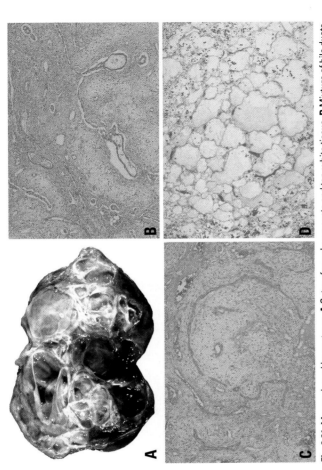

Fig. 8.61 Mesenchymal hamartoma. **A** Cut surface shows cysts and tan-white tissue. **B** Mixture of bile ducts, mesenchymal tissue and blood vessels. **C** Bile ducts display a ductal plate malformation; the primitive mesenchymal tissue consists of loosely arranged stellate cells. In addition to blood vessels, the tumour also contains liver cells (top). **D** Fluid accumulation in the mesenchyme mimics lymphangioma, but the spaces lack an endothelial lining.

Table 8.05
Presentation of mesenchymal tumours of the liver.

Mode of Presentation	Examples
Asymptomatic (incidental finding)	Any
Upper abdominal mass +/- hepatomegaly	Any
Sudden increase in size of tumour	Mesenchymal hamartoma, cavernous haemangioma
Febrile illness with weight loss	Inflammatory pseudotumour, embryonal sarcoma, angiosarcoma
Acute abdominal crisis from rupture	Cavernous haemangioma, angiosarcoma, epithelioid haemangioendothelioma
Budd-Chiari syndrome	Epithelioid haemangioendothelioma
Congestive heart failure	Infantile haemangioendothelioma
Cardiac tumour syndrome	Embryonal sarcoma
Consumption coagulopathy	Cavernous haemangioma, infantile haemangioendothelioma
Hypoglycaemia	Solitary fibrous tumour
Portal hypertension	Epithelioid haemangioendothelioma, inflammatory pseudotumour
Liver failure	Epithelioid haemangioendothelioma, angiosarcoma
Obstructive jaundice	Inflammatory pseudotumour
Lung metastases	Epithelioid haemangioendothelioma, angiosarcoma

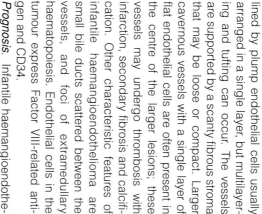

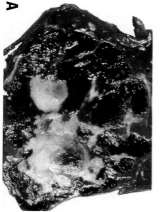

mation' that develops *in utero*. There may be a variety of associated congenital anomalies, including hemihypertrophy

Infantile haemangioendothelioma

This lesion is defined as a benign tumour composed of vessels lined by plump endothelial cells, intermingled with bile ducts, that are set in a fibrous stroma. Infantile haemangioendothelioma accounts for about one fifth of all liver tumours and pseudotumours from birth to 21 years of age. It usually presents in the first two years of life, when it represents 40% of all tumours and pseudotumours and 70% of the benign ones {1839}. It occurs more frequently in females (63%) than in males. Infantile haemangioendothelioma is a localized 'tumour malfor-

saccharide, or it is collagenous and arranged concentrically around the ducts. Fluid accumulation leads to separation of the fibres with formation of lymphangioma-like areas and larger cavities. The epithelial component consists of bile ducts that may be tortuous and occasionally dilated. The ducts often are arranged in a ductal-plate-malformation pattern. Islets of liver cells without an acinar architecture may be present. Numerous arteries and veins are scattered throughout, as are foci of extramedullary haematopoiesis.

Fig. 8.62 Infantile haemangioendothelioma. **A** Red and brown tumour with focal hemorrhage. **B** Multiple brown cavitary lesions. **C** The tumour is well circumscribed but not encapsulated, and consists of small vessels. **D** Masson trichrome stain shows vessels lined by a single layer of plump endothelial cells surrounded by a scant fibrous stroma. Note the scattered bile ducts.

and Cornelia de Lange syndrome. Patients may develop congestive heart failure or consumption coagulopathy, with or without an abdominal mass {397, 1708}, and about 10% have haemangiomas of the skin.

Grossly, infantile haemangioendothelioma forms a single large mass (55%) or involves the entire liver by multiple lesions (45%). The single tumours have a maximum diameter up to 14 cm while the multiple lesions are often less than a centimeter. The large, single lesions are red-brown or red-tan, often with haemorrhagic or fibrotic centers and focal calcification. The small lesions appear spongy and red-brown on sectioning.

Histopathology. Lesions are composed of numerous small vascular channels

lined by plump endothelial cells usually arranged in a single layer, but multilayering and tufting can occur. The vessels are supported by a scanty fibrous stroma that may be loose or compact. Larger cavernous vessels with a single layer of flat endothelial cells are often present in the centre of the larger lesions; these vessels may undergo thrombosis with infarction, secondary fibrosis and calcification. Other characteristic features of infantile haemangioendothelioma are small bile ducts scattered between the vessels, and foci of extramedullary haematopoiesis. Endothelial cells in the tumour express Factor VIII-related antigen and CD34.

Prognosis. Infantile haemangioendothelioma has an overall survival of 70%; adverse risk factors include congestive heart failure, jaundice and the presence of multiple tumours {1708}. Single tumours are generally resected although some 5-10% undergo spontaneous regression. Hepatic artery ligation or transarterial embolization are other therapeutic modalities. There are occasional reports of transformation of infantile haemangioendothelioma to angiosarcoma {1708}.

Cavernous haemangioma

This is the most frequently occurring benign tumour of the liver. The reported incidence varies from 0.4 to 20%, the highest figure being the result of a thorough prospective search {892}. It is more frequent in females, and occurs at all ages but is least common in the paediatric age group. Although it usually presents in adults, it is thought to be a hamartomatous lesion. It is known to increase in size or even rupture during pregnancy, and also may enlarge or recur in patients on oestrogen therapy. Consumption coagulopathy may occur. Cavernous

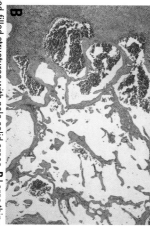

Fig. 8.63 Cavernous haemangioma. **A** Multilocular blood-filled structures with pale solid areas. **B** Large thin-walled vascular spaces.

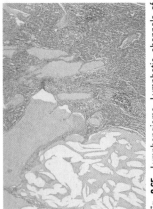

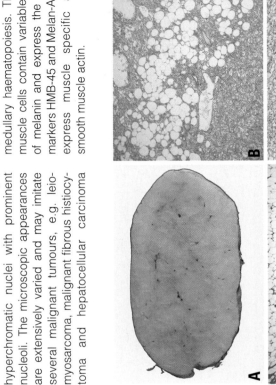

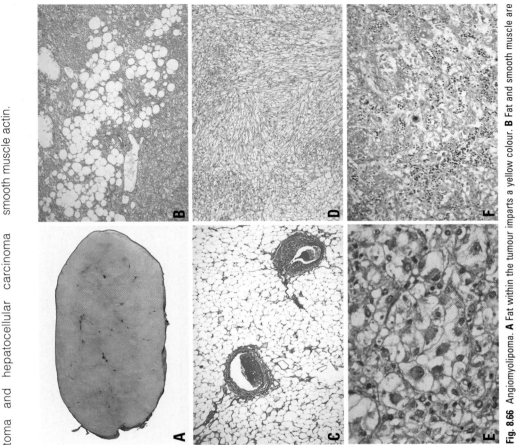

haemangiomas are not known to undergo malignant change. Only large symptomatic tumours require surgical excision.

Macroscopically, cavernous haemangiomas vary from a few millimeters to huge tumours ('giant' haemangiomas) that can replace most of the liver. They are usually single, and soft or fluctuant. When sectioned they partially collapse due to the escape of blood and have a spongy appearance. Recent haemorrhages, organized thrombi, fibrosis and calcification may be seen.

Histopathology. Lesions are typically composed of blood-filled vascular channels of varied size lined by a single layer of flat endothelial cells supported by fibrous tissue. Thrombi in various stages of organization with areas of infarction may be present, and older lesions show dense fibrosis and calcification. In sclerosed haemangiomas, most or all of the vessels are occluded and sometimes are only demonstrable by stains for elastic tissue.

Fig. 8.64 Sclerosed haemangioma. Pale hyalinized nodule with remnants of obliterated vessels.

Fig. 8.65 Lymphangioma. Lymphatic channels of variable size contain clear pink fluid.

gated with blunt ends, but the larger smooth muscle cells can have large, hyperchromatic nuclei with prominent nucleoli. The microscopic appearances are extensively varied and may imitate several malignant tumours, e.g. leiomyosarcoma, malignant fibrous histiocytoma and hepatocellular carcinoma

{1971}. A characteristic feature of angiomyolipoma is the presence of extramedullary haematopoiesis. The smooth muscle cells contain variable quantities of melanin and express the melanoma markers HMB-45 and Melan-A. They also express muscle specific actin and smooth muscle actin.

Angiomyolipoma

The lesion is defined as a benign tumour composed of variable admixtures of adipose tissue, smooth muscle (spindled or epithelioid), and thick-walled blood vessels. The age range of angiomyolipoma is from 30-72 years, with a mean of 50 years {1373}. It is seen equally in males and females {604}. A small number are associated with tuberous sclerosis.

Angiomyolipomas are usually single, with 60% located in the right lobe, 30% in the left lobe, 20% in both lobes and 8% in the caudate lobe {1373}. They are sharply demarcated but not encapsulated, fleshy or firm and, when sectioned, with a homogeneous yellow, yellow-tan or tan appearance, depending on their content of fat.

Histopathology. Angiomyolipomas are composed of adipose tissue, smooth muscle and thick-walled, sometimes hyalinized blood vessels in varying proportions. Morphologically and phenotypically they are believed to belong to a family of lesions characterized by proliferation of perivascular epithelioid cells {2197}. The smooth muscle is composed of spindle-shaped cells arranged in bundles, or larger more rounded cells with an 'empty' (glycogen-rich) cytoplasm or an eosinophilic, epithelioid appearance. The nuclei of the spindle cells are elon-

Fig. 8.66 Angiomyolipoma. **A** Fat within the tumour imparts a yellow colour. **B** Fat and smooth muscle are present. **C** Two characteristically thick-walled arteries are surrounded by fat. **D** This tumour is composed predominantly of smooth muscle. The clear cytoplasm is due to glycogen that was lost during processing. **E** Large smooth muscle cells show perinuclear condensation of cytoplasm. **F** Marked extramedullary haematopoiesis.

Solitary fibrous tumour

Solitary fibrous tumour has an age range from 32-83 years (mean, 57 years) {1270}. Its aetiology is unknown. Lesions vary considerably in size, from 2-20 cm in diameter {1270}. They arise in either lobe and are occasionally pedunculated. The external surface is smooth and the consistency firm. They are sharply demarcated but not encapsulated. Gross sections show a light tan to almost white colour with a whorled texture.

Histopathology. Solitary fibrous tumour often shows alternating cellular and relatively acellular areas. The cellular areas consist of bundles of spindle cells arranged haphazardly or in a storiform pattern. There is a well-developed reticulin network. In some cases the cells are arranged around ectatic vessels in a haemangiopericytoma-like pattern. Nuclei of the spindle cells are uniform and lack pleomorphism, but these tumours may undergo malignant change as evidenced by the presence of foci of necrosis, prominent cellular atypia, and mitotic activity in the range of 2-4 mitoses/10 hpf {1270, 514}. The relatively acellular areas of solitary fibrous tumour contain abundant collagen bundles with thin, stretched-out tumour cells. The tumour cells characteristically express CD34.

Inflammatory pseudotumour

This lesion is defined as a benign, non-neoplastic, non-metastasizing mass composed of fibrous tissue and proliferated myofibroblasts, with a marked inflammatory infiltration, predominantly plasma cells {318}.

The mean age at presentation of inflammatory pseudotumour of the liver is 56 years (range, 3-77) {438}; it is commoner in males (70%) than in females {1270}. Inflammatory pseudotumours are solitary (81%) or less often multiple (19%) {1275} and usually intrahepatic, but some can involve the hepatic hilum. About half of the solitary tumours are located in the right lobe. They vary in size from 1 cm to large masses involving an entire lobe, and are firm, tan, yellow-white or white. Some inflammatory pseudotumours are probably the residuum of a resolved bacterial abscess, while others may be related to Epstein-Barr virus infection {82, 318}.

Histopathology. The lesions are similar to those occurring in other sites. They are composed of inflammatory cells in a stroma of interlacing bundles of myofibro-blasts, fibroblasts, and collagen bundles. The majority of inflammatory cells are mature plasma cells, but lymphocytes (and occasional lymphoid aggregates or follicles), as well as eosinophils and neutrophils, may be present. Macrophages, sometimes showing xanthomatous changes, occasional granulomas and, rarely, phlebitis involving portal vein branches or outflow veins, may be seen.

Lymphangioma and lymphangiomatosis

Lymphangioma is a benign tumour characterized by multiple endothelial-lined spaces that vary in size from capillary channels to large, cystic spaces containing lymph. The vascular spaces are lined by a single layer of endothelial cells, though papillary projections or tufting may be seen.

The cells rest on a basement membrane and the supporting stroma is usually scanty. Clear, pink-staining lymph fills the lymphatic channels.

Hepatic lymphangiomatosis, often accompanied by lymphangiomatosis of the spleen, skeleton, and other tissues, may represent a malformation syndrome. Diffuse lymphangiomatosis involving the liver and multiple organs is associated with a poor prognosis. Single lesions have been successfully resected.

Pseudolipoma

Pseudolipoma is believed to represent an appendix epiploica attached to the Glisson capsule after becoming detached from the large bowel {1609}. Lesions are usually a small, encapsulated mass of fat located in a concavity on the surface of the liver, the fat typically showing necrosis and calcification {891}.

Focal fatty change

Focal fatty change of the liver is characterized by multiple, contiguous acini showing macrovesicular steatosis of hepatocytes, with preservation of acinar architecture {804}. About 45% of cases of a series of focal fatty change occurred in patients with diabetes mellitus {632}.

Embryonal sarcoma

A malignant tumour composed of mesenchymal cells that, by light microscopy, are undifferentiated.

Embryonal sarcoma ('undifferentiated' sarcoma) comprises 6% of all primary hepatic tumours in childhood {2082}. It usually occurs between 5 and 20 years of age {1840}. Rarely, cases have occurred in middle and even old age. The incidence in males and females is equal {1840}. Embryonal sarcoma is of unknown aetiology, although one patient had a past history of prenatal exposure

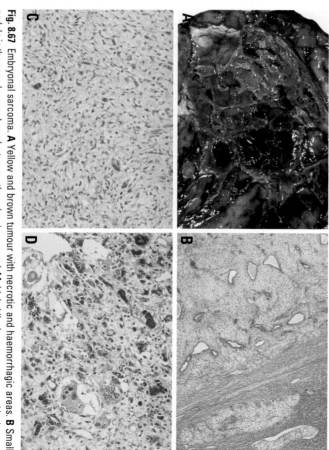

Fig. 8.67 Embryonal sarcoma. **A** Yellow and brown tumour with necrotic and haemorrhagic areas. **B** Small nodule in the pseudocapsule and a tumour thrombus in a vessel. Multiple bile ducts are entrapped in the sarcomatous tissue. **C** Spindle and stellate cells together with giant cells in a loose myxoid stroma. **D** Pleomorphic cells with eosinophillic cytoplasmic globules.

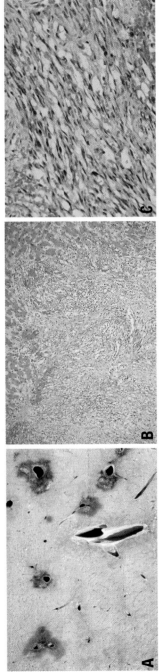

Fig. 8.68 Kaposi sarcoma. **A** Multiple dark brown lesions centered in large portal areas. **B, C** Spindle cells and slit-like vascular spaces.

to phenytoin {148}. Symptoms include abdominal enlargement, fever, weight loss, and nonspecific gastrointestinal complaints {1840}. Rarely, the tumour invades the vena cava and grows into the right atrium, mimicking a cardiac tumour {561}.

Macroscopy. Embryonal sarcoma is usually located in the right lobe of the liver, and varies from 10-20 cm in diameter. It is typically well-demarcated but not encapsulated. Gross sections reveal a variegated surface with glistening, solid, grey-white tumour tissue alternating with cystic, gelatinous areas and/or red and yellow foci of haemorrhage or necrosis.

Histopathology. Embryonal sarcoma is composed of malignant stellate or spindle cells that are compactly or loosely arranged in a myxoid stroma. Tumour cells often show prominent anisonucleosis with hyperchromasia; giant cells that may be multinucleated are seen in many cases. A characteristic feature is the presence of eosinophilic globules of varied size, sometimes many per cell, in the cytoplasm. They are PAS-positive, resist diastase digestion, and express alpha-1 antitrypsin, though the larger globules may only be immunoreactive at the periphery. Entrapped bile ducts and hepatocellular elements are often present in the peripheral areas of these tumours. The spindle, stellate and giant cells typically show no morphological evidence of differentiation, but immunohistochemical studies in a few cases have demonstrated widely divergent differentiation into both mesenchymal and epithelial phenotypes, probably from a primitive stem cell {1460}.

Prognosis. Until recently the prognosis of embryonal sarcoma has been very poor, with a median survival of less than one year after diagnosis {1840}. The survival has greatly improved in the last sev-

eral years with some patients living five or more years after combined modality therapy (surgical resection, radiotherapy, and chemotherapy).

Kaposi sarcoma

This lesion is defined as a tumour composed of slit-like vascular channels, spindle cells, mononuclear inflammatory cells, with an admixture of haemosiderin-laden macrophages.

Kaposi sarcoma involves the liver in 12-25% of fatal cases of the acquired immunodeficiency syndrome (AIDS), but is not known to contribute significantly to its morbidity and mortality. In patients with AIDS, it is aetiologically related to HHV-8 infection {276, 1367}. It involves portal areas but can infiltrate the adjacent parenchyma for short distances, and is characterized grossly by irregular, variably-sized, red-brown lesions scattered throughout the liver.

Histologically, lesions resemble those occurring in other sites with spindle cells showing elongated or ovoid, vesicular nuclei with rounded ends and inconspicuous nucleoli. Eosinophilic, PAS-positive globules may be seen in the cytoplasm. The tumour cells are separated by slit-like vascular spaces . Aggregates of haemosiderin granules may be present. The spindle cells express endothelial cell markers (CD31, CD34).

Epithelioid haemangioendothelioma

A tumour of variable malignant potential that is composed of epithelioid or spindle cells growing along preformed vessels or forming new vessels.

Epithelioid haemangioendothelioma presents between 12 and 86 years (mean 47 years) {807, 1150}. Its overall incidence is unknown, but more are reported in females (61%) than in males (39%) {807, 1150}. Risk factors are not known; the

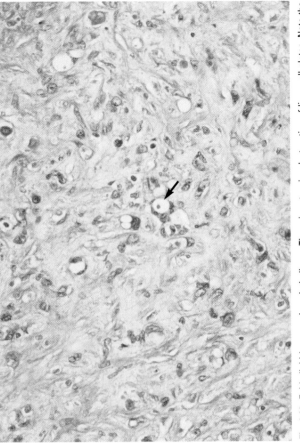

Fig. 8.69 Epithelioid haemangioendothelioma. There is extensive destruction of liver cell plates. Note the intracellular vascular lumina (arrow).

suggestion of a relationship to oral contraceptive use has not been validated {1270}. Epithelioid haemangioendothelioma causes systemic symptoms (weakness, malaise, anorexia, episodic vomiting, upper abdominal pain, and weight loss) and hepato-splenomegaly {807, 1150}. Some patients develop jaundice and liver failure. Uncommon modes of presentation include the Budd-Chiari syndrome {2040} or portal hypertension.

Macroscopy. Macroscopically, lesions are usually multifocal; ill-defined lesions scattered throughout the liver vary from a few millimeters to several centimeters in greatest dimension. They are firm, tan to white on sectioning, and often have a hyperaemic periphery; calcification may be evident grossly.

Histopathology. The tumour nodules are ill-defined, and often involve multiple contiguous acini. In actively proliferating lesions the acinar landmarks, such as terminal hepatic venules (THV) and portal areas, can be recognized despite extensive infiltration by the tumour. The cells grow along preexisting sinusoids, THV, and portal vein branches, and often invade Glisson capsule. Growth within the acini is associated with gradual atrophy and eventual disappearance of liver cell plates. Intravascular growth may be in the form of a solid plug, or a polypoid or tuft-like projection.

Neoplastic cell are either 'dendritic', with spindle or irregular shapes and multiple interdigitating processes, 'epithelioid', with a more rounded shape and an abundant cytoplasm, or 'intermediate'. Nuclear atypia and mitoses are mainly observed in the epithelioid cells. Cytoplasmic vacuoles, representing intracellular vascular lumens, are often identified and may contain erythrocytes. The tumour cells synthesize factor VIII-related antigen (von Willebrand factor), which can be demonstrated in the cytoplasm or in the neoplastic vascular lumens. Other endothelial cell markers, such as CD31 and CD34 are also positive.

The stroma can have a myxoid appearance due to an abundance of sulphated mucopolysaccharide. Reticulin fibres surround nests of tumour cells. Basement membrane can be demonstrated around the cells by the PAS stain, as well as ultrastructurally and immunohistochemically. Variable numbers of smooth muscle cells surround the basement membrane.

As the lesions evolve they are associated with progressive fibrosis and calcification. Eventually, tumour cells (and indeed, the vascular nature of the lesion) may be difficult if not impossible to recognize in the densely sclerosed areas. Needle biopsy specimens taken from such areas often pose diagnostic problems. The histopathological differential diagnosis includes

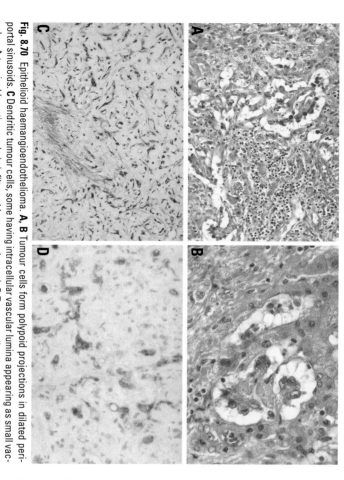

Fig. 8.70 Epithelioid haemangioendothelioma. **A, B** Tumour cells form polypoid projections in dilated periportal sinusoids. **C** Dendritic tumour cells, some having intracellular vascular lumina appearing as small vacuoles. A terminal hepatic venule is infiltrated by tumour (arrow). **D** Tumour cells express factor VIII-related antigen.

angiosarcoma and cholangiocarcinoma. Angiosarcoma is much more destructive than epithelioid haemangioendothelioma, obliterates acinar landmarks and results in cavity formation. Cells of cholangiocarcinoma are arranged in a tubular or glandular pattern, and often produce mucin; the cells are cytokeratin positive and do not express endothelial cell markers.

Prognosis. The clinical outcome of epithelioid haemangioendothelioma is unpredictable, with some patients having a fulminant course and others surviving many years with no therapy. A recent study {1150} showed a correlation between high cellularity of the tumour with a poor clinical outcome. Successful treatment includes resection, when feasible, and liver transplantation.

Angiosarcoma

A malignant tumour composed of spindle or pleomorphic cells that line, or grow into, the lumina of preexisting vascular spaces, such as liver sinusoids and small veins.

Worldwide, about 200 cases of angiosarcoma are diagnosed annually {848, 59}. During the period 1973-87, the SEER database of the US National Cancer Institute contained 6,391 histologically-confirmed primary liver cancers; of these only 65 (1%) were angiosarcomas {252}. The peak incidence is in the 6th and 7th decades of life. The male to female ratio is 3:1 {1085}.

75% of angiosarcomas of the liver have no known aetiology {484}. The remainder have been linked to prior administration of Thorotrast (a radioactive material containing thorium dioxide, that was used as an angiography contrast medium from the 1930s to the early 1950s), exposure to vinyl chloride monomer (VCM) or inorganic arsenic, and the use of androgenic-anabolic steroids {484}.

Patients with angiosarcoma present in one of several ways: 61% have symptoms referable to the liver (e.g. hepatomegaly, abdominal pain, ascites); 15% have an acute abdominal crisis due to haemoperitoneum from rupture of the tumour; 15% have splenomegaly, often with pancytopenia; and 9% present due to distant metastases {804}. The prognosis of angiosarcoma is very poor, with most patients dying within 6 months of diagnosis.

Macroscopy. Angiosarcoma typically affects the entire liver. Grayish-white

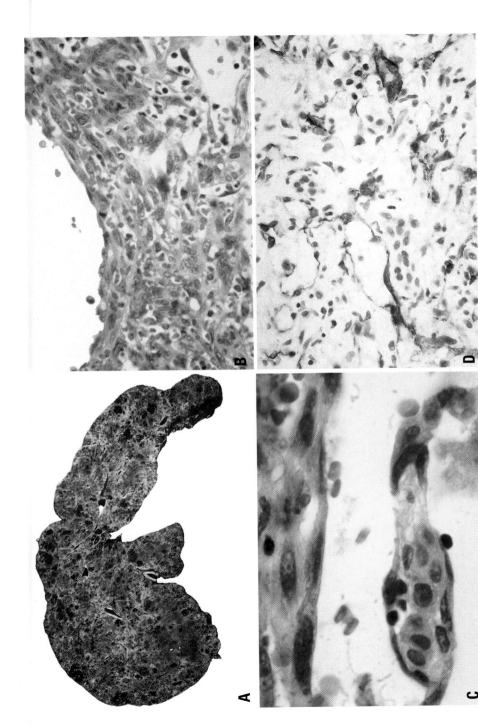

Fig. 8.71 Angiosarcoma. **A** Multiple dark brown tumour foci scattered throughout the liver. **B** Solid portion showing spindle cells and numerous small vascular channels. **C** Intravascular papillary structure covered by neoplastic endothelial cells. **D** Tumour cells express CD34.

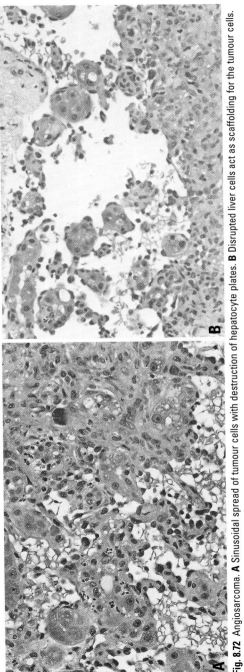

Fig. 8.72 Angiosarcoma. **A** Sinusoidal spread of tumour cells with destruction of hepatocyte plates. **B** Disrupted liver cells act as scaffolding for the tumour cells.

tumour alternates with red-brown haemorrhagic areas. Large cavities with ragged edges, filled with liquid or clotted blood, may be present. A reticular pattern of fibrosis is seen in cases related to prior exposure to Thorotrast.

Histopathology. Tumour cells grow along preformed vascular channels (sinusoids, THV and portal vein branches). Sinusoidal growth is associated with progressive atrophy of liver cells and disruption of the plates, with formation of larger vascular channels and eventually the development of cavities of varied size. These cavities have ragged walls lined by tumour cells, sometimes with polypoid or papillary projections, and are filled with clotted blood and tumour debris. Reti-

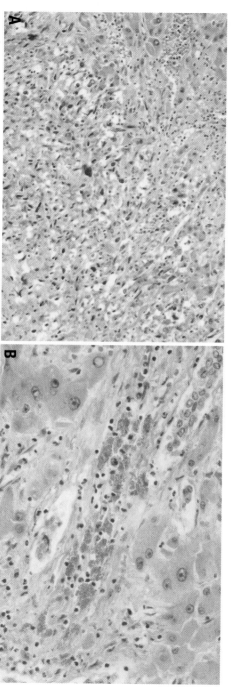

Fig. 8.73 Angiosarcoma. **A** Closely packed elongated tumour cells. **B** Pink-brown granular deposits of Thorotrast in a portal area adjacent to an angiosarcoma.

culin fibres and, less often, collagen fibres support the tumour cells. Perithelial cells, reactive for alpha-smooth muscle actin, may also be present. The tumour cells are sometimes packed solidly in nodules that resemble fibrosarcoma. The cells of angiosarcoma are spindle-shaped, rounded or irregular in outline, and often have ill-defined borders. The cytoplasm is lightly eosinophilic, and nuclei are hyperchromatic and elongated or irregular in shape. Nucleoli can be small, or large and eosinophilic. Large, bizarre nuclei and multinucleated cells may be seen, and mitotic figures are frequently identified. The spindled cells have ill-defined outlines, a lightly eosinophilic cytoplasm, and vesicular nuclei with blunt ends. Factor VIII-related antigen can be identified in tumour cells immunohistochemically. Other useful markers include CD31 and CD34; the former is believed to be the most sensitive immunostain {1224}.

Invasion of THV and portal vein branches leads to progressive obstruction of the lumen, and readily explains the frequently encountered areas of haemorrhage, infarction, and necrosis. Haematopoietic activity is observed in the majority of tumours.

Cases related to Thorotrast and vinyl chloride monomer are often associated with considerable periportal and subcapsular fibrosis. Thorotrast deposits are readily recognized in reticuloendothelial cells, in connective tissue of portal areas, in Glisson capsule, or in the walls of THV. The deposits are coarsely granular and refractile, and in an H&E-stained section they have a pink-brown hue. They are readily visualized by scanning electron microscopy, and thorium can be definitively identified by energy dispersive X-ray microanalysis {804}.

Genetics. Analysis of six hepatic angiosarcomas associated with VCM exposure found three *TP53* mutations, all A:T→T:A transversions, which are otherwise uncommon in human cancers {728}. Another study of 21 sporadic angiosarcomas not associated with vinyl chloride

exposure found *TP53* mutations to be uncommon, thus supporting previous evidence of the carcinogenic potential of chloroethylene oxide, a metabolite of VCM {1776}. A high rate of *KRAS-2* mutations has been found in both sporadic and Thorotrast-induced angiosarcomas of the liver {1542}.

Malignant mesenchymal tumours other than angiosarcoma may have cytogenetic aberrations similar to those of soft tissue tumours {513, 1812}.

Carcinosarcoma

This neoplasm is defined as a malignant tumour containing an intimate mixture of carcinomatous (either hepatocellular or cholangiocellular) and sarcomatous elements; such lesions have also been called 'malignant mixed tumour' of the liver. Carcinosarcoma should be distinguished from carcinomas with foci of spindled epithelial cells and from the rare true 'collision' tumours.

Secondary tumours of the liver

P.P. Anthony
P. DeMatos

Definition

Malignant neoplasms metastasized to the liver from extrahepatic primary tumours.

Epidemiology

In Europe and North America, metastases predominate over primary hepatic tumours in a ratio of 40:1 {130, 1517}. In Japan the ratio is 2.6:1 {1517}. In South-East Asia and sub-Saharan Africa, primary hepatic tumours are more common than metastases {1909} owing to the high incidence of hepatocellular carcinoma, a shorter life span (common extrahepatic carcinomas affect older age groups) and the low incidence of certain tumour types (e.g. carcinomas of the lung and colorectum). Autopsy studies in the USA and Japan have shown that about 40% of patients with extrahepatic cancer have hepatic metastases {351, 1517}.

Aetiopathogenesis

The liver has a rich systemic (arterial) and portal (venous) blood supply, providing a potentially abundant source of circulating neoplastic cells. Circulating tumour cell arrest is controlled by Kupffer cells in the sinusoids {881, 121} and may be enhanced by growth factors such as transforming growth factor alpha (TGFα) {385}, tumour necrosis factor (TNF) {1431}, and insulin-like growth factor-1 (IGF-1) {1091}. As tumour deposits enlarge, they induce angiogenesis using native sinusoidal endothelium; this enhances their chances of survival and is often macroscopically evident {1919}. Most metastases from unpaired abdominal organs reach the liver via the portal vein, and from other sites via the systemic arterial circulation. Lymphatic spread is less common and extension to the liver via the peritoneal fluid is rare {351}.
Cirrhosis provides some relative protection against seeding by secondary tumours {1983, 1211}. It has also been suggested that metastasis is rare in fatty livers {676}, but excess alcohol consumption apparently enhances hepatic metastases {1140}.

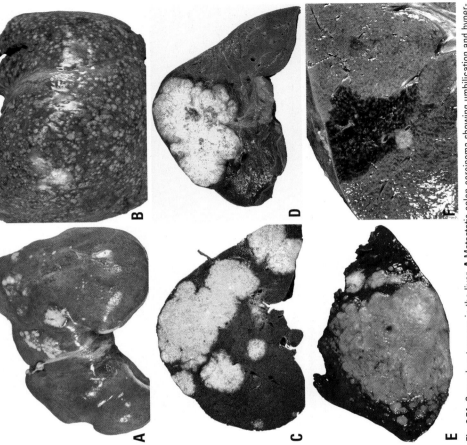

Fig. 8.74 Secondary tumours in the liver. **A** Metastatic colon carcinoma showing umbilication and hyperemic borders. **B** Metastatic small cell carcinoma of lung forming innumerable small nodules. **C, D** Metastatic large intestinal carcinoma, cut surfaces. **E** Metastatic gastric adenocarcinoma, cut surface. **F** A metastasis lies adjacent to a Zahn infarct.

In the majority of cases, metastases to the liver are a manifestation of systemic, disseminated disease. Colorectal carcinoma, neuroendocrine tumours, and renal cell carcinoma are exceptions as these neoplasms sometimes produce isolated, even solitary deposits {1517}.

Origin of metastases

The majority of secondary liver neoplasms are carcinomas, involvement by lymphomas is next and sarcomas are uncommon. The order of frequency by primary site in Western populations is: upper gastrointestinal tract (stomach,

gallbladder, pancreas): 44-78%; colon: 56-58%; lung 42-43%; breast 52-53%; oesophagus 30-32% and genito-urinary organs 24-38% {130, 1517, 351}. Carcinomas of the prostate and the ovaries preferentially spread to the lymph nodes and the spine, and to the peritoneal cavity, respectively.

Hodgkin and non-Hodgkin lymphomas may involve the liver in up to 20% of cases on presentation and 55% at autopsy {1620, 826}. Sarcomas are much less common but 6% had hepatic metastases at presentation (mostly intra-abdominal leiomyosarcomas) in one study {833},

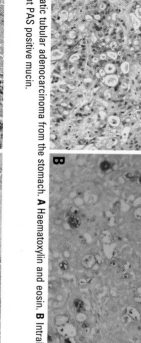
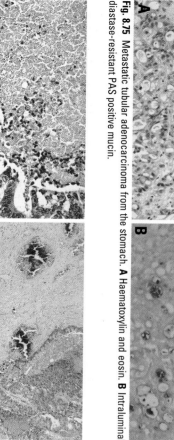

Fig. 8.75 Metastatic tubular adenocarcinoma from the stomach. **A** Haematoxylin and eosin. **B** Intraluminal diastase-resistant PAS positive mucin.

Fig. 8.76 Metastatic colorectal carcinoma. **A** Tumour is necrotic and cell type is typically columnar. **B** Necrosis may result in calcification.

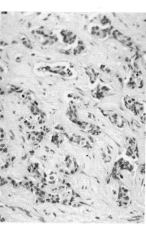

Fig. 8.77 Metastatic breast carcinoma.

while 34% had hepatic metastases at autopsy in another {1517}. In a study of randomly selected liver biopsies from England and Wales {852}, the commonest histological type of metastasis was adenocarcinoma (39%), followed by carcinoma not otherwise specified (36%); the rest were undifferentiated small cell carcinoma, other special types of carcinoma, and lymphomas.

Clinical features

Symptoms and signs

Hepatic metastases produce clinical manifestations in about two-thirds of cases and they generally reveal themselves through symptoms referable to the liver. Afflicted patients often present with ascites, hepatomegaly or abdominal fullness, hepatic pain, jaundice, anorexia, and weight loss. Constitutional symptoms, such as malaise, fatigue, and fever may be present. On examination, nodules or a mass are felt in up to 50% of the cases, and a friction bruit may be heard on auscultation. Unfortunately, symptomatic presentation is associated with a bulky, rapidly progressive tumours with a poor prognosis {2035}.

Rarely, patients present with fulminant hepatic failure, obstructive jaundice, or intraperitoneal haemorrhage. Functioning neuroendocrine tumours produce syndromes of hormonal excess. 'Carcinomatous cirrhosis' with jaundice, ascites, and bleeding varices due to diffuse infiltration of the liver, usually by metastatic breast carcinoma, has been described {174}.

Laboratory studies

The alkaline phosphatase (ALP) and serum glutamic-oxaloacetic transaminase (SGOT) levels, although non-specific, are elevated in approximately 80% and 67% of patients respectively, and most likely represent the effects of hepatic parenchymal infiltration by tumour and of generalized wasting. Elevated lactic dehydrogenase (LDH) levels are relatively specific for the presence of metastatic breast carcinoma. Tests of synthetic function, e.g. serum albumin levels and the prothrombin time, may be normal despite extensive metastatic involvement. Alphafetoprotein (AFP) levels may be slightly to moderately elevated but very high concentrations are more consistent with a diagnosis of hepatocellular carcinoma {904}. Carcinoembryonic antigen (CEA) levels, which are raised in as many as 90% of patients with metastases from colorectal carcinoma, can be useful in monitoring patients after primary tumour resection. However, CEA levels do not correlate well with prognosis {2043, 1821}.

Imaging

Ultrasound (US) can identify tumours measuring 1-2 cm in size, can differentiate solid from cystic lesions, and provide guidance for percutaneous needle biopsy. However, it provides poor anatomical definition and frequently misses smaller lesions.

Computed tomography (CT), using both contrasted and non-contrasted images, can also serve as a screening tool. The administration of intravenous contrast permits the detection of tumours as small as 0.5 cm in diameter {1763}. Most metastases display decreased vascularity in comparison to the surrounding hepatic parenchyma and appear as hypodense defects. Tumours that are hypervascular (e.g. melanoma, carcinoids and some breast cancers) or calcified (e.g. colorectal carcinoma) are better delineated by noncontrast views.

Magnetic resonance imaging (MRI) is more sensitive than CT in the detection of hepatic tumours and can demonstrate additional lesions, too small to be seen on CT.

Positron emission tomography (PET) can detect metastatic disease in the liver and elsewhere. Using 2-(18)fluoro-2-deoxy-D-glucose (F-18 FDG), a radiolabeled glucose analogue, PET highlights metabolically active tissues. Through co-registration with anatomical studies like CT or MRI, viable malignant tumours can be differentiated from benign or necrotic lesions {54}.

CT arterial portography performed preoperatively, and intraoperative ultrasound are associated with the highest sensitivities {1796}. The former is capable of detecting lesions as small as 15 mm, although a false positive rate of

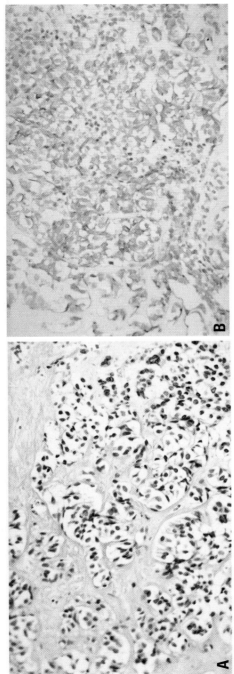

Fig. 8.78 Metastatic islet cell carcinoma of pancreas. **A** Haematoxylin and eosin. **B** Somatostatin immunoreactivity.

17% has been reported {1795}. Its success relies on the fact that tumours are not fed by portal vein blood, so that metastases appear as filling defects. The latter, capable of detecting lesions 2-4 mm in diameter delineates the anatomical location of tumours in relationship to major vascular and biliary structures and provides guidance for intraoperative needle biopsies. It is the definitive step in determining resectability at the time of exploratory laparotomy or laparoscopy. *Angiography* use has declined in recent years. It remains useful for defining vascular anatomy for planned hepatic resections, selective chemotherapy, chemoembolization, or devascularization procedures, for assessing whether there is metastatic involvement of the portal venous system and/or hepatic veins, and for differentiating between benign vascular lesions, such as haemangiomas and metastases, when other imaging studies have yielded equivocal results.

Macroscopy

The distribution of metastases from colorectal carcinoma was found to be homogenous, regardless of the primary site of origin {1695} but in another study, it was suggested that right sided cancers predominantly metastasize to the right lobe of the liver and left sided cancers to both lobes {1749}.

Metastases are nearly always multinodular or diffusely infiltrative, but may rarely be solitary and massive (e.g. from colorectal and renal cell carcinomas). Umbilication (a central depression on the surface of a metastatic deposit) is due to necrosis or scarring and is typical of an adenocarcinoma from stomach, pancreas or colorectum. A vascular rim around the periphery is often seen. Highly mucin secreting adenocarcinomas appear as glistening, gelatinous masses whilst well differentiated keratinizing squamous cell carcinomas are granular. Metastatic carcinoid tumours can form pseudocysts {401}. Haemorrhagic secondary deposits suggest angiosarcoma, choriocarcinoma, carcinoma of thyroid or kidney, neuroendocrine tumour, or vascular leiomyosarcoma. Some diffusely infiltrating carcinomas (e.g. small cell carcinoma), lymphomas and sarcomas may have a soft, opaque 'fish flesh' appearance. Metastatic breast carcinoma in particular can produce an intensely fibrous, granular liver ('carcinomatous cirrhosis') either before {174} or after {1693} treatment.

Calcification of secondary deposits is a feature of colorectal carcinoma but it is seldom excessive and has no effect on prognosis {653}. Metastatic melanoma is often, but not always, of a brown-black colour. Secondary tumours may appear in the liver long after the removal of the primary.

Histopathology

Liver biopsy samples can be obtained by percutaneous or transjugular routes with or without imaging techniques for guidance, as a wedge during laparotomy, or a fine needle can be used to aspirate material for cytology. Each of these methods has advantages and drawbacks but a guided percutaneous needle biopsy producing a core of liver for histology is the one most frequently used. It produces a tissue sample that is usually adequate for all purposes, including the use of special stains, immunohistochemistry and molecular biological techniques. Touch preparations for cytology can also be prepared from needle cores before fixation and may provide an instant diagnosis {1523}.

Differential diagnosis

Hepatocellular carcinoma can usually be distinguished from metastatic tumours by its trabecular structure, sinusoids, lack of stroma, bile production, absence of mucin secretion, and the demonstration of bile canaliculi by polyclonal CEA antisera, which is specific for a liver cell origin. Other useful immunophenotypic features in this differentiation are the presence of liver export proteins (albumin, fibrinogen, alpha-1-antitrypsin), the cytokeratin pattern, and the expression of Hep Par 1 antigen {1046}. Metastatic tumours that often mimic hepatocellular carcinoma are adrenal cortical and renal cell carcinomas. Amelanotic melanoma may also cause difficulties but it is easily identified by positive immunostaining for S100 protein and HMB45.

The distinction between primary cholangiocarcinoma and metastatic adenocar-

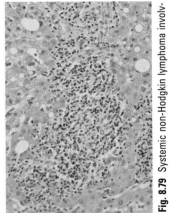

Fig. 8.79 Systemic non-Hodgkin lymphoma involving the liver.

cinomas is much more difficult and may be impossible {351}. Cholangiocarcinoma may take on any of the histological patterns of an adenocarcinoma; it is usually tubular but may be mucinous, signet-ring, papillary, cystic, or undifferentiated. Mucin secretion and production of CEA are nearly always demonstrable in both primary and secondary adenocarcinomas. Metastases from many sites form similar patterns. However, small tubular or tubulo-papillary glands frequently derive from the stomach, gallbladder and extrahepatic biliary tree, and a signet-ring cell appearance suggests a gastric primary. Perhaps the easiest pattern to recognize as metastatic in origin is that exhibited by adenocarcinomas of the colon and rectum, which nearly always show glands of variable size and shape that are lined by tall columnar cells and contain debris within the lumina. Metastases from the colorectum frequently have well defined edges whereas those from other glandular sites tend to be more diffuse. Colorectal metastases are also frequently necrotic and may show calcification {653}.

The presence of carcinoma-in-situ in intrahepatic bile ducts in the vicinity of an adenocarcinoma is evidence that it is a cholangiocarcinoma. However, this may be mimicked by intrabiliary ductal growth of metastatic colonic adenocarcinoma {1593}. Analysis of cytokeratin expression may be useful in the distinction of primary and metastatic gastrointestinal adenocarcinomas. The former express cytokeratins 7 and 19 but not 20, whereas the latter are negative for 7 and positive for 20 {1141}.

Carcinoma of the breast often produces a diffuse sinusoidal infiltrate that on imaging studies may mimic cirrhosis and, indeed, may be associated with splenomegaly, ascites and oesophageal varices {174}; sclerosis following systemic chemotherapy may exaggerate this effect. Metastases from the breast may be identified by the combined use of a zinc-α2-glycoprotein, gross cystic disease fluid protein 15 and oestrogen receptor {283}. However, occult breast carcinoma presenting with metastases is rare and most patients with liver involvement have a past history of a primary tumour.

Most hepatic metastases from the lung in clinical practice are undifferentiated small cell carcinomas, characteristically producing an enlarged liver due to diffuse or miliary spread. The primary tumour may still be small, asymptomatic and undetected. Squamous cell and adenocarcinomas will metastasize to the liver but their existence is usually known already. The same applies to squamous cell carcinomas of the oesophagus and cervix. Squamous cell carcinomas of the head and neck seldom involve the liver. Neuroendocrine/islet cell/carcinoid tumours are easily identified by their

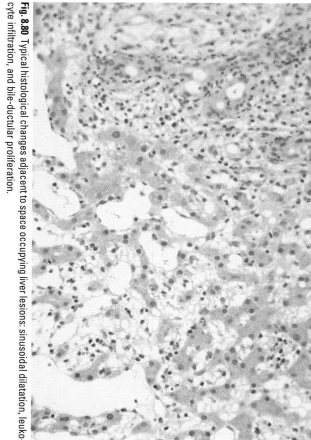

Fig. 8.80 Typical histological changes adjacent to space occupying liver lesions: sinusoidal dilatation, leukocyte infiltration, and bile-ductular proliferation.

organoid nesting pattern, uniform cytology and vascularity, and positive immunostaining for chromogranin, synaptophysin and neuron specific enolase; islet cell tumours also produce specific hormones such as insulin, glucagon, gastrin, vasoactive intestinal peptide and somatostatin, which either give rise to clinical syndromes or can be demonstrated in the blood or tumour tissue.

Most sarcomas that metastasize to the liver are gastrointestinal stromal tumours that are positive for CD34 and c-kit, or leiomyosarcomas of the uterus that may be positive for desmin or muscle-specific actin. Some carcinomas, notably of the kidney, may be sarcomatoid in their morphology.

Many haematological malignancies, e.g. leukaemias, myeloproliferative disorders and both Hodgkin and non-Hodgkin lymphomas, involve the liver. Leukaemias tend to produce diffuse sinusoidal infiltrates. Hodgkin and high-grade non-Hodgkin lymphomas produce tumour-like masses, while low-grade non-Hodgkin lymphomas produce diffuse portal infiltrates.

Rare secondary tumours include those from the thyroid, prostate, and gonads. The diagnosis can be confirmed by the immunohistochemical demonstration of thyroglobulin, prostate specific antigen and AFP and βHCG, respectively.

A triad of histological features, namely proliferating bile ducts, leukocytes and focal sinusoidal dilatation, is found in the liver adjacent to space-occupying lesions. Their presence in a core biopsy suggests the possibility of a metastatic deposit missed by the biopsy needle. Three lesions, bile duct adenoma, sclerosed haemangioma, and larval granuloma may resemble metastatic tumours at laparotomy.

Prognosis

In most cases, disseminated disease is present which precludes surgical intervention. Due to recent improvements in imaging techniques, more metastatic carcinomas are being diagnosed early, providing the possibility of surgical resection in a greater number of patients. When curative resection is feasible, 5-year survival can be as high as 40%; without surgical therapy, median survivals of less than 12 months should be expected {1817}.

CHAPTER 9

Tumours of the Gallbladder and Extrahepatic Bile Ducts

These two closely related tumour sites show remarkable differences in terms of epidemiology, aetiology, and clinical presentation. The incidence of gallbladder carcinoma shows prominent geographic, gender, and racial differences, while extrahepatic bile duct carcinomas show none of these variations. Aetiologic associations include gall stones, sclerosing cholangitis, ulcerative colitis, abnormal choledochopancreatic junction, choledochal cysts, and infestation with liver flukes.

WHO histological classification of tumours of the gallbladder and extrahepatic bile ducts

Epithelial tumours

Benign		
Adenoma		8140/0[1]
Tubular		8211/0
Papillary		8260/0
Tubulopapillary		8263/0
Biliary cystadenoma		8161/0
Papillomatosis (adenomatosis)		8264/0

Intraepithelial neoplasia (dysplasia and carcinoma in situ)

Malignant	
Carcinoma	
Adenocarcinoma	8140/3
Papillary adenocarcinoma	8260/3
Adenocarcinoma, intestinal type	8144/3
Adenocarcinoma, gastric foveolar type	
Mucinous adenocarcinoma	8480/3
Clear cell adenocarcinoma	8310/3
Signet-ring cell carcinoma	8490/3
Adenosquamous carcinoma	8560/3
Squamous cell carcinoma	8070/3
Small cell carcinoma	8041/3
Large cell neuroendocrine carcinoma	8013/3
Undifferentiated carcinoma	8020/3
Biliary cystadenocarcinoma	8161/3
Carcinoid tumour	8240/3
Goblet cell carcinoid	8243/3
Tubular carcinoid	8245/1
Mixed carcinoid-adenocarcinoma	8244/3
Others	

Non-epithelial tumours	
Granular cell tumour	9580/0
Leiomyoma	8890/0
Leiomyosarcoma	8890/3
Rhabdomyosarcoma	8900/3
Kaposi sarcoma	9140/3
Malignant lymphoma	

Secondary tumours

[1] Morphology code of the International Classification of Diseases for Oncology (ICD-O) {542} and the Systematized Nomenclature of Medicine (http://snomed.org). Behaviour is coded /0 for benign tumours, /1 for unspecified, borderline, or uncertain behaviour, /2 for in situ carcinomas and grade III intraepithelial neoplasia and /3 for malignant tumours.

TNM classification of tumours of the gallbladder

TNM classification[1,2]

T – Primary Tumour

TX	Primary tumour cannot be assessed
T0	No evidence of primary tumour
Tis	Carcinoma in situ
T1	Tumour invades lamina propria or muscle layer
T1a	Tumour invades lamina propria
T1b	Tumour invades muscle layer
T2	Tumour invades perimuscular connective tissue, no extension beyond serosa or into liver
T3	Tumour perforates serosa (visceral peritoneum) or directly invades into one adjacent organ or both (extension 2 cm or less into liver)
T4	Tumour extends more than 2 cm into liver and/or into two or more adjacent organs (stomach, duodenum, colon, pancreas, omentum, extrahepatic bile ducts, any involvement of liver)

N – Regional Lymph Nodes

NX	Regional lymph nodes cannot be assessed
N0	No regional lymph node metastasis
N1	Metastasis in cystic duct, pericholedochal, and/or hilar lymph nodes (i.e., in the hepatoduodenal ligament)
N2	Metastasis in peripancreatic (head only), periduodenal, peripor- tal, coeliac, and/or superior mesenteric lymph nodes

M – Distant Metastasis

MX	Distant metastasis cannot be assessed
M0	No distant metastasis
M1	Distant metastasis

Stage Grouping

Stage 0	Tis	N0	M0	
Stage I	T1	N0	M0	
Stage II	T2	N0	M0	
Stage III	T1	N1	M0	
	T2	N1	M0	
	T3	N0, N1	M0	
Stage IVA	T4	N0, N1	M0	
Stage IVB	Any T	N2	M0	
	Any T	Any N	M1	

[1] {66, 361}. The classification applies only to carcinomas.
[2] A help desk for specific questions about the TNM classification is available at http://tnm.uicc.org.

TNM classification of tumours of the extrahepatic bile ducts

TNM classification[1,2]

T – Primary Tumour

TX Primary tumour cannot be assessed
T0 No evidence of primary tumour
Tis Carcinoma in situ
T1 Tumour invades subepithelial connective tissue or fibromuscular layer
T1a Tumour invades subepithelial connective tissue
T1b Tumour invades fibromuscular layer
T2 Tumour invades perifibromuscular connective tissue
T3 Tumour invades adjacent structures: liver, pancreas, duodenum, gallbladder, colon, stomach

N – Regional Lymph Nodes

NX Regional lymph nodes cannot be assessed
N0 No regional lymph node metastasis
N1 Metastasis in cystic duct, pericholedochal, and/or hilar lymph nodes (i.e., in the hepatoduodenal ligament)
N2 Metastasis in peripancreatic (head only), periduodenal, periportal, coeliac, superior mesenteric, posterior peripancreatico-duodenal lymph nodes

M – Distant Metastasis

MX Distant metastasis cannot be assessed
M0 No distant metastasis
M1 Distant metastasis

Stage Grouping

Stage 0	Tis	N0	M0
Stage I	T1	N0	M0
Stage II	T2	N0	M0
Stage III	T1	N1, N2	M0
	T2	N1, N2	M0
Stage IVA	T3	Any N	M0
Stage IVB	Any T	Any N	M1

[1]{66, 361}. The classification applies to carcinomas of extrahepatic bile ducts and those of choledochal cysts.
[2]A help desk for specific questions about the TNM classification is available at http://tnm.uicc.org.

TNM classification of tumours of the Ampulla of Vater

TNM classification[1,2]

T – Primary Tumour

TX Primary tumour cannot be assessed
T0 No evidence of primary tumour
Tis Carcinoma in situ
T1 Tumour limited to ampulla of Vater or sphincter of Oddi
T2 Tumour invades duodenal wall
T3 Tumour invades 2 cm or less into pancreas
T4 Tumour invades more than 2 cm into pancreas and/or into other adjacent organs

N – Regional Lymph Nodes

NX Regional lymph nodes cannot be assessed
N0 No regional lymph node metastasis
N1 Regional lymph node metastasis

M – Distant Metastasis

MX Distant metastasis cannot be assessed
M0 No distant metastasis
M1 Distant metastasis

Stage Grouping

Stage 0	Tis	N0	M0
Stage I	T1	N0	M0
Stage II	T2	N0	M0
	T3	N0	M0
Stage III	T1	N1	M0
	T2	N1	M0
	T3	N1	M0
Stage IV	T4	Any N	M0
	Any T	Any N	M1

[1]{66, 361}. The classification applies only to carcinomas.
[2]A help desk for specific questions about the TNM classification is available at http://tnm.uicc.org.

Carcinoma of the gallbladder and extrahepatic bile ducts

J. Albores-Saavedra
J.C. Scoazec
C. Wittekind
B. Sripa

H.R. Menck
N. Soehendra
P.V.J. Sriram

Definition

A malignant epithelial tumour with glandular differentiation, arising in the gallbladder or extrahepatic biliary system.

Epidemiology

Most tumours of the gallbladder and extrahepatic bile ducts are carcinomas. Only a small proportion are adenomas, carcinoid and stromal tumours {35}.

Geographic distribution

The incidence of carcinoma of the gallbladder varies in different parts of the world and also differs among different ethnic groups within the same country. In the United States, carcinoma of the gallbladder is more common in Native Americans and Hispanic Americans than in whites or blacks; the rate among female Native Americans is 21 per 100,000 compared with 1.4 per 100,000 among white females. In Latin American countries, the highest rates are found in Chile, Mexico and Bolivia. In Japan, the incidence rates are intermediate. In the general population of the United States cancer of the gallbladder accounts for 0.17% for all cancers in males and 0.49% in females.

There are no geographic variations in the incidence of extrahepatic bile duct carcinoma which accounts for 0.16% of all invasive cancers in males and 0.15% in females in the general population of the United States {35}.

Age and sex distribution

Carcinomas of the gallbladder and extrahepatic bile ducts are diseases of older age groups. Most patients are in the 6th or 7th decades of life. Gallbladder carcinomas have a strong female predominance, whereas extrahepatic bile duct carcinomas occur more frequently in males.

Aetiology

Unlike carcinoma of the extrahepatic bile ducts, gallbladder carcinomas are not associated with primary sclerosing cholangitis or ulcerative colitis.

Gallbladder carcinoma

Gallstones. The incidence of gallbladder cancer is higher in patients with gallstones than in patients without stones {35}, and stones are present in over 80% of gallbladder carcinomas. The incidence of gallbladder carcinoma parallels that of gallstones, being more frequent in females and in certain ethnic groups, e.g. Native Americans, who have a high incidence of stones. Nevertheless, although gall stones are considered a risk factor, the overall incidence of carcinoma of the gallbladder in patients with cholelithiasis is less than 0.2%; this percentage varies with race, sex, and length of exposure to the stones {35}. While some authors have reported a correlation between gallstone size and the risk of cancer, others have not found such a correlation {35}.

Abnormal choledochopancreatic junction. Data largely reported from Japan indicate an association between gallbladder cancer and an abnormal junction of the pancreatic and common bile ducts {1248}. Normally, the main pancreatic duct and the common bile duct unite within the sphincter to form the pancreaticobiliary duct. The abnormal junction is defined as the union of the pancreatic and common bile ducts outside the wall of the duodenum beyond the influence of the sphincter of Oddi. As a result, pancreatic juice can reflux into the common bile duct, resulting in hyperplastic, meta-

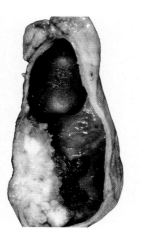

Fig. 9.01 Gallbladder carcinoma with a white, irregular cut surface next to a large gall stone.

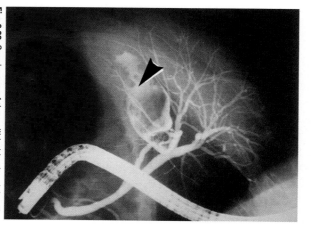

Fig. 9.02 Carcinoma of the gallbladder involving the fundus (arrow). Bile ducts are normal.

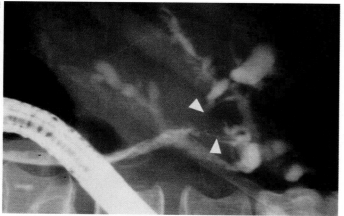

Fig. 9.03 Hilar cholangiocarcinoma extending beyond both the right and left hepatic bile ducts (Klatskin type III) (arrows).

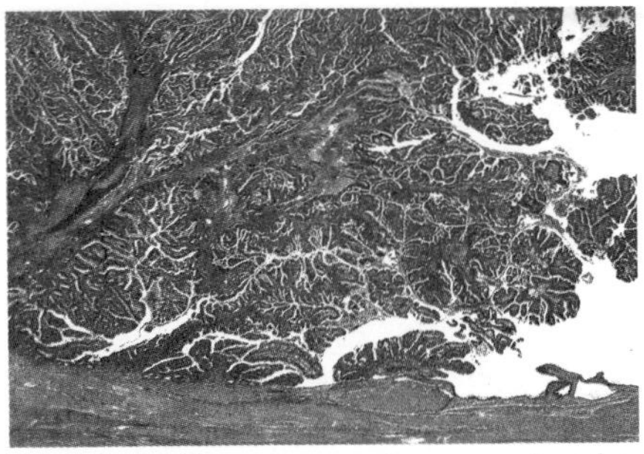

Computed tomography and ultrasonography can be used to demonstrate the lesion.

Carcinomas of the extrahepatic bile ducts usually present relatively early with obstructive jaundice, which can rapidly progress or fluctuate. Jaundice usually appears while the tumour is relatively small before widespread dissemination has occurred. Other symptoms include right upper quadrant pain, malaise, weight loss, pruritus, anorexia, nausea, and vomiting. If cholangitis develops, chills and fever appear. In patients with carcinoma of the proximal bile ducts (right and left hepatic ducts, common hepatic duct), the intrahepatic bile ducts are dilated, the gallbladder is not palpable and the common duct often collapses. Patients with carcinoma in the common or cystic ducts have a distended and palpable gallbladder as well as a markedly dilated proximal duct system, as may be shown by ultrasonography and computerised tomography. Transhepatic cholangiograms and endoscopic retrograde cholangiopancreatography are essential for exact localization of carcinomas of the extrahepatic bile ducts.

Macroscopy

Carcinoma of the gallbladder appears as an infiltrating grey white mass. Some carcinomas may cause diffuse thickening and induration of the entire gallbladder wall. The gallbladder may be distended by the tumour, or collapsed due to obstruction of the neck or cystic duct. It can also assume an hourglass deformity when the tumour arises in the body and constricts the lateral walls. Papillary carcinomas are usually sessile and exhibit a polypoid or cauliflower-like appearance. Mucinous and signet ring cell carcinomas have a mucoid or gelatinous cut surface. Although any type of gallbladder

cancer may show necrosis, undifferentiated giant cell and small cell carcinomas are usually the most necrotic. Submucosal growth is an important feature of signet ring and small cell carcinomas. Carcinomas of the extrahepatic bile ducts have been divided into polypoid, nodular, scirrhous constricting, and diffusely infiltrating types. This separation can provide a guide to the operative procedure, extent of resection, and prognosis. However, except for the polypoid tumours, this separation is rarely possible in practice because of overlapping gross features. The nodular and scirrhous types tend to infiltrate surrounding tissues and are difficult to resect. The diffusely infiltrating types tend to spread linearly along the ducts.

Tumour staging

There are separate TNM classifications for carcinomas of the gallbladder, extrahepatic bile ducts, and the ampulla of Vater.

Histopathology

The histological classification of tumours of the gallbladder and extrahepatic bile ducts is essentially similar to the previous WHO classification published in 1991 {1774} and to the classification adopted by the AFIP fascicle published in 2000 {35}.

Adenocarcinoma

Well to moderately differentiated adenocarcinomas are the most common malignant epithelial tumours of the gallbladder and extrahepatic bile ducts. They are composed of short or long tubular glands lined by cells that vary in height from low cuboidal to tall columnar, superficially resembling biliary epithelium. Mucin is frequently present in the cells and glands. Rarely, the extracellular mucin may

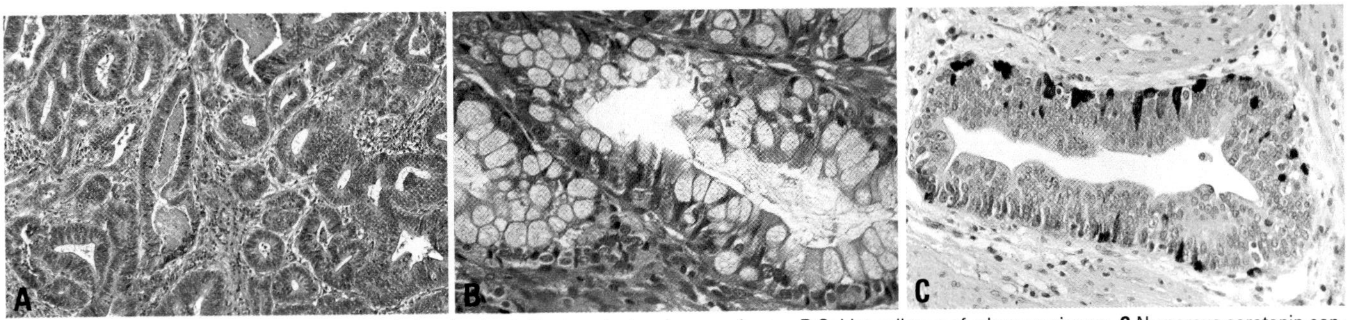

plastic, and neoplastic changes in the gallbladder epithelium.

Porcelain gallbladder. Diffuse calcification of the gallbladder wall (porcelain gallbladder) is associated with carcinoma in 10-25% of cases.

Genetic susceptibility. As discussed above, carcinoma of the gallbladder is concentrated in certain racial and ethnic groups. Familial aggregation of gallbladder cancer has been recorded in the US and in other countries {35}.

Carcinoma of extrahepatic bile ducts

Well established risk factors for carcinomas of the extrahepatic bile ducts are sclerosing cholangitis, ulcerative colitis, abnormal choledochopancreatic junction, choledochal cysts and infestation with the liver flukes *C. sinensis* and *O. viverrini.* Choledocholithiasis does not seem to play a role in the pathogenesis of carcinomas of the extrahepatic bile ducts.

Clinical features

Cancer of the gallbladder usually presents late in its course. The signs and symptoms are not specific, often resembling those of chronic cholecystitis. Right upper quadrant pain is common.

Fig. 9.04 Papillary adenocarcinoma, non-invasive. The tumour projects into the lumen, but does not invade the wall of the gallbladder.

Fig. 9.05 Intestinal type adenocarcinoma. **A** Tubular glands similar to colonic adenocarcinoma. **B** Goblet cell type of adenocarcinoma. **C** Numerous serotonin containing cells in a neoplastic gland.

become calcified {1465, 1606}. About one-third of the well differentiated tumours show focal intestinal differentiation and contain goblet and endocrine cells {36, 2152, 2158}. The endocrine cells may be numerous and show immunoreactivity for serotonin and peptide hormones, but a diagnosis of neuroendocrine neoplasm is not warranted. Paneth cells may rarely be seen. An extremely well differentiated adenocarcinoma with gastric foveolar phenotype that simulates adenoma has been described in the extrahepatic bile ducts {39}. Adenocarcinomas may show cribriform or angiosarcomatous patterns. They may also contain cyto- and synctio-trophoblast cells.

Extrahepatic bile duct adenocarcinomas tend to be better differentiated than their gallbladder counterparts. Many gallbladder carcinomas are immunoreactive for TP53 {1907, 2125}

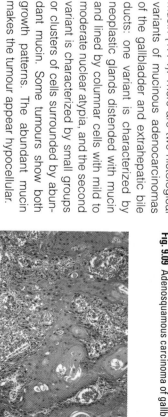

Fig. 9.08 Signet-ring cell carcinoma of gallbladder.

Mucinous adenocarcinoma. Mucinous adenocarcinomas of the biliary tree are similar to those that arise in other anatomic sites. By definition, more than 50% of the tumour contains extracellular mucin {1774}. There are two histological variants of mucinous adenocarcinomas of the gallbladder and extrahepatic bile ducts: one variant is characterized by neoplastic glands distended with mucin and lined by columnar cells with mild to moderate nuclear atypia, and the second variant is characterized by small groups or clusters of cells surrounded by abundant mucin. Some tumours show both growth patterns. The abundant mucin makes the tumour appear hypocellular.

Cystadenocarcinoma refers to a unilocular or multilocular glandular tumour that may be the result of malignant transformation of a cystadenoma.

Clear cell adenocarcinoma. This rare malignant tumour is composed predominantly of glycogen-rich clear cells having well-defined cytoplasmic borders and hyperchromatic nuclei. In addition to clear cells, a variable number of cells contain eosinophilic granular cytoplasm. The clear cells line glands or are arranged in nests, sheets, cords, trabeculae or papillary structures {40, 145, 1856}. Foci of conventional adenocarci-

Fig. 9.07 Mucinous adenocarcinoma of gallbladder.

Fig. 9.06 Well differentiated adenocarcinoma infiltrating gallbladder wall.

Histological variants of adenocarcinoma

Papillary adenocarcinoma. This malignant tumour is composed predominantly of papillary structures lined by cuboidal or columnar epithelial cells often containing variable amounts of mucin. Some tumours show intestinal differentiation with collections of goblet, endocrine, and Paneth cells. Papillary adenocarcinomas may fill the lumen before invading the wall. Papillary adenocarcinomas appear to be more frequent in the gallbladder than in the extrahepatic biliary tree {2150}. In addition, skip lesions may be observed in approximately 10% of cases {1989}.

Adenocarcinoma, intestinal type. This unusual variant of adenocarcinoma is composed of tubular glands or papillary structures lined predominantly by cells with an intestinal phenotype, namely goblet cells or colonic-type epithelium or both, with or without a variable number of endocrine and Paneth cells {41}.

Signet-ring cell carcinoma. Cells containing intracytoplasmic mucin displacing the nuclei toward the periphery predominate in this variant of adenocarcinoma. A variable amount of extracellular mucin is usually present. Lateral spread through the lamina propria is a common feature.

noma with focal mucin production are usually found and are useful in separating primary from metastatic clear cell carcinomas. In some clear cell adenocarcinomas of the biliary tree the columnar cells contain subnuclear and supranuclear vacuoles similar to those seen in secretory endometrium. Focal hepatoid differentiation with production of alpha-fetoprotein has been documented in clear cell carcinomas of the gallbladder {2000}.

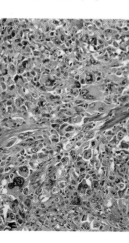
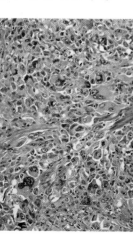
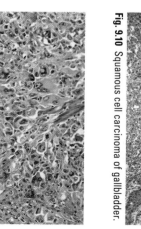

Fig. 9.11 Undifferentiated carcinoma of gallbladder, spindle and giant cell type. No glandular differentiation.

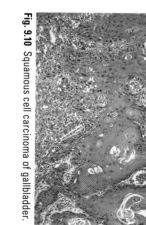

Fig. 9.10 Squamous cell carcinoma of gallbladder.

Fig. 9.09 Adenosquamous carcinoma of gallbladder.

A diffusely infiltrating linear pattern resembling linitis plastica of the stomach is observed in some cases.

Adenosquamous carcinoma

This tumour consists of two malignant components, one glandular and the other squamous. The extent of differentiation of the two components varies, but in general they tend to be moderately differentiated {1357, 1867}. Keratin pearls are often present in the squamous component, and mucin is usually demonstrable in the neoplastic glands.

Squamous cell carcinoma

This malignant epithelial tumour is composed entirely of squamous cells. The extent of differentiation varies considerably. Keratinizing and non-keratinizing types exist. Spindle cells predominate in some poorly differentiated tumours, which may be confused with sarcomas. Immunostains for cytokeratin may clarify the diagnosis in these spindle cell cases. The tumour may arise from areas of squamous metaplasia. Intraepithelial neoplasia can be found in the metaplastic squamous mucosa {35}.

Small cell carcinoma

This lesion is covered in the chapter on endocrine tumours of the gallbladder and extrahepatic bile ducts.

Undifferentiated carcinoma

Undifferentiated carcinomas are more common in the gallbladder than in the extrahepatic bile ducts. Characteristically, glandular structures are absent in undifferentiated carcinomas. There are four histological variants {40, 411, 643, 1360}.
Undifferentiated carcinoma, spindle and giant cell type. The spindle and giant cell type is the most common and resembles a sarcoma. These tumours have been referred to as pleomorphic spindle and giant cell adenocarcinomas or sarcomatoid carcinomas. They consist of variable proportions of spindle, giant and polygonal cells, but foci of well-differentiated neoplastic glands are usually found in some of these tumours after extensive sampling. Areas of squamoid differentiation may also be seen. Rarely, foci of osteoclast-like multinucleated giant cells are present. The presence of cytokeratin in the spindle cells may help to distinguish this tumour from carcinosarcoma.
Undifferentiated carcinoma with osteoclast-like giant cells. This variant contains mononuclear cells and numerous evenly spaced osteoclast-like giant cells resembling giant cell tumour of bone. The mononuclear cells show immunoreactivity for cytokeratin and epithelial membrane antigen while the osteoclast-like giant cells are positive for histiocytic markers such as CD68.
Undifferentiated carcinoma, small cell type. The tumour is composed of sheets of round cells with vesicular nuclei and prominent nucleoli that occasionally contain cytoplasmic mucin.
Undifferentiated carcinoma, nodular or lobular type. The fourth variant consists of well defined nodules or lobules of neoplastic cells superficially resembling breast carcinoma.

Carcinosarcoma

This malignant tumour consists of a mixture of two components: carcinomatous and sarcomatous. The epithelial elements usually predominate in the form of glands but may be arranged in cords or sheets. Foci of malignant squamous cells are occasionally seen. The mesenchymal component includes foci of heterologous elements such as chondrosarcoma, osteosarcoma, and rhabdomyosarcoma. Cytokeratin and carcinoembryonic antigen are absent from the mesenchymal

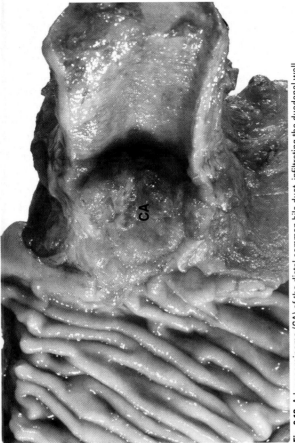

Fig. 9.13 Adenocarcinoma (CA) of the distal common bile duct, infiltrating the duodenal wall.

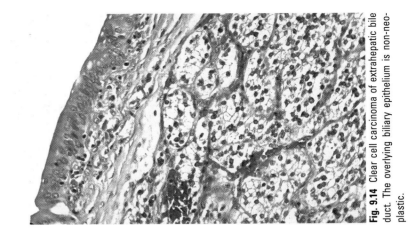

Fig. 9.14 Clear cell carcinoma of extrahepatic bile duct. The overlying biliary epithelium is non-neoplastic.

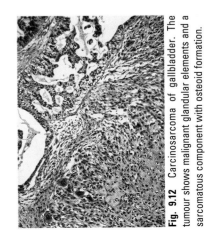

Fig. 9.12 Carcinosarcoma of gallbladder. The tumour shows malignant glandular elements and a sarcomatous component with osteoid formation.

component, which helps to distinguish carcinosarcomas from spindle and giant cell carcinomas.

Grading

Adenocarcinomas can be divided into well, moderately, or poorly differentiated types. The diagnosis of well differentiated adenocarcinoma requires that 95% of the tumour contains glands. For moderately differentiated adenocarcinoma 40 to 94% of the tumour should be composed of glands and for poorly differentiated adenocarcinomas 5 to 39% of the tumour should contain glands. Undifferentiated carcinomas display less than 5% of glandular structures.

Precursor lesions

Adenoma

Adenoma

Adenomas are benign neoplasms of glandular epithelium (intraepithelial neoplasia) that are typically polypoid, single and well-demarcated. They are more common in women than in men {42}. There is a wide age range; although mostly a disease of adults rare gallbladder adenomas occur in children {1256, 2126}. They are more common in the gallbladder than in the extrahepatic bile ducts, and are found in 0.3-0.5% of gallbladders removed for cholelithiasis or chronic cholecystitis. A small proportion of adenomas progress to carcinoma {42, 909, 967}.

Adenomas are often small, asymptomatic, and usually discovered incidentally during cholecystectomy, but they can be multiple, fill the lumen of the gallbladder and be symptomatic. Occasionally, adenomas of the gallbladder occur in

association with the Peutz-Jeghers syndrome {521} or with Gardner syndrome {1900, 2041}. Adenomas of the extrahepatic bile ducts are usually symptomatic and cause biliary obstruction. These benign tumours are not associated with lithiasis.

According to their pattern of growth, they are divided into three types: tubular, papillary, and tubulopapillary. Cytologically, they are classified as: pyloric gland type, intestinal type, and biliary type. Tubular adenomas of pyloric gland type are more common in the gallbladder while intestinal type adenomas are more common in the extrahepatic bile ducts {42}.

Tubular adenoma, pyloric-gland type. A benign tumour composed of closely packed short tubular glands that are similar to pyloric glands. Early lesions appear as well demarcated nodules embedded in the lamina propria and covered with normal biliary epithelium. They are composed of lobules that contain closely packed pyloric-type glands, some of which may be cystically dilated. The epithelial cells are columnar or cuboidal with vesicular or hyperchromatic nuclei and small nucleoli and variable amounts of cytoplasmic mucin. Nodular aggregates of cytologically bland spindle cells with eosinophilic cytoplasm but without keratinization or intercellular bridges known as squamoid morules {984, 1361} are present in about 10% of the cases, whereas frank squamous metaplasia is exceedingly rare. Paneth cells and endocrine cells are often present. By immunohistochemistry, serotonin and a variety of peptide hormones

including somatostatin, pancreatic polypeptide, and gastrin have been detected in the cytoplasm of these cells. Smaller lesions show low-grade intraepithelial neoplasia, but larger adenomas may have high-grade changes or foci of invasive carcinoma. As they enlarge, most adenomas develop a pedicle and project into the lumen. Rarely, they extend into or arise from Rokitansky-Aschoff sinuses, a finding that should not be mistaken for carcinoma {42}.

Tubular adenoma, intestinal type. This benign tumour is composed of tubular glands lined by cells with an intestinal phenotype, and closely resembles colonic adenomas. It consists of tubular glands lined by pseudostratified columnar cells with elongated hyperchromatic nuclei, and high-grade dysplastic changes are frequent. The glands lack invasive properties and focally are arranged in well defined lobules. The adenomatous epithelium may extend into the Rokitansky-Aschoff sinuses, a finding that should not be confused with stromal invasion. Clusters of goblet, Paneth, and endocrine cells are usually mixed with the columnar cells. Serotonin and, less frequently, peptide hormones have been identified in the endocrine cells by immunohistochemistry. Hyperplasia of metaplastic pyloric type glands is often seen at the base of the adenomas.

Papillary adenoma, intestinal type. This benign tumour consists predominantly of papillary structures lined by dysplastic cells with an intestinal phenotype. These adenomas, which usually arise in a background of pyloric gland metaplasia, may

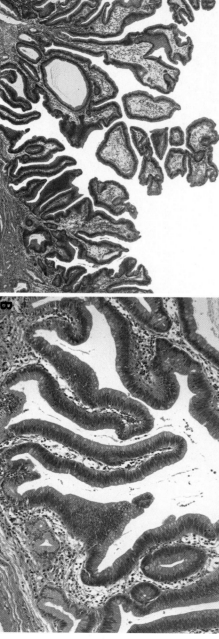

Fig. 9.15 Papillary adenoma of gallbladder, intestinal type. **A** Numerous papillary structures project into lumen. **B** Pseudostratified columnar cells with scattered goblet and Paneth cells.

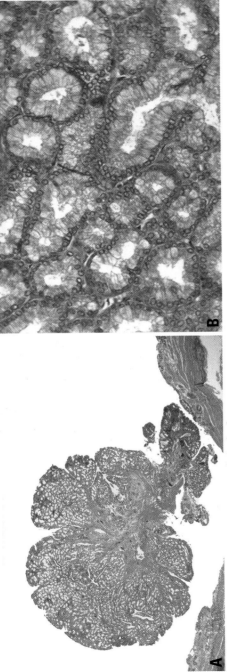

Fig. 9.16 A, B Tubular adenoma of gallbladder, pyloric gland type.

occur in the gallbladder or the extrahepatic bile ducts. In a series of five intestinal type papillary adenomas of the gallbladder, one progressed to invasive carcinoma {42}. The predominant cell is columnar with elongated hyperchromatic nuclei and little or no cytoplasmic mucin. The cells are pseudostratified, mitotically active, and indistinguishable from those of villous adenomas arising in the large intestine. Tubular glands lined by the same type of epithelium, but representing less than 20% of the tumour, may also be found. Dysplastic changes are more extensive than in pyloric-gland type adenomas. Also present are goblet, Paneth, and serotonin-containing cells. Some of the endocrine cells are immunoreactive for peptide hormones.

Papillary adenoma, biliary type. This lesion consists predominantly of papillary structures lined by cells with a biliary phenotype. It is well demarcated and consists of papillary structures lined by tall columnar cells, which except for the presence of more cytoplasmic mucin show minimal variation from normal gallbladder epithelium. Endocrine or Paneth cells are not found. Only mild dysplastic changes are noted. In situ or invasive carcinoma has not been reported in association with these adenomas. This is the rarest form of adenoma of the gallbladder; we have seen only one case. Most papillary lesions composed of normal-appearing gallbladder epithelium are examples of hyperplasia secondary to chronic cholecystitis.

Tubulo-papillary adenoma. When tubular glands and papillary structures each

comprise more than 20% of the tumour, the term tubulo-papillary adenoma is applied. Two subtypes are recognized: one is composed of tubular glands and papillary structures similar to those of tubulovillous intestinal adenomas; the other subtype consists of tubular glands similar to pyloric glands and papillary structures often lined by foveolar epithelium. Paneth and endocrine cells are present in some. Rarely, tubulo-papillary adenomas arise from the epithelial invaginations of adenomyomatous hyperplasia.

Other benign biliary lesions

Biliary cystadenoma. These lesions resemble their intrahepatic counterparts (see chapter on bile duct cystadenoma and cystadenocarcinoma). Cystadenomas are seen predominantly among adult females and are usually symptomatic. Some of the tumours may measure up to 20 cm in diameter leading to obstructive jaundice or cholecystitis-like symptoms. More common in the extrahepatic bile ducts than in the gallbladder, cystadenomas are multiloculated neoplasms that contain mucinous or serous fluid and are lined by columnar epithelium reminiscent of bile duct or foveolar gastric epithelium {404}. Occasionally endocrine cells are present. The cellular subepithelial stroma resembles ovarian stroma and shows immunoreactivity for estrogen and progesterone receptors {2029}. The stroma also shows variable fibrosis. Malignant transformation (cystadenocarcinoma) can occur {404}.

Papillomatosis (adenomatosis). Papillomatosis is a clinicopathological condition

characterized by multiple recurring papillary adenomas, that may involve extensive areas of the extrahepatic bile ducts and even extend into the gallbladder and intrahepatic bile ducts. The disease affects both sexes equally. Most patients are adults between 50 and 60 years. Complete excision of the multicentric lesions is difficult and local recurrence is common. The lesion consists of numerous papillary structures as well as complex glandular formations. Because severe dysplasia is often present, papillomatosis is difficult to distinguish from papillary carcinoma. Some regard this lesion as a form of low-grade multicentric intraductal papillary carcinoma. Papillomatosis has a greater potential for malignant transformation than solitary adenomas.

Intraepithelial neoplasia (dysplasia)

If intraepithelial neoplasia is found, multiple sections should be taken to exclude invasive cancer. Cholecystectomy is a curative surgical procedure for patients with in situ carcinoma or with carcinoma extending into the lamina propria {35}.

Epidemiology. The rate of intraepithelial neoplasia of the gallbladder reflects that of invasive carcinoma. In countries in which carcinoma of the gallbladder is endemic, the prevalence is higher than in countries in which this tumour is sporadic. Studies from different countries have shown that the incidence of high-grade dysplasia or carcinoma in situ in gallbladders with lithiasis has varied from 0.5-3% {35}. This variation in the incidence of intraepithelial neoplasia is also attributable to other factors such as lack of uniformity in morphological criteria and sampling methods.

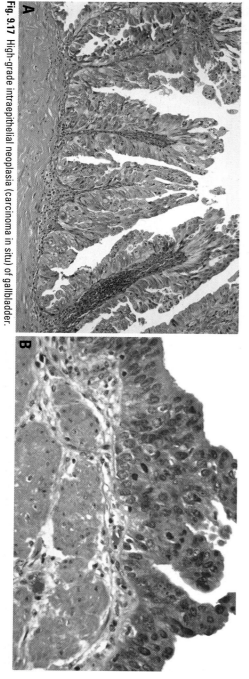

Fig. 9.17 High-grade intraepithelial neoplasia (carcinoma in situ) of gallbladder.

Macroscopic features.

Intraepithelial neoplasia is usually not recognized on macroscopic examination because it often occurs in association with chronic cholecystitis. The mucosa may appear granular, nodular, plaque-like, or trabeculated. The papillary type of intraepithelial neoplasia usually appears as a small, cauliflower-like excrescence that projects into the lumen and can be recognized on close inspection. However, in most cases, the gallbladder shows only a thickened and indurated wall, the result of chronic inflammation and fibrosis.

Microscopic features.

Microscopically two types of intraepithelial neoplasia are recognized: papillary and flat, the latter being more common. The papillary type is characterized by short fibrovascular stalks that are covered by dysplastic or neoplastic cells.

Intraepithelial neoplasia usually begins on the surface epithelium and subsequently extends downward into the Rokitansky-Aschoff sinuses and into metaplastic pyloric glands. Columnar, cuboidal, and elongated cells with variable degrees of nuclear atypia, loss of polarity, and occasional mitotic figures are characteristic. The dysplastic cells are usually arranged in a single layer, but can be pseudostratified. Later, papillary structures covered by dysplastic epithelium may form. The large nuclei of dysplastic cells may be round, oval, or fusiform, with one or two nucleoli that are more prominent than those of normal cells.

The cytoplasm is usually eosinophilic and contains non-sulphated acid and neutral mucin. Goblet cells are found in one third of cases. An abrupt transition

between normal-appearing columnar cells and intraepithelial neoplasia is seen in nearly all cases. In general, the cell population of dysplasia is homogeneous, unlike the heterogeneous cell population of the epithelial atypia of repair. Widespread involvement of the mucosa by intraepithelial neoplasia often occurs. For this reason, we have suggested that some, if not most, invasive carcinomas of the gallbladder arise from a field change within the epithelium.

The cells of intraepithelial neoplasia are reactive for CEA and for the carbohydrate antigen CA19-9 {35}. Expression of p53 occurs in some lesions {2125}.

Differential diagnosis.

Reactive epithelial changes ('atypia of repair') differs from intraepithelial neoplasia in consisting of a heterogeneous cell population in which columnar mucus-secreting cells, low cuboidal cells, atrophic-appearing epithelium, and pencil-like cells are present. In addition, there is a gradual transition of the cellular abnormalities, in contrast with the abrupt transition seen in intraepithelial neoplasia. The extent of nuclear atypia is less pronounced in reactive changes and immunoreactivity for p53 protein is absent, while usually positive in intraepithelial neoplasia.

High-grade intraepithelial neoplasia and carcinoma in situ

In cases where the cells have all the cytological features of malignancy with frequent mitotic figures, nuclear crowding and prominent pseudostratification, the term carcinoma in situ may be used. Neoplastic cells first appear along the surface epithelium and later spread into the epithelial invaginations and antral-

type metaplastic glands. In the late stages of carcinoma in situ, the histological picture is that of back-to-back glands located in the lamina propria but often connected with the surface epithelium. However, not all in situ carcinomas exhibit this type of growth pattern. Some show distinctive papillary features with small fibrovascular stalks lined by neoplastic cells. Not infrequently, a combination of these growth patterns is seen.

The differential diagnosis between high-grade intraepithelial neoplasia (severe dysplasia) and carcinoma in situ is difficult and often impossible in many cases. This is not important because the two lesions, which vary only in degree histologically, are closely related biologically.

Histological variants of carcinoma in situ.

An in situ carcinoma composed of goblet cells, columnar cells, Paneth cells, and endocrine cells, has been described, which may represent an in situ phase of intestinal-type adenocarcinoma {35, 41}. Another type of in situ intestinal-type carcinoma is composed of cells closely resembling those of colonic carcinomas at the light and electron microscopic lev-

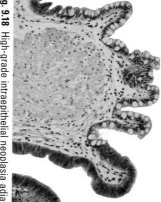

Fig. 9.18 High-grade intraepithelial neoplasia adjacent to intestinal metaplasia with numerous mature goblet cells.

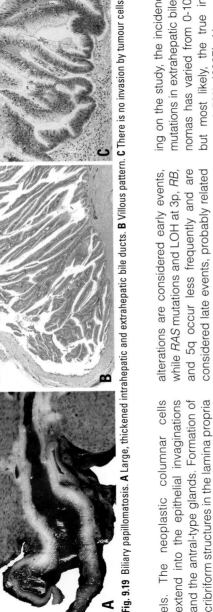

Fig. 9.19 Biliary papillomatosis. **A** Large, thickened intrahepatic and extrahepatic bile ducts. **B** Villous pattern. **C** There is no invasion by tumour cells.

els. The neoplastic columnar cells extend into the epithelial invaginations and the antral-type glands. Formation of cribriform structures in the lamina propria occurs. This tumour also has scattered endocrine cells, most of which are immunoreactive for serotonin.

Two examples of in situ signet-ring cell carcinoma confined to the surface epithelium and to the epithelial invaginations of the gallbladder have been reported {40}. These in situ signet ring cell carcinomas represented incidental findings in cholecystectomy specimens and were cytologically similar to those reported in the stomach. This unusual form of carcinoma in situ should be distinguished from epithelial cells which acquire signet-ring cell morphology when desquamated within the lumen of dilated metaplastic pyloric glands in cases of chronic cholecystitis and from mucin-containing histiocytes (muciphages).

The morphological type of in situ carcinoma does not always correspond with that of the invasive carcinoma. For example, we have seen conventional adenocarcinoma in situ in the mucosa adjacent to invasive squamous, small cell, and undifferentiated carcinomas.

The wall of the gallbladder with dysplasia or carcinoma in situ usually shows variable inflammatory changes, typically with a predominance of lymphocytes and plasma cells, although lymphoid follicles with germinal centers, xanthogranulomatous inflammation or an acute inflammatory reaction may be present.

Molecular pathology

Mutations of *TP53* are found in the vast majority of invasive gallbladder carcinomas {2124, 2127}. Loss of heterozygosity (LOH) at chromosomal loci 8p (44%), 9p (50%) and 18q (31%) are also frequently detected {2127}. These genetic

alterations are considered early events, while *RAS* mutations and LOH at 3p, *RB*, and 5q occur less frequently and are considered late events, probably related to tumour progression. Amplification of the *c-erbB-2* gene, that codes for a glycoprotein structurally similar to the epidermal growth factor receptor was detected in 30 of 43 invasive gallbladder carcinomas {1036}. However, no correlation between *c-erbB-2* gene amplification and prognosis was found.

In contrast to lesions of the gallbladder, the incidence of *TP53* mutations in extrahepatic bile duct carcinomas is lower and appears to be a late molecular event.

Although the frequency of *KRAS* mutations in gallbladder carcinomas has ranged from 0%-34% in different studies, most investigators have found these mutations to be significantly higher in extrahepatic bile duct tumours than in gallbladder carcinomas {2067}. Depending on the study, the incidence of *KRAS* mutations in extrahepatic bile duct carcinomas has varied from 0-100% {1586}, but most likely, the true incidence is around 56% {2067}. However, the incidence of *KRAS* mutations is greater in gallbladder carcinomas associated with an anomalous junction of the pancreaticobiliary duct than in carcinomas not associated with this congenital anomaly {661}. These molecular pathology findings support the concept that gallbladder carcinogenesis requires a number of genetic alterations involving activation of oncogenes or inactivation of tumour suppressor genes.

The molecular pathology of adenomas of the gallbladder differs from that of carcinomas. None of 16 adenomas showed *TP53* or p16 *Ink4/CDKN2a* gene mutations, which are common in carcinomas {2126}. Four adenomas had *KRAS* mutations (2 in codon 12 and 2 in codon 61) which are considered rare and late

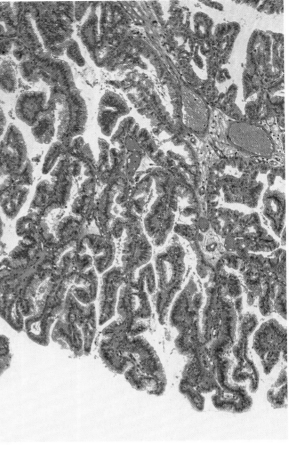
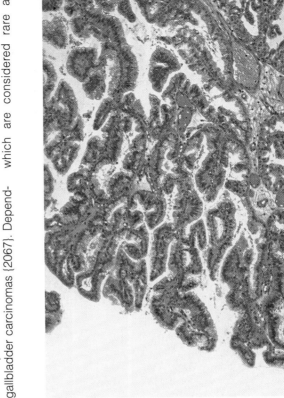
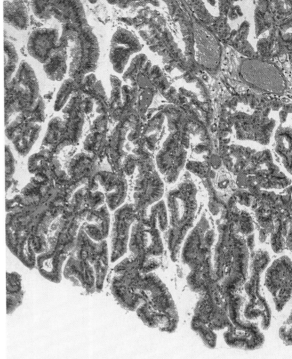

Fig. 9.20 Papillomatosis of extrahepatic bile duct.

Endocrine tumours of the gallbladder and extrahepatic bile ducts

C. Capella
E. Solcia
L.H. Sobin
R. Arnold

Definition

Tumours with endocrine differentiation arising from the extrahepatic bile ducts and gallbladder.

Epidemiology

In an analysis of 8305 cases of carcinoids of all sites, 19 cases of gallbladder and one case of biliary tract carcinoids were recorded, representing 0.2% and 0.01% of cases {1251}. The average age of presentation (60 years) is lower than the average age of presentation of non-carcinoid neoplasms (71 years). The reported male/female ratio is 1:1.2 {1251}. Small cell carcinomas of the gallbladder, like other carcinomas, are more common in females (M/F ratio: 1:1.8) {1359}. The reported average age of presentation is 65 years (range, 43-83 years) {1359}. Small cell carcinomas represent about 4% of all malignant tumours of the gallbladder {1359, 37}.

Aetiology

Small cell carcinomas are more common in females and are almost always associ-

ated with stones {34, 1524}. There is no available information on the aetiology of the very rare carcinoid tumours of the extrahepatic biliary tree.

Localization

All types of endocrine tumours are more often located in the gallbladder than in extrahepatic bile ducts {1251, 2157, 1639, 34}.

Clinical features

Gallbladder carcinoids can cause recurrent upper quadrant pain. Carcinoids of extrahepatic bile ducts typically produce the sudden onset of biliary colic and/or sometimes painless jaundice {1639}. In the majority of cases of small cell carcinoma, the chief complaint is abdominal pain. Other clinical features include abdominal mass, jaundice, and ascites {1359}. A case of primary gastrinoma of the common hepatic duct with Zollinger-Ellison syndrome {1175}, and a patient with Cushing syndrome due to an ACTH-secreting small cell carcinoma have been reported {1801}.

Macroscopy

Carcinoids are usually small grey-white or yellow submucosal nodules or polyps, sometimes infiltrating the muscular wall, that may be located in any part of the gallbladder or the extrahepatic biliary tree {1639, 34}. Small cell carcinomas appear as a nodular mass or diffusely invade the gallbladder wall {1359}. A significant proportion of mixed endocrine-exocrine carcinomas have a polypoid or protruding aspect {2157, 2030}.

Histopathology

Carcinoid (well differentiated endocrine tumour)

The cells forming this tumour are uniform in size, with round or oval nuclei, inconspicuous nucleolus, and eosinophilic cytoplasm. Neoplastic cells are arranged in combined patterns with trabecular anastomosing structures, tubular structures and solid nests {1639, 299, 603, 177}. Tumour cells show positive staining for Grimelius silver {1639, 195, 115, 926, 1205}, chromogranin {1639, 57}, neuron-specific enolase {195, 115, 57}, and sev-

events in the pathogenesis of carcinomas of the gallbladder. Only one adeno-ma of intestinal type showed loss of heterozygosity at 5q22 {2126}.

Intraepithelial neoplasia (both dysplasia and carcinoma in situ) shows a high incidence of loss of heterozygosity at the TP53 gene locus. Other molecular abnormalities include loss of heterozygosity at 9p and 8p loci and the 18q gene. These abnormalities are also early events and

most likely contributing factors in the pathogenesis of gallbladder carcinoma. However, KRAS mutations were not detected in intraepithelial neoplasia {2125}.

Prognosis and predictive factors

The prognosis of tumours of the extrahepatic biliary tract depends primarily on the extent of disease and histological type (694, 695). Polypoid tumours (which

histologically often prove to be papillary carcinomas) have the best prognosis. Non-invasive papillary carcinomas are associated with a better prognosis than other types of invasive carcinomas. Perineural invasion and lymphatic permeation are common in the extrahepatic bile duct carcinoma and are significant prognostic factors {2150, 376}.

eral hormones including serotonin {115, 57}, gastrin {1175, 1156}, and somatostatin {603, 57}.
Cases showing regional or distant metastases {177, 926, 1205, 57} or signs of local aggressive growth, including invasion of the entire wall {1205, 57} and neural invasion {1205}, should be considered as well differentiated endocrine carcinomas (malignant carcinoids).

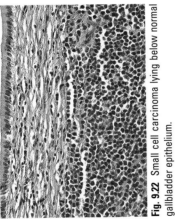

Fig. 9.22 Small cell carcinoma lying below normal gallbladder epithelium.

Small cell carcinoma (poorly differentiated endocrine carcinoma)

The cell population and growth patterns of this tumour are similar to those of small cell carcinoma of the lung {38, 40, 1359}. Small cell carcinomas appear to be more common in the gallbladder than in the extrahepatic bile ducts. Some mimic carcinoid tumours.

Most tumours are composed of round or fusiform cells arranged in sheets, nests, cords, and festoons. Rosette-like structures and tubules are occasionally present. Extensive necrosis and subepithelial growth are constant features. In necrotic areas, intense basophilic staining of the blood vessels occurs. The tumour cells have round or ovoid hyperchromatic nuclei with inconspicuous nucleoli. A few tumour giant cells can be observed in some cases {1359, 34}. Occasionally, focal glandular configurations similar to those of adenocarcinomas, and foci of squamous differentiation are seen {40, 774, 40, 1359}. Mitotic figures are frequently observed and they are reported to range from 15 to 206 (mean 75) per 10 high power fields {1359}.

Most small cell carcinomas show scattered Grimelius positive cells. In addition, tumour cells immunoexpress epithelial markers such as EMA, AE1/AE3 and CEA, and endocrine markers such as NSE, chromogranin A, Leu7, serotonin, somatostatin, and ACTH {1359, 34}. Ultrastructurally, a small number of dense core secretory granules can be found {34, 37}.

Mixed endocrine-exocrine carcinoma

A significant number of cases reported in the older literature as carcinoids, including the cases reviewed by Yamamoto et al. {2157}, are in fact mixed endocrine-exocrine carcinomas. These are composite tumours in which areas of adenocarcinoma intermingle with areas of endocrine cell carcinoma formed by solid and/or trabecular structures with cells which are argyrophilic and immunoreactive for endocrine markers, including NSE, chromogranin, serotonin and gastrin {2157, 2030, 1405, 1575}. The adenocarcinoma component is usually tubular or papillary, formed by columnar cells, goblet cells and sometimes Paneth cells, but a case of a combined diffuse type tumour in which mucin-containing signet-ring cells were admixed with clear endocrine cells has also been reported {1455}.

These tumours behave as adenocarcinomas and, therefore, are clinically more aggressive than carcinoids. Adenocarcinoma with endocrine cells should not be included in this category.

Genetic susceptibility

Carcinoids of the gallbladder and extrahepatic bile ducts are infrequently associated with the Zollinger-Ellison, MEN I, or the carcinoid syndromes. One patient with von Hippel-Lindau syndrome and a carcinoid tumour of the extrahepatic bile ducts has been reported.

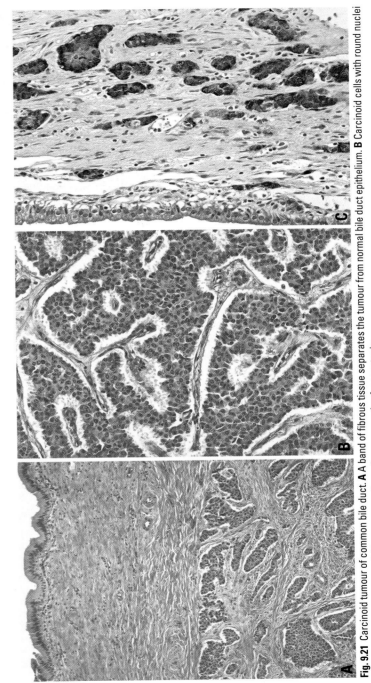

Fig. 9.21 Carcinoid tumour of common bile duct. **A** A band of fibrous tissue separates the tumour from normal bile duct epithelium. **B** Carcinoid cells with round nuclei and eosinophilic cytoplasm. **C** The tumour cells are immunoreactive for serotonin.

Genetics

Overexpression of TP53 has been found in 64% of small cell carcinomas of the gallbladder {1359}, compared with a frequency of 44% in small cell carcinomas of the lung {773} and 75% in small cell carcinomas of the stomach {1589}.

Prognostic factors

The percentage of gallbladder carcinoids showing regional and distant metastases has been estimated as approximately 44% and 11%, respectively {1251}. The 5-year survival rate was 41% in SEER data. Carcinoid tumours larger than 2 cm often extend into the liver or metastasize. Complete excision of small tumours is usually curative. The prognosis of small cell carcinoma of the gallbladder is poor, with only one of 18 patients {34} surviving 11 months following cholecystectomy, radiotherapy, and chemotherapy. In one study, the survival rates differed significantly between stages I, II, III and stage IV {1359}. The survival of patients with small cell carcinoma of the gallbladder appears to be shorter than that of patients with papillary adenocarcinoma {1359}.

Neural and mesenchymal tumours

J. Albores-Saavedra
J.C. Scoazec
C. Wittekind
B. Sripa
H.R. Menck
N. Soehendra
P.V.J. Sriram

Paraganglioma

This benign tumour is composed of chief cells and sustentacular cells arranged in a nesting or zellballen pattern. The chief cells are argyrophilic and stain for neuron-specific enolase and chromogranin. The sustentacular cells are S-100 protein positive. The tumour is located in either the subserosa or muscular wall of the gallbladder and apparently arises from normal paraganglia. This rare and small tumour is usually an incidental finding in cholecystectomy specimens. Paragangliomas also occur in the extrahepatic bile ducts, where they may be symptomatic.

Granular cell tumour

Granular cell tumours are the most common benign non-epithelial tumours of the extrahepatic biliary tract. They are more common in the bile ducts than in the gallbladder. Although usually single, granular cell tumours may be multicentric or may coexist with one or more granular cell tumours in other sites, especially the skin.

Ganglioneuromatosis

Ganglioneuromatosis of the gallbladder is a component of the type IIb multiple endocrine neoplasia syndrome. The histological changes consist of Schwann cell and ganglion cell proliferation in the lamina propria as well as enlarged and distorted nerves in the muscle layer and subserosa. Neurofibromatosis is exceedingly rare in the gallbladder but has been reported in association with multiple neurofibromatosis.

Embryonal rhabdomyosarcoma ('sarcoma botryoides') is the most common malignant neoplasm of the biliary tract in childhood. It occurs more frequently in the bile ducts than in the gallbladder. Kaposi sarcoma of the extrahepatic biliary tract is an incidental autopsy finding in the acquired immune deficiency syndrome. The haemorrhagic lesions are usually located in the subserosa or muscular wall of the gallbladder or in the periductal connective tissue of the bile ducts. Other malignant non-epithelial tumours are leiomyosarcoma, malignant fibrous histiocytoma and angiosarcoma. Leiomyoma, lipoma, haemangioma, and lymphangioma have been described. A benign stromal tumour of the gallbladder with interstitial cells of Cajal phenotype has been reported recently {35}.

Lymphoma of the gallbladder

A. Wotherspoon

In common with lymphoma elsewhere in the digestive system, primary lymphoma of the gallbladder is defined as an extranodal lymphoma arising in the gallbladder with the bulk of the disease localized to this site {796}. Contiguous lymph node involvement and distant spread may be seen but the primary clinical presentation is in the gallbladder with therapy directed at this site.

Primary lymphoma of the gallbladder is extremely rare, with only about 13 cases reported {282, 1201, 94, 138}. Two cases of low-grade B-cell MALT lymphoma have been described {1201, 138}, while the majority of the remainder have been large B-cell lymphomas. MALT lymphomas may arise within acquired MALT that is frequently encountered within gallbladders associated with chronic cholecystitis {1943}. The morphology of primary MALT lymphoma of the gallbladder resembles that seen elsewhere in the digestive tract. Lymphoid follicles are surrounded by an infiltrate of centrocyte-like (CCL) cells showing variable plasma cell differentiation. Infiltration of the epithelium with the formation of lymphoepithelial lesions is a typical feature. Characteristically, the CCL cells show expression of the pan-B-cell markers CD20 and CD79a, and there is frequent expression of bcl-2 protein. Tumour cells are usually negative for CD5 and CD10 but there may be expression of CD43.

Secondary tumours and melanoma

P. DeMatos
P.P. Anthony

Incidence and origins

Although rare in clinical practice, gallbladder and extrahepatic bile duct metastases were encountered in 15% and 6% of cases respectively in an autopsy study of melanoma patients {373}. Indeed, malignant melanoma accounts for more than 50% of all reported cases of gallbladder and intrabiliary metastases {100}. Other metastatic lesions include carcinomas of the kidney, lung, breast, ovary and oesophagus {35, 1674, 2085}; some examples result from transcoelomic spread in the setting of peritoneal carcinomatosis. The gallbladder and extrahepatic bile ducts may also be involved by direct extension from carcinomas of the pancreas, stomach, colon and liver.

Metastatic infiltration of the common bile duct by carcinoma of the breast, giving rise to obstructive jaundice, has been reported {471}. Certain types of non-Hodgkin lymphoma (e.g. mantle cell lymphoma) may also involve the common bile duct.

Malignant melanoma

Primary malignant melanoma is exceedingly rare in the gallbladder. Junctional activity in the epithelium adjacent to the tumour, absence of a primary melanoma elsewhere in the body and long term survival are important features to distinguish primary from the more commonly occurring metastatic melanoma. However, junctional activity has been reported in metastatic melanoma in the gallbladder.

Clinical features

Involvement of the gallbladder by metastatic tumour rarely produces symptoms, which could explain the paucity of clinical reports published in the literature {373, 427}. When symptoms are present, they are usually those of acute cholecystitis {1433, 1013, 427}. Patients with bile duct metastases may present with obstructive jaundice {180}.

Ultrasound may be used to evaluate metastatic lesions within the gallbladder. Computed tomography is also helpful especially for assessing the extent of tumour when therapeutic intervention is contemplated {1013}. The common bile duct is best imaged through the use of ultrasound, endoscopic retrograde cholangiography, and percutaneous transhepatic cholangiography.

Macroscopy

Intraluminal metastases of melanoma tend to be polypoid whilst metastatic carcinoma of the breast and lymphoma produce diffuse infiltrates and strictures.

Histopathology

The features are similar to those observed in other organs.

CHAPTER 10

Tumours of the Exocrine Pancreas

Pancreatic carcinoma is a highly malignant neoplasm that still carries a very poor prognosis. Ductal adenocarcinoma is the most frequent type. Although cigarette smoking has been established as a causative factor, the risk attributable to tobacco abuse amounting to approximately 30%. An increased risk is also associated with hereditary pancreatitis, but additional aetiological factors remain to be identified.

Significant progress has been made in the understanding of the molecular basis of ductal carcinomas. *KRAS* point mutations and inactivation of the tumour suppressor genes *p16*, *TP53* and *DPC4* have been identified as most frequent genetic alterations.

Non-ductal pancreatic neoplasms span a wide range of histological features that need to be recognized by pathologists as several entities are associated with distinct opportunities for therapy.

WHO histological classification of tumours of the exocrine pancreas

Epithelial tumours

Benign	
Serous cystadenoma	8441/0[1]
Mucinous cystadenoma	8470/0
Intraductal papillary-mucinous adenoma	8453/0
Mature teratoma	9080/0
Borderline (uncertain malignant potential)	
Mucinous cystic neoplasm with moderate dysplasia	8470/1
Intraductal papillary-mucinous neoplasm with moderate dysplasia	8453/1
Solid-pseudopapillary neoplasm	8452/1
Malignant	
Ductal adenocarcinoma	8500/3
Mucinous noncystic carcinoma	8480/3
Signet ring cell carcinoma	8490/3
Adenosquamous carcinoma	8560/3
Undifferentiated (anaplastic) carcinoma	8020/3
Undifferentiated carcinoma with osteoclast-like giant cells	8035/3
Mixed ductal-endocrine carcinoma	8154/3
Serous cystadenocarcinoma	8441/3
Mucinous cystadenocarcinoma	8470/3
– non-invasive	8470/2
– invasive	8470/3
Intraductal papillary-mucinous carcinoma	8453/3
– non-invasive	8453/2
– invasive (papillary-mucinous carcinoma)	8453/3
Acinar cell carcinoma	8550/3
Acinar cell cystadenocarcinoma	8551/3
Mixed acinar-endocrine carcinoma	8154/3
Pancreatoblastoma	8971/3
Solid-pseudopapillary carcinoma	8452/3
Others	
Non-epithelial tumours	
Secondary tumours	

[1] Morphology code of the International Classification of Diseases for Oncology (ICD-O) {542} and the Systematized Nomenclature of Medicine (http://snomed.org). Behaviour is coded /0 for benign tumours, /1 for unspecified, borderline or uncertain behaviour, /2 for in situ carcinomas and /3 for malignant tumours.

TNM classification of tumours of the exocrine pancreas

TNM classification[1,2]

Primary Tumour (T)

TX Primary tumour cannot be assessed
T0 No evidence of primary tumour
Tis Carcinoma in situ
T1 Tumour limited to the pancreas, 2 cm or less in greatest dimension
T2 Tumour limited to the pancreas, more than 2 cm in greatest dimension
T3 Tumour extends directly into any of the following: duodenum, bile duct, peripancreatic tissues[3]
T4 Tumour extends directly into any of the following: stomach, spleen, colon, adjacent large vessels[4]

Regional Lymph Nodes (N)

NX Regional lymph nodes cannot be assessed
N0 No regional lymph node metastasis
N1 Regional lymph node metastasis
    N1a Metastasis in a single regional lymph node
    N1b Metastasis in multiple regional lymph nodes

Distant Metastasis (M)

MX Distant metastasis cannot be assessed
M0 No distant metastasis
M1 Distant metastasis

Stage grouping

Stage 0	Tis	N0	M0
Stage I	T1	N0	M0
	T2	N0	M0
Stage II	T3	N0	M0
Stage III	T1	N1	M0
	T2	N1	M0
	T3	N1	M0
Stage IVA	T4	Any N	M0
Stage IVB	Any T	Any N	M1

[1] {66, 361}. This classification applies only to carcinomas of the exocrine pancreas.
[2] A help desk for specific questions about the TNM classification is available at http://tnm.uicc.org.
[3] Peripancreatic tissues include the surrounding retroperitoneal soft tissue or retroperitoneal space), including mesentery (mesenteric fat), mesocolon, greater and lesser omentum, and peritoneum. Direct invasion to bile ducts and duodenum includes involvement of ampulla of Vater.
[4] Adjacent large vessels are the portal vein, coeliac artery, and superior mesenteric and common hepatic arteries and veins (not splenic vessels).

Ductal adenocarcinoma of the pancreas

G. Klöppel
R.H. Hruban
D.S. Longnecker
G. Adler
S.E. Kern
T.J. Partanen

Definition

A carcinoma occurring almost exclusively in adults that probably arises from and is phenotypically similar to, pancreatic duct epithelia, with mucin production and expression of a characteristic cytokeratin pattern.

ICD-O codes

Ductal adenocarcinoma	8500/3
Mucinous noncystic carcinoma	8480/3
Signet ring cell carcinoma	8490/3
Adenosquamous carcinoma	8560/3
Undifferentiated (anaplastic) carcinoma	8020/3
Undifferentiated carcinoma with osteoclast-like giant cells	8035/3
Mixed ductal-endocrine carcinoma	8154/3

Epidemiology

Incidence and geographical distribution

Ductal adenocarcinoma and its variants are the most common neoplasms in the pancreas, representing 85-90% of all pancreatic neoplasms {359, 941, 1781}. In developed countries, the annual age-adjusted incidence rates (world standard population) range from 3.1 (Herault, France) to 20.8 (central Louisiana, USA, blacks) per 100,000 males and from 2.0 (Herault, France) to 11.0 (San Francisco, CA, USA, blacks) per 100,000 females {1471}. Rates from most developing countries range from 1.0 to close to 10 per 100,000. Incidence and mortality rates are almost identical, since survival rates for pancreatic carcinoma are very low.

Time trends

After a steady increase between 1930 and 1980, the incidence rates have levelled off {593}. It is currently the fifth leading cause of cancer death in Western countries, second only to colon cancer among malignancies of the digestive tract.

Age and sex distribution

Approximately 80% of cases manifest clinically in patients 60-80 years; cases below the age of 40 years are rare {1781}. The incidence of pancreatic carcinoma is slightly higher among men than women,

with a male/female ratio of 1.6 in developed nations and 1.1 in developing countries. Blacks have distinctly higher rates than whites {593}.

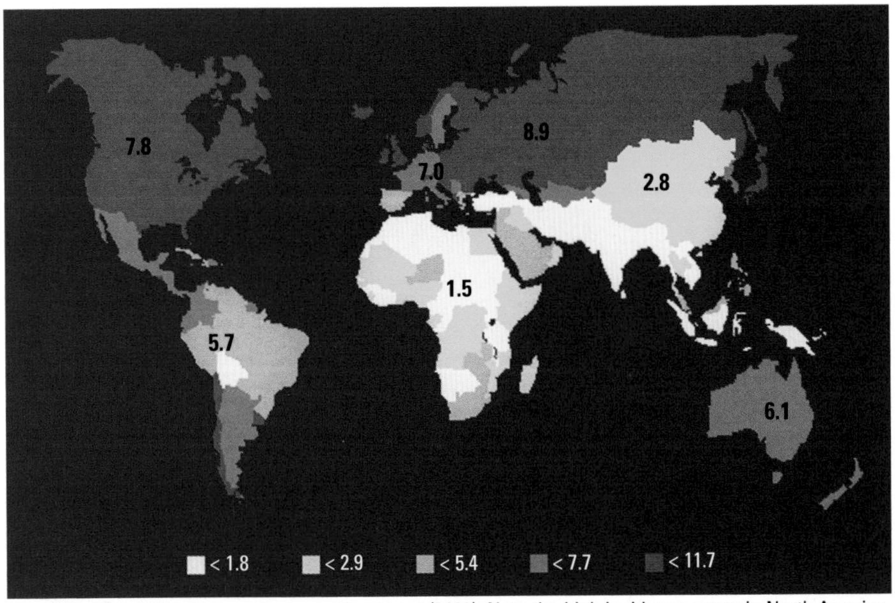

Aetiology

The development of pancreatic carcinoma is strongly related to cigarette smoking, which carries a 2-3 fold relative risk (RR) that increases with the number of pack-years of smoking {21}. Although the association between cigarette smoking and pancreatic carcinoma is not as strong as that between cigarette smoking and lung cancer (RR > 20), it has been estimated that a substantial reduction of the number of smokers in the European Union could save as many as 68,000 lives that would otherwise be lost to pancreatic cancer during the next 20 years {1293}. Chronic pancreatitis, past gastric surgery, occupational exposure to chemicals such as chlorinated hydrocarbon solvents, radiation exposure, and diabetes mellitus have also been associated with the development of pancreatic carcinoma {593, 1100, 2080}. A markedly increased risk has been observed in hereditary pancreatitis {1101}.

A number of dietary factors have been putatively connected with pancreatic cancer, including a diet low in fibre and high in meat and fat {593}. Coffee consumption was once thought to be a risk factor for pancreatic carcinoma, but recent studies showed no significant associations {593}.

Localization

60-70% of pancreatic ductal adenocarcinomas are found in the head of the gland, the remainder occur in the body and/or tail. Pancreatic head tumours are mainly localized in the upper half, rarely in the uncinate process {1781}. Rarely, heterotopic pancreatic tissue gives rise to a carcinoma {596, 1898}.

Clinical features

Symptoms and signs

Clinical features include abdominal pain, unexplained weight loss, jaundice and pruritus. Diabetes mellitus is present in

Fig. 10.01 Global distribution of pancreatic cancer (2000). Note the high incidence areas in North America, Europe, and the Russian Federation.

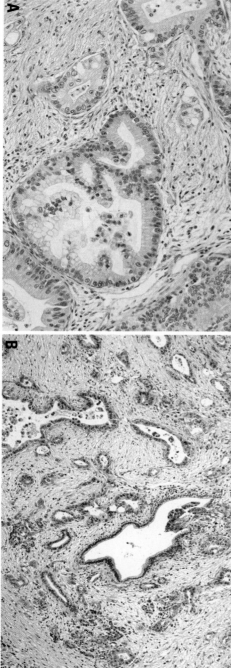

Fig. 10.03 Ductal adenocarcinoma. **A** Well differentiated tumour with desmoplasia and irregular gland formation. **B** Well differentiated neoplasm involving a normal duct (right part).

70% of patients, usually with a diabetes history of less than 2 years. Later symptoms are related to liver metastasis and/or invasion of adjacent organs (stomach, colon) or of the peritoneal cavity (ascites). Occasionally, patients present with acute pancreatitis {621}, migratory thrombophlebitis, hypoglycaemia, or hypercalcaemia {1261}.

Imaging and laboratory tests

Currently, the most important tests for establishing the diagnosis of pancreatic carcinoma are ultrasonography (US) and computerised tomography (CT) or magnetic resonance imaging (MRI), with or without guided percutaneous fine-needle biopsy, endoscopic retrograde cholangiography (ERCP), endoscopic ultrasonography (EUS) and tumour marker determination (CA 19-9, Du-Pan 2, CEA, Span-1). The sensitivity and specificity of any of these tests alone ranges between 55 and 95%. By applying combinations of these tests, accuracy rates of more than 95% have been achieved {2061}. On transabdominal US and on EUS, pancreatic ductal adenocarcinomas are characterised as echo-poor and inhomogeneous mass lesions in about 80% of cases. About 10% of the tumours appear echo-rich. With increasing size, tumours tend to become inhomogeneous, with cystic and echo-rich areas. Indirect signs of a pancreatic tumour (dilatation of pancreatic and/or common bile duct) are usually found proximal to tumours larger than 3 cm. On EUS lymph node metastases appear as enlarged echo-poor nodes. ERPC may demonstrate dis-

placement, narrowing, or obstruction of the pancreatic duct. Angiography is helpful in preoperative management. CT shows pancreatic adenocarcinomas as hypodense masses in up to 92% of cases {528}. Diffuse tumour involvement of the pancreas is found in about 4%. In up to 4% the pancreatic and common bile duct are dilated without an identifiable mass.

KRAS mutations. Mutations in codon 12 of the *KRAS* gene have been detected in the stool, in pancreatic juice and/or blood samples from patients with proven ductal adenocarcinoma of the pancreas {224, 960, 1876}, but their diagnostic value in is still controversial.

Fine needle aspiration (FNA)

FNA can be performed percutaneously with guidance by imaging techniques or under direct visualisation at surgery. Aspirates from a typical, well to moderately differentiated ductal adenocarcinoma show a cellular aspirate {32, 940}. Pancreatic juice cytology obtained from ERCP is less sensitive than percutaneous or intraoperative FNA (76 versus 90 to 100%) {32, 1242, 1311}.

Macroscopy

Ductal adenocarcinomas are firm and poorly defined masses. The cut surfaces are yellow to white. Haemorrhage and necrosis are uncommon, but microcystic areas may occur. In surgical series, the size of most carcinomas of the head of the pancreas ranges from 1.5 to 5 cm, with a mean diameter between 2.5 and 3.5 cm. Carcinomas of the body/tail are

usually somewhat larger at diagnosis. Tumours with a diameter less than 2 cm are infrequent {697} and may be difficult to recognise by gross inspection. Carcinomas of the head of the pancreas usually invade the common bile duct and/or the main pancreatic duct and produce stenosis that results in proximal dilatation of both duct systems. Complete obstruction of the main pancreatic duct leads to extreme prestenotic duct dilatation with duct haustration and fibrous atrophy of the parenchyma (i.e. obstructive chronic pancreatitis). More advanced pancreatic head carcinomas involve the duodenal wall, causing ulcerations. Carcinomas in the pancreatic body or tail obstruct the main pancreatic duct, but typically do not involve the common bile duct.

Tumour spread and staging

It is an exception to find a resected carcinoma that is still limited to the pancreas {1414}. In head carcinomas, peripancre-

Fig. 10.02 Ductal adenocarcinoma. An ill-defined pale carcinoma in the head of the pancreas.

atic tumour invasion, often via perineural sheaths, primarily involves the retroperitoneal fatty tissue. Subsequently, retroperitoneal veins and nerves are invaded. Direct extension into neighbouring organs and/or the peritoneum is seen in advanced cases. In carcinomas of the body and tail, local extension is usually greater, because of delayed tumour detection, and includes invasion of the spleen, stomach, left adrenal gland, colon, and peritoneum {359, 941}.

Lymphatic spread of pancreatic head carcinomas involves, in descending order of frequency, the retroduodenal (posterior pancreaticoduodenal) and the superior pancreatic head groups, the inferior head and the superior body groups, and the anterior pancreaticoduodenal and the inferior body groups {359}. This lymph node compartment is usually resected together with the head of the pancreas, using a standard Whipple procedure {1955}. More distal nodal metastases may occur in the ligamentum hepatoduodenale, at the coeliac trunk, the root of the superior mesenteric artery, and in para-aortic nodes at the level of the renal arteries. These lymph node compartments are only removed if an extended Whipple procedure is performed. Carcinomas of the body and tail metastasise especially to the superior and inferior body and tail lymph node groups and the splenic hilus lymph nodes. They may also spread via lymphatic channels to pleura and lung.

Haematogenous metastasis occurs, in approximate order of frequency, to the liver, lungs, adrenals, kidneys, bones, brain, and skin {359, 941, 1231}.

Staging

The 1997 TNM classification {66} is presented on page 220. Another staging system has been published by the Japan Pancreas Society {832}.

Histopathology

Most ductal adenocarcinomas are well to moderately differentiated. They are characterized by well-developed glandular structures, which more or less imitate normal pancreatic ducts, embedded in desmoplastic stroma. The large amount of fibrous stroma accounts for their firm consistency. Variations in the degree of differentiation within the same neoplasm are frequent, but well differentiated carcinomas with foci of poor differentiation are uncommon.

Well differentiated carcinomas consist of large duct-like structures, combined with medium-sized neoplastic glands. Tubular or cribriform patterns are typical; there may also be small irregular papillary projections without a distinct fibrovascular stalk, particularly in large duct-like structures. Mitotic activity is low. In between the neoplastic glands there may be a few non-neoplastic ducts as well as remnants of acini and individual islets.

Sometimes, the neoplastic duct-like glands are so well differentiated that they are difficult to distinguish from non-neoplastic ducts. However, the mucin-containing neoplastic glands may be ruptured or incompletely formed, a feature that is not seen in normal ducts. The mucin-producing neoplastic cells tend to be columnar, have eosinophilic and occasionally pale or even clear cytoplasm, and are usually larger than those of non-neoplastic ducts. They contain large round to ovoid nuclei which may vary in size, with sharp nuclear membranes and distinct nucleoli that are not found in normal duct cells. Moreover, although the neoplastic cell nuclei tend to be situated at the base of the cell, they always show some loss of polarity.

Moderately differentiated carcinomas predominantly show a mixture of medium-sized duct-like and tubular structures of variable shape, embedded in desmoplastic stroma. Incompletely formed glands are common. Compared with the well differentiated carcinoma, there is a

greater variation in nuclear size, chromatin structure and prominence of nucleoli. Mitotic figures are rather frequent. The cytoplasm is usually slightly eosinophilic, but clear cells are occasionally abundant. Mucin production appears to be decreased and intraductal in situ components are somewhat less frequent than in well differentiated carcinomas. Foci of poor and irregular glandular differentiation are often found at the leading edge of the neoplasm, particularly where it invades the peripancreatic tissue.

Poorly differentiated ductal carcinomas are infrequent. They are composed of a mixture of densely packed, small irregular glands as well as solid tumour cell sheets and nests, which entirely replace the acinar tissue. While typical large, duct-like structures and intraductal tumour components are absent, there may be small squamoid, spindle cell, or anaplastic foci (comprising by definition less than 20% of the tumour tissue). There may be some scattered inflammatory cells. Foci of necrosis and haemorrhage occur. The neoplastic cells show marked pleomorphism, little or no mucin production, and brisk mitotic activity. At the advancing edge of the carcinoma, the gland and the peripancreatic tissue are infiltrated by small clusters of neoplastic cells.

Changes in non-neoplastic pancreas

All ductal adenocarcinomas are associated with more or less developed fibrosclerotic and inflammatory changes

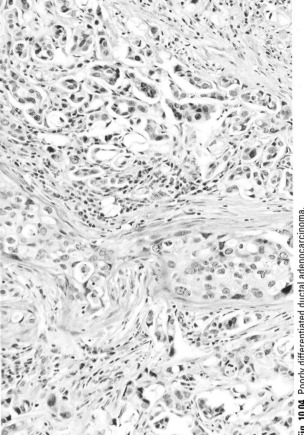

Fig. 10.04 Poorly differentiated ductal adenocarcinoma.

Fig. 10.05 Undifferentiated carcinoma exhibiting extreme pleomorphism with giant cells.

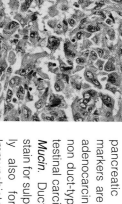

in the adjoining non-neoplastic pancreas, due to carcinomatous duct obstructions (obstructive chronic pancreatitis). In cases of complete occlusion of the main duct, there is marked upstream dilatation of the duct and almost complete fibrotic atrophy of the parenchyma. In contrast to chronic pancreatitis due to alcoholism, intraductal calcifications are generally absent. Poorly differentiated carcinomas usually destroy the islets. In the well and moderately differentiated neoplasms, however, islets may be found entrapped in neoplastic tissue. In addition, scattered endocrine cells occur attached to or intermingled between neoplastic columnar cells. Only in exceptional cases do the endocrine cells constitute a second cell component of the ductal carcinoma (see mixed ductal-endocrine carcinoma).

Histochemistry and immunohistochemistry

Although no histochemical or immunohistochemical marker is able to unequivocally distinguish pancreatic from extra-

pancreatic adenocarcinoma, some markers are useful in separating ductal adenocarcinoma of the pancreas from non duct-type tumours or other gastrointestinal carcinomas.

Mucin. Ductal adenocarcinomas mainly stain for sulphated acid mucins but focally also for neutral mucins {1714}. Immunohistochemically, most ductal adenocarcinomas express MUC1, MUC3 and MUC5/6 (but not MUC2) {1918, 2179}, CA 19-9, Du-Pan 2, Span-1, CA 125 and TAG72 {1714, 1884}. The expression patterns of CA 19-9, Du-Pan 2, Span-1, CA 125 and TAG 72 are largely comparable in their immunoreactivity and specificity. These markers also label the epithelium of normal pancreatic ducts to some extent, particularly in chronic pancreatitis, and the tumour cells of some serous cystadenomas and acinar cell carcinomas {1282}.

Carcinoembryonic antigen (CEA). Monospecific antibodies against CEA that do not recognise other members of the CEA family are capable of discriminating between non-neoplastic duct changes, such as ductal papillary hyperplasia, and a variety of neoplasms {119}. CEA is negative in serous cystadenoma.

Cytokeratins, vimentin, endocrine markers and enzymes. Normal pancreatic and biliary ductal cells and pancreatic centroacinar cells express the cytokeratins (CK) 7, 8, 18, 19 and occasionally also 4 {1696}. Acinar cells contain only CK 8 and 18, and islet cells 8, 18 and occasionally also 19. Ductal adenocarcinomas express the same set of cytokeratins as the normal duct epithelium, i.e. CK 7, 8, 18 and 19. More than 50% of

the carcinomas also express CK 4 {1696}, but are usually negative for CK 20 {1259}. As the usual keratin patterns of non-duct-type pancreatic neoplasms (i.e. acinar carcinomas and endocrine tumours, CK 8, 18 and 19) and gut carcinomas (i.e. CK 8, 18, 19 and 20) differ from that of ductal carcinoma, it is possible to distinguish these tumours on the basis of their CK profile.

Ductal adenocarcinomas are usually negative for vimentin {1696}. With rare exceptions (see mixed ductal-endocrine carcinoma), they also fail to label with endocrine markers such as synaptophysin and the chromogranins, but may contain, particularly if well differentiated, some scattered (possibly non-neoplastic) endocrine cells in close association with the neoplastic cells {167}. They are generally negative for pancreatic enzymes such as trypsin, chymotrypsin and lipase {739, 1282}.

Growth factors and adhesion molecules. Pancreatic carcinomas overexpress epidermal growth factor and its receptor, c-erbB-2, transforming growth factor alpha {380, 1676, 2163}, metallothionein {1409}, CD44v6 {259, 1880} and membranous E-cadherin {1519}.

Ultrastructure

Ductal adenocarcinoma cells are characterized by mucin granules in the apical cytoplasm, irregular microvilli on the luminal surface, and a more or less polarised arrangement of the differently sized nuclei {359, 901, 1714}. The content of the mucin granules (0.4-2.0 μm) varies from solid-electron dense to filamentous and punctate; often there is a dense

A

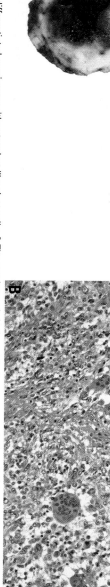

B

Fig. 10.06 Undifferentiated carcinoma with osteoclast-like giant cells. **A** The carcinoma is in the uncinate process and shows haemorrhagic necrosis. **B** There is marked cellular pleomorphism with scattered osteoclast-like giant cells and a well-differentiated ductal carcinoma component (left upper corner).

eccentric core. Some cells have features of gastric foveolar cells, showing granules with a punctate-cerebroid structure {1714}. Loss of tumour differentiation is characterized by loss of cell polarity, disappearance of a basal lamina, appearance of irregular luminal spaces, and loss of mucin granules {901}.

Histological variants

Adenosquamous carcinoma and undifferentiated (anaplastic) carcinoma (including osteoclast-like giant cell tumours), mucinous noncystic adenocarcinoma and signet-ring cell carcinoma are considered variants of ductal adenocarcinoma because most of these carcinomas, even if poorly differentiated, contain some foci showing neoplastic glands with ductal differentiation {288, 359, 941, 947, 1781}.

Adenosquamous carcinoma

This rare neoplasm, relative frequency 3-4% {941, 359, 813, 1415}, is characterized by the presence of variable proportions of mucin-producing glandular elements and squamous components. The squamous component should account for at least 30% of the tumour tissue. In addition, there may be anaplastic and spindle cell carcinoma foci. Pure squamous carcinomas are very rare.

Undifferentiated (anaplastic) carcinoma

Also called giant cell carcinoma, pleomorphic large cell carcinoma, and sarcomatoid carcinoma, these tumours have a relative frequency of 2-7%. They are composed of large eosinophilic pleomorphic cells and/or ovoid to spindle-shaped cells that grow in poorly cohesive formations supported by scanty fibrous stroma. Commonly the carcinomas contain small foci of atypical glandular elements {359, 941, 1786, 1962}. Carcinomas consisting predominantly of spindle cells may also contain areas of squamoid differentiation. High mitotic activity as well as perineural, lymphatic, and blood vessel invasion is found in almost all cases. Immunohistochemically, some or most tumour cells express cytokeratins and usually also vimentin {740}. Electron microscopy reveals microvilli and mucin granules in some cases {359}. Undifferentiated carcinomas with a neoplastic mesenchymal component (carcinosarcoma) have so far not been described.

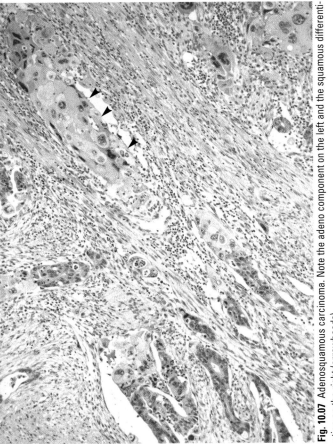

Fig. 10.07 Adenosquamous carcinoma. Note the adeno component on the left and the squamous differentiation on the right (arrowheads).

Undifferentiated carcinoma with osteoclast-like giant cells

This rare neoplasm is composed of pleomorphic to spindle-shaped cells and scattered non-neoplastic osteoclast-like giant cells with usually more than 20 uniformly small nuclei. In many cases there is an associated in situ or invasive adenocarcinoma {359}. The osteoclast-like giant cells are often concentrated near areas of haemorrhage and may contain haemosiderin and, occasionally, phagocytosed mononuclear cells. Osteoid formation may also be found.

Immunohistochemically, at least some of the neoplastic cells express cytokeratin, vimentin and p53 {740, 2095}. The osteoclast-like giant cells, in contrast, are negative for cytokeratin and p53, but positive for vimentin, leukocyte common antigen (CD56) and macrophage markers such as KP1 {740, 1258, 2095}.

The mean age of patients with osteoclast-like giant cell tumours is 60 years but there is a wide age range from 32 to 82 years {1370}. Some tumours are found in association with mucinous cystic neoplasms {1258, 2095, 2198}. In the early reports on this tumour it was suggested that they may have a more favourable prognosis than the usual ductal adenocarcinoma {359}. More recently a mean survival of 12 months has been reported.

Mucinous noncystic carcinoma

This uncommon carcinoma (relative frequency: 1-3%) {941} has also been called 'colloid' or gelatinous carcinoma. Mucin accounts for > 50% of the tumour. The large pools of mucin are partially lined by well-differentiated cuboidal cells and contain clumps or strands of tumour cells. Some floating cells may be of the signet-ring cell type.

Sex and age distribution are similar to those of ductal adenocarcinoma. The tumours may be very large and are usually well demarcated. The development of pseudomyxoma peritonei has been described {285}. It is of interest that the invasive component of some of the intraductal papillary-mucinous tumours resembles mucinous noncystic carcinoma. Mucinous noncystic carcinoma should not be confused with mucinous cystic tumour because of the much better prognosis of the latter (see chapter on mucinous cystic neoplasms).

Signet-ring cell carcinoma

The extremely rare signet-ring cell carcinoma is an adenocarcinoma composed almost exclusively of cells filled with mucin {1781, 1951}. The prognosis is extremely poor; a gastric primary should always be excluded before making this diagnosis.

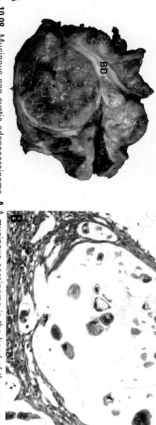

Fig. 10.08 Mucinous non-cystic adenocarcinoma. **A** A mucinous carcinoma in the head of the pancreas obstructs the main pancreatic duct and impinges on the bile duct (BD). **B** The neoplastic cells float in pools of mucin.

Mixed ductal-endocrine carcinoma

Mixed ductal-endocrine carcinoma {947} has also been referred to as mixed carcinoid-adenocarcinoma, mucinous carcinoid tumour {359}, or simply mixed exocrine-endocrine tumour. This neoplasm is characterized by an intimate admixture of ductal and endocrine cells in the primary tumour as well as in its metastases. By definition, the endocrine cells should comprise at least one third to one half of the tumour tissue. The ductal differentiation is defined by mucin production and the presence of a duct type marker such as CEA. The endocrine cells are characterized by the presence of neuroendocrine markers and/or hormonal products; immunoexpression of all four islet hormones, amylin (IAPP), serotonin, pancreatic polypeptide (PP), and occasionally gastrin have been described {167}.

Mixed ductal-endocrine carcinomas, as defined above, seem to be exceptionally rare in the pancreas {1714, 1781}. Biologically, the mixed carcinoma behaves like the usual ductal adenocarcinoma.

Acinar cell carcinomas {739, 1694, 1985} and pancreatoblastomas {741} with some endocrine and ductal elements, and endocrine tumours with ductal components {1372, 1941} are not discussed here, because their behaviour is dictated by their acinar and endocrine elements.

Mixed ductal-endocrine carcinomas should also be distinguished from ductal adenocarcinomas with scattered endocrine cells, since scattered endocrine cells are found in 40-80% of ductal adenocarcinomas {167, 289} and seem to be particularly frequent in the well differentiated tumours, where they are either lined up along the base of the neoplastic

ductal structures or lie between the neoplastic columnar cells. 'Collision tumours' composed of two topographically separate components are not included in the mixed ductal-endocrine category.

Other rare carcinomas

Other very rare carcinomas of probable ductal phenotype include clear cell carcinoma {359, 882, 1908, 1121} and ciliated cell carcinoma (see chapter on miscellaneous carcinomas) {1276, 1786}. Carcinomas with 'medullary' histology have recently been described {590}; these lesions are associated with wild-type *KRAS* status and microsatellite instability.

The so-called *microglandular carcinomas* {359} or microadenocarcinomas are distinguished by a microglandular to solid-cribriform pattern. They most likely do not form an entity of their own but belong to either the ductal, endocrine, or acinar carcinomas.

Grading

A few formal grading systems have been described. Miller et al. graded pancreatic tumours using the system of Broder, which distinguishes four grades of cellular atypia. High-grade carcinomas (Broder grades 3 and 4) were larger and the frequency of venous thrombosis and metastasis higher than in low-grade tumours.

A more recent grading system is based on combined assessment of histological and cytological features and mitotic activity {944, 1119}. If there is intratumour heterogeneity, i.e. a variation in the degree of differentiation and mitotic activity, the higher grade and mitotic activity is assigned. This rule also applies if only a minor component (less than half of the tumour) was of lower grade. Using this system, there is a correlation between grade and survival and grade is an independent prognostic variable {944, 1119}.

Precursor lesions
Pancreatic neoplasms

Mucinous cystic neoplasms and intraductal papillary mucinous neoplasms may progress to invasive cancer. In the case of mucinous cystic neoplasms, the invasive component usually resembles ductal adenocarcinoma {1781}. In the case of intraductal papillary-mucinous

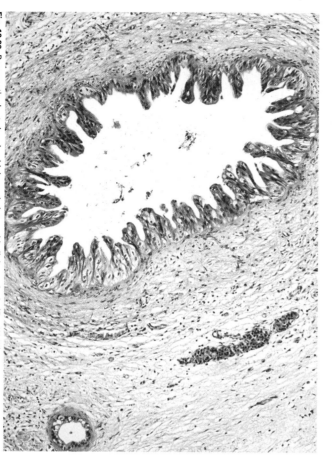

Fig. 10.09 Pancreatic duct showing high-grade intraepithelial neoplasia (PanIN III).

Table 10.01
List of recommended terms with synonyms for focal hyperplastic and metaplastic duct lesions in the human exocrine pancreas.

Recommended WHO term	Previous WHO classification {1202}	Other synonyms
Squamous metaplasia Incomplete squamous metaplasia	Squamous metaplasia Incomplete squamous metaplasia	Epidermoid metaplasia, multilayered metaplasia focal epithelial hyperplasia, focal atypical epithelial hyperplasia, multilayered metaplasia
PanIN-IA	Mucinous cell hypertrophy	Mucinous cell hyperplasia, mucinous ductal hyperplasia, mucoid transformation, simple hyperplasia, flat ductal hyperplasia, mucous hypertrophy, hyperplasia with pyloric gland metaplasia, ductal hyperplasia grade 1, non-papillary epithelial hypertrophy, nonpapillary ductal hyperplasia
PanIN-IB	Ductal papillary hyperplasia Adenomatoid ductal hyperplasia	Papillary ductal hyperplasia, ductal hyperplasia grade 2 Adenomatous hyperplasia, ductular cell hyperplasia
PanIN-II	Any PanIN-I lesion with moderate dysplasia as defined in the text	
PanIN-III	Severe ductal dysplasia	Ductal hyperplasia grade 3, atypical hyperplasia Carcinoma in situ

carcinoma, the invasive component either corresponds to a usual ductal adenocarcinoma or to mucinous noncystic carcinoma {1781}.

Severe ductal dysplasia – carcinoma in situ

This change of the ductal epithelium is characterized by irregular epithelial budding and bridging, small papillae lacking fibrovascular stalks, and severe nuclear abnormalities such as loss of polarity, pleomorphism, coarse chromatin, dense nucleoli and mitotic figures. The lesion is often surrounded by one or two layers of fibrosclerotic tissue. Here, no attempt is made to distinguish between severe dysplasia and carcinoma in situ, since it is very difficult, if not impossible, to draw a clear distinction between these two

changes, which both represent high-grade intraepithelial neoplasia. The lesion corresponds to PanIN III in the proposed terminology of pancreatic intraepithelial neoplasia (Table 10.01). High-grade intraepithelial neoplasia is commonly found in association with an invasive ductal adenocarcinoma {358, 555, 943}, and may represent either a precursor to invasive carcinoma or continuous intraductal extensions of the invasive tumour. Similar duct changes have also been described remote from the macroscopic tumour {1781} or years before the development of an invasive ductal carcinoma {185, 191}.

Duct changes

With the exception of high-grade intraepithelial neoplasia, the precursors to infil-

trating ductal adenocarcinomas are still ill-defined. Putative precursor lesions (Table 10.01) include mucinous cell hypertrophy, ductal papillary hyperplasia with mucinous cell hypertrophy (papillary duct lesion without atypia), adenomatoid (adenomatous) ductal hyperplasia, and squamous metaplasia {1781, 947}. All these lesions may show mild nuclear atypia.

The evidence that some of these duct lesions (i.e. mucinous cell hypertrophy and papillary hyperplasia) may be precursors to invasive carcinoma comes from three areas: morphological studies, clinical reports, and genetic analyses. At the light microscopic level, ductal papillary hyperplasia was found adjacent to invasive carcinomas more frequently than it was in pancreases without cancer {290, 358, 943, 965}. It was also noted

Table 10.02
Histopathological grading of pancreatic ductal adenocarcinoma {1119}.

Tumour grade	Glandular differentiation	Mucin production	Mitoses (per 10 HPF)	Nuclear features
Grade 1	Well differentiated	Intensive	≤ 5	Little polymorphism, polar arrangement
Grade 2	Moderately differentiated duct like structures and tubular glands	Irregular	6-10	Moderate polymorphism
Grade 3	Poorly differentiated glands, mucoepidermoid and pleomorphic structures	Abortive	> 10	Marked polymorphism and increased size

Table 10.03
Genetic alterations in pancreatic ductal carcinoma.

Gene	Chromosome	Mechanism of alteration	% of cancers
Oncogenes			
KRAS	12p	Point mutation	> 90
MYB, AKT2, AIB1	6q, 19q, 20q	Amplification¹	10-20
HER/2-neu	17q	Overexpression	70
Tumor suppressor genes			
p16	9p	Homozygous deletion	40
		Loss of heterozygosity and intragenic mutation	40
		Promotor hypermethylation	15
TP53	17p	Loss of heterozygosity and intragenic mutation	50-70
DPC4	18q	Homozygous deletion	35
		Loss of heterozygosity and intragenic mutation	20
BRCA2	13q	Inherited intragenic mutation and loss of heterozygosity	7
LKB1/STK11	19p	Loss of heterozygosity and intragenic mutation, homozygous deletion	5
MKK4	17p	Homozygous deletion, loss of heterozygosity and intragenic mutation	4
ALK5 and TGFβR2	9q, 3p	Homozygous deletion	4
DNA Mismatch Repair			
MSH2, MLH1, others	2p, 3p, others	Unknown	< 5

¹In cases of amplification, it is generally not possible to unambiguously identify the key oncogene due to the participation of multiple genes in an amplicon.

that ductal papillary hyperplasia is similar to severe dysplasia-carcinoma in situ lesions seen in the vicinity of invasive ductal carcinomas {358}. Clinically, Brat et al. {185} and Brockie et al. {191} have reported a total of five patients who developed infiltrating ductal adenocarcinomas years after the identification of atypical duct lesions in their pancreas. Finally, molecular genetic analyses of duct lesions have demonstrated that they contain some of the same genetic alterations seen in infiltrating ductal carcinomas. For example, activating point muta-tions in codon 12 of the KRAS genealterations of the p16 and TP53 tumour suppressor genes and loss of BRCA2 and DPC4 have all been reported in duct lesions {1286, 1875, 2166, 2105, 589}. Duct lesions and infiltrating cancers from the same pancreas may harbour identical mutations {1120, 1286}. Only a minority of duct lesions may progress to invasive cancer, as demonstrated by recent data from a study on normal pancreases, which showed that all types of duct lesions and even normal epithelium may harbour KRAS mutations, and that the lesions are evenly distributed in the pancreas and do not concentrate in the head region where the carcinoma is most frequent {647}. It has recently been suggested that the term 'Pancreatic Intraepithelial Neoplasia (PanIN)' be adopted for these duct lesions (see http://pathology.jhu.edu/pancreas.panin) {937}. Table 10.01 indicates the general relationship between the previous WHO terminology and this new proposed PanIN terminology.

Genetic susceptibility

Between 3% and 10% of cases of pancreatic cancer are familial {754, 1125, 1126, 499}. Some arise in patients with recognized genetic syndromes, as discussed below, but in most instances the genetic basis for the familial aggregation of pancreatic carcinomas has not been identified. A confounding factor is the possibility of shared environmental factors, such as tobacco use. Nevertheless, some studies show familial aggregations suggestive of a genetic aetiology {485, 577, 499, 1207} Studies of extended families have shown a pattern suggestive of an autosomal dominant mode of inheritance.

Hereditary pancreatitis

This disease is caused by germline mutations in the cationic trypsinogen gene on 7q35 {2098}. This syndrome is characterized by the early onset of severe recurrent bouts of acute pancreatitis, and affected individuals have as high as a 40% lifetime risk of developing pancreatic carcinoma {1101}.

FAMMM syndrome

Familial atypical multiple mole melanoma (FAMMM) is associated with germline mutations in the p16 tumour suppressor gene on 9p. Affected individuals have an increased risk of developing both melanoma and pancreatic carcinoma {601, 1127, 1285, 2097}. The lifetime risk for developing pancreatic carcinoma is about 10%.

BRCA2

The discovery of the second breast cancer gene (BRCA2) on 13q was made possible in large part by the discovery of a homozygous deletion in a pancreatic carcinoma {1697}. Pancreatic carcinomas have been reported in some kindred with BRCA2 mutations and familial breast cancer {1514, 1934, 591, 479} identified germline mutations in *BRCA2* in about 7% of patients with pancreatic ductal carcinoma. Remarkably, most pancreatic ductal carcinoma patients with such mutations do not have a strong family history of breast or pancreatic carcinoma. A number of them are, however, of Ashkenazi Jewish ancestry {591, 1442}.

Peutz-Jeghers syndrome

Patients with the Peutz-Jeghers syndrome have an increased risk of developing pancreatic carcinoma, and recently the biallelic inactivation of the *LKB1/STK11* gene has been demonstrated in a pancreatic carcinoma which arose in a patient with the Peutz-Jeghers syndrome {579, 1851}.

Hereditary nonpolyposis colon cancer (HNPCC)

This syndrome is associated with an increased risk of developing carcinoma of the colon, endometrium, stomach, and ovary {2071}. It can be caused by germline mutations in any one of a number of DNA mismatch repair genes, including *MSH2* on 2p and *MLH1* on 3p {1029, 1078, 2071}. Lynch et al. have reported pancreatic carcinomas in some kindred with HNPCC, and Goggins et al. have recently reported microsatellite instability, a genetic change associated with defects in DNA mismatch repair genes, in about 4% of pancreatic carcinomas {590, 1130, 1487}.

Genetics

Genetic alterations are listed in Table 10.03. At the chromosome level, they include losses and gains of genetic material as well as generalised chromosome instability {608, 625, 626}. The most frequent gains identified cytogenetically include those of chromosomes 12 and 7; the most common recurrent structural abnormalities involve chromosome arms 1p, 6q, 7q, 17p, 1q, 3p, 11p, and 19q, and the most frequent losses involve chromosomes 18, 13, 12, 17, and 6 {626, 625}. Similar patterns of loss have been identified at the molecular level {184, 1716}, using highly polymorphic microsatellite markers. These include very high rates of loss at chromosomes 18q (90%), 17p (90%), 1p (60%), and 9p (85%) and moderately frequent losses at 3p, 6p, 8p, 10q, 12q, 13q, 18p, 21q, and 22q (25-50% of cases).

Recurrent losses of genetic material at specific loci in a carcinoma suggest that these loci harbour tumour suppressor genes which are inactivated in the carcinoma, and, indeed, the *p16* gene on 9p, the *Tp53* gene on 17p, and the *DPC4* gene on 18q are all frequently inactivated in pancreatic carcinoma {1716}. The *p16* tumour suppressor gene is inactivated in 40% of pancreatic carcinomas by homozygous deletion, in 40% by loss of one allele coupled with an intragenic mutation in the second, and by hypermethylation of the *p16* promoter in an additional 15% {223, 1698, 2104}. The *Tp53* is inactivated in 75% of pancreatic carcinomas by loss of one allele coupled with an intragenic mutation in the second allele {1570, 1624}. The *DPC4* tumour suppressor gene is inactivated in 55% of pancreatic carcinomas {651}, in 35% of the carcinomas by homozygous deletion and in 20% by loss of one allele coupled with an intragenic mutation in the second allele. The *BRCA2* tumour suppressor gene on 13q is inactivated in about 7% of pancreatic carcinomas {591, 1442, 1697}. Remarkably, in almost all of these cases one allele of *BRCA2* is inactivated by a germline (inherited) mutation in the gene {591}. Other tumour suppressor genes which have been shown to be occasionally inactivated in pancreatic carcinoma include the genes *MKK4, RB1, LKB1/STK11*, and the transforming growth factor β receptors I and II {592, 761, 1850, 1851}.

Several oncogenes have been shown to be activated in ductal adenocarcinomas of the pancreas. These include the *KRAS* gene on chromosome 12p, which is activated by point mutations in over 90% of the carcinomas, overexpression of the *HER2-neu* gene on 17q in 70% of the carcinomas, and amplification of the *AKT2* gene on chromosome 19q in 10-20% of the carcinomas, the nuclear receptor coactivator gene *AIB1* on chromosome 20q, and the *MYB* gene on chromosome 6q {47, 292, 380, 576, 761, 1242, 2039}. Compared to normal pancreas, *Smad2* mRNA levels are increased in pancreatic carcinoma, which might lead to the over-expression of components of the TGF-beta signalling pathway that is observed in these lesions {931}. DNA mismatch repair genes, such as *MLH1* and *MSH2*, can also play a role. Microsatellite instability resulting from the inactivation of both alleles of a DNA mis-

match repair gene has been identified in 4% of pancreatic carcinomas {590}. They had wild-type *KRAS* genes and a characteristic 'medullary' histological appearance, forming a distinct subset of pancreatic adenocarcinomas (see section on other rare carcinomas).

Prognosis and predictive factors

Ductal adenocarcinoma is fatal in most cases {639}. The mean survival time of the untreated patient is 3 months, while the mean survival after radical resection varies from 10-20 months {560, 692, 814, 1955}. The overall 5-year survival rate of patients treated by resection is 3-4% {639}, although in selected and stage-stratified series survival figures approaching 25 or even 46% have been reported {560, 1955, 1966, 1976}. Unresectable carcinomas are treated with palliative bypass operations. Response to chemotherapy with 5-fluorouracil or gemcitabine may be seen in up to approximately 10% of patients. Radiotherapy alone is largely ineffective {2061}.

Site, size, and stage

The survival time is longer in patients with carcinomas confined to the pancreas and less than 3 cm in diameter (17-29 months) than in patients with tumours of greater size or retroperitoneal invasion (6-15 months) {2172}. Carcinomas of the body or the tail of the pancreas tend to present at a more advanced stage than those of the head {560, 1955, 1966, 1976}. Some have found that lymph node metastases significantly worsen prognosis, while others have not {710, 1955, 2172}.

Residual tumour tissue

Patients with no residual tumour following resection (R0) have the most favourable prognosis of all patients undergoing surgical resection {2108}. This implies that local spread to peripancreatic tissues, i.e. the retroperitoneal resection margin, is of utmost importance in terms of prognosis {1122}.

Recurrence

Local recurrence seems to be the major factor determining survival after resection of pancreatic ductal carcinoma. The most common sites of recurrences are the tissues surrounding the large mesenteric vessels {646}. Clear retroperitoneal resection margin or margins are therefore

Table 10.04
Genetic syndromes with an increased risk of pancreatic cancer.

Syndrome (MIM No)¹	Mode of inheritance	Gene (chromosomal location)	Lifetime risk of pancreatic cancer
Early onset familial pancreatic adenocarcinoma associated with diabetes (Seattle family) {479}	Autosomal dominant	Unknown	About 30%; 100-fold increased risk of pancreatic cancer; high risk of diabetes and pancreatitis
Hereditary pancreatitis (167800)	Autosomal dominant	Cationic trypsinogen (7q35)	30%; 50-fold increased risk of pancreatic cancer {1101, 499}
FAMMM: familial atypical multiple mole melanoma (155600)	Autosomal dominant	p16/CMM2 (9p21)	10% {601, 1127, 2097}
Familial breast cancer (600185)	Autosomal dominant	BRCA2 (13q12-q13)	5-10%; 6174delT in Ashkenazi Jews {1442}; 999del5 in Iceland {1934}
Ataxia-telangiectasia (208900) (heterozygote state)	Autosomal recessive	ATM, ATB, others (11q22-q23)	Unknown; somewhat increased
Peutz-Jeghers (175200)	Autosomal dominant	STK11/LKB1 (19p)	Unknown; somewhat increased {579}
HNPCC: hereditary non-polyposis colorectal cancer (120435)	Autosomal dominant	MSH2 (2p), MLH1 (3p), others	Unknown; somewhat increased {1130, 2071}
Familial pancreatic cancer	Possibly autosomal dominant	Unknown	Unknown; 5-10fold increased risk if a first-degree relative has pancreatic cancer {499, 1128, 755}

¹ Mendelian Inheritance in Man: www.ncbi.nlm.nih.gov/omim

required, if a 'curative' resection (R0) is to be achieved {1122}. Second in frequency are recurrences arising from lymph node or liver metastases that were too small to be detected during surgery. The peritoneum and the bone marrow are rare sites of recurrence, although malignant cells are detected cytologically in one quarter of the patients during laparoscopy and one half of the patients when bone marrow trepanation is performed during a Whipple procedure {870}.

Grading

Based on the criteria of the grading system summarised in Table 10.02, it was found that median postoperative survival correlated significantly with tumour grade {944}, mitotic index, and severity of cellular atypia. As grading systems are, however, to a great extent subjective, reproducibility may be low {1119}. Other studies found no relationship between grade and survival {2079}. Nuclear parameters such as median nuclear size, nuclear area, and nuclear perimeter have been shown to be of prognostic value for ductal adenocarcinoma {477, 944}.

DNA content and proliferation

Nondiploid and/or aneuploid DNA content is associated with advanced tumour stage and shorter survival {46, 105, 476, 2079}. Tumours with low argyrophylic nucleolar organizer region (AgNOR) counts per cell (< 3.25) have been reported to have a better prognosis than tumours with a high AgNOR count {1413}. High Ki-67 labeling index is an indicator of poor prognosis, but does not seem to be an independent prognostic parameter {1111, 1119}. The immunohistochemical expression of a number of growth factors has shown weak association with survival {21, 535}.

Serous cystic neoplasms
of the pancreas

C. Capella
E. Solcia
G. Klöppel
R.H. Hruban

Serous cystic pancreatic tumours are cystic epithelial neoplasms composed of glycogen-rich, ductular-type epithelial cells that produce a watery fluid similar to serum. Most are benign (serous cystadenomas), either serous microcystic adenoma or serous oligocystic adenoma. Only very rare cases exhibit signs of malignancy (serous cystadenocarcinoma). A solid variant of serous cystadenoma (solid serous cystadenoma) has been described {1499} but remains to be established as a separate disease entity.

ICD-O codes

Serous cystadenoma   8441/0
Serous cystdenocarcinoma   8441/3

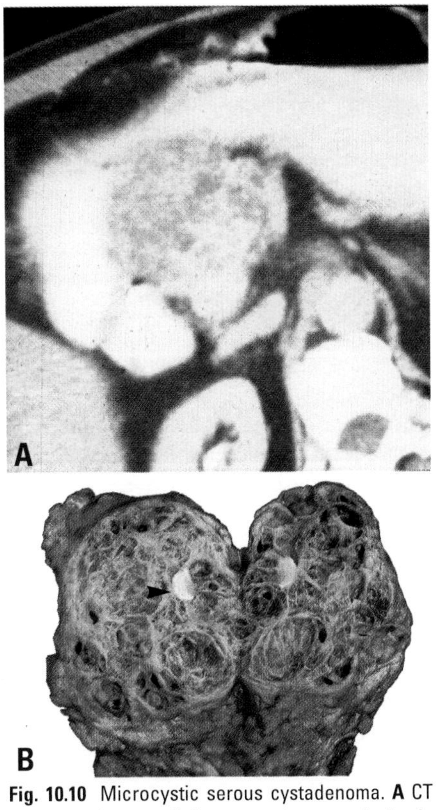

Serous microcystic adenoma

Definition
A benign neoplasm composed of numerous small cysts lined by uniform glycogen-rich cuboidal epithelial cells, disposed around a central stellate scar.

Epidemiology
This is a rare neoplasm, accounting for 1 to 2% of all exocrine pancreatic tumours {1280}. The mean age at presentation is 66 years (range, 34-91 years), with a predominance in women (70%) {1781}. It has been reported in patients with different ethnicity {327, 2151}.

Aetiology
The aetiology and pathogenesis of the neoplasm are unknown. The striking predilection for women suggests that sex hormones or genetic factors may play a role. An association with Von Hippel-Lindau disease has been reported {327, 2026} and confirmed by recent genetic molecular investigations {2026}.

Localization
The neoplasms occur most frequently (50-75%) in the body or tail; the remaining tumours involve the head of the pancreas {49, 327}.

Clinical features
About one third of the neoplasms present as an incidental finding at routine physical examination or at autopsy {445}. Approximately two thirds of patients exhibit symptoms related to local mass effects, including abdominal pain, palpable mass, nausea and vomiting, and weight loss {1544}. Jaundice due to obstruction of the common bile duct is unusual, even in neoplasms originating from the head of the pancreas.

Pancreatic serum tumour markers are generally normal. Calcifications are found in a few patients on plain abdominal roentgenograms. Ultrasonography (US) and computed tomography (CT) reveal a well circumscribed, multilocular cyst, occasionally with an evident central stellate scar and a sunburst type calcification {532, 817, 1544}. On angiography, the tumours are usually hypervascular.

Macroscopy
Serous microcystic adenomas are single, well-circumscribed, slightly bosselated, round lesions, with diameters ranging from 1-25 cm in greatest dimension (average, 6-10 cm). On section, the neoplasms are sponge-like and are made up of numerous tiny cysts filled with serous (clear watery) fluid. The cysts range from 0.01-0.5 cm, with a few larger cysts of up to 2 cm in diameter. Often, the cysts are arranged around a more or less centrally located, dense fibronodular core from which thin fibrous septa radiate to the periphery (central stellate scar).

Histopathology
At low magnification, the pattern of the cysts is similar to a sponge. The cysts contain proteinaceous fluid and are lined by a single layer of cuboidal or flattened epithelial cells. Their cytoplasm is clear and only rarely eosinophilic and granular. The nuclei are centrally located, round to oval in shape, uniform, and have an inconspicuous nucleolus. Due to the presence of abundant intracytoplasmic glycogen, the periodic acid-Schiff (PAS) stain without diastase digestion is positive, whereas PAS-diastase and Alcian blue stains are negative {160}. Mitoses are practically absent and there is no cytological atypia. Occasionally, the neoplastic cells form intracystic papillary projections, usually without a fibrovascular stalk. The central fibrous stellate core is formed of hyalinized tissue with a few clusters of tiny cysts.

Immunohistochemistry
The epithelial nature of these neoplasms is reflected in their immunoreactivity for epithelial membrane antigen and cytokeratins 7, 8, 18, and 19. In addition, the neoplastic cells may focally express CA19-9 and B72.3 {815, 1752}. They are uniformly negative for carcinoembryonic

Fig. 10.10 Microcystic serous cystadenoma. **A** CT scan showing a well demarcated, spongy lesion in the head of the pancreas. **B** Cut surface showing a typical honeycomb appearance and a (para-)central stellate scar (arrowhead).

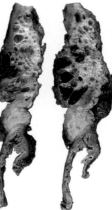

Fig. 10.11 Serous oligocystic adenoma. This CT scan shows a macrocystic neoplasm in the head of the pancreas.

Fig. 10.13 Serous cystadenoma. A cystic neoplasm replaces the head of the pancreas; a portion of duodenum is on the right.

Genetics

Loss of heterozygosity at the von Hippel-Lindau (VHL) gene locus, mapped to chromosome 3p25, was found in 2/2 serous microcystic adenomas associated with VHL disease and in 7/10 sporadic cases {2026}. In contrast to ductal adenocarcinomas, serous microcystic adenomas have wild-type *KRAS* and lack immunoreactivity for TP53 {815}.

Prognosis

The prognosis of patients with this neoplasm is excellent, since there is only a minimal risk of malignant transformation {1159}.

Serous oligocystic adenoma

Definition

A benign neoplasm composed of few, relatively large cysts, lined by uniform glycogen-rich cuboidal epithelial cells.

Synonyms

This tumour category includes macrocystic serous cystadenoma {257, 1062}, serous oligocystic and ill-demarcated adenoma {445}, and some cystadenomas observed in children {2057}. Whether these neoplasms form a homogeneous group remains to be established.

Epidemiology

Serous oligocystic adenomas are much less common than serous microcystic adenomas {445, 1062}. There is no sex predilection. Adults are usually 60 years and over (age range, 30-69 years; mean, 65 years); the tumour has been described in two male and two female infants, aged between 2 and 16 months {1781}.

Macroscopy

These neoplasms typically appear as a cystic mass with a diameter of 4-10 cm (mean, 6 cm) {1781}. On cut surface,

Aetiology

The aetiology of this neoplasm is not known. In children, it has been suggested that the lesions may be of malformative origin and not true neoplasms since in two cases there was a cytomegalovirus infection in the adjacent pancreas {52, 273}.

Localization

Most serous oligocystic adenomas are located in the head and body of the pancreas {1781}. In the head, they may obstruct the periampullary portion of the common bile duct.

Clinical features

In most cases reported in adult patients, the neoplasms caused symptoms that led to their discovery and removal. The most common symptom was upper abdominal discomfort or pain {1781}. Other symptoms included jaundice and steatorrhoea. In infants, the tumours presented as a palpable abdominal mass {52, 273}.

Fig. 10.12 Serous microcystic cystadenoma. **A** The lesion is well demarcated from the adjacent pancreas. **B** Cysts of varying size. **C** The epithelium is cuboidal and focally PAS-positive.

antigen (CEA), trypsin, chromogranin A, synaptophysin, S-100 protein, desmin, vimentin, factor VIII-related antigen and actin {49, 119, 445, 689, 815, 1752, 1781, 2151}.

Ultrastructure

Electron microscopy shows a single row of uniform epithelial cells lining the cysts and resting on a basal lamina {49, 160, 915}. The apical surfaces have poorly developed or no microvilli. The cytoplasm contains numerous glycogen granules but only a few mitochondria, short profiles of endoplasmic reticulum, lipid droplets, and multivesicular bodies. Golgi complexes are rarely identified. Zymogen granules and neurosecretory granules are absent.

there are few (occasionally only one) macroscopically visible cysts filled with watery clear or brown fluid. The cysts usually vary between 1 and 2 cm in diameter, but cysts as large as 8 cm have been reported {1062}. The irregularly arranged cysts, sometimes separated by broad septa, lie within a fibrous stroma that lacks a central stellate scar. The cysts and the supporting fibrous tissue may extend into the adjoining pancreatic tissue so that the tumours are poorly demarcated.

Histopathology

Serous oligocystic adenoma has generally the same histological features as serous microcystic adenoma. Occasionally, however, the lining epithelium may be more cuboidal and less flattened, and the nuclei are generally larger. The cytoplasm is either clear, due to the presence of glycogen, or eosinophilic. The stromal framework is well developed and often hyalinized. The tumour border is not well defined and small cysts often extend into the adjoining pancreatic tissue. The immunohistochemical and ultrastructural features are the same as for serous microcystic adenoma {445, 2057}.

Prognosis

There is no evidence of malignant potential {445}.

Serous cystadenocarcinoma

Definition

A malignant cystic epithelial neoplasm composed of glycogen-rich cells.

Epidemiology

So far, only eight cases have been reported {573, 815, 1781}. These patients

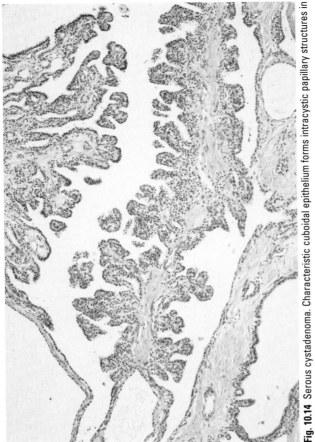

Fig. 10.14 Serous cystadenoma. Characteristic cuboidal epithelium forms intracystic papillary structures in this field.

were between 63 and 72 years of age; there were four women and four men. Three patients were Caucasian and four were from Japan {8, 815, 1781}.

Clinical features

Clinical symptoms reported in the cases so far observed include bleeding from gastric varices due to tumour invasion of the wall of the stomach and the splenic vein, a palpable upper abdominal mass, and jaundice. Ultrasonography and CT revealed a hyperechoic mass. CEA and CA19-9 were normal or slightly increased.

Macroscopy

These neoplasms have a spongy appearance {573, 879, 2182}. Their reported size has varied between 2.5 and 12 cm. Liver and lymph node metastases have been reported {573, 815, 1781, 2182}.

Invasion of the spleen and metastasis to the gastric wall were found in one case.

Histopathology

The histological features in the primary tumour as well as in the metastases are remarkably similar to those of serous microcystic adenoma, although focal mild nuclear pleomorphism can be found {573, 2182}. One carcinoma reported showed neural invasion and aneuploid nuclear DNA content {879}, while other cases showed vascular and perivascular invasion {1412} or involvement of a lymph node and adipose tissue {8}.

Prognosis

Serous cystadenocarcinomas are slowly growing neoplasms and palliative resection may be helpful even in advanced stages {2182}.

Mucinous cystic neoplasms of the pancreas

G. Zamboni
G. Klöppel
R.H. Hruban

D.S. Longnecker
G. Adler

Definition

Cystic epithelial neoplasms occurring almost exclusively in women, showing no communication with the pancreatic ductal system and composed of columnar, mucin-producing epithelium, supported by ovarian-type stroma. According to the grade of intraepithelial neoplasia (dysplasia), tumours may be classified as adenoma, borderline (low-grade malignant) and non-invasive or invasive carcinoma.

ICD-O codes

Mucinous cystadenoma	8470/0
Mucinous cystic neoplasm with moderate dysplasia	8470/1
Mucinous cystadenocarcinoma	
non-invasive	8470/2
invasive	8470/3

Epidemiology

Although more than 500 cases have been reported in the literature {328, 2198}, mucinous cystic neoplasm (MCN) is still considered a rare lesion, representing approximately 2-5% of all exocrine pancreatic tumours {1781, 1932}. Changes in diagnostic criteria over the years and the high resectability rate compared to that of ductal adenocarcinoma may have led to an overrepresentation of MCNs in histopathology series. The increasing number of these lesions seen in recent years is most likely due to advances in diagnostic techniques, allowing early and correct recognition of MCN.

In a recent study, in which MCNs were defined by the lack of a communication with the pancreatic duct system and the presence of an ovarian type stroma, all occurred in women {2198}. It is likely that many of the cases reported in men in the early literature were intraductal papillary mucinous neoplasms (IPMNs) {328, 1932, 2198}.

The mean age at diagnosis is 49 years (range, 20-82 years) {1781}. Patients with mucinous cystadenocarcinomas are about 10 years older than patients with adenomatous or borderline tumours

noma (54 versus 44 years), suggesting an adenoma - carcinoma sequence {2198}. MCTNs seem to occur in patients with different ethnic background {1781}.

Aetiology

Pancreatic MCNs share many features with their counterparts in the liver and retroperitoneum, including their morphology and their almost exclusive occurrence in women {328, 2139, 404, 2198}. The possible derivation of the stromal component of MCNs from the ovarian primordium is supported by morphology, tendency to undergo luteinization, presence of hilar-like cells, and immunophenotypic sex cord-stromal differentiation. It has been hypothesized that ectopic ovarian stroma incorporated during embryogenesis in the pancreas, along the biliary tree or in the retroperitoneum may release hormones and growth factors causing nearby epithelium to proliferate and form cystic tumours {2198}. Since the left primordial gonad and the dorsal pancreatic anlage lie side by side during the fourth and fifth weeks of development, this hypothesis could explain the predilection of MCN for the body-tail region of the pancreas {1977}.

Localization

The overwhelming majority of cases occur in the body-tail of the pancreas {328, 1932, 2148, 2198}. The head is only rarely involved, with a predilection for mucinous cystadenocarcinomas {1932, 2198}.

Fig. 10.15 Mucinous cystic neoplasm. The pancreatic duct, which does not communicate with the cyst lumen, has been opened over the surface of the tumour (left, arrowheads). The thick wall and irregular lining of the bisected neoplasm are shown on the right.

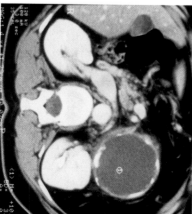

Fig. 10.16 Mucinous cystic neoplasm in the tail of the pancreas. The thick wall shows focal calcification.

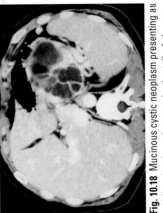

Preoperative diagnosis of MCN is important, since other types of cystic neoplasm may be treated differently. Furthermore, MCNs must be distinguished from an inflammatory pseudocyst, because drainage may be appropriate for patients with a pseudocyst, but is disastrous for patients with MCN, since apparently histologically benign mucinous cystic tumours can recur after drainage as invasive cystadenocarcinomas {328, 2194}. The best approach to obtain an exact preoperative diagnosis is the combined evaluation of all available clinical, serological, radiological, and biopsy findings.

Clinical features
Symptoms and signs
The clinical presentation depends on the size of the tumour. Small tumours (< 3 cm) are usually found incidentally. Larger tumours may produce symptoms that are usually due to compression of adjacent structures, and are often accompanied by a palpable abdominal mass. An association with diabetes mellitus is relatively frequent, whereas jaundice is uncommon {1781}.

Serum tumour markers
An increase in the peripheral blood serum tumour markers CEA, CA 19-9, or high cyst fluid levels of CEA, CA 19-9, TAG-72, CA-15-3 or MCA (mucin-like carcinoma-associated antigen) together with a low amylase level is suggestive of MCN. The highest levels of these markers are seen in cystadenocarcinoma {1063, 1804}.

Imaging
Abdominal X-ray may demonstrate nodular calcifications in the tumour capsule and compression or displacement of the stomach, duodenum or colon. US and CT reveal a sharply demarcated hypoechoic or low density mass with one or more large loculations {1461}. Features suggestive of malignant transformation include an irregular thickening of the cyst wall and/or papillary excrescences projecting into the cystic cavity {201, 2060}. Magnetic resonance imaging may have a complementary role. Endoscopic retrograde cholangiography (RCP) shows a displacement of the main pancreatic duct and the absence of communication with the cystic cavity, a very important finding for the differential diagnosis with IPMN.
Fine needle aspiration cytology (FNAC) can be performed percutaneously with CT or US guidance, or intraoperatively {1019}.

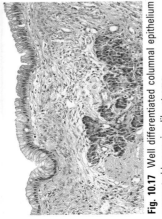

Fig. 10.17 Well differentiated columnar epithelium supported by ovarian-like stroma.

dostratifications and crypt-like invaginations. The columnar cells are characterized by basally located nuclei and abundant intracellular mucin which is diastase-PAS and Alcian blue positive. Pseudopyloric, gastric foveolar, small and large intestinal, and squamous differentiation can also be found. About half of the tumours contain scattered argyrophil and argentaffin endocrine cells at the bases of the columnar cells {33, 36, 328, 2151}.

Macroscopy
MCNs typically present as a round mass with a smooth surface and a fibrous pseudocapsule with variable thickness and frequent calcifications. The size of the tumour ranges from 2-35 cm in greatest dimension, with an average size between 6 and 10 cm. The cut surfaces demonstrate a unilocular or multilocular tumour with cystic spaces ranging from a few millimetres to several centimeters in diameter, containing either thick mucin or a mixture of mucin and haemorrhagic-necrotic material. The internal surface of unilocular tumours is usually smooth and glistening, whereas the multilocular tumours often show papillary projections and mural nodules. Malignant tumours are likely to show papillary projections and/or mural nodules and multilocularity {2198}. As a rule, there is no communication of the tumour with the pancreatic duct system, but exceptions have been reported {2148}.

Tumour spread and staging
Invasive mucinous cystadenocarcinoma follows the same pathways of local spread as ductal adenocarcinoma. The first metastases are typically found in the regional peripancreatic lymph nodes and the liver {1781}. Staging follows the protocol for ductal adenocarcinomas.

Histopathology
MCNs show two distinct components: an inner epithelial layer and an outer densely cellular ovarian-type stromal layer. Large locules can be extensively denuded and many sections are often needed to demonstrate the epithelial lining. The epithelium may be flat or it may form papillary or polypoid projections, pseu-

Spectrum of differentiation
This ranges from histologically benign appearing columnar epithelium to severely atypical epithelium. According to the grade of intraepithelial neoplasia (dysplasia), tumours may be classified as adenoma, borderline (low-grade malignant) and non-invasive or invasive carcinoma {947}.
Mucinous cystadenomas show only a slight increase in the size of the basally located nuclei and the absence of mitosis. Mucinous cystic neoplasms of borderline malignant potential exhibit papillary projections or crypt-like invaginations, cellular pseudostratification with crowding of slightly enlarged nuclei, and mitoses.
Mucinous cystadenocarcinomas may be invasive or non-invasive. They show changes of high-grade intraepithelial neoplasia which are usually focal and may be detected only after careful search of multiple sections from different regions. The epithelial cells, which often form papillae with irregular branching and budding, show nuclear stratification, severe nuclear atypia and frequent mitoses.
Invasive mucinous cystadenocarcinoma is characterized by invasion of the malignant epithelium into the stroma. The invasive component usually resembles the common ductal adenocarcinoma. How-

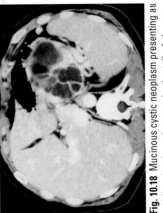

Fig. 10.18 Mucinous cystic neoplasm presenting as multiloculated cystic mass in the tail of the pancreas.

ever, mucinous cystadenocarcinomas with invasive adenosquamous carcinoma, osteoclast-like giant cell or choriocarcinoma have been reported {328, 1530, 1571, 2194}. Invasive foci may be focal and require careful search.

Stroma

The ovarian-type stroma consists of densely packed spindle-shaped cells with round or elongated nuclei and sparse cytoplasm. It frequently displays a variable degree of luteinization, characterized by the presence of single or clusters of epithelioid cells with round to oval nuclei and abundant clear or eosinophilic cytoplasm. Occasionally, these cells, resembling ovarian hilar cells, can be found associated with (or present in) nerve trunks. Stromal luteinization is found in decreasing order of frequency from adenomatous to carcinomatous cases {2194}. The stroma of large MCNs may become fibrotic and hypocellular. Rare MCNs show mural nodules with a sarcomatous stroma or an associated sarcoma {1932, 2088, 2198}.

Immunohistochemistry

The epithelial component is immunoreactive with epithelial markers including EMA, CEA, cytokeratins 7, 8, 18 and 19 {2151}, and it may show gastroenteropancreatic differentiation, as is also observed in ovarian and retroperitoneal MCN {1714, 1910}. With increasing degrees of epithelial atypia the character of mucin production changes from sulphated to sialated or neutral mucin {1932}. The neoplastic cells express gas-

tric type mucin marker M1 and PGII, the intestinal mucin markers CAR-5 and M3SI, and the pancreatic type mucin marker DUPAN-2 and CA19-9 {119, 1714, 2151, 2190}. Furthermore, pancreatic, hepatobiliary, and retroperitoneal MCNs share the same types of intraepithelial endocrine cells {613, 1911, 1910}. p-53 nuclear positivity in more than 10% of neoplastic cells, found in 20% of MCN, strongly correlates with mucinous cystadenocarcinoma {2198}.

The stromal component expresses vimentin, alpha smooth muscle actin, desmin and, in a high proportion, progesterone and estrogen receptors {2198}. The luteinized cells are labeled with antibodies against tyrosine hydroxylase, calretinin, which have been shown to recognize testicular Leydig cells and hilar ovarian cells, and the sex cord-stromal differentiation marker inhibin {2198, 2206}.

Ultrastructure

Electron microscopy of tumours with only mild to moderate dysplasia demonstrates columnar epithelial cells resting on a thin basement membrane. The cells may have well-developed microvilli and mucin granules {33}.

Genetics

Activating point mutations in codon 12 of KRAS were found in invasive mucinous cystic neoplasms (MCNs) {117} and mucinous cystic neoplasms associated with osteoclast-like giant cells {1485}. Mutations of KRAS and allelic losses of 6q, 9p, 8p have been reported in MCNs with sarcomatous stroma {1998}.

Prognosis and predictive factors

The prognosis of MCN, regardless of the degree of cellular atypia, is excellent if the tumour is completely removed {328, 410, 2060, 2198}. The prognosis of invasive mucinous cystadenocarcinoma depends on the extent of tumour invasion. Tumour recurrence and poor outcome correlate with invasion of the stroma and peritumoural tissues {2198}. Patients older than 50 years appear to have a lower survival rate {2198}. Other variables such as site, tumour size, macroscopic appearance, grade of differentiation, luteinization of the stroma and p53 positivity have no prognostic significance.

Aneuploidy is a rare event in MCNs, is largely restricted to mucinous cystadenocarcinomas and carries a worse prognosis {1792, 1932, 512}.

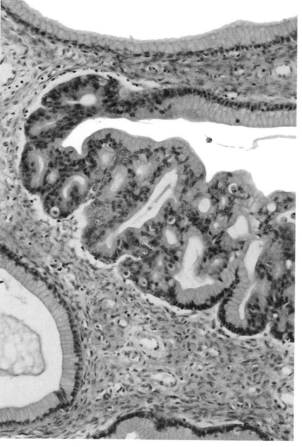

Fig. 10.19 Mucinous cystadenocarcinoma. The neoplasm exhibits well differentiated and poorly differentiated mucinous epithelium.

Fig. 10.20 Mucinous cystadenocarcinoma. The thick wall of this cystic neoplasm is invaded by mucinous carcinoma at upper left.

D.S. Longnecker
G. Adler

R.H. Hruban
G. Klöppel

Intraductal papillary-mucinous neoplasms of the pancreas

Definition

An intraductal papillary mucin-producing neoplasm, arises in the main pancreatic duct or its major branches. The papillary epithelium component, and the degree of mucin secretion, cystic duct dilatation, and invasiveness are variable. Intraductal papillary-mucin neoplasms are divided into benign, borderline, and malignant non-invasive or invasive lesions.

ICD-O codes

Intraductal papillary-mucinous adenoma
8453/0

Intraductal papillary-mucinous neoplasm
with moderate dysplasia   8453/1
Intraductal papillary-mucinous carcinoma
    non-invasive   8453/2
    invasive   8453/3

Synonyms and historical annotation

Papillary pancreatic neoplasms have been recognized for many years {247, 1532}, but the distinction between mucinous cystic neoplasms and intraductal papillary neoplasms was not made until the last two decades {947, 1781, 65, 1404}. Interest in IPMNs was first stimulated when they were recognized clinically {1281}, and pathological descriptions quickly followed {2164, 1093}. The incidence appears to have risen since the first reports, but this may reflect the combined effects of new diagnostic techniques, and progress in recognition and classification of IPMNs {1138, 918}. It is likely that many IPMNs were classified among the mucinous cystic neoplasms as recently as a decade ago.

Epidemiology

The incidence is low and not precisely known because IPMNs are not accurately identified in large population-based registries. Nomenclature and classification have been highly variable until recently, and are not yet standardized worldwide. IPMNs have been estimated to amount to 1-3% of exocrine pancreatic neoplasms, with an incidence rate well below 1 per 100,000 per year {1280, 1095}.

IPMNs are found in a broad age range (30-94) with a median age of diagnosis in the 6-7th decade {1443, 2148, 556}. They occur more frequently in males than in females {1138, 2148}. IPMNs were first reported from France and Japan, but subsequent reports have come from all parts of the world. Two studies provide some evidence that the incidence may be higher among Asians than among whites, but issues of consistency of classification require that this be further evaluated {1095, 941}.

Aetiology

The low incidence and imprecise identification of IPMN in large databases has hindered recognition of aetiological factors. In one series, most patients with IPMNs were cigarette smokers {550}. There is no consistent association with other types of pancreatic neoplasm {2198}.

Localization

The majority of these neoplasms occur in the main pancreatic duct and its branches in the head of the pancreas {1781, 330, 97}. A single cystic mass or segmental involvement of the duct is usual, but diffuse involvement is also described {1093, 1751, 1953}. Multicentric origin is suspected because of recurrence in pancreatic remnants following surgical removal of IPMNs {1088}. IPMNs may extend to the ampulla of Vater, commonly in association with involvement of the duct of Wirsung or the common bile duct {1781}.

Clinical features

Clinical presentation includes epigastric pain, pancreatitis, weight loss, diabetes, and jaundice {2169, 1953, 942}; some patients have no symptoms. Some cases are detected because of dilatation of the pancreatic duct seen incidentally in imaging studies. Serum amylase and lipase are commonly elevated. Endoscopic ultrasound, ERCP, and endoscopic examination of the pancreatic duct {1596} may all contribute to pre-

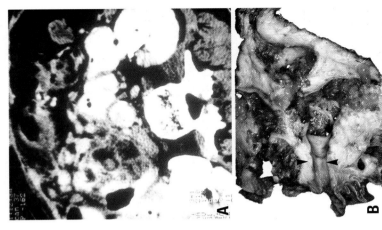

Fig. 10.21 Intraductal papillary-mucinous neoplasm. **A** Large neoplasm in the head of the pancreas containing multiple cystic spaces. **B** The lesion illustrated in A sectioned to demonstrate the dilated, mucin-filled main pancreatic duct (arrowheads).

operative diagnosis. Endoscopic biopsy or cytology may provide histological confirmation, but definitive diagnosis requires surgical removal and extensive histological sampling. Serum markers such as CEA and CA19-9 are too insensitive to be of value {2148, 1953}.

Macroscopy

Depending on the degree of ductal dilatation, IPMNs vary in size from 1 to 8 cm in maximum dimension {17}. They are cystic and may appear multiloculated if branch ducts are involved. The mucin found in IPMN is viscous or sticky and can dilate parts of the duct that are lined by normal appearing epithelium. The lining of cystic spaces may be smooth and glistening, granular, or velvet-like, the latter reflecting papillary growth. When

resection {1953}. Invasive neoplasms are staged as ductal adenocarcinomas.

Histopathology

IPMN tumour cells are usually tall columnar mucin-containing epithelial cells that line dilated ducts or cystic spaces arising from dilated branch ducts. The epithelium typically forms papillary or pseudopapillary structures, but portions of the neoplasm may be lined by non-papillary epithelium or be denuded of epithelium. The amount of mucin production varies widely, as does the degree of duct dilatation {97, 872}. Goblet or Paneth cells may be present as a manifestation of intestinal metaplasia in the neoplastic epithelium, and neuroendocrine cells have also been demonstrated.

The recently described intraductal oncocytic papillary neoplasm probably represents a rare related phenotype that is similar macroscopically {1244, 1860}. Oncocytic IPMNs are composed of stratified oncocytic cells with pale pink cytoplasmic granules that are much finer than those seen in Paneth cells. Goblet cells may be interspersed among the oncocytic cells. A characteristic feature of the oncocytic papillary neoplasms is the formation of 'intraepithelial lumina', which are spaces in the epithelium about one quarter the size of the cells.

Histochemistry and immunohistochemistry

A variety of abnormalities have been demonstrated in IPMNs using mucin and immunohistochemical stains.

Most IPMNs express epithelial membrane antigen (EMA) as well as several cytokeratins {1917}. A variety of endocrine cell types occur in most tumours but account for fewer than 5 per cent of the tumour cells {1676}. A change in type of mucin has been suggested as a marker of progression since normal duct cells characteristically secrete sulfated mucin, intraductal papillary-mucinous adenomas characteristically secrete neutral mucin, and dysplastic epithelium secretes predominantly sialomucin {1138, 1916, 1186}. Nearly all IPMNs express MUC2 {2179}.

Overexpression of c-erbB-2 protein occurs in a high fraction of IPMNs {1939, 1675, 1877, 380}.

A study of cell proliferation, as shown by PCNA and Ki67 labelling indices, demonstrated a progressive increase in cell proliferation from normal duct epithelium, to adenomas, to borderline tumours, to carcinomas {1917}. The labeling index in IPM carcinomas was lower than in ductal adenocarcinomas. Although immunostaining of p53 protein was detected in a lower fraction of IPM (31%) than is usually seen in solid ductal adenocarcinomas, it was found only in borderline and malignant IPMN and therefore may be a marker of progression {1939}.

Failure of IPMN to elicit the production of a collagenase that mediates invasion was reported {2193}.

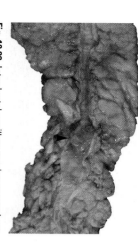

Fig. 10.24 Intraductal papillary-mucinous neoplasm within the dilated main pancreatic duct and branch ducts.

papillary growths are large, the dilated ducts may show localized excrescences or be filled with soft papillary masses of tissue.

The pancreatic parenchyma surrounding and retrograde to the tumour is often pale and firm, reflecting changes of chronic obstructive pancreatitis. When there is invasion, gelatinous areas may be identified in fibrotic tissue.

Tumour spread and staging

Adenomas, borderline tumours and non-invasive carcinomas may extend intraductally into adjacent portions of the duct system, and evidence of such extension is often encountered adjacent to IPMNs. Recurrence following surgical resection has been reported in patients that had IPMNs extending into the margin of

Fig. 10.22 Intraductal papillary mucinous neoplasm in the main pancreatic duct (arrowhead).

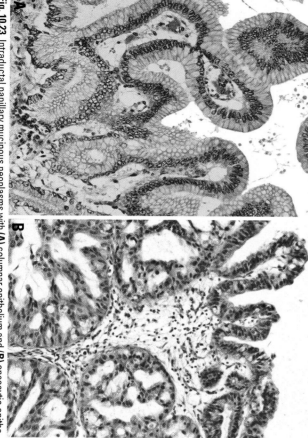

Fig. 10.23 Intraductal papillary mucinous neoplasms with **(A)** columnar epithelium and **(B)** oncocytic epithelium.

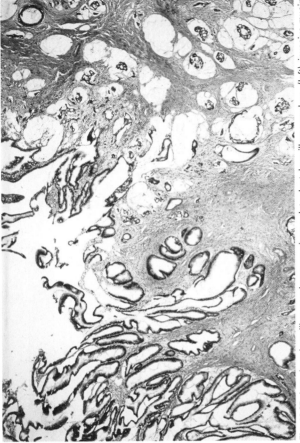

Fig. 10.25 Intraductal papillary-mucinous carcinoma. Intraductal papillary neoplasm (left), invasive mucin secreting carcinoma (right).

Classification and grading of IPMNs

IPMNs have been the source of great confusion that is reflected in a diverse nomenclature found in case and series reports and in standard references {1781}. Because of the variability within a tumour, it is important to sample IPMNs well, giving special emphasis to papillary areas because this is where the highest degree of intraepithelial neoplasia (dysplasia) is likely to occur, and to sclerotic areas that may reflect invasion.

IPMNs are classified as benign, borderline, or malignant on the basis of the greatest degree of dysplasia present. In accordance with the previous WHO classification, lesions are specifically designated as intraductal papillary-mucinous adenoma, borderline intraductal papillary-mucinous neoplasm, and intraductal papillary-mucinous carcinoma, with or without invasion {947, 1781}.

A slightly different histopathological classification has been proposed by the Japan Pancreas Society (JPS) {65}, intraductal tumours are designated as intraductal papillary adenoma or adenocarcinoma. The degree of cellular atypia in adenomas is designated as slight, moderate, or severe. The JPS category of adenoma with severe atypia corresponds to the WHO borderline lesion, although some authors also utilize a borderline category {2148}

Intraductal papillary-mucinous adenoma

The epithelium is comprised of tall columnar mucin-containing cells that show slight or no dysplasia, i.e. the epithelium maintains a high degree of differentiation in adenomas.

Borderline intraductal papillary-mucinous neoplasm

IPMNs with moderate dysplasia are placed in the borderline category. The epithelium shows no more than moderate loss of polarity, nuclear crowding, nuclear enlargement, pseudostratification, and nuclear hyperchromatism. Papillary areas maintain identifiable stromal cores, but pseudopapillary structures may be present.

Intraductal papillary-mucinous carcinoma

IPMNs with severe dysplastic epithelial change are designated as carcinoma even in the absence of invasion. Carcinomas are papillary or micropapillary. Cribriform growth and budding of

small clusters of epithelial cells into the lumen support the diagnosis of carcinoma. Severe dysplasia is manifest cytologically as loss of polarity, loss of differentiated cytoplasmic features including diminished mucin content, cellular and nuclear pleomorphism, nuclear enlargement, and the presence of mitoses (especially if suprabasal or luminal in location). Severely dysplastic cells may lack mucin. Non-invasive lesions are termed non-invasive intraductal papillary-mucinous carcinoma. When invasive, an IPMN may be called a papillary-mucinous carcinoma since it is no longer only intraductal. When IPMNs become invasive, the invasive component may assume the appearance of a tubular ductal adenocarcinoma or a mucinous noncystic carcinoma {17}. If the invasive component is dominant, and is a ductal

or mucinous noncystic carcinoma, then that diagnosis may be used, descriptively noting the association with an IPMN component.

Differential diagnosis

Historically, IPMNs and mucinous cystic neoplasms (MCNs) have been confused because they are both cystic and have a similar epithelial component. However, IPMNs and MCNs are distinct entities and can be separated easily, because MCNs typically occur in women with a median age in the fifth decade, almost always are located in the tail or body of the pancreas, typically exhibit a thick wall with a cellular 'ovarian' stroma, and typically fail to communicate with the pancreatic duct system.

Precursor lesions

The criteria for classifying pancreatic intraepithelial neoplasia (PanIN) lesions (including papillary hyperplasia, see chapter on ductal adenocarcinoma of the pancreas) in IPMNs are not well established {1144, 1744}, and need to be defined. PanIN lesions characteristically occur in intralobular ducts, are not detected macroscopically, and are clinically silent {17}. It seems likely that the earliest stage of development of the IPMN would involve the progression from a flat area of mucous metaplasia to a papillary lesion in a main or branch pancreatic duct as suggested by Nagai et al.

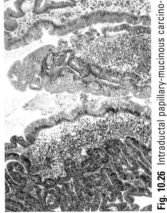

Fig. 10.26 Intraductal papillary-mucinous carcinoma. This tumour shows moderately differentiated (left) and well differentiated (right) areas.

Table 10.05
Summary of mucin histochemistry and immunostaining of IPMN.

Antibody or epitope	Comments on staining in IPMN	Reference
Differentiation markers		
Alcian blue stain	Adenomas contain neutral mucin, carcinomas contain sialomucin	{1138, 1916}
MUC1	Negative>>positive	{2179}
MUC2	Positive>>negative	{2179}
Endocrine markers	< 5% of cells positive in most IPMN	{1676}
Epithelial membrane antigen	Positive	{1917}
Cytokeratins 7, 8, 18, 19	Positive	{1917}
CEA	Positive	{1939}
CA-19-9	Positive	{1939}
B72.3	Positive	{1939}
DUPAN-2	Seen in a minority	{1939}
Oncogene products		
c-erbB-2	13/17 IPMN positive, including all with moderate or severe dysplasia	{1675} {1939}
p27	p27 staining exceeds cyclin E	{556}
Tumour suppressor gene products		
TP53	Often positive in borderline tumours and carcinomas	{1939}
Proliferation markers		
PCNA and Ki67	Labeling index increases with progression from adenoma to carcinoma	{1917}

{1306}. Thus, it will be difficult to recognize the initial stage of an intraductal papillary-mucinous adenoma unless a distinctive molecular marker is identified.

Genetic susceptibility

Excessive rates of colonic and gastric epithelial neoplasms were reported in a group of 42 patients with IPMNs {106}. This suggests the possibility of a predisposing genetic susceptibility, but no specific hereditary syndrome was identified.

Genetics

Activating point mutations in codon 12 of the KRAS gene have been reported in 40-60% of intraductal papillary mucinous neoplasms {1939, 544}. Fujii et al. examined a series of IPMNs using polymorphic microsatellite markers and found allelic loss at 9p in 62% of the cases and at 17p and at 18q in ~40% {544}. These allelic losses include the loci of the p16, TP53, and DPC4 tumour-suppressor genes. In addition to immunohistochemical evidence of p53 abnormality in IPMN {544}, mutations have been demonstrated in two adenomas {876}. Overexpression of anti-apoptotic genes in IPMN is reported {1247}.
Mutations of KRAS and TP53 genes have been detected in DNA from pancreatic juice of patients with IPMN {875}.

Prognosis and predictive factors

The overall 5-year survival rate for a composite series was 83% {2148}. The prognosis is excellent for adenomas and borderline tumours with 3 and 5-year survivals approaching 100%. The survival rates are high for non-invasive carcinomas, and survival rates for patients with invasive IPMNs may also be higher than for patients with typical ductal adenocarcinomas {2148, 97, 2169}. The histological classification, with major emphasis on the presence or absence of invasion, and stage remain the best predictors for survival.
As the distinction between IPMNs and MCNs has been refined, some authors report that MCNs are more often malignant than IPMNs and that the latter have a better prognosis following treatment {97}, but this was not confirmed in other series {1953, 551}. Expression of MUC2 and MUC5AC mucins are associated with a good prognosis relative to ductal adenocarcinomas that do not express these mucins {2179, 2178}.

D.S. Klimstra
D. Longnecker

Acinar cell carcinoma

Definition

A carcinoma occurring mainly in adults, composed of relatively uniform neoplastic cells that are arranged in solid and acinar patterns and produce pancreatic enzymes.

ICD-O codes

Acinar cell carcinoma   8550/3
Acinar cell cystadenocarcinoma   8551/3
Mixed acinar-endocrine carcinoma 8154/3

Epidemiology

Acinar cell carcinomas represent 1-2% of all exocrine pancreatic neoplasms in adults {739, 936}. Most occur in late adulthood, with a mean age of 62 years {825, 979, 2073}. The tumour is rare in adults under the age of 40. Pediatric cases do occur, usually manifesting in patients 8 to 15 years of age {979, 1282}. Males are affected more frequently than females, with an M:F ratio of 2:1 {739, 936}.

Aetiology

The aetiology is unknown.

Localization

Acinar cell carcinomas may arise in any portion of the pancreas but are somewhat more common in the head.

Clinical features

Symptoms and signs

Most acinar cell carcinomas present clinically with relatively non-specific symptoms including abdominal pain, weight loss, nausea, or diarrhoea {739, 936, 979, 2073}. Because they generally push rather than infiltrate into adjacent structures, biliary obstruction and jaundice are infrequent presenting complaints.
A well-described syndrome occurring in 10-15% of patients is the lipase hypersecretion syndrome {1781, 213, 936, 975}. It is most commonly encountered in patients with hepatic metastases, and is characterized by excessive secretion of lipase into the serum, with clinical symptoms including subcutaneous fat necrosis and polyarthralgia. Peripheral blood

eosinophilia may also be noted. In some patients, the lipase hypersecretion syndrome is the first presenting sign of the tumour, while in others it develops following tumour recurrence. Successful surgical removal of the neoplasm may result in the normalization of the serum lipase levels and resolution of the symptoms.

Laboratory analyses

Other than an elevation of serum lipase levels associated with the lipase hypersecretion syndrome, there are no specific laboratory abnormalities in patients with acinar cell carcinoma. A few cases show increased serum alpha-fetoprotein {819, 1426, 1369, 1747}.

Imaging

Acinar cell carcinomas are generally bulky with a mean size of 11 cm {979}. On abdominal CT scans, they are circumscribed and have a similar density to the surrounding pancreas. Because of their larger size and relatively sharp circumscription, acinar cell carcinomas can generally be distinguished from ductal adenocarcinomas radiographically.

Fine needle aspiration cytology

There is usually a high cellular yield from fine needle aspiration {1446, 1978, 2015}. The cytological appearances of acinar cell carcinomas closely mimic of pancreatic endocrine neoplasms, although the latter are more likely to exhibit a plasmacytoid appearance to the cells and a speckled chromatin pattern. Immunohistochemistry may be used on cytological specimens to confirm the diagnosis of acinar cell carcinoma {1446, 1978}.

Macroscopy

Acinar cell carcinomas are generally circumscribed and may be multinodular {739, 936}. Individual nodules are soft and vary from yellow to brown. Areas of necrosis and cystic degeneration may be present. Occasionally, the neoplasm is found attached to the pancreatic surface. Extension into adjacent structures, such as duodenum, spleen, or major

vessels may occur. Multicystic examples of acinar cell carcinoma have been reported as acinar cell cystadenocarcinoma {229, 739, 1815}.

Tumour spread and staging

Metastases most commonly affect regional lymph nodes and the liver, although distant spread to other organs occurs occasionally. Acinar cell carcinomas are staged using the same protocol as ductal adenocarcinomas.

Histopathology

Large nodules of cells are separated by hypocellular fibrous bands. The desmoplastic stroma characteristic of ductal adenocarcinoma is generally absent. Tumour necrosis may occur and is generally infarct-like in appearance. Within the tumour cell islands, there is an abundant fine microvasculature.
Several architectural patterns have been described. The most characteristic is the acinar pattern, with neoplastic cells arranged in small glandular units; there are numerous small lumina within each island of cells giving a cribriform appearance. In some instances, the lumina are more dilated, resulting in a glandular pattern, although separate glandular structures surrounded by stroma are usually not encountered. A number of the micro-

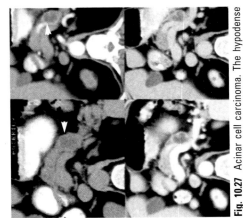

Fig. 10.27 Acinar cell carcinoma. The hypodense lobulated tumour occupies the tail of the pancreas.

glandular tumours previously reported as 'microadenocarcinoma' were more recently shown to have been acinar cell carcinomas (see chapter on miscellaneous carcinomas). The second most common pattern in acinar cell carcinomas is the solid pattern: solid nests of cells lacking luminal formations are separated by small vessels. Within these nests, cellular polarization is generally not evident, but there may be an accentuation of polarization at the interface with the vessels, resulting in basal nuclear localization in these regions and a palisading of nuclei along the microvasculature. In rare instances, a trabecular arrangement of tumour cells may be present, with exceptional cases also showing a gyriform appearance {936}. The neoplastic cells contain minimal to moderate amounts of cytoplasm that may be more abundant in cells lining lumina. The cytoplasm varies from amphophilic to eosinophilic and is characteristically granular, reflecting the presence of zymogen granules. In many instances, however, only minimal cytoplasmic granularity may be detectable. The nuclei are generally round to oval and relatively uniform, with marked nuclear pleomorphism being exceptional. A single, prominent, central nucleolus is a characteristic finding but not invariably present. The mitotic rate is variable (mean 14 per 10 high power fields, range 0 to > 50 per 10 high power fields). Zymogen granules are weakly positive with PAS staining, and resistant to diastase. Mucin production is generally not detectable with mucicarmine or Alcian blue stains and, if present, is limited to the luminal membrane in acinar or glandular formations. The histochemical stain for butyrate esterase can be used to identify active lipase within the tumour cells {936, 938}. Due to the scarcity of zymogen granules in many examples of acinar cell carcinoma, histochemical stains are relatively insensitive for documenting acinar differentiation, and very focal staining may be difficult to interpret with confidence.

Immunohistochemistry

Immunohistochemical identification of pancreatic enzyme production is helpful in confirming the diagnosis of acinar cell carcinoma. Antibodies against trypsin, chymotrypsin, lipase, and elastase have all been used {739, 810, 936, 1282}. Both

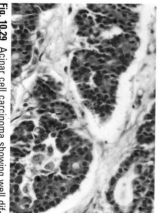

Fig. 10.29 Acinar cell carcinoma showing well differentiated acinar structures.

trypsin and chymotrypsin are detectable in over 95% of cases; lipase is less commonly identified (approximately 70% of cases) {936}. Pancreatic stone protein is also commonly expressed {739}. In solid areas, immunohistochemical staining for enzymes may show diffuse cytoplasmic positivity, whereas the reaction product is restricted to the apical cytoplasm in acinar areas.

Immunohistochemical markers of endocrine and ductal differentiation may also be detected in acinar cell carcinomas, generally in a minor cell population {739, 936}. Scattered individual cells stain for chromogranin or synaptophysin are found in over one third of lesions. Over half exhibit focal CEA and B72.3 expression {739, 936}. Uncommonly, there is immunohistochemical positivity for alpha-fetoprotein, generally in cases associated with elevations in serum alpha-fetoprotein {819}.

Ultrastructure

Electron microscopy provides further evidence of enzyme production {675, 408, 936, 1978}. Exocrine secretory features are consistently found, with abundant rough endoplasmic reticulum arranged in parallel arrays and relatively abundant

mitochondria. Cellular polarization is generally evident, with basal basement membranes and apical lumina. Adjacent cells are joined by tight junctions. Although the distribution varies from cell to cell, most acinar cell carcinomas exhibit electron dense zymogen granules. In polarized cells, they are located in the apical cytoplasm, and the secretory contents may be seen within the luminal spaces where granules have fused with the apical membrane. The size range of zymogen granules in acinar cell carcinomas (125-1000 nm) is somewhat greater than that found in non-neoplastic acinar cells (250-1000 nm). In addition to typical zymogen granules, a second granule type, the irregular fibrillary granule, is detected ultrastructurally in many cases {302, 936, 938, 1477}. It has been suggested that irregular fibrillary granules may represent a recapitulation of the fetal zymogen granules, although attempts to document the presence of pancreatic enzymes within them by immunohistochemistry have been unconvincing {936, 938, 1032}.

Fig. 10.28 An acinar cell carcinoma (AC) lies near the spleen (SP). The tumour's cut surface is lobulated.

Acinar cell carcinoma variants

Acinar cell cystadenocarcinoma

Acinar cell cystadenocarcinomas are rare, grossly cystic neoplasms with cytoarchitectural features of acinar cell carcinomas {229, 825, 739, 1815}.

Mixed acinar-endocrine carcinoma

Rare neoplasms have shown a substantial (greater than 25%) proportion of more than one cell type. These neoplasms have been designated 'mixed carcinomas', and, depending upon the cell types identified, as 'mixed acinar-endocrine carcinoma', 'mixed acinar-ductal carcinoma', or 'mixed acinar-endocrine-ductal carcinoma' {997, 1369, 2015}. Of these, the best characterized is the mixed acinar-endocrine carcinoma {997}. In many mixed acinar-endocrine carcinomas, the evidence for divergent differentiation is only provided by immunohistochemical staining. Although different regions of the tumours may suggest acinar or endocrine differentiation morphologically, many areas have intermediate features, and immunohistochemistry generally shows a mixture of cells expressing acinar or endocrine markers (or both). In exceptional cases, however, there is also morphological evidence of multiple lines of differentiation,

KRAS mutations and *TP53* immunoreactivity {739, 1485, 1920, 1921}.

Prognosis and predictive factors

These neoplasms are aggressive, with a median survival of 18 months and a 5-year survival rate of less than 10% {739, 936}. Approximately 50% of patients have metastases at the time of diagnosis, and an additional 25% develop metastatic disease following surgical resection of the primary tumour {936}.

The most important prognostic factor is tumour stage, with patients lacking lymph node or distant metastases surviving longer {936}. Patients with the lipase hypersecretion syndrome were shown to have a particularly short survival, because most of these patients had widespread metastatic disease. Despite poor overall survival rates, there are anecdotal reports of survival for several years in the presence of metastatic disease, and responses to chemotherapy have been noted {936}. Thus, the prognosis of acinar cell carcinoma may be somewhat less poor than that of ductal adenocarcinoma.

No specific grading system for acinar cell carcinomas has been proposed. No association between the extent of acinus formation and prognosis has been observed.

There is an insufficient number of pediatric acinar cell carcinomas to allow an accurate assessment of the biological behaviour in children. Available data suggest that acinar cell carcinomas occurring under the age of 20 may be less aggressive than their adult counterparts {936, 1446}.

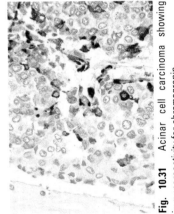

Fig. 10.31 Acinar cell carcinoma showing immunoreactivity for chromogranin.

with some regions exhibiting obvious acinar features and other areas endocrine features. Most reported acinar-endocrine carcinomas have been composed predominantly of acinar elements based on the proportion of cells staining immunohistochemically {997}. There are insufficient cases recorded to suggest that the biological behaviour of mixed acinar-endocrine carcinomas differs from that of pure acinar cell carcinomas.

Precursor lesions

No documented precursor lesions for acinar cell carcinomas have been defined. Initial suggestions that so-called atypical acinar cell nodules may represent preneoplastic lesions of acinar cells have not been substantiated by later studies {1094}. Atypical acinar cell nodules occur either because of dilatation of the rough endoplasmic reticulum (resulting in reduced basophilia of the basal

cytoplasm) or depletion of zymogen granules (resulting in reduced eosinophilia of the apical cytoplasm and an increase in nuclear:cytoplasmic ratio); these lesions are relatively common incidental findings in resected pancreases.

Genetics

In contrast to ductal adenocarcinomas, acinar cell carcinomas very rarely show

Fig. 10.30 Acinar cell carcinoma. Solid pattern with uniform round nuclei.

Pancreatoblastoma

D.S. Klimstra
D. Longnecker

Definition

A malignant epithelial tumour, generally affecting young children, composed of well-defined solid nests of cells with acinar formations and squamoid corpuscles, separated by stromal bands. Acinar differentiation prevails, often associated with lesser degrees of endocrine or ductal differentiation.

ICD-O code

8971/3

Epidemiology

Incidence

Pancreatoblastoma is an exceedingly rare tumour, less than 75 cases having been reported {782, 939, 2117}. However, it is among the most frequent pancreatic tumours in childhood, probably accounting for 30-50% of pancreatic neoplasms occurring in young children {631}.

Age and sex distribution

The majority of pancreatoblastomas occur in children, most being under the age of 10. The median age of pediatric patients is approximately 4 years {742, 939}, and only a few cases have been described in the second decade of life {782}. A number of congenital examples have also been documented {939}. Rarely, tumours histologically indistinguishable from pancreatoblastomas occur in adult patients ranging between 19 and 56 years of age {939, 1053, 1452}. There is a slight male predominance, with an M:F ratio of 1.3:1 {939}.

Aetiology

The aetiology is unknown.

Localization

The head of the gland is affected in about 50% of cases, the remainder being equally divided between the body and the tail.

Clinical features

The presenting features of pancreatoblastoma are generally non-specific. Especially in the pediatric age group, many patients present with an incidentally detected abdominal mass {782, 939}. Related symptoms include pain, weight loss, and diarrhoea. The paraneoplastic syndromes associated with acinar cell carcinoma (lipase hypersecretion syndrome) and pancreatic endocrine neoplasms have not been described, but one patient developed Cushing syndrome {1478}.

Radiologically, pancreatoblastomas are large, well-defined, lobulated tumours which may show calcifications on CT scan {1833, 2027, 2117}. There is no consistent elevation of serum tumour markers, but some cases have exhibited increased alpha-fetoprotein levels {802, 939}.

Macroscopy

The size of pancreatoblastomas varies from 1.5-20 cm. Most tumours are solitary, solid neoplasms composed of well-defined lobules of soft, fleshy tissue separated by fibrous bands. Areas of necrosis may be prominent. Uncommonly the

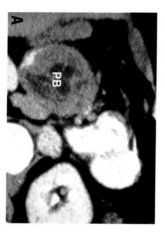

A

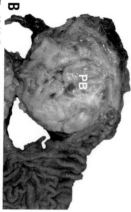

B

Fig. 10.32 Pancreatoblastoma. **A** CT image showing a large tumour (PB) in the head of the pancreas, with hypodense areas. **B** The cut surface of the neoplasm demonstrates a lobulated structure.

tumours are grossly cystic, a phenomenon not reported in all cases associated with the Beckwith-Wiedeman syndrome {432}.

Histopathology

The epithelial elements of pancreatoblastomas are highly cellular and arranged in well-defined islands separated by stromal bands, producing a 'geographic' low power appearance. Solid, hypercellular areas composed of nests of polygonal cells alternate with regions showing more obvious acinar differentiation, with polarized cells surrounding small luminal spaces. In rare tumours, larger glandular spaces lined by mucin-containing cells may be seen {939}. Nuclear atypia is generally minimal.

Squamoid corpuscles. One of the most characteristic features of pancreatoblastoma is the 'squamoid corpuscle'. These enigmatic structures vary from large islands of plump, epithelioid cells to whorled nests of spindled cells to frankly keratinizing squamous islands. The nuclei of the squamoid corpuscles are larger and more oval than those of the surrounding cells; nuclear clearing due to the accumulation of biotin may be seen {1895}. The frequency and composition of the squamoid corpuscles varies in different regions of the tumour and between different cases.

Stroma. Especially in pediatric cases, the stroma of pancreatoblastomas is often hypercellular, in some instances achieving a neoplastic appearance. Rarely, the presence of heterologous stromal elements, including neoplastic bone and cartilage, has been reported {127, 939}.

Histochemistry and immunohistochemistry

Over 90% of pancreatoblastomas exhibit evidence of acinar differentiation in the form of PAS-positive, diastase resistant cytoplasmic granules as well as immunohistochemical staining for pancreatic enzymes, including trypsin, chymotrypsin, and lipase {939, 1282, 1400}. The staining may be focal, often limited to the apical cytoplasm in areas of the tumour with acinar formations. At least focal

nar differentiation {939, 1758}, with relatively abundant rough endoplasmic reticulum and mitochondria, and apically located dense zymogen granules. The zymogen granules may be round and uniform, resembling those of non-neoplastic cells. In addition, irregular fibrillary granules similar to those described in acinar cell carcinomas may be found {936, 939}. In rare cases, dense-core neurosecretory-type granules and mucigen granules have also been observed {939}. Examination of the squamoid corpuscles has revealed tonofilaments but no evidence of a specific line of differentiation.

Genetic susceptibility

In several reported cases (all congenital examples), pancreatoblastomas have been a component of the Beckwith-Wiedeman syndrome {432}.

Prognosis

Pancreatoblastomas are malignant tumours. Nodal or hepatic metastases are present in 35% of patients {782, 939}. More widespread dissemination may also occur. In pediatric patients lacking evidence of metastatic disease at first presentation, the prognosis is very good, most patients being cured by a combination of surgery and chemotherapy {894, 1299}. In the presence of metastatic disease or in adult patients with pancreatoblastomas, the outcome is usually fatal {312, 939}, the mean survival being 1.5 years {939}. However, a favourable response to chemotherapy has been noted in some children {235, 2027}.

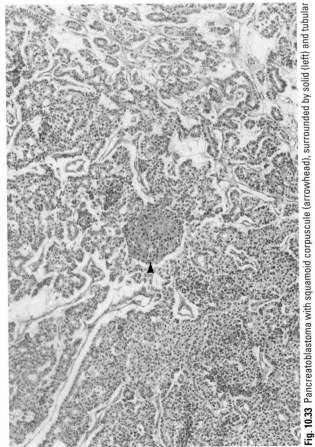

Fig. 10.33 Pancreatoblastoma with squamoid corpuscle (arrowhead), surrounded by solid (left) and tubular (right) structures.

immunoreactivity for markers of endocrine differentiation (chromogranin or synaptophysin) is found in over two-thirds of cases, and expression of markers of ductal differentiation such as CEA, DUPAN-2, or B72.3 is found in more than half of cases {939}. In most instances, the proportion of cells expressing acinar markers outnumbers the proportion expressing endocrine or ductal markers. In cases associated with elevations in the serum levels of alpha-fetoprotein, immunohistochemical positivity for AFP has been detectable {802, 939}. Immunohistochemical evaluation of the squamoid corpuscles has failed to define a reproducible line of differentiation for this component {939}.

Relationship to acinar cell carcinoma

Both pancreatoblastomas and acinar cell carcinomas consistently exhibit acinar differentiation and may exhibit lesser degrees of endocrine and ductal differentiation. {936, 939}. Histologically, acinar formations are characteristic of pancreatoblastoma, and the solid areas resemble the solid pattern of acinar cell carcinoma. Biologically, the two tumours are also similar, with a relatively favorable prognosis in childhood, but a very poor prognosis in adulthood. For these reasons, some observers have suggested that pancreatoblastoma represents the paediatric counterpart of acinar cell carcinoma. Although this proposal is attractive in many ways, pancreatoblastoma remains a separately definable neoplasm with characteristic histologic, immunohistochemical, and clinical features.

Ultrastructure

By electron microscopy, pancreatoblastomas generally exhibit evidence of aci-

Solid-pseudopapillary neoplasm

G. Klöppel
J. Lüttges
D. Klimstra

R. Hruban
S. Kern
G. Adler

Definition

A usually benign neoplasm with predominant manifestation in young women, composed of monomorphic cells forming solid and pseudopapillary structures, frequently showing haemorrhagic-cystic changes and variably expressing epithelial, mesenchymal and endocrine markers.

ICD-O codes

Solid pseudopapillary neoplasm   8452/1
Solid pseudopapillary carcinoma   8452/3

Synonyms

Solid-cystic tumour {946}, papillary-cystic tumour {170}, solid and papillary epithelial neoplasm.

Epidemiology

Solid-pseudopapillary neoplasm is uncommon but has been recognized with increasing frequency in recent years {946, 1192, 1358}. It accounts for approximately 1-2% of all exocrine pancreatic tumours {359, 941, 1280}.

Localization

There is no preferential localization within the pancreas {1282, 1358}.

Clinical features

Usually, the neoplasms are found incidentally on routine physical examination or they cause abdominal discomfort and pain {1358}, occasionally after abdominal trauma {945}. Jaundice is rare {1427}, even in tumours that originate from the head of the pancreas, and there is no associated functional endocrine syndrome. All known tumour markers are normal.

Ultrasonography (US) and computed tomography (CT) reveal a sharply demarcated, variably solid and cystic mass without any internal septation {300}. The tumour margin may contain calcifications. Administration of contrast medium results in enhancement of the solid tumour parts. On angiography, the neoplasms are usually hypovascular or mildly hypervascular lesions with displacement of surrounding vessels {2153}. Fine needle aspiration cytology performed under radiological control shows monomorphic cells with round nuclei and eosinophilic or foamy cytoplasm {234, 2119, 2140}.

Macroscopy

The neoplasms present as large, round,

Aetiology

The aetiology is unknown. The striking sex and age distribution point to genetic and hormonal factors, but there are no reports indicating an association with endocrine disturbances including overproduction of oestrogen or progesterone. Moreover, only very few women developed a solid pseudopapillary neoplasm after long-term use of hormonal contraceptives {359, 436, 1655}.

It occurs predominantly in adolescent girls and young women (mean 35 years; range 8-67 years) {1781, 1072}. It is rare in men (mean, 35 years; range 25-72 years) {945, 1193, 1975}. There is no apparent ethnic preference {978, 1395}.

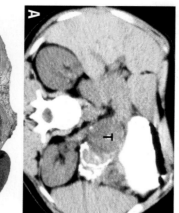

Fig. 10.35 Solid-pseudopapillary neoplasm. The pseudopapillary structures are lined by small monomorphic cells.

Tumour spread

Only few metastasizing solid-pseudopapillary neoplasms have been reported {359, 1358}. Common metastatic sites include regional lymph nodes, the liver, peritoneum, and greater omentum {300, 2209, 1358}.

Histopathology

In large neoplasms, extensive necrosis is typical and the preserved tissue is usually found in the tumour periphery under the fibrous capsule. This tissue exhibits a solid monomorphic pattern with variable sclerosis. More centrally there is a pseudopapillary pattern, and these components often gradually merge into each

solitary masses (average size 8-10 cm; range, 3-18 cm), and are often fluctuant. They are usually encapsulated and well demarcated from the surrounding pancreas. Multiple tumours are exceptional {1427}. The cut surfaces reveal lobulated, light brown solid areas, zones of haemorrhage and necrosis, and cystic spaces filled with necrotic debris. Occasionally, the haemorrhagic-cystic changes involve almost the entire lesion so that the neoplasm may be mistaken for a pseudocyst. The tumour wall may contain calcifications {1358}. A few tumours have been found to be attached to the pancreas or even in extrapancreatic locations {812, 914, 945}. Invasion of adjacent organs or the portal vein is rare {1655, 1684, 1701}.

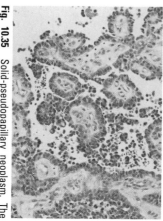

Fig. 10.34 Solid-pseudopapillary neoplasm. **A** The round hypodense tumour (T) replaces the tail of the pancreas. **B** The pseudocystic neoplasm is attached to the spleen, and shows haemorrhagic necrosis.

other. In both patterns, the uniform polyhedral cells are arranged around delicate, often hyalinized fibrovascular stalks with small vessels {1395}. Neoplastic cells that are arranged radially around the minute fibrovascular stalks may resemble 'ependymal' rosettes. Luminal spaces are consistently absent. In the solid parts, disseminated aggregates of neoplastic cells with foamy cytoplasm or cholesterol crystals surrounded by foreign body cells may be found. The spaces between the pseudopapillary structures are filled with red blood cells. The hyalinized connective tissue strands may contain foci of calcification and even ossification {1193}.

The neoplastic cells have either eosinophilic or clear vacuolar cytoplasm. Occasionally they contain eosinophilic, diastase-resistant PAS-positive globules of varying size, which may also occur outside the cells. Glycogen or mucin cannot be detected. Grimelius positive cells may occur. The round to oval nuclei have finely dispersed chromatin and are often grooved or indented. Mitoses are usually rare, but in a few instances prominent mitotic activity is observed {1358}. In rare cases, there is also vessel invasion {2140}. The neoplastic tissue is usually well demarcated from the normal pancreas, although a fibrous capsule may be absent and invasion of tumour cell nests into the surrounding pancreatic tissue may occur {1193, 1358}.

Criteria of malignancy

Although criteria of malignancy have not yet been clearly established, it appears that unequivocal perineural invasion, angioinvasion, or deep invasion into the surrounding tissue indicate malignant behaviour, and such lesions should be classified as solid-pseudopapillary carcinoma. Nishihara et al. {1358} compared the histological features of three metastasizing and 19 nonmetastasizing solid-pseudopapillary neoplasms, and found that venous invasion, degree of nuclear atypia, mitotic count and prominence of necrobiotic cell nests (cells with pyknotic nuclei and eosinophilic cytoplasm) were associated with malignancy. However, neoplasms in which the above-mentioned histological criteria of malignancy are not detected may also give rise to metastases. Consequently, benign appearing solid-pseudopapillary neoplasms must be classified as lesions of uncertain malignant potential.

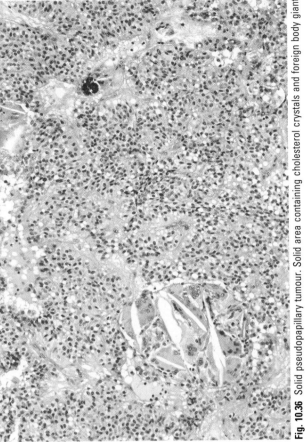

Fig. 10.36 Solid pseudopapillary tumour. Solid area containing cholesterol crystals and foreign body giant cells.

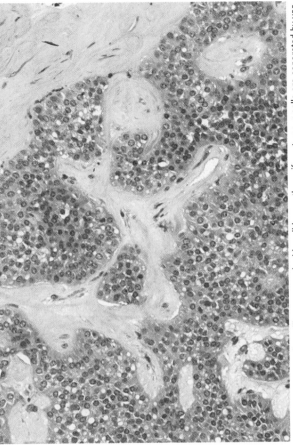

Fig. 10.37 Solid pseudopapillary tumour. In this solid area, the uniform tumour cells are separated by vascular hyalinized stroma.

Histochemistry and immunohistochemistry

The most consistently positive markers for solid-pseudopapillary neoplasms are alpha-1-antitrypsin, alpha-1-antichymotrypsin, neuron specific enolase (NSE), vimentin and progesterone receptors {306, 945, 963, 1226}. The cellular reaction for alpha-1-antitrypsin and alpha-1-antichymotrypsin is always intense, but only involves small cell clusters or single cells, a finding that is characteristic of this neoplasm. Alpha-1-antitrypsin also stains the PAS-positive globules. Staining for NSE and vimentin, in contrast, is usually diffuse.

Inconsistent results have been reported for epithelial markers, synaptophysin, pancreatic enzymes, islet cell hormones and other antigens such as CEA or CA 19.9. Most authors report negative results for chromogranin A, CEA, CA 19.9 and AFP. A few neoplasms have been found to express S-100 {945, 1226, 1358}. Cytokeratin is detected in 30% {946} to 70% {963, 2195}, depending on the method of antigen retrieval applied.

Usually, the staining for keratin is focal and faint. The keratin profile (CK 7, 8, 18 and 19) is that of the ductal cell {740, 1844}. Positive immunoreactivity for trypsin, chymotrypsin, amylase and/or phospholipase A2 has been reported {166, 1072, 1192, 1226, 1844}, but has not been confirmed by most other authors {812, 945, 1282}. Similarly, focal positivity for glucagon, somatostatin and/or insulin has been described in some tumours {1226, 2021, 2147}, but was not detected in most other cases {1072, 1282, 1844}.

Ultrastructure

The neoplastic cells have round or markedly indented nuclei containing a small single nucleolus and a narrow rim of marginated heterochromatin. The cells show abundant cytoplasm, which is rich in mitochondria. Zymogen-like granules of variable sizes (500-3000 nm) are conspicuous, probably representing deposits of alpha-1-antitrypsin. The contents of these granules commonly dis-

integrate, forming multilamellated vesicles and lipid droplets {946, 1031, 1226, 2154}. Neurosecretory-like granules have been described in a few tumours {867, 880, 1684, 2119, 2147}. Intermediate cell junctions are rarely observed and microvilli are lacking, but small intercellular spaces are frequent.

Genetics

In contrast to infiltrating ductal carcinomas, solid-pseudopapillary neoplasms appear to have wild-type KRAS genes and do not immunoexpress p53 {512, 1007, 1039}. An unbalanced translocation between chromosomes 13 and 17 resulting in a loss of 13q14→qter and 17p11→pter has been described in one solid-pseudopapillary neoplasm {616}.

Prognosis and predictive factors

In general, the prognosis is good. After complete removal more than 95% of the patients are cured. Local spread or dissemination to the peritoneal cavity has been reported in the context of abdomi-

nal trauma and rupture of the tumour {1060}. Even in patients who had local spread, recurrences {359, 999}, or metastases {234, 1192, 1642}, long disease-free periods have been recorded after initial diagnosis and resection. Only a few patients have died of a metastasizing solid-pseudopapillary neoplasm {1192, 1395}.

Histological criteria. Perineural invasion, angioinvasion, or deep invasion into the surrounding tissue indicate malignant behaviour, and such lesions are classified as solid-pseudopapillary carcinoma. Venous invasion, a high degree of nuclear atypia, mitotic activity and prominence of necrobiotic cell nests (cells with pyknotic nuclei and eosinophilic cytoplasm) were reported to be associated with malignancy {1358}.

DNA content. There is evidence that an aneuploid DNA content assessed by flow cytometry is associated with malignant behaviour, although the number of cases studied is small {867, 1358, 234}.

G. Zamboni
G. Klöppel

Miscellaneous carcinomas of the pancreas

Oncocytic carcinoma

These lesions are characterized by large cells with granular eosinophilic cytoplasm and large nuclei with well-defined nucleoli. Ultrastructurally, the cells show abundant mitochondria and lack zymogen and neuroendocrine granules. Local invasiveness, lymph node and pulmonary metastasis can occur {1781}. Differential diagnosis includes endocrine tumour {1454} and solid pseudopapillary tumour.

Nonmucinous, glycogen-poor cystadenocarcinoma

A large, encapsulated mass with cystic spaces lined by serous adenoma like component and malignant-appearing columnar epithelium. The tumour cells are negative for mucins and show oncocytic features by electron microscopy {533}.

Choriocarcinoma

An aggressive tumour, associated with elevated levels of serum human chorionic gonadotrophin (hCG), composed of cytotrophoblastic cells intermingled with syncytiotrophoblastic cells immunoreactive for hCG. Choriocarcinoma can be 'pure' or associated with mucinous cystadenocarcinoma {1781, 2194}.

Clear cell carcinoma

A carcinoma composed of clear cells, rich in glycogen and poor in mucin, morphologically resembling renal cell carcinoma {941}. Adenocarcinomatous, anaplastic, or intraductal papillary components can be found {1781}. A ductal phenotype has been suggested by the pattern of immunoreactivity for cytokeratins, the lack of vimentin expression, and the presence of *KRAS* mutation {1121}.

Ciliated cell carcinoma

This lesion shows the pattern of ductal adenocarcinoma, but contains many ciliated cells, as demonstrated at the ultrastructural level {1781}.

Microglandular carcinoma

Also known as microadenocarcinoma, this lesion is characterized by cribriform or microglandular pattern of growth {941}. The same cases were reclassified with immunohistochemistry as adenocarcinoma, acinar cell carcinoma and endocrine carcinoma {1090}. Microglandular carcinoma is best regarded as a pattern of growth rather than a distinctive entity.

Medullary carcinoma

This recently described carcinoma shows a syncytial growth pattern and lymphoepithelioma-like features (see chapter on ductal adenocarcinoma, other rare carcinomas) {590}.

M. Miettinen
J.Y. Blay
L.H. Sobin

Mesenchymal tumours of the pancreas

Primary mesenchymal tumours of the pancreas are exceedingly rare. Leiomyosarcomas and malignant gastrointestinal stromal tumours appear to be the least uncommon.

Recently, solitary fibrous tumours, similar to those more commonly seen on the serosal surfaces of the pleura and peritoneum, have been described {1118}. Histologically they show bland spindle cells in a collagenous background. The lesional cells are positive for CD34 but negative for KIT and desmin; focal actin positivity may occur.

Lymphoma of the pancreas

H.K. Müller-Hermelink
A. Chott
R.D. Gascoyne
A. Wotherspoon

Definition

Primary lymphoma of the pancreas is defined as an extranodal lymphoma arising in the pancreas with the bulk of the disease localized to this site. Contiguous lymph node involvement and distant spread may be seen but the primary clinical presentation is in the pancreas with therapy directed to this site.

Epidemiology

Primary lymphoma of the pancreas is very rare accounting for less than 0.5% of pancreatic tumours. As with primary lymphomas occurring elsewhere in the digestive tract, patients are more frequently elderly {796}.

Aetiology

Immunodeficiency predisposes to pancreatic lymphoma, both in the setting of HIV infection {866} and as post-transplant lymphoproliferative disorders following solid organ transplantation {240}. Familial pancreatic lymphoma has been reported in a sibling pair (brother and sister) who each presented with a high-grade B-cell lymphoma {830}. Pancreatic lymphoma in their seventh decade {830}. Pancreatic lymphoma has also been described in a patient with short bowel syndrome {903}.

Clinical features

The presentation of primary pancreatic lymphoma may mimic that of carcinoma or pancreatitis {240}. Pain free jaundice can occur {1330}. Ultrasonography may show an echo-poor lesion {1330}.

Histopathology

Primary pancreatic lymphomas are usually of B phenotype. Lymphomas of various types have been described, including low-grade lymphomas of diffuse small cell type {903, 1480}, follicle centre cell lymphoma {1330, 1238}, low-grade MALT lymphoma {1925}, and large B-cell lymphoma {1529, 830}. Only extremely rare cases of pancreatic T-cell lymphoma have been reported, including a single case of anaplastic large cell lymphoma (CD30 positive) of T-cell type {1179} and a case of pancreatic involvement by adult T-cell leukaemia/lymphoma {1408}. The histology of these cases varies little from that seen where these lymphoma types are encountered more frequently.

Prognosis

The distinction between lymphoma and carcinoma is important, as pancreatic lymphomas are associated with better prognosis and may be curable even in advanced stages. Occasional cases of relapse following prolonged remission have been reported in cases treated by chemotherapy {1529}.

Secondary tumours of the pancreas

E. Paál
A. Kádár

Definition

Secondary tumours of the pancreas are in most cases part of an advanced metastatic disease. They account for 3-16% of all pancreatic malignancies, affecting males and females equally {1190, 1012, 1597, 1781}. In our experience based on combined autopsy and histology material, out of 610 neoplasms involving the pancreas 26 (4.25%) were secondary. Any age may be affected, but the highest incidence is in the 6th decade.

Epidemiology

Secondary tumours of the pancreas are in most cases part of an advanced metastatic disease. They account for 3-16% of all pancreatic malignancies, affecting males and females equally {1190, 1012, 1597, 1781}. In our experience based on combined autopsy and histology material, out of 610 neoplasms involving the pancreas 26 (4.25%) were secondary. Any age may be affected, but the highest incidence is in the 6th decade.

Localization

Any anatomic region of the pancreas may be involved and there is no site predilection {934}. Lesions can be solitary, multiple, or diffuse {502}.

Clinical features

There are no specific symptoms for secondary tumours of the pancreas. Abdominal pain, jaundice, and diabetes might be the first sign, or in some cases an attack of acute pancreatitis {1290, 1608, 1772}.

The lesions are most commonly detected by imaging studies {934}. Fine needle aspiration can provide a rapid diagnosis {905, 645, 1250}.

Origin

Both epithelial and non-epithelial secondary tumours occur in the pancreas. The pancreas may be involved by direct spread (e.g. from stomach, liver, adrenal gland, retroperitoneum) or by lymphatic or haematogenous spread from distant sites {905}. Renal cell carcinoma is

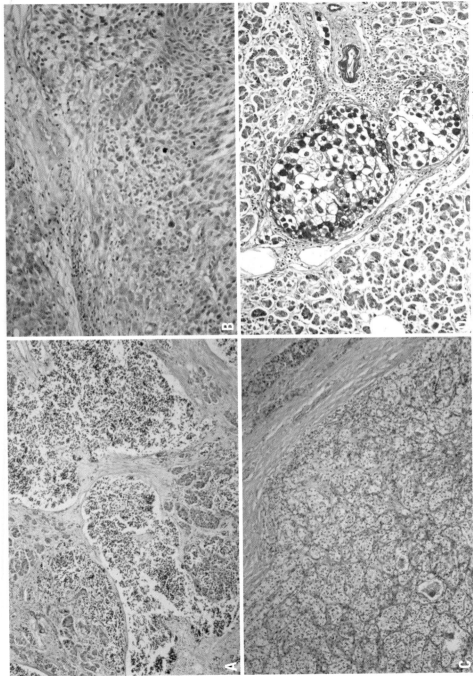

Fig. 10.38 Secondary tumours in the pancreas. **A** Metastatic small cell lung carcinoma. **B** Metastatic melanoma. **C** Metastatic renal cell carcinoma. **D** Metastatic gastric signet ring cell carcinoma.

unique as a primary site since it might give rise to late solitary metastases {1644, 218}.

Histopathology

The main differential diagnostic problem is to distinguish metastases from primary pancreatic neoplasms. The most problematic tumours are metastases from the gastrointestinal tract, renal cell carcino-

mas, small cell carcinoma, and lymphomas {240, 645, 1781}. Apart from the clinical and radiological signs {934}, multiple tumour foci with an abrupt transition from normal pancreas to the neoplastic tissue without signs of chronic pancreatitis in the surrounding parenchyma support metastatic origin {2089}. Immunohistochemistry specific for certain primary tumours may also be helpful {1190, 1707}.

Prognosis

Since in most cases pancreatic metastases indicate an advanced neoplastic disease, the prognosis is generally poor. In cases of solitary metastases, combined adjuvant therapy and surgical resection might be beneficial {360, 674, 218, 1597}.

Contributors

Dr Lauri A. AALTONEN *
Department of Medical Genetics
Haartman Institute, University of Helsinki
PO Box 21 (Haartmaninkatu 3)
SF-00014 Helsinki
FINLAND
Tel. +358 9 1912 6278
Fax +358 9 1912 6677
lauri.aaltonen@helsinki.fi

Dr Guido ADLER
Department of Medicine I
University of Ulm
Robert Koch Strasse 8
D-89070 Ulm
GERMANY
Tel. +49 731 50 24300/24301
Fax +49 731 50 24302
guido.adler@medizin.uni-ulm.de

Dr Jorge ALBORES-SAAVEDRA *
Dept. of Pathology, Univ. of Texas
Southwestern Medical Center
5323 Harry Hines Blvd
Dallas, TX 75235-9072
USA
Tel. +1 214 590 6585
Fax +1 214 590 1411
rmuril@mednet.swmed.edu

Dr Peter P. ANTHONY *
Histopathology Department
Royal Devon and Exeter Hospital
Church Lane
Exeter EX2 5AD
UNITED KINGDOM
Tel. +44 1392 402942
Fax +44 1392 402964
peter.anthony@ukgateway.net

Dr Mark J. ARENDS
Dept of Histopathology, Box 235
Addenbrooke's Hospital
Hills Road
CB2 2QQ Cambridge
UNITED KINGDOM
Tel. +44 1223 217176
Fax +44 1223 216980
mja40@cam.ac.uk

Dr Rudolf ARNOLD
Zentrum für Innere Medizin
Klinikum der Philipps Universitat Marburg
Baldingerstrasse, P.O.B. 2360
D-35033 Marburg
GERMANY
Tel. +49 6421 286 6460
Fax +49 6421 286 8922
arnoldr@mailer.uni-marburg.de

Dr Marc Billaud
Faculté de Médecine
Lab. de Génétique et Cancer, UMR 5641
8 avenue Rockefeller
69373 Lyon
FRANCE
Tel. +33 4 78 77 72 14
Fax +33 4 78 77 72 20
billaud@univ-lyon1.fr

Dr Jean-Yves BLAY
Centre Leon Berard
Université Lyon I
28 rue Laennec
69008 Lyon
FRANCE
Tel. +33 4 78 78 27 57
Fax +33 4 78 78 28 16
blay@lyon.fnclcc.fr

Dr Hubert E. BLUM
Department of Medicine II
University Hospital
Hugstetter Strasse, 55
D-79106 Freiburg
GERMANY
Tel. +49 7612 703403
Fax +49 7612 703610
heblum@ukl.uni.freiburg.de

Dr Randall W. BURT
Div. of Gastroenterology, Rm 4R118
University of Utah Health Science Ctr.
50 North Medical Drive
Salt Lake City, UT 84132
USA
Tel. +1 801 581 7802
Fax +1 801 581 7476
randall.burt@hsc.utah.edu

Dr Carlo CAPELLA *
Department of Pathology
University of Pavia at Varese
Ospedale di Circolo
I-21100 Varese
ITALY
Tel. +39 0332 278231 or 272
Fax +39 0332 278599
carlo.capella@ospedale.varese.it

Dr Fatima CARNEIRO
IPATIMUP
Medical Faculty, University of Porto
Rua Roberto Frias s/n
4200 Porto
PORTUGAL
Tel. +351 2509 0591
Fax +351 2550 3940
fcarneiro@ipatimup.pt

Dr Norman J. CARR *
Department of Cellular Pathology
Southampton General Hospital
Tremona Road
Southampton S016 6YD
UNITED KINGDOM
Tel. +44 2380 796051
Fax +44 2380 796869

Dr Andreas CHOTT
Department of Clinical Pathology
University of Vienna
Waehringer Guertel 18-20
A 1090 Vienna
AUSTRIA
Tel. +43 1 405 3402
Fax +43 1 405 3402
andreas.chott@akh-wien.ac.at

* The asterisk indicates participation in
the Working Group Meeting on the WHO
Classification of Tumours of the Digestive
System that was held in Lyon, France,
Nov 6-9, 1999.

Dr W.H. CHOW
National Cancer Institute
EPS 8100
6120 Executive Blvd.
Bethesda, MD 20892-7182
USA
Tel. +1 301 435 4708
Fax +1 301 402 1819
choww@exchange.nih.gov

Dr Pelayo CORREA
Department of Pathology,
Louisiana State Univ. Medical Center
1901 Perdido Street
New Orleans, LA 70112
USA
Tel. +1 504 568 6035
Fax +1 504 599 1278
correa@isuhsc.edu

Dr G.T. DEANS
Consulting Surgeon
Stepping Hill Hospital
Poplar Gr.
Stockport SK2 7JE
UNITED KINGDOM
Tel. +44 161 440 8820
Fax +44 161 483 8576
gtdeans@uk.gateway.net

Dr Pierre DEMATOS
Department of Surgery, Box 37049
Duke University Medical Center
Erwin Road
Durham, NC 27710
USA
Tel. +1 919 681 2559
Fax +1 919 681 2779
demat001@mc.duke.edu

Dr Yves DEUGNIER
Centre Hospitalier Régional Ponchaillou
Université de Rennes
2 rue Henri Le Guilloux
35033 Rennes
FRANCE
Tel. +33 2 99 28 42 97
Fax +33 2 99 28 41 12
yves.deugnier@univ-rennes1.fr

Dr Michael F. DIXON
Academic Unit of Pathology
University of Leeds
Algernon Firth Building
LS2 9JT Leeds
UNITED KINGDOM
Tel. +44 113 243 1751
Fax +44 113 292 2834
miked@pathology.leeds.ac.uk

Dr Charis ENG
Human Cancer Genetics Program
Ohio State University Cancer Ctr.
420 W 12th Avenue, 690 MRF
Columbus, OH 43210
USA
Tel. +1 614 688 4508
Fax +1 614 688 3205
eng-1@medctr.osu.edu

Dr Claus FENGER *
Dept. of Pathology
Odense University Hospital
Winsloewparken 15
DK-5000 Odense C
DENMARK
Tel. +45 6541 4807
Fax +45 6591 2943
claus.fenger@ouh.dk

Dr Cecilia FENOGLIO-PREISER *
Department of Pathology
University of Cincinnati, School of Medicine
231 Bethesda Ave, POB 670529
Cincinnati, OH 45267-0529
USA
Tel. +1 513 558 4500
Fax +1 513 558 2289
cecilia.fenogliopreiser@uc.edu

Dr J.K. FIELD
Molecular Genetics and Oncology Group
Clinical and Dental Sciences
University of Liverpool
Liverpool L69 3BX
UNITED KINGDOM
Tel. +44 151 794 8900
Fax +44 151 794 8989
j.k.field@liv.ac.uk

Dr Hans-Peter FISCHER
Institute of Pathology
University Hospital
Sigmund Freud Str. 25
D-53127 Bonn
GERMANY
Tel. +49 228 287 6340
Fax +49 228 287 5030
fischer@mailer.meb.uni-bonn.de

Dr Jean-François FLEJOU
Serv. d'Anatomie et de Cytologie
Pathologiques, Hôpital Saint Antoine
184 rue du Faubourg St Antoine
75012 Paris
FRANCE
Tel. +33 1 40 87 54 59
Fax +33 1 40 87 00 77
jean-francois.flejou@bjn.ap-hop-paris.fr

Dr Franz FOGT
Department of Pathology, Presbyterian
Med. Center, Univ of Pennsylvania
39th & Market Streets
Philadelphia, PA 19104-2699
USA
Tel. +1 215 662 8077
Fax +1 215 662 1694
fogt@mail.med.upenn.edu

Dr M. FRISCH
Viral Epidemiology Branch
National Cancer Institute
6120 Executive Blvd, EPS / 8015
Bethesda, MD 20852
USA
Tel. +1 301 594 7825
Fax +1 301 402 0817
frischm@mail.nih.gov

Dr Helmut GABBERT *
Institute of Pathology
Heinrich Heine University
Moorenstr. 5
40225 Düsseldorf
GERMANY
Tel. +49 211 811 8339
Fax +49 211 811 8353
gabbert@med.uni-duesseldorf.de

Dr Randy D. GASCOYNE
Department of Pathology
British Columbia Cancer Agency
600 West 10th Avenue
Vancouver, BC V5Z 4E6
CANADA
Tel. +1 604 877 6000, ext. 2097
Fax +1 604 877 6178
rgascoyn@bccancer.bc.ca

Dr Robert M. GENTA
Department of Pathology - 113
Veterans Affairs Medical Center
2002 Holcombe Blvd
Houston, TX 77030
USA
Tel. +1 713 794 7113
Fax +1 713 794 7810
rmgenta@bcm.tmc.edu

Dr David GOLDGAR
International Agency for
Research on Cancer (IARC)
150 Cours Albert Thomas
69372 Lyon
FRANCE
Tel. +33 4 72 73 85 33
Fax +33 4 72 73 83 42
goldgar@iarc.fr

Dr Stephen B. GRUBER
Division of Molecular Medicine and Genetics
University of Michigan
4301 MSRB III
Ann Arbor, MI 48109-0652
USA
Tel. +1 734 763 2532
Fax +1 734 763 7672
sgruber@umich.edu

Dr Parry GUILFORD
Cancer Genetics, Lab. of Biochemistry
University of Otago
PO Box 56
Dunedin, Aorearoa
NEW ZEELAND
Tel. +64 3 479 7868
Fax +64 3 479 7738
parry.guilford@otago.ac.nz

Dr Pierre HAINAUT
International Agency for
Research on Cancer (IARC)
150 Cours Albert Thomas
69372 Lyon
FRANCE
Tel. +33 4 72 73 85 32
Fax +33 4 72 73 83 22
hainaut@iarc.fr

Dr Stanley R. HAMILTON *
Department of Pathology
M.D. Anderson Cancer Center
1515 Holcombe Boulevard
Houston, TX 77030, USA
Tel. +1 713 792 6313
Fax +1 713 794 1824
shamilto@notes.mdacc.tmc.ed
shamilto@md.anderson.org

Dr Setsuo HIROHASHI *
National Cancer Center
Research Institute
1-1, Tsukiji 5-chome, Chuo-ku
104-0045 Tokyo
JAPAN
Tel. +81 3 3542 2511 (ext 4101)
Fax +81 3 3248 0326
shirohas@gan2.ncc.go.jp

Dr Heinz HÖFLER
Institute of Pathology
Technische Universität München
Ismaninger Str. 22
D-81675 München
GERMANY
Tel. +49 89 4140 4160
Fax +49 89 4140 4865
hoefler@lrz.tu-muenchen.de

Dr James R. HOWE
Department of Surgery
University of Iowa, College of Medicine
200 Hawkins Drive
Iowa City, IA 52242-
USA
Tel. +1 319 356 7945
Fax +1 319 356 8378
james-howe@uiowa.edu

Dr Ralph H. HRUBAN
GI Liver Pathology, Meyer 7-181
Johns Hopkins Univ. School of Medicine
600 N. Wolfe Street
Baltimore, MD 21287
USA
Tel. +1 410 955 9132
Fax +1 410 955 0115
rhruban@jhmi.edu

Dr Gyorgy ILLYES
Department of Pathology
Semmelweiss University of Medicine
Ulloi ut 93
1061 Budapest
HUNGARY
Tel. +36 1 215 6921
Fax +36 1 215 6921
igy@korb2.sote.hu

Dr Haruhiro INOUE *
Department of Surgery
Tokyo Medical & Dental University
1-5-45 Yushima, Bunkyo-ku
113-8519 Tokyo
JAPAN
Tel. +81 3 5803 5225
Fax +81 3 3817 4126
hiro.inoue.srg1@med.tmd.ac.jp

Dr Kamal G. ISHAK *
Dept. of Hepatic and GI Pathology
Armed Forces Institute of Pathology
Alaska Avenue at 14th St
Washington, DC 20306
USA
Tel. +1 202 782 1707
Fax +1 202 782 9020
ishak@afip.osd.mil

Dr Heikki J. JÄRVINEN
Department of Surgery
Helsinki University Central Hospital
Haartmaninkatu 4, PO Box 260
00029 HUCH Helsinki
Finland
Tel. +358 9 4717 3852
Fax +358 9 4717 4675

Dr Jeremy R. JASS *
Pathology Department, Grad Med School
University of Queensland
Herston Rd.
4006 Brisbane, Queensland
Australia
Tel. +61 7 3365 5340
Fax +61 7 3365 5511
j.jass@mailbox.uq.edu.au

Dr Anna KADAR
Department of Pathology
Semmelweiss University of Medicine
Ulloi ut 93
1061 Budapest
HUNGARY
Tel. +36 1 215 6921
Fax +36 1 215 6921
kadann@korb2.sote.hu

Dr G. KELLER
Institute of Pathology
Technische Universität München
Ismaninger Str 22
D-81675 München
GERMANY
Tel. +49 89 4140 4592
Fax +49 89 4140 4915
gisela.keller@irz.tum.de

Dr S.E. KERN
Department of Pathology
Johns Hopkins Univ School of Medicine
1650 Orleans Street - CRB 451
Baltimore, MD 21205-2196
USA
Tel. +1 410 614 33 14
Fax +1 410 614 97 05
sk@jhmi.edu

Dr Lars G. KINDBLOM
Department of Pathology
University of Gothenburg
Sahlgren University Hospital
41345 Gothenburg
SWEDEN
Tel. +46 31 342 1928
Fax +46 31 827194
lars-gunnar.kindblom@llcr.med.gu.se

Dr Paul KLEIHUES *
International Agency for
Research on Cancer (IARC)
150 Cours Albert Thomas
69372 Lyon
FRANCE
Tel. +33 4 72 73 85 77
Fax +33 4 72 73 85 64
kleihues@iarc.fr

Dr David S. KLIMSTRA
Department of Pathology
Memorial Sloan Kettering Cancer Center
1275 York Avenue
New York, NY 10021
USA
Tel. +1 212 639 2410
Fax +1 212 717 3203
klimstrd@mskcc.org

Dr Günter KLÖPPEL *
Institute of Pathology
University of Kiel
Michaelisstrasse 11
D-24105 Kiel
GERMANY
Tel. +49 431 597 3400
Fax +49 431 597 3462
gkloeppel@path.uni-kiel.de

Dr Masamichi KOJIRO
Department of Pathology
School of Medicine, Kurume Univ.
67 Asahi-machi
8030-0001 Kurume
JAPAN
Tel. +81 942 317546
Fax +81 942 320905
kojiro@med.kurume-u.ac.jp

Dr Shin-ei KUDO *
Department of Gastroenterology
Akita Red Cross Hospital
222-1 Naeshirosawa-aza Saruta, Kamikitade
010-1495 Akita-City
JAPAN
Tel. +81 18 829 5000, ext 3325
Fax +81 18 829 5115
kudo-s@synap.ne.jp

Dr René LAMBERT *
International Agency for
Research on Cancer (IARC)
150 Cours Albert Thomas
69372 Lyon
FRANCE
Tel. +33 4 72 73 85 14
Fax +33 4 72 73 86 50
lambert@iarc.fr

Dr Pierre LAURENT PUIG
U490 Laboratoire de Toxicol. Moleculaire
Faculté de Médicine, Université Paris V
45 rue des Saints Pères
75006 Paris, FRANCE
Tel. +33 1 42 86 20 81
Fax +33 1 42 86 20 72
pierre.laurent-puig@biomedicale.univ-
paris5.fr

Dr Anthony S.Y. LEONG
Discipline of Anatomical Pathology
University of Newcastle, Locked Bag 1
Hunter Regional Mail Centre
Newcastle 2310
AUSTRALIA
Tel. +61 2 4921 4000
Fax +61 2 4921 4440
aleong@mail.newcastle.edu.au

Dr Daniel S. LONGNECKER *
Department of Pathology
Dartmouth-Hitchcock
Medical Center
Lebanon, NH 03756
USA
Tel. +1 603 650 7899
Fax +1 603 650 6120
daniel.s.longnecker@dartmouth.edu

Dr Jutta LÜTTGES
Institute of Pathology
University of Kiel
Michaelisstrasse 11
D-24105 Kiel
GERMANY
Tel. +49 431 597 3422
Fax +49 431 597 3428
jluettges@path.uni-kiel.de

Dr Marc-Claude MARTI
Policlinique de Chirurgie
Hôpital Cantonal Universitaire
Rue Michel Servet
CH-1211 Geneva 4
SWITZERLAND
Tel. +41 22 372 790?
Fax +41 22 372 7909
marc-claude.marti@hcuge.ch

Dr Francis MEGRAUD
Laboratoire de Bactériologie
Hôpital Pellegrin
Place Amélie Raba Léon
33076 Bordeaux
FRANCE
Tel. +33 5 56 79 59 10
Fax +33 5 56 79 60 18
francis.megraud@chu-aquitaine.fr

Dr Herman R. MENCK
Commission on Cancer
American College of Surgeons
633 N Saint Clair Street
Chicago, IL 60611
USA
Tel. +1 312 664 4050
Fax +1 312 202 5009
mencky@aol.com

Dr Markku MIETTIENEN *
Dept. of Soft Tissue Pathology
Armed Forces Institute of Pathology
Alaska Avenue at 14th St
Washington, DC 20306
USA
Tel. +1 202 782 2793
Fax +1 202 782 9182
miettienen@afip.osd.mil

Dr Ruggero MONTESANO
International Agency for
Research on Cancer (IARC)
150 Cours Albert Thomas
69372 Lyon
FRANCE
Tel. +33 4 72 73 84 63
Fax +33 4 72 73 83 22
montesano@iarc.fr

Dr Hans K. MÜLLER-HERMELINK
Pathologisches Institut
der Universität Würzburg
Josef-Schneider-Str. 2
D-97080 Würzburg
GERMANY
Tel. +49 931 201 3776
Fax +49 931 201 3440 /3505
path062@mail.uni-wuerzburg.de

Dr Nubia MUNOZ
International Agency for
Research on Cancer (IARC)
150 Cours Albert Thomas
69372 Lyon
FRANCE
Tel. +33 4 72 73 84 04
Fax +33 4 72 73 83 45
munoz@iarc.fr

Dr Yusuke NAKAMURA
Laboratory of Molecular Medicine
Inst. of Medical Science, Univ. of Tokyo
4-6-1 Shirokanedai Minato-ku
Tokyo 108,
JAPAN
Tel. +81 3 5449 5372
Fax +81 3 5449 5433
yusuke@ims.u-tokyo.ac.jp

Dr Shin-ichi NAKAMURA
Division of Pathology
School of Medicine, Iwate Medical University
19-1 Uchimaru
020 Morioka,
JAPAN
Tel. +81 19 651 5111
Fax +81 19 629 1437
nakamurashin@ma2.justnet.ne.jp

Dr Yasuni NAKANUMA *
Second Department of Pathology
Kanazawa Univ. School of Medicine
Takaramachi 13-1
920-8640 Kanazawa
JAPAN
Tel. +81 76 265 2195
Fax +81 76 234 4229
pbcpsc@kenroku.kanazawa-u.ac.jp

Dr Claus NIEDERAU
St. Joseph Hospital, Academic Teaching
Hospital. Dpt of Medicine
Mühlheimerstrasse 83
46045 Oberhausen
GERMANY
Tel. +49 208 837301
Fax +49 208 837309
claus.niederau@uni-duesseldorf.de

Dr Edina PAAL
Department of Pathology
Semmelweiss University of Medicine
Ulloi ut 93
1061 Budapest
HUNGARY
Tel. +36 1 215 6921
Fax +36 1 215 6921

Dr Rolland PARC
Service de Chirurgie Digestive
Hôpital Saint Antoine
184 rue du Faubourg St Antoine
75571 Paris
FRANCE
Tel. +33 1 49 28 25 46
Fax +33 1 49 28 25 48
rolland.parc@sat.ap-hop-paris.fr

Dr Timo J. PARTANEN
Dept. of Epidemiology and Biostatistics
Finnish Institute of Occupational Health
Topeliuksenkatu 41 A
FIN-00250 Helsinki
FINLAND
Tel. +358 9 474 7392
Fax +358 9 474 7423
tpar@occuphealth.fi

Dr Paivi PELTOMAKI
Division of Human Cancer Genetics
Ohio State University
420 W. 12th Avenue, 690 MRF
Columbus, OH 43210
USA
Tel. +1 614 688 4493
Fax +1 614 688 4245
peltomaki-1@medctr.osu.edu

Dr Marco PENNAZIO
Servizio de Gastroenterologia
Ospedale San Giovanni
Via Cavour, 31
10123 Torino
ITALY
Tel. +39 011 566 4065
Fax +39 011 817 3869
mpen60@yahoo.com

Dr Thierry PONCHON
Gastroentérologie, Pavillon 0
Hôpital Edouard Herriot
Place d'Arsonval
69347 Lyon
FRANCE
Tel. +33 4 72 11 01 46
Fax +33 4 72 11 01 47
thierry.ponchon@chu-lyon.fr

Dr Steven M. POWELL
Department of Internal Medicine
University of Virginia
Health Sciences Center, Box 10013
Charlottesville, VA 22906-0013
USA
Tel. +1 804 243 2655
Fax +1 804 243 6169
smp8n@virginia.edu

Dr Elio RIBOLI
International Agency for
Research on Cancer (IARC)
150 Cours Albert Thomas
69372 Lyon
FRANCE
Tel. +33 4 72 73 84 38
Fax +33 4 72 73 83 61
riboli@iarc.fr

Dr Francesco P. ROSSINI
Servizio de Gastroenterologia
Ospedale San Giovanni
Via Cavour 31
10123 Torino
ITALY
Tel. +39 011 566 4065
Fax +39 011 817 3869
fprossini@yahoo.com

Dr Carlos A. RUBIO *
Gastrointestinal and Liver Pathology
Department of Pathology
Karolinska Institute
171 76 Stockholm
SWEDEN
Tel. +46 8 5177 4527
Fax +46 8 5177 4524
carlos.rubio@onkpat.ki.se

Dr Massimo RUGGE *
Immunohistochemistry and Pathology
Universita degli Studi di Padova
Via Aristide Gabelli, 61
35121 Padova
ITALY
Tel. +39 049 942 4970
Fax +39 049 942 4981
rugge@ux1.unipd.it

Dr Michiie SAKAMOTO
Chief, Pathology Division
National Cancer Center Research Institute
1-1, Tsukiji 5-chome, Chuo-ku
104-0045 Tokyo
JAPAN
Tel. +81 3 3542 2511, ext. 4200
Fax +81 3 3248 2737
msakamot@gan2.ncc.go.jp

Dr Mitsuru SASAKO *
WHO CC for Gastric Cancer
National Cancer Center Hospital
5-1-1, Tsukiji, Chuo-ku
104-0045 Tokyo
JAPAN
Tel. +81 3 3542 2511
Fax +81 3 3542 3815
msasako@gan2.ncc.go.jp

Dr Dietmar SCHMIDT
Institute of Pathology
A 2, 2
D-68159 Mannheim
GERMANY
Tel. +49 621 22779
Fax +49 621 153288
dschmi@t-online.de

Dr Jean-Yves SCOAZEC *
Service d'Anatomie Pathologique,
Batiment 10, Univ. Lyon I
Hôpital Edouard Herriot
69437 Lyon
FRANCE
Tel. +33 4 72 11 07 50
Fax +33 4 72 11 68 91
jscoazec@worldnet.fr

Dr Neil A. SHEPHERD
Department of Histopathology
Gloucestershire Royal Hospital
Great Western Road
Gloucester GL1 3NN
UNITED KINGDOM
Tel. +44 1452 395263
Fax +44 1452 395285
n.shepherd@virgin.net

Dr Tadakazu SHIMODA *
Department of Clinical Laboratory
National Cancer Center Hospital
5-1-1 Tsukiji Chuo Ku
104-0045 Tokyo
JAPAN
Tel. +81 3 3542 2511
Fax +81 3 5565 7029
tshimoda@gan2.ncc.gao.jp

Dr Rüdiger J. SIEWERT
Chirurgische Klinik
Klinikum rechts der Isar
Ismaningerstrasse 22
81675 München
GERMANY
Tel. +49 89 4140/2120
Fax +49 89 470 6298
catharina@nt1.chir.med.tu-muenchen.de

Dr Leslie H. SOBIN *
Division of Gastrointestinal Pathology
Armed Forces Institute of Pathology
Alaska Avenue at 14th St
Washington, DC 20306-6000
USA
Tel. +1 202 782 2880
Fax +1 202 782 9020
sobin@afip.osd.mil

Dr Nib SOEHENDRA
University Hospital of Hamburg-Eppendorf
Department of Interdisciplinary Endoscopy
Martinistrasse 52
20246 Hamburg
GERMANY
Tel. +49 40 4280 33424
Fax +49 40 4280 34420
soehendr@uke.uni-hamburg.de

Dr Enrico SOLCIA
Department of Human Pathology
University of Pavia
Policlinico San Matteo
I-27100 Pavia
ITALY
Tel. +39 038 252 8474
Fax +39 038 252 5866
apat@unipv.it

Dr Stuart J. SPECHLER *
Medical Center 111B1
Department of Veterans Affairs
4500 South Lancaster Road
Dallas, TX 75216
USA
Tel. +1 214 374 7799
Fax +1 214 857 1571
sjspechler@aol.com

Dr Bancboh SRIPA
Department of Pathology
Faculty of Medicine
Khon Kaen University
Khon Kaen 40002
THAILAND
Tel. +66 43 348388
Fax +66 43 348375
banchob@kkul.kku1.ac.th

Dr Parupudi V.J. SRIRAM
University Hospital Hamburg-Eppendorf
Department of Interdisciplinary Endoscopy
Martinistrasse 52
20246 Hamburg
GERMANY
Tel. +49 40 4280 33424
Fax +49 40 4280 34420

Dr H.J. STEIN
Department of Surgery
Technische Universität München
Ismaninger Str 22
D-81675 München
GERMANY
Tel. +49 89 4140 2120
Fax +49 89 4140 4865
stein@1.chir.med.tu-muenchen.de

Dr J. Thomas STOCKER *
Department of Pathology, Uniformed
Services Univ of Health Sciences
4301 Jones Bridge Road
Bethesda, MD 20814-4799
USA
Tel. +1 301 295 3480
Fax +1 301 295 1640
jstocker@usuhs.mil

Dr Manfred STOLTE
Institut fur Pathologie
Klinikum Bayreuth
Preuschwitzer Str. 101
D-95445 Bayreuth
GERMANY
Tel. +49 921 400 5600
Fax +49 921 400 5609
pathologie.klinikum@bnbt.de

Dr Ian C. TALBOT *
Academic Dept. of Pathology
Imperial Cancer Research Fund
St Mark's Hospital, Watford Road
Harrow, Middlesex HAL 3UJ
UNITED KINGDOM
Tel. +44 181 235 4220
Fax +44 181 235 4277
i.talbot@icrf.icnet.uk

Dr Vanchai VATANASAPT
Mekong Institute
Medical Faculty
Khon Kaen University
Khon Kaen 40002
THAILAND
Tel. +66 4324 1479
Fax +66 4334 3131
kambro@kkul.kku.ac.th

Dr Neil D. THEISE
Department of Pathology, Room 461
New York University Medical Center
560 First Avenue
New York, NY 10016
USA
Tel. + 1 212 263 8944
Fax +1 212 263 7916
neitheise@aol.com

Dr Gilles THOMAS
Molecular Genetics
Fondation Jean Dausset
27 rue J Dodu
75010 Paris
FRANCE
Tel. +33 1 53 72 51 50
Fax +33 1 53 72 51 58
thomas@cephb.fr

Dr Hideaki TSUKUMA
Osaka Medical Center for Cancer and
Cardiovascular Diseases
3-3 Nokamishi, 1 chome, Higashinari-ku
Osaka 537 - 8511
JAPAN
Tel. +81 6 6972 1181
Fax +81 6 6978 2821
xtukuma@iph.pref.osaka.jp

Dr Hans F.A. VASEN
The Netherlands Hereditary Tumour
Foundation c/o Medipark BV, Building 5, 2333
Rijnsburgerweg, 10
2333 AA Leiden,
THE NETHERLANDS
Tel. +31 71 526 1955
Fax +31 71 521 2137
nfdht@xs4all.nl

Dr Bert VOGELSTEIN
Johns Hopkins Oncology Center
424 North Bond Street
Baltimore, MD 21205
USA
Tel. +1 410 955 8877
Fax +1 410 955 0548
vogelbe@welchlink.welch.jhu.edu

Dr Peter VOGT
Department of Pathology
University Hospital USZ
Schmelzbergstr. 12
8091 Zürich
SWITZERLAND
Tel. +41 1 255 2524
Fax +41 1 255 4400

Dr Ian R. WANLESS
Department of Pathology
Toronto General Hospital
200 Elisabeth Street
Toronto, Ontario M5G 2C4
CANADA
Tel. +1 416 340 3330
Fax +1 416 586 9901
ian.wanless@utoronto.ca

Dr Hidenobu WATANABE
1st Department of Pathology
Niigata University School of Medicine
1-757 Asahimachi-dori
Niigata 951-8510
JAPAN
Tel. +81 25 227 2093
Fax +81 25 227 0760
watahide@med.niigata-u.ac.jp

Dr Martin WERNER *
Institute of Pathology
Technische Universität München
Ismaninger Str 22
D-81675 München
GERMANY
Tel. +49 89 4140 4170
Fax +49 89 4140 4865
martin.werner@lrz.tu-muenchen.de

Dr Sidney J. WINAWER
Gastroenterology-Nutrition Service
Memorial Sloan Kettering Cancer Center
1275 York Avenue
New York, NY 10021
USA
Tel. +1 212 639 7678
Fax +1 212 639 2766
winawer@mskcc.org

Dr Christian WITTEKIND *
Institute of Pathology
University of Leipzig
Liebigstrasse 26
D-04103 Leipzig
GERMANY
Tel. +49 34 1971 5000
Fax +49 34 1971 5009
wittc@medizin.uni-leipzig.de

Dr Andrew WOTHERSPOON *
Histopathology Department
The Royal Marsden NHS Trust
Fulham Road
London SW3 6JJ
UNITED KINGDOM
Tel. +44 171 352 7348
Fax +44 171 352 7348
andrew.wotherspoon@rmh.nthames.nhs.uk

Dr Nick A. WRIGHT
Imperial College
School of Medicine
Hammersmith Hospital
London W12 0NN
UNITED KINGDOM
Tel. +44 181 383 3200 or 171 269 3038
Fax +44 181 383 3203
n.wright@ic.ac.uk

Dr Guiseppe ZAMBONI *
Department of Pathology
University of Verona
Strada Le Grazie
37134 Verona
ITALY
Tel. +39 045 807 4815
Fax +39 045 809 8136
zamboni@anpat.univr.it

Source of charts and photographs

1.

1.01	IARC Press, Lyon
1.02	IARC Press, Lyon
1.03 A-F	T. Shimoda
1.04	H. Inoue
1.05 A, B	H. Inoue
1.06	T. Shimoda
1.07	L.H. Sobin
1.08	H.E. Gabbert
1.09 A, B	H. Watanabe
1.10 A	L.H. Sobin
1.10 B, C	T. Shimoda
1.11 A	L.H. Sobin
1.11 B	T. Shimoda
1.12	H.E. Gabbert
1.13 A	I.C. Talbot
1.13 B	T. Shimoda
1.13 C	H.E. Gabbert
1.13 D	I.C. Talbot
1.14	N.J. Carr
1.15 A-C	H.E. Gabbert
1.16	J.K. Field
1.17	P. Hainaut
1.18	P. Hainaut
1.19	C. Fenoglio-Preiser
1.20	C. Fenoglio-Preiser
1.21	C. Fenoglio-Preiser
1.22	R. Lambert
1.23 A, B	M. Werner
1.24	C. Fenoglio-Preiser
1.25 A	L.H. Sobin
1.25 B	M. Werner
1.26	L.H. Sobin
1.27	M. Werner
1.28 A, C	M. Werner
1.28 B	C. Fenoglio-Preiser
1.29	P. Anthony
1.30	M. Werner
1.31 A, B	M. Miettinen
1.32	M. Miettinen
1.33	M. Miettinen
1.34	C. Fenoglio-Preiser
1.35	C. Fenger
1.36	N.J. Carr

2.

2.01	S.J. Spechler
2.02	H.J. Stein
2.03	S.J. Spechler
2.04	R. Lambert
2.05 A	F. Fogt
2.05 B	C.A. Rubio
2.06	M. Werner

3.

3.01	IARC Press, Lyon
3.02	IARC Press, Lyon
3.03	P. Correa
3.04	C. Fenoglio-Preiser
3.05 A, B	H. Inoue
3.06 A-D	H. Inoue
3.07	C. Fenoglio-Preiser
3.08 A	I.C. Talbot
3.08 B	N.A. Sheperd
3.09 A, B	C. Fenoglio-Preiser
3.09 C	M. Sasako
3.09 D-F	C. Fenoglio-Preiser
3.10 A	M. Sasako
3.10 B	F. Carneiro
3.10 C	C. Fenoglio-Preiser
3.11 A	I.C. Talbot
3.11 B	C. Fenoglio-Preiser
3.12 A	H. Watanabe
3.12 B	C. Fenoglio-Preiser
3.13 A	M. Sasako
3.13 B	H. Watanabe
3.13 C	M. Sasako
3.13 D	L.H. Sobin
3.14	C. Fenoglio-Preiser
3.15	L.H. Sobin
3.16 A, B	L.H. Sobin
3.17 A, B	F. Carneiro
3.18 A, B	M. Sasako
3.18 C	H. Watanabe
3.19 A, B	M. Sasako
3.20	M. Rugge
3.21	I.C. Talbot
3.22	C.A. Rubio
3.23 A	I.C. Talbot
3.23 B	M. Rugge
3.24 A	C. Fenoglio-Preiser
3.24 B	I.C. Talbot
3.24 C	M. Rugge
3.25 A-D	N.J. Carr
3.26 A, B	N.J. Carr
3.27	J.R. Jass
3.28 A, B	F. Carneiro
3.28 C	H.E. Gabbert
3.29	H.E. Gabbert
3.30	C. Fenoglio-Preiser
3.31	L.H. Sobin
3.32	C. Capella
3.33 A	J.R. Jass
3.33 B	C. Capella
3.34	C. Capella
3.35 A	S.R. Hamilton
3.35 B	C. Capella
3.36	C. Capella
3.37	I.C. Talbot
3.38	K. Ishak
3.39	A. Wotherspoon
3.40	S.R. Hamilton
3.41 A, B	A. Wotherspoon
3.42 A, B	J.R. Jass
3.42 C, D	A. Wotherspoon
3.43	M. Miettinen
3.44	C. Fenoglio-Preiser
3.45 A, B	C. Fenger
3.46 A-C	M. Miettinen
3.47	Lasota
3.48 A, B	M. Miettinen
3.49	H. Watanabe
3.50	J.R. Jass
3.51	N.J. Carr
3.52	C. Fenoglio-Preiser
3.53	K. Ishak
3.54	L.H. Sobin
3.55	L.H. Sobin

4.

4.01 A	L.H. Sobin
4.01 B	S.R. Hamilton
4.02	C. Fenoglio-Preiser
4.03 A, B	N.J. Carr
4.04 A	L.H. Sobin
4.04 B	N.J. Carr
4.05	I.C. Talbot
4.06	L.H. Sobin
4.07 A	L. Aaltonen
4.07 B	L.H. Sobin
4.08 A, B	J.R. Jass
4.09 A, B	L.H. Sobin
4.10	L.H. Sobin
4.11	L. Aaltonen
4.12	C. Capella
4.13 A-D	N.J. Carr
4.14	C. Capella
4.15 A	N.J. Carr
4.15 B	C. Capella
4.16	P. Vogt

4.17 A-c C. Capella
4.18 J.R. Jass
4.19 A, B L.H. Sobin
4.20 A I.C. Talbot
4.20 B J.R. Jass
4.21 J.R. Jass
4.22 A-c A. Chott
4.23 A-c A. Chott
4.24 J.R. Jass
4.25 A, B C. Fenger
4.26 M. Miettinen
4.27 A, B C. Fenoglio-Preiser
4.28 A I.C. Talbot
4.28 B C. Fenoglio-Preiser
4.29 L.H. Sobin
4.30 C. Niederau
4.31 L.H. Sobin

5.

5.01 L.H. Sobin
5.02 N.J. Carr
5.03 A, B N.J. Carr
5.04 N.J. Carr
5.05 K. Ishak
5.06 J.R. Jass
5.07 J.R. Jass
5.08 L.H. Sobin
5.09 N.J. Carr
5.10 A I.C. Talbot
5.10 B C. Capella
5.11 C. Capella
5.12 C. Fenger
5.13 N.J. Carr
5.14 A, B N.J. Carr
5.15 C. Capella
5.16 C. Capella
5.17 N.J. Carr
5.18 A L.H. Sobin
5.18 B L.H. Sobin
5.18 C J.R. Jass
5.19 C. Capella

6.

6.01 IARC Press, Lyon
6.02 IARC Press, Lyon
6.03 C. Fenoglio-Preiser
6.04 A, B S. Kudo
6.05 A-c C.A. Rubio
6.06 A-D S. Kudo
6.07 A, B S. Kudo
6.08 A, B S. Kudo
6.08 c H.E. Gabbert
6.09 C.A. Rubio
6.10 L.H. Sobin
6.11 C.A. Rubio
6.12 A, B C. Fenoglio-Preiser
6.12 c I.C. Talbot
6.12 D H.E. Gabbert
6.13 A C.A. Rubio
6.13 B L.H. Sobin
6.14 C.A. Rubio
6.15 C.A. Rubio

6.16 C.A. Rubio
6.17 A I.C. Talbot
6.17 B, D C.A. Rubio
6.17 C C.A. Rubio
6.18 C.A. Rubio
6.19 J.R. Jass
6.20 A I.C. Talbot
6.20 B L.H. Sobin
6.20 C C.A. Rubio
6.21 J.R. Jass
6.22 S.R. Hamilton
6.23 C. Fenoglio-Preiser
6.24 L.H. Sobin
6.25 A, B C. Capella
6.26 A, B L.H. Sobin
6.27 N.J. Carr
6.28 J.R. Jass
6.29 A C.A. Rubio
6.29 B C.A. Rubio
6.30 A C.A. Rubio
6.30 B J.R. Jass
6.30 C L.H. Sobin
6.31 C.A. Rubio
6.32 C.A. Rubio
6.33 N.J. Carr
6.34 L.H. Sobin
6.35 A, B C.A. Rubio
6.36 C.A. Rubio
6.37 L.H. Sobin
6.38 A L.H. Sobin
6.38 B I.C. Talbot
6.39 I.C. Talbot
6.40 A I.C. Talbot
6.40 B I.C. Talbot
6.41 J.R. Jass
6.42 A I.C. Talbot
6.42 B L.H. Sobin
6.43 A I.C. Talbot
6.43 B, C L.H. Sobin
6.44 A I.C. Talbot
6.44 B F. Fogt
6.45 L.H. Sobin
6.46 S.R. Hamilton
6.47 A C. Fenger
6.47 B I.C. Talbot
6.48 I.C. Talbot
6.49 I.C. Talbot
6.50 J.R. Jass
6.51 N.J. Carr
6.52 A, C P. Vogt
6.52 B C. Fenger
6.52 D I.C. Talbot
6.53 A, B L.H. Sobin
6.54 I.C. Talbot
6.55 I.C. Talbot
6.56 I.C. Talbot
6.57 I.C. Talbot
6.58 A, B I.C. Talbot
6.59 I.C. Talbot
6.60 A, B P. Polakis
6.61 I.C. Talbot
6.62 J.R. Jass
6.63 A, B J.R. Jass
6.64 J.R. Jass
6.65 A, B J.R. Jass
6.66 J.R. Jass

6.67 A, C I.C. Talbot
6.67 B J.R. Jass
6.68 A L.H. Sobin
6.68 B I.C. Talbot
6.69 C.A. Rubio
6.70 A, B F. Fogt
6.72 A J.R. Jass
6.72 B F. Fogt
6.73 I.C. Talbot
6.74 J.R. Jass
6.75 J.R. Jass
6.76 A, B J.R. Jass
6.77 L.H. Sobin
6.78 A C. Capella
6.78 B L.H. Sobin
6.79 C. Capella
6.80 N.J. Carr
6.81 A C. Fenoglio-Preiser
6.81 B L.H. Sobin
6.82 I.C. Talbot
6.83 I.C. Talbot
6.84 A. Wotherspoon
6.85 L.H. Sobin
6.86 J.R. Jass
6.87 L.H. Sobin
6.88 A, B M. Miettinen
6.89 C. Fenger
6.90 M. Miettinen
6.91 A, B L.H. Sobin

7.

7.01 Lippincott-Raven Publishers {490}
7.02 C. Fenger
7.03 C. Fenoglio-Preiser
7.04 C. Fenger
7.05 L.H. Sobin
7.06 C. Fenger
7.07 C. Fenger
7.08 C. Fenger
7.09 A, B C. Fenger
7.10 C. Fenger
7.11 I.C. Talbot
7.12 C. Fenger
7.13 C. Fenger
7.14 L.H. Sobin
7.15 C. Fenger
7.16 C. Fenger
7.17 A, B L.H. Sobin
7.18 L.H. Sobin
7.19 C. Fenger
7.20 J.R. Jass
7.21 A, B L.H. Sobin
7.22 I.C. Talbot
7.23 A-c I.C. Talbot

8.

8.01 IARC, Lyon
8.02 IARC, Lyon
8.03 IARC Press, Lyon
8.04 {1471}
8.05 P. Hainaut

8.06 A	A. Kadar
8.06 B, C	S. Hirohashi
8.06 D	P. Vogt
8.07	S. Hirohashi
8.08 A-E, I	S. Hirohashi
8.08 G, H	K. Ishak
8.09 A	K. Ishak
8.09 B	S. Hirohashi
8.10 A, B	S. Hirohashi
8.11 A, B	H.P. Fischer
8.12	K. Ishak
8.13	K. Ishak
8.14 A-C	S. Hirohashi
8.15 A, B	S. Hirohashi
8.16 A, B	S. Hirohashi
8.17	S. Hirohashi
8.18 A, B	I.R. Wanless
8.19	S. Hirohashi
8.20 A, B	I.R. Wanless
8.21 A, B	I.R. Wanless
8.22	S. Hirohashi
8.23	S. Hirohashi
8.24	R. Montesano
8.25	H. Ohgaki
8.26	H. Ohgaki
8.27	S. Hirohashi
8.28	V. Vatanasapt
8.29	IARC Press, Lyon {1471}
8.30	S. Kudo
8.31 A, B	Y. Nakanuma
8.32 A-C	Y. Nakanuma
8.33 A, B	Y. Nakanuma
8.34 A, B	Y. Nakanuma
8.35	Y. Nakanuma
8.36 A	Y. Nakanuma
8.36 B-D	K. Ishak
8.37	Y. Nakanuma
8.38 A, B	H.P. Fischer
8.39	H.P. Fischer
8.40 A, B	P. Anthony
8.41	Y. Nakanuma
8.42 A, B	H.P. Fischer
8.43 A, B	K. Ishak
8.44	J. Albores-Saavedra
8.45	Y. Nakanuma
8.46 A, B	Y. Nakanuma
8.47	K. Ishak
8.48	J.T. Stocker
8.49	J.T. Stocker
8.50 A, B	J.T. Stocker
8.51 A, B	J.T. Stocker
8.52	J.T. Stocker
8.53	K. Ishak
8.54	J.T. Stocker
8.55	J.T. Stocker
8.56	J.T. Stocker
8.57	J.T. Stocker
8.58 A, B	J.T. Stocker
8.59	J.T. Stocker
8.60	K. Ishak
8.61 A	J.T. Stocker
8.61 B-D	K. Ishak
8.62 A-D	K. Ishak
8.63 A, B	K. Ishak
8.64	P. Anthony

8.65	K. Ishak
8.66 A-F	K. Ishak
8.67 A-D	K. Ishak
8.68 A-C	K. Ishak
8.69	K. Ishak
8.70 A-D	K. Ishak
8.71 A	C. Wittekind
8.71 B-D	H.P. Fischer
8.72 A, B	K. Ishak
8.73 A, B	K. Ishak
8.74 A, B	P. Anthony
8.74 C	C. Fenoglio-Preiser
8.74 D	P. Anthony
8.74 E, F	A. Kadar
8.75 A, B	P. Anthony
8.76 A, B	P. Anthony
8.77	P. Anthony
8.78 A, B	P. Anthony
8.79	P. Anthony
8.80	P. Anthony

9.

9.01	J. Albores-Saavedra
9.02	N. Soehendra
9.03	N. Soehendra
9.04	J. Albores-Saavedra
9.05 A-C	J. Albores-Saavedra
9.06	J. Albores-Saavedra
9.07	J. Albores-Saavedra
9.08	J. Albores-Saavedra
9.09	J. Albores-Saavedra
9.10	J. Albores-Saavedra
9.11	J. Albores-Saavedra
9.12	J. Albores-Saavedra
9.13	J. Albores-Saavedra
9.14	J. Albores-Saavedra
9.15 A, B	J. Albores-Saavedra
9.16 A, B	J. Albores-Saavedra
9.17 A, B	J. Albores-Saavedra
9.18	H.P. Fischer
9.19 A-C	J. Albores-Saavedra
9.20	J. Albores-Saavedra
9.21 A-C	J. Albores-Saavedra
9.22	J. Albores-Saavedra

10.

10.01	IARC Press, Lyon
10.02	G. Kloppel
10.03 A, B	G. Kloppel
10.04	G. Kloppel
10.05	D.S. Longnecker
10.06 A	G. Kloppel
10.06 B	G. Kloppel
10.07	P. Vogt
10.08 A	P. Vogt
10.08 B	P. Vogt
10.09	P. Vogt
10.10 A	G. Zamboni
10.10 B	P. Vogt
10.11	G. Zamboni
10.12 A	G. Kloppel
10.12 B, C	N. J. Carr

10.13	G. Kloppel
10.14	G. Kloppel
10.15	G. Zamboni
10.16	G. Zamboni
10.17	P. Vogt
10.18	G. Zamboni
10.19	G. Kloppel
10.20	G. Zamboni
10.21 A, B	G. Zamboni
10.22	G. Kloppel
10.23 A	D.S. Longnecker
10.23 B	P. Vogt
10.24	G. Zamboni
10.25	G. Kloppel
10.26	G. Kloppel
10.27	G. Kloppel
10.28	G. Zamboni
10.29	D.S. Longnecker
10.30	D.S. Longnecker
10.31	G. Zamboni
10.32 A, B	G. Zamboni
10.33	D.S. Longnecker
10.34 A, B	G. Zamboni
10.35	D.S. Longnecker
10.36	P. Vogt
10.37	G. Kloppel
10.38 A-C	A. Kadar
10.38 D	P. Vogt

References

1. AJCC Cancer Staging Manual (1997). Fifth edition. Lippincott: Philadelphia.

2. Aaltonen LA, Peltomaki P, Mecklin JP, Jarvinen H, Jass JR, Green JS, Lynch HT, Watson P, Tallqvist G, Juhola M, et al. (1994). Replication errors in benign and malignant tumors from hereditary nonpolyposis colorectal cancer patients. *Cancer Res* 54: 1645-1648.

3. Aaltonen LA, Salovaara R, Kristo P, Canzian F, Hemminki A, Peltomaki P, Chadwick RB, Kaariainen H, Eskelinen M, Jarvinen H, Mecklin JP, de-la-Chapelle A (1998). Incidence of hereditary nonpolyposis colorectal cancer and the feasibility of molecular screening for the disease. *N Engl J Med* 338: 1481-1487.

4. Aarnio M, Salovaara R, Aaltonen LA, Mecklin JP, Jarvinen HJ (1997). Features of gastric cancer in hereditary non-polyposis colorectal cancer syndrome. *Int J Cancer* 74: 551-555.

5. Aarnio M, Sankila R, Pukkala E, Salovaara R, Aaltonen LA, de-la-Chapelle A, Peltomaki P, Mecklin JP, Jarvinen HJ (1999). Cancer risk in mutation carriers of DNA-mismatch-repair genes. *Int J Cancer* 81: 214-218.

6. Abbas Z, Hussainy AS, Ibrahim F, Jafri SM, Shaikh H, Khan AH (1995). Barrett's oesophagus and Helicobacter pylori. *J Gastroenterol Hepatol* 10: 331-333.

7. Abdelwahab IF, Klein MJ (1983). Granular cell tumor of the stomach: a case report and review of the literature. *Am J Gastroenterol* 78: 71-76.

8. Abe H, Kubota K, Mori M, Miki K, Minagawa M, Noie T, Kimura W, Makuuchi M (1998). Serous cystadenoma of the pancreas with invasive growth: benign or malignant? *Am J Gastroenterol* 93: 1963-1966.

9. Abel ME, Chiu YS, Russell TR, Volpe PA (1993). Adenocarcinoma of the anal glands. Results of a survey. *Dis Colon Rectum* 36: 383-387.

10. Abenoza P, Manivel JC, Wick MR, et a (1987). Hepatoblastoma: an immunohistochemical and ultrastructural study. *Hum Pathol* 18: 1025-1035.

11. Aberle H, Bauer A, Stappert J, Kispert A, Kemler R (1997). beta-catenin is a target for the ubiquitin-proteasome pathway. *EMBO J* 16: 3797-3804.

12. Abou SM, Baer HU, Friess H, Berberat P, Zimmermann A, Graber H, Gold LI, Korc M, Buchler MW (1999). Transforming growth factor betas and their signaling receptors in human hepatocellular carcinoma. *Am J Surg* 177: 209-215.

13. Acharya S, Wilson T, Gradia S, Kane MF, Guerrette S, Marsischky GT, Kolodner R, Fishel R (1996). hMSH2 forms specific mispair-binding complexes with hMSH3 and hMSH6. *Proc Natl Acad Sci U S A* 93: 13629-13634.

14. Achille A, Baron A, Zamboni G, Orlandini S, Bogina G, Bassi C, Iacono C, Scarpa A (1998). Molecular pathogenesis of sporadic duodenal cancer. *Br J Cancer* 77: 760-765.

15. Adam IJ (1994). Role of circumferential margin involvement in the local recurrence of rectal cancer. *Lancet* 344: 707-711.

16. Adler SN, Lyon DT, Sullivan PD (1982). Adenocarcinoma of the small bowel. Clinical features, similarity to regional enteritis, and analysis of 338 documented cases. *Am J Gastroenterol* 77: 326-330.

17. Adsay NV, Adair CF, Heffess CS, Klimstra DS (1996). Intraductal oncocytic papillary neoplasms of the pancreas. *Am J Surg Pathol* 20: 980-994.

18. Agarwal SK, Guru SC, Heppner C, Erdos MR, Collins RM, Park SY, Saggar S, Chandrasekharappa SC, Collins FS, Spiegel AM, Marx SJ, Burns AL (1999). Menin interacts with the AP1 transcription factor JunD and represses JunD-activated transcription. *Cell* 96: 143-152.

19. Agha FP, Weatherbee L, Sams JS (1984). Verrucous carcinoma of the esophagus. *Am J Gastroenterol* 79: 844-849.

20. Aghazarian SG, Birely BC (1993). Adenocarcinoma of the small intestine. *South Med J* 86: 1067-1069.

21. Ahlgren JD (1996). Epidemiology and risk factors in pancreatic cancer. *Semin Oncol* 23: 241-250.

22. Ahlman H, Wangberg B, Nilsson O (1993). Growth regulation in carcinoid tumors. *Endocrinol Metab Clin North Am* 22: 889-915.

23. Ahn YO, Park BJ, Yoo KY, Lee HS, Kim CY, Shigematsu T (1989). Incidence estimation of primary liver cancer among Koreans. *J Korean Cancer Assoc* 21: 241-248.

24. Ahnen DJ, Feigl P, Quan G, Fenoglio PC, Lovato LC, Bunn-PA J, Stemmerman G, Wells JD, Macdonald JS, Meyskens-FL J (1998). Ki-ras mutation and p53 overexpression predict the clinical behavior of colorectal cancer: a Southwest Oncology Group study. *Cancer Res* 58: 1149-1158.

25. Aiello A, Giardini R, Tondini C, Balzarotti M, Diss T, Peng H, Delia D, Pilotti S (1999). PCR-based clonality analysis: a reliable method for the diagnosis and follow-up monitoring of conservatively treated B-cell MALT lymphomas? *Histopathology* 34: 326-330.

26. Aikou T, Shimazu H (1989). Difference in main lymphatic pathways from the lower esophagus and gastric cardia. *Jpn J Surg* 19: 290-295.

27. Aird I, Bentall H (1953). A relationship between cancer of the stomach and ABO groups. *BMJ* 1: 799.

28. Akiyama H, Tsurumaru M, Udagawa H, Kajiyama Y (1994). Radical lymph node dissection for cancer of the thoracic esophagus. *Ann Surg* 220: 364-372.

29. Akiyama Y, Sato H, Yamada T, Nagasaki H, Tsuchiya A, Abe R, Yuasa Y (1997). Germ-line mutation of the hMSH6/GTBP gene in an atypical hereditary nonpolyposis colorectal cancer kindred. *Cancer Res* 57: 3920-3923.

30. Aktas D, Ayhan A, Tuncbilek E, Ozdemir A, Uzunalimoglu B (1998). No evidence for overexpression of the p53 protein and mutations in exons 4-9 of the p53 gene in a large family with adenomatous polyposis. *Am J Gastroenterol* 93: 1524-1526.

31. Akwari OE, Dozois RR, Weiland LH, Beahrs OH (1978). Leiomyosarcoma of the small and large bowel. *Cancer* 42: 1375-1384.

32. Al-Kaisi N, Siegler EE (1989). Fine needle aspiration cytology of the pancreas. *Acta Cytol* 33: 145-152.

33. Albores-Saavedra J, Angeles AA, Nadji M, Henson E, Alvarez L (1987). Mucinous cystadenocarcinoma of the pancreas. Morphologic and immunohistochemical observations. *Am J Surg Pathol* 11: 11-20.

34. Albores-Saavedra J, Henson DE (1986). Tumors of the Gallbladder and Extrahepatic Bile Ducts. AFIP: Washington, D.C.

35. Albores-Saavedra J, Henson DE, Klimstra D (1999). Tumors of the Gallbladder and Extrahepatic Bile Ducts. Atlas of Tumor Pathology. Third series, AFIP: Washington, D.C.

36. Albores-Saavedra J, Nadji M, Henson D, Angeles AA (1988). Enteroendocrine cell differentiation in carcinomas of the gallbladder and mucinous cystadenocarcinomas of the pancreas. *Pathol Res Pract* 183: 169-175.

37. Albores-Saavedra J, Soriano J, Larazza-Hernandez O, Aguirre J, Henson DE (1984). Oat cell carcinoma of the gallbladder. *Hum Pathol* 15: 639-646.

38. Albores SJ, Cruz OH, Alcantara VA, Henson DE (1981). Unusual types of gallbladder carcinoma. A report of 16 cases. *Arch Pathol Lab Med* 105: 287-293.

39. Albores SJ, Delgado R, Henson DE (1999). Well-differentiated adenocarcinoma, gastric foveolar type, of the extrahepatic bile ducts: A previously unrecognized and distinctive morphologic variant of bile duct carcinoma. *Ann Diagn Pathol* 3: 75-80.

40. Albores SJ, Molberg K, Henson DE (1996). Unusual malignant epithelial tumors of the gallbladder. *Semin Diagn Pathol* 13: 326-338.

41. Albores SJ, Nadji M, Henson DE (1986). Intestinal-type adenocarcinoma of the gallbladder. A clinicopathologic study of seven cases. *Am J Surg Pathol* 10: 19-25.

42. Albores-Saavedra J, Vardaman CJ, Vuitch F (1993). Non-neoplastic polypoid lesions and adenomas of the gallbladder. *Pathol Annu* 28 Pt 1: 145-177.

43. Albrecht S, von-Schweinitz D, Waha A, Kraus JA, von-Deimling A, Pietsch T (1994). Loss of maternal alleles on chromosome arm 11p in hepatoblastoma. *Cancer Res* 54: 5041-5044.

44. Allaire GS, Rabin L, Ishak KG, Sesterhenn IA (1988). Bile duct adenoma. A study of 152 cases. *Am J Surg Pathol* 12: 708-715.

45. Allgaier HP, Deibert P, Olschewski M, Spamer C, Blum U, Gerok W, Blum HE (1998). Survival benefit of patients with inoperable hepatocellular carcinoma treated by a combination of transarterial chemoembolization and percutaneous ethanol injection - a single-center analysis including 132 patients. *Int J Cancer* 79: 601-605.

46. Allison DC, Piantadosi S, Hruban RH, Dooley WC, Fishman EK, Yeo CJ, Lillemoe KD, Pitt HA, Lin P, Cameron JL (1998). DNA content and other factors associated with ten-year survival after resection of pancreatic carcinoma. *J Surg Oncol* 67: 151-159.

47. Almoguera C, Shibata D, Forrester K, Martin J, Arnheim N, Perucho M (1988). Most human carcinomas of the exocrine pancreas contain mutant c-K-ras genes. *Cell* 53: 549-554.

48. Alonsozana EL, Stamberg J, Kumar D, Jaffe ES, Medeiros LJ, Frantz C, Schiffer CA, O'Connell BA, Kernan S, Stass SA, Abruzzo LV (1997). Isochromosome 7q: the primary cytogenetic abnormality in hepatosplenic gammadelta T cell lymphoma. *Leukemia* 11: 1367-1372.

49. Alpert LC, Truong LD, Bossart MI, Spjut HJ (1988). Microcystic adenoma (serous cystadenoma) of the pancreas. A study of 14 cases with immunohistochemical and electron-microscopic correlation. *Am J Surg Pathol* 12: 251-263.

50. Alvarez CM, Fernandez FA, Rodilla IG, Val BJ (1996). Perianal basal cell carcinoma: a comparative histologic, immunohistochemical, and flow cytometric study with basaloid carcinoma of the anus. *Am J Dermatopathol* 18: 371-379.

51. Ambs S, Merriam WG, Bennett WP, Felley BE, Oguntusika MO, Oser SM, Klein S, Shields PG, Billiar TR, Harris CC (1998). Frequent nitric oxide synthase-2 expression in human colon adenomas: implication for tumor angiogenesis and colon cancer progression. *Cancer Res* 58: 334-341.

52. Amir G, Hurvitz H, Neeman Z, Rosenmann E (1986). Neonatal cytomegalovirus infection with pancreatic cystadenoma and nephrotic syndrome. *Pediat Pathol* 6: 393-401.

53. Andant C, Puy H, Deybach JC, Soule JC, Nordmann Y (1997). Occurrence of hepatocellular carcinoma in a case of hereditary coproporphyria. *Am J Gastroenterol* 92: 1389-1390.

54. Andersson JL, Sundin A, Valind S (1995). A method for coregistration of PET and MR brain images. *J Nucl Med* 36: 1307-1315.

55. Andoh A, Takaya H, Bamba M, Sakumoto H, Inoue T, Tujikawa T, Koyama S, Fujiyama Y, Bamba T (1998). Primary gastric Burkitt's lymphoma presenting with c-myc gene rearrangement. *J Gastroenterol* 33: 710-715.

56. Andres E, Herbrecht R, Campos F, Marcellin L, Oberling F (1997). Primary hepatic lymphoma associated with chronic hepatitis C. *Ann Med Intern* 148: 280-283.

57. Angeles AA, Quintanilla ML, Lariiva SJ (1991). Primary carcinoid of the common bile duct. Immunohistochemical characterization of a case and review of the literature. *Am J Clin Pathol* 96: 341-344.

58. Anon. (1976). Japanese Society for Esophageal Diseases. Guidelines for clinical and pathologic studies on carcinoma of the esophagus. *Jpn J Surg* 6: 69-78.

59. Anon. (1981). Angiosarcoma of the liver: a growing problem? *Br Med J Clin Res Ed* 282: 504-505.

60. Anon. (1987). Surveillance Epidemiology and End Results (SEER) Program: Division of cancer prevention and control. National Cancer Institute:

61. Anon. (1990). Primary liver cancer in Japan. Clinicopathologic features and results of surgical treatment. Liver Cancer Study Group of Japan. *Ann Surg* 211: 277-287.

62. Anon. (1993). American Joint Committee on Cancer. Manual for staging of cancer. 4th ed, JB Lippincott: Philadelphia.

63. Anon. (1995). Japanese Research Society for Gastric Cancer, Japanese Classification of Gastric Carcinoma. Kanehara: Tokyo.

64. Anon. (1995). Terminology of hepatocellular lesions. International Working Party. *Hepatology* 22: 983-993.

65. Anon. (1996). Classification of Pancreatic Carcinoma. Kanehara & Co., Ltd.: Tokyo.

66. Anon. (1997). UICC: TNM classification of malignant tumors. Wiley Press: New York.

67. Anon. (1998). Age-adjusted death rates by Prefecture, Special Report on Vital Statistics. In: *Statistics and Information Department, Minister's Secretariat, Ministry of Health and Welfare*, Health and Welfare Statistics Association: Tokyo.

68. Anon. (1998). Terminologia Anatomica: International Anatomical Terminology/FCAT. Thieme: Stuttgart.

69. Anon. (1999). Breast Cancer Linkage Consortium: Cancer risks in BRCA2 mutation carriers. *J Natl Cancer Inst* 91: 1310-1316.

70. Anon. (1999). SEER 1973-1996 Public Use CD-ROM. *http://www-seer.ims.nci.nih.gov/*

71. Anthony PP (1994). Tumours and tumour-like lesions of the liver and biliary tract. In: *Pathology of the liver*, MacSween RNM, Anthony PP, Scheuer PJ, Burt AD, Portmann BC (eds), Churchill Livingstone: Edinburgh, London, Madrid, Melbourne, New York, Tokyo.

72. Anthony PP, Drury RA (1970). Elastic vascular sclerosis of mesenteric blood vessels in argentaffin carcinoma. *J Clin Pathol* 23: 110-118.

73. Anthony PP, Vogel CL, Barker LF (1973). Liver cell dysplasia: a premalignant condition. *J Clin Pathol* 26: 217-223.

74. Anthony T, Simmang C, Lee EL, Turnage RH (1997). Perianal mucinous adenocarcinoma. *J Surg Oncol* 64: 218-221.

75. Antonioli DA, Wang HH (1997). Morphology of Barrett's esophagus and Barrett's-associated dysplasia and adenocarcinoma. *Gastroenterol Clin North Am* 26: 495-506.

76. Appelman HD (1990). Mesenchymal tumors of the gut: historical perspectives, new approaches, new results, and does it make any difference? *Monogr Pathol* 220-246.

77. Appelman HD, Helwig EB (1969). Glomus tumors of the stomach. *Cancer* 23: 203-213.

78. Appelman HD, Helwig EB (1976). Gastric epithelioid leiomyoma and leiomyosarcoma (leiomyoblastoma). *Cancer* 38: 708-728.

79. Appelman HD, Helwig EB (1977). Cellular leiomyomas of the stomach in 49 patients. *Arch Pathol Lab Med* 101: 373-377.

80. Appelman HD, Helwig EB (1977). Sarcomas of the stomach. *Am J Clin Pathol* 67: 2-10.

81. Arakawa M, Kage M, Sugihara S, Nakashima T, Suenaga M, Okuda K (1986). Emergence of malignant lesions within an adenomatous hyperplastic nodule in a cirrhotic liver. Observations in five cases. *Gastroenterology* 91: 198-208.

82. Arber DA, Kanel OW, van-de-Rijn M, Davis RE, Medeiros LJ, Jaffe ES, Weiss LM (1995). Frequent presence of the Epstein-Barr virus in inflammatory pseudotumor. *Hum Pathol* 26: 1093-1098.

83. Arber N, Neugut AI, Weinstein IB, Holt P (1997). Molecular genetics of small bowel cancer. *Cancer Epidemiol Biomarkers Prev* 6: 745-748.

84. Argatoff LH, Connors JM, Klasa RJ, Horsman DE (1997). Mantle cell lymphoma: a clinicopathologic study of 80 cases. *Blood* 89: 2067-2078.

85. Armitage NC, Jass JR, Richman PI, Thomson JP, Phillips RK (1989). Paget's disease of the anus: a clinicopathological study. *Br J Surg* 76: 60-63.

86. Arnulf B, Copie BC, Delfau LM, Lavergne SA, Bosq J, Wechsler J, Wassef M, Matuchansky C, Epardeau B, Stern M, Bagot M, Reyes F, Gaulard P (1998). Nonhepatosplenic gammadelta T-cell lymphoma: a subset of cytotoxic lymphoma with mucosal or skin localization. *Blood* 91: 1723-1731.

87. Arslan PC, Rugge M (1982). Gastric cancer: problems in histological diagnosis. *Histopathology* 6: 391-398.

88. Asaka M, Takeda H, Sugiyama T, Kato M (1997). What role does Helicobacter pylori play in gastric cancer? *Gastroenterology* 113: S56-S60.

89. Asbun J, Asbun HJ, Padilla A, Lang A, Bloch J (1992). Leiomyosarcoma of the rectum. *Am Surg* 58: 311-314.

90. Ascoli V, Lo Coco F, Artini M, Levrero M, Martelli M, Negro F (1998). Extranodal lymphomas associated with hepatitis C virus infection. *Am J Clin Pathol* 109: 600-609.

91. Ashida K, Terada T, Kitamura Y, Kaibara N (1998). Expression of E-cadherin, alpha-catenin, beta-catenin, and CD44 (standard and variant isoforms) in human cholangiocarcinoma: an immunohistochemical study. *Hepatology* 27: 974-982.

92. Ashton KM, Diss TC, Pan L, Du MQ, Isaacson PG (1997). Molecular analysis of T-cell clonality in ulcerative jejunitis and enteropathy-associated T-cell lymphoma. *Am J Pathol* 151: 493-498.

93. Attar BM, Levendoglu H, Rhee H (1990). Small cell carcinoma of the esophagus. Report of three cases and review of the literature. *Dig Dis Sci* 35: 145-152.

94. Au E, Ang PT, Tan P, Sng I, Fong CM, Chua EJ, Ong YW (1997). Gastrointestinal lymphoma- a review of 54 patients in Singapore. *Ann Acad Med (Singapore)* 26: 758-761.

95. Auer IA, Gascoyne RD, Connors JM, Cotter FE, Greiner TC, Sanger WG, Horsman DE (1997). t(11;18)(q21;q21) is the most common translocation in MALT lymphomas. *Ann Oncol* 8: 979-985.

96. Austin DF (1982). Etiological clues from descriptive epidemiology: squamous carcinoma of the rectum or anus. *Natl Cancer Inst Monogr* 62: 89-90.

97. Azar C, Van-de-Stadt J, Rickaert F, Deviere M, Baize M, Kloppel G, Gelin M, Cremer M (1996). Intraductal papillary mucinous tumours of the pancreas. Clinical and therapeutic issues in 32 patients. *Gut* 39: 457-464.

98. Azuma M, Sunagawa M, Shida S (1994). [Metastatic carcinoma of the appendix]. *Nippon Rinsho Suppl* 6: 725-727.

99. Bach N, Kahn H, Thung SN, Schaffner F, Kilon FM, Miller CM (1991). Hepatocellular carcinoma in a long-term survivor of intrahepatic biliary duct hypoplasia. *Am J Gastroenterol* 86: 1527-1530.

100. Backman H (1969). Metastases of malignant melanoma in the gastrointestinal tract. *Geriatrics* 24: 112-120.

101. Baert AL, Casteels-Van-Daele M, Broeckx J, Wijndaele L, Wilms G, Eggermont E (1983). Generalized juvenile polyposis with pulmonary arteriovenous malformations and hypertrophic osteoarthropathy. *Am J Roentgenol* 141: 661-

102. Baffa R, Veronese ML, Santoro R, Mandes B, Palazzo JP, Rugge M, Santoro E, Croce CM, Huebner K (1998). Loss of FHIT expression in gastric carcinoma. *Cancer Res* 58: 4708-4714.

103. Bagdi E, Diss TC, Munson P, Isaacson PG (1999). Mucosal intra-epithelial lymphocytes in enteropathy-associated T-cell lymphoma, ulcerative jejunitis, and refractory celiac disease constitute a neoplastic population. *Blood* 94: 260-264.

104. Bailey FW (1916). Pseudomyxoma cysts of the appendix and ruptured pseudomyxomatous ovarian cyst. *Surg Gynec Obstet* 23: 219-221.

105. Baisch H, Kloppel G, Reinke B (1990). DNA ploidy and cell-cycle analysis in pancreatic and ampullary carcinoma: flow cytometric study of formalin-fixed paraffin-embedded tissue. *Virchows Arch A Pathol Anat Histopathol* 417: 145-150.

106. Bakotic BW, Robinson MJ, Sturm PD, Hruban RH, Offerhaus GJ, Albores SJ (1999). Pyloric gland adenoma of the main pancreatic duct. *Am J Surg Pathol* 23: 227-231.

107. Bale SJ, Bale AE, Stewart K, Dachowski L, McBride OW, Glaser T, Green JE, Mulvihill JJ, Brandi ML, Sakaguchi K, et a (1989). Linkage analysis of multiple endocrine neoplasia type 1 with INT2 and other markers on chromosome 11. *Genomics* 4: 320-322.

108. Bando K, Nagai H, Matsumoto S, Koyama M, Kawamura N, Onda M, Emi M (1999). Identification of a 1-cM region of common deletion on 4q35 associated with progression of hepatocellular carcinoma. *Genes Chromosomes Cancer* 25: 284-289.

109. Banks ER, Frierson-HF J, Mills SE, George E, Zarbo RJ, Swanson PE (1992). Basaloid squamous cell carcinoma of the head and neck. A clinicopathologic and immunohistochemical study of 40 cases. *Am J Surg Pathol* 16: 939-946.

110. Banks PM, Chan J, Cleary ML, Delsol G, De-Wolf-Peeters C, Gatter K, Grogan TM, Harris NL, Isaacson PG, Jaffe ES, et a (1992). Mantle cell lymphoma. A proposal for unification of morphologic, immunologic, and molecular data. *Am J Surg Pathol* 16: 637-640.

111. Barnhill M, Hess E, Guccion JG, Nam LH, Bass BL, Patterson RH (1994). Tripartite differentiation in a carcinoma of the duodenum. *Cancer* 73: 266-272.

112. Barrett MT, Sanchez CA, Prevo LJ, Wong DJ, Galipeau C, Paulson TG, Rabinovitch PS, Reid BJ (1999). Evolution of neoplastic cell lineages in Barrett oesophagus. *Nat Genet* 22: 106-109.

113. Barrett WL, Callahan TD, Orkin BA (1998). Perianal manifestations of human immunodeficiency virus infection: experience with 260 patients. *Dis Colon Rectum* 41: 606-611.

114. Barrison IG, Foster S, Harris JW, Pinching AJ, Walker JG (1988). Upper gastrointestinal Kaposi's sarcoma in patients positive for HIV antibody without cutaneous disease. *Br Med J Clin Res Ed* 296: 92-93.

115. Barron RL, Manivel JC, Mendez SN, Jessurun J (1991). Carcinoid tumor of the common bile duct: evidence for its origin in metaplastic endocrine cells. *Am J Gastroenterol* 86: 1073-1076.

116. Barry RE, Read AE (1973). Coeliac disease and malignancy. *Q J Med* 42: 665-675.

117. Bartsch D, Bastian D, Bart P, Schudy A, Nies C, Kisker O, Wagner H, Rothmund M (1998). K-ras oncogene mutations indicate pancreatic duct type carcinomas as well as nonduct type neoplasias. *Virchows Arch A Pathol Anat Histopathol* 408: 361-374.

118. Basik M, Rodriguez BM, Penetrante R, Petrelli NJ (1995). Prognosis and recurrence patterns of anal adenocarcinoma. *Am J Surg* 169: 233-237.

119. Batge B, Bosslet K, Sedlacek HH, Kern HF, Kloppel G (1986). Monoclonal antibodies against CEA-related components discriminate between pancreatic duct type carcinomas and nonneoplastic duct lesions as well as ductal adenomas. *Virchows Arch A Pathol Anat Histopathol* 408: 361-374.

120. Battles OE, Page DL, Johnson JE (1997). Cytokeratins, CEA, and mucin histochemistry in the diagnosis and characterization of extramammary Paget's disease. *Am J Clin Pathol* 108: 6-12.

121. Bayon LG, Izquierdo MA, Sirovich I, van-Rooijen N, Beelen RH, Meijer S (1996). Role of Kupffer cells in arresting circulating tumor cells and controlling metastatic growth in the liver. *Hepatology* 23: 1224-1231.

122. Beck PL, Gill MJ, Sutherland LR (1996). HIV-associated non-Hodgkin's lymphoma of the gastrointestinal tract. *Am J Gastroenterol* 91: 2377-2381.

123. Beckers A, Abs R, Reyniers E, De-Boulle K, Stevenaert A, Heller FR, Kloppel G, Meurisse M, Willems PJ (1994). Variable regions of chromosome 11 loss in different pathological tissues of a patient with the multiple endocrine neoplasia type I syndrome. *J Clin Endocrinol Metab* 79: 1498-1502.

124. Behrens J, Jerchow BA, Wurtele M, Grimm J, Asbrand C, Wirtz R, Kuhl M, Wedlich D, Birchmeier W (1998). Functional interaction of an axin homolog, conductin, with beta-catenin, APC, and GSK3beta. *Science* 280: 596-599.

125. Benatti P, Roncucci L, Percesepe A, Viel A, Pedroni M, Tamassia MG, Vaccina F, Fante R, De-Pietri S, Ponz-de LM (1998). Small bowel carcinoma in hereditary nonpolyposis colorectal cancer. *Am J Gastroenterol* 93: 2219-2222.

126. Bengoechea O, Martinez P, Larrinaga B, Valerdi J, Borda F (1987). Hyperplastic polyposis of the colorectum and adenocarcinoma in a 24-year-old man. *Am J Surg Pathol* 11: 323-327.

127. Benjamin E, Wright DH (1980). Adenocarcinoma of the pancreas in childhood: a report of two cases. *Histopathology* 4: 87-104.

128. Berardi RS (1972). Carcinoid tumors of the colon (exclusive of the rectum): review of the literature. *Dis Colon Rectum* 15: 383-391.

129. Berezowski K, Stastny JF, Kornstein MJ (1996). Cytokeratins 7 and 20 and carcinoembryonic antigen in ovarian and colonic carcinoma. *Mod Pathol* 9: 426-429.

130. Berge T, Lundberg S (1977). Cancer in Malmo 1958-69. *Acta Pathol Microbiol Scand* S260: 140-149.

131. Bertoni F, Cazzaniga G, Bosshard G, Roggero E, Barbazza R, de-Boni M, Capella C, Pedrinis E, Cavalli F, Biondi A, Zucca E (1997). Immunoglobulin heavy chain diversity genes rearrangement pattern indicates that MALT-type gastric lymphoma B cells have undergone an antigen selection process. *Br J Haematol* 97: 830-836.

132. Bertoni G, Sassatelli R, Nigrisoli E, et al. (1995). First observation of microadenomas in the ileal mucosa of patients with familial adenomatous polyposis and colectomies. *Gastroenterology* 109: 374-380.

133. Bertram P, Treutner KH, Rubben A, Hauptmann S, Schumpelick V (1995). Invasive squamous-cell carcinoma in giant anorectal condyloma (Buschke-Lowenstein tumor). *Langenbecks Arch Chir* 380: 115-118.

134. Bertrand P, Tishkoff DX, Filosi N, Dasgupta R, Kolodner RD (1998). Physical interaction between components of DNA mismatch repair and nucleotide excision repair. *Proc Natl Acad Sci U S A* 95: 14278-14283.

135. Berx G, Becker KF, Hofler H, van-Roy F (1998). Mutations of the human E-cadherin (CDH1) gene. *Hum Mutat* 12: 226-237.

136. Bhathal PS, Hughes NR, Goodman ZD (1996). The so-called bile duct adenoma is a peribiliary gland hamartoma. *Am J Surg Pathol* 20: 858-864.

137. Bianchi L (1993). Glycogen storage disease I and hepatocellular tumours. *Eur J Pediatr* 152 Suppl 1: 1995.

138. Bickel A, Eitan A, Tsilman B, Cohen HI (1999). Low-grade B cell lymphoma of mucosa-associated lymphoid tissue (MALT) arising in the gallbladder. *Hepatogastroenterology* 46: 1643-1646.

139. Bierner-Huttmann AE, Walsh MD, McGuckin MA, Ajkioka Y, Watanabe H, Leggett BA, Jass JR (1999). Immunohistochemical staining patterns of MUC1, MUC2, MUC4, and MUC5AC mucins in hyperplastic polyps, serrated adenomas, and traditional adenomas of the colorectum. *J Histochem Cytochem* 47: 1039-1047.

140. Binkley GE, Derrick WA (1945). The association of squamous cancer with anal manifestations of lymphogranuloma venereum. *Am J Dig Dis* 12: 46-47.

141. Birch JM (1994). Li-Fraumeni syndrome. *Eur J Cancer* 30A: 1935-1941.

142. Birch JM, Blair V, Kelsey AM, Evans DG, Harris M, Tricker KJ, Varley JM (1998). Cancer phenotype correlates with constitutional TP53 genotype in families with the Li-Fraumeni syndrome. *Oncogene* 17: 1061-1068.

143. Bisgaard ML, Fenger K, Bulow S, Niebuhr E, Mohr J (1994). Familial adenomatous polyposis (FAP): frequency, penetrance, and mutation rate. *Hum Mutat* 3: 121-125.

144. Bishop AE, Hamid QA, Adams C, Bretherton WD, Jones PM, Denny P, Stamp GW, Hurt RL, Grimelius L, Harmar AJ, et a (1989). Expression of tachykinins by ileal and lung carcinoid tumors assessed by combined in situ hybridization, immunocytochemistry, and radioimmunoassay. *Cancer* 63: 1129-1137.

145. Bittinger A, Altekruger I, Barth P (1995). Clear cell carcinoma of the gallbladder. A histological and immunohistochemical study. *Pathol Res Pract* 191: 1259-1265.

146. Black WC (1968). Enterochromaffin cell types and corresponding carcinoid tumors. *Lab Invest* 19: 473-486.

147. Blackman E, Nash SV (1985). Diagnosis of duodenal and ampullary epithelial neoplasms by endoscopic biopsy: a clinicopathologic and immunohistochemical study. *Hum Pathol* 16: 901-910.

148. Blattner WA, Henson DE, Young RC, Fraumeni-JF J (1977). Malignant mesenchymoma and birth defects. Prenatal exposure to phenytoin. *JAMA* 238: 334-335.

149. Bloch MJ, Iozzo RV, Edmunds-LH J, Brooks JJ (1987). Polypoid synovial sarcoma of the esophagus. *Gastroenterology* 92: 229-233.

150. Blohme I, Brynger H (1985). Malignant disease in renal transplant patients. *Transplantation* 39: 23-25.

151. Blomjous JG, Hop WC, Langenhorst BL, ten-Kate FJ, Eykenboom WM, Tilanus HW (1992). Adenocarcinoma of the gastric cardia. Recurrence and survival after resection. *Cancer* 70: 569-574.

152. Blot WJ, Devesa SS, Kneller RW, Fraumeni-JF J (1991). Rising incidence of adenocarcinoma of the esophagus and gastric cardia. *JAMA* 265: 1287-1289.

153. Blot WJ, Dhillon AP, Fraumeni-JF J (1993). Continuing climb in rates of esophageal adenocarcinoma: an update. *JAMA* 270: 1320-1320.

154. Boardman LA, Thibodeau SN, Schaid DJ, Lindor NM, McDonnell SK, Burgart LJ, Ahlquist DA, Podratz KC, Pittelkow M, Hartmann LC (1998). Increased risk for cancer in patients with the Peutz-Jeghers syndrome. *Ann Intern Med* 128: 896-899.

155. Boch JA, Shields HM, Antonioli DA, Zwas F, Sawhney RA, Trier JS (1997). Distribution of cytokeratin markers in Barrett's specialized columnar epithelium. *Gastroenterology* 112: 760-765.

156. Bodmer WF, Bailey CJ, Bodmer J, Bussey HJ, Ellis A, Gorman P, Lucibello FC, Murday VA, Rider SH, Scambler P, et a (1987). Localization of the gene for familial adenomatous polyposis on chromosome 5. *Nature* 328: 614-616.

157. Boey J, Choi TK, Wong J, Ong GB (1981). The surgical management of anorectal malignant melanoma. *Aust N Z J Surg* 51: 132-136.

158. Bognel C, Lasser P, Zimmermann P (1992). [Gastric metastases. Apropos of 17 cases]. *Ann Chir* 46: 436-441.

159. Bogomoletz WV (1992). Solitary rectal ulcer syndrome. Mucosal prolapse syndrome. *Pathol Annu* 27 Pt 1: 1995.

160. Bogomoletz WV, Adnet JJ, Widgren S, Stavrou M, McLaughlin JE (1980). Cystadenoma of the pancreas: a histological, histochemical and ultrastructural study of seven cases. *Histopathology* 4: 309-320.

161. Bogomoletz WV, Molas G, Gayet B, Potet F (1989). Superficial squamous cell carcinoma of the esophagus. A report of 76 cases and review of the literature. *Am J Surg Pathol* 13: 535-546.

162. Bogomoletz WV, Potet F, Molas G (1985). Condylomata acuminata, giant condyloma acuminatum (Buschke-Loewenstein tumour) and verrucous squamous carcinoma of the perianal and anorectal region: a continuous precancerous spectrum? *Histopathology* 9: 155-169.

163. Boige V, Laurent PP, Fouchet P, Flejou JF, Monges G, Bedossa P, Bioulac SP, Capron F, Schmitz A, Olschwang S, Thomas G (1997). Concerted nonsyntenic allelic losses in hyperploid hepatocellular carcinoma as determined by a high-resolution allelotype. *Cancer Res* 57: 1986-1990.

164. Boland CR, Thibodeau SN, Hamilton SR, Sidransky D, Eshleman JR, Burt RW, Meltzer SJ, Rodriguez BM, Fodde R, Ranzani GN, Srivastava S (1998). A National Cancer Institute Workshop on Microsatellite Instability for cancer detection and familial predisposition: development of international criteria for the determination of microsatellite instability in colorectal cancer. *Cancer Res* 58: 5248-5257.

165. Boman BM, Moertel CG, O'Connell MJ, Scott M, Weiland LH, Beart RW, Gunderson LL, Spencer RJ (1984). Carcinoma of the anal canal. A clinical and pathologic study of 188 cases. *Cancer* 54: 114-125.

166. Bombi JA, Milla A, Badal JM, Piulachs J, Estape J, Cardesa A (1984). Papillary-cystic neoplasm of the pancreas. Report of two cases and review of the literature. *Cancer* 54: 780-784.

167. Bommer G, Friedel U, Heitz PU, Kloppel G (1980). Pancreatic PP cell distribution and hyperplasia: immunocytochemical morphology in normal pancreas, chronic pancreatitis and pancreatic carcinoma. *Virchows Arch A Pathol Anat Histopathol* 387: 319-331.

168. Bonavina L, Fociani P, Asnaghi D, Ferrero S (1998). Synovial sarcoma of the esophagus simulating achalasia. *Dis Esophagus* 11: 268-271.

169. Bonin SR, Pajak TF, Russell AH, Coia LR, Paris KJ, Flam MS, Sauter ER (1999). Overexpression of p53 protein and outcome of patients treated with chemoradiation for carcinoma of the anal canal: a report of randomized trial RTOG 87-04. Radiation Therapy Oncology Group. *Cancer* 85: 1226-1233.

170. Boor PJ, Swanson MR (1979). Papillary-cystic neoplasm of the pancreas. *Am J Surg Pathol* 3: 69-75.

171. Bordi C, D'Adda T, Azzoni C, Canavese G, Brandi ML (1998). Gastrointestinal endocrinetumors: recent developments. *Endocr Pathol* 9: 99-115.

172. Bordi C, D'Adda T, Azzoni C, Pilato FP, Caruana P (1995). Hypergastrinemia and gastric enterochromaffin-like cells. *Am J Surg Pathol* 19 Suppl 1: S8-19.

173. Bordi C, Falchetti A, Azzoni C, D'Adda T, Canavese G, Guariglia A, Santini D, Tomassetti P, Brandi ML (1997). Aggressive forms of gastric neuroendocrine tumors in multiple endocrine neoplasia type I. *Am J Surg Pathol* 21: 1075-1082.

174. Borja ER, Hori JM, Pugh RP (1975). Metastatic carcinomatosis of the liver mimicking cirrhosis: case report and review of the literature. *Cancer* 35: 445-449.

175. Borrmann R (1926). Geshwulste des Magens und Duodenums. In: *Handbuch der Speziellen Pathologischen Anatomie und Histologie*, Henke F, Lubarsch O (eds), Springer-Verlag: Berlin.

176. Bosch FX (1997). Global epidemiology in hepatocellular carcinoma. In: *Liver Cancer*, Okuda K, Tabor E (eds), Churchill Livingstone: New York.

177. Bosl GJ, Yagoda A, Camara LL (1980). Malignant carcinoid of the gallbladder: third reported case and review of the literature. *J Surg Oncol* 13: 215-222.

178. Bouzourene H, Haefliger T, Delacretaz F, Saraga E (1999). The role of Helicobacter pylori in primary gastric MALT lymphoma. *Histopathology* 34: 118-123.

179. Bove KE, Soukup S, Ballard ET, Ryckman F (1996). Hepatoblastoma in a child with trisomy 18: cytogenetics, liver anomalies, and literature review. *Pediatr Pathol Lab Med* 16: 253-262.

180. Bowdler DA, Leach RD (1982). Metastatic intrabiliary melanoma. *Clin Oncol* 8: 251-255.

181. Bradbear RA, Bain C, Siskind V, Schofield FD, Webb S, Axelsen EM, Halliday JW, Bassett ML, Powell LW (1985). Cohort study of internal malignancy in genetic hemochromatosis and other chronic nonalcoholic liver diseases. *J Natl Cancer Inst* 75: 81-84.

182. Brady MS, Kavolius JP, Quan SH (1995). Anorectal melanoma. A 64-year experience at Memorial Sloan-Kettering Cancer Center. *Dis Colon Rectum* 38: 146-151.

183. Brainard JA, Goldblum JR (1997). Stromal tumors of the jejunum and ileum: a clinicopathologic study of 39 cases. *Am J Surg Pathol* 21: 407-416.

184. Brat DJ, Hahn SA, Griffin CA, Yeo CJ, Kern SE, Hruban RH (1997). The structural basis of molecular genetic deletions. An integration of classical cytogenetic and molecular analyses in pancreatic adenocarcinoma. *Am J Pathol* 150: 383-391.

185. Brat DJ, Lillemoe KD, Yeo CJ, Warfield PB, Hruban RH (1998). Progression of pancreatic intraductal neoplasias to infiltrating adenocarcinoma of the pancreas. *Am J Surg Pathol* 22: 163-169.

186. Breivik J, Gaudernack G (1999). Genomic instability, DNA methylation, and natural selection in colorectal carcinogenesis. *Semin Cancer Biol* 9: 245-254.

187. Brenes F, Ruiz B, Correa P, Hunter F, Rhamakrishnan T, Fontham E, Shi TY (1993). Helicobacter pylori causes hyperproliferation of the gastric epithelium: pre- and post-eradication indices of proliferating cell nuclear antigen. *Am J Gastroenterol* 88: 1870-1875.

188. Bressac B, Kew M, Wands J, Ozturk M (1991). Selective G to T mutations of p53 gene in hepatocellular carcinoma from southern Africa. *Nature* 350: 429-431.

189. Bridge MF, Perzin KH (1975). Primary adenocarcinoma of the jejunum and ileum. A clinicopathologic study. *Cancer* 36: 1876-1887.

190. Briggs JC, Ibrahim NB (1983). Oat cell carcinomas of the oesophagus: a clinicopathological study of 23 cases. *Histopathology* 7: 261-277.

191. Brockie E, Anand A, Albores SJ (1998). Progression of atypical ductal hyperplasia/carcinoma in situ of the pancreas to invasive adenocarcinoma. *Ann Diagn Pathol* 2: 286-292.

192. Brofeldt SA (1927). Zur Pathogenese des Plattenepithelkrebses der Pars analis recti. *Acta Soc Med Fenn Duodecim* 8: 3-15.

193. Bronner CE, Baker SM, Morrison PT, Warren G, Smith LG, Lescoe MK, Kane M, Earabino C, Lipford J, Lindblom A, et a (1994). Mutation in the DNA mismatch repair gene homologue hMLH1 is associated with hereditary non-polyposis colon cancer. *Nature* 368: 258-261.

194. Broome U, Lofberg R, Veress B, Eriksson LS (1995). Primary sclerosing cholangitis and ulcerative colitis: evidence for increased neoplastic potential. *Hepatology* 22: 1404-1408.

195. Brown WM, Henderson JM, Kennedy JC (1990). Carcinoid tumor of the bile duct. A case report and literature review. *Am Surg* 56: 343-346.

196. Brownstein MH, Wolf M, Bikowski JB (1978). Cowden's disease: a cutaneous marker of breast cancer. *Cancer* 41: 2393-2398.

197. Buchler M, Malfertheiner P, Baczako K, Krautzberger W, Beger HG (1985). A metastatic endocrine-neurogenic tumor of the ampulla of Vater with multiple endocrine immunoreaction - malignant paraganglioma? *Digestion* 31: 54-59.

198. Buchwalter JA, Jurayi MN (1957). Relationship of chronic anorectal disease to carcinoma. *Arch Surg* 75: 352-361.

199. Buckley JA, Fishman EK (1998). CT evaluation of small bowel neoplasms: spectrum of disease. *Radiographics* 18: 379-392.

200. Buetow KH, Murray JC, Israel JL, London WT, Smith M, Kew M, Blanquet V, Brechot C, Redeker A, Govindarajah S (1989). Loss of heterozygosity and tumor suppressor gene responsible for primary hepatocellular carcinoma. *Proc Natl Acad Sci U S A* 86: 8852-8856.

201. Buetow PC, Rao P, Thompson LD (1998). From the Archives of the AFIP. Mucinous cystic neoplasms of the pancreas: radiologic-pathologic correlation. *Radiographics* 18: 433-449.

202. Bulow C, Bulow S (1997). Is screening for thyroid carcinoma indicated in familial adenomatous polyposis? The Leeds Castle Polyposis Group. *Int J Colorectal Dis* 12: 240-242.

203. Bulow S (1987). Familial polyposis coli. *Dan Med Bull* 34: 1-15.

204. Bulow S, Alm T, Fausa O, Hultcrantz R, Jarvinen H, Vasen H (1995). Duodenal adenomatosis in familial adenomatous polyposis. DAF Project Group. *Int J Colorectal Dis* 10: 43-46.

205. Bulow S, Holm NV, Hauge M (1986). The incidence and prevalence of familial polyposis coli in Denmark. *Scand J Soc Med* 14: 67-74.

206. Burke AP, Helwig EB (1989). Gangliocytic paraganglioma. *Am J Clin Pathol* 92: 1-9.

207. Burke AP, Shekitka KM, Sobin LH (1991). Small cell carcinoma of the large intestine. *Am J Clin Pathol* 95: 315-321.

208. Burke AP, Sobin LH, Federspiel BH, Shekitka KM, Helwig EB (1990). Carcinoid tumors of the duodenum. A clinicopathologic study of 99 cases. *Arch Pathol Lab Med* 114: 700-704.

209. Burke AP, Sobin LH, Federspiel BH, Shekitka KM, Helwig EB (1990). Goblet cell carcinoids and related tumors of the vermiform appendix. *Am J Clin Pathol* 94: 27-35.

210. Burke AP, Sobin LH, Shekitka KM, Federspiel BH, Helwig EB (1990). Somatostatin-producing duodenal carcinoids in patients with von Reckinghausen's neurofibromatosis. A predilection for black patients. *Cancer* 65: 1591-1595.

211. Burke AP, Thomas RM, Elsayed AM, Sobin LH (1997). Carcinoids of the jejunum and ileum: an immunohistochemical and clinicopathologic study of 167 cases. *Cancer* 79: 1086-1093.

212. Burke AP, Shepherd N, Mann CV (1987). Carcinoid tumours of the rectum and anus. *Br J Surg* 74: 358-361.

213. Burns WA, Matthews MJ, Hamosh M, Weide GV, Blum R, Johnson FB (1974). Lipase-secreting acinar cell carcinoma of the pancreas with polyarthropathy. A light and electron microscopic, histochemical, and biochemical study. *Cancer* 33:

214. Burt EC, McGown G, Thorncroft M, James LA, Birch JM, Varey JM (1999). Exclusion of the genes CDKN2 and PTEN as causative gene defects in Li-Fraumeni syndrome. *Br J Cancer* 80: 9-10.

215. Burt RW, Bishop DT, Lynch HT, Rozen P, Winawer SJ (1990). Risk and surveillance of individuals with heritable factors for colorectal cancer. WHO Collaborating Centre for the Prevention of Colorectal Cancer. *Bull World Health Organ* 68: 655-665.

216. Bussey HJ (1975). Familial polyposis coli. Family studies, histopathology, differential diagnosis and results of treatment. The John Hopkins University Press: Baltimore.

217. Bussey HJ, Veale AM, Morson BC (1978). Genetics of gastrointestinal polyposis. *Gastroenterology* 74: 1325-1330.

218. Butturini G, Bassi C, Falconi M, Salvia R, Caldiron E, Iannucci A, Zamboni G, Graziani R, Procacci C, Pederzoli P (1998). Surgical treatment of pancreatic metastases from renal cell carcinomas. *Dig Surg* 15: 241-246.

219. Cadiot G, Laurent PP, Thuille B, Lehy T, Mignon M, Olschwang S (1993). Is the multiple endocrine neoplasia type I gene a suppressor for fundic argyrophil tumors in the Zollinger-Ellison syndrome? *Gastroenterology* 105: 579-582.

220. Cagir B, Nagy MW, Topham A, Rakinic J, Fry RD (1999). Adenosquamous carcinoma of the colon, rectum, and anus: epidemiology, distribution, and survival characteristics. *Dis Colon Rectum* 42: 258-263.

221. Calaluce R (1998). Micrometastasis in colorectal carcinoma: a review. *J Surg Oncol* 67: 194-202.

222. Caldarola VT, Jackman RJ, Moertel GC, Dockerty MB (1964). Carcinoid tumors of rectum. *Am J Surg* 107: 844-849.

223. Caldas C, Hahn SA, da-Costa LT, Redston MS, Schutte M, Seymour AB, Weinstein CL, Hruban RH, Yeo CJ, Kern SE (1994). Frequent somatic mutations and homozygous deletions of the p16 (MTS1) gene in pancreatic adenocarcinoma [published erratum in Nat Genet;8: 410]. *Nat Genet* 8: 27-32.

224. Caldas C, Hahn SA, Hruban RH, Redston MS, Yeo CJ, Kern SE (1994). Detection of K-ras mutations in the stool of patients with pancreatic adenocarcinoma and pancreatic ductal hyperplasia. *Cancer Res* 54: 3568-3573.

225. Calvert RJ, Evans PA, Randerson JA, Jack AS, Morgan GJ, Dixon MF (1996). The significance of B-cell clonality in gastric lymphoid infiltrates. *J Pathol* 180: 26-32.

226. Cameron AJ, Carpenter HA (1997). Barrett's esophagus, high-grade dysplasia, and early adenocarcinoma: a pathological study. *Am J Gastroenterol* 92: 586-591.

227. Cammarota G, Fedeli G, Tursi A, Corazza GR, Gasbarrini G (1996). Coeliac disease and follicular gastritis. *Lancet* 347: 268

228. Campbell WJ, Spence RA, Parks TG (1994). Familial adenomatous polyposis. *Br J Surg* 81: 1722-1733.

229. Cantrell BB, Cubilla AL, Erlandson RA, Fortner J, Fitzgerald PJ (1981). Acinar cell cystadenocarcinoma of human pancreas. *Cancer* 47: 410-416.

230. Cantril ST, Green JP, Schall GL, Schaupp WC (1983). Primary radiation therapy in the treatment of anal carcinoma. *Int J Radiat Oncol Biol Phys* 9: 1271-1278.

231. Cantu JM, Rivera H, Ocampo-Campos R, Bedolla N, Cortes-Gallegos V, Gonzalez-Mendoza A, Diaz M, Hernandez A (1980). Peutz-Jeghers syndrome with feminizing sertoli cell tumor. *Endocr Pathol* 2: 92-110.

232. Capella C, Polak JM, Timson CM, Frigerio B, Solcia E (1980). Gastric carcinoids of argyrophil ECL cells. *Ultrastruct Pathol* 1: 411-418.

233. Capella C, Riva C, Rindi G, Sessa F, Usellini L, Chiaravalli A, Carnevali L, Solcia E (1991). Histopathology, hormone products and clinico-pathologic profile of endocrine tumours of the upper small intestine. A study of 44 cases. *Endocr Pathol* 2: 92-110.

234. Capellari JO, Geisinger KR, Albertson DA, Wolfman NT, Kute TE (1990). Malignant papillary cystic tumor of the pancreas. *Cancer* 66: 193-198.

235. Caracciolo G, Vicedomini D, Di-Blasi A, Indolfi P, Casale F, De-Dominicis G, Saggiomo G, Greco N (1995). Adenocarcinoma of the pancreas in childhood (pancreatoblastoma): report of a case with good response to chemotherapy. *Tumori* 81: 391-394.

236. Carbone A, Gloghini A, Gaidano G, Cilia AM, Bassi P, Polito P, Vaccher E, Saglio G, Tirelli U (1995). AIDS-related Burkitt's lymphoma. Morphologic and immunophenotypic study of biopsy specimens. *Am J Clin Pathol* 103: 561-567.

237. Carbone A, Gloghini A, Gaidano G, Franceschi S, Capello D, Drexler HG, Falini B, Dalla FR (1998). Expression status of BCL-6 and syndecan-1 identifies distinct histogenetic subtypes of Hodgkin's disease. *Blood* 92: 2220-2228.

238. Carbonnel F, Grollet BL, Brouet JC, Teilhac MF, Cosnes J, Angonin R, Deschaseaux M, Chatelet FP, Gendre JP, Sigaux F (1998). Are complicated forms of celiac disease cryptic T-cell lymphomas? *Blood* 92: 3879-3886.

239. Carbonnel F, Lavergne A, Messing B, Tsapis A, Berger R, Galian A, Nemeth J, Brouet JC, Rambaud JC (1994). Extensive small intestinal T-cell lymphoma of low-grade malignancy associated with a new chromosomal translocation. *Cancer* 73: 1286-1291.

240. Cario E, Runzi M, Metz K, Layer P, Goebell H (1997). Diagnostic dilemma in pancreatic lymphoma. Case report and review. *Int J Pancreatol* 22: 67-71.

241. Carl W, Sullivan MA, Herrera L (1990). Dental abnormalities and bone lesions in patients with familial adenomatous polyposis. In: *Familial Adenomatous Polyposis*, Herrera L (ed), Alan R. Liss, Inc.: New York.

242. Carlson GJ, Nivatvongs S, Snover DC (1984). Colorectal polyps in Cowden's disease (multiple hamartoma syndrome). *Am J Surg Pathol* 8: 763-770.

243. Carneiro F (1997). The distinction between dysplasia and truly invasive cancer. Classification of gastric carcinomas. *Curr Diagn Pathol* 4: 51-59.

244. Carneiro F, Amado M, Lago P, Taveira GA, Amil M, Barreira R, Soares J, Pinho C (1996). Helicobacter pylori infection and blood groups. *Am J Gastroenterol* 91: 2646-2647.

245. Carneiro F, Sobrinho SM (1996). Metastatic pattern of gastric carcinoma. *Hum Pathol* 27: 213-214.

246. Carney JA (1972). The triad of gastric epithelioid leiomyosarcoma, pulmonary chondroma and functioning extra-adrenal paraganglioma. *Medicine* 62: 159-169.

247. Caroli J, Hadchouel P, Mercadier M, Lageron A (1975). [Benign papilloma of Wirsung's duct? Diagnosis by retrograde catheterization]. *Med Chir Dig* 4: 163-166.

248. Carr NJ, Bratthauer GL, Lichy JH, Taubenberger JK, Monihan JM, Sobin LH (1994). Squamous cell papillomas of the esophagus: a study of 23 lesions for human papillomavirus by in situ hybridazation and the polymerase chain reaction. *Hum Pathol* 25: 536-540.

249. Carr NJ, Monihan JM, Sobin LH (1994). Squamous cell papilloma of the esophagus: a clinicopathologic and follow-up study of 25 cases. *Am J Gastroenterol* 89: 245-248.

250. Carr NJ, Sobin LH (1995). Epithelial noncarcinoid tumors and tumor-like lesions of the appendix. *Cancer* 76: 2383-2384.

251. Carr NJ, Sobin LH (1996). Unusual tumors of the appendix and pseudomyxoma peritonei. *Semin Diagn Pathol* 13: 314-325.

252. Carriaga MT, Henson DE (1995). Liver, gallbladder, extrahepatic bile ducts, and pancreas. *Cancer* 75: 171-190.

253. Carter KJ, Schaffer HA, Ritchie WP Jr (1984). Early gastric cancer. *Ann Surg* 199: 604-609.

254. Carter PS, Sheffield JP, Shepherd N, Melcher DH, Jenkins D, Ewings P, Talbot I, Northover JM (1994). Interobserver variation in the reporting of the histopathological grading of anal intraepithelial neoplasia. *J Clin Pathol* 47: 1032-1034.

255. Carvalho B, Seruca R, Carneiro F, Buys CH, Kok K (1999). Substantial reduction of the gastric carcinoma critical region at 6916.3-923.1. *Genes Chromosomes Cancer* 26: 29-34.

256. Cary NR, Barron DJ, McGoldrick JP, Wells FC (1993). Combined oesophageal adenocarcinoma and carcinoid in Barrett's oesophagitis: potential role of enterochromaffin-like cells in oesophageal malignancy. *Thorax* 48: 404-405.

257. Casadei R, Santini D, Greco VM, Piana S, Okoro HU, Conti A, Marrano D (1997). Macrocystic serous cystadenoma of the pancreas. Diagnostic, therapeutic and pathological considerations of three cases. *Ital J Gastroenterol Hepatol* 29: 54-57.

258. Caspari R, Olschwang S, Friedl W, Mandl M, Boisson C, Boker T, Augustin A, Kadmon M, Moslein G, Thomas G, et a (1995). Familial adenomatous polyposis: desmoid tumours and lack of ophthalmic lesions (CHRPE) associated with APC mutations beyond codon 1444. *Hum Mol Genet* 4: 337-340.

259. Castella EM, Ariza A, Ojanguren I, Mate JL, Roca X, Fernandez VA, Navas PJ (1996). Differential expression of CD44v6 in adenocarcinoma of the pancreas: an immunohistochemical study. *Virchows Arch* 429: 191-195.

260. Castrillo JM, Montalban C, Abraira V, Carrion R, Cruz MA, Larana JG, Menarguez J, Bellas C, Piris MA, Gomez MF, Serrano M, Rivas C (1996). Evaluation of the international index in the prognosis of high grade gastric malt lymphoma. *Leuk Lymphoma* 24: 159-163.

261. Castroagudin JF, Gonzalez-Quintela A, Fraga M, Forteza J, Barrio E (1999). Presentation of T-cell-rich B-cell lymphoma mimicking acute hepatitis. *Hepatogastroenterology* 46: 1710-1713.

262. Cavenee WK, Burger PC, van Meir EG (2000). Turcot Syndrome. In: *Pathology and Genetics of Tumours of the Nervous System*, Kleihues P, Cavenee WK (eds), pp. 238-239, IARC Press: Lyon.

263. Celli A, Que FG (1998). Dysregulation of apoptosis in the cholangiopathies and cholangiocarcinoma. *Semin Liver Dis* 18: 177-185.

264. Censini S, Lange C, Xiang Z, Crabtree JE, Ghiara P, Borodovsky M, Rappuoli R, Covacci A (1996). cag, a pathogenicity island of Helicobacter pylori, encodes type I-specific and disease-associated virulence factors. *Proc Natl Acad Sci U S A* 93: 14648-14653.

265. Cerar A, Jutersek A, Vidmar S (1991). Adenoid cystic carcinoma of the esophagus. A clinicopathologic study of three cases. *Cancer* 67: 2159-2164.

266. Cerottini JP, Caplin S, Pampallona S, Givel JC (1999). Prognostic factors in colorectal cancer. *Oncol Rep* 6: 409-414.

267. Cetta F, Montalto G, Petracci M (1997). Hepatoblastoma and APC gene mutation in familial adenomatous polyposis. *Gut* 41: 417.

268. Cetta F, Toti P, Petracci M, Montalto G, Disanto A, Lore F, Fusco A (1997). Thyroid carcinoma associated with familial adenomatous polyposis. *Histopathology* 31: 231-236.

269. Chalasani N, Wo JM, Hunter JG, Waring JP (1997). Significance of intestinal metaplasia in different areas of esophagus including esophagogastric junction. *Dig Dis Sci* 42: 603-607.

270. Chan WY, Wong N, Chan AB, Chow JH, Lee JC (1998). Consistent copy number gain in chromosome 12 in primary diffuse large cell lymphomas of the stomach. *Am J Pathol* 152: 11-16.

271. Chandrasekharappa SC, Guru SC, Manickam P, Olufemi SE, Collins FS, Emmert BM, Debelenko LV, Zhuang Z, Lubensky IA, Crabtree JS, Wang Y, Roe BA, Weisemann J, Boguski MS, Agarwal SK, Kester MB, Kim YS, Heppner C, Dong Q, Spiegel AM, Burns AL, Marx SJ (1997). Positional cloning of the gene for multiple endocrine neoplasia-type 1. *Science* 276: 404-407.

272. Chandrasoma P (1997). Pathophysiology of Barrett's esophagus. *Semin Thorac Cardiovasc Surg* 9: 270-278.

273. Chang CH, Perrin EV, Hertzler J, Brough AJ (1980). Cystadenoma of the pancreas with cytomegalovirus infection in a female infant. *Arch Pathol Lab Med* 104: 7-8.

274. Chang CS, Chen LT, Yang YC, Lin JT, Chang KC, Wang JT (1999). Isolation of Helicobacter pylori protein, FldA, associated with mucosa-associated lymphoid tissue lymphoma of the stomach. *Gastroenterology* 117: 82-88.

275. Chang MH, Chen CJ, Lai MS, Hsu HM, Wu TC, Kong MS, Liang DC, Shau WY, Chen DS (1997). Universal hepatitis B vaccination in Taiwan and the incidence of hepatocellular carcinoma in children. Taiwan Childhood Hepatoma Study Group. *N Engl J Med* 336: 1855-1859.

276. Chang Y, Cesarman E, Pessin MS, Lee F, Culpepper J, Knowles DM, Moore PS (1994). Identification of herpesvirus-like DNA sequences in AIDS-associated Kaposi's sarcoma. *Science* 266: 1865-1869.

277. Chanvitan A, Nekarda H, Casson AG (1995). Prognostic value of DNA index, S-phase fraction and p53 protein accumulation after surgical resection of esophageal squamous-cell carcinomas in Thailand. *Int J Cancer* 63: 381-386.

278. Chao DT, Korsmeyer SJ (1998). BCL-2 family: regulators of cell death. *Annu Rev Immunol* 16: 1998.

279. Chapman CJ, Dunn-Walters DK, Stevenson FK, Hussell T, Isaacson PG, Spencer J (1996). Sequence analysis of immunoglobulin genes that encode autoantibodies expressed by lymphomas of mucosa associated lymphoid tissue. *J Clin Mol Biol* 49: M29-M32.

280. Chapman PD, Church W, Burn J, Gunn A (1989). The detection of congenital hypertrophy of retinal pigment epithelium (CHRPE) by indirect ophthalmoscopy: a reliable clinical feature of familial adenomatous polyposis. *Br Med J* 298: 353-354.

281. Charlotte F, L'Hermine A, Martin N, Geleyn Y, Nollet M, Gaulard P, Zafrani ES (1994). Immunohistochemical detection of bcl-2 protein in normal and pathological human liver. *Am J Pathol* 144: 460-465.

282. Chatila R, Fiedler PN, Vender RJ (1996). Primary lymphoma of the gallbladder: case report and review of the literature. *Am J Gastroenterol* 91: 2242-2244.

283. Chaubert P, Hurlimann J (1992). Mammary origin of metastases. Immunohistochemical determination. *Arch Pathol Lab Med* 116: 1181-1188.

284. Chaudhry A, Papanicolaou V, Oberg K, Heldin CH, Funa K (1992). Expression of platelet-derived growth factor and its receptors in neuroendocrine tumors of the digestive system. *Cancer Res* 52: 1006-1012.

285. Chejfec G, Rieker WJ, Jablokow VR, Gould VE (1986). Pseudomyxoma peritonei associated with colloid carcinoma of the pancreas. *Gastroenterology* 90: 202-205.

286. Chen C, Cook LS, Li XY, Hallagan S, Madeleine MM, Daling JR, Weiss NS (1999). CYP2D6 genotype and the incidence of anal and vulvar cancer. *Cancer Epidemiol Biomarkers Prev* 8: 317-321.

287. Chen C, Madeleine MM, Lubinski C, Weiss NS, Tickman EW, Daling JR (1996). Glutathione S-transferase M1 genotypes and the risk of anal cancer: a population-based case-control study. *Cancer Epidemiol Biomarkers Prev* 5: 985-991.

288. Chen J, Baithun SI (1985). Morphological study of 391 cases of exocrine pancreatic tumours with special reference to the classification of exocrine pancreatic carcinoma. *J Pathol* 146: 17-29.

289. Chen J, Baithun SI, Pollock DJ, Berry CL (1988). Argyrophilic and hormone immunoreactive cells in normal and hyperplastic pancreatic ducts and exocrine pancreatic carcinoma. *Virchows Arch A Pathol Anat Histopathol* 413: 399-405.

290. Chen J, Baithun SI, Ramsay MA (1985). Histogenesis of pancreatic carcinomas: a study based on 248 cases. *J Pathol* 146: 65-76.

291. Chen MF, Jan YY, Jeng LB, Hwang TL, Wang CS, Chen SC, Chao TC, Chen HM, Lee WC, Yeh TS, Lo YF (1999). Intrahepatic cholangiocarcinoma in Taiwan. *J Hepato biliary Pancreat Surg* 6: 136-141.

292. Cheng JQ, Ruggeri B, Klein WM, Sonoda G, Altomare DA, Watson DK, Testa JR (1996). Amplification of AKT2 in human pancreatic cells and inhibition of AKT2 expression and tumorigenicity by anti-sense RNA. *Proc Natl Acad Sci U S A* 93: 3636-3641.

293. Cheng WS, Govindarajan S, Redeker AG (1992). Hepatocellular carcinoma in a case of Wilson's disease. *Liver* 12: 42-45.

294. Chetritt J, Sagan C, Heymann MF, Le-Bodic MF (1996). [Immunohistochemical study of 17 cases of rectal neuroendocrine tumors]. *Ann Pathol* 16: 98-103.

295. Chetty R, Arendse MP (1999). Gastrointestinal Kaposi's sarcoma, with special reference to the appendix. *S Afr J Surg* 37: 9-11.

296. Chetty R, Bhathal PS, Slavin JL (1993). Prolapse-induced inflammatory polyps of the colorectum and anal transitional zone. *Histopathology* 23: 63-67.

297. Chevrel JP, Amouroux J, Gueraud JP (1975). [3 cases of familial juvenile polyposis]. *Chirurgie* 101: 708-721.

298. Chinyama CN, Marshall REK, Owen WJ, Mason RC, Kothari D, Wilkinson ML, Sanderson JD (1999). Expression of MUC1 and MUC2 mucin gene products in Barrett's metaplasia, dysplasia and adenocarcinoma: an immunopathological study with clinical correlation. *Histopathology* 35: 517-524.

299. Chittal SM, Ra PM (1989). Carcinoid of the cystic duct. *Histopathology* 15: 643-646.

300. Choi BI, Kim KW, Han MC, Kim YI, Kim CW (1988). Solid and papillary epithelial neoplasms of the pancreas: CT findings. *Radiology* 166: 413-416.

301. Chong FK, Graham JH, Madoff IM (1979). Mucin-producing carcinoid ("composite tumor") of upper third of esophagus: a variant of carcinoid tumor. *Cancer* 44: 1853-1859.

302. Chong JM, Fukayama M, Shiozawa Y, Hayashi Y, Funata N, Takizawa T, Koike M (1996). Fibrillary inclusions in neoplastic and fetal acinar cells of the pancreas. *Virchows Arch* 428: 261-266.

303. Chott A, Dragosics B, Radaszkiewicz T (1992). Peripheral T-cell lymphomas of the intestine. *Am J Pathol* 141: 1361-1371.

304. Chott A, Gerdes D, Spooner A, Mosberger I, Kummer JA, Ebert EC, Blumberg RS, Balk SP (1997). Intraepithelial lymphocytes in normal human intestine do not express proteins associated with cytolytic function. *Am J Surg Pathol* 21: 435-442.

305. Chott A, Haedicke W, Mosberger I, Fodinger M, Winkler K, Mannhalter C, Muller HH (1998). Most CD56+ intestinal lymphomas are CD8+CD5-T-cell lymphomas of monomorphic small to medium size histology. *Am J Pathol* 153: 1483-1490.

306. Chott A, Kloppel G, Buxbaum P, Heitz PU (1987). Neuron specific enolase demonstration in the diagnosis of a solid-cystic (papillary cystic) tumour of the pancreas. *Virchows Arch A Pathol Anat Histopathol* 410: 397-402.

307. Chott A, Vesely M, Simonitsch I, Mosberger I, Hanak H (1999). Classification of intestinal T-cell neoplasms and their differential diagnosis. *Am J Clin Pathol* 111: S68-S74.

308. Chou ST, Chan CW (1980). Recurrent pyogenic cholangitis: a necropsy study. *Pathology* 12: 415-428.

309. Chow WH, Blaser MJ, Blot WJ, Gammon MD, Vaughan TL, Risch HA, Perez PG, Schoenberg JB, Stanford JL, Rotterdam H, West AB, Fraumeni-JF J (1998). An inverse relation between cagA+ strains of Helicobacter pylori infection and risk of esophageal and gastric cardia adenocarcinoma. *Cancer Res* 58: 588-590.

310. Chow WH, Blot WJ, Vaughan TL, Risch HA, Gammon MD, Stanford JL, Dubrow R, Schoenberg JB, Mayne ST, Farrow DC, Ahsan H, West AB, Rotterdam H, Niwa S, Fraumeni-JF J (1998). Body mass index and risk of adenocarcinomas of the esophagus and gastric cardia. *J Natl Cancer Inst* 90: 150-155.

311. Chowla A, Malhi-Chowla N, Chidambaram A, Surick B (1999). Primary hepatic lymphoma in hepatitis C: case report and review of the literature. *Am Surg* 65: 881-883.

312. Chun Y, Kim W, Park K, Lee S, Jung S (1997). Pancreatoblastoma. *J Pediatr Surg* 32: 1612-1615.

313. Chung DC (1998). Molecular prognostic markers and colorectal cancer: the search goes on. *Gastroenterology* 114: 1330-1332.

314. Clark GW, Smyrk TC, Burdiles P, Hoeft SF, Peters JH, Kiyabu M, Hinder RA, Brenner CG, DeMeester TR (1994). Is Barrett's metaplasia the source of adenocarcinomas of the cardia? *Arch Surg* 129: 609-614.

315. Clark SK, Phillips RK (1996). Desmoids in familial adenomatous polyposis. *Br J Surg* 83: 1494-1504.

316. Coburn MC, Pricolo VE, DeLuca FG, Bland KI (1995). Malignant potential in intestinal juvenile polyposis syndromes. *Ann Surg Oncol* 2: 386-391.

317. Cochet B, Carrel J, Desbaillets L, Widgren S (1979). Peutz-Jeghers syndrome associated with gastrointestinal carcinoma. Report of two cases in a family. *Gut* 20: 169-175.

318. Coffin CM, Watterson J, Priest JR, Dehner LP (1995). Extrapulmonary inflammatory myofibroblastic tumor (inflammatory pseudotumor). A clinicopathologic and immunohistochemical study of 84 cases. *Am J Surg Pathol* 19: 859-872.

319. Coggi G, Bosari S, Roncalli M, Graziani D, Bossi P, Viale G, Buffa R, Ferrero S, Piazza M, Blandamura S, Segalin A, Bonavina L, Peracchia A (1997). p53 protein accumulation and p53 gene mutation in esophageal carcinoma. A molecular and immunohistochemical study with clinico-pathologic correlations. *Cancer* 79: 425-432.

320. Cogliatti SB, Schmid U, Schumacher U, Eckert F, Hansmann ML, Hedderich J, Takahashi H, Lennert K (1991). Primary B-cell gastric lymphoma: a clinicopathological study of 145 patients. *Gastroenterology* 101: 1159-1170.

321. Cohen J (1999). The scientific challenge of hepatitis C. *Science* 285: 26-30.

322. Cohen PR, Kohn SR, Kurzrock R (1991). Association of sebaceous gland tumors and internal malignancy: the Muir-Torre syndrome. *Am J Med* 90: 606-613.

323. Coire CI, Qizilbash AH, Castelli MF (1987). Hepatic adenomata in type Ia glycogen storage disease. *Arch Pathol Lab Med* 111: 166-169.

324. Collins DC (1963). 71,000 human appendix specimens: a final report summarizing forty years' study. *Am J Proctol* 14: 365-381.

325. Collins SP, Reoma JL, Gamm DM, Uhler MD (2000). LKB1, a novel serine/threonine protein kinase and potential tumour suppressor, is phosphorylated by cAMP-dependent protein kinase (PKA) and prenylated in vivo. *Biochemistry* 345: 673-680.

326. Colombari R, Tsui WM (1995). Biliary tumors of the liver. *Semin Liver Dis* 15: 402-413.

327. Compagno J, Oertel JE (1978). Microcystic adenomas of the pancreas (glycogen-rich cystadenomas): a clinicopathologic study of 34 cases. *Am J Clin Pathol* 69: 289-298.

328. Compagno J, Oertel JE (1978). Mucinous cystic neoplasms of the pancreas with overt and latent malignancy (cystadenocarcinoma and cystadenoma). A clinicopathologic study of 41 cases. *Am J Clin Pathol* 69: 573-580.

329. Conias S, Strutton G, Stephenson G (1998). Adult cutaneous Langerhans cell histiocytosis. *Australas J Dermatol* 39: 106-108.

330. Conley CR, Scheithauer BW, van-Heerden JA, Weiland LH (1987). Diffuse intraductal papillary adenocarcinoma of the pancreas. *Ann Surg* 205: 246-249.

331. Conrad RJ, Gribbin D, Walker NI, Ong TH (1993). Combined cystic teratoma and hepatoblastoma of the liver. Probable divergent differentiation of an uncommitted hepatic precursor cell. *Cancer* 72: 2910-2913.

332. Conran RM, Hitchcock CL, Waclawiw MA, Stocker JT, Ishak KG (1992). Hepatoblastoma: the prognostic significance of histologic type. *Pediatr Pathol* 12: 167-183.

333. Conte WJ, Rotter JI, Schwartz AG, Congleton JE (1982). Hereditary generalized juvenile polyposis, arteriovenous malformations and colonic carcinoma. *Clin Res* 30: 93A-.

334. Cooke CB, Krenacs, Stetler-Stevenson M, Greiner TC, Raffeld M, Kingma DW, Abruzzo L, Frantz C, Kaviani M, Jaffe ES (1996). Hepatosplenic T-cell lymphoma: a distinct clinicopathologic entity of cytotoxic gamma delta T-cell origin. *Blood* 88: 4265-4274.

335. Cooney BS, Levine MS, Schnall MD (1995). Metastatic thyroid carcinoma presenting as an expansile intraluminal esophageal mass. *Abdom Imaging* 20: 20-22.

336. Cooper GS, Yuan Z, Stange KC, Rimm AA (1998). Use of Medicare claims data to measure county-level variations in the incidence of colorectal carcinoma. *Cancer* 83: 673-678.

337. Cooper HS, Patchefsky AS, Marks G (1979). Adenomatous and carcinomatous changes within hyperplastic colonic epithelium. *Dis Colon Rectum* 22: 152-156.

338. Cooper PN, Quirke P, Hardy GJ, Dixon MF (1992). A flow cytometric, clinical, and histological study of stromal neoplasms of the gastrointestinal tract. *Am J Surg Pathol* 16: 163-170.

339. Cooper P, Mills SE, Allen M (1982). Malignant melanoma of the anus: report of 12 patients and analysis of 255 additional cases. *Dis Colon Rectum* 25(7): 693-703.

340. Cormier RT, Hong KH, Halberg RB, Hawkins TL, Richardson P, Mulherkar R, Dove WF, Lander ES (1997). Secretory phospholipase Pla2g2a confers resistance to intestinal tumorigenesis. *Nat Genet* 17: 88-91.

341. Corrao G, Arico S (1998). Independent and combined action of hepatitis C virus infection and alcohol consumption on the risk of symptomatic liver cirrhosis. *Hepatology* 27: 914-919.

342. Correa P (1992). Human gastric carcinogenesis: a multistep and multifactorial process - First American Cancer Society Award Lecture on Cancer Epidemiology and Prevention. *Cancer Res* 52: 6735-6740.

343. Correa P (1995). Helicobacter pylori and gastric carcinogenesis. *Am J Surg Pathol* 19 Suppl 1: 1995.

344. Correa P, Miller MJ (1998). Carcinogenesis, apoptosis and cell proliferation. *Br Med Bull* 54: 151-162.

345. Cortina R, McCormick J, Kolm P, Perry RR (1995). Management and prognosis of adenocarcinoma of the appendix. *Dis Colon Rectum* 38: 848-852.

346. Costa MJ (1994). Pseudomyxoma peritonei. Histologic predictors of patient survival. *Arch Pathol Lab Med* 118: 1215-1219.

347. Cox CL, Butts DR, Roberts MP, Wessels RA, Bailey HR (1997). Development of invasive adenocarcinoma in a long-standing Kock continent ileostomy: report of a case. *Dis Colon Rectum* 40: 500-503.

348. Cox KL, Frates-RC J, Wong A, Gandhi G (1980). Hereditary generalized juvenile polyposis, arteriovenous malformation. *Gastroenterology* 78: 1566-1570.

349. Cox LS (1997). Multiple pathways control cell growth and transformation: overlapping and independent activities of p53 and p21Cip1/WAF1/Sdi1. *J Pathol* 183: 134-140.

350. Craanen ME, Blok P, Dekker W, Ferwerda J, Tytgat GN (1992). Subtypes of intestinal metaplasia and Helicobacter pylori. *Gut* 33: 597-600.

351. Craig JR, Peters RL, Edmondson HA (1989). Tumours of the Liver and Intrahepatic Bile Ducts. AFIP: Washington, D.C.

352. Craig JR, Peters RL, Edmondson HA, Omata M (1980). Fibrolamellar carcinoma of the liver: a tumor of adolescents and young adults with distinctive clinicopathologic features. *Cancer* 46: 372-379.

353. Craig SR, Wallce WH, Ramesar KC, Cameron EW (1996). Primary malignant melanoma of the esophagus. *Hepatogastroenterology* 43: 519-520.

354. Crespi M, Munoz N, Grassi A, Qiong S, Jing WK, Jien LJ (1984). Precursor lesions of oesophageal cancer in a low-risk population in China: comparison with high-risk populations. *Int J Cancer* 34: 599-602.

355. Crook T, Wrede D, Tidy J, Scholefield J, Crawford L, Vousden KH (1991). Status of c-myc, p53 and retinoblastoma genes in human papillomavirus positive and negative squamous carcinomas of the anus. *Oncogene* 6: 1251-1257.

356. Crook T, Wrede D, Tidy JA, Mason WP, Evans DJ, Vousden KH (1992). Clonal p53 mutation in primary cervical cancer: association with human-papillomavirus-negative tumours. *Lancet* 339: 1070-1073.

357. Crump M, Gospodarowicz M, Shepherd FA (1999). Lymphoma of the gastrointestinal tract. *Semin Oncol* 26: 324-337.

358. Cubilla AL, Fitzgerald PJ (1976). Morphological lesions associated with human primary invasive nonendocrine pancreas cancer. *Cancer Res* 36: 2690-2698.

359. Cubilla AL, Fitzgerald PJ (1984). Tumours of the Exocrine Pancreas. AFIP: Washington, D.C.

360. Cunningham JD, Cirincione E, Ryan A, Canin EJ, Brower S (1998). Indications for surgical resection of metastatic ocular melanoma. A case report and review of the literature. *Int J Pancreatol* 24: 49-53.

361. Cunningham JM, Christensen ER, Tester DJ, Kim CY, Roche PC, Burgart LJ, Thibodeau SN (1998). Hypermethylation of the hMLH1 promoter in colon cancer with microsatellite instability. *Cancer Res* 58: 3455-3460.

362. Cunningham RE, Federspiel BH, McCarthy WF, Sobin LH, O'Leary TJ (1993). Predicting prognosis of gastrointestinal smooth muscle tumors. Role of clinical and histologic evaluation, flow cytometry, and image cytometry. *Am J Surg Pathol* 17: 588-594.

363. D'Adda T, Keller G, Bordi C, Hofler H (1999). Loss of heterozygosity in 11q13-14 regions in gastric neuroendocrine tumors not associated with multiple endocrine neoplasia type 1 syndrome. *Lab Invest* 79: 671-677.

364. Dahia PL, Aguiar RC, Alberta J, Kum JB, Caron S, Sill H, Marsh DJ, Ritz J, Freedman A, Stiles C, Eng C (1999). PTEN is inversely correlated with the cell survival factor Akt/PKB and is inactivated via multiple mechanismsin haematological malignancies. *Hum Mol Genet* 8: 185-193.

365. Daigo Y, Nishiwaki T, Kawasoe T, Tamari M, Tsuchiya E, Nakamura Y (1999). Molecular cloning of a candidate tumor suppressor gene, DLC1, from chromosome 3p21.3. *Cancer Res* 59: 1966-1972.

366. Daimaru Y, Kido H, Hashimoto H, Enjoji M (1988). Benign schwannoma of the gastrointestinal tract: a clinicopathologic and immunohistochemical study. *Hum Pathol* 19: 257-264.

367. Daling JR, Sherman KJ, Hislop TG, Maden C, Mandelson MT, Beckmann AM, Weiss NS (1992). Cigarette smoking and the risk of anogenital cancer. *Am J Epidemiol* 135: 180-189.

368. Daling JR, Weiss NS, Hislop TG, Maden C, Coates RJ, Sherman KJ, Ashley RL, Beagrie M, Ryan JA, Corey L (1987). Sexual practices, sexually transmitted diseases, and the incidence of anal cancer. *N Engl J Med* 317: 973-977.

369. Daling JR, Weiss NS, Klopfenstein LL, Cochran LE, Chow WH, Daifuku R (1982). Correlates of homosexual behavior and the incidence of anal cancer. *JAMA* 247: 1988-1990.

370. Daly JM, Karnell LH, Menck HR (1996). National Cancer Data Base report on esophageal carcinoma. *Cancer* 78: 1820-1828.

371. Dammacco F, Gatti P, Sansonno D (1998). Hepatitis C virus infection, mixed cryoglobulinemia, and non-Hodgkin's lymphoma: an emerging picture. *Leuk Lymphoma* 31: 463-476.

372. Darmstadt GL (1996). Perianal lymphangioma circumscriptum mistaken for genital warts. *Pediatrics* 98: 461-463.

373. DasGupta T, Brasfield R (1964). Metastatic melanoma: a clinicopathologic study. *Cancer* 17: 1323-1339.

374. Daum S, Foss HD, Anagnostopoulos I, Dederke B, Demel G, Araujo I, Riecken EO, Stein H (1997). Expression of cytotoxic molecules in intestinal T-cell lymphomas. The German Study Group on Intestinal Non-Hodgkin Lymphoma. *J Pathol* 182: 311-317.

375. David L, Seruca R, Nesland JM, Soares P, Sansonetty F, Holm R, Borresen AL, Sobrinho SM (1992). c-erbB-2 expression in primary gastric carcinomas and their metastases. *Mod Pathol* 5: 384-390.

376. Davis RI, Sloan JM, Hood JM, Maxwell P (1988). Carcinoma of the extrahepatic biliary tract: a clinicopathological and immunohistochemical study. *Histopathology* 12: 623-631.

377. Dawsey SM, Lewin KJ, Wang GQ, Liu FS, Nieberg RK, Yu Y, Li JY, Blot WJ, Li B, Taylor PR (1994). Squamous esophageal histology and subsequent risk of squamous cell carcinoma of the esophagus. A prospective follow-up study from Linxian, China. *Cancer* 74: 1686-1692.

378. Dawson IMP, Cornes JS, Morson BC (1961). Primary malignant lymphoid tumours of the intestinal tract. Report of 37 cases with a study of factors influencing prognosis. *Br J Surg* 49: 80-89.

379. Dawson PM, Hershman MJ, Wood CB (1985). Metastatic carcinoma of the breast in the anal canal. *Postgrad Med J* 61: 1081.

380. Day JD, Digiuseppe JA, Yeo C, Lai GM, Anderson SM, Goodman SN, Kern SE, Hruban RH (1996). Immunohistochemical evaluation of HER-2/neu expression in pancreatic adenocarcinoma and pancreatic intraepithelial neoplasms. *Hum Pathol* 27: 119-124.

381. Dayal Y, Tallberg KA, Nunnemacher G, DeLellis RA, Wolfe HJ (1986). Duodenal carcinoids in patients with and without neurofibromatosis. A comparative study. *Am J Surg Pathol* 10: 348-357.

382. de-Bruin PC, Kummer JA, van d, V, van-Heerde P, Kluin PM, Willemze R, Ossenkoppele GJ, Radaszkiewicz T, Meijer CJ (1994). Granzyme B-expressing peripheral T-cell lymphomas: neoplastic equivalents of activated cytotoxic T cells with preference for mucosa-associated lymphoid tissue localization. *Blood* 84: 3785-3791.

383. de-Jong D, Boot H, van-Heerde P, Hart GA, Taal BG (1997). Histological grading in gastric lymphomas: pretreatment criteria and clinical relevance. *Gastroenterology* 112: 1466-1474.

384. de-Jong D, van-der-Hulst RW, Pals G, van-Dijk WC, van-der-Ende A, Tytgat GN, Taal BG, Boot H (1996). Gastric non-associated lymphoid tissue are not associated with more aggressive Helicobacter pylori strains as identified by CagA. *Am J Clin Pathol* 106: 670-675.

385. De-Jong KP, Stellema R, Karrenbeld A, Koudstaal J, Gouw AS, Sluiter WJ, Peeters PM, Slooff MJ, De-Vries EG (1998). Clinical relevance of transforming growth factor alpha, epidermal growth factor receptor, p53, and Ki67 in colorectal liver metastases and corresponding primary tumors. *Hepatology* 28: 971-979.

386. de-La-Coste A, Romagnolo B, Billuart P, Renard CA, Buendia MA, Soubrane O, Fabre M, Chelly J, Beldjord C, Kahn A, Perret C (1998). Somatic mutations of the beta-catenin gene are frequent in mouse and human hepatocellular carcinomas. *Proc Natl Acad Sci U S A* 95: 8847-8851.

387. De-Stefani E, Munoz N, Esteve J, Vasallo A, Victora CG, Teuchmann S (1990). Mate drinking, alcohol, tobacco, diet, and esophageal cancer in Uruguay. *Cancer Res* 50: 426-431.

388. de Mascarel A, Dubus P, Belleannee G, Megraud F, Merlio JP (1998). Low prevalence of the extra-nodal B cells in Helicobacter pylori gastritis patients with duodenal ulcer. *Hum Pathol* 29: 784-790.

389. De Quay N, Cerottini JP, Albe X, Saraga E, Givel JC, Caplin S (1999). Prognosis in Duke's B colorectal carcinoma: the Jass classification revisited. *Eur J Surg* 165: 577–592.

390. De Vita S, Sacco C, Sansonno D, Gloghini A, Dammacco F, Crovatto M, Santini G, Dolcetti R, Boiocchi M, Carbone A, Zagonel V (1997). Characterization of overt B-cell lymphomas in patients with hepatitis C virus infection. *Blood* 90: 776–782.

391. De Vos Irvine H, Goldberg D, Hole DJ, McMenamin J (1998). Trends in primary liver cancer. *Lancet* 351: 500–508.

392. Deans GT, McAleer JJ, Spence RA (1994). Malignant anal tumours. *Br J Surg* 81: 500–508.

393. Deans GT, Spence RA (1995). Neoplastic lesions of the appendix. *Br J Surg* 82: 299–306.

394. Debelenko LV, Emmert BM, Zhuang Z, Epshteyn E, Moskaluk CA, Jensen RT, Liotta LA, Lubensky IA (1997). The multiple endocrine neoplasia type I gene locus is involved in the pathogenesis of type II gastric carcinoids. *Gastroenterology* 113: 773–781.

395. Debelenko LV, Zhuang Z, Emmert BM, Chandrasekharappa SC, Manickam P, Guru SC, Marx SJ, Skarulis MC, Spiegel AM, Collins FS, Jensen RT, Liotta LA, Lubensky IA (1997). Allelic deletions on chromosome 11q13 in multiple endocrine neoplasia type 1-associated and sporadic gastrinomas and pancreatic endocrine tumors. *Cancer Res* 57: 2238–2243.

396. DeCastro M, Sanchez J, Herrera A, Chaves A, Duran R, Garcia BL, Garcia MC, Seguí J, Moreno OR (1993). Hepatitis C virus antibodies and liver disease in patients with porphyria cutanea tarda. *Hepatology* 17: 551–557.

397. Dehner LP, Ishak KG (1971). Vascular tumors of the liver in infants and children. A study of 30 cases and review of the literature. *Arch Pathol* 92: 101–111.

398. Delcore R, Cheung LY, Friesen SR (1988). Outcome of lymph node involvement in patients with the Zollinger-Ellison syndrome. *Ann Surg* 208: 291–298.

399. Delevett AF, Cheung R (1975). True villous adenoma of the jejunum. *Gastroenterology* 69: 217–219.

400. DeMatos P, Wolfe WG, Shea CR, Prieto VG, Siegler HF (1997). Primary malignant melanoma of the esophagus. *J Surg Oncol* 66: 201–206.

401. Dent GA, Feldman JM (1984). Pseudocystic liver metastases in patients with carcinoid tumors: report of three cases. *Am J Clin Pathol* 82: 275–279.

402. Deuffic S, Poynard T, Buffat L, Valleron AJ (1998). Trends in primary liver cancer. *Lancet* 351: 214–215.

403. Deugnier YM, Guyader D, Crantock L, Lopez JM, Turlin B, Yaouanq J, Jouanolle H, Campion JP, Launois B, Halliday JW, et a (1993). Primary liver cancer in genetic hemochromatosis: a clinical, pathological, and pathogenetic study of 54 cases. *Gastroenterology* 104: 228–234.

404. Devaney K, Goodman Z, Ishak K (1994). Hepatobiliary cystadenoma and cystadenocarcinoma. A light microscopic and immunohistochemical study of 70 patients. *Am J Surg Pathol* 18: 1078–1091.

405. Devesa SS, Blot WJ, Fraumeni-JF J (1998). Changing patterns in the incidence of esophageal and gastric carcinoma in the United States. *Cancer* 83: 2049–2053.

406. Deziel DJ, Saclarides TJ, Marshall JS, Yaremko LM (1991). Appendiceal Kaposi's sarcoma: a cause of right lower quadrant pain in the acquired immune deficiency syndrome. *Am J Gastroenterol* 86: 901–903.

407. Di-Cristofano A, Pesce B, Cordon CC, Pandolfi PP (1998). Pten is essential for embryonic development and tumour suppression. *Nat Genet* 19: 348–355.

408. di-Sant'Agnese PA (1991). Acinar cell carcinoma of the pancreas. *Ultrastruct Pathol* 15: 573–577.

409. DiConstanzo DP, Urmacher C (1987). Primary malignant melanoma of the esophagus. *Am J Surg Pathol* 11: 46–52.

410. Didolkar M, Malhotra Y, Holyoke E, Elias E (1975). Cystadenoma of the pancreas. *Surg Gynec Obstet* 140: 925–928.

411. Diebold BS, Vaiton JC, Pache JC, d'Amore ES (1995). Undifferentiated carcinoma of the gallbladder. Report of a case with immunohistochemical findings. *Arch Pathol Lab Med* 119: 279–282.

412. Dierlamm J, Baens M, Wlodarska I, Stefanova OM, Hernandez JM, Hossfeld DK, De-Wolf-Peeters C, Hagemeijer A, Van-den-Berghe H, Marynen P (1999). The apoptosis inhibitor gene API2 and a novel 18q gene, MLT, are recurrently rearranged in the t(11;18)(q21;q21)p associated with mucosa-associated lymphoid tissue lymphomas. *Blood* 93: 3601–3609.

413. Dierlamm J, Michaux L, Wlodarska I, Pittaluga S, Zeller W, Stul M, Criel A, Thomas J, Boogaerts M, Delaere P, Cassiman JJ, De-Wolf-Peeters C, Mecucci C, Van-den-Berghe H (1996). Trisomy 3 in marginal zone B-cell lymphoma: a study based on cytogenetic analysis and fluorescence in situ hybridization. *Br J Haematol* 93: 242–249.

414. Dihlmann S, Gebert J, Siermann A, Herfarth C, von-Knebel-Doeberitz M (1999). Dominant negative effect of the APC1309 mutation: a possible explanation for genotype-phenotype correlations in familial adenomatous polyposis. *Cancer Res* 59: 1857–1860.

415. Ding HF, Fisher DE (1998). Mechanisms of p53-mediated apoptosis. *Crit Rev Oncog* 9: 83–98.

416. Dingley KH, Curtis KD, Nowell S, Felton JS, Lang NP, Turteltaub KW (1999). DNA and protein adduct formation in the colon and blood of humans after exposure to a dietary-relevant dose of 2-amino-1-methyl-6-phenylimidazo[4,5-b]pyridine. *Cancer Epidemiol Biomarkers Prev* 8: 507–512.

417. Diss TC, Pan L, Peng H, Wotherspoon AC, Isaacson PG (1994). Sources of DNA for detecting B cell monoclonality using PCR. *J Clin Pathol* 47: 493–496.

418. Diss TC, Peng H, Wotherspoon AC, Isaacson PG, Pan L (1993). Detection of monoclonality in low-grade B-cell lymphomas using the polymerase chain reaction is dependent on primer selection and lymphoma type. *J Pathol* 169: 291–295.

419. Dixon MF, Martin IG, Sue LH, Wyatt JI, Quirke P, Johnston D (1994). Goseki grading in gastric cancer: comparison with existing systems of grading and its reproducibility. *Histopathology* 25: 309–316.

420. Doglioni C, Wotherspoon AC, Moschini A, de-Boni M, Isaacson PG (1992). High incidence of primary gastric lymphoma in northeastern Italy. *Lancet* 339: 834–835.

421. Doherty MA, McIntyre M, Arnott SJ (1984). Oat cell carcinoma of the esophagus: a case report of six British patients with a review of the literature. *Int J Radiat Oncol Biol Phys* 10: 147–152.

422. Doki Y, Shiozaki H, Tahara H, Kobayashi K, Miyata M, Oka H, Iihara K, Mori T (1993). Prognostic value of DNA ploidy in squamous cell carcinoma of esophagus. Analyzed with improved flow cytometric measurement. *Cancer* 72: 1813–1818.

423. Dolcetti R, Viel A, Doglioni C, Russo A, Guidoboni M, Capozzi E, Vecchiato N, Macrì S, Fornasarig M, Boiocchi M (1999). High prevalence of activated intraepithelial cytotoxic T lymphocytes and increased neoplastic cell apoptosis in colorectal carcinomas with microsatellite instability. *Am J Pathol* 154: 1805–1813.

424. Domizio P, Owen RA, Shepherd NA, Talbot IC, Norton AJ (1993). Primary lymphoma of the small intestine. A clinicopathological study of 119 cases. *Am J Surg Pathol* 17: 429–442.

425. Domizio P, Talbot IC, Spigelman AD, Williams CB, Phillips RK (1991). Upper gastrointestinal pathology in familial adenomatous polyposis: results from a prospective study of 102 patients. *J Clin Pathol* 43: 738–743.

426. Donato F, Tagger A, Chiesa R, Ribero ML, Tomasoni V, Fasola M, Gelatti U, Portera G, Boffetta P, Nardi G (1997). Hepatitis B and C virus infection, alcohol drinking, and hepatocellular carcinoma: a case-control study in Italy. Brescia HCC Study. *Hepatology* 26: 579–584.

427. Dong XD, DeMatos P, Prieto VG, Seigler HF (1999). Melanoma of the gallbladder. *Cancer* 85: 32–39.

428. Donnelly WH, Sieber WK, Yunis EJ (1969). Polypoid ganglioneurofibromatosis of the large bowel. *Arch Pathol* 87: 537–541.

429. Donow C, Pipeleers MM, Schroder S, Stamm B, Heitz PU, Kloppel G (1991). Surgical pathology of gastrinoma. Site, size, multicentricity, association with multiple endocrine neoplasia type 1, and malignancy. *Cancer* 68: 1329–1334.

430. dos Santos NR, Seruca R, Constancia M, Seixas M, Sobrinho SM (1996). Microsatellite instability at multiple loci in gastric carcinoma: clinicopathologic implications and prognosis. *Gastroenterology* 110: 38–44.

431. Dozois RR, Judd ES, Dahlin DC, Bartholomew LG (1969). The Peutz-Jeghers syndrome. Is there a predisposition to the development of intestinal malignancy? *Arch Surg* 98: 509–517.

432. Drut R, Jones MC (1988). Congenital pancreatoblastoma in Beckwith-Wiedemann syndrome: an emerging association. *Pediatr Pathol* 8: 331–339.

433. Du Plessis DG, Louw JA, B Wranz PA (1999). Mucinous epithelial cysts of the spleen associated with pseudomyxoma peritonei. *Histopathology* 35(6): 551–557.

434. Du M, Diss TC, Xu C, Peng H, Isaacson PG, Pan L (1996). Ongoing mutation in MALT lymphoma immunoglobulin gene suggests that antigen stimulation plays a role in the clonal expansion. *Leukemia* 10: 1190–1197.

435. Du M, Peng H, Singh N, Isaacson PG, Pan L (1995). The accumulation of p53 abnormalities is associated with progression of mucosa-associated lymphoid tissue lymphoma. *Blood* 86: 4587–4593.

436. Duff P, Greene VP (1985). Pregnancy complicated by solid-papillary epithelial tumor of the pancreas, pulmonary embolism, and pulmonary embolectomy. *Am J Obstet Gynecol* 152: 80–81.

437. Dumas A, Thung SN, Lin CS (1998). Diffuse hyperplasia of the peribiliary glands. *Arch Pathol Lab Med* 122: 87–89.

438. Dunkelberg J, Goodman Z, Brewer T, Ishak KG (1991). Hepatic inflammatory pseudotumor (HIP): clinicopathologic correlation in 31 cases. *Gastroenterology* 100: A738-

439. Dunn J, Garde J, Dolan K, Gosney JR, Sutton R, Meltzer SJ, Field JK (1999). Multiple target sites of allelic imbalance on chromosome 17 in Barrett's oesophageal cancer. *Oncogene* 18: 987–993.

440. Dyson N, Howley PM, Munger K, Harlow E (1989). The human papilloma virus-16 E7 oncoprotein is able to bind to the retinoblastoma gene product. *Science* 243: 934–937.

441. Eck M, Schmausser B, Haas R, Greiner A, Czub S, Muller HH (1997). MALT-type lymphoma of the stomach is associated with Helicobacter pylori strains expressing the CagA protein. *Gastroenterology* 112: 1482–1486.

442. Edmonds P, Merino MJ, Livolsi VA, Duray PH (1984). Adenocarcinoid (mucinous carcinoid) of the appendix. *Gastroenterology* 86: 302–309.

443. Edwards JM, Hillier VF, Lawson RA, Moussalli H, Hasleton PS (1989). Squamous carcinoma of the oesophagus: histological criteria and their prognostic significance. *Br J Cancer* 59: 429–433.

444. Egan LJ, Walsh SV, Stevens FM, Connolly CE, Egan EL, McCarthy CF (1995). Celiac-associated lymphoma. A single institution experience of 30 cases in the combination chemotherapy era. *J Clin Gastroenterol* 21: 123–129.

445. Egawa N, Maillet B, Schroder S, Foulis A, Mukai K, Kloppel G (1994). Serous oligocystic and ill-demarcated adenoma of the pancreas: a variant of serous cystic adenoma. Virchows Arch 424: 13-17.

446. Ehrlich PF, Greenberg ML, Filler RM (1997). Improved long-term survival with preoperative chemotherapy for hepatoblastoma. J Pediatr Surg 32: 999-1002.

447. Eidt S, Stolte M, Fischer R (1994). Helicobacter pylori gastritis and primary gastric non-Hodgkin's lymphomas. J Clin Pathol 47: 436-439.

448. Ekbom A, et al (1992). Survival and causes of death in patients with inflammatory bowel disease: a population-based study. Gastroenterology 103: 954-960.

449. el-Rifai W, Harper JC, Cummings OW, Hytinen ER, Frierson-HF J, Knuutila S, Powell SM (1998). Consistent genetic alterations in xenografts of proximal stomach and gastro-esophageal junction adenocarcinomas. Cancer Res 58: 34-37.

450. el-Rifai W, Sarlomo RM, Andersson LC, Miettinen M, Knuutila S (1998). DNA copy number changes in gastrointestinal stromal tumors - a distinct genetic entity. Ann Chir Gynaecol 87: 287-290.

451. el-Rifai W, Sarlomo RM, Miettinen M, Knuutila S, Andersson LC (1996). DNA copy number losses in chromosome 14: an early change in gastrointestinal stromal tumors. Cancer Res 56: 3230-3233.

452. El-Serag HB, Mason AC (1999). Rising incidence of hepatocellular carcinoma in the United States. N Engl J Med 340: 745-750.

453. El-Serag HB, Sonnenberg A (1999). Ethnic variations in the occurrence of gastroesophageal cancers. J Clin Gastroenterol 28: 135-139.

454. Elliott GB, Fisher BK (1967). Perianal keratoacanthoma. Arch Dermatol 95: 81-82.

455. Elliott LA, Hall GD, Perren TJ, Spencer JA (1995). Metastatic breast carcinoma involving the gastric antrum and duodenum: computed tomography appearances. Br J Radiol 68: 970-972.

456. Ellis A, Field JK, Field EA, Friedmann PS, Fryer A, Howard P, Leigh IM, Risk J, Shaw JM, Whittaker J (1994). Tylosis associated with carcinoma of the oesophagus and oral leukoplakia in a large Liverpool family - a review of six generations. Eur J Cancer B Oral Oncol 30B: 102-112.

457. Elmore LW, Hancock AR, Chang SF, Wang XW, Chang S, Callahan CP, Geller DA, Will H, Harris CC (1997). Hepatitis B virus X protein and p53 tumor suppressor interactions in the modulation of apoptosis. Proc Natl Acad Sci U S A 94: 14707-14712.

458. Elsayed AM, Albahra M, Nzeako UC, Sobin LH (1996). Malignant melanomas in the small intestine: a study of 103 patients. Am J Gastroenterol 91: 1001-1006.

459. Emi M, Fujiwara Y, Nakajima T, Tsuchiya E, Tsuda H, Hirohashi S, Maeda Y, Tsuruta K, Miyaki M, Nakamura Y (1992). Frequent loss of heterozygosity for loci on chromosome 8p in hepatocellular carcinoma, colorectal cancer, and lung cancer. Cancer Res 52: 5368-5372.

460. Emi M, Fujiwara Y, Ohata H, Tsuda H, Hirohashi S, Koike M, Miyaki M, Monden M, Nakamura Y (1993). Allelic loss at chromosome band 8p21.3-p22 is associated with progression of hepatocellular carcinoma. Genes Chromosomes Cancer 7: 152-157.

461. Emory TS, Derringer GA, Sobin LH, O'Leary TJ (1997). Ki-67 (MIB-1) immunohistochemistry as a prognostic factor in gastrointestinal smooth-muscle tumors. J Surg Pathol 2: 239-242.

462. Emory TS, Sobin LH, Lukes L, Lee DH, O'Leary TJ (1999). Prognosis of gastrointestinal smooth-muscle (stromal) tumors. Am J Surg Pathol 23: 82-87.

463. Endo EG, Walton DS, Albert DM (1996). Neonatal hepatoblastoma metastatic to the choroid and iris. Arch Ophthalmol 114: 757-761.

464. Endo M, Takeshita K, Yoshida M (1986). How can we diagnose the early stage of esophageal cancer? Endoscopic diagnosis. Endoscopy 18 Suppl 3: 1989.

465. Endo M, Yoshino K, Takeshita K, Kawano T (1991). Analysis of 1125 cases of early esophageal carcinoma in Japan. Dis Esophagus 2: 71-76.

466. Endoh Y, Tamura G, Motoyama T, Ajioka Y, Watanabe H (1999). Well-differentiated adenocarcinoma mimicking complete-type intestinal metaplasia in the stomach. Hum Pathol 30: 826-832.

467. Eng C (1997). Cowden syndrome. J Genet Counsel 6: 181-191.

468. Eng C, Murday V, Seal S, Mohammed S, Hodgson SV, Chaudary MA, Fentiman IS, Ponder BA, Eeles RA (1994). Cowden syndrome and Lhermitte-Duclos disease in a family: a single genetic syndrome with pleiotropy? J Med Genet 31: 458-461.

469. Eng C, Peacocke M (1998). PTEN and inherited hamartoma-cancer syndromes. Nat Genet 19: 223

470. Eng C, Spechler SJ, Ruben R, Li FP (1993). Familial Barrett esophagus and adenocarcinoma of the gastroesophageal junction. Cancer Epidemiol Biomarkers Prev 2: 397-399.

471. Engel JJ, Trujillo Y, Spellberg M (1980). Metastatic carcinoma of the breast: a cause of obstructive jaundice. Gastroenterology 78: 132-135.

472. Enzan H, Himeno H, Iwamura S, Onishi S, Saibara T, Yamamoto Y, Hara H (1994). Alpha-smooth muscle actin-positive perisinusoidal stromal cells in human hepatocellular carcinoma. Hepatology 19: 895-903.

473. Eriksson S, Carlson J, Velez R (1986). Risk of cirrhosis and primary liver cancer in alpha 1-antitrypsin deficiency. N Engl J Med 314: 736-739.

474. Erlandson RA, Klimstra DS, Woodruff JM (1996). Subclassification of gastrointestinal stromal tumors based on evaluation by electron microscopy and immunohistochemistry. Ultrastruct Pathol 20: 373-393.

475. Ernst SI, Hubbs AE, Przygodzki RM, Emory TS, Sobin LH, O'Leary TJ (1998). KIT mutation portends poor prognosis in gastrointestinal stromal/smooth muscle tumors. Lab Invest 78: 1633-1636.

476. Eskelinen M, Lipponen P, Collan Y, Marin S, Alhava E, Nordling S (1991). Relationship between DNA ploidy and survival in patients with exocrine pancreatic cancer. Pancreas 6: 90-95.

477. Eskelinen M, Lipponen P, Marin S, Haapasalo H, Makinen K, Ahtola H, Puittinen J, Nuutinen P, Alhava E (1991). Prognostic factors in human pancreatic cancer, with special reference to quantitative histology. Scand J Gastroenterol 26: 483-490.

478. Espinosa A, Berga C, Martin P, V, Sanchez V, Diaz J, Segura J, Escuder J, Barbod A (1998). Hemangiopericytoma ischiorectal. Report of a case. J Cardiovasc Surg Torino 39: 577-581.

478A. Evans HL (1985). Smooth muscle tumors of the gastrointestinal tract. A study of 56 cases followed for a minimum of 10 years. Cancer 56: 2242-2250.

479. Evans JP, Burke W, Chen R, Bennett RL, Schmidt RA, Dellinger EP, Kimmey M, Crispin D, Brentnall TA, Byrd DR (1995). Familial pancreatic adenocarcinoma: association with diabetes and early molecular diagnosis. J Med Genet 32: 330-335.

480. Everhart-CW J, Holtzapple PG, Humphries TJ (1983). Barrett's esophagus: an acquired condition with genetic predisposition. Am J Gastroenterol 88: 1262-1265.

481. Fagundes RB, de-Barros SG, Putten AC, Mello ES, Wagner M, Bassi LA, Bombassaro MA, Gobbi D, Souto EB (1999). Occult dysplasia is disclosed by Lugol chromoendoscopy in alcoholics at high risk for squamous cell carcinoma of the esophagus. Endoscopy 31: 281-285.

482. Fahmy N, King JF (1993). Barrett's esophagus: an acquired condition with genetic predisposition. Am J Gastroenterol 5: 357-358.

483. Falk GW, Rice TW, Goldblum JR, Richter JE (1999). Jumbo biopsy forceps protocol still misses unsuspected cancer in Barrett's esophagus with high-grade dysplasia. Gastrointest Endosc 49: 170-176.

484. Falk H, Herbert J, Crowley S, Ishak KG, Thomas LB, Popper H, Caldwell GG (1981). Epidemiology of hepatic angiosarcoma in the United States: 1964-1974. Environ Health Perspect 41: 107-113.

485. Falk RT, Pickle LW, Fontham ET, Correa P, Fraumeni-JF J (1988). Life-style risk factors for pancreatic cancer in Louisiana: a case-control study. Am J Epidemiol 128: 324-336.

486. Farcet JP, Gaulard P, Marolleau JP, Le Couedic JP, Henni T, Gourdin MF, Divine M, Haioun C, Zafrani S, Goossens M, Hercend T, Reyes F (1990). Hepatosplenic T-cell lymphoma: sinusal/sinusoidal localization of malignant cells expressing the T-cell receptor gammadelta. Blood 75: 2213-2219.

487. Fargion S, Mandelli C, Piperno A, Cesana B, Fracanzani AL, Fraquelli M, Bianchi PA, Fiorelli G, Conte D (1992). Survival and prognostic factors in 212 Italian patients with genetic hemochromatosis. Hepatology 15: 655-659.

488. Federspiel BH, Burke AP, Sobin LH, Shekitka KM (1990). Rectal and colonic carcinoids. A clinicopathologic study of 84 cases. Cancer 65: 135-140.

489. Fenger C (1989). Surgical pathology of the anal canal: a review of the recent literature on the anatomy and pathology. In: Prog Surg Pathol, Fenoglio-Preiser CM, Wolff M, Rilke F (eds). Springer-Verlag: Berlin.

490. Fenger C (1997). Anal canal. In: Histology for Pathologists, Sternberg SS (eds), 2nd ed. Lippincott Raven: New York.

491. Fenger C, Filipe MI (1981). Mucin histochemistry of the anal canal epithelium. Studies of normal anal mucosa and mucosa adjacent to carcinoma. Histochem J 13: 921-930.

492. Fenger C, Frisch M, Jass JR, Williams GT, Hilden J (2000). Anal cancer subtype reproducibility study. Virchows Arch 463(3): 229-233.

493. Fenger C, Lyon H (1982). Endocrine cells and melanin-containing cells in the anal canal epithelium. Histochem J 14: 631-639.

494. Fenger C, Nielsen VT (1986). Intraepithelial neoplasia in the anal canal. The appearance and relation to genital neoplasia. Acta Pathol Microbiol Immunol Scand A 94: 343-349.

495. Fenger C, Schroder HD (1990). Neuronal hyperplasia in the anal canal. Histopathology 16: 481-485.

496. Fenoglio-Preiser CM, Lantz PE, Listrom MB, Davis M, Rilke FO (1989). Tumors of the small intestine. In: Gastrointestinal Pathology. An Atlas and Text, Raven Press: New York.

497. Fenoglio-Preiser CM, Noffsinger AE, Belli J, Stemmermann GN (1996). Pathologic and phenotypic features of gastric cancer. Semin Oncol 23: 292-306.

498. Fenoglio-Preiser CM, Pascal RR, Perzin KH (1990). Adenocarcinoma of the small intestine, including ampulla of Vater. In: Tumors of the Intestines, 2nth ed. AFIP: Washington.

499. Fernandez E, La-Vecchia C, D'Avanzo B, Negri E, Franceschi S (1994). Family history and the risk of liver, gallbladder, and pancreatic cancer. Cancer Epidemiol Biomarkers Prev 3: 209-212.

500. Ferrell LD, Beckstead JH (1991). Paneth-like cells in an adenoma and adenocarcinoma in the ampulla of Vater. Arch Pathol Lab Med 115: 956-958.

501. Ferreres JC, Fernandez F, Rodriguez VA, Gonzalez R, I, Ursua I, Ramos R, Val BJ (1991). Helicobacter pylori in Barrett's esophagus. *Histol Histopathol/6:* 403-408.

502. Ferrozzi F, Bova D, Campodonico F, Chiara FD, Passari A, Bassi P (1997). Pancreatic metastases: CT assessment. *Eur Radiol 7:* 241-245.

503. Fetsch JF, Laskin WB, Lefkowitz M, Kindblom LG, Meis KJ (1996). Aggressive angiomyxoma: a clinicopathologic study of 29 female patients. *Cancer 78:* 79-90.

504. Filipe MI, Munoz N, Matko I, Kato I, Pompe K, V, Jutersek A, Teuchmann S, Benz M, Prijon T (1994). Intestinal metaplasia types and the risk of gastric cancer: a cohort study in Slovenia. *Int J Cancer 57:* 324-329.

505. Fink D, Nebel S, Aebi S, Zheng H, Kim HK, Christen RD, Howell SB (1997). Expression of the DNA mismatch repair proteins hMLH1 and hPMS2 in normal human tissues. *Br J Cancer 76:* 890-893.

506. Fiocca R, Capella C, Buffa R, Fontana P, Solcia E, Hage E, Chance RE, Moody RL (1980). Glucagon, glicentin and pancreatic polypeptide-like immunoreactivities in rectal carcinoids and related non-tumor cells. *Am J Pathol 100:* 81-92.

507. Fiocca R, Rindi G, Capella C, Grimelius L, Polak JM, Schwartz TW, Yanaihara N, Solcia E (1987). Glucagon, glicentin, proglucagon, PYY, PP and proPP-icosapeptide immunoreactivities of rectal carcinoid tumors and related islet cells. *Regul Pept 17:* 9-29.

508. Fischbach W, Kestel W, Kirchner T, Mossner J, Wilms K (1992). Malignant lymphomas of the upper gastrointestinal tract. Results of a prospective study in 103 patients. *Cancer 70:* 1075-1080.

509. Fishel R, Lescoe MK, Rao MR, Copeland NG, Jenkins NA, Garber J, Kane M, Kolodner R (1993). The human mutator gene homolog MSH2 and its association with hereditary nonpolyposis colon cancer. *Cell/75:* 1027-1038.

510. Fleisher AS, Esteller M, Wang S, Tamura G, Suzuki H, Yin J, Zou TT, Abraham JM, Kong D, Smolinski KN, Shi YQ, Rhyu MG, Powell SM, James SP, Wilson KT, Herman JG, Meltzer SJ (1999). Hypermethylation of the hMLH1 gene promoter in human gastric cancers with microsatellite instability. *Cancer Res 59:* 1090-1095.

511. Flejou JF, Barge J, Menu Y, Degott C, Bismuth H, Potet F, Benhamou JP (1985). Liver adenomatosis. An entity distinct from liver adenoma? *Gastroenterology 89:* 1132-1138.

512. Flejou JF, Boulange B, Bernandes P, Belghiti J, Henin D (1996). p53 protein expression and DNA ploidy in cystic tumors of the pancreas. *Pancreas 13:* 247-252.

513. Fletcher JA, Kozakewich HP, Hoffer FA, Lage JM, Weidner N, Tepper R, Pinkus GS, Morton CC, Corson JM (1991). Diagnostic relevance of clonal cytogenetic aberrations in malignant soft-tissue tumors. *N Engl J Med 324:* 436-442.

514. Flint A, Weiss SW (1995). CD-34 and keratin expression distinguishes solitary fibrous tumor (fibrous mesothelioma) of pleura from desmoplastic mesothelioma. *Hum Pathol/6:* 428-431.

515. Fogt F, Vortmeyer AO, Stolte M, Mueller E, Mueller J, Noffsinger A, Poremba C, Zhuang Z (1998). Loss of heterozygosity of p53 in ulcerative colitis-associated dysplasia and carcinoma. *Hum Pathol 29:* 961-964.

516. Fogt F, Zhuang Z, Poremba C, Dockhorn-Dworniczak B, Vortmeyer A (1998). Comparison of p53 immunoexpression with allelic loss of p53 in ulcerative colitis-associated dysplasia and carcinomas. *Oncol Rep 5:* 477-480.

517. Fondrinier E, Guerin O, Lorimier G (1997). [A comparative study of metastatic patterns of ductal and lobular carcinoma of the breast from two matched series (376 patients)]. *Bull Cancer 84:* 1101-1107.

518. Ford D, Easton DF, Bishop DT, Narod SA, Goldgar DE (1994). Risks of cancer in BRCA1-mutation carriers. Breast Cancer Linkage Consortium. *Lancet 343:* 692-695.

519. Forman D, Newell DG, Fullerton F, Yarnell JW, Stacey AR, Wald N, Sitas F (1991). Association between infection with Helicobacter pylori and risk of gastric cancer: evidence from a prospective investigation. *BMJ 302:* 1302-1305.

520. Foss HD, Schmitt GA, Daum S, Anagnostopoulos I, Assaf C, Hummel M, Stein H (1999). Origin of primary gastric T-cell lymphomas from intraepithelial T-lymphocytes: report of two cases. *Histopathology 34:* 9-15.

521. Foster DR, Foster DB (1980). Gall-bladder polyps in Peutz-Jeghers syndrome. *Postgrad Med J 56:* 373-376.

522. Foucar E, Kaplan LR, Gold JH, Kiang DT, Sibley RK, Bosl G (1979). Well-differentiated peripheral cholangiocarcinoma with an unusual clinical course. *Gastroenterology 77:* 347-353.

523. Franceschi S, Bidoli E, Negri E, Barbone F, La-Vecchia C (1994). Alcohol and cancers of the upper aerodigestive tract in men and women. *Cancer Epidemiol Biomarkers Prev 3:* 299-304.

524. Francois A, Lesesve JF, Stamatoullas A, Comoz F, Lenormand B, Etienne I, Mendel I, Hemet J, Bastard C, Tilly H (1997). Hepatosplenic gamma/delta T-cell lymphoma: report of two cases in immunocompromised patients, associated with isochromosome 7q. *Am J Surg Pathol 21:* 781-790.

525. Franquemont DW (1995). Differentiation and risk assessment of gastrointestinal stromal tumors. *Am J Clin Pathol 103:* 41-47.

526. Franquemont DW, Frierson-HF J (1992). Muscle differentiation and clinicopathologic features of gastrointestinal stromal tumors. *Am J Surg Pathol 16:* 947-954.

527. Freeman C, Berg JW, Cutler SJ (1972). Occurrence and prognosis of extranodal lymphomas. *Cancer 29:* 252-260.

528. Freeny PC (1988). Radiology of the pancreas: two decades of progress in imaging and intervention. *AJR Am J Roentgenol/150:* 975-981.

529. Freni SC, Keeman JN (1977). Leiomyomatosis of the colon. *Cancer 39:* 263-266.

530. Friberg B, Svensson C, Goldman S, Glimelius B (1998). The Swedish National Care Programme for Anal Carcinoma - implementation and overall results. *Acta Oncol 37:* 25-32.

531. Friedl W, Kruse R, Uhlhaas S, Stolte M, Schartmann B, Keller KM, Jungck M, Stern M, Loff S, Back W, Propping P, Jenne DE (1999). Frequent 4-bp deletion in exon 9 of the SMAD4/MADH4 gene in familial juvenile polyposis patients. *Genes Chromosomes Cancer 25:* 403-406.

532. Friedman AC, Lichtenstein JE, Dachman AH (1983). Cystic neoplasms of the pancreas. Radiological-pathological correlation. *Radiology 149:* 45-50.

533. Friedman HD (1990). Nonmucinous, glycogen-poor cystadenocarcinoma of the pancreas. *Arch Pathol Lab Med 114:* 888-891.

534. Friedman SL, Wright TL, Altman DF (1985). Gastrointestinal Kaposi's sarcoma in patients with acquired immunodeficiency syndrome. Endoscopic and autopsy findings. *Gastroenterology 89:* 102-108.

535. Friess H, Buchler MW, Korc M (1996). Growth factors and growth factor receptors in pancreatic cancer. In: *Pancreatic Cancer, Molecular and Clinical Advances.* Neoptolemos JP, Lemoine NR (eds), Blackwell Science: Oxford.

536. Frisch M, Fenger C, van-den-Brule AJ, Sorensen P, Meijer CJ, Walboomers JM, Adami HO, Melbye M, Glimelius B (1999). Variants of squamous cell carcinoma of the anal canal and perianal skin and their relation to human papillomaviruses. *Cancer Res 59:* 753-757.

537. Frisch M, Glimelius B, van-den-Brule AJ, Wohlfahrt J, Meijer CJ, Walboomers JM, Adami HO, Melbye M (1998). Benign anal lesions, inflammatory bowel disease and risk for high-risk human papillomavirus-positive and -negative anal carcinoma. *Br J Cancer 78:* 1534-1538.

538. Frisch M, Glimelius B, van-den-Brule AJ, Wohlfahrt J, Meijer CJ, Walboomers JM, Goldman S, Svensson C, Adami HO, Melbye M (1997). Sexually transmitted infection as a cause of anal cancer. *N Engl J Med 337:* 1350-1358.

539. Frisch M, Glimelius B, Wohlfahrt J, Adami HO, Melbye M (1999). Tobacco smoking as a risk factor in anal carcinoma: an antiestrogenic mechanism? *J Natl Cancer Inst 91:* 708-715.

540. Frisch M, Melbye M, Moller H (1993). Trends in incidence of anal cancer in Denmark. *Br Med J 306:* 419-422.

541. Frisch M, Olsen JH, Bautz A, Melbye M (1994). Benign anal lesions and the risk of anal cancer. *N Engl J Med 331:* 300-302.

542. Fritz A, Percy C, Jack A, Shanmugaratnam K, Sobin L, Parkin DM, Whelan S (2000). International Classification of Diseases for Oncology (ICD-O), 3rd ed, WHO: Geneva.

543. Froelicher P, Miller G (1986). The European experience with esophageal cancer limited to the mucosa and submucosa *Gastrointest Endosc 32:* 88-90.

544. Fujii H, Inagaki H, Kasai S, Miyokawa N, Tokusashi Y, Gabrielson E, Hruban RH (1997). Genetic progression and heterogeneity in intraductal papillary-mucinous neoplasms of the pancreas. *Am J Pathol 151:* 1447-1454.

545. Fujii H, Nakanishi Y, Ochiai A, Tsuda H, Yamaguchi H, Tachimori Y, Kato H, Watanabe H, Shimoda T (1997). Solitary esophageal metastasis of breast cancer with 15 years' latency: a case report and review of the literature. *Pathol Int 47:* 614-617.

546. Fujimori M, Tokino T, Hino O, Kitagawa T, Imamura T, Okamoto E, Mitsunobu M, Ishikawa T, Nakagama H, Harada H, et al (1991). Allelotype study of primary hepatocellular carcinoma. *Cancer Res 51:* 89-93.

547. Fujisawa S, Motomura S, Fujimaki K, Tanabe J, Tomita N, Hara M, Mohri H (1999). Primary esophageal T cell lymphoma. *Leuk Lymphoma 33:* 199-202.

548. Fujiwara T, Stolker JM, Watanabe T, Rashid A, Longo P, Eshleman JR, Booker S, Lynch HT, Jass JR, Green JS, Kim H, Jen J, Vogelstein B, Hamilton SR (1998). Accumulated clonal genetic alterations in familial and sporadic colorectal carcinomas with widespread instability in microsatellite sequences. *Am J Pathol/153:* 1063-1078.

549. Fukino K, Iida A, Teramoto A, Sakamoto G, Kasumi F, Nakamura Y, Emi M (1999). Frequent allelic loss at the TOC locus on 17q25.1 in primary breast cancers. *Genes Chromosomes Cancer 24:* 345-350.

550. Fukushima N, Mukai K (1999). Pancreatic neoplasms with abundant mucus production: emphasis on intraductal papillary-mucinous tumors and mucinous cystic tumors. *Adv Anat Pathol 6:* 65-77.

551. Fukushima N, Mukai K, Kanai Y, Hasebe T, Shimada K, Ozaki H, Kinoshita T, Kosuge T (1997). Intraductal papillary tumors and mucinous cystic tumors of the pancreas: clinicopathologic study of 38 cases. *Hum Pathol 28:* 1010-1017.

552. Fung CY, Grossbard ML, Linggood RM, Younger J, Flieder A, Harris NL, Graeme CF (1999). Mucosa-associated lymphoid tissue lymphoma of the stomach: long term outcome after local treatment. *Cancer 85:* 9-17.

553. Furnari FB, Huang HJ, Cavenee WK (1998). The phosphoinositol phosphatase activity of PTEN mediates a serum-sensitive G1 growth arrest in glioma cells. *Cancer Res 58:* 5002-5008.

554. Furnari FB, Lin H, Huang HS, Cavenee WK (1997). Growth suppression of glioma cells by PTEN requires a functional phosphatase catalytic domain. *Proc Natl Acad Sci U S A* 94: 12479-12484.

555. Furukawa T, Chiba R, Kobari M, Matsuno S, Nagura H, Takahashi T (1994). Varying grades of epithelial atypia in the pancreatic ducts of humans. Classification based on morphometry and multivariate analysis and correlated with positive reactions of carcinoembryonic antigen . *Arch Pathol Lab Med* 118: 227-234.

556. Furukawa T, Takahashi T, Kobari M, Matsuno S (1992). The mucus-hypersecreting tumor of the pancreas. Development and extension visualized by three-dimensional computerized mapping. *Cancer* 70: 1505-1513.

557. Gabbert HE, Muller W, Schneiders A, Meier S, Hommel G (1995). The relationship of p53 expression to the prognosis of 418 patients with gastric carcinoma. *Cancer* 76: 720-726.

558. Gadacz TR, McFadden DW, Gabrielson EW, Ullah A, Berman JJ (1990). Adenocarcinoma of the ileostomy: the latent risk of cancer after colectomy for ulcerative colitis and familial polyposis. *Surgery* 107: 698-703.

559. Gagliardi G, Stepniewska KA, Hershman MJ, Hawley PR, Talbot IC (1995). New grade-related prognostic variable for rectal cancer. *Br J Surg* 82: 599-602.

560. Gall FP, Kessler H, Hermanek P (1991). Surgical treatment of ductal pancreatic carcinoma. *Eur J Surg Oncol* 17: 173-181.

561. Gallivan MV, Lack EE, Chun B, Ishak KG (1983). Undifferentiated ("embryonal") sarcoma of the liver: ultrastructure of a case presenting as a primary intracardiac tumor. *Pediatr Pathol* 1: 291-300.

562. Gammon MD, Schoenberg JB, Ahsan H, Risch HA, Vaughan TL, Chow WH, Rotterdam H, West AB, Dubrow R, Stanford JL, Mayne ST, Farrow DC, Niwa S, Blot WJ, Fraumeni-JF (1997). Tobacco, alcohol, and socioeconomic status and adenocarcinomas of the esophagus and gastric cardia. *J Natl Cancer Inst* 89: 1277-1284.

563. Garber JE, Li FP, Kingston JE, Krush AJ, Strong LC, Finegold MJ, Bertario L, Bulow S, Filippone A, Gedde DTJ, et a (1988). Hepatoblastoma and familial adenomatous polyposis. *J Natl Cancer Inst* 80: 1626-1628.

564. Garcia SB, Park HS, Novelli M, Wright NA (1999). Field cancerization, clonality, and epithelial stem cells: the spread of mutated clones in epithelial sheets. *J Pathol* 187: 61-81.

565. Gardner EJ, Richards RC (1953). Multiple cutaneous lesions occurring simultaneously with hereditary polyposis and osteomatosis. *Am J Hum Genet* 5: 139-148.

566. Garfinkel L, Mushinski M (1999). U.S. cancer incidence, mortality and survival: 1973-1996. *Stat Bull Metrop Insur Co* 80: 23-32.

567. Gascoyne RD, Adomat SA, Krajewski S, Krajewska M, Horsman DE, Tolcher AW, O'Reilly SE, Hoskins P, Coldman AJ, Reed JC, Connors JM (1997). Prognostic significance of Bcl-2 protein expression and Bcl-2 gene rearrangement in diffuse aggressive non-Hodgkin's lymphoma. *Blood* 90: 244-251.

568. Gayther SA, Gorringe KL, Ramus SJ, Huntsman D, Roviello F, Grehan N, Machado JC, Pinto E, Seruca R, Halling K, MacLeod P, Powell SM, Jackson CE, Ponder BA, Caldas C (1998). Identification of germ-line E-cadherin mutations in gastric cancer families of European origin. *Cancer Res* 58: 4086-4089.

569. Gelfand MD (1983). Barrett esophagus in sexagenarian identical twins. *J Clin Gastroenterol* 5: 251-253.

570. Gembala RB, Hare JL, Meilahn J (1993). Intraabdominal metastatic thymoma. *AJR Am J Roentgenol* 161: 1331-

571. Genna M, Leopardi F, Fambri P, Postorino A (1997). [Neurogenic tumors of the ano-rectal region]. *Ann Ital Chir* 68: 351-353.

572. Genta RM, Hamner HW, Graham DY (1993). Gastric lymphoid follicles in Helicobacter pylori infection: frequency, distribution, and response to triple therapy. *Hum Pathol* 24: 577-583.

573. George DH, Murphy F, Michalski R, Ulmer BG (1989). Serous cystadenocarcinoma of the pancreas: a new entity? *Am J Surg Pathol* 13: 61-66.

574. Ger R, Reuben J (1968). Squamous-cell carcinoma of the anal canal: a metastatic lesion. *Dis Colon Rectum* 11: 213-219.

575. Gerard JP, Romestaing P, Ardiet JM, Baillargeon J, Maisonneuve P, Perret C (1991). [Current treatment of cancers of the anal canal]. *Ann Chir* 49: 363-368.

576. Ghadimi BM, Schrock E, Walker RL, Wangsa D, Jauho A, Meltzer PS, Ried T (1999). Specific chromosomal aberrations and amplification of the AIB1 nuclear receptor coactivator gene in pancreatic carcinomas. *Am J Pathol* 154: 525-536.

577. Ghadirian P, Boyle P, Simard A, Baillargeon J, Maisonneuve P, Perret C (1991). Reported family aggregation of pancreatic cancer within a population-based case-control study in the Francophone community in Montreal, Canada. *Int J Pancreatol* 10: 183-196.

578. Giardiello FM, Petersen GM, Brensinger JD, Luce MC, Cayouette MC, Bacon J, Booker SV, Hamilton SR (1996). Hepatoblastoma and APC gene mutation in familial adenomatous polyposis . *Gut* 39: 867-869.

579. Giardiello FM, Welsh SB, Hamilton SR, Offerhaus GJ, Gittelsohn AM, Booker SV, Krush AJ, Yardley JH, Luk GD (1987). Increased risk of cancer in the Peutz-Jeghers syndrome. *N Engl J Med* 316: 1511-1514.

580. Gifaldi AS, Petros JG, Wolfe GR (1992). Metastatic breast carcinoma presenting as persistent diarrhea. *J Surg Oncol* 51: 211-215.

581. Gillen CD, Walmsley RS, Prior P, Andrews HA, Allan RN (1994). Icerative colitis and Crohn's disease: a comparison of the colorectal cancer risk in extensive colitis. *Gut* 35: 1590-1592.

582. Gillen CD, Wilson CA, Walmsley RS, Sanders DS, O'Dwyer ST, Allan RN (1995). Occult small bowel adenocarcinoma complicating Crohn's disease: a report of three cases. *Postgrad Med J* 71: 172-174.

583. Gisbertz IA, Jonkers DM, Arends JW, Bot FJ, Stockbrugger RW, Vrints LW, Schouten HC (1997). Specific detection of Helicobacter pylori and non-Helicobacter pylori flora in small- and large-cell primary gastric B-cell non-Hodgkin's lymphoma. *Ann Oncol* 8 Suppl 2: 33-36.

584. Gledhill A, Hall PA, Cruse JP, Pollock DJ (1986). Enteroendocrine cell hyperplasia, carcinoid tumours and adenocarcinoma in long-standing ulcerative colitis. *Histopathology* 10: 501-508.

585. Gleeson CM, Sloan JM, McManus DT, Maxwell P, Arthur K, McGuigan JA, Ritchie AJ, Russell SE (1998). Comparison of p53 and DNA content abnormalities in adenocarcinoma of the oesophagus and gastric cardia. *Br J Cancer* 77: 277-286.

586. Goddard MJ, Lonsdale RN (1992). The histogenesis of appendiceal carcinoid tumours. *Histopathology* 20: 345-349.

587. Godwin JD (1975). Carcinoid tumors. An analysis of 2,837 cases. *Cancer* 36: 560-569.

588. Goedert M, Otten U, Suda K, Heitz PU, Stalder GA, Obrecht JP, Holzach P, Allgower M (1980). Dopamine, norepinephrine and serotonin production by an intestinal carcinoid tumor. *Cancer* 45: 104-107.

589. Goggins M, Hruban RH, Kern SE (2000). BRCA2 is inactivated late in the development of pancreatic intraepithelial neoplasia: evidence and implications 3. *Am J Pathol* 156: 1767-1771.

590. Goggins M, Offerhaus GJ, Hilgers W, Griffin CA, Shekher M, Tang D, Sohn TA, Yeo CJ, Kern SE, Hruban RH (1998). Pancreatic adenocarcinomas with DNA replication errors (RER+) are associated with wild-type K-ras and characteristic histopathology. Poor differentiation, a syncytial growth pattern, and pushing borders suggest RER+. *Am J Pathol* 152: 1501-1507.

591. Goggins M, Schutte M, Lu J, Moskaluk CA, Weinstein CL, Petersen GM, Yeo CJ, Jackson CE, Lynch HT, Hruban RH, Kern SE (1996). Germline BRCA2 gene mutations in patients with apparently sporadic pancreatic carcinomas. *Cancer Res* 56: 5360-5364.

592. Goggins M, Shekher M, Turnacioglu K, Yeo CJ, Hruban RH, Kern SE (1998). Genetic alterations of the transforming growth factor beta receptor genes in pancreatic and biliary adenocarcinomas. *Cancer Res* 58: 5329-5332.

593. Gold EB, Goldin SB (1998). Epidemiology of and risk factors for pancreatic cancer. *Surg Oncol Clin N Am* 7: 67-91.

594. Goldblum JR, Appelman HD (1995). Stromal tumors of the duodenum. A histologic and immunohistochemical study of 20 cases. *Am J Surg Pathol* 19: 71-80.

595. Goldblum JR, Hart WR (1998). Perianal Paget's disease: a histologic and immunohistochemical study of 11 cases with and without associated rectal adenocarcinoma. *Am J Surg Pathol* 22: 170-179.

596. Goldfarb WB, Bennett D, Monafo W (1963). Carcinoma in heterotopic gastric pancreas. *Ann Surg* 158: 56-58.

597. Goldgar DE, Easton DF, Cannon AL, Skolnick MH (1994). Systematic population-based assessment of cancer risk in first-degree relatives of cancer probands. *J Natl Cancer Inst* 86: 1600-1608.

598. Goldie SJ, Kuntz KM, Weinstein MC, Freedberg KA, Welton ML, Palefsky JM (1999). The clinical effectiveness and cost-effectiveness of screening for anal squamous intraepithelial lesions in homosexual and bisexual HIV-positive men. *JAMA* 281: 1822-1829.

599. Goldman S, Auer G, Erhardt K, Seligson U (1987). Prognostic significance of clinical stage, histologic grade, and nuclear DNA content in squamous-cell carcinoma of the anus. *Dis Colon Rectum* 30: 444-448.

600. Goldman S, Glimelius B, Nilsson B, Pahlman L (1989). Incidence of anal epidermoid carcinoma in Sweden 1970-1984. *Acta Chir Scand* 155: 191-197.

601. Goldstein AM, Fraser MC, Struewing JP, Hussussian CJ, Ranade K, Zametkin DP, Fontaine LS, Organic SM, Dracopoli NC, Clark-WH J, et al (1995). Increased risk of pancreatic cancer in melanoma-prone kindreds with p16INK4 mutations. *N Engl J Med* 333: 970-974.

602. Gonzalez CF (1991). Undifferentiated small cell ("anaplastic") hepatoblastoma. *Pediatr Pathol* 11: 155-161.

603. Goodman ZD, Albores SJ, Lundblad DM (1984). Somatostatinoma of the cystic duct. *Cancer* 53: 498-502.

604. Goodman ZD, Ishak KG (1984). Angiomyolipomas of the liver. *Am J Surg Pathol* 8: 745-750.

605. Goodman ZD, Ishak KG, Langloss JM, Sesterhenn IA, Rabin L (1985). Combined hepatocellular-cholangiocarcinoma. A histologic and immunohistochemical study. *Cancer* 55: 124-135.

606. Goodnight J, Venook A, Ames M, Taylor C, Gilden R, Figlin RA (1996). Practice guidelines for esophageal cancer. *Cancer J Scie Am* 2: S37-S43.

607. Gopez EV, Mourelatos Z, Rosato EF, Livolsi VA (1997). Acute appendicitis secondary to metastatic bronchogenic adenocarcinoma. *Am Surg* 63: 778-780.

608. Gorunova L, Johansson B, Dawiskiba S, Andren SA, Jin Y, Mandahl N, Heim S, Mitelman F (1995). Massive cytogenetic heterogeneity in a pancreatic carcinoma: fifty-four karyotypically unrelated clones. *Genes Chromosomes Cancer* 14: 259-266.

609. Goseki N, Koike M, Yoshida M (1992). Histopathologic characteristics of early stage esophageal carcinoma. A comparative study with gastric carcinoma. *Cancer* 69: 1088-1093.

610. Goseki N, Takizawa T, Koike M (1992). Differences in the mode of the extension of gastric cancer classified by histological type: new histological classification of gastric carcinoma. *Gut* 33: 606-612.

611. Gottieb CA, Meinl E, Maeda KM (1990). Rectal non-Hodgkin's lymphoma: a clinicopathologic study and review. *Henry Ford Hosp Med* J 38: 255-258.

612. Gough DB, Donohue JH, Schutt AJ, Gonchoroff N, Goellner JR, Wilson TO, Naessens JM, O'Brien PC, van-Heerden JA (1994). Pseudomyxoma peritonei. Long-term patient survival with an aggressive regional approach. *Am J Surg* 219: 112-119.

613. Gourley WK, Kumar D, Bouton MS, Fish JC, Nealon W (1992). Cystadenoma and cystadenocarcinoma with mesenchymal stroma of the liver. Immunohistochemical analysis. *Arch Pathol Lab Med* 116: 1047-1050.

614. Grady WM, Myeroff LL, Swinler SE, Rajput A, Thiagalingam S, Lutterbaugh JD, Neumann A, Brattain MG, Chang J, Kim SJ, Kinzler KW, Vogelstein B, Willson JK, Markowitz S (1999). Mutational inactivation of transforming growth factor beta receptor type II in microsatellite stable colon cancers. *Cancer Res* 59: 320-324

615. Graham DY, Yamaoka Y (1998). H. pylori and cagA: relationships with gastric cancer, duodenal ulcer, and reflux esophagitis and its complications. *Helicobacter* 3: 145-151.

616. Grant LD, Lauwers GY, Meloni AM, Stone JF, Betz JL, Vogel S, Sandberg AA (1996). Unbalanced chromosomal translocation, der(17)t(13;17)(q14;p11) in a solid and cystic papillary epithelial neoplasm of the pancreas. *Am J Surg Pathol* 20: 339-345.

617. Grapin C, Audry G, Josset P, Patte C, Sorrel DE, Gruner M (1994). Histiocytosis X revealed by complex anal fistula. *Eur J Pediatr Surg* 4: 184-185.

618. Green LK (1990). Hematogenous metastases to the stomach. A review of 67 cases. *Cancer* 65: 1596-1600.

619. Green LK, Silva EG (1989). Hepatoblastoma in an adult with metastasis to the ovaries. *Am J Clin Pathol* 92: 110-115.

620. Green PH, O'Toole KM, Weinberg LM, Goldfarb JP (1981). Early gastric cancer. *Gastroenterology* 81: 247-256.

621. Greenberg RE, Bank S, Stark B (1990). Adenocarcinoma of the pancreas producing pancreatitis and pancreatic abscess. *Pancreas* 5: 108-113.

622. Greenstein AJ, Balasubramanian S, Harpaz N, Rizwan M, Sachar DB (1997). Carcinoid tumor and inflammatory bowel disease: a study of eleven cases and review of the literature. *Am J Gastroenterol* 92: 682-685.

623. Greenstein AJ, Sachar DB, Smith H, Janowitz HD, Aufses-AH J (1981). A comparison of cancer risk in Crohn's disease and ulcerative colitis. *Cancer* 48: 2742-2745.

624. Griesser GH, Schumacher U, Elfeldt R, Horny HP (1985). Adenosquamous carcinoma of the ileum. Report of a case and review of the literature. *Virchows Arch A Pathol Anat Histopathol* 406: 483-487.

625. Griffin CA, Hruban RH, Long PP, Morsberger LA, Douna IF, Yeo CJ (1995). Consistent chromosome abnormalities in adenocarcinoma of the pancreas. *Genes Chromosomes Cancer* 9: 93-100.

626. Griffin CA, Hruban RH, Morsberger LA, Ellingham T, Long PP, Jaffee EM, Hauda KM, Bohlander SK, Yeo CJ (1995). Chromosome abnormalities in pancreatic adenocarcinoma. *Genes Chromosomes Cancer* 55: 2394-2399.

627. Grigioni WF, D'errico A, Milani M, Villanacci V, Avellini C, Miglioli M, Blasco G, Barbara L, Possati L (1984). Early gastric cancer. Clinico-pathological analysis of 125 cases of early gastric cancer (EGC). *Acta Pathol Jpn* 34: 979-989.

628. Grisham MB, Ware K, Gilleland-HE J, Gilleland LB, Abell CL, Yamada T (1992). Neutrophil-mediated nitrosamine formation: role of nitric oxide in rats. *Gastroenterology* 103: 1260-1266.

629. Groden J, Thliveris A, Samowitz W, Carlson M, Gelbert L, Albertsen H, Joslyn G, Stevens J, Spirio L, Robertson M (1991). Identification and characterization of familial adenomatous polyposis coli gene. *Cell* 66: 589-600.

630. Groisman GM, Polak CS (1998). Fibroepithelial polyps of the anus: a histologic, immunohistochemical, and ultrastructural study, including comparison with the normal anal subepithelial layer. *Am J Surg Pathol* 22: 70-76.

631. Grosfeld JL, Vane DW, Rescorla FJ, McGuire W, West KW (1990). Pancreatic tumors in childhood: analysis of 13 cases. *J Pediatr Surg* 25: 1057-1062.

632. Grove A, Vyberg B, Vyberg M (1991). Focal fatty change of the liver. A review and a case associated with continuous ambulatory peritoneal dialysis. *Virchows Arch A Pathol Anat Histopathol* 419: 69-75.

633. Gruber SB, Entius MM, Petersen GM, Laken SJ, Longo PA, Boyer R, Levin AM, Mujumdar UJ, Trent JM, Kinzler KW, Vogelstein B, Hamilton SR, Polymeropoulos MH, Offerhaus GJ, Giardiello FM (1998). Pathogenesis of adenocarcinoma in Peutz-Jeghers syndrome. *Cancer Res* 58: 5267-5270.

634. Grunewald M, Vieth M, Kreibich H, Bethke B, Stolte M (1997). [The status of diagnosis of Barrett esophagus: An analysis of 1000 histologically diagnosed cases]. *Dtsch Med Wochenschr* 122: 427-431.

635. Grussendorf CE (1997). Anogenital premalignant and malignant tumors (including Buschke-Lowenstein tumors). *Clin Dermatol* 15: 377-388.

636. Gryfe R, Swallow C, Bapat B, Redston M, Gallinger S, Couture J (1997). Molecular biology of colorectal cancer. *Curr Probl Cancer* 21: 233-300.

637. Gu J, Tamura M, Yamada KM (1998). Tumor suppressor PTEN inhibits integrin- and growth factor-mediated mitogen-activated protein (MAP) kinase signaling pathways. *J Cell Biol* 143: 1375-1383.

638. Guanrei Y, Sungjian Q (1987). Incidence rate of adenocarcinoma of the gastric cardia, and endoscopic classification of early cardial carcinoma in Henan Province, the People's Republic of China. *Endoscopy* 19: 7-10.

639. Gudjonsson B (1987). Cancer of the pancreas, 50 years of surgery. *Cancer* 60: 2284-2303.

640. Guilford P, Hopkins J, Grady W, Markowitz S, Willis J, Lynch H, Rajput A, Wiesner G, Lindor N, Burgart L, Toro T, Lee D, Limacher JM, Shaw D, Findlay M, Reeve A (1999). E-cadherin germline mutations define an inherited cancer syndrome dominated by diffuse gastric cancer. *Hum Mutat* 14(3): 249-255.

641. Guilford P, Hopkins J, Harraway J, McLeod M, McLeod N, Harawira P, Taite H, Scoular R, Miller A, Reeve AE (1998). E-cadherin germline mutations in familial gastric cancer. *Nature* 392: 402-405.

642. Guillem JG, Smith AJ, Calle JP, Ruo L (1999). Gastrointestinal polyposis syndromes. *Curr Probl Surg* 36: 217-323.

643. Guo KJ, Yamaguchi K, Enjoji M (1988). Undifferentiated carcinoma of the gallbladder. A clinicopathologic, histochemical, and immunohistochemical study of 21 patients with a poor prognosis. *Cancer* 61: 1872-1879.

644. Gupta NM, Goenka MK, Jindal A, Behera A, Vaiphei K (1996). Primary lymphoma of the esophagus. *J Clin Gastroenterol* 23: 203-206.

645. Gupta RK, Lallu S, Delahunt B (1998). Fine-needle aspiration cytology of metastatic clear-cell renal carcinoma presenting as a solitary mass in the head of the pancreas. *Diagn Cytopathol* 19: 194-197.

646. Guthoff A, Rothe B, Klapdor R, Kloppel G, Greten H (1987). Site of recurrence after resection for pancreatic carcinoma. *Dig Dis Sci* 32: 1168-

647. Gyde SN, et al (1988). Colorectal cancer un ulcerative colitis: a cohort study of primary referrals from three centres. *Gut* 29: 206-217.

648. Haas JE, Muczynski KA, Krailo M, Ablin A, Land V, Vietti TJ, Hammond GD (1989). Histopathology and prognosis in childhood hepatoblastoma and hepatocarcinoma. *Cancer* 64: 1082-1095.

649. Haenszel W, Kurihara M, Locke FB, Shimuzu K, Segi M (1976). Stomach cancer in Japan. *J Natl Cancer Inst* 56: 265-274.

650. Hagihara P, Vazquez MD, Parker-JC J, Griffen WO (1976). Carcinoma of anal-ductal origin: report of a case. *Dis Colon Rectum* 19: 694-701.

651. Hahn SA, Schutte M, Hoque AT, Moskaluk CA, da-Costa LT, Rozenblum E, Weinstein CL, Fischer A, Yeo CJ, Hruban RH, Kern SE (1996). DPC4, a candidate tumor suppressor gene at human chromosome 18q21.1. *Science* 271: 350-353.

652. Hakanson R, Ekelund M, Sunder F (1984). Activation and proliferation of gastric endocrine cells. In: *Evolution and Tumor Pathology of the Neuroendocrine System*, Falkmer S, Hakanson R, Sunder F (eds), Elsevier: Amsterdam.

653. Hale HL, Husband JE, Gossios K, Norman AR, Cunningham D (1998). CT of calcified liver metastases in colorectal carcinoma. *Clin Radiol* 53: 735-741.

654. Halling KC, Harper JC, Moskaluk CA, Thibodeau SN, Petroni GR, Yustein AS, Tosi P, Minacci C, Roviello F, Piva P, Hamilton SR, Jackson CE, Powell SM (1999). Origins of microsatellite instability in gastric cancer. *Am J Pathol* 155: 205-

655. Hamid QA, Bishop AE, Rode J, Dhillon AP, Rosenberg BF, Reed RJ, Sibley RK, Polak JM (1986). Duodenal gangliocytic paragangliomas: a study of 10 cases with immunocytochemical neuroendocrine markers. *Hum Pathol* 17: 1151-1157.

656. Hamilton SR (1985). Colorectal carcinomas in patients with Crohn's disease. *Gastroenterology* 89: 398-407.

657. Hamilton SR (1986). Pathologic diagnosis of colorectal and anal malignancies: classification and prognostic features of pathologic findings. In: *Colorectal Tumors*, Beahrs OH, Higgins GA, Weinstein JJ (eds), J.B. Lipincott: Philadelphia.

658. Hamilton SR, Liu B, Parsons RE, Papadopoulos N, Jen J, Powell SM, Krush AJ, Berk T, Cohen Z, Tetu B, et al (1995). The molecular basis of Turcot's syndrome. *N Engl J Med* 332: 839-847.

659. Hammond C, Jeffers L, Carr BI, Simon D (1999). Multiple genetic alterations, 4q28, a new suppressor region, and potential gender differences in human hepatocellular carcinoma. *Hepatology* 29: 1479-1485.

660. Han HJ, Maruyama M, Baba S, Park JG, Nakamura Y (1995). Genomic structure of human mismatch repair gene, hMLH1, and its mutation analysis in patients with hereditary non-polyposis colorectal cancer (HNPCC). *Hum Mol Genet* 4: 237-242.

661. Hanada K, Itoh M, Fujii K, Tsuchida A, Ooishi H, Kaiiyama G (1996). K-ras and p53 mutations in stage I gallbladder carcinoma with an anomalous junction of the pancreaticobiliary duct. *Cancer* 77: 452-458.

662. Hanada M, Nakano K, Ii Y, Yamashita H (1984). Carcinosarcoma of the esophagus with osseous and cartilagenous production. A combined study of keratin immunohistochemistry and electron microscopy. *Acta Pathol Jpn* 34: 669-678.

663. Hanby AM, Poulsom R, Singh S, Jankowski J, Hopwood D, Elia G, Rogers L, Patel K, Wright NA (1993). Hyperplastic polyps: a cell lineage which both synthesizes and secretes trefoil-peptides and has phenotypic similarity with the ulcer- associated cell lineage. *Am J Pathol* 142: 663-668.

664. Hansen S, Whg J, Giercksky KE, Tretli S (1997). Esophageal and gastric carcinoma in Norway 1958-1992: incidence trend variability according to morphological subtypes and organ subsites. *Int J Cancer* 72: 340-344.

665. Hanssen AM, Fryns JP (1995). Cowden syndrome. *J Med Genet* 32: 117-119.

666. Haque S, Modlin IM, West AB (1992). Multiple glomus tumors of the stomach with intravascular spread. *Am J Surg Pathol* 16: 291-299.

667. Haratake J, Hashimoto H (1995). An immunohistochemical analysis of 13 cases with combined hepatocellular and cholangiocellular carcinoma. *Liver* 15: 9-15.

668. Harris AC, Ben-Ezra JM, Contos MJ, Kornstein MJ (1996). Malignant lymphoma can present as hepatobiliary disease. *Cancer* 78: 2011-2019.

669. Harris KM, Kelly S, Berry E, Hutton J, Roderick P, Cullingworth J (1998). Systematic review of endoscopic ultrasound in gastro-oesophageal cancer. *Health Technol Assess* 2: 1-134.

670. Harris NL, Jaffe ES, Stein H, Banks PM, Chan JK, Cleary ML, Delsol G, DeWolf-Peeters C, Falini B, Gatter KC (1994). A revised European-American classification of lymphoid neoplasms: a proposal from the International Lymphoma Study Group. *Blood* 84: 1361-1392.

671. Harrison JC, Dean PJ, Vander ZR, elZeky F, Wruble LD (1991). Adenocarcinoma of the stomach with invasion limited to the muscularis propria. *Hum Pathol* 22: 111-117.

672. Harrison PM (1999). Prevention of bile duct cancer in primary sclerosing cholangitis. *Ann Oncol* 10: 208-211.

673. Hasebe T, Sakamoto M, Mukai K, Kawano N, Konishi M, Ryu M, Fukamachi S, Hirohashi S (1995). Cholangiocarcinoma arising in bile duct adenoma with focal area of bile duct hamartoma. *Virchows Arch* 426: 209-213.

674. Hashimoto M, Watanabe G, Matsuda M, Dohi T, Tsurumaru M (1998). Management of the pancreatic metastases from renal cell carcinoma: report of four resected cases. *Hepatogastroenterology* 45: 1150-1154.

675. Hassan MO, Gogate PA (1993). Malignant mixed exocrine-endocrine tumor of the pancreas with unusual intracytoplasmic inclusions. *Ultrastruct Pathol* 17: 483-493.

676. Hayashi S, Masuda H, Shigematsu M (1997). Liver metastasis rare in colorectal cancer patients with fatty liver. *Hepatogastroenterology* 44: 1069-1075.

677. Hayes J, Dunn E (1989). Has the incidence of primary gastric lymphoma increased? *Cancer* 63: 2073-2076.

678. Hayward J (1961). The lower end of the oesophagus. *Thorax* 16: 36-41.

679. He D, Zhang DK, Lam KY, Ma L, Ngan HY, Liu SS, Tsao SW (1997). Prevalence of HPV infection in esophageal squamous cell carcinoma in Chinese patients and its relationship to the p53 gene mutation. *Int J Cancer* 72: 959-964.

680. He TC, Sparks AB, Rago C, Hermeking H, Zawel L, da-Costa LT, Morin PJ, Vogelstein B, Kinzler KW (1998). Identification of c-MYC as a target of the APC pathway. *Science* 281: 1509-1512.

681. Heathcote J, Knauer CM, Oakes D, Archibald RW (1980). Perforation of an adenocarcinoma of the small bowel affected by regional enteritis. *Gut* 21: 1093-1096.

682. Heenan PJ, Elder DE, Sobin LH (1996). Histological Typing of Skin Tumours. 2nd ed, Springer-Verlag: Berlin - New York.

683. Heidet L, Boye E, Cai Y, Sado Y, Zhang X, Flejou JF, Fekete F, Ninomiya Y, Gubler MC, Antignac C (1998). Somatic deletion of the 5' ends of both the COL4A5 and COL4A6 genes in a sporadic leiomyoma of the esophagus. *Am J Pathol* 152: 673-678.

684. Heidl G, Langhans P, Krieg V, Mellin W, Schilke R, Bunte H (1993). Comparative studies of cardia carcinoma and infracardial gastric carcinoma. *J Cancer Res Clin Oncol* 120: 91-94.

685. Heiman TM, Cohen LB, Bolnick K, Szporn AH (1985). Villous polyposis of the ileum. *Am J Gastroenterol* 80: 983-985.

686. Heinimann K, Scott RJ, Chappuis P, Weber W, Muller H, Dobbie Z, Hutter P (1999). N-acetyltransferase 2 influences cancer prevalence in hMLH1/hMSH2 mutation carriers. *Cancer Res* 59: 3038-3040.

687. Heise W, Arasteh K, Mostertz P, Skorde J, Schmidt W, Obst C, Koeppen M, Weiss R, Grosse G, Niedobitek F, L'Age M (1997). Malignant gastrointestinal lymphomas in patients with AIDS. *Digestion* 58: 218-224.

688. Heiskanen I, Kellokumpu I, Jarvinen H (1999). Management of duodenal adenomas in 98 patients with familial adenomatous polyposis. *Endoscopy* 31(6): 412-416.

689. Helpap B, Vogel J (1988). Immunohistochemical studies on cystic pancreatic neoplasms. *Pathol Res Pract* 184: 39-45.

690. Hemminki A, Markie D, Tomlinson I, Avizienyte E, Roth S, Loukola A, Bignell G, Warren W, Aminoff M, Hoglund P, Jarvinen H, Kristo P, Pelin K, Ridanpaa M, Salovaara R, Toro T, Bodmer W, Olschwang S, Olsen AS, Stratton MR, de la Chapelle A, Aaltonen LA (1998). A serine/threonine kinase gene defective in Peutz-Jeghers syndrome. *Nature* 391: 184-187.

691. Hemminki A, Tomlinson I, Markie D, Jarvinen H, Sistonen P, Bjorkqvist AM, Knuutila S, Salovaara R, Bodmer W, Shibata D, de la Chapelle A, Aaltonen LA (1997). Localization of a susceptibility locus for Peutz-Jeghers syndrome to 19p using comparative genomic hybridization and targeted linkage analysis. *Nat Genet* 15: 87-90.

692. Henne BD, Vogel I, Luttges J, Kloppel G, Kremer B (1998). Ductal adenocarcinoma of the pancreas head: survival after regional versus extended lymphadenectomy. *Hepatogastroenterology* 45: 855-866.

693. Hennies HC, Hagedorn M, Reis A (1995). Palmoplantar keratoderma in association with carcinoma of the esophagus maps to chromosome 17q distal to the keratin gene cluster. *Genomics* 29: 537-540.

694. Henson DE, Albores SJ, Corle D (1992). Carcinoma of the extrahepatic bile ducts. Histologic types, stage of disease, grade, and survival rates. *Cancer* 70: 1498-1501.

695. Henson DE, Albores SJ, Corle D (1992). Carcinoma of the gallbladder. Histologic types, stage of disease, grade, and survival rates. *Cancer* 70: 1493-1497.

696. Herman JG, Umar A, Polyak K, Graff JR, Ahuja N, Issa JP, Markowitz S, Willson JK, Hamilton SR, Kinzler KW, Kane MF, Kolodner RD, Vogelstein B, Kunkel TA, Baylin SB (1998). Incidence and functional consequences of hMLH1 promoter hypermethylation in colorectal carcinoma. *Proc Natl Acad Sci U S A* 95: 6870-6875.

697. Hermanek P (1991). Staging of exocrine pancreatic carcinoma. *Eur J Surg Oncol* 17: 167-172.

698. Hermanek P, Henson D, Sobin LH (1993). TNM supplement 1993: a commentary on uniform use. Springer Verlag: Berlin-New York.

699. Hernandez-Boussard T, Rodriguez-Tome P, Montesano R, Hainaut P (1999). IARC p53 database: a relational database to compile and analyse p53 mutations in human tumors and cell lines. *Hum Mutat* 14: 1-8.

700. Hernandez L, Fest T, Cazorla M, Teruya FJ, Bosch F, Peinado MA, Piris MA, Montserrat E, Cardesa A, Jaffe ES, Campo E, Raffeld M (1996). p53 gene mutations and protein overexpression are associated with aggressive variants of mantle cell lymphomas. *Blood* 87: 3351-3359.

701. Herrera GA, Cerezo L, Jones JE, Sack J, Grizzle WE, Pollack WJ, Lott RL (1989). Gastrointestinal autonomic nerve tumors. 'Plexosarcomas'. *Arch Pathol Lab Med* 113: 846-853.

702. Herrera GA, Pinto-de MH, Grizzle WE, Han SG (1984). Malignant small bowel neoplasm of enteric plexus derivation (plexosarcoma). Light and electron microscopic study confirming the origin of the neoplasm. *Dig Dis Sci* 29: 275-284.

703. Herzog U, Boss M, Spichtin HP (1994). Endoanal ultrasonography in the follow-up of anal carcinoma. *Surg Endosc* 8: 1186-1189.

704. Heselmeyer K, du MS, Blegen H, Friberg B, Svensson C, Schrock E, Veldman T, Shah K, Auer G, Ried T (1997). A recurrent pattern of chromosomal aberrations and immunophenotypic appearance defines anal squamous cell carcinomas. *Br J Cancer* 76: 1271-1278.

705. Hibi K, Kondo K, Akiyama S, Ito K, Takagi H (1995). Frequent genetic instability in small intestinal carcinomas. *Jpn J Cancer Res* 86: 357-360.

706. Higa E, Rosai J, Pizzimbono CA, Wise L (1973). Mucosal hyperplasia, mucinous cystadenoma, and mucinous cystadenocarcinoma of the appendix. A re-evaluation of appendiceal "mucocele". *Cancer* 32: 1525-1541.

707. Hinson FL, Ambrose NS (1998). Pseudomyxoma peritonei. *Br J Surg* 85: 1332-1339.

708. Hiorns LR, Scholefield JH, Palmer JG, Shepherd NA, Kerr IB (1990). Ki-ras oncogene mutations in non-HPV-associated anal carcinoma. *J Pathol* 161: 99-103.

709. Hippelainen M, Eskelinen M, Lipponen P, Chang F, Syrjanen K (1993). Mitotic activity index, volume corrected mitotic index and human papilloma-virus suggestive morphology are not prognostic factors in carcinoma of the oesophagus. *Anticancer Res* 13: 677-681.

710. Hirata K, Sato T, Mukaiya M, Yamashiro K, Kimura M, Sasaki K, Denno R (1997). Results of 1001 pancreatic resections for invasive ductal adenocarcinoma of the pancreas. *Arch Surg* 132: 771-776.

711. Hirata Y, Sakamoto N, Yamamoto H, Matsukura S, Imura H, Okada S (1976). Gastric carcinoid with ectopic production of ACTH and beta-MSH. *Cancer* 37: 377-385.

712. Hirohashi S (1992). Pathology and molecular mechanisms of multistage hepatocarcinogenesis. In: *Multistage Carcinogenesis*, Harris CC (eds), Japan Sci Soc Press/CRC Press: Tokyo/Boca Raton.

713. Hirota S, Isozaki K, Moriyama Y, Hashimoto K, Nishida T, Ishiguro S, Kawano K, Hanada M, Kurata A, Takeda M, Muhammad TG, Matsuzawa Y, Kanakura Y, Shinomura Y, Kitamura Y (1998). Gain-of-function mutations of c-kit in human gastrointestinal stromal tumors. *Science* 279: 577-580.

714. Hirota T, Nishimaki T, Suzuki T, Komukai S, Kuwabara S, Aizawa K, Hatakeyama K (1998). Esophageal intramural metastasis from an adenocarcinoma of the gastric cardia: report of a case. *Surg Today* 28: 1160-1162.

715. Hirota WK, Loughney TM, Lazas DJ, Maydonovitch CL, Rholl V, Wong RK (1999). Specialized intestinal metaplasia, dysplasia, and cancer of the esophagus and esophagogastric junction: prevalence and clinical data. *Gastroenterology* 116: 277-285.

716. Hirota WK, Loughney TM, Lazas DJ, Maydonovitch CL, Wong RK (1997). Is Helicobacter pylori associated with specialized metaplasia of the esophagus or stomach? A prospective study of 889 patients. *Gastroenterology* A149.

717. Hisada M, Garber JE, Fung CY, Fraumeni-JF J, Li FP (1998). Multiple primary cancers in families with Li-Fraumeni syndrome. *J Natl Cancer Inst* 90: 606-611.

718. Hisamichi S, Sugawara N (1984). Mass screening for gastric cancer by X-ray examination. *Jpn J Clin Oncol* 14: 211-223.

719. Hiyama E, Yokoyama T, Tatsumoto N, Hiyama K, Imamura Y, Murakami Y, Kodama T, Piatyszek MA, Shay JW, Matsuura Y (1995). Telomerase activity in gastric cancer. Cancer Res 55: 3258-3262.

720. Hiyama T, Yokozaki H, Shinamoto F, Haruma K, Yasui W, Kajiyama G, Tahara E (1998). Frequent p53 gene mutations in serrated adenomas of the colorectum. J Pathol 186: 131-139.

721. Hizawa K, Iida M, Matsumoto T, Kohrogi N, Yao T, Fujishima M (1993). Neoplastic transformation arising in Peutz-Jeghers polyposis. Dis Colon Rectum 36: 953-957.

722. Hock YL, Scott KW, Grace RH (1993). Mixed adenocarcinoma/carcinoid tumour of large bowel in a patient with Crohn's disease. J Clin Pathol 46: 183-185.

723. Hoda SA, Hajdu SI (1992). Small cell carcinoma of the esophagus. Cytology and immunohistology in four cases. Acta Cytol 36: 113-120.

724. Hoffman JW, Fox PS, Milwauke SDW (1973). Duodenal wall tumors and the Zollinger-Ellison syndrome. Arch Surg 107: 334-338.

725. Hofler H, Kloppel G, Heitz PU (1984). Combined production of mucus, amines and peptides by goblet-cell carcinoids of the appendix and ileum. Pathol Res Pract 178: 555-561.

726. Hofmann JW, Fox PS, Wilson SD (1973). Duodenal wall tumors and the Zollinger-Ellison syndrome. Surgical management. Arch Surg 107: 334-339.

727. Hofting I, Pott G, Stolte M (1993). [The syndrome of juvenile polyposis]. Leber Magen Darm 23: 107-2.

728. Hollstein M, Marion MJ, Lehman T, Welsh J, Harris CC, Martel PG, Kusters I, Montesano R (1994). p53 mutations at A:T base pairs in angiosarcomas of vinyl chloride-exposed factory workers. Carcinogenesis 15: 1-3.

729. Hollstein M, Shomer B, Greenblatt M, Soussi T, Hovig E, Montesano R, Harris CC (1996). Somatic point mutations in the p53 gene of human tumors and cell lines: updated compilation. Nucleic Acids Res 24: 141-146.

730. Holly EA, Whittemore AS, Aston DA, Ahn DK, Nickoloff BJ, Kristiansen JJ (1989). Anal cancer incidence: genital warts, anal fissure or fistula, hemorrhoids, and smoking. J Natl Cancer Inst 81: 1726-1731.

731. Holm R, Tanum G (1996). Evaluation of the prognostic significance of nm23/NDP kinase and cathepsin D in anal carcinomas. An immunohistochemical study. Virchows Arch 428: 85-89.

732. Holm R, Tanum G, Karlsen F, Nesland JM (1994). Prevalence and physical state of human papillomavirus DNA in anal carcinomas. Mod Pathol 7: 449-453.

733. Holmes F, Borek D, Owen KM, Hassanein R, Fishback J, Behbehani A, Baker A, Holmes G (1988). Anal cancer in women. Gastroenterology 95: 107-111.

734. Holscher AH, Bollschweiler E, Bumm R, Bartels H, Hofler H, Siewert JR (1995). Prognostic factors of resected adenocarcinoma of the esophagus. Surgery 118: 845-855.

735. Holscher AH, Bollschweiler E, Schneider PM, Siewert JR (1995). Prognosis of early esophageal cancer. Comparison between adeno- and squamous cell carcinoma. Cancer 76: 178-186.

736. Honda N, Cobb C, Lechago J (1986). Bile duct carcinoma associated with multiple von Meyenburg complexes in the liver. Hum Pathol 17: 1287-1290.

737. Honda T, Kai I, Ohi G (1999). Fat and dietary fiber intake and colon cancer mortality: a chronological comparison between Japan and the United States. Nutr Cancer 33: 95-99.

738. Hong MK, Laskin WB, Herman BE, Johnston MH, Vargo JJ, Steinberg SM, Allegra CJ, Johnston PG (1995). Expansion of the Ki-67 proliferative compartment correlates with degree of dysplasia in Barrett's esophagus. Cancer 75: 423-429.

739. Hoorens A, Lemoine NR, McLellan E, Morohoshi T, Kamisawa T, Heitz PU, Stamm B, Ruschoff J, Wiedenmann B, Kloppel G (1993). Pancreatic acinar cell carcinoma. An analysis of cell lineage markers, p53 expression, and Ki-ras mutation. Am J Pathol 143: 685-698.

740. Hoorens A, Prenzel K, Lemoine NR, Kloppel G (1998). Undifferentiated carcinoma of the pancreas: analysis of intermediate filament profile and Ki-ras mutations provides evidence of a ductal origin. J Pathol 185: 53-60.

741. Horie A, Haratake J, Jimi A, Matsumoto M, Ishii N, Tsutsumi Y (1987). Pancreatoblastoma in Japan, with differential diagnosis from papillary cystic tumor (ductuloacinar adenoma) of the pancreas. Acta Pathol Jpn 37: 47-63.

742. Horie A, Yano Y, Kotoo Y, Miwa A (1977). Morphogenesis of pancreatoblastoma, infantile carcinoma of the pancreas: report of two cases. Cancer 39: 247-254.

743. Horio Y, Suzuki H, Ueda R, Koshikawa T, Sugiura T, Ariyoshi Y, Shimokata K, Takahashi T (1994). Predominantly tumor-limited expression of a mutant allele in a Japanese family carrying a germline p53 mutation. Oncogene 9: 1231-1235.

744. Horsch D, Fink T, Goke B, Arnold R, Buchler M, Weihe E (1994). Distribution and chemical phenotypes of neuroendocrine cells in the human anal canal. Regul Pept 54: 527-542.

745. Horton KM, Jones B, Bayless TM, Lazenby AJ, Fishman EK (1994). Mucinous adenocarcinoma at the ileocecal valve mimicking Crohn's disease. Dig Dis Sci 39: 2276-2281.

745A. Hosokova O, Tsuda S, Kidani E, Watanabe K, Tanigawa Y, Shirazaki S, Hayashi H, Hinoshita T (1998). Diagnosis of gastric cancer up to three years after negative upper GI endoscopy. Endoscopy 30: 669-674.

746. Hou PC (1955). The pathology of Clonorchis sinesis infestation in the liver. J Pathol Bacteriol 70: 53-64.

747. Hou PC (1959). Relationship between primary carcinoma of the liver and infection with Clonorchis sinesis. J Pathol Bacteriol 72: 239-246.

748. Houlston R, Bevan S, Williams A, Young J, Dunlop M, Rozen P, Eng C, Markie D, Woodford RK, Rodriguez BM, Leggett B, Neale K, Phillips R, Sheridan E, Hodgson S, Iwama T, Eccles D, Bodmer W, Tomlinson I (1998). Mutations in DPC4 (SMAD4) cause juvenile polyposis syndrome, but only account for a minority of cases. Hum Mol Genet 7: 1907-1912.

749. Howe JR, Mitros FA, Summers RW (1998). The risk of gastrointestinal carcinoma in familial juvenile polyposis. Ann Surg Oncol 5: 751-756.

750. Howe JR, Ringold JC, Summers RW, Mitros FA, Nishimura DY, Stone EM (1998). A gene for familial juvenile polyposis maps to chromosome 18q21.1. Am J Hum Genet 62: 1129-1136.

751. Howe JR, Roth S, Ringold JC, Summers RW, Jarvinen HJ, Sistonen P, Tomlinson IP, Houlston RS, Bevan S, Mitros FA, Stone EM, Aaltonen LA (1998). Mutations in the SMAD4/DPC4 gene in juvenile polyposis. Science 280: 1086-1088.

752. Howel-Evans W, McConnell RB, Clarke CA, Sheppard PM (1958). Carcinoma of the oesophagus with keratosis palmaris et plantaris (tylosis): A study of two families. Quart J Med 27: 413-429.

753. Howell WM, Leung ST, Jones DB, Nakshabendi I, Hall MA, Lanchbury JS, Ciclitira PJ, Wright DH (1995). HLA-DRB, DQA, and -DQB polymorphism in celiac disease and enteropathy-associated T-cell lymphoma. Common features and additional risk factors for malignancy. Hum Immunol 43: 29-37.

754. Hruban RH, Petersen GM, Ha PK, Kern SE (1998). Genetics of pancreatic cancer. From genes to families. Surg Oncol Clin N Am 7: 1-23.

755. Hruban RH, Petersen GM, Ha PK, Kern SE (1998). Genetics of pancreatic cancer. From genes to families. Surg Oncol Clin N Am 7: 1-23.

756. Hsia CC, Axiotis CA, Di-Bisceglie AM, Tabor E (1992). Transforming growth factor-alpha in human hepatocellular carcinoma and coexpression with hepatitis B surface antigen in adjacent liver. Cancer 70: 1049-1056.

757. Hsu HC, Chen CC, Huang GT, Lee PH (1996). Clonal Epstein-Barr virus associated cholangiocarcinoma with lymphoepithelioma-like component. Hum Pathol 27: 848-850.

758. Hsu IC, Metcalf RA, Sun T, Welsh JA, Wang NJ, Harris CC (1991). Mutational hotspot in the p53 gene in human hepatocellular carcinomas. Nature 350: 427-428.

759. Huang CB, Eng HL, Chuang JH, Cheng YF, Chen WJ (1997). Primary Burkitt's lymphoma of the liver: report of a case with long-term survival after surgical resection and combination chemotherapy. J Pediatr Hematol Oncol 19: 135-138.

760. Huang H, Fuji H, Sankila A, Mahler-Araujo BM, Matsuda M, Cathomas G, Ohgaki H (1999). Beta-catenin mutations are frequent in human hepatocellular carcinomas associated with hepatitis C virus infection. Am J Pathol 155(6): 1795-1801.

761. Huang L, Lang D, Geradts J, Obara T, Klein SA, Lynch HT, Ruggeri BA (1996). Molecular and immunochemical analyses of RB1 and cyclin D1 in human ductal pancreatic carcinomas and cell lines. Mol Carcinog 15: 85-95.

762. Hui AM, Kanai Y, Sakamoto M, Tsuda H, Hirohashi S (1997). Reduced p21(WAF1/CIP1) expression and p53 mutation in hepatocellular carcinomas. Hepatology 25: 575-579.

763. Hui AM, Sakamoto M, Kanai Y, Ino Y, Gotoh M, Yokota J, Hirohashi S (1996). Inactivation of p16INK4 in hepatocellular carcinoma. Hepatology 24: 575-579.

764. Hui AM, Sun L, Kanai Y, Sakamoto M, Hirohashi S (1998). Reduced p27Kip1 expression in hepatocellular carcinomas. Cancer Lett 132: 67-73.

765. Huncharek M, Muscat J (1995). Small cell carcinoma of the esophagus. The Massachusetts General Hospital experience, 1978 to 1993. Chest 107: 179-181.

766. Hurlimann J, Saraga EP (1994). Expression of p53 protein in gastric carcinomas. Association with histologic type and prognosis. Am J Surg Pathol 18: 1247-1253.

767. Husemann B (1989). Cardia carcinoma considered as a distinct clinical entity. Br J Surg 76: 136-139.

768. Hussell T, Isaacson PG, Crabtree JE, Spencer J (1993). The response of cells from low-grade gastric lymphomas of mucosa-associated lymphoid tissue to Helicobacter pylori. Lancet 342: 571-574.

769. Hussell T, Isaacson PG, Crabtree JE, Spencer J (1996). Helicobacter pylori-specific tumour-infiltrating T cells provide contact dependent help for the growth of malignant B cells in low-grade gastric lymphoma of mucosa-associated lymphoid tissue. J Pathol 178: 122-127.

770. Ichikawa A, Kinoshita T, Watanabe T, Kato H, Nagai H, Tsushita K, Saito H, Hotta T (1997). Mutations of the p53 gene as a prognostic factor in aggressive B-cell lymphoma. N Engl J Med 337: 529-534.

771. Ichinohasama R, Miura I, Takahashi T, Yaginuma Y, Myers J, DeCoteau JF, Yee C, Kadin ME, Mori S, Sawai T (1996). Peripheral CD4+ CD8- gammadelta T cell lymphoma: a case report with multiparameter analyses. Hum Pathol 27: 1370-1377.

772. Ide H, Nakamura T, Hayashi K, Endo T, Kobayashi A, Eguchi R, Hanyu F (1994). Esophageal squamous cell carcinoma. Esophageal pathology and prognosis. World J Surg 18: 321-330.

773. Iggo R, Gatter K, Bartek J, Lane D, Harris AL (1990). Increased expression of mutant forms of p53 oncogene in primary lung cancer. *Lancet* 335: 675-679.

774. Iida Y, Tsutsumi Y (1992). Small cell (endocrine cell) carcinoma of the gallbladder with squamous and adenocarcinomatous components. *Acta Pathol Jpn* 42: 119-125.

775. Iino H, Jass JR, Simms LA, Young J, Leggett B, Ajioka Y, Watanabe H (1999). DNA microsatellite instability in hyperplastic colonic polyps, serrated adenomas, and mixed polyps: a mild mutator pathway for colorectal cancer? *J Clin Pathol* 52: 5-9.

776. Ikeda H, Hachitanda Y, Tanimura M, Maruyama K, Koizumi T, Tsuchida Y (1998). Development of unfavorable hepatoblastoma in children of very low birth weight: results of a surgical and pathologic review. *Cancer* 82: 1789-1796.

777. Ikeda H, Matsuyama S, Tanimura M (1997). Association between hepatoblastoma and very low birth weight: a trend or a chance? *J Pediatr* 130: 557-560.

778. Ikeda Y, Ozawa S, Ando N, Kitagawa Y, Ueda M, Kitajima M (1996). Meanings of c-erbB and int-2 amplification in superficial esophageal squamous cell carcinomas. *Ann Thorac Surg* 62: 835-838.

779. Ikeguchi M, Saito H, Katano K, Tsujitani S, Maeta M, Kaibara N (1997). Clinicopathologic significance of the expression of mutated p53 protein and the proliferative activity of cancer cells in patients with esophageal squamous cell carcinoma. *J Am Coll Surg* 185: 398-403.

780. Imai T, Kubo T, Watanabe H (1971). Chronic gastritis in Japanese with reference to high incidence of gastric carcinoma. *J Natl Cancer Inst* 47: 179-195.

781. Imai T, Sannohe Y, Okano H (1978). Oat cell carcinoma (apudoma) of the esophagus: a case report. *Cancer* 41: 358-364.

782. Imamura T, Nakagawa A, Okuno M, Takai S, Komada H, Kwon AH, Uetsuji S, Kamiyama Y, Sakaida N, Okamura A (1998). Pancreatoblastoma in an adolescent girl: case report and review of 26 Japanese cases. *Eur J Surg* 164: 309-312.

783. Inai K, Kobuke T, Yonehara S, Tokuoka S (1989). Duodenal gangliocytic paraganglioma with lymph node metastasis in a 17-year-old boy. *Cancer* 63: 2540-2545.

784. Indinnimeo M, Cicchini C, Stazi A, Limiti MR, Giarnieri E, Ghini C, Vecchione A (1998). The prevalence of p53 immunoreactivity in anal canal carcinoma. *Oncol Rep* 5: 1455-1457.

785. Indinnimeo M, Cicchini C, Stazi A, Mingazzini P, Ghini C, Pavone P (1998). Trans anal full thickness tru-cut needle biopsies in anal canal tumors after conservative treatment. *Oncol Rep* 5: 325-327.

786. Ioachim HL, Antonescu C, Giancotti F, Dorsett B, Weinstein MA (1997). EBV-associated anorectal lymphomas in patients with acquired immune deficiency syndrome. *Am J Surg Pathol* 21: 997-1006.

787. Ioachim HL, Dorsett B, Cronin W, Maya M, Wahl S (1991). Acquired immunodeficiency syndrome-associated lymphomas: clinical, pathologic, immunologic, and viral characteristics of 111 cases. *Hum Pathol* 22: 659-673.

788. Ionov Y, Peinado MA, Malkhosyan S, Shibata D, Perucho M (1993). Ubiquitous somatic mutations in simple repeated sequences reveal a new mechanism for colonic carcinogenesis. *Nature* 363: 558-561.

789. Ireland AP, Clark GW, DeMeester TR (1997). Barrett's esophagus. The significance of p53 in clinical practice. *Ann Surg* 225: 17-30.

790. Isaacson P (1981). Crypt cell carcinoma of the appendix (so-called adenocarcinoid tumor). *Am J Surg Pathol* 5: 213-224.

791. Isaacson P, MacLennan KA, Subbuuswamy SG (1984). Multiple lymphomatous polyposis of the gastrointestinal tract. *Histopathology* 8: 641-656.

792. Isaacson P, Notron AJ (1994). Extranodal lymphomas. 1st ed, Churchill Livingstone: New York.

793. Isaacson P, Spencer J (1987). Malignant lymphoma of mucosa-associated lymphoid tissue. *Histopathology* 11: 445-462.

794. Isaacson P, Wright DH (1978). Intestinal lymphoma associated with malabsorption. *Lancet* 1: 67-70.

795. Isaacson PG (1995). Intestinal lymphoma and enteropathy. *J Pathol* 177: 111-113.

796. Isaacson PG (1999). Gastrointestinal lymphomas of T- and B-cell types. *Mod Pathol* 12: 151-158.

797. Isaacson PG, Banks PM, Best PV, McClure SP, Muller HH, Wyatt JI (1995). Primary low-grade hepatic B-cell lymphoma of mucosa-associated lymphoid tissue (MALT)-type. *Am J Surg Pathol* 19: 571-575.

798. Isaacson PG, Dogan A, Price SK, Spencer J (1989). Immunoproliferative small-intestinal disease. An immunohistochemical study. *Am J Surg Pathol* 13: 1023-1033.

799. Isaacson PG, O'Connor NT, Spencer J, Bevan DH, Connolly CE, Kirkham N, Pollock DJ, Wainscoat JS, Stein H, Mason DY (1985). Malignant histiocytosis of the intestine: a T-cell lymphoma. *Lancet* 2: 688-691.

800. Isaacson PG, Wotherspoon AC, Diss T, Pan LX (1991). Follicular colonization in B-cell lymphoma of mucosa-associated lymphoid tissue. *Am J Surg Pathol* 15: 819-828.

801. Isaacson PG, Wotherspoon AC, Diss TC, Barbazzi R, de-Boni M, Doglioni C (1999). Long term follow-up of gastric MALT lymphoma treated by eradication of Helicobacter pylori with antibiotics. *Gastroenterology* 117: 750-751.

802. Iseki M, Suzuki T, Koizumi Y, Hirose M, Laskin WB, Nakazawa S, Ohaki Y (1986). Alpha-fetoprotein-producing pancreatoblastoma. A case report. *Cancer* 57: 1833-1835.

803. Ishak KG (1988). Benign tumors and pseudotumors of the liver. *Appl Pathol* 6: 82-104.

804. Ishak KG (1997). Malignant mesenchymal tumours of the liver. In: *Liver Cancer*, Okuda K, Tabor E (eds), Churchill Livingstone: New York.

805. Ishak KG (2000). Liver. In: *The pathology of incipient neoplasia*, Henson DE, Albores-Saavedra J (eds), 3rd ed Oxford University Press: New York.

806. Ishak KG, Anthony PP, Sobin LH (1999). WHO International Classification of Tumours: Histological Typing of Tumours of the Liver. Springer: Berlin, Heidelberg, New York, Tokyo.

807. Ishak KG, Sesterhenn IA, Goodman ZD, Rabin L, Stromeyer FW (1984). Epithelioid hemangioendothelioma of the liver: a clinicopathologic and follow-up study of 32 cases. *Hum Pathol* 15: 839-852.

808. Ishak KG, Sharp H (1994). Metabolic errors and liver disease. In: *Pathology of the liver*, MacSween RNM, Anthony PP, Scheuer PJ, Burt AD, Portmann BC (eds), Churchill Livingstone: Edinburgh, London, Madrid, Melbourne, New York, Tokyo.

809. Ishak KG, Willis GW, Cummins SD, Bullock AA (1977). Biliary cystadenoma and cystadenocarcinoma: report of 14 cases and review of the literature. *Cancer* 39: 322-338.

810. Ishihara A, Sanda T, Takanari H, Yatani R, Liu PI (1989). Elastase-1-secreting acinar cell carcinoma of the pancreas. A cytologic, electron microscopic and histochemical study. *Acta Cytol* 33: 157-163.

811. Ishihara M, Mehregan DR, Hashimoto K, Yotsumoto S, Toi Y, Pietruk T, Mehregan AH, Mehregan DA (1998). Staining of eccrine and apocrine neoplasms and metastatic adenocarcinoma with IKH-4, a monoclonal antibody specific for the eccrine gland. *J Cutan Pathol* 25: 100-105.

812. Ishikawa O, Ishiguro S, Ohhigashi H, Sasaki Y, Yasuda T, Imaoka S, Iwanaga T, Nakaizumi A, Fujita M, Wada A (1990). Solid and papillary neoplasm arising from an ectopic pancreas in the mesocolon. *Am J Gastroenterol* 85: 597-601.

813. Ishikawa O, Matsui Y, Aoki I, Iwanaga T, Terasawa T, Wada A (1980). Adenosquamous carcinoma of the pancreas: a clinicopathologic study and report of three cases. *Cancer* 46: 1192-1196.

814. Ishikawa O, Ohigashi H, Imaoka S, Furukawa H, Sasaki Y, Fujita M, Kuroda C, Iwanaga T (1992). Preoperative indications for extended pancreatectomy for locally advanced pancreas cancer involving the portal vein. *Ann Surg* 215: 231-236.

815. Ishikawa T, Nakao A, Nomoto S, Hosono M, Harada A, Nonami T, Takagi H (1998). Immunohistochemical and molecular biological studies of serous cystadenoma of the pancreas. *Pancreas* 16: 40-44.

816. Isolauri J, Mattila J, Kallioniemi OP (1991). Primary undifferentiated small cell carcinoma of the esophagus: clinicopathological and flow cytometric evaluation of eight cases. *J Surg Oncol* 46: 174-177.

817. Itai Y, Ohhashi K, Furui S, Araki T, Murakami Y, Ohtomo K, Atomi Y (1988). Microcystic adenoma of the pancreas: spectrum of computed tomographic findings. *J Comput Assist Tomogr* 12: 797-803.

818. Ito N, Kawata S, Tamura S, Takaishi K, Shirai Y, Kiso S, Yabuuchi I, Matsuda Y, Nishioka M, Tarui S (1991). Elevated levels of transforming growth factor beta messenger RNA and its polypeptide in human hepatocellular carcinoma. *Cancer Res* 51: 4080-4083.

819. Itoh T, Kishi K, Tojo M, Kitajima N, Kinoshita Y, Inatome T, Fukuzaki H, Nishiyama N, Tachibana H, Takahashi H, et a (1992). Acinar cell carcinoma of the pancreas with elevated serum alpha-fetoprotein levels: a case report and a review of 28 cases reported in Japan. *Gastroenterol Jpn* 27: 785-791.

820. Iwafuchi M, Watanabe H, Ajioka Y, Shimoda T, Iwashita A, Ito S (1990). Immunohistochemical and ultrastructural studies of twelve argentaffin and six argyrophil carcinoids of the appendix vermiformis. *Hum Pathol* 21: 773-780.

821. Iwafuchi M, Watanabe H, Ishihara N, Enjoji M, Iwashita A, Yanaihara N, Ito S (1987). Neoplastic endocrine cells in carcinomas of the small intestine: histochemical and immunohistochemical studies of 24 tumors. *Hum Pathol* 18: 185-194.

822. Iwama T, Konishi M, Iijima T, Yoshinaga K, Tominaga T, Koike M, Miyaki M (1999). Somatic mutation of the APC gene in thyroid carcinoma associated with familial adenomatous polyposis. *Jpn J Cancer Res* 90: 372-376.

823. Iwaya T, Maesawa C, Ogasawara S, Tamura G (1998). Tylosis esophageal cancer locus on chromosome 17q25.1 is commonly deleted in sporadic human esophageal cancer. *Gastroenterology* 114: 1206-1210.

824. Izbicki JR, Hosch SB, Pichlmeier U, Rehders A, Busch C, Niendorf A, Passlick B, Broelsch CE, Pantel K (1997). Prognostic value of immunohistochemically identifiable tumor cells in lymph nodes of patients with completely resected esophageal cancer. *N Engl J Med* 337: 1188-1194.

825. Jackson SA, Savidge RS, Stein L, Varley H (1952). Carcinoma of the pancreas associated with fat necrosis. *Lancet* 263: 962-967.

826. Jaffe ES (1987). Malignant lymphomas: pathology of hepatic involvement. *Semin Liver Dis* 7: 257-268.

827. Jaffe ES (1995). Surgical pathology of the lymph nodes and related organs. 2nd ed, W. B. Saunders Company: Philadelphia.

828. Jager AC, Bisgaard ML, Myrhoj T, Bernstein I, Rehfeld JF, Nielsen FC (1997). Reduced frequency of extracolonic cancers in hereditary nonpolyposis colorectal cancer families with monoallelic hMLH1 expression. *Am J Hum Genet* 61: 129-138.

829. Jakobovitz O, Nass D, DeMarco L, Barbosa AJ, Simoni FB, Rechavi G, Friedman E (1996). Carcinoid tumors frequently display genetic abnormalities involving chromosome 11. *J Clin Endocrinol Metab* 81: 3164-3167.

830. James JA, Milligan DW, Morgan GJ, Crocker J (1998). Familial pancreatic lymphoma. *J Clin Pathol* 51: 80-82.

831. Jameson CF (1989). Primary hepatocellular carcinoma in hereditary haemorrhagic telangiectasia: a case report and literature review. *Histopathology* 15: 550-552.

832. Japan Pancreas Society (1996). Classification of Pancreatic Carcinoma. First English Edition. Kanehara & Co., Ltd.: Tokio.

833. Jaques DP, Coit DG, Casper ES, Brennan MF (1995). Hepatic metastases from soft-tissue sarcoma. *Ann Surg* 221: 392-397.

834. Jarvinen H (1993). Juvenile gastrointestinal polyposis. *Prob Gen Surg* 10: 749.

835. Jarvinen HJ (1985). Time and type of prophylactic surgery for familial adenomatosis coli. *Ann Surg* 202: 93-97.

836. Jarvinen HJ (1992). Epidemiology of familial adenomatous polyposis in Finland: impact of family screening on the colorectal cancer rate and survival. *Gut* 33: 357-360.

837. Jass JR (1981). Mucin histochemistry of the columnar epithelium of the oesophagus: a retrospective study. *J Clin Pathol* 34: 866-870.

838. Jass JR (1994). Juvenile polyposis. In: *Familial Adenomatous Polyposis and Other Polyposis Syndromes*, Phillips RK, Spigelman AD, Thomson JPS (eds), Edward Arnold: London.

839. Jass JR (1998). Diagnosis of hereditary non-polyposis colorectal cancer. *Histopathology* 32: 491-497.

840. Jass JR (1999). Serrated adenoma and colorectal cancer. *J Pathol* 187: 499-502.

841. Jass JR, Biden KG, Cummings MC, Simms LA, Walsh M, Schoch E, Meltzer SJ, Wright C, Searle J, Young J, Leggett BA (1999). Characterisation of a subtype of colorectal cancer combining features of the suppressor and mild mutator pathways. *J Clin Pathol* 52: 455-460.

842. Jass JR, Do KA, Simms LA, Iino H, Wynter C, Pillay SP, Searle J, Radford SG, Young J, Leggett B (1998). Morphology of sporadic colorectal cancer with DNA replication errors. *Gut* 42: 673-679.

843. Jass JR, Filipe MI (1980). Sulphomucins and precancerous lesions of the human stomach. *Histopathology* 4: 271-279.

844. Jass JR, Ino H, Ruszkiewicz A, Painter D, Solomon MJ, Koorey DJ, Cohn D, Furlong KL, Walsh MD, Palazzo J, Bocker Edmonston T, Fishel R, Young J, Leggett BA (2000). Neoplastic progression occurs through mutator pathways in hyperplastic polyposis of the colorectum. *Gut* 47: 43-49.

845. Jass JR, Sobin LH (1989). WHO: Histological Typing of Intestinal Tumours. 2nd ed, Springer-Verlag: Berlin.

846. Jass JR, Stewart SM, Stewart J, Lane MR (1994). Hereditary non-polyposis colorectal cancer - morphologies, genes and mutations. *Mutat Res* 310: 125-133.

847. Jass JR, Williams CB, Bussey HJ, Morson BC (1988). Juvenile polyposis - a precancerous condition. *Histopathology* 13: 619-630.

848. Jawhari A, Jordan S, Poole S, Browne P, Pignatelli M, Farthing MJ (1997). Abnormal immunoreactivity of the E-cadherin-catenin complex in gastric carcinoma: relationship with patient survival. *Gastroenterology* 112: 46-54.

849. Jeevaratnam P, Cotter DS, Browett PJ, Van-De-Water NS, Pokos V, Jass JR (1996). Familial giant hyperplastic polyposis predisposing to colorectal cancer: a new hereditary bowel cancer syndrome. *J Pathol* 179: 20-25.

850. Jeghers H, McKusick VA, Katz KH (1949). Generalized intestinal polyposis and melanin spots of the oral mucosa, lips and digits. *N Engl J Med* 241: 1031-1036.

851. Jen J, Powell SM, Papadopoulos N, Smith KJ, Hamilton SR, Vogelstein B, Kinzler KW (1994). Molecular determinants of dysplasia in colorectal lesions. *Cancer Res* 54: 5523-5526.

852. Jenkins D, Gilmore IT, Doel C, Gallivan S (1995). Liver biopsy in the diagnosis of malignancy. *QJM* 88: 819-825.

853. Jenne DE, Reimann H, Nezu J, Friedel W, Loff S, Jeschke R, Muller O, Back W, Zimmer M (1998). Peutz-Jeghers syndrome is caused by mutations in a novel serine threonine kinase. *Nat Genet* 18: 38-43.

854. Jensen RT (1993). Gastrinoma as a model for prolonged hypergastrinemia in man. In: *Gastrin*, Walsh JH (eds), Raven Press: New York.

855. Jensen SL, Hagen K, Shokouh AM, Nielsen OV (1987). Does an erroneous diagnosis of squamous-cell carcinoma of the anal canal and anal margin at first physician visit influence prognosis? *Dis Colon Rectum* 30: 345-351.

856. Jessurun J, Romero GM, Manivel JC (1999). Medullary adenocarcinoma of the colon: clinicopathologic study of 11 cases. *Hum Pathol* 30: 843-848.

857. Jetmore AB, Ray JE, Gathright-JB J, McMullen KM, Hicks TC, Timmcke AE (1992). Rectal carcinoids: the most frequent carcinoid tumor. *Dis Colon Rectum* 35: 717-725.

858. Jia L, Wang XW, Harris CC (1999). Hepatitis B virus X protein inhibits nucleotide excision repair. *Int J Cancer* 80: 875-879.

859. Jiang W, Zhang YJ, Kahn SM, Hollstein MC, Santella RM, Lu SH, Harris CC, Montesano R, Weinstein IB (1993). Altered expression of the cyclin D1 and retinoblastoma genes in human esophageal cancer. *Proc Natl Acad Sci U S A* 90: 9026-9030.

860. Jiricny J (1998). Replication errors: challenging the genome. *EMBO J* 17: 6427-6436.

861. Jochem VJ, Fuerst PA, Fromkes JJ (1992). Familial Barrett's esophagus associated with adenocarcinoma. *Gastroenterology* 102: 1400-1402.

862. Johnston J, Helwig EB (1981). Granular cell tumors of the gastrointestinal tract and perianal region: a study of 74 cases. *Dig Dis Sci* 26: 807-816.

863. Jones EA, Morson BC (1984). Mucinous adenocarcinoma in anorectal fistulae. *Histopathology* 8: 279-292.

864. Jones EG (1964). Familial gastric cancer. *N Z Med J* 63: 287-290.

865. Jones PA (1979). Leiomyosarcoma of the appendix: report of two cases. *Dis Colon Rectum* 22: 175-178.

866. Jones WF, Sheikh MY, McClave SA (1997). AIDS-related non-Hodgkin's lymphoma of the pancreas. *Am J Gastroenterol* 92: 335-338.

866A. Jonsson T, Johansson JH, Hallgrimsson JG (1989). Carcinoid tumors of the appendix in children younger than 16 years. A retrospective clinical and pathologic study. *Acta Chir Scand* 155: 113-116.

867. Jorgensen LJ, Hansen AB, Burcharth F, Philipsen E, Horn T (1992). Solid and papillary neoplasm of the pancreas. *Ultrastruct Pathol* 16: 659-666.

868. Joslyn G, Carlson M, Thliveris A, Albertsen H, Gelbert L, Samowitz W, Groden J, Stevens J, Spirio L, Robertson M, et al (1991). Identification of deletion mutations and three new genes at the familial polyposis locus. *Cell* 66: 601-613.

869. Jossens JV, Geboers J (1981). Nutrition and gastric cancer. *Nutr Cancer* 2: 250-261.

870. Juhl H, Stritzel M, Wroblewski A, Henne BD, Kremer B, Schmiegel W, Neumaier M, Wagener C, Schreiber HW, Kalthoff H (1994). Immunocytological detection of micrometastatic cells: comparative evaluation of findings in the peritoneal cavity and the bone marrow of gastric, colorectal and pancreatic cancer patients. *Int J Cancer* 57: 330-335.

871. Jung MY, Shin HR, Lee CU, Sui SY, Lee SW, Park BC (1993). A study of the ratio of hepatocellular carcinoma over cholangiocarcinoma and their risk factors. *J Korean Med Assoc* 29: 29-37.

872. Jyotheeswaran S, Zotalis G, Penmetsa P, Levea CM, Schoeniger LO, Shah AN (1998). A newly recognized entity: intraductal "oncocytic" papillary neoplasm of the pancreas. *Am J Gastroenterol* 93: 2539-2543.

873. Kadakia SC, Parker A, Canales L (1992). Metastatic tumors to the upper gastrointestinal tract: endoscopic experience. *Am J Gastroenterol* 87: 1418-1423.

874. Kader HA, Ruchelli E, Maller ES (1998). Langerhans' cell histiocytosis with stool retention caused by a perianal mass. *J Pediatr Gastroenterol Nutr* 26: 226-228.

875. Kaino M, Kondoh S, Okita S, Hatano S, Shiraishi K, Okita K (1999). Detection of K-ras and p53 gene mutations in pancreatic juice for the diagnosis of intraductal papillary mucinous tumors. *Pancreas* 18: 294-299.

876. Kaino M, Kondoh S, Okita S, Ryozawa S, Hatano S, Shiraishi K, Kaino S, Akiyama T, Okita K, Kawano T (1996). p53 mutations in two patients with intraductal papillary adenoma of the pancreas. *Jpn J Cancer Res* 87: 1195-1198.

877. Kalish RJ, Clancy PE, Orringer MB, Appelman HD (1984). Clinical, epidemiologic, and morphologic comparison between adenocarcinoma arising in Barrett's esophageal mucosa and in the gastric cardia. *Gastroenterology* 86: 461-467.

878. Kamb A, Gruis NA, Weaver-Feldhaus J, Liu Q, Harshman K, Tavtigian SV, Stockert E, Day RSI, Johnson BE, Skolnick MH (1994). A cell cycle regulator potentially involved in genesis of many tumor types. *Science* 264: 436-439.

879. Kamei K, Funabiki T, Ochiai M, Amano H, Kasahara M, Sakamoto T (1991). Multifocal pancreatic serous cystadenoma with atypical cells and focal perineural invasion. *Int J Pancreatol* 10: 161-172.

880. Kamisawa T, Fukayama M, Koike M, Tabata I, Okamoto A (1987). So-called "papillary and cystic neoplasm of the pancreas". An immunohistochemical and ultrastructural study. *Acta Pathol Jpn* 37.

881. Kan Z, Ivancev K, Lunderquist A, McCuskey PA, McCuskey RS, Wallace S (1995). In vivo microscopy of hepatic metastases: dynamic observation of tumor cell invasion and interaction with Kupffer cells. *Hepatology* 21: 487-494.

882. Kanai N, Nagaki S, Tanaka T (1987). Clear cell carcinoma of the pancreas. *Acta Pathol Jpn* 37: 1521-1526.

883. Kanai Y, Hui AM, Sun L, Ushijima S, Sakamoto M, Tsuda H, Hirohashi S (1999). DNA hypermethylation at the D17S5 locus and reduced HIC-1 mRNA expression are associated with hepatocarcinogenesis. *Hepatology* 29: 703-709.

884. Kanai Y, Ushijima S, Hui AM, Ochiai A, Tsuda H, Sakamoto M, Hirohashi S (1997). The E-cadherin gene is silenced by CpG methylation in human hepatocellular carcinomas. *Int J Cancer* 71: 355-359.

885. Kanai Y, Ushijima S, Tsuda H, Sakamoto M, Sugimura T, Hirohashi S (1996). Aberrant DNA methylation on chromosome 16 is an early event in hepatocarcinogenesis. *Jpn J Cancer Res* 87: 1210-1217.

886. Kane MF, Loda M, Gaida GM, Lipman J, Mishra R, Goldman H, Jessup JM, Kolodner R (1997). Methylation of the hMLH1 promoter correlates with lack of expression of hMLH1 in sporadic colon tumors and mismatch repair-defective human tumor cell lines. *Cancer Res* 57: 808-811.

887. Kang YK, Kim WH, Lee HW, Lee HK, Kim YI (1999). Mutation of p53 and K-ras, and loss of heterozygosity of APC in intrahepatic cholangiocarcinoma. *Lab Invest* 79: 477-483.

888. Kanhouwa S, Burns W, Matthews M, Chisholm R (1975). Anaplastic carcinoma of the lung with metastasis to the anus: report of a case. *Dis Colon Rectum* 18: 42-48.

889. Kao JH, Chen DS (2000). Overview of hepatitis B and C viruses. In: *Infectious causes of cancer*, Goedert JJ (eds), Humana Press: New Jersey.

890. Karat D, O'Hanlon DM, Hayes N, Scott D, Raimes SA, Griffin SM (1995). Prospective study of Helicobacter pylori infection in primary gastric lymphoma. *Br J Surg* 82: 1369-1370.

891. Karhunen PJ (1985). Hepatic pseudolipoma. *J Clin Pathol* 38: 877-879.

892. Karhunen PJ (1986). Benign hepatic tumours and tumour like conditions in men. *J Clin Pathol* 39: 183-188.

893. Kastury K, Baffa R, Druck T, Ohta M, Cotticelli MG, Inoue H, Negrini M, Rugge M, Huang D, Croce CM, Palazzo J, Huebner K (1996). Potential gastrointestinal tumor suppressor locus at the 3p14.2 FRA3B site identified by homozygous deletions in tumor cell lines. *Cancer Res* 56: 978-983.

894. Kataria R, Bhatnagar V, Agarwala S, Sharma MC, Gupta AK, Mitra DK (1998). Clinical course and management of pancreatoblastoma in children. *Trop Gastroenterol* 19: 67-69.

895. Kato H, Tachimori Y, Watanabe H, Iizuka T (1993). Evaluation of the new (1987) TNM classification for thoracic esophageal tumors. *Int J Cancer* 53: 220-223.

896. Kato H, Tachimori Y, Watanabe H, Itabashi M, Hirota T, Yamaguchi H, Ishikawa T (1992). Intramural metastasis of thoracic esophageal carcinoma. *Int J Cancer* 50: 49-52.

897. Kawanishi K, Shiozaki H, Doki Y, Sakita I, Inoue M, Yano M, Tsujinaka T, Shamma A, Monden M (1999). Prognostic significance of heat shock proteins 27 and 70 in patients with squamous cell carcinoma of the esophagus. *Cancer* 85: 1649-1657.

898. Keeffe EB, Pinson CW, Ragsdale J, Zonana J (1993). Hepatocellular carcinoma in arteriohepatic dysplasia. *Am J Gastroenterol* 88: 1446-1449.

899. Kelsell DP, Risk JM, Leigh IM, Stevens HP, Ellis A, Hennies HC, Reis A, Weissenbach J, Bishop DT, Spurr NK, Field JK (1996). Close mapping of the focal non-epidermolytic palmoplantar keratoderma (PPK) locus associated with oesophageal cancer (TOC). *Hum Mol Genet* 5: 857-860.

900. Kenmochi K, Sugihara S, Kojiro M (1987). Relationship of histologic grade of hepatocellular carcinoma (HCC) to tumor size, and demonstration of tumor cells of multiple different grades in single small HCC. *Liver* 7: 18-26.

901. Kern HF, Roher HD, von-Bulow M, Kloppel G (1987). Fine structure of three major grades of malignancy of human pancreatic adenocarcinoma. *Pancreas* 2: 2-13.

902. Kessler KJ, Kerlakian GM, Welling RE (1996). Perineal and perirectal sarcomas: report of two cases. *Dis Colon Rectum* 39: 468-472.

903. Keung YK, Cobos E, Trowers E (1997). Primary pancreatic lymphoma associated with short bowel syndrome: review of carcinogenesis of gastrointestinal malignancies. *Leuk Lymphoma* 26: 405-408.

904. Kew MC (1989). Tumour markers of hepatocellular carcinoma. *J Gastroenterol Hepatol* 4: 373-384.

905. Khalbuss WE, Gherson J, Zaman M (1999). Pancreatic metastasis of cardiac rhabdomyosarcoma diagnosed by fine needle aspiration. A case report. *Acta Cytol* 43: 447-451.

906. Kheir SM, Halpern NB (1984). Paraganglioma of the duodenum in association with congenital neurofibromatosis. Possible relationship. *Cancer* 53: 2491-2496.

907. Kiba T, Tsuda H, Pairojkul C, Inoue S, Sugimura T, Hirohashi S (1993). Mutations of the p53 tumor suppressor gene and the ras gene family in intrahepatic cholangiocellular carcinomas in Japan and Thailand. *Mol Carcinog* 8: 312-318.

908. Kidokoro T (1972). Frequency of resection, metastasis, and five-year survival rate of early gastric carcinoma in a surgical clinic. In: *Early Gastric Cancer*, Murakami T (ed), University Park Press: Baltimore.

909. Kijima H, Watanabe H, Iwafuchi M, Ishihara N (1989). Histogenesis of gallbladder carcinoma from investigation of early carcinoma and microcarcinoma. *Acta Pathol Jpn* 39: 235-244.

910. Kikuchi YR, Konishi M, Ito S, Seki M, Tanaka K, Maeda Y, Iino H, Fukayama M, Koike M, Mori T, et a (1992). Genetic changes of both p53 alleles associated with the conversion from colorectal adenoma to early carcinoma in familial adenomatous polyposis and non-familial adenomatous polyposis patients. *Cancer Res* 52: 3965-3971.

911. Kilgore SP, Ormsby AH, Gramlich TL, Rice TW, Richter JE, Falk GW, Goldblum JR (2000). The gastric cardia: fact or fiction? *Am J Gastroenterol* 95: 921-924.

912. Killinger-WA J, Rice TW, Adelstein DJ, Medendorp SV, Zuccaro G, Kirby TJ, Goldblum JR (1996). Stage II esophageal carcinoma: the significance of T and N. *J Thorac Cardiovasc Surg* 111: 935-940.

913. Kim YI (1984). Liver carcinoma and liver fluke infection. *Arzneimittelforschung* 34: 1121-1126.

914. Kim YI, Kim ST, Lee GK, Choi BI (1990). Papillary cystic tumor of the liver. A case report with ultrastructural observation. *Cancer* 65: 2740-2746.

915. Kim YI, Seo JW, Suh JS, Lee KU, Choe KJ (1990). Microcystic adenomas of the pancreas. Report of three cases with of multicentric origin. *Am J Clin Pathol* 94: 150-156.

916. Kimura H, Konishi K, Maeda K, Yabushita K, Tsuji M, Miwa A (1999). Highly aggressive behavior and poor prognosis of small-cell carcinoma in the alimentary tract: flow-cytometric analysis and immunohistochemical staining for the p53 protein and proliferating cell nuclear antigen. *Dig Surg* 16: 152-157.

917. Kimura H, Nakajima T, Kagawa K, Deguchi T, Kakusui M, Katagishi T, Okanoue T, Kashima K, Ashihara T (1998). Angiogenesis in hepatocellular carcinoma as evaluated by CD34 immunohistochemistry. *Liver* 18: 14-19.

918. Kimura W, Makuuchi M, Kuroda A (1998). Characteristics and treatment of mucin-producing tumor of the pancreas. *Hepatogastroenterology* 45: 2001-2008.

919. Kin M, Torimura T, Ueno T, Inuzuka S, Tanikawa K (1994). Sinusoidal capillarization in small hepatocellular carcinoma. *Pathol Int* 44: 771-778.

920. Kindblom LG, Remotti HE, Aldenborg F, Meis KJ (1998). Gastrointestinal pacemaker cell tumor (GIPACT): gastrointestinal stromal tumors show phenotypic characteristics of the interstitial cells of Cajal. *Am J Pathol* 152: 1259-1269.

921. Kinzler KW, Nilbert MC, Su LK, Vogelstein B, Bryan TM, Levy DB, Smith KJ, Preisinger AC, Hedge P, McKechnie D, et a (1991). Identification of FAP locus genes from chromosome 5q21. *Science* 253: 661-665.

922. Kinzler KW, Vogelstein B (1996). Lessons from hereditary colorectal cancer. *Cell* 87: 159-170.

923. Kirk CM, Lewin D, Lazarchick J (1999). Primary hepatic B-cell lymphoma of mucosa-associated lymphoid tissue. *Arch Pathol Lab Med* 123: 716-719.

924. Kirk GD, Camus-Randon AM, Mendy M, Goedert JJ, Merle P, Trepo C, Brechot C, Hainaut P, Montesano R (2000). Ser-249 p53 mutations in plasma DNA of patients with hepatocellular carcinoma from The Gambia. *J Natl Cancer Inst* 19;92(2): 148-153.

925. Kiss A, Szepesi A, Lotz G, Nagy P, Schaff Z (1998). Expression of transforming growth factor-alpha in hepatoblastoma. *Cancer* 83: 690-697.

926. Kitagawa K, Takashima T, Matsui O, Kadoya M, Haratake KJ, Tsuji M (1986). Angiographic findings in two carcinoid tumors of the gallbladder. *Gastrointest Radiol* 11: 55-55.

927. Kitagawa Y, Ueda M, Ando N, Ozawa S, Shimizu N, Kitajima M (1996). Further evidence for prognostic significance of epidermal growth factor receptor gene amplification in patients with esophageal squamous cell carcinoma. *Clin Cancer Res* 2: 909-914.

928. Kitamura Y, Hirota S, Nishida T (1998). Molecular pathology of c-kit proto-oncogene and development of gastrointestinal stromal tumors. *Am Chir Gynaecol* 87: 282-286.

929. Kiyabu MT, Bishop PC, Parker JW, Turner RR, Fitzgibbons PL (1988). Smooth muscle tumors of the gastrointestinal tract. Flow cytometric quantitation of DNA and nuclear antigen content and correlation with histologic grade. *Am J Surg Pathol* 12: 954-960.

930. Klas JV, Rothenberger DA, Wong WD, Madoff RD (1999). Malignant tumors of the anal canal: the spectrum of disease, treatment, and outcomes. *Cancer* 85: 1686-1693.

931. Kleef J, Friess H, Simon P, Susmallian S, Buchler P, Zimmermann A, Buchler MW, Korc M (1999). Overexpression of Smad2 and colocalization with TGF-beta1 in human pancreatic cancer. *Dig Dis Sci* 44(9): 1793-1802.

932. Kleihues P, Cavenee WK (2000). *Pathology and Genetics of Tumours of the Nervous System*, 2nd ed, IARC Press: Lyon.

933. Klein A, Clemens J, Cameron J (1989). Periampullary neoplasms in von Recklinghausen's disease. *Surgery* 106: 815-819.

934. Klein KA, Stephens DH, Welch TJ (1998). CT characteristics of metastatic disease of the pancreas. *Radiographics* 18: 369-378.

935. Klimstra DS (1994). Pathologic prognostic factors in esophageal carcinoma. *Semin Oncol* 21: 425-430.

936. Klimstra DS, Heffess CS, Oertel JE, Rosai J (1992). Acinar cell carcinoma of the pancreas. A clinicopathologic study of 28 cases. *Am J Surg Pathol* 16: 815-837.

937. Klimstra DS, Longnecker DS (1994). K-ras mutations in pancreatic ductal proliferative lesions. *Am J Pathol* 145: 1547-1548.

938. Klimstra DS, Rosai J, Heffess CS (1994). Mixed acinar-endocrine carcinomas of the pancreas. *Am J Surg Pathol* 18: 765-778.

939. Klimstra DS, Wenig BM, Adair CF, Heffess CS (1995). Pancreatoblastoma. A clinicopathologic study and review of the literature. *Am J Surg Pathol* 19: 1371-1389.

940. Kloppel G (1984). Pancreatic biopsy. In: *Pancreatic Pathology*, Kloppel G, Heitz PU (eds), Churchill Livingstone: Edinburgh.

941. Kloppel G (1994). Pancreatic, non-endocrine tumours. In: *Pancreatic Pathology*, Kloppel G, Heitz PU (eds), Churchill Livingstone: Edinburgh.

942. Kloppel G (1998). Clinicopathologic view of intraductal papillary-mucinous tumor of the pancreas. *Hepatogastroenterology* 45: 1981-1985.

943. Kloppel G, Bommer G, Ruckert K, Seifert G (1980). Intraductal proliferation in the pancreas and its relationship to human and experimental carcinogenesis. *Virchows Arch Pathol Anat* 387: 221-233.

944. Kloppel G, Lingenthal G, von-Bulow M, Kern HF (1985). Histological and fine structural features of pancreatic ductal adenocarcinomas in relation to growth and prognosis: studies in xenografted tumours and clinico-histopathological correlation in a series of 75 cases. *Histopathology* 9: 841-856.

945. Kloppel G, Maurer R, Hofmann E, Luthold K, Oscarson J, Forsby N, Ihse I, Ljungberg O, Heitz PU (1991). Solid-cystic (papillary-cystic) tumours within and outside the pancreas in men: report of two patients. *Virchows Arch A Pathol Anat Histopathol* 418: 179-183.

946. Kloppel G, Morohoshi T, John HD, Oehmichen W, Opitz K, Angelkort A, Lietz H, Ruckert K (1981). Solid and cystic acinar cell tumour of the pancreas. *Virchows Arch A Pathol Anat Histopathol* 392: 171-183.

947. Kloppel G, Solcia E, Longnecker DS, Capella C, Sobin LH (1996). WHO: Histological Typing of Tumours of the Exocrine Pancreas. 2nd ed, Springer-Verlag: Berlin.

948. Klump B, Hsieh CJ, Holzmann K, Gregor M, Porschen R (1998). Hypermethylation of the CDKN2/p16 promoter during neoplastic progression in Barrett's esophagus. *Gastroenterology* 115: 1381-1386.

949. Kodama I, Kofuji K, Yano S, Shinozaki K, Murakami N, Hori H, Takeda J, Shirouzu K (1998). Lymph node metastasis and lymphadenectomy for carcinoma in the gastric cardia: clinical experience. *Int Surg* 83: 205-209.

950. Kodama Y, Inokuchi K, Soeijima K, Matsusaka T, Okamura T (1983). Growth patterns and prognosis in early gastric carcinoma. Superficially spreading and penetrating growth types. *Cancer* 51: 320-326.

951. Kohler HH, Hohler T, Kusel U, Kirkpatrick CJ, Schirmacher P (1999). Hepatocellular carcinoma in a patient with hereditary hemochromatosis and noncirrhotic liver. A case report. *Pathol Res Pract* 195: 509-513.

952. Kojiro M (1997). Pathology of hepatocellular carcinoma. In: *Liver Cancer*, Okuda K, Tabor E (eds), Churchill Livingstone: New York.

953. Kojiro M, Sugihara S, Kakizoe S, Nakashima O, Kiyomatsu K (1989). Hepatocellular carcinoma with sarcomatous change: a special reference to the relationship with anticancer therapy. *Cancer Chemother Pharmacol* 23 Suppl: S4-S8.

954. Kok TC, Nooter K, Tjong AH-S, Smits HL, Ter-Schegget JT (1997). No evidence of known types of human papillomavirus in squamous cell cancer of the oesophagus in a low-risk area. Rotterdam Oesophageal Tumour Study Group. *Eur J Cancer* 33: 1865-1868.

955. Kolodner RD, Hall NR, Lipford J, Kane MF, Morrison PT, Finan PJ, Burn J, Chapman P, Earabino C, Merchant E et al (1995). Structure of the human MLH1 locus and analysis of a large hereditary nonpolyposis colorectal carcinoma kindred for mlh1 mutations. *Cancer Res* 55: 242-248.

956. Kolodner RD, Hall NR, Lipford J, Kane MF, Rao MR, Morrison P, Wirth L, Finan PJ, Burn J, Chapman P (1994). Structure of the human MSH2 locus and analysis of two Muir-Torre kindreds for msh2 mutations. *Genomics* 24: 516-526.

957. Kolodner RD, Marsischky GT (1999). Eukaryotic DNA mismatch repair. *Curr Opin Genet Dev* 9: 89-96.

958. Komorowski RA, Cohen EB (1981). Villous tumors of the duodenum: a clinicopathologic study. *Cancer* 47: 1377-1386.

959. Kondo F, Wada K, Nagato Y, Nakajima T, Kondo Y, Hirooka N, Ebara M, Ohto M, Okuda K (1989). Biopsy diagnosis of well-differentiated hepatocellular carcinoma based on new morphologic criteria. *Hepatology* 9: 751-755.

960. Kondo H, Sugano K, Fukayama N, Kyogoku A, Nose H, Shimada K, Ohkura H, Ohtsu A, Yoshida S, Shimosato Y (1994). Detection of point mutations in the K-ras oncogene at codon 12 in pure pancreatic juice for diagnosis of pancreatic carcinoma. *Cancer* 73: 1589-1594.

961. Kondo Y, Kanai Y, Sakamoto M, Mizokami M, Ueda R, Hirohashi S (1999). Microsatellite instability associated with hepatocarcinogenesis. *J Hepatol* 31: 529-536.

962. Konishi M, Kikuchi YR, Tanaka K, Muraoka M, Onda A, Okumura Y, Kishi N, Iwama T, Mori T, Koike M, Ushio K, Chiba M, Nomizu S, Konishi F, Utsunomiya J, Miyaki M (1996). Molecular nature of colon tumors in hereditary nonpolyposis colon cancer, familial polyposis, and sporadic colon cancer. *Gastroenterology* 111: 307-317.

963. Kosmahl M, Seada LS, Janig U, Harms D, Kloppel G (1999). Solid-pseudopapillary tumor of the pancreas: its origin revisited. *Virchows Arch*

964. Koura AN, Giacco GG, Curley SA, Skibber JM, Feig BW, Ellis LM (1997). Carcinoid tumors of the rectum: effect of size, histopathology, and surgical treatment on metastasis free survival. *Cancer* 79: 1294-1298.

965. Kozuka S, Sassa R, Taki T, Masamoto K, Nagasawa S, Saga S, Hasegawa K, Takeuchi M (1979). Relation of pancreatic duct hyperplasia to carcinoma. *Cancer* 43: 1418-1428.

966. Kozuka S, Tsubone M, Yamaguchi A, Hachisuka K (1981). Adenomatous residue in cancerous papilla of Vater. *Gut* 22: 1031-1034.

967. Kozuka S, Tsubone N, Yasui A, Hachisuka K (1982). Relation of adenoma to carcinoma in the gallbladder. *Cancer* 50: 2226-2234.

968. Kramer-MD, Gibb SP, Ellis-FH J (1986). Giant leiomyoma of esophagus. *J Surg Oncol* 33: 166-169.

969. Kraus FT, Perezmesa C (1966). Verrucous carcinoma. Clinical and pathologic study of 105 cases involving oral cavity, larynx and genitalia. *Cancer* 19: 26-38.

970. Kraus JA, Albrecht S, Wiestler OD, von-Schweinitz D, Pietsch T (1996). Loss of heterozygosity on chromosome 1 in human hepatoblastoma. *Int J Cancer* 67: 467-471.

971. Kruse R, Rutten A, Lamberti C, Hosseiny MH, Wang Y, Ruelfs C, Jungck M, Mathiak M, Ruzicka T, Hartschuh W, Bisceglia M, Friedl W, Propping P (1998). Muir-Torre phenotype has a frequency of DNA mismatch-repair-gene mutations similar to that in hereditary nonpolyposis colorectal cancer families defined by the Amsterdam criteria. *Am J Hum Genet* 63: 63-70.

972. Kubo A, Kato Y, Yanagisawa A, Rubio CA, Hiratsuka H (1997). Serrated adenoma. *Endosc Digest* 9: 559-563.

973. Kudo S (1993). Endoscopic mucosal resection of flat and depressed types of early colorectal cancer. *Endoscopy* 25: 455-461.s

974. Kudo S, Kashida H, Tamura S, Kudo Nakajima T (1997). The problem of "flat" colonic adenoma. *Gastrointest Endosc Clin N Am* 7: 87-98.

975. Kuerer H, Shim H, Pertsemlidis D, Unger P (1997). Functioning pancreatic acinar cell carcinoma: immunohistochemical and ultrastructural analyses. *Am J Clin Oncol* 20: 101-107.

976. Kuniyasu H, Yasui W, Kitadai Y, Yokozaki H, Ito H, Tahara E (1992). Frequent amplification of the c-met gene in scirrhous type stomach cancer. *Biochem Biophys Res Commun* 189: 227-232.

977. Kuniyasu H, Yasui W, Shimamoto F, Fujii K, Nakahara M, Asahara T, Dohi K, Tahara E (1996). Hepatoblastoma in an adult associated with c-met proto-oncogene imbalance. *Pathol Int* 46: 1005-1010.

978. Kuo TT, Su IJ, Chien CH (1984). Solid and papillary neoplasm of the pancreas. Report of three cases from Taiwan. *Cancer* 54: 1469-1474.

979. Kuopio T, Ekfors TO, Nikkanen V, Nevalainen TJ (1995). Acinar cell carcinoma of the pancreas. Report of three cases. *APMIS* 103: 69-78.

980. Kurahashi H, Takami K, Oue T, Kusafuka T, Okada A, Tawa A, Okada S, Nishisho I (1995). Biallelic inactivation of the APC gene in hepatoblastoma. *Cancer Res* 55: 5007-5011.

981. Kurita M, Komatsu H, Hata Y, Shiina S, Ota S, Terano A, Sugimoto T, Oka T, Nanba Y (1994). Pseudomyxoma peritonei due to adenocarcinoma of the lung: case report. *J Gastroenterol* 29: 344-348.

982. Kuroishi T, Nishikawa Y, Tominaga S, Aoki K (1999). Cancer mortality statistics in 33 countries (1953-1992). In: *Cancer Mortality and Morbidity Statistics*, Tominaga S, Oshima A (eds), Japan Scientific Societies Press: Tokyo.

983. Kurose K, Araki T, Matsunaka T, Takada Y, Emi M (1999). Variant manifestation of Cowden disease in Japan: hamartomatous polyposis of the digestive tract with mutation of the PTEN gene. *Am J Hum Genet* 64: 308-310.

984. Kushima R, Remmele W, Stolte M, Borchard F (1996). Pyloric gland type adenoma of the gallbladder with squamoid spindle cell metaplasia. *Pathol Res Pract* 192: 963-969.

985. Kusumoto H, Yoshitake H, Mochida K, Kumashiro R, Sano C, Inutsuka S (1992). Adenocarcinoma in Meckel's diverticulum: report of a case and review of 30 cases in the English and Japanese literature. *Am J Gastroenterol* 87: 910-913.

986. Kusunoki M, Fujita S, Sakanoue Y, Shoji Y, Yanagi H, Yamamura T, Utsunomiya J (1991). Disappearance of hyperplastic polyposis after resection of rectal cancer. Report of two cases. *Dis Colon Rectum* 34: 829-832.

987. Kuwano H (1998). Peculiar histopathologic features of esophageal cancer. *Surg Today* 28: 573-575.

988. Kuwano H, Ohno S, Matsuda H, Mori M, Sugimachi K (1988). Serial histologic evaluation of multiple primary squamous cell carcinomas of the esophagus. *Cancer* 61: 1635-1638.

989. Kuwano H, Matsuda H, Matsuoka H, Kai H, Okudaira Y, Sugimachi K (1987). Intra-epithelial carcinoma concomitant with esophageal squamous cell carcinoma. *Cancer* 59: 783-787.

990. Kvist N, et al (1989). Malignancy in ulcerative colitis. *Scand J Gastroenterol* 24: 497-506.

991. Kwekkeboom DJ, Krenning EP (1996). Somatostatin receptor scintigraphy in patients with carcinoid tumors. *World J Surg* 20: 157-161.

992. Ky A, Sohn N, Weinstein MA, Korelitz BI (1998). Carcinoma arising in anorectal fistulas of Crohn's disease. *Dis Colon Rectum* 41: 992-996.

993. La-Rosa S, Chiaravalli AM, Capella C, Uccella S, Sessa F (1997). Immunohistochemical localization of acidic fibroblast growth factor in normal human enterochromaffin cells and related gastrointestinal tumours. *Virchows Arch* 430: 117-124.

994. La-Rosa S, Uccella S, Billo P, Facco C, Sessa F, Capella C (1999). Immunohistochemical localization of alpha- and betaA-subunits of inhibin/activin in human normal endocrine cells and related tumors of the digestive system. *Virchows Arch* 434: 29-36.

995. La-Rosa S, Uccella S, Capella C, Chiaravalli A, Sessa F (1998). Localization of acidic fibroblast growth factor, fibroblast growth factor receptor-4, transforming growth factor alpha, and epidermal growth factor receptor in human endocrine cells of the gut and related tumors: an immunohistochemical study. *Appl Immunohistochem* 6: 199-208.

996. La-Vecchia C, Negri E, Franceschi S, Gentile A (1992). Family history and the risk of stomach and colorectal cancer. *Cancer* 70: 50-55.

997. Labate AM, Klimstra DL, Zakowski MF (1997). Comparative cytologic features of pancreatic acinar cell carcinoma and islet cell tumor. *Diagn Cytopathol* 16: 112-116.

998. Labenz J, Blum AL, Bayerdorffer E, Meining A, Stolte M, Borsch G (1997). Curing Helicobacter pylori infection in patients with duodenal ulcer may provoke reflux esophagitis. *Gastroenterology* 112: 1442-1447.

999. Lack EE, Cassady JR, Levey R, Vawter GF (1983). Tumors of the exocrine pancreas in children and adolescents. A clinical and pathologic study of eight cases. *Am J Surg Oncol* 38: 19-21.

1000. Laferla G, Kaye SB, Crean GP (1988). Hepatocellular and gastric carcinoma associated with familial polyposis coli.

1001. Lagergren J, Bergstrom R, Lindgren A, Nyren O (1999). Symptomatic gastroesophageal reflux as a risk factor for esophageal adenocarcinoma. *N Engl J Med* 340: 825-831.

1002. Lagergren J, Bergstrom R, Nyren O (1999). Association between body mass and adenocarcinoma of the esophagus and gastric cardia. *Ann Intern Med* 130: 883-890.

1003. Laken SJ, Papadopoulos N, Petersen GM, Gruber SB, Hamilton SR, Giardiello FM, Brensinger JD, Vogelstein B, Kinzler KW (1999). Analysis of masked mutations in familial adenomatous polyposis. *Proc Natl Acad Sci U S A* 96: 2322-2326.

1004. Laken SJ, Petersen GM, Gruber SB, Oddoux C, Ostrer H, Giardiello FM, Hamilton SR, Hampel H, Markowitz A, Klimstra D, Jhanwar S, Winawer S, Offit K, Luce MC, Kinzler KW, Vogelstein B (1997). Familial colorectal cancer in Ashkenazim due to a hypermutable tract in APC. *Nat Genet* 17: 79-83.

1005. Lam KY, Law SY, So MK, Fok M, Ma LT, Wong J (1996). Prognostic implication of proliferative markers MIB-1 and PC10 in esophageal squamous cell carcinoma. *Cancer* 77: 7-13.

1006. Lam KY, Leung CY, Ho JW (1996). Sarcomatoid carcinoma of the small intestine. *Aust N Z J Surg* 66: 636-639.

1007. Lam KY, Lo CY, Fan ST (1999). Pancreatic solid-cystic-papillary tumor: clinicopathologic features in eight patients from Hong Kong and review of the literature. *World J Surg* 23: 1045-1050.

1008. Lam KY, Tsao SW, Zhang D, Law S, He D, Ma L, Wong J (1997). Prevalence and predictive value of p53 mutation in patients with oesophageal squamous cell carcinomas: a prospective clinico-pathological study and survival analysis of 70 patients. *Int J Cancer* 74: 212-219.

1009. Lambert R (1999). Diagnosis of esophagogastric tumors: a trend toward virtual biopsy. *Endoscopy* 31: 38-46.

1010. Lambert R (1999). Diagnosis of esophagogastric tumors: a trend toward virtual biopsy. *Endoscopy* 31: 38-46.

1011. Lambert R (1999). The role of endoscopy in the prevention of esophagogastric cancer. *Endoscopy* 31: 180-199.

1012. Lampert K, Nemcsik J, Paal E (1999). Metastatic tumours of the pancreas. A clinicopathological study of 62 cases. *Dig Surg* 16 (Suppl 1): 36

1013. Langley RG, Bailey EM, Sober AJ (1997). Acute cholecystitis from metastatic melanoma to the gall-bladder in a patient with a low-risk melanoma. *Br J Dermatol* 136: 279-282.

1014. Lapner PC, Chou S, Jimenez C (1997). Perianal fetal rhabdomyoma: case report. *Pediatr Surg Int* 12: 544-547.

1015. Larsson C, Skogseid B, Oberg K, Nakamura Y, Nordenskjold M (1988). Multiple endocrine neoplasia type 1 gene maps to chromosome 11 and is lost in insulinoma. *Nature* 332: 85-87.

1016. Lashner BA (1992). Risk factors for small bowel cancer in Crohn's disease. *Dig Dis Sci* 37: 1179-1184.

1017. Lashner BA, Riddell RH, Winans CS (1986). Ganglioneuromatosis of the colon and extensive glycogenic acanthosis in Cowden's disease. *Dig Dis Sci* 31: 213-216.

1018. Lasota J, Jasinski M, Sarlomo RM, Miettinen M (1999). Mutations in exon 11 of c-Kit occur preferentially in malignant versus benign gastrointestinal stromal tumors and do not occur in leiomyomas or leiomyosarcomas. *Am J Pathol* 154: 53-60.

1019. Laucirica R, Schwartz M, Ramzy Y (1992). Fine needle aspiration of cystic epithelial neoplasms. *Acta Cytol* 36: 881-886.

1020. Launoy G, Milan CH, Faivre J, Pienkowski P, Milan Cl, Gignoux M (1997). Alcohol, tobacco and oesophageal cancer: effects of the duration of consumption, mean intake and current and former consumption. *Br J Cancer* 75: 1389-1396.

1021. Lauren T (1965). The two histologic main types of gastric carcinoma. *Acta Pathol Microbiol Scand* 64: 34.

1022. Laurent JC, Filoche B, Depadt G, Proye C, Combemale B, Lagache G (1972). [Study of a series of 32 tumors of the small intestine]. *Lille Med* 17: 104-110.

1023. Lauwers GY, Erlandson RA, Casper ES, Brennan MF, Woodruff JM (1993). Gastrointestinal autonomic nerve tumors. A clinicopathological, immunohistochemical, and ultrastructural study of 12 cases. *Am J Surg Pathol* 17: 887-897.

1024. Lauwers GY, Scott GV, Vauthey JN (1998). Adenocarcinoma of the upper esophagus arising in cervical ectopic gastric mucosa: rare evidence of malignant potential of so-called "inlet patch". *Dig Dis Sci* 43: 901-907.

1025. Lauwers GY, Shimizu M, Correa P, Riddell RH, Kato Y, Lewin KJ, Yamabe H, Sheahan DG, Lewin D, Sipponen P, Kubilis PS, Watanabe H (1999). Evaluation of gastric biopsies for neoplasia: differences between Japanese and Western pathologists. *Am J Surg Pathol* 23: 511-518.

1026. Law SY, Fok M, Lam KY, Loke SL, Ma LT, Wong J (1994). Small cell carcinoma of the esophagus. *Cancer* 73: 2894-2899.

1027. Law SY, Fok M, Wong J (1996). Pattern of recurrence after oesophageal resection for cancer: clinical implications. *Br J Surg* 83: 107-111.

1028. Le-Bail B, Bioulac SP, Arnoux R, Perissat J, Saric J, Balabaud C (1990). Late recurrence of a hepatocellular carcinoma in a patient with incomplete Alagille syndrome. *Gastroenterology* 99: 1514-1516.

1029. Leach FS, Nicolaides NC, Papadopoulos N, Liu B, Jen J, Parsons R, Peltomaki P, Sistonen P, Aaltonen LA, Nystrom LM, et a (1993). Mutations of a mutS homolog in hereditary nonpolyposis colorectal cancer. *Cell* 75: 1215-1225.

1030. Leach FS, Polyak K, Burrell M, Johnson KA, Hill D, Dunlop MG, Wyllie AH, Peltomaki P, de-la-Chapelle A, Hamilton SR, Kinzler KW, Vogelstein B (1996). Expression of the human mismatch repair gene hMSH2 in normal and neoplastic tissues. *Cancer Res* 56: 235-240.

1031. Learmonth GM, Price SK, Visser AE, Emms M (1985). Papillary and cystic neoplasm of the pancreas - an acinar cell tumour? *Histopathology* 9: 63-79.

1032. Lebenthal E, Lev R, Lee PC (1986). Prenatal and postnatal development of the human exocrine pancreas. In: *The Exocrine Pancreas. Biology, Pathobiology, and Diseases*, Go VLW, Brooks FP, Dimagno EP, et al (eds), Raven Press: New York.

1033. LeBrun DP, Silver MM, Fredman MH, Philips MJ (1991). Fibrolamellar carcinoma of the liver in a patient with Fanconi anemia. *Hum Pathol* 22: 396-398.

1034. LeBrun DP, Kamel OW, Cleary ML, Dorfman RF, Warnke RA (1992). Follicular lymphomas of the gastrointestinal tract. Pathologic features in 31 cases and bcl-2 oncogenic protein expression. *Am J Pathol* 140: 1327-1335.

1035. Lecoin L, Gabella G, Le-Douarin N (1996). Origin of the c-kit-positive interstitial cells in the avian bowel. *Development* 122: 725-733.

1036. Lee CS, Pirdas A (1995). Epidermal growth factor receptor immunoreactivity in gallbladder and extrahepatic biliary tract tumours. *Pathol Res Pract* 191: 1087-1091.

1037. Lee JC, Lin PW, Lin YJ, Lai J, Yang HB, Lai MD (1995). Analysis of K-ras gene mutations in periampullary cancers, gallbladder cancers and cholangiocarcinomas from paraffin-embedded tissue sections. *J Formos Med Assoc* 94: 719-723.

1038. Lee SS, Jang JJ, Cho KJ, Khang SK, Kim CW (1997). Epstein-Barr virus-associated primary gastrointestinal lymphoma in non-immunocompromised patients in Korea. *Histopathology* 30: 234-242.

1039. Lee WY, Tzeng CC, Chen RM, Tsao CJ, Jin YT (1997). Papillary cystic tumors of the pancreas: assessment of malignant potential by analysis of progesterone receptor, flow cytometry, and ras oncogene mutation. *Anticancer Res* 17: 2587-2591.

1040. Lee YY, Wilczynski SP, Chumakov A, Chih D, Koeffler HP (1994). Carcinoma of the vulva: HPV and p53 mutations. *Oncogene* 9: 1655-1659.

1041. Legoix P, Bluteau O, Bayer J, Perret C, Balabaud C, Belghiti J, Franco D, Thomas G, Laurent PP, Zucman RJ (1999). Beta-catenin mutations in hepatocellular carcinoma correlate with a low rate of loss of heterozygosity. *Oncogene* 18: 4044-4046.

1042. Lehy T, Cadiot G, Mignon M, Ruszniewski P, Bonfils S (1992). Influence of multiple endocrine neoplasia type 1 on gastric endocrine cells in patients with the Zollinger-Ellison syndrome. *Gut* 33: 1275-1279.

1043. Lei KI (1998). Primary non-Hodgkin's lymphoma of the liver. *Leuk Lymphoma* 29: 293-299.

1044. Lengauer C, Kinzler KW, Vogelstein B (1998). Genetic instabilities in human cancers. *Nature* 396: 643-649.

1045. Lennard-Jones JE, Melville DM, Morson BC, Ritchie JK, Williams CB (1990). Precancer and cancer in extensive ulcerative colitis: findings among 401 patients over 22 years. *Gut* 31: 800-806.

1046. Leong AS, Sormunen RT, Tsui WM, Liew CT (1998). Hep Par 1 and selected antibodies in the immunohistological distinction of hepatocellular carcinoma from cholangiocarcinoma, combined tumours and metastatic carcinoma. *Histopathology* 33: 318-324.

1047. Leppert M, Dobbs M, Scambler P, O'Connell P, Nakamura Y, Stauffer D, Woodward S, Burt R, Hughes J, Gardner E, et a (1987). The gene for familial polyposis coli maps to the long arm of chromosome 5. *Science* 238: 1411-1413.

1048. Lerma E, Oliva E, Tugues D, Prat J (1994). Stromal tumours of the gastrointestinal tract: a clinicopathological and ploidy analysis of 33 cases. *Virchows Arch* 424: 19-24.

1049. Lerut T, Coosemans W, Van-Raemdonck D, Dillemans B, De-Leyn P, Marnette JM, Geboes K (1994). Surgical treatment of Barrett's carcinoma. Correlations between morphological findings and prognosis. *J Thorac Cardiovasc Surg* 107: 1059-1065.

1050. Leung SY, Yuen ST, Chung LP, Chu KM, Chan AS, Ho JC (1999). hMLH1 promoter methylation and lack of hMLH1 expression in sporadic gastric carcinomas with high-frequency microsatellite instability. *Cancer Res* 59: 159-164.

1051. Levchenko AM, Vasechko VN, Erusalimskii EL (1985). [Metastasis of small-cell lung cancer to the appendix]. *Klin Khir* 56-57.

1052. Levey JM, Banner B, Darrah J, Bonkovsky HL (1994). Inflammatory cloacogenic polyp: three cases and literature review. *Am J Gastroenterol* 89: 438-441.

1053. Levey JM, Banner BF (1996). Adult pancreatoblastoma: a case report and review of the literature. *Am J Gastroenterol* 91: 1841-1844.

1054. Levi S, Urbano IA, Gill R, Thomas DM, Gilbertson J, Foster C, Marshall CJ (1991). Multiple K-ras codon 12 mutations in cholangiocarcinomas demonstrated with a sensitive polymerase chain reaction technique. *Cancer Res* 51: 3497-3502.

1055. Levin KJ, Appelman HD (1996). Atlas of Tumor Pathology. Tumors of the oesophagus and stomach. AFIP: Washington, D.C.

1056. Levine AJ (1997). p53, the cellular gatekeeper for growth and division. *Cell* 88: 323-331.

1057. Levine AM (1992). Acquired immunodeficiency syndrome-related lymphoma. *Blood* 80: 8-20.

1058. Levine MS, Chu P, Furth EE, Rubesin SE, Laufer I, Herlinger H (1997). Carcinoma of the esophagus and esophagogastric junction: sensitivity of radiographic diagnosis. *AJR Am J Roentgenol* 168: 1423-1426.

1059. Levine MS, Pantongrag BL, Aguilera NS, Buck JL, Buetow PC (1996). Non-Hodgkin lymphoma of the stomach: a cause of linitis plastica. *Radiology* 201: 375-378.

1060. Levy P, Bougaran J, Gayet B (1997). [Diffuse peritoneal carcinosis of pseudopapillary and solid tumor of the pancreas. Role of abdominal injury]. *Gastroenterol Clin Biol* 21: 789-793.

1061. Levy R, Czernobilsky B, Geiger B (1991). Cytokeratin polypeptide expression in a cloacogenic carcinoma and in the normal anal canal epithelium. *Virchows Arch A Pathol Anat Histopathol* 418: 447-455.

1062. Lewandrowski K, Warshaw A, Compton C (1992). Macrocystic serous cystadenoma of the pancreas: a morphologic variant differing from microcystic adenoma. *Hum Pathol* 23: 871-875.

1063. Lewandrowski KB, Southern JF, Pins MR, Compton CC, Warshaw AL (1993). Cyst fluid analysis in the differential diagnosis of pancreatic cysts. A comparison of pseudocysts, serous cystadenomas, mucinous cystic neoplasms, and mucinous cystadenocarcinoma. *Ann Surg* 217: 41-47.

1064. Lewis BS, Kornbluth A, Waye JD (1991). Small bowel tumours: yield of enteroscopy. *Gut* 32: 763-765.

1065. Li DM, Sun H (1997). TEP1, encoded by a candidate tumor suppressor locus, is a novel protein tyrosine phosphatase regulated by transforming growth factor beta. *Cancer Res* 57: 2124-2129.

1066. Li FP, Fraumeni-JF J, Mulvihill JJ, Blattner WA, Dreyfus MG, Tucker MA, Miller RW (1988). A cancer family syndrome in twenty-four kindreds. *Cancer Res* 48: 5358-5362.

1067. Li J., Simpson L, Takahashi M, Miliaresis C, Myers MP, Tonks N, Parsons R (1998). The PTEN/MMAC1 tumor suppressor induces cell death that is rescued by the AKT/protein kinase B oncogene. *Cancer Res* 58: 5667-5672.

1068. Li J, Yen C, Liaw D, Podsypanina K, Bose S, Wang SI, Puc J, Miliaresis C, Rodgers L, McCombie R, Bigner SH, Giovanella BC, Ittmann M, Tycko B, Hibshoosh H, Wigler MH, Parsons R (1997). PTEN, a putative protein tyrosine phosphatase gene mutated in human brain, breast, and prostate cancer. *Science* 275: 1943-1947.

1069. Liang JT, Yu SC, Lee PH, Chang KJ, Fang CL, Lin WJ, Chuang SM (1995). Endoscopic diagnosis of malignant melanoma in the gastric cardia - report of a case without a detectable primary lesion. *Endoscopy* 27: 409.

1070. Liang R, Chan WP, Kwong YL, Chan AC, Xu WS, Au WY, Srivastava G, Ho FC (1997). Bcl-6 gene hypermutations in diffuse large B-cell lymphoma of primary gastric origin. *Br J Haematol* 99: 668-670.

1071. Liaw D, Marsh DJ, Li J., Dahia PL, Wang SI, Zheng Z, Bose S, Call KM, Tsou HC, Peacocke M, Eng C, Parsons R (1997). Germline mutations of the PTEN gene in Cowden disease, an inherited breast and thyroid cancer syndrome. *Nat Genet* 16: 64-67.

1072. Lieber MR, Lack EE, Roberts JRJ, Solomon D, Chandra R, Triche TJ (1987). Solid and papillary epithelial neoplasm of the pancreas. An ultrastructural and immunocytochemical study of six cases. *Am J Surg Pathol* 11: 85-93.

1073. Lim HW, Mascaro JM (1995). The porphyrias and hepatocellular carcinoma. *Dermatol Clin* 13: 135-142.

1074. Lin AY, Gridley G, Tucker M (1995). Benign anal lesions and anal cancer. *N Engl J Med* 332: 190-191.

1075. Lindblom A, Tannergard P, Werelius B, Nordenskjold M (1993). Genetic mapping of a second locus predisposing to hereditary non-polyposis colon cancer. *Nat Genet* 5: 279-282.

1076. Liston R, Pitt MA, Banerjee AK (1996). Reflux oesophagitis and Helicobacter pylori infection in elderly patients. *Postgrad Med J* 72: 221-223.

1077. Liu B, Nicolaides NC, Markowitz S, Willson JK, Parsons RE, Jen J, de-la-Papadopolous N, Peltomaki P, de-la-Chapelle A, Hamilton SR, Vogelstein B, Kinzler KW (1995). Mismatch repair gene defects in sporadic colorectal cancers with microsatellite instability. *Nat Genet* 9: 48-55.

1078. Liu B, Parsons R, Papadopoulos N, Nicolaides NC, Lynch HT, Watson P, Jass JR, Dunlop M, Wyllie A, Peltomaki P, de-la-Chapelle A, Hamilton SR, Vogelstein B, Kinzler KW (1996). Analysis of mismatch repair genes in hereditary nonpolyposis colorectal cancer patients. *Nat Med* 2: 169-174.

1079. Liu B, Parsons RE, Hamilton SR, Petersen GM, Lynch HT, Watson P, Markowitz S, Willson JK, Green J, de-la-Chapelle A, et a (1994). hMSH2 mutations in hereditary nonpolyposis colorectal cancer kindreds. *Cancer Res* 54: 4590-4594.

1079A. Liu W, Dong X, Mai M, Seelan RS, Taniguchi K, Krishnadath KK, Halling KC, Cunningham JM, Qian C, Christensen E, Roche PC, Smith DI, Thibodeau SN (2000). *Nat Genet* 26: 146-147.

1080. Liver Cancer Study Group of Japan (1997). Classification of Primary Liver Cancer. Kanehara-Shuppan: Tokyo.

1081. Lloyd KM, Denis M (1963). Cowden's disease: a possible new symptom complex with multiple system involvement. *Ann Intern Med* 58: 136-142.

1082. Loane J, Kealy WF, Mulcahy G (1998). Perianal hidradenoma papilliferum occurring in a male: a case report. *Ir J Med Sci* 167: 26-27.

1083. Lobert PF, Appelman HD (1981). Inflammatory cloacogenic polyp. A unique inflammatory lesion of the anal transitional zone. *Am J Surg Pathol* 5: 761-766.

1084. Lock MR, Thomson JP (1977). Fissure-in-ano: the initial management and prognosis. *Br J Surg* 64: 355-358.

1085. Locker GY, Doroshow JH, Zwelling LA, Chabner BA (1979). The clinical features of hepatic angiosarcoma: a report of four cases and a review of the English literature. *Medicine Baltimore* 58: 48-64.

1086. Loeffler M, Grossmann B (1991). A stochastic branching model with formation of subunits applied to the growth of intestinal crypts. *J Theor Biol* 150: 175-191.

1087. Loffeld RJ, Ten-Tije BJ, Arends JW (1992). Prevalence and significance of Helicobacter pylori in patients with Barrett's esophagus. *Am J Gastroenterol* 87: 1598-1600.

1088. Loftus-EV J, Olivares PB, Batts KP, Adkins MC, Stephens DH, Sarr MG, Dimagno EP (1996). Intraductal papillary-mucinous tumors of the pancreas: clinicopathologic features, outcome, and nomenclature. Members of the Pancreas Clinic, and Pancreatic Surgeons of Mayo Clinic. *Gastroenterology* 110: 1909-1918.

1089. Loke TK, Lo SS, Chan CS (1997). Case report: Krukenberg tumours arising from a primary duodenojejunal adenocarcinoma. *Clin Radiol* 52: 154-155.

1090. Lonardo F, Cubilla AL, Klimstra DS (1996). Microadenocarcinoma of the pancreas - morphologic pattern or pathologic entity? A reevaluation of the original series. *Am J Surg Pathol* 20: 1385-1393.

1091. Long L, Nip J, Brodt P (1994). Paracrine growth stimulation by hepatocyte-derived insulin-like growth factor-1: a regulatory mechanism for carcinoma cells metastatic to the liver. *Cancer Res* 54: 3732-3737.

1092. Longacre TA, Fenoglio PC (1990). Mixed hyperplastic adenomatous polyps/serrated adenomas. A distinct form of colorectal neoplasia. *Am J Surg Pathol* 14: 524-537.

1093. Longnecker DS (1998). Observations on the etiology and pathogenesis of intraductal papillary-mucinous neoplasms of the pancreas. *Hepatogastroenterology* 45: 1973-1980.

1094. Longnecker DS, Shinozuka H, Dekker A (1980). Focal acinar cell dysplasia in human pancreas. *Cancer* 45: 534-540.

1095. Longnecker DS, Tosteson TD, Karagas MF, Mott LA (1998). Incidence of pancreatic intraductal papillary-mucinous carcinomas in Japanese and Caucasians in SEER data. *Pancreas* 17: 446.

1096. Longy M, Lacombe D (1996). Cowden disease. Report of a family and review. *Ann Genet* 39: 35-42.

1097. Lorimier G, Binelli C, Burtin P, Maillart P, Bertrand G, Verriele V, Fondrinier E (1992). Metastatic gastric cancer arising from breast carcinoma: endoscopic ultrasonographic aspects. *Eur J Gynaecol Oncol* 13: S85-S88.

1098. Lothe RA, Peltomaki P, Meling GI, Aaltonen LA, Nystrom LM, Pylkkanen L, Heimdal K, Andersen TI, Moller P, Rognum TO, et a (1993). Genomic instability in colorectal cancer: relationship to clinicopathological variables and family history. *Cancer Res* 53: 5849-5852.

1099. Louie DC, Offit K, Jaslow R, Parsa NZ, Murty VV, Schluger A, Chaganti RS (1995). p53 overexpression as a marker of poor prognosis in mantle cell lymphomas with t(11;14)(q13;q32). *Blood* 86: 2892-2899.

1100. Lowenfels AB, Maisonneuve P, Cavallini G, Ammann RW, Lankisch PG, Andersen JR, Dimagno EP, Andren SA, Domellof L (1993). Pancreatitis and the risk of pancreatic cancer. International Pancreatitis Study Group. *N Engl J Med* 328: 1433-1437.

1101. Lowenfels AB, Maisonneuve P, Dimagno EP, Elitsur Y, Gates-LK J, Perrault J, Whitcomb DC (1997). Hereditary pancreatitis and the risk of pancreatic cancer. International Hereditary Pancreatitis Study Group. *J Natl Cancer Inst* 89: 442-446.

1102. Lowitt MH, Karineimi AL, Niemi KM, Kao GF (1996). Cutaneous malakoplakia: a report of two cases and review of the literature. *J Am Acad Dermatol* 34: 325-332.

1103. Lu SL, Kawabata M, Imamura T, Akiyama Y, Nomizu T, Miyazono K, Yuasa Y (1998). HNPCC associated with germline mutation in the TGF-beta type II receptor gene. *Nat Genet* 19: 17-18.

1104. Lu YK, Li YM, Gu YZ (1987). Cancer of esophagus and esophagogastric junction: analysis of results of 1,025 resections after 5 to 20 years. *Ann Thorac Surg* 43: 176-181.

1105. Lubensky IA, Debelenko LV, Zhuang Z, Emmert BM, Dong Q, Chandrasekharappa S, Guru SC, Manickam P, Olufemi SE, Marx SJ, Spiegel AM, Collins FS, Liotta LA (1996). Allelic deletions on chromosome 11q13 in multiple tumors from individual MEN1 patients. *Cancer Res* 56: 5272-5278.

1106. Luck A, Hensman C, Hewett P (1998). Laparoscopic colectomy for cancer: a review. *Aust N Z J Surg* 68: 318-327.

1107. Ludwig J, Wahlstrom HE, Batts KP, Wiesner RH (1992). Papillary bile duct dysplasia in primary sclerosing cholangitis. *Gastroenterology* 102: 2134-2138.

1108. Luk GD (1993). Gastrointestinal malignancy. *Aliment Pharmacol Ther* 7: 661-669.

1109. Lukish JR, Muro K, DeNobile J, Katz R, Williams J, Cruess DF, Drucker W, Kirsch I, Hamilton SR (1998). Prognostic significance of DNA replication errors in young patients with colorectal cancer. *Ann Surg* 227: 51-56.

1110. Luna PP, Rodriguez DF, Lujan L, Alvarado I, Kelly J, Rojas ME, Labastida S, Gonzalez JL (1998). Colorectal sarcoma: analysis of failure patterns. *J Surg Oncol* 69: 36-40.

1111. Lundin J., Nording S., von-Boguslawsky K, Roberts PJ, Haglund C (1995). Prognostic significance of DNA ploidy and S-phase fraction in patients with pancreatic cancer. *Anticancer Res* 15: 2659-2668.

1112. Lundquist K, Kohler S, Rouse RV (1999). Intraepidermal cytokeratin 7 expression is not restricted to Paget cells but is also seen in Toker cells and Merkel cells. *Am J Surg Pathol* 23: 212-219.

1113. Lundqvist C, Baranov V, Hammarstrom S, Athin L, Hammarstrom ML (1995). Intra-epithelial lymphocytes. Evidence for regional specialization and extrathymic T cell maturation in the human gut epithelium. *Int Immunol* 7: 1473-1487.

1114. Lundqvist M, Eriksson B, Oberg K, Wilander E (1989). Histogenesis of a duodenal carcinoid. *Pathol Res Pract* 184: 217-222.

1115. Lundqvist M, Wilander E (1987). A study of the histopathogenesis of carcinoid tumors of the small intestine and appendix. *Cancer* 60: 201-206.

1116. Lung ML, Chan WC, Zong YS, Tang CM, Fok CL, Wong KT, Chan LK, Lau KW (1996). p53 mutational spectrum of esophageal carcinomas from five different geographical locales in China. *Cancer Epidemiol Biomarkers Prev* 5: 277-284.

1117. Lunniss PJ, Sheffield JP, Talbot IC, Thomson JP, Phillips RK (1995). Persistence of idiopathic anal fistula may be related to epithelialization. *Br J Surg* 82: 32-33.

1118. Luttges J, Mentzel T, Hubner G, Kloppel G (1999). Solitary fibrous tumour of the pancreas: a new member of the small group of mesenchymal pancreatic tumours. *Virchows Arch* 435/1: 37-42.

1119. Luttges J, Schemm S, Vogel I, Hedderich J, Kremer B, Kloppel G (2000). The grade of pancreatic ductal adenocarcinoma is an independent prognostic factor and is superior to the immunohistochemical cell proliferation. *J Pathol* 191: 154-161.

1120. Luttges J, Schlehe B, Menke MA, Vogel I, Henne BD, Kloppel G (1999). The K-ras mutation pattern in pancreatic ductal adenocarcinoma usually is identical to that in associated normal, hyperplastic, and metaplastic ductal epithelium. *Cancer* 85: 1703-1710.

1121. Luttges J, Vogel I, Menke M, Henne BD, Kremer B, Kloppel G (1998). Clear cell carcinoma of the pancreas: an adenocarcinoma with ductal phenotype. *Histopathology* 32: 444-448.

1122. Luttges J, Vogel I, Menke M, Henne BD, Kremer B, Kloppel G (1998). The retroperitoneal resection margin and vessel involvement are important factors determining survival after pancreaticoduodenectomy for ductal adenocarcinoma of the head of the pancreas. *Virchows Arch* 433: 237-242.

1123. Lyda MH, Noffsinger A, Belli J, Fischer J, Fenoglio PC (1998). Multifocal neoplasia involving the colon and appendix in ulcerative colitis: pathological and molecular features. *Gastroenterology* 115: 1566-1573.

1124. Lynch ED, Ostermeyer EA, Lee MK, Arena JF, Ji H, Dann J, Swisshelm K, Suchard D, MacLeod PM, Kvinnsland S, Gjertsen BT, Heimdal K, Lubs H, Moller P, King MC (1997). Inherited mutations in PTEN that are associated with breast cancer, cowden disease, and juvenile polyposis. *Am J Hum Genet* 61: 1254-1260.

1125. Lynch HT, Fitzsimmons ML, Smyrk TC, Lanspa SJ, Watson P, McClellan J, Lynch JF (1990). Familial pancreatic cancer: clinicopathologic study of 18 nuclear families. *Am J Gastroenterol* 85: 54-60.

1126. Lynch HT, Fusaro L, Smyrk TC, Watson P, Lanspa S, Lynch JF (1995). Medical genetic study of eight pancreatic cancer-prone families. *Cancer Invest* 13: 141-149.

1127. Lynch HT, Fusaro RM (1991). Pancreatic cancer and the familial atypical multiple mole melanoma (FAMMM) syndrome. *Pancreas* 6: 127-131.

1128. Lynch HT, Smyrk T, Kern SE, Hruban RH, Lightdale CJ, Lemon SJ, Lynch JF, Fusaro LR, Fusaro RM, Ghadirian P (1996). Familial pancreatic cancer: a review. *Semin Oncol* 23: 251-275.

1129. Lynch HT, Smyrk T, Lynch J (1997). An update of HNPCC (Lynch syndrome). *Cancer Genet Cytogenet* 93: 84-99.

1130. Lynch HT, Smyrk TC, Watson P, Lanspa SJ, Lynch JF, Lynch PM, Cavalieri RJ, Boland CR (1993). Genetics, natural history, tumor spectrum, and pathology of hereditary nonpolyposis colorectal cancer: an updated review. *Gastroenterology* 104: 1535-1549.

1131. Lyss AP (1988). Appendiceal malignancies. *Semin Oncol* 15: 129-137.

1132. Mac Donald RA (1956). A study of 356 carcinoids of the gastrointestinal tract. Report of four new cases of carcinoid syndrome. *Am J Med* 21: 867-878.

1133. MacDonald WC, MacDonald JB (1987). Adenocarcinoma of the esophagus and/or gastric cardia. *Cancer* 60: 1094-1098.

1134. MacGillivray DC, Heaton RB, Rushin JM, Cruess DF (1992). Distant metastasis from a carcinoid tumor of the appendix less than one centimeter in size. *Surgery* 111: 466-471.

1135. Machado JC, Carneiro F, Beck S, Rossi S, Lopes J, Taveira GA (1998). E-cadherin expression is correlated with the isolated cell/diffuse histotype and with the features of biological aggressiveness of gastric carcinoma. *Int J Surg Pathol* 6: 135-144.

1136. Machado JC, Soares P, Carneiro F, Rocha A, Beck S, Blin N, Berx G, Sobrinho SM (1999). E-cadherin gene mutations provide a genetic basis for the phenotypic divergence of mixed gastric carcinomas. *Lab Invest* 79: 459-465.

1137. Macpherson N, Lesack D, Klasa R, Horsman D, Connors JM, Barnett M, Gascoyne RD (1999). Small noncleaved, non-Burkit's (Burkit-Like) lymphoma: cytogenetics predict outcome and reflect clinical presentation. *J Clin Oncol* 17: 1558-1567.

1138. Madura JA, Wiebke EA, Howard TJ, Cummings OW, Hull MT, Sherman S, Lehman GA (1997). Mucin-hypersecreting intraductal neoplasms of the pancreas: a precursor to cystic pancreatic malignancies. *Surgery* 122: 786-792.

1139. Maeda H, Yamagata A, Nishikawa S, Yoshinaga K, Kobayashi S, Nishi K (1992). Requirement of c-kit for development of intestinal pacemaker system. *Development* 116: 369-375.

1140. Maeda M, Nagawa H, Maeda T, Koike H, Kasai H (1998). Alcohol consumption enhances liver metastasis in colorectal carcinoma patients. *Cancer* 83: 1483-1488.

1141. Maeda T, Kajiyama K, Adachi E, Takenaka K, Sugimachi K, Tsuneyoshi M (1996). The expression of cytokeratins 7, 19, and 20 in primary and metastatic carcinomas of the liver. *Mod Pathol* 9: 901-909.

1142. Maehama T, Dixon JE (1998). The tumor suppressor, PTEN/MMAC1, dephosphorylates the lipid second messenger, phosphatidylinositol 3,4,5-trisphosphate. *J Biol Chem* 273: 13375-13378.

1143. Maes M, Depardieu C, Dargent JL, Hermans M, Verhaeghe JL, Delabie J, Pittaluga S, Troufleau P, Verhest A, De-Wolf-Peeters C (1997). Primary low-grade B-cell lymphoma of MALT-type occurring in the liver: a study of two cases. *J Hepatol* 27: 922-927.

1144. Maeshiro K, Nakayama Y, Yasunami Y, Furuta K, Ikeda S (1998). Diagnosis of mucin-producing tumor of the pancreas by balloon-catheter endoscopic retrograde pancreatography - compression study. *Hepatogastroenterology* 45: 1986-1995.

1145. Maglinte DT, Reyes BL (1997). Small bowel cancer. Radiologic diagnosis. *Radiol Clin North Am* 35: 361-380.

1146. Mah PT, Loo DC, Tock EP (1974). Pancreatic acinar cell carcinoma in childhood. *Am J Dis Child* 128: 101-104.

1147. Maimon S, Zinninger M (1953). Familial gastric cancer. *Gastroenterology* 25: 139-

1148. Majerus B, Timmermans M (1990). [Gastric metastases of ovarian adenocarcinoma. Apropos of a case]. *Acta Chir Belg* 90: 166-171.

1149. Makhlouf HR, Burke AP, Sobin LH (1999). Carcinoid tumors of the ampulla of Vater. A comparison with duodenal carcinoid tumors. *Cancer* 85: 1241-1249.

1150. Makhlouf HR, Ishak KG, Goodman ZD (1999). Epithelioid hemangioendothelioma of the liver: a clinicopathologic study of 137 cases. *Cancer* 85: 562-582.

1151. Malkin D, Li FP, Strong LC, Fraumeni JF J, Nelson CE, Kim DH, Kassel J, Gryka MA, Bischoff FZ, Tainsky MA, et a (1990). Germ line p53 mutations in a familial syndrome of breast cancer, sarcomas, and other neoplasms. *Science* 250: 1233-1238.

1152. Mallory SB (1995). Cowden syndrome (multiple hamartoma syndrome). *Dermatol Clin* 13: 27-31.

1153. Mandard AM, Chasle J, Marnay J, Villedieu B, Bianco C, Roussel A, Elie H, Vernhes JC (1981). Autopsy findings in 111 cases of esophageal cancer. *Cancer* 48: 329-335.

1154. Mandard AM, Marnay J, Gignoux M, Segol P, Blanc L, Ollivier JM, Borel B, Mandard JC (1984). Cancer of the esophagus and associated lesions: detailed pathologic study of 100 esophagectomy specimens. *Hum Pathol* 15: 660-669.

1155. Mandishona E, MacPhail AP, Gordeuk VR, Kedda MA, Paterson AC, Rouault TA, Kew MC (1998). Dietary iron overload as a risk factor for hepatocellular carcinoma in Black Africans. *Hepatology* 27: 1563-1566.

1156. Mandujano VG, Angeles AA, de-la-Cruz-Hernandez J, Sansores PM, Larriva SJ (1995). Gastrinoma of the common bile duct: immunohistochemical and ultrastructural study of a case. *J Clin Gastroenterol* 20: 321-324.

1157. Mannick EE, Bravo LE, Zarama G, Realpe JL, Zhang XJ, Ruiz B, Fontham ET, Mera R, Miller MJ, Correa P (1996). Inducible nitric oxide synthase, nitrotyrosine, and apoptosis in Helicobacter pylori gastritis: effect of antibiotics and antioxidants. *Cancer Res* 56: 3238-3243.

1158. Mant JW, Vessey MP (1995). Trends in mortality from primary liver cancer in England and Wales 1975-92: influence of oral contraceptives. *Br J Cancer* 72: 800-803.

1159. Mao C, Guvendi M, Domenico DR, Kim K, Thomford NR, Howard JM (1995). Papillary cystic and solid tumors of the pancreas: a pancreatic embryonic tumor? Studies of three cases and cumulative review of the world's literature. *Surgery* 118: 821-828.

1160. Marchesa P, Fazio VW, Church JM, McGannon E (1997). Adrenal masses in patients with familial adenomatous polyposis. *Dis Colon Rectum* 40: 1023-1028.

1161. Marchesa P, Fazio VW, Oliart S, Goldblum JR, Lavery IC (1997). Perianal Bowen's disease: a clinicopathologic study of 47 patients. *Dis Colon Rectum* 40: 1286-1293.

1162. Marchesa P, Fazio VW, Oliart S, Goldblum JR, Lavery IC, Milsom JW (1997). Long-term outcome of patients with perianal Paget's disease. *Ann Surg Oncol* 4: 475-480.

1163. Marchio A, Meddeb M, Pineau P, Danglot G, Trollais P, Bernheim A, Dejean A (1997). Recurrent chromosomal abnormalities in hepatocellular carcinoma detected by comparative genomic hybridization. *Genes Chromosomes Cancer* 18: 59-65.

1164. Markowitz AJ, Winawer SJ (1999). Screening and surveillance for colorectal cancer. *Semin Oncol* 26: 485-498.

1165. Markowitz S, Wang J, Myeroff L, Parsons R, Sun L, Lutterbaugh J, Fan RS, Zborowska E, Kinzler KW, Vogelstein B, et a (1995). Inactivation of the type II TGF-beta receptor in colon cancer cells with microsatellite instability. *Science* 268: 1336-1338.

1166. Marra G, Boland CR (1995). Hereditary nonpolyposis colorectal cancer: the syndrome, the genes, and historical perspectives. *J Natl Cancer Inst* 87: 1114-1125.

167. Marsh DJ, Coulon V, Lunetta KL, Rocca SP, Dahia PL, Zheng Z, Liaw D, Caron S, Duboue B, Lin AY, Richardson AL, Bonnetblanc JM, Bressieux JM, Cabarrot MA, Chompret A, Demange L, Eeles RA, Yahanda AM, Fearon ER, Fricker JP, Gorlin RJ, Hodgson SV, Huson S, Lacombe D, LePrat F, Odent S, Toulouse C, Olapade OI, Sobol H, Tishler S, Woods CG, Robinson BG, Weber HC, Parsons R, Peacocke M, Longy M, Eng C (1998). Mutation spectrum and genotype-phenotype analyses in Cowden disease and Bannayan-Zonana syndrome, two hamartoma syndromes with germline PTEN mutation. *Hum Mol Genet* 7:507-515.

168. Marsh DJ, Dahia PL, Caron S, Kum JB, Frayling IM, Tomlinson IP, Hughes KS, Eeles RA, Hodgson SV, Murday VA, Houlston R, Eng C (1998). Germline PTEN mutations in Cowden syndrome-like families. *J Med Genet* 35: 881-885.

169. Marsh DJ, Dahia PL, Zheng Z, Liaw D, Parsons R, Gorlin RJ, Eng C (1997). Germline mutations in PTEN are present in Bannayan-Zonana syndrome. *Nat Genet* 16: 333-334.

170. Marsh DJ, Kum JB, Lunetta KL, Bennett MJ, Gorlin RJ, Ahmed SF, Bodurtha J, Crowe C, Curtis MA, Dazouki M, Dunn T, Feit H, Geraghty MT, Graham JM, Hodgson SV, Hunter A, Korf BR, Manchester D, Miesfeldt S, Murday VA, Nathanson KA, Parisi M, Pober B, Romano C, Tolmie JL, Trembath R, Winter RM, Zackai EH, Zori RT, Weng LP, Dahia PLM, Eng C (1999). PTEN mutation spectrum and genotype-phenotype correlations in Bannayan-Riley-Ruvalcaba syndrome suggest a single entity with Cowden syndrome. *Hum Mol Genet* 8: 1461-1472.

171. Marsh DJ, Roth S, Lunetta KL, Hennninki A, Dahia PL, Sistonen P, Zheng Z, Caron S, van-Orsouw NJ, Bodmer WF, Cottrell SE, Dunlop MG, Eccles D, Hodgson SV, Jarvinen H, Kellokumpu I, Markie D, Neale K, Phillips R, Rozen P, Syngal S, Vijg J, Tomlinson IP, Aaltonen LA, Eng C (1997). Exclusion of PTEN and 10q22-24 as the susceptibility locus for juvenile polyposis syndrome. *Cancer Res* 57: 5017-5021.

172. Marsh MN, Crowe PT (1995). Morphology of the mucosal lesion in gluten sensitivity. *Baillieres Clin Gastroenterol* 9: 273-293.

173. Martensson H, Nobin A, Sundler F, Falkmer S (1985). Endocrine tumors of the ileum. Cytochemical and clinical aspects. *Pathol Res Pract* 180: 356-363.

174. Marti MC (1991). Cancer de l'anus: considerations anatomo-cliniques. *Lyon Chir* 87: 49-52.

175. Martignoni ME, Friess H, Lubke D, Uhl W, Maurer C, Muller M, Richard H, Reubi JC, Buchler MW (1999). Study of a primary gastrinoma in the common hepatic duct - a case report. *Digestion* 60: 187-190.

176. Martin AR, Chan WC, Perry DA, Greiner TC, Weisenburger DD (1995). Aggressive natural killer cell lymphoma of the small intestine. *Mod Pathol* 8: 467-472.

177. Martin IG, Dixon MF, Sue LH, Axon AT, Johnston D (1994). Goseki histological grading of gastric cancer is an important predictor of outcome. *Gut* 35: 758-763.

178. Martinez ME, McPherson RS, Levin B, Glober GA (1997). A case-control study of dietary intake and other lifestyle factors for hyperplastic polyps. *Gastroenterology* 113: 423-429.

179. Maruyama H, Nakatsuji N, Sugihara S, Atsumi M, Shimamoto K, Hayashi K, Tsutsumi M, Konishi Y (1997). Anaplastic Ki-1-positive large cell lymphoma of the pancreas: a case report and review of the literature. *Jpn J Clin Oncol* 27: 51-57.

180. Maruyama M, Baba Y (1994). Gastric carcinoma. *Radiol Clin North Am* 32: 1233-1252.

181. Masaki T, Sheffield JP, Talbot IC, Williams CB (1994). Non-polypoid adenoma of the large intestine. *Int J Colorectal Dis* 9: 180-183.

182. Masson P (1928). Carcinoids (argentaffin-cell tumors) and nerve hyperplasia of the appendicular mucosa. *Am J Pathol* 4: 181-211.

183. Matano S, Nakamura S, Annen Y, Hattori N, Kiyohara K, Kakuta K, Kyoda K, Sugimoto T (1998). Primary hepatic lymphoma in a patient with chronic hepatitis B. *Am J Gastroenterol* 93: 2301-2302.

184. Matolcsy A, Nagy M, Kisfaludy N, Kelenyi G (1999). Distinct clonal origin of low-grade MALT-type and high-grade lesions of a multifocal gastric lymphoma. *Histopathology* 34: 6-8.

185. Matsubara T, Ueda M, Takahashi T, Nakajima T, Nishi M (1996). Localization of recurrent disease after extended lymph node dissection for carcinoma of the thoracic esophagus. *J Am Coll Surg* 182: 340-346.

186. Matsubayashi H, Watanabe H, Nishikura K, Ajioka Y, Kijima H, Saito T (1998). Determination of pancreatic ductal carcinoma histogenesis by analysis of mucous quality and K-ras mutation. *Cancer* 82: 651-660.

187. Matsuda Y, Ichida T, Matsuzawa J, Sugimura K, Asakura H (1999). A fallopian tube lesion of borderline malignancy associated with pseudo-myxoma peritonei. *Histopathology* 13: 223-225.

188. Matsui K, Jin XM, Kitagawa M, Miwa A (1998). Clinicopathologic features of neuroendocrine carcinomas of the stomach: appraisal of small cell and large cell variants. *Arch Pathol Lab Med* 122: 1010-1017.

189. Matsui S, Shiozaki H, Inoue M, Tamura S, Doki Y, Kadowaki T, Iwazawa T, Shimaya K, Nagafuchi A, Tsukita S, et a (1994). Immunohistochemical evaluation of alpha-catenin expression in human gastric cancer. *Virchows Arch* 424: 375-381.

190. Matsukuma S, Suda A, Abe H, Ogata S, Wada R (1997). Metastatic cancer involving pancreatic duct epithelium and its mimicry of primary pancreatic cancer. *Histopathology* 30: 208-213.

191. Matsumoto T, Mizuno M, Shimizu M, Manabe T, Iida M, Fujishima M (1999). Serrated adenoma of the colorectum: colonoscopic and histologic features. *Gastrointest Endosc* 49: 736-742.

192. Matsunou H, Konishi F (1990). Papillary-cystic neoplasm of the pancreas. A clinicopathologic study concerning the tumor aging and malignancy of nine cases. *Cancer* 65: 2747-2757.

193. Matsunou H, Konishi F, Yamamichi N, Takayanagi N, Mukai M (1990). Solid, infiltrating variety of papillary cystic neoplasm of the pancreas. *Cancer* 65: 2747-2757.

194. Matsuoka Y, Masumoto T, Suzuki K, Terada K, Ushimi T, Yokoyama Y, Abe K, Kamata N, Yasuno M, Hishima T (1999). Pseudomyxoma retroperitonei. *Eur Radiol* 9: 457-459.

195. Matsuura H, Sugimachi K, Ueo H, Kuwano H, Koga Y, Okamura T (1986). Malignant potentiality of squamous cell carcinoma of the esophagus predictable by DNA analysis. *Cancer* 57: 1810-1814.

196. Mayer B, Johnson JP, Leitl F, Jauch KW, Heiss MM, Schildberg FW, Birchmeier W, Funke I (1993). E-cadherin expression in primary and metastatic gastric cancer: down-regulation correlates with cellular dedifferentiation and glandular disintegration. *Cancer Res* 53: 1690-1695.

197. McArdle JE, Lewin KJ, Randall G, Weinstein W (1992). Distribution of dysplasias and early invasive carcinoma in Barrett's esophagus. *Hum Pathol* 23: 479-482.

198. McCann BG (1998). A case of metaplastic polyposis of the colon associated with focal adenomatous change and metachronous adenocarcinomas. *Histopathology* 13: 700-702.

199. McCarthy JH, Aga R (1988). A fallopian tube lesion of borderline malignancy with focal adenomatous change and metachronous adenocarcinomas. *Histopathology* 13: 700-702.

200. McClave SA, Boyce-HW J, Gottfried MR (1987). Early diagnosis of columnar-lined esophagus: a new endoscopic diagnostic criterion. *Gastrointest Endosc* 33: 413-416.

201. McCluggage W, Mackel E, McCusker G (1996). Primary low grade malignant lymphoma of mucosa-associated lymphoid tissue of gallbladder. *Histopathology* 29: 285-287.

202. McColl I, Bussey HJ, Veale AM, Morson BC (1964). Juvenile polyposis coli. *Proc Roy Soc Med* 57: 896-897.

203. McDermott VG, Low VH, Keogan MT, Lawrence JA, Paulson EK (1996). Malignant melanoma metastatic to the gastrointestinal tract. *AJR Am J Roentgenol* 166: 809-813.

204. McGarrity TJ, Ruggiero FM, Chey WY, Bajaj R, Kelly JE, Kauffman GL, Jr. (2000). Giant fundic polyp complicating attenuated familial adenomatous polyposis. *Am J Gastroenterol* 95: 1824-1828.

205. McLean CA, Pedersen JS (1991). Endocrine cell carcinoma of the gallbladder. *Histopathology* 19: 173-176.

206. McLeod HL, Murray GI (1999). Tumour markers of prognosis in colorectal cancer. *Br J Cancer* 79: 191-203.

207. McNamara PJ (1996). Familial pancreatic cancer: an aggregation analysis. [*Masters of Science*]

208. McNeely B, Owen DA, Pezim M (1992). Multiple microcarcinoids arising in chronic ulcerative colitis. *Am J Clin Pathol* 98: 112-116.

209. McNeill PM, Wagman LD, Neifeld JP (1987). Small bowel metastases from primary carcinoma of the lung. *Cancer* 59: 1486-1489.

210. Mehenni H, Gehrig C, Nezu J, Oku A, Shimane M, Rossier C, Guex N, Blouin JL, Scott HS, Antonarakis SE (1998). Loss of LKB1 kinase activity in Peutz-Jeghers syndrome, and evidence for allelic and locus heterogeneity. An autopsy study. *Am J Hum Genet* 63: 1641-1650.

211. Melato M, Laurino L, Mudi E, Valente M, Okuda K (1989). Relationship between cirrhosis, liver cancer, and hepatic metastases. An autopsy study. *Cancer* 64: 455-459.

212. Melbye M, Cote TR, Kessler L, Gail M, Biggar RJ (1994). High incidence of anal cancer among AIDS patients. The AIDS/Cancer Working Group. *Lancet* 343: 636-639.

213. Melbye M, Rabkin C, Frisch M, Biggar RJ (1994). Changing patterns of anal cancer incidence in the United States, 1940-1989. *Am J Epidemiol* 139: 772-780.

214. Mellemkjaer L, et al (1995). Cancer in patients with ulcerative colitis. *Int J Cancer* 60: 330-333.

215. Mellon I, Rajpal DK, Koi M, Boland CR, Champe GN (1996). Transcription-coupled repair deficiency and mutations in human mismatch repair genes. *Science* 272: 557-560.

216. Melo CR, Melo IS, Schmitt FC, Fagundes R, Amendola D (1993). Multicentric granular cell tumor of the colon: report of a patient with 52 tumors. *Am J Gastroenterol* 88: 1785-1787.

217. Memeo L, Pecorello I, Ciardi A, Aiello E, De Quarto A, Di Tondo U (1999). Primary non-Hodgkin's lymphoma of the liver. *Acta Oncol* 38: 655-658.

218. Mendelsohn G, Diamond MP (1984). Familial ganglioneuromatous polyposis of the large bowel. Report of a family with associated juvenile polyposis. *Am J Surg Pathol* 8: 515-520.

219. Menke PM, Schoute NW, Mulder AH, Hop WC, van-Blankenstein M, Tilanus HW (1992). Outcome of surgical treatment of adenocarcinoma in Barrett's oesophagus. *Gut* 33: 1454-1458.

220. Menuck LS, Amberg JR (1975). Metastatic disease involving the stomach. *Am J Dig Dis* 20: 903-913.

221. Messerini L, Ciantelli M, Baglioni S, Palomba A, Zampi G, Papi L (1999). Prognostic significance of microsatellite instability in sporadic mucinous colorectal cancers. *Hum Pathol* 30: 629-634.

1222. Michael D, Beer DG, Wilke CW, Miller DE, Glover TW (1997). Frequent deletions of FHIT and FRA3B in Barrett's metaplasia and esophageal adenocarcinomas. Oncogene 15: 1653-1659.

1223. Michelassi F, Testa G, Pomidor WJ, Lashner BA, Block GE (1993). Adenocarcinoma complicating Crohn's disease. Dis Colon Rectum 36: 654-661.

1224. Miettinen M, Holthofer H, Lehto VP, Miettinen A, Virtanen I (1983). Ulex europaeus I lectin as a marker for tumors derived from endothelial cells. Am J Clin Pathol 79: 32-36.

1225. Miettinen M, Monihan JM, Sarlomo-Rikala M, Kovatich AJ, Carr NJ, Emory TS, Sobin LH (1999). Gastrointestinal stromal tumors/smooth muscle tumors (GISTs) primary in the omentum and mesentery: clinicopathologic and immunohistochemical study of 26 cases. Am J Surg Pathol 23(9): 1109-1118.

1226. Miettinen M, Partanen S, Fraki O, Kivilaakso E (1987). Papillary cystic tumor of the pancreas. An analysis of cellular differentiation by electron microscopy and immunohistochemistry. Am J Surg Pathol 11: 855-865.

1227. Miettinen M, Sarlomo RM, Lasota J (1999). Gastrointestinal stromal tumors: recent advances in understanding of their biology. Hum Pathol 30: 1213-1220.

1228. Miettinen M, Sarlomo RM, Sobin LH, Lasota J (2000). Esophageal stromal tumors - a clinicopathologic, immunohistochemical and molecular genetic study of seventeen cases and comparison with esophageal leiomyomas and leiomyosarcomas. Am J Surg Pathol 24: 211-222.

1229. Miettinen M, Virolainen M, Maarit SR (1995). Gastrointestinal stromal tumors - value of CD34 antigen in their identification and separation from true leiomyomas and schwannomas. Am J Surg Pathol 19: 207-216.

1230. Migasena P, Reaunsuwan W, Changbumrung S (1980). Nitrates and nitrites in local Thai preserved protein foods. J Med Assoc Thai 63: 500-505.

1231. Mikal S, Campbell AJA (1950). Carcinoma of the pancreas. Diagnostic and operative criteria based on one hundred consecutive autopsies. Surgery 28: 963-969.

1232. Mikhael AI, Bacchi CE, Zarbo RJ, Ma CK, Gown AM (1999). CD34 expression in stromal tumors of the gastrointestinal tract. Appl Immunohistochem 2: 89-93.

1233. Miller JH, Greenspan BS (1985). Integrated imaging of hepatic tumors in childhood. Part I: Malignant lesions (primary and metastatic). Radiology 154: 83-90.

1234. Minardi-AJ, Zibari GB, Aultman DF, McMillan RW, McDonald JC (1998). Small-bowel tumors. J Am Coll Surg 186: 664-668.

1235. Ming KW (1992). Small intestinal stromal tumors with skeinoid fibers. Clinicopathological, immunohistochemical, and ultrastructural investigations. Am J Surg Pathol 16: 145-155.

1236. Ming SC (1973). Atlas of Tumor Pathology. Tumors of the esophagus and stomach. 2nd ed, AFIP: Washington, D.C.

1237. Mingazzini PL, Malchiodi AF, Blandamura V (1982). Villous adenoma of the duodenum: cellular composition and histochemical findings. Histopathology 6: 235-244.

1238. Misdraji J, Fernandez-del CC, Ferry JA (1997). Follicle center lymphoma of the ampulla of Vater presenting with jaundice: report of a case. Am J Surg Pathol 21: 484-488.

1239. Mise M, Arii S, Higashituji H, Furutani M, Niwano M, Harada T, Ishigami S, Toda Y, Nakayama H, Fukumoto M, Fujita J, Imamura M (1996). Clinical significance of vascular endothelial growth factor and basic fibroblast growth factor gene expression in liver tumor. Hepatology 23: 455-464.

1240. Misumi A, Murakami A, Harada K, Baba K, Akagi M (1989). Definition of carcinoma of the gastric cardia. Langenbecks Arch Chir 374: 221-226.

1241. Miwa K, Hattori T, Miyazaki I (1995). Duodenogastric reflux and foregut carcinogenesis. Cancer 75: 1426-1432.

1242. Miwa W, Yasuda J, Murakami Y, Yashima K, Sugano K, Sekine T, Kono A, Egawa S, Yamaguchi K, Hayashizaki Y, Sekiya T (1996). Isolation of DNA sequences amplified at chromosome 19q13.1-q13.2 including the AKT2 locus in human pancreatic cancer. Biochem Biophys Res Commun 225: 968-974.

1243. Miyahara M, Saito T, Etoh K, Shimoda K, Kitano S, Kobayashi M, Yokoyama S (1995). Appendiceal intussusception due to an appendiceal malignant polyp - an association in a patient with Peutz-Jeghers syndrome: report of a case. Surg Today 25: 834-837.

1244. Miyakawa S, Horiguchi A, Hayakawa M, Ishihara S, Miura K, Horiguchi Y, Imai H, Mizoguchi Y, Kuroda M (1996). Intraductal papillary adenocarcinoma with mucin hypersecretion and coexistent invasive ductal carcinoma of the pancreas with apparent topographic separation. J Gastroenterol 31: 889-893.

1245. Miyaki M, Konishi M, Kikuchi YR, Enomoto M, Tanaka K, Takahashi H, Muraoka M, Mori T, Konishi F, Iwama T (1993). Coexistence of somatic and germline mutations of APC gene in desmoid tumors from patients with familial adenomatous polyposis. Cancer Res 53: 5079-5082.

1246. Miyaki M, Seki M, Okamoto M, Yamanaka A, Maeda Y, Tanaka K, Kikuchi R, Iwama T, Ikeuchi T, Tonomura A, et a (1990). Genetic changes and histopathological types in colorectal tumors from patients with familial adenomatous polyposis. Cancer Res 50: 7166-7173.

1247. Miyamoto Y, Hosotani R, Wada M, Lee JU, Koshiba T, Fujimoto K, Tsuji S, Nakajima S, Doi R, Kato M, Shimada Y, Imamura M (1999). Immunohistochemical analysis of Bcl-2, Bax, Bcl-X, and Mcl-1 expression in pancreatic cancers. Oncology 56: 73-82.

1248. Miyazaki K, Date K, Imamura S, Ogawa Y, Nakayama F (1989). Familial occurrence of anomalous pancreaticobiliary duct union associated with gallbladder neoplasms. Am J Gastroenterol 84: 176-181.

1249. Mizobuchi S, Tachimori Y, Kato H, Watanabe H, Nakanishi Y, Ochiai A (1997). Metastatic esophageal tumors from distant primary lesions: report of three esophagectomies and study of 1835 autopsy cases. Jpn J Clin Oncol 27: 410-414.

1250. Mockli GC, Silversmith M (1997). Squamous cell carcinoma of the lung metastatic to the pancreas: diagnosis by fine-needle aspiration biopsy. Diagn Cytopathol 16: 287-288.

1251. Modlin IM, Sandor A (1997). An analysis of 8305 cases of carcinoid tumors. Cancer 79: 813-829.

1252. Moertel CG, Dockerty MB, Judd ES (1968). Carcinoid tumors of the vermiform appendix. Cancer 21: 270-278.

1252A. Moertel CG, Dockerty MB (1973). Familial occurrence of metastasizing carcinoid tumors. Ann Intern Med 78: 389-390.

1253. Moertel CG, Sauer W, Dockerty M, Baggenstoss A (1961). Life history of carcinoid tumor of the small intestine. Cancer 14: 901-912.

1254. Moertel CG, Weiland LH, Nagorney DM, Dockerty MB (1987). Carcinoid tumor of the appendix: treatment and prognosis. N Engl J Med 317: 1699-1701.

1255. Moertel CL, Weiland LH, Telander RL (1990). Carcinoid tumor of the appendix in the first two decades of life. J Pediatr Surg 25: 1073-1075.

1256. Mogilner JG, Dharan M, Siplovich L (1991). Adenoma of the gallbladder in childhood. J Pediatr Surg 26: 223-224.

1257. Mohler M, Gutzler F, Kallinowski B, Goeser T, Stremmel W (1997). Primary hepatic high-grade non-Hodgkin's lymphoma and chronic hepatitis C infection. Dig Dis Sci 42: 2241-2245.

1258. Molberg KH, Heffess C, Delgado R, Albores SJ (1998). Undifferentiated carcinoma with osteoclast-like giant cells of the pancreas and periampullary region. Cancer 82: 1279-1287.

1259. Moll R, Lowe A, Laufer J, Franke WW (1992). Cytokeratin 20 in human carcinomas. A new histodiagnostic marker detected by monoclonal antibodies. Am J Pathol 140: 427-447.

1260. Monihan JM, Carr NJ, Sobin LH (1994). CD34 immunoexpression in stromal tumours of the gastrointestinal tract and in mesenteric fibromatoses. Histopathology 25: 469-473.

1261. Monno S, Nagata A, Homma T, Oguchi H, Kawa S, Kaji R, Furuta S (1984). Exocrine pancreatic cancer with humoral hypercalcemia. Am J Gastroenterol 79: 128-132.

1262. Montalban C, Castrillo JM, Abraira V, Serrano M, Bellas C, Piris MA, Carrion R, Cruz MA, Larana JG, Menarguez J, et a (1995). Gastric B-cell mucosa-associated lymphoid tissue (MALT) lymphoma. Clinicopathological study and evaluation of the prognostic factors in 143 patients. Ann Oncol 6: 355-362.

1263. Montalban C, Manzanal A, Castrillo JM, Escribano L, Bellas C (1995). Low grade gastric B-cell MALT lymphoma progressing into high grade lymphoma. Clonal identity of the two stages of the tumour, unusual bone involvement and leukemic dissemination. Histopathology 27: 89-91.

1264. Montesano R, Hainaut P (1998). Molecular precursor lesions in oesophageal cancer. Cancer Surv 32: 53-68.

1265. Montesano R, Hainaut P, Wild CP (1997). Hepatocellular carcinoma: from gene to public health. J Natl Cancer Inst 89: 1844-1851.

1266. Montesano R, Hollstein M, Hainaut P (1996). Genetic alterations in esophageal cancer and their relevance to etiology and pathogenesis: a review. Int J Cancer 69: 225-235.

1267. Moody F, Thornbjarnason B (1964). Carcinoma of the ampulla of Vater. Am J Surg 107: 572-579.

1268. Moore SD, Gold RP, Lebwohl O, Price JB, Lefkowitch S (1984). Adenosquamous carcinoma of the liver arising in biliary cystadenocarcinoma: clinical, radiologic, and pathologic features with review of the literature. J Clin Gastroenterol 6: 267-275.

1269. Morales TG, Sampliner RE, Bhattacharyya A (1997). Intestinal metaplasia of the gastric cardia. Am J Gastroenterol 92: 414-418.

1270. Moran CA, Ishak KG, Goodman ZD (1998). Solitary fibrous tumor of the liver: a clinicopathologic and immunohistochemical study of nine cases. Ann Diagn Pathol 2: 19-24.

1271. Mori M, Kitagawa S, Iida M, Sakurai T, Enjoji M, Sugimachi K, Ooiwa T (1987). Early carcinoma of the gastric cardia. A clinicopathologic study of 21 cases. Cancer 59: 1758-1766.

1272. Mori M, Matsukuma A, Adachi Y, Miyagahara T, Matsuda H, Kuwano H, Sugimachi K, Enjoji M (1989). Small cell carcinoma of the esophagus. Cancer 63: 564-573.

1273. Mori M, Sakaguchi H, Akazawa K, Tsuneyoshi M, Sueishi K, Sugimachi K (1995). Correlation between metastatic site, histological type, and serum tumor markers of gastric carcinoma. Hum Pathol 26: 504-508.

1274. Mori T, Yanagisawa A, Kato Y, Miura K, Nishihira T, Mori S, Nakamura Y (1994). Accumulation of genetic alterations during esophageal carcinogenesis. Hum Mol Genet 3: 1969-1971.

1275. Morimitsu Y, Hsia CC, Kojiro M, Tabor E (1995). Nodules of less-differentiated tumor within or adjacent to hepatocellular carcinoma: relative expression of transforming growth factor-alpha and its receptor in the different areas of tumor. *Hum Pathol* 26: 1126-1132.

1276. Morinaga S, Tsumuraya M, Nakajima T, Shimosato Y, Okazaki N (1986). Ciliated-cell adenocarcinoma of the pancreas. *Acta Pathol Jpn* 36: 1905-1910.

1277. Morishita Y, Tanaka T, Kato K, Kawamori T, Amano K, Funato T, Tarao M, Mori H (1991). Gastric collision tumor (carcinoid and adenocarcinoma) with gastrinal stromal tumors. *Oncogene* 18: 711-719.

1278. Morita M, Kuwano H, Nakashima T, Taketomi A, Baba H, Saito T, Tomoda H, Egashira A, Kawaguchi H, Kitamura K, Sugimachi K (1998). Family aggregation of carcinoma of the hypopharynx and cervical esophagus: special reference to multiplicity of cancer in upper aerodigestive tract. *Int J Cancer* 76: 468-471.

1279. Morita M, Kuwano H, Ohno S, Sugimachi K, Seo Y, Tomoda H, Furusawa M, Nakashima T (1994). Multiple occurrence of carcinoma in the upper aerodigestive tract associated with esophageal cancer: reference to smoking, drinking and family history. *Int J Cancer* 58: 207-210.

1280. Morohoshi T, Held G, Kloppel G (1983). Exocrine pancreatic tumours and their histological classification. A study based on 167 autopsy and 97 surgical cases. *Histopathology* 7: 645-661.

1281. Morohoshi T, Kanda M, Asanuma K, Kloppel G (1989). Intraductal papillary neoplasms of the pancreas. A clinicopathologic study of six patients. *Cancer* 64: 1329-1335.

1282. Morohoshi T, Kanda M, Horie A, Chott A, Dreyer T, Kloppel G, Heitz PU (1987). Immunocytochemical markers of uncommon pancreatic tumors. Acinar cell carcinoma, pancreatoblastoma, and solid cystic (papillary-cystic) tumor. *Cancer* 59: 739-747.

1283. Moser AR, Pitot HC, Dove WF (1990). A dominant mutation that predisposes to multiple intestinal neoplasia in the mouse. *Science* 247: 322-324.

1284. Moser AR, Shoemaker AR, Connelly CS, Clipson L, Gould KA, Luongo C, Dove WF, Siggers PH, Gardner RL (1995). Homozygosity for the Min allele of Apc results in disruption of mouse development prior to gastrulation. *Dev Dyn* 203: 422-433.

1285. Moskaluk C, Hruban RH, Lietman A, Smyrk T, Fusaro L, Fusaro R, Lynch J, Yeo CJ, Jackson C, Kern SE (1998). Novel germline p16INK4 allele (Asp145Cys) in a family with multiple pancreatic carcinomas. *Hum Mutat* 12: 70.

1286. Moskaluk CA, Hruban RH, Kern SE (1997). p16 and K-ras gene mutations in the intraductal precursors of human pancreatic adenocarcinoma. *Cancer Res* 57: 2140-2143.

1287. Moskaluk CA, Hu J, Perlman EJ (1998). Comparative genomic hybridization of esophageal and gastroesophageal adenocarcinomas shows consensus areas of DNA gain and loss. *Genes Chromosomes Cancer* 22: 305-311.

1288. Moskaluk CA, Rumpel CA (1998). Allelic deletion in 11p15 is a common occurrence in esophageal and gastric adenocarcinoma. *Cancer* 83: 232-239.

1289. Moskaluk CR, Tian Q, Marshall CR, Rumpel CA, Franquemont DW, Frierson HF J (1999). Mutations of c-kit JM domain are found in a minority of human gastrointestinal stromal tumors. *Oncogene* 18: 1897-1902.

1290. Mountney J, Maury AC, Jackson AM, Coleman RE, Johnson AG (1997). Pancreatic metastases from breast cancer: an unusual cause of biliary obstruction. *Eur J Surg Oncol* 23: 574-576.

1291. Moyana TN, Satkunam N (1992). A comparative immunohistochemical study of jejunoileal and appendiceal carcinoids. Implications for histogenesis and pathogenesis. *Cancer* 70: 1081-1088.

1292. Moynihan MJ, Bast MA, Chan WC, Delabie J, Wickert RS, Wu G, Weisenburger DD (1996). Lymphomatous polyposis. A neoplasm of either follicular mantle or germinal center cell origin. *Am J Surg Pathol* 20: 442-452.

1293. Mulder I, van-Genugten ML, Hoongenveen RT, de-Hollander AE, Bueno-de-Mesquita HB (1999). The impact of smoking on future pancreatic cancer: a computer simulation. *Ann Oncol* 10: 74-78.

1294. Muleris M, Salmon RJ, Girodet J, Zafrani B, Dutrillaux B (1987). Recurrent deletions of chromosomes 11q and 3p in anal canal carcinoma. *Int J Cancer* 39: 595-598.

1295. Muller G, Dargent JL, Duwel V, D'Olne D, Vanvuchelen J, Haot J, Hustin J (1997). Leukaemia and lymphoma of the appendix presenting as acute appendicitis or acute abdomen. Four case reports with a review of the literature. *J Cancer Res Clin Oncol* 123: 560-564.

1296. Munoz N (1988). Descriptive epidemiology of stomach cancer. In: *Gastric Carcinogenesis*, Reed PI, Hill MJ (eds), Excerpta Medica: Amsterdam, New York, Oxford.

1297. Murakami H, Furihata M, Ohtsuki Y, Ogoshi S (1999). Determination of the prognostic significance of cyclin B1 overexpression in patients with esophageal squamous cell carcinoma. *Virchows Arch* 434: 153-158.

1298. Murakami T (1971). Pathomorphological diagnosis. Definition and gross classification of early gastric cancer. *Gann Monogr* 11: 53.

1299. Murakami T, Ueki K, Kawakami H, Gondo T, Kuga T, Esato K, Furukawa S (1996). Pancreatoblastoma: case report and review of treatment in the literature. *Med Pediatr Oncol* 27: 193-197.

1300. Murata M, Tagawa M, Watanabe S, Kimura H, Takeshita T, Morimoto K (1999). Genotype difference of aldehyde dehydrogenase 2 gene in alcohol drinkers influences the incidence of Japanese colorectal cancer patients. *Jpn J Cancer Res* 90: 711-719.

1301. Murata Y, Oguma H, Kitamura Y, Ide H, Suzuki S, Takasaki T (1998). [The role of endoscopic ultrasonography for gastric cancer in the cardiac area]. *Nippon Geka Gakkai Zasshi* 99: 564-568.

1302. Murata Y, Suzuki S, Ohta M, Mitsunaga A, Hayashi K, Yoshida K, Ide H (1996). Small ultrasonic probes for determination of the depth of superficial esophageal cancer. *Gastrointest Endosc* 44: 23-28.

1303. Murray GI, Duncan ME, O'Neil P, McKay JA, Melvin WT, Fothergill JE (1998). Matrix metalloproteinase-1 is associated with poor prognosis in oesophageal cancer. *J Pathol* 185: 256-261.

1304. Myers MP, Stolarov JP, Eng C, Li J, Wang SI, Wigler MH, Parsons R, Tonks NK (1997). PTEN, the tumor suppressor from human chromosome 10q23, is a dual-specificity phosphatase. *Proc Natl Acad Sci U S A* 94: 9052-9057.

1305. Myerson RJ, Karnell LH, Menck HR (1997). The National Cancer Data Base report on carcinoma of the anus. *Cancer* 80: 805-815.

1306. Nagai E, Ueki T, Chijiiwa K, Tanaka M, Tsuneyoshi M (1995). Intraductal papillary mucinous neoplasms of the pancreas associated with so-called "mucinous ductal ectasia". Histochemical and immunohistochemical analysis of 29 cases. *Am J Surg Pathol* 19: 576-589.

1307. Nagai H, Pineau P, Tiollais P, Buendia MA, Dejean A (1997). Comprehensive allelotyping of human hepatocellular carcinoma. *Oncogene* 14: 2927-2933.

1308. Nagase H, Miyoshi Y, Horii A, Aoki T, Ogawa M, Utsunomiya J, Baba S, Sasazuki T, Nakamura Y (1992). Correlation between the location of germ-line mutations in the APC gene and the number of colorectal polyps in familial adenomatous polyposis patients. *Cancer Res* 52: 4055-4057.

1309. Nagase H, Nakamura Y (1993). Mutations of the APC (adenomatous polyposis coli) gene. *Hum Mutat* 2: 425-434.

1310. Nakahara M, Isozaki K, Hirota S, Miyagawa J, Hase SN, Taniguchi M, Nishida T, Kanayama S, Kitamura Y, Shinomura Y, Matsuzawa Y (1998). A novel gain-of-function mutation of c-kit gene in gastrointestinal stromal tumors. *Gastroenterology* 115: 1090-1095.

1311. Nakaizumi A, Tatsuta M, Uehara H, Yamamoto R, Takenaka A, Kishigami Y, Takemura K, Kitamura T, Okuda S (1992). Cytologic examination of pure pancreatic juice in the diagnosis of pancreatic carcinoma. The endoscopic retrograde intraductal catheter aspiration cytologic technique. *Cancer* 70: 2610-2614.

1312. Nakajima T, Kondo Y (1990). A clinicopathological study of intrahepatic cholangiocarcinoma containing a component of squamous cell carcinoma. *Cancer* 65: 1401-1404.

1313. Nakajima T, Tajima Y, Sugano I, Nagao K, Kondo Y, Wada K (1993). Intrahepatic cholangiocarcinoma with sarcomatous change. Clinicopathologic and immunohistochemical evaluation of seven cases. *Cancer* 72: 1872-1877.

1314. Nakamura S, Aoyagi K, Furuse M, Suekane H, Matsumoto T, Yao T, Sakai Y, Fuchigami T, Yamamoto I, Tsuneyoshi M, Fujishima M (1998). B-cell monoclonality precedes the development of gastric MALT lymphoma in Helicobacter pylori-associated chronic gastritis. *Am J Pathol* 152: 1271-1279.

1314A. Nakamura S, Kino I (1984). Morphogenesis of minute adenomas in familial polyposis coli. *J Natl Cancer Inst* 73: 41-49.

1315. Nakamura S, Kino I, Baba S (1988). Cell kinetics analysis of background colonic mucosa of patients with intestinal neoplasms by ex vivo autoradiography. *Gut* 29: 997-1002.

1316. Nakamura S, Yao T, Aoyagi K, Iida M, Fujishima M, Tsuneyoshi M (1997). Helicobacter pylori and primary gastric lymphoma. A histopathologic and immunohistochemical analysis of 237 patients. *Cancer* 79: 3-11.

1317. Nakamura T, Kimura H, Nakano G (1986). Adenomatosis of small intestine: case report. *J Clin Pathol* 39: 981-986.

1318. Nakamura T, Mohri H, Shimazaki M, Ito Y, Ohnishi T, Nishino K, Fujihiro S, Shima H, Matsushita T, Yasuda M, Moriwaki H, Muto Y, Deguchi T (1997). Esophageal metastasis from prostate cancer: diagnostic use of reverse transcriptase-polymerase chain reaction for prostate-specific antigen. *Microsc Res Tech* 38: 552-570.

1319. Nakamura Y, Hoso M, Sanzen T, Sasaki M (1997). Microstructure and development of the normal and pathologic biliary tract in humans, including blood supply. *Microsc Res Tech* 38: 552-570.

1320. Nakamura Y, Kurumaya H, Ohta G (1984). Multiple cysts in the hepatic hilum and their pathogenesis. A suggestion of periductal gland origin. *Virchows Arch A Pathol Anat Histopathol* 404: 341-350.

1321. Nakanuma Y, Ohta G (1982). Pathological study of hepatolithiasis associated with intrahepatic cholangiocarcinoma. *Annual Report of Japanese Hepatolithiasis Study Group* 208-216.

1322. Nakanuma Y, Terada T, Tanaka Y, Ohta G (1985). Are hepatolithiasis and cholangiocarcinoma aetiologically related? A morphological study of 12 cases of hepatolithiasis associated with cholangiocarcinoma. *Virchows Arch A Pathol Anat Histopathol* 406: 45-58.

1323. Nakanuma Y, Yamaguchi K, Ohta G, Terada T (1988). Pathologic features of hepatolithiasis in Japan. *Hum Pathol* 19: 1181-1186.

1324. Nakashima O, Sugihara S, Kage M, Kojiro M (1995). Pathomorphologic characteristics of small hepatocellular carcinoma: a special reference to small hepatocellular carcinoma with indistinct margins. *Hepatology* 22: 101-105.

1324A. Nakayama M, Okamoto Y, Morita T, Matsumoto M, Fukui H, Nakano H, Tsujii T (1990). Promoting effects of citrulline in hepatocarcinogenesis: possible mechanism in hypercitrullinemia. *Hepatology* 11: 819-823.

1325. Nandurkar S, Talley NJ (1999). Barrett's esophagus: the long and the short of it. *Am J Gastroenterol* 94: 30-40.

1326. Nascimbeni R, Villanacci V, Mariani PP, Di Betta E, Ghirardi M, Donato F, Salerni B (1999). Aberrant crypt foci in the human colon: frequency and histologic patterns in patients with colorectal cancer or diverticular disease. *Am J Surg Pathol* 23: 1256-1263.

1327. Natsugoe S, Mueller J, Stein HJ, Feith M, Hofler H, Siewert JR (1998). Micrometastasis and tumor cell microinvolvement of lymph nodes from esophageal squamous cell carcinoma: frequency, associated tumor characteristics, and impact on prognosis. *Cancer* 83: 858-866.

1328. Naunheim KS, Zeitels J, Kaplan EL, Sugimoto J, Shen KL, Lee CH, Straus FH (1983). Rectal carcinoid tumors - treatment and prognosis. *Surgery* 94: 670-676.

1329. Nawroz IM (1987). Malignant carcinoid tumour of oesophagus. *Histopathology* 11: 879-880.

1330. Neef B, Kunzig B, Sinn I, Kieninger G, von Gaisberg U (1997). [Primary pancreatic lymphoma. A rare cause of pain-free icterus]. *Deut Med Wochenschrift* 122: 12-17.

1331. Negri E, La-Vecchia C, Levi F, Franceschi S, Serra ML, Boyle P (1996). Comparative descriptive epidemiology of oral and oesophageal cancers in Europe. *Eur J Cancer Prev* 5: 267-279.

1332. Nehal KS, Levine VJ, Ashinoff R (1998). Basal cell carcinoma of the genitalia. *Dermatol Surg* 24: 1361-1363.

1333. Nelen MR, Kremer H, Konings IB, Schoute F, van-Essen AJ, Koch R, Woods CG, Fryns JP, Hamel B, Hoefsloot LH, Peeters EA, Padberg GW (1999). Novel PTEN mutations in patients with Cowden disease: absence of clear genotype-phenotype correlations. *Eur J Hum Genet* 7: 267-273.

1334. Nelen MR, Padberg GW, Peeters EA, Lin AY, van-den-Helm B, Frants RR, Coulon V, Goldstein AM, van-Reen MM, Easton DF, Eeles RA, Hodgsen S, Mulvihill JJ, Murday VA, Tucker MA, Mariman EC, Starink TM, Ponder BA, Ropers HH, Kremer H, Longy M, Eng C (1996). Localization of the gene for Cowden disease to chromosome 10q22-23. *Nat Genet* 13: 114-116.

1335. Nelen MR, van-Staveren WC, Peeters EA, Hassel MB, Gorlin RJ, Hamm H, Lindboe CF, Fryns JP, Sijmons RH, Woods DG, Mariman EC, Padberg GW, Kremer H (1997). Germline mutations in the PTEN/MMAC1 gene in patients with Cowden disease. *Hum Mol Genet* 6: 1383-1387.

1336. Neoptolemos JP, Talbot IC, Shaw DC, Carr LD (1988). Long-term survival after resection of ampullary carcinoma is associated independently with tumor grade and a new staging classification that assesses local invasiveness. *Cancer* 61: 1403-1407.

1337. Neshat K, Sanchez CA, Galipeau PC, Blount PL, Levine DS, Joslyn G, Reid BJ (1994). p53 mutations in Barrett's adenocarcinoma and high-grade dysplasia. *Gastroenterology* 106: 1589-1595.

1338. Neubauer A, Thiede C, Morgner A, Alpen B, Ritter M, Neubauer B, Wundisch T, Ehninger G, Stolte M, Bayerdorffer E (1997). Cure of Helicobacter pylori infection and duration of remission of low-grade gastric mucosa-associated lymphoid tissue lymphoma. *J Natl Cancer Inst* 89: 1350-1355.

1339. Neugut AI, Jacobson JS, Suh S, Mukherjee R, Arber N (1998). The epidemiology of cancer of the small bowel. *Cancer Epidemiol Biomarkers Prev* 7: 243-251.

1340. Neumann RD, Livolsi VA, Rosenthal NS, Burrell M, Ball TJ (1976). Adenocarcinoma in biliary papillomatosis. *Gastroenterology* 70: 779-782.

1341. Neumeister P, Hoefler G, Beham SC, Schmidt H, Apfelbeck U, Schaider H, Linkesch W, Sill H (1997). Deletion analysis of the p16 tumor suppressor gene in gastrointestinal mucosa-associated lymphoid tissue lymphomas. *Gastroenterology* 112: 1871-1875.

1342. Newman DH, Doerhoff CR, Bunt TJ (1984). Villous adenoma of the duodenum. *Am Surg* 50: 26-28.

1343. Nezu JI, Oku A, Shimane M (1999). Loss of cytoplasmic retention ability of mutant LKB1 found in Peutz-Jeghers syndrome patients. *Biochem Biophys Res Commun* 261: 750-755.

1344. Ng EH, Pollock RE, Romsdahl MM (1992). Prognostic implications of patterns of failure for gastrointestinal leiomyosarcomas. *Cancer* 69: 1334-1341.

1345. Ng FC, Ang HK, Chng HC (1993). Adenosquamous carcinoma of the ileum - a case report. *Singapore Med J* 34: 361-362.

1346. Nguyen T, Brunson D, Crespi CL, Penman BW, Wishnok JS, Tannenbaum SR (1992). DNA damage and mutation in human cells exposed to nitric oxide in vitro. *Proc Natl Acad Sci U S A* 89: 3030-3034.

1347. Nicolaides NC, Carter KC, Shell BK, Papadopoulos N, Vogelstein B, Kinzler KW (1995). Genomic organization of the human PMS2 gene family. *Genomics* 30: 195-206.

1348. Nicolaides NC, Littman SJ, Modrich P, Kinzler KW, Vogelstein B (1998). A naturally occurring hPMS2 mutation can confer a dominant negative mutator phenotype. *Mol Cell Biol* 18: 1635-1641.

1349. Nicolaides NC, Palombo F, Kinzler KW, Vogelstein B, Jiricny J (1996). Molecular cloning of the N-terminus of GTBP. *Genomics* 31: 395-397.

1350. Nicolaides NC, Papadopoulos N, Liu B, Wei YF, Carter KC, Ruben SM, Rosen CA, Haseltine WA, Fleischmann RD, Fraser CM, et a (1994). Mutations of two PMS homologues in hereditary nonpolyposis colon cancer. *Nature* 371: 75-80.

1351. Niederau C, Fischer R, Sonnenberg A, Stremmel W, Trampisch HJ, Strohmeyer G (1985). Survival and causes of death in cirrhotic and in noncirrhotic patients with primary hemochromatosis. *N Engl J Med* 313: 1256-1262.

1352. Nielsen HJ, Hansen U, Christensen IJ, Reimert CM, Brunner N, Moesgaard F (1999). Independent prognostic value of eosinophil and mast cell infiltration in colorectal cancer tissue. *J Pathol* 189: 487-495.

1353. Nielsen OV, Jensen SL (1981). Basal cell carcinoma of the anus-a clinical study of 34 cases. *Br J Surg* 68: 856-857.

1354. Nielsen SN, Wold LE (1986). Adenocarcinoma of jejunum in association with nontropical sprue. *Arch Pathol Lab Med* 110: 822-824.

1355. Nishida N, Fukuda Y, Komeda T, Kita R, Sando T, Furukawa M, Amenomori M, Shibagaki I, Nakao K, Ikenaga M, et a (1994). Amplification and overexpression of the cyclin D1 gene in aggressive human hepatocellular carcinoma. *Cancer Res* 54: 3107-3110.

1356. Nishida T, Hirota S, Taniguchi M, Hashimoto K, Isozaki K, Nakamura H, Kanakura Y, Tanaka T, Takabayashi A, Matsuda H, Kitamura Y (1998). Familial gastrointestinal stromal tumours with germline mutation of the KIT gene. *Nat Genet* 19: 323-324.

1357. Nishihara K, Nagai E, Izumi Y, Yamaguchi K, Tsuneyoshi M (1994). Adenosquamous carcinoma of the gallbladder: a clinicopathological, immunohistochemical and flow-cytometric study of twenty cases. *Jpn J Cancer Res* 85: 389-399.

1358. Nishihara K, Nagoshi M, Tsuneyoshi M, Yamaguchi K, Hayashi Y (1993). Papillary cystic tumors of the pancreas. Assessment of their malignant potential. *Cancer* 71: 82-92.

1359. Nishihara K, Tsuneyoshi M (1993). Small cell carcinoma of the gallbladder: a clinicopathological, immunohistochemical and flow cytometric study of 15 cases. *Int J Oncol* 3: 901-908.

1360. Nishihara K, Tsuneyoshi M (1993). Undifferentiated spindle cell carcinoma of the gallbladder: a clinicopathologic, immunohistochemical, and flow cytometric study of 11 cases. *Hum Pathol* 24: 1298-1305.

1361. Nishihara K, Yamaguchi K, Hashimoto H, Enjioji M (1991). Tubular adenoma of the gallbladder with squamoid spindle cell metaplasia. Report of three cases with immunohistochemical study. *Acta Pathol Jpn* 41: 41-45.

1362. Nishikura K, Watanabe H (1997). Gastric microcarcinoma. Its histopathological characteristics. In: *Progress in Gastric Cancer Research 1997*, Siewert JR, Roder JD (eds), Monduzzi Editore: Bologna, Italy.

1363. Nishimata H, Setoyama S, Nishimata Y, et al (1992). Natural history of gastric cancer in cardia. *Stom Intest* 27: 25-38.

1364. Nishisho I, Nakamura Y, Miyoshi Y, Miki Y, Ando H, Horii A, Koyama K, Utsunomiya J, Baba S, Hedge P (1991). Mutations of chromosome 5q21 genes in FAP and colorectal cancer patients. *Science* 253: 665-669.

1365. Nitecki SS, Wolff BG, Schlinkert R, Sarr MG (1994). The natural history of surgically treated primary adenocarcinoma of the appendix. *Ann Surg* 219: 51-57.

1366. Noda Y, Watanabe H, Iida M, Narisawa R, Kurosaki I, Iwafuchi M, Satoh M, Ajioka Y (1992). Histologic follow-up of ampullary adenomas in patients with familial adenomatosis coli. *Cancer* 70: 1847-1856.

1367. Noel JC, Hermans P, Andre J, Fayt I, Simonart T, Verhest A, Haot J, Burny A (1996). Herpesvirus-like DNA sequences and Kaposi's sarcoma: relationship with epidemiology, clinical spectrum, and histologic features. *Cancer* 77: 2132-2136.

1368. Noffsinger AE, Miller MA, Cusi MV, Fenoglio-Preiser CM (1996). The pattern of cell proliferation in neoplastic and nonneoplastic lesions of ulcerative colitis. *Cancer* 78: 2307-2312.

1369. Nojima T, Kojima T, Kato H, Sato T, Koito K, Nagashima K (1992). Alpha-fetoprotein-producing acinar cell carcinoma of the pancreas. *Hum Pathol* 23: 828-830.

1370. Nojima T, Nakamura F, Ishikura M, Inoue K, Nagashima K, Kato H (1993). Pleomorphic carcinoma of the pancreas with osteoclast-like giant cells. *Int J Pancreatol* 14: 275-281.

1371. Nomura A, Stemmermann GN, Chyou PH, Kato I, Perez PG, Blaser MJ (1991). Helicobacter pylori infection and gastric carcinoma among Japanese Americans in Hawaii. *N Engl J Med* 325: 1132-1136.

1372. Nonomura A, Kono N, Mizukami Y, Nakanuma Y, Matsubara F (1992). Duct-acinar-islet cell tumor of the pancreas. *Ultrastruct Pathol* 16: 317-329.

1373. Nonomura A, Mizukami Y, Kodaya N (1994). Angiomyolipoma of the liver. *J Gastroenterol* 29: 95-105.

1374. Nowak MA, Guerriere KP, Pathan A, Campbell TE, Deppisch LM (1998). Perianal Paget's disease: distinguishing primary and secondary lesions using immunohistochemical studies including gross cystic disease fluid protein-15 and cytokeratin 20 expression. *Arch Pathol Lab Med* 122: 1077-1081.

1375. Nucci MR, Robinson CR, Longo P, Campbell P, Hamilton SR (1997). Phenotypic and genotypic characteristics of aberrant crypt foci in human colorectal mucosa. *Hum Pathol* 28: 1396-1407.

1376. Nugent KP, Spigelman AD, Nicholls RJ, Talbot IC, Neale K, Phillips RK (1993). Pouch adenomas in patients with familial adenomatous polyposis. Br J Surg 80: 1620.

1377. Nugent KP, Spigelman AD, Talbot IC, Phillips RK (1994). Gallbladder dysplasia in patients with familial adenomatous polyposis. Br J Surg 81: 291-292.

1378. Nyberg B, Sonnenfeld T (1986). Metastatic breast carcinoma causing intestinal obstruction. Acta Chir Scand Suppl 530: 95-96.

1379. Nystrom LM, Wu Y, Mosio AL, Hofstra RM, Osinga J, Mecklin JP, Jarvinen HJ, Leisti J, Buys CH, de-la-Chapelle A, Peltomaki P (1996). DNA mismatch repair gene mutations in 55 kindreds with verified or putative hereditary non-polyposis colorectal cancer. Hum Mol Genet 5: 763-769.

1380. O'Brian DS, Kennedy MJ, Daly PA, O'Brien AA, Tanner WA, Rogers P, Lawlor E (1989). Multiple lymphomatous polyposis of the gastrointestinal tract. A clinicopathologically distinctive form of non-Hodgkin's lymphoma of B-cell centrocytic type. Am J Surg Pathol 13: 691-699.

1381. O'Connor HJ, Cunnane K (1994). Helicobacter pylori and gastro-oesophageal reflux disease - a prospective study. Ir J Med Sci 163: 369-373.

1382. O'Connor PM, Jackman J, Bae I, Myers TG, Fan S, Mutoh M, Scudiero DA, Monks A, Sausville EA, Weinstein JN, Friend S, Fornace-AJ J, Kohn KW (1997). Characterization of the p53 tumor suppressor pathway in cell lines of the National Cancer Institute anticancer drug screen and correlations with the growth-inhibitory potency of 123 anticancer agents. Cancer Res 57: 4285-4300.

1383. O'Farrelly C, Feighery C, O'Briain DS, Stevens F, Connolly CE, McCarthy C, Weir DG (1986). Humoral response to wheat protein in patients with coeliac disease and enteropathy associated T cell lymphoma. Br Med J Clin Res Ed 293: 908-910.

1384. O'Hara BJ, McCue PA, Miettinen M (1992). Bile duct adenomas with endocrine component. Immunohistochemical study and comparison with conventional bile duct adenomas. Am J Surg Pathol 16: 21-25.

1385. O'Mahony S, Howdle PD, Losowsky MS (1996). Review article: management of patients with non-responsive coeliac disease. Aliment Pharmacol Ther 10: 671-680.

1386. Oates JA, Sjoerdsma A (1962). A unique syndrome associated with secretion of 5-hydroxytryptophan by metastatic gastric carcinoids. Am J Med 32: 333-342.

1387. Oberg A, Stenling R, Tavelin B, Lindmark G (1998). Are lymph node micrometastases of any clinical significance in Dukes Stages A and B colorectal cancer? Dis Colon Rectum 41: 1244-1249.

1388. Oberg S, Peters JH, DeMeester TR, Chandrasoma P, Hagen JA, Ireland AP, Ritter MP, Mason RJ, Crookes P, Bremner CG (1997). Inflammation and specialized intestinal metaplasia of cardiac mucosa is a manifestation of gastroesophageal reflux disease. Ann Surg 226: 522-530.

1389. Ochiai T, Morishima T, Kondo M (1997). Symptomatic porphyria secondary to hepatocellular carcinoma. Br J Dermatol 136: 129-131.

1390. Oda T, Imai Y, Nakatsuru Y, Hata J, Ishikawa T (1996). Somatic mutations of the APC gene in sporadic hepatoblastomas. Cancer Res 56: 3320-3323.

1391. Oda T, Tsuda H, Sakamoto M, Hirohashi S (1994). Different mutations of the p53 gene in nodule-in-nodule hepatocellular carcinoma as an evidence for multistage progression. Cancer Lett 83: 197-200.

1392. Oda T, Tsuda H, Scarpa A, Sakamoto M, Hirohashi S (1992). Mutation pattern of the p53 gene as a diagnostic marker for multiple hepatocellular carcinoma. Cancer Res 52: 3674-3678.

1393. Oda T, Tsuda H, Scarpa A, Sakamoto M, Hirohashi S (1992). p53 gene mutation spectrum in hepatocellular carcinoma. Cancer Res 52: 6358-6364.

1394. Odze RD, Medline P, Cohen Z (1994). Adenocarcinoma arising in an appendix involved with chronic ulcerative colitis. Am J Gastroenterol 89: 1905-1907.

1395. Oertel JE, Mendelsohn G, Compagno J (1982). Solid and papillary epithelial neoplasms of the pancreas. In: Pancreatic Tumours in Children, Humphrey GB, Grindey GB, Dehner LP, Acton RT, Pysher TJ (eds), Martinus Nijhoff: Den Haag.

1396. Oetting G, Franz HB (1998). Mapping of androgen, estrogen and progesterone receptors in the anal continence organ. Eur J Obstet Gynecol Reprod Biol 77: 211-216.

1397. Offerhaus GJ, Giardiello FM, Krush AJ, Booker SV, Tersmette AC, Kelley NC, Hamilton SR (1992). The risk of upper gastrointestinal cancer in familial adenomatous polyposis. Gastroenterology 102: 1980-1982.

1398. Offner FA, Lewin KJ, Weinstein WM (1996). Metaplastic columnar cells in Barrett's esophagus: a common and neglected cell type. Hum Pathol 27: 885-889.

1399. Oguzkurt L, Karabulut N, Cakmakci E, Besim A (1997). Primary non-Hodgkin's lymphoma of the esophagus. Abdom Imaging 22: 8-10.

1400. Ohaki Y, Misugi K, Fukuda J, Okudaira M, Hirose M (1987). Immunohistochemical study of pancreatoblastoma. Acta Pathol Jpn 37: 1581-1590.

1401. Ohashi K, Nakajima Y, Kanehiro H, Tsutsumi M, Taki J, Aomatsu Y, Yoshimura A, Ko S, Kin T, Yagura K, et al (1995). Ki-ras mutations and p53 protein expressions in intrahepatic cholangiocarcinomas: relation to gross tumor morphology. Gastroenterology 109: 1612-1617.

1402. Ohashi K, Tsutsumi M, Nakajima Y, Noguchi O, Okita S, Kitada H, Tsujiuchi T, Kobayashi E, Nakano H, Konishi Y (1994). High rates of Ki-ras point mutation in both intra- and extra-hepatic cholangiocarcinomas. Jpn J Clin Oncol 24: 305-310.

1403. Ohgaki H, Hernandez-Boussard T, Kleihues P, Hainaut P (1999). p53 germline mutations and the molecular basis of the Li-Fraumeni syndrome. In: Molecular biology in cancer medicine, Kurzrock R, Talpaz M (eds), 2nd ed. Martin Dunitz Ltd.: London.

1404. Ohhashi K, Murakami Y, Maruyama M (1982). Four cases of mucous secreting pancreatic cancer. Prog Dig Endosc 20: 348-351.

1405. Ohmori T, Furuya K, Okada K, Tabei R, Tao S (1993). Adenoendocrine cell carcinoma of the gallbladder: a histochemical and immunohistochemical study. Acta Pathol Jpn 43: 268-274.

1406. Ohnishi H, Kawamura M, Hanada R, Kaneko Y, Tsunoda A, Hongo T, Bessho F, Yokomori K, Hayashi Y (1996). Infrequent mutations of the TP53 gene and no amplification of the MDM2 gene in hepatoblastomas. Genes Chromosomes Cancer 15: 187-190.

1407. Ohnishi S, Hoh E, Kodama T, Moriyama T, Imawari M, Takaku F, Aoyama H, Sunouchi H, Wada Y (1986). [A case of gallbladder carcinoma metastatic to the appendix associated with acute peritonitis]. Nippon Shokakibyo Gakkai Zasshi 83: 1540-1543.

1408. Ohnishi Y, Akashi T, Kuniyoshi M, Fukutomi M, Yokota M, Iguchi H, Funakoshi A, Wakasugi H (1999). [A case of adult T-cell leukemia (lymphoma type) involving the pancreas]. Nippon Shokakibyo Gakkai Zasshi 96: 64-69.

1409. Ohshio G, Imamura T, Okada N, Wang ZH, Yamaki K, Kyogoku T, Suwa H, Yamabe H, Imamura M (1996). Immunohistochemical study of metallothionein in pancreatic carcinomas. J Cancer Res Clin Oncol 122: 351-355.

1410. Ohta H, Noguchi Y, Takagi K, Nishi M, Kajitani T, Kato Y (1987). Early gastric carcinoma with special reference to macroscopic classification. Cancer 60: 1099-1106.

1411. Ohta M, Inoue H, Cotticelli MG, Kastury K, Baffa R, Palazzo J, Siprashvili Z, Mori M, McCue P, Druck T, et a (1996). The FHIT gene, spanning the chromosome 3p14.2 fragile site and renal carcinoma-associated t(3;8) breakpoint, is abnormal in digestive tract cancers. Cell 84: 587-597.

1412. Ohta T, Nagakawa T, Itoh H, Fonseca L, Miyazaki I, Terada T (1993). A case of serous cystadenoma of the pancreas with focal malignant changes. Int J Pancreatol 14: 283-289.

1413. Ohta T, Nagakawa T, Tsukioka Y, Mori K, Takeda T, Kayahara M, Ueno K, Fonseca L, Miyazaki I, Terada T (1993). Expression of argyrophilic nucleolar organizer regions in ductal adenocarcinoma of the pancreas and its relationship to prognosis. Int J Pancreatol 13: 193-200.

1414. Ohta T, Nagakawa T, Ueno K, Kayahara M, Mori K, Kobayashi H, Takeda T, Miyazaki I (1993). The mode of lymphatic and local spread of pancreatic carcinomas less than 4.0 cm in size. Int Surg 78: 208-212.

1415. Ohtsuki Y, Yoshino T, Takahashi K, Sonobe H, Kohno K, Akagi T (1987). Electron microscopic study of mucoepidermoid carcinoma in the pancreas. Acta Pathol Jpn 37: 1175-1182.

1416. Oka T, Ayabe H, Kawahara K, Tagawa Y, Hara S, Tsuji H, Kusano H, Nakano M, Tomita M (1993). Esophagectomy for metastatic carcinoma of the esophagus from lung cancer. Cancer 71: 2958-2961.

1417. Okuda K (1997). Hepatitis C virus and hepatocellular carcinoma. In: Liver Cancer, Okuda K, Tabor E (eds), Churchill Livingstone: New York.

1418. Okuda K, Kubo Y, Okazaki N, Arishima T, Hashimoto M (1977). Clinical aspects of intrahepatic bile duct carcinoma including hilar carcinoma: a study of 57 autopsy-proven cases. Cancer 39: 232-246.

1419. Okuda K, Liver Cancer Study Group of Japan (1980). Primary liver cancer in Japan. Cancer 45: 7663-7669.

1420. Oliveira C, Seruca R, Seixas M, Sobrinho-Simoes M (1998). The clinicopathological features of gastric carcinomas with microsatellite instability may be mediated by mutations of different "target genes": a study of the TGFbeta RII, IGFII R, and BAX genes. Am J Pathol 153: 1211-1219.

1421. Olschwang S, Serova SO, Lenoir GM, Thomas G (1998). PTEN germ-line mutations in juvenile polyposis coli. Nat Genet 18: 12-14.

1422. Olschwang S, Tiret A, Laurent PP, Muleris M, Parc R, Thomas G (1993). Restriction of ocular fundus lesions to a specific subgroup of APC mutations in adenomatous polyposis coli patients. Cell 75: 959-968.

1423. Olsen BS, Holck S (1987). Neurogenous hyperplasia leading to appendiceal obliteration: an immunohistochemical study of 237 cases. Histopathology 11: 843-849.

1424. Omata M, Peters RL, Tatter D (1981). Sclerosing hepatic carcinoma: relationship to hypercalcemia. Liver 1: 33-49.

1425. Omonishi K, Yoshino T, Sakuma I, Kobayashi K, Moriyama M, Akagi T (1998). bcl-6 protein is identified in high-grade but not low-grade mucosa-associated lymphoid tissue lymphomas of the stomach. Mod Pathol 11: 181-185.

1426. Ono J, Sakamoto H, Sakoda K, Yagi Y, Hagio S, Sato E, Katsuki T (1984). Acinar cell carcinoma of the pancreas with elevated serum alpha-fetoprotein. Int Surg 69: 361-364.

1427. Orlando CA, Bowman RL, Loose JH (1991). Multicentric papillary-cystic neoplasm of the pancreas. Arch Pathol Lab Med 115: 958-960.

1428. Orlowska J, Jarosz D, Gugulski A, Pachlewski J, Butruk E (1994). Squamous cell papillomas of the esophagus: report of 20 cases and literature review. Am J Gastroenterol 89: 434-437.

1429. Ormsby AH, Goldblum JR, Rice TW, Richter JE, Falk GW, Vaezi MF, Gramlich TL (1999). Cytokeratin subsets can reliably distinguish Barrett's esophagus from intestinal metaplasia of the stomach. *Hum Pathol* 30: 288-294.

1430. Ormsby AH, Kilgore SP, Goldblum JR, Richter JE, Rice TW, Gramlich TL (1999). The location and frequency of intestinal metaplasia at the esophagogastric junction in 223 consecutive autopsies; implications for patient treatment and preventive strategies in Barrett's esophagus. *Mod Pathol* 13: 614-620.

1431. Orosz P, Kruger A, Hubbe M, Ruschoff J, Von-Hoegen P, Mannel DN (1995). Promotion of experimental liver metastasis by tumor necrosis factor. *Int J Cancer* 60: 867-871.

1432. Ostapowicz G, Watson KJ, Locarnini SA, Desmond PV (1998). Role of alcohol in the progression of liver disease caused by hepatitis C virus infection. *Hepatology* 27: 1730-1735.

1433. Ostick DG, Haqqani MT (1976). Obstructive cholecystitis due to metastatic melanoma. *Postgrad Med J* 52: 710-712.

1434. Ott G, Kalla J, Steinhoff A, Rosenwald A, Katzenberger T, Roblick U, Ott MM, Muller HH (1998). Trisomy 3 is not a common feature in malignant lymphomas of mucosa-associated lymphoid tissue type. *Am J Pathol* 153: 689-694.

1435. Ott G, Katzenberger T, Greiner A, Kalla J, Rosenwald A, Heinrich U, Ott MM, Muller HH (1997). The t(11;18)(q21;q21) chromosome translocation is a frequent and specific aberration in low-grade but not high-grade malignant non-Hodgkin's lymphomas of the mucosa-associated lymphoid tissue (MALT) type. *Cancer Res* 57: 3944-3948.

1436. Ott G, Katzenberger T, Siebert R, DeCoteau JF, Fletcher JA, Knoll JH, Kalla J, Rosenwald A, Ott MM, Weber MK, Kadin ME, Muller HH (1998). Chromosomal abnormalities in nodal and extranodal CD30+ anaplastic large cell lymphomas: infrequent detection of the t(2;5) in extranodal lymphomas. *Genes Chromosomes Cancer* 22: 114-121.

1437. Ott G, Kirchner T, Seidl S, Müller-Hermelink HK (1993). Primary gastric lymphoma is rarely associated with Epstein-Barr virus. *Virchows Arch B Cell Pathol Incl Mol Pathol* 64: 287-291.

1438. Otter R, Bieger R, Kluin PM, Hermans J, Willemze R (1989). Primary gastrointestinal non-Hodgkin's lymphoma in a population-based registry. *Br J Cancer* 60: 745--750.

1439. Owen RW (1998). Dietary and chemopreventive strategies. *Recent Results Cancer Res* 146: 195-213.

1440. Ozaki S, Harada K, Sanzen T, Watanabe K, Tsui WS, Nakanuma Y (1999). In situ nucleic acid detection of human telomerase in intrahepatic cholangiocarcinoma and its preneoplastic lesion. *Hepatology* 30: 914-919.

1441. Ozaki S, Ogasahara K, Kosaka M, Inoshita T, Wakatsuki S, Uehara H, Matsumoto T (1998). Hepatosplenic gamma delta T-cell lymphoma associated with hepatitis B virus infection. *J Med Invest* 44: 215-217.

1442. Ozcelik H, Schmocker B, Di-Nicola N, Shi XH, Langer B, Moore M, Taylor BR, Narod SA, Darlington G, Andrulis IL, Gallinger S, Redston M (1997). Germline BRCA2 6174delT mutations in Ashkenazi Jewish pancreatic cancer patients. *Nat Genet* 16: 17-18.

1443. Paal E, Thompson LD, Przygodzki RM, Bratthauer GL, Heffess CS (1999). A clinicopathologic and immunohistochemical study of 22 intraductal papillary mucinous neoplasms of the pancreas, with a review of the literature. *Mod Pathol* 12: 518-528.

1444. Padberg B, Schroder S, Capella C, Frilling A, Kloppel G, Heitz PU (1995). Multiple endocrine neoplasia type 1 (MEN 1) revisited. *Virchows Arch* 426: 541-548.

1445. Padberg GW, Schot JD, Vielvoye GJ, Bots GT, de-Beer FC (1991). Lhermitte-Duclos disease and Cowden disease: a single phakomatosis. *Ann Neurol* 29: 517-523.

1446. Pairojkul C, Shirai T, Hirohashi S, Thamavit W, Bhudisawasd W, Uttaravicien T, Itoh M, Ito N (1991). Multistage carcinogenesis of liver-fluke-associated cholangiocarcinoma in Thailand. *Princess Takamatsu Symp* 22: 77-86.

1447. Palefsky JM (1994). Anal human papillomavirus infection and anal cancer in HIV-positive individuals: an emerging problem. *AIDS* 8: 283-295.

1448. Palefsky JM, Holly EA, Gonzales J, Berline J, Ahn DK, Greenspan JS (1991). Detection of human papillomavirus DNA in anal intraepithelial neoplasia and anal cancer. *Cancer Res* 51: 1014-1019.

1449. Palefsky JM, Holly EA, Ralston ML, Jay N, Berry JM, Darragh TM (1998). High incidence of anal high-grade squamous intra-epithelial lesions among HIV-positive and HIV-negative homosexual and bisexual men. *AIDS* 12: 495-503.

1450. Palli D (1994) Gastric carcinogenesis dietary factors. *Eur J Gastroenterol Hepatol* 6: 1076-7082.

1451. Palombo F, Gallinari P, Iaccarino I, Lettieri T, Hughes M, D'Arrigo A, Truong O, Hsuan JJ, Jiricny J (1995). GTBP, a 160-kilodalton protein essential for mismatch-binding activity in human cells. *Science* 268: 1912-1914.

1452. Palosaari D, Clayton F, Seaman J (1986). Pancreatoblastoma in an adult. *Arch Pathol Lab Med* 110: 650-652.

1453. Papadopoulos N, Nicolaides NC, Wei YF, Ruben SM, Carter KC, Rosen CA, Haseltine WA, Fleischmann RD, Fraser CM, Adams MD, et a (1994). Mutation of a mutL homolog in hereditary colon cancer. *Science* 263: 1625-1629.

1454. Papotti M, Cassoni P, Taraglio S, Bussolati G (1999). Oncocytic and oncocytoid tumors of the exocrine pancreas, liver and gastrointestinal tract. *Semin Diagn Pathol* 16: 126-134.

1455. Papotti M, Galliano D, Monga G (1990). Signet-ring cell carcinoid of the gallbladder. *Histopathology* 17: 255-259.

1456. Papotti M, Sambataro D, Marchesa P, Negro F (1997). A combined hepatocellular/cholangiocellular carcinoma with sarcomatoid features. *Liver* 17: 47-52.

1457. Paraf F, Brocheriou C (1988). [Metastatic tumors of the small intestine]. *Presse Med* 17: 1495-

1458. Paraf F, Flejou JF, Pignon JP, Fekete F, Potet F (1995). Surgical pathology of adenocarcinoma arising in Barrett's esophagus. Analysis of 67 cases. *Am J Surg Pathol* 19: 183-191.

1459. Paraf F, Flejou JF, Potet F, Molas G, Fekete F (1992). Adenomas arising in Barrett's esophagus with adenocarcinoma. Report of three cases. *Pathol Res Pract* 188: 1028-1032.

1460. Parham DM, Kelly DR, Donnelly WH, Douglass EC (1991). Immunohistochemical and ultrastructural spectrum of hepatic sarcomas of childhood: evidence for a common histogenesis. *Mod Pathol* 4: 648-653.

1461. Parienty R, Ducellier R, Lubrano J, Piccard J, Pradel J, Solarski N (1980). Cystadenomas of the pancreas: diagnosis by computed tomography. *J Comput Assist Tomogr* 4: 364-3676.

1462. Park K, Kim SJ, Bang YJ, Park JG, Kim NK, Roberts AB, Sporn MB (1994). Genetic changes in the transforming growth factor beta (TGF-beta) type II receptor gene in human gastric cancer cells: correlation with sensitivity to growth inhibition by TGF-beta. *Proc Natl Acad Sci U S A* 91: 8772-8776.

1463. Park WS, Pham T, Wang C, Pack S, Mueller E, Mueller J, Vortmeyer AO, Zhuang Z, Fogt F (1998). Loss of heterozygosity and microsatellite instability in non-neoplastic mucosa from patients with chronic ulcerative colitis. *Int J Molecul Med* 2: 221-224.

1464. Parker GM, Stollman NH, Rogers A (1996). Adenomatous polyposis coli presenting as adenocarcinoma of the appendix. *Am J Gastroenterol* 91: 801-802.

1465. Parker GW, Joffe N (1972). Calcifying primary mucus-producing adenocarcinoma of the gall-bladder. *Br J Radiol* 45: 468-469.

1466. Parker JA, Kalnins VI, Deck JH, Cohen Z, Berk T, Cullen JB, Kiskis AA, Ke WJ (1990). Histopathological features of congenital fundus lesions in familial adenomatous polyposis. *Can J Ophthalmol* 25: 159-163.

1467. Parkin DM, Ohshima H, Srivatanakul P, Vatanasapt V (1993). Cholangiocarcinoma: epidemiology, mechanisms of carcinogenesis and prevention. *Cancer Epidemiol Biomarkers Prev* 2: 537-544.

1468. Parkin DM, Ohshima H, Srivatanakul P, Vatanasapt V (1993). Cholangiocarcinoma: epidemiology, mechanisms of carcinogenesis and prevention. *Cancer Epidemiol Biomarkers Prev* 2: 537-544.

1469. Parkin DM, Pisani P, Ferlay J (1999). Estimates of the worldwide incidence of 25 major cancers in 1990. *Int J Cancer* 80: 827-841.

1470. Parkin DM, Srivatanakul P, Khlat M, Chenvidhya D, Chotiwan P, Insiripong S, L'Abbe KA, Wild CP (1991). Liver cancer in Thailand. I. A case-control study of cholangiocarcinoma. *Int J Cancer* 48: 323-328.

1471. Parkin DM, Whelan SL, Ferlay J, Raymond L, Young J (1997). Cancer Incidence in Five Continents. IARC Press: Lyon.

1472. Parks TG (1970). Mucus-secreting adenocarcinoma of anal gland origin. *Br J Surg* 57: 434-436.

1473. Parsonnet J, Friedman GD, Vandersteen DP, Chang Y, Vogelman JH, Orentreich N, Sibley RK (1991). Helicobacter pylori infection and the risk of gastric carcinoma. *N Engl J Med* 325: 1127-1131.

1474. Parsonnet J, Hansen S, Rodriguez L, Gelb AB, Warnke RA, Jellum E, Orentreich N, Vogelman JH, Friedman GD (1994). Helicobacter pylori infection and gastric lymphoma. *N Engl J Med* 330: 1267-1271.

1475. Parsons R, Li GM, Longley M, Modrich P, Liu B, Berk T, Hamilton SR, Kinzler KW, Vogelstein B (1995). Mismatch repair deficiency in phenotypically normal human cells. *Science* 268: 738-740.

1476. Pascal RR, Clearfield HR (1987). Mucoepidermoid (adenosquamous) carcinoma arising in Barrett's esophagus. *Dig Dis Sci* 32: 428-432.

1477. Pasquinelli G, Preda P, Martinelli GN, Galassi A, Santini D, Venza E (1995). Filamentous inclusions in nonneoplastic and neoplastic pancreas: an ultrastructural and immunogold labeling study. *Ultrastruct Pathol* 19: 495-500.

1478. Passmore SJ, Berry PJ, Oakhill A (1988). Recurrent pancreatoblastoma with inappropriate adrenocorticotrophic hormone secretion. *Arch Dis Child* 63: 1494-1496.

1479. Paull A, Trier JS, Dalton MD, Camp RC, Loeb P, Goyal RK (1976). The histologic spectrum of Barrett's esophagus. *N Engl J Med* 295: 476-480.

1480. Pecorari P, Gorji N, Melato M (1999). Primary non-Hodgkin's lymphoma of the head of the pancreas: a case report and review of the literature. *Oncol Rep* 6: 1111-1115.

1481. Peek-RM J, Moss SF, Tham KT, Perez PG, Wang S, Miller GG, Atherton JC, Holt PR, Blaser MJ (1997). Helicobacter pylori cagA+ strains and dissociation of gastric epithelial cell proliferation from apoptosis. *J Natl Cancer Inst* 89: 863-868.

1482. Peers F, Bosch X, Kaldor J, Linsell A, Plujimen M (1987). Aflatoxin exposure, hepatitis B virus infection and liver cancer in Swaziland. *Int J Cancer* 39: 545-553.

1483. Peiffert D, Bey P, Pernot M, Guillemin F, Luporsi E, Hoffstetter S, Aletti P, Boissel P, Bigard MA, Dartois D, Baylac F (1997). Conservative treatment by irradiation of epidermoid cancers of the anal canal: prognostic factors of tumoral control and complications. *Int J Radiat Oncol Biol Phys* 37: 313-324.

1484. Peiffert D, Bey P, Pernot M, Hoffstetter S, Marchal C, Beckendorf V, Guillemin F (1997). Conservative treatment by irradiation of epidermoid carcinomas of the anal margin. *Int J Radiat Oncol Biol Phys* 39: 57-66.

1485. Pellegata NS, Sessa F, Renault B, Bonato M, Leone BE, Solcia E, Ranzani GN (1994). K-ras and p53 gene mutations in pancreatic cancer: ductal and nonductal tumors progress through different genetic lesions. *Cancer Res* 54: 1556-1560.

1486. Peltomaki P, Aaltonen LA, Sistonen P, Pylkkanen L, Mecklin JP, Jarvinen H, Green JS, Jass JR, Weber JL, Leach FS, et a (1993). Genetic mapping of a locus predisposing to human colorectal cancer. *Science* 260: 810-812.

1487. Peltomaki P, Lothe RA, Aaltonen LA, Pylkkanen L, Nystrom-Lahti M, Seruca R, David L, Holm R, Ryberg D, Haugen A, et a (1993). Microsatellite instability is associated with tumors that characterize the hereditary non-polyposis colorectal carcinoma syndrome. *Cancer Res* 53: 5853-5855.

1488. Peltomaki P, Vasen HF (1997). Mutations predisposing to hereditary nonpolyposis colorectal cancer: database and results of a collaborative study. The International Collaborative Group on Hereditary Nonpolyposis Colorectal Cancer. *Gastroenterology* 113: 1146-1158.

1489. Peng H, Chen G, Du M, Singh N, Isaacson PG, Pan L (1996). Replication error phenotype and p53 gene mutation in lymphomas of mucosa-associated lymphoid tissue. *Am J Pathol* 148: 643-648.

1490. Peng H, Diss T, Isaacson PG, Pan L (1997). c-myc gene abnormalities in mucosa-associated lymphoid tissue (MALT) lymphomas. *J Pathol* 181: 381-386.

1491. Peng H, Du M, Diss TC, Isaacson PG, Pan L (1997). Genetic evidence for a clonal link between low and high-grade components in gastric MALT B-cell lymphoma. *Histopathology* 30: 425-429.

1492. Peng H, Ranaldi R, Diss TC, Isaacson PG, Bearzi I, Pan L (1998). High frequency of CagA+ Helicobacter pylori infection in high-grade gastric MALT lymphomas. *J Pathol* 185: 409-412.

1493. Peng SS, Tsang YM, Lin JT, Wang HH, Chiang IP, Hsu JC (1998). Radiographic and computed tomographic findings of gastric mucosa-associated lymphoid tissue lymphomas. *J Formos Med Assoc* 97: 261-265.

1494. Penn I (1986). Cancers of the anogenital region in renal transplant recipients. Analysis of 65 cases. *Cancer* 58: 611-616.

1495. Pennazio M, Arrigoni A, Risio M, Spandre M, Rossini FP (1995). Clinical evaluation of push-type enteroscopy. *Endoscopy* 27: 164-170.

1496. Pera M, Cameron AJ, Trastek VF, Carpenter HA, Zinsmeister AR (1993). Increasing incidence of adenocarcinoma of the esophagus and esophagogastric junction. *Gastroenterology* 104: 510-513.

1497. Peralta RC, Casson AG, Wang RN, Keshavjee S, Redston M, Bapat B (1998). Distinct regions of frequent loss of heterozygosity of chromosome 5p and 5q in human esophageal cancer. *Int J Cancer* 78: 600-605.

1498. Pereira AD, Suspiro A, Chaves P, Saraiva A, Gloria L, de-Almeida JC, Leitao CN, Soares J, Mira FC (1998). Short segments of Barrett's epithelium and intestinal metaplasia in normal appearing oesophagogastric junctions: the same or two different entities? *Gut* 42: 659-662.

1499. Perez-Ordonez B, Naseem A, Lieberman PH, Klimstra DS (1996). Solid serous adenoma of the pancreas. The solid variant of serous cystadenoma? *Am J Surg Pathol* 20: 1401-1405.

1500. Perkins JT, Blackstone MO, Riddell RH (1985). Adenomatous polyposis coli and multiple endocrine neoplasia type 2b. A pathogenetic relationship. *Cancer* 55: 375-381.

1501. Perlmutter DH (1998). Alpha-1-antitrypsin deficiency. *Semin Liver Dis* 18: 217-225.

1502. Perrone T, Sibley RK, Rosai J (1985). Duodenal gangliocytic paraganglioma. An immunohistochemical and ultrastructural study and a hypothesis concerning its origin. *Am J Surg Pathol* 9: 31-41.

1503. Perry RE, Christensen MA, Thorson AG, Williams T (1989). Familial polyposis: colon cancer in the absence of rectal polyps. *Br J Surg* 76: 744-

1504. Persson PG, et al (1996). Survival and cause-specific mortality in inflammatory bowel disease: a population-based cohort study. *Gastroenterology* 110: 1339-1345.

1505. Perzin KH, Bridge MF (1981). Adenomas of the small intestine: a clinicopathologic review of 51 cases and a study of their relationship to carcinoma. *Cancer* 48: 799-819.

1506. Perzin KH, Bridge MF (1982). Adenomatous and carcinomatous changes in hamartomatous polyps of the small intestine (Peutz-Jeghers syndrome): report of a case and review of the literature. *Cancer* 49: 971-983.

1507. Pesko P, Rakic S, Milicevic M, Bulajic P, Gerzic Z (1994). Prevalence and clinicopathologic features of multiple squamous cell carcinoma of the esophagus. *Cancer* 73: 2687-2690.

1508. Pessione F, Degos F, Marcellin P, Duchatelle V, Njapoum C, Martinot PM, Degott C, Valla D, Erlinger S, Rueff B (1998). Effect of alcohol consumption on serum hepatitis C virus RNA and histological lesions in chronic hepatitis C. *Hepatology* 27: 1717-1722.

1509. Peters JH, Hoeft SF, Heimbucher J, Bremner RM, DeMeester TR, Bremner CG, Clark GW, Kiyabu M, Parisky Y (1994). Selection of patients for curative or palliative resection of esophageal cancer based on preoperative endoscopic ultrasonography. *Arch Surg* 129: 534-539.

1510. Petmitr S (1997). Cancer genes and cholangiocarcinoma. *Southeast Asian J Trop Med Public Health* 28 Suppl 1: 80-84.

1511. Petmitr S, Pinlaor S, Thousungnoen A, Karalak A, Migasena P (1998). K-ras oncogene and p53 gene mutations in cholangiocarcinoma from Thai patients. *Southeast Asian J Trop Med Public Health* 29: 71-75.

1512. Peutz JL (1921). [A very remarkable case of familial polyposis of mucous membrane of intestinal tract and accompanied by peculiar pigmentations of skin and mucous membrane]. *Netherlands Tijdschrift voor Geneeskunde* 10: 134-146.

1513. Pham BN, Villanueva RP (1989). Ganglioneuromatous proliferation associated with juvenile polyposis coli. *Arch Pathol Lab Med* 113: 91-94.

1514. Phelan CM, Lancaster JM, Tonin P, Gumbs C, Cochran C, Carter R, Ghadirian P, Perret C, Moslehi R, Dion F, Faucher MC, Dole K, Karimi S, Foulkes W, Lounis H, Warner E, Goss P, Anderson D, Larsson C, Narod SA, Futreal PA (1996). Mutation analysis of the BRCA2 gene in 49 site-specific breast cancer families. *Nat Genet* 13: 120-122.

1515. Piao Z, Park C, Park JH, Kim H (1998). Allelotype analysis of hepatocellular carcinoma. *Int J Cancer* 75: 29-33.

1516. Picciocchi A, Coppola R, Pallavicini F, Riccioni ME, Cileti S, Marino-Cosentino LM, Marasca G, Ortona L (1998). Major liver resection for non-Hodgkin's lymphoma in an HIV-positive patient: report of a case. *Surg Today* 28: 1257-1260.

1517. Pickren JW, Tsukada Y, Lane WW (1982). Liver metastases: analysis of autopsy data. In: *Liver Metastases*, Weiss L, Gilbert HA (eds), Hall Medical Publishers: Boston.

1518. Picus D, Balfe DM, Koehler RE, Roper CL, Owen JW (1983). Computed tomography in the staging of esophageal carcinoma. *Radiology* 146: 433-438.

1519. Pignatelli M, Ansari TW, Gunter PJ, Liu D, Hirano S, Takeichi M, Kloppel G, Lemoine NR (1994). Loss of membranous E-cadherin expression in pancreatic cancer: correlation with lymph node metastasis, high grade, and advanced stage. *J Pathol* 174: 243-248.

1520. Pinotti G, Zucca E, Roggero E, Pascarella A, Bertoni F, Savio A, Savio E, Capella C, Pedrinis E, Saletti P, Morandi E, Santandrea G, Cavalli F (1997). Clinical features, treatment and outcome in a series of 93 patients with low-grade gastric MALT lymphoma. *Leuk Lymphoma* 26: 527-537.

1521. Pipeleers MM, Somers G, Willems G, Foulis A, Imrie C, Bishop AE, Polak JM, Hacki WH, Stamm B, Heitz PU, et a (1990). Gastrinomas in the duodenums of patients with multiple endocrine neoplasia type 1 and the Zollinger-Ellison syndrome. *N Engl J Med* 322: 723-727.

1522. Pisani P, Parkin DM, Ferlay J (1999). Estimates of the worldwide mortality from twenty-five major cancers in 1990. *Int J Cancer* 83(1): 18-29.

1523. Pitman MB, Szyfelbein WM (1994). Fine Needle Aspiration Biopsy of the Liver. Butterworth-Heinemann: Boston.

1524. Pitt HA, Dooley WC, Yeo CJ, Cameron JL (1995). Malignancies of the biliary tree. *Curr Probl Surg* 32: 1-90.

1525. Platt CC, Haboubi NY, Schofield PF (1991). Primary squamous cell carcinoma of the terminal ileum. *J Clin Pathol* 44: 253-254.

1526. Podsypanina K, Ellenson LH, Nemes A, Gu J, Tamura M, Yamada KM, Cordon CC, Catoretti G, Fisher PE, Parsons R (1999). Mutation of Pten/Mmac1 in mice causes neoplasia in multiple organ systems. *Proc Natl Acad Sci U S A* 96: 1563-1568.

1527. Poe R, Snover DC (1988). Adenomas in glycogen storage disease type 1. Two cases with unusual histologic features. *Am J Surg Pathol* 12: 477-483.

1528. Polyak K, Hamilton SR, Vogelstein B, Kinzler KW (1996). Early alteration of cell-cycle-regulated gene expression in colorectal neoplasia. *Am J Pathol* 149: 381-387.

1529. Popescu RA, Wotherspoon AC, Cunningham D (1998). Local recurrence of a primary pancreatic lymphoma 18 years after complete remission. *Hematol Oncol* 16: 29-32.

1530. Posen J (1981). Giant cell tumor of the pancreas of the osteoclastic type associated with a mucinous secreting cystadenocarcinoma. *Hum Pathol* 12: 944-947.

1531. Potter JD (1999). Colorectal cancer: molecules and populations. *J Natl Cancer Inst* 91: 916-932.

1532. Pour PM, Konishi Y, Kloppel G, Longnecker DS (1994). Atlas of Exocrine Pancreatic Tumors. Springer-Verlag: Tokyo.

1533. Powers C, Ros PR, Stoupis C, Johnson WK, Segel KH (1994). Primary liver neoplasms: MR imaging with pathologic correlation. *Radiographics* 14: 459-482.

1534. Poynard T, Bedossa P, Opolon P (1997). Natural history of liver fibrosis progression in patients with chronic hepatitis C. The OBSVIRC, METAVIR, CLINIVIR, and DOSVIRC groups. *Lancet* 349: 825-832.

1535. Prabhu RM, Medeiros LJ, Kumar D, Drachenberg CI, Papadimitriou JC, Appelman HD, Johnson LB, Laurin J, Heyman M, Abruzzo LV (1998). Primary hepatic low-grade B-cell lymphoma of mucosa-associated lymphoid tissue (MALT) associated with primary biliary cirrhosis. *Mod Pathol* 11: 404-410.

1536. Prayson RA, Hart WR, Petras RE (1994). Pseudomyxoma peritonei. A clinicopathologic study of 19 cases with emphasis on site of origin and nature of associated ovarian tumors. *Am J Surg Pathol* 18: 591-603.

1537. Prior A, Whorwell PJ (1986). Familial Barrett's oesophagus? *Hepatogastroenterology* 33: 86-87.

1538. Pritchard BN, Youngberg GA (1993). Atypical mitotic figures in basal cell carcinoma. A review of 208 cases. *Am J Dermatopathol* 15: 549-552.

1539. Proctor DD, Fraser JL, Mangano MM, Calkins DR, Rosenberg SJ (1992). Small cell carcinoma of the esophagus in a patient with longstanding primary achalasia. *Am J Gastroenterol* 87: 664-667.

1540. Prolla TA (1998). DNA mismatch repair and cancer. *Curr Opin Cell Biol* 10: 311-316.

1541. Pruneri G, Graziadei G, Ermellino L, Baldini L, Neri A, Buffa R (1998). Plasmablastic lymphoma of the stomach. A case report. *Haematologica* 83: 87-89.

1542. Przygodzki RM, Finkelstein SD, Keohavong P, Zhu D, Bakker A, Swalsky PA, Soini Y, Ishak KG, Bennett WP (1997). Sporadic and Thorotrast-induced angiosarcomas of the liver manifest frequent and multiple point mutations in K-ras-2. *Lab Invest* 76: 153-159.

1543. Purdie CA, Piris J (2000). Histopathological grade, mucinous differentiation and DNA ploidy in relation to prognosis in colorectal carcinoma. *Histopathology* 36: 121-126.

1544. Pyke CM, van Heerden JA, Colby TV, Sarr MG, Weaver AL (1992). The spectrum of serous cystadenoma of the pancreas. Clinical, pathologic, and surgical aspects. *Ann Surg* 215: 132-139.

1545. Qiao ZK, Halliday ML, Rankin JG, Coates RA (1988). Relationship between hepatitis B surface antigen prevalence, per capita alcohol consumption and primary liver cancer death rate in 30 countries. *J Clin Epidemiol* 41: 787-792.

1546. Qin Y, Greiner A, Trunk MJ, Schmausser B, Ott MM, Muller HH (1995). Somatic hypermutation in low-grade mucosa-associated lymphoid tissue-type B-cell lymphoma. *Blood* 86: 3528-3534.

1547. Qiu SL, Yang GR (1988). Precursor lesions of esophageal cancer in high-risk populations in Henan Province, China. *Cancer* 62: 551-557.

1548. Qizilbash AH (1975). Mucoceles of the appendix. Their relationship to hyperplastic polyps, mucinous cystadenomas, and cystadenocarcinomas. *Arch Pathol* 99: 548-555.

1549. Queiroz DM, Mendes EN, Rocha GA, Oliveira AM, Oliveira CA, Magalhaes PP, Moura SB, Cabral MM, Nogueira AM (1998). cagA-positive Helicobacter pylori and risk for developing gastric carcinoma in Brazil. *Int J Cancer* 78: 135-139.

1550. Quillin SP, Brink JA (1992). Hepatoma complicating Byler disease. *AJR Am J Roentgenol* 159: 432-433.

1551. Quint LE, Hepburn LM, Francis IR, Whyte RI, Orringer MB (1995). Incidence and distribution of distant metastases from newly diagnosed esophageal carcinoma. *Cancer* 76: 1120-1125.

1552. Quintanilla ML, Lome MC, Ott G, Gschwendtner A, Gredler E, Reyes E, Angeles AA, Fend F (1997). Primary non-Hodgkin's lymphoma of the intestine: high prevalence of Epstein-Barr virus in Mexican lymphomas as compared with European cases. *Blood* 89: 644-651.

1553. Radford DM, Ashley SW, Wells-SA.J, Gerhard DS (1990). Loss of heterozygosity of markers on chromosome 11 in tumors from patients with multiple endocrine neoplasia syndrome type 1. *Cancer Res* 50: 6529-6533.

1554. Radi MJ, Fenoglio PC, Bartow SA, Key CR, Pathak DR (1986). Gastric carcinoma in the young: a clinicopathological and immunohistochemical study. *Am J Gastroenterol* 81: 747-756.

1555. Rafter J, Glinghammar B (1998). Interactions between the environment and genes in the colon. *Eur J Cancer Prev* 7: S69-S74.

1556. Ramnani DM, Wistuba II, Behrens C, Gazdar AF, Sobin LH, Albores SJ (1999). K-ras and p53 mutations in the pathogenesis of classical and goblet cell carcinoids of the appendix. *Cancer* 86: 14-21.

1557. Ramos G, Murao M, de Oliveira BM, de Castro LP, Viana MB (1997). Primary hepatic non-Hodgkin's lymphoma in children: a case report and review of the literature. *Med Pediatr Oncol* 28: 370-372.

1558. Rampino N, Yamamoto H, Ionov Y, Li Y, Sawai H, Reed JC, et a (1997). Somatic frameshift mutations in the BAX gene in colon cancers of the microsatellite mutator phenotype. *Science* 275: 967-969.

1559. Ranchod M, Kempson RL (1977). Smooth muscle tumors of the gastrointestinal tract and retroperitoneum: a pathologic analysis of 100 cases. *Cancer* 39: 255-262.

1560. Raney-RB J, Crist W, Hays D, Newton W, Ruymann F, Tefft M, Beltangady M (1990). Soft tissue sarcoma of the perineal region in childhood. A report from the Intergroup Rhabdomyosarcoma Studies I and II, 1972 through 1984. *Cancer* 65: 2787-2792.

1561. Rappel S, Altendorf HA, Stolte M (1995). Prognosis of gastric carcinoid tumours. *Digestion* 56: 455-462.

1562. Rashid A, Hamilton SR (1997). Genetic alterations in sporadic and Crohn's-associated adenocarcinomas of the small intestine. *Gastroenterology* 113: 127-135.

1563. Rashid A, Zahurak M, Goodman SN, Hamilton SR (1999). Genetic epidemiology of mutated K-ras proto-oncogene, altered suppressor genes, and microsatellite instability in colorectal adenomas. *Gut* 44: 826-833.

1564. Ratto C, Sofo L, Ippoliti M, Merico M, Bossola M, Vecchio FM, Doglietto GB, Crucitti F (1999). Accurate lymph-node detection in colorectal specimens resected for cancer is of prognostic significance. *Dis Colon Rectum* 42: 143-154.

1565. Rawlinson J, Skehan S (1999). Pathologist's guide to the radiology of nodules in the liver. *Pathol Case Rev* 4: 147-159.

1566. Ray GS, Lee JR, Nwokeji K, Mills LR, Goldenring JR (1997). Increased immunoreactivity for Rab11, a small GTP-binding protein, in low-grade dysplastic Barrett's epithelia. *Lab Invest* 77: 503-511.

1567. Ready AR, Soul JO, Newman J, Matthews HR (1989). Malignant carcinoid tumour of the oesophagus. *Thorax* 44: 594-596.

1568. Redel CA, Zwiener RJ (1998). Anatomy and anomalies of the stomach and duodenum. In: *Sleisenger and Fordtran's Gastrointestinal and Liver Disease*, Feldman F, Scharschmidt BF, Sleidenger MH (eds), 6th ed. W.B. Saunders Company: Philadelphia.

1569. Redleaf MI, Moran WJ, Gruber B (1993). Mycosis fungoides involving the cervical esophagus. *Arch Otolaryngol Head Neck Surg* 119: 690-693.

1570. Redston MS, Caldas C, Seymour AB, Hruban RH, da-Costa L, Yeo CJ, Kern SE (1994). p53 mutations in pancreatic carcinoma and evidence of common involvement of homocopolymer tracts in DNA microdeletions. *Cancer Res* 54: 3025-3033.

1571. Rego J, Ruvira L, Garcia A, Freijanes P, Penaranda J, Soto J (1991). Pancreatic mucinous cystadenocarcinoma with pseudosarcomatous mural nodules. A report of a case with immunohistochemical study. *Cancer* 67: 494-498.

1572. Reid BJ, Haggitt RC, Rubin CE, Roth G, Surawicz CM, Van-Belle G, Lewin K, Weinstein WM, Antonioli DA, Goldman H, et a (1988). Observer variation in the diagnosis of dysplasia in Barrett's esophagus. *Hum Pathol* 19: 166-178.

1573. Reid BJ, Weinstein WM, Lewin KJ, Haggitt RC, VanDeventer G, DenBesten L, Rubin CE (1988). Endoscopic biopsy can detect high-grade dysplasia or early adenocarcinoma in Barrett's esophagus without grossly recognizable neoplastic lesions. *Gastroenterology* 94: 81-90.

1574. Reis CA, David L, Correa P, Carneiro F, de-Bolos C, Garcia E, Mandel U, Clausen H, Sobrinho SM (1999). Intestinal metaplasia of human stomach displays distinct patterns of mucin (MUC1, MUC2, MUC5AC, and MUC6) expression. *Cancer Res* 59: 1003-1007.

1575. Resnick MB, Jacobs DO, Brodsky GL (1994). Multifocal adenocarcinoma in situ with underlying carcinoid tumor of the gallbladder. *Arch Pathol Lab Med* 118: 933-934.

1576. Restrepo C, Moreno J, Duque E, Cuello C, Amsel J, Correa P (1978). Juvenile colonic polyposis in Colombia. *Dis Colon Rectum* 21: 600-612.

1577. Rhyu MG, Park WS, Jung YJ, Choi SW, Meltzer SJ (1994). Allelic deletions of MCC/APC and p53 are frequent late events in human gastric carcinogenesis. *Gastroenterology* 106: 1584-1588.

1578. Ribeiro MB, Greenstein AJ, Heimann TM, Yamazaki Y, Aufses-AH J (1991). Adenocarcinoma of the small intestine in Crohn's disease. *Surg Gynecol Obstet* 173: 343-349.

1579. Ricaurte O, Flejou JF, Vissuzaine C, Goldfain D, Rotenberg A, Cadiot G, Potet F (1996). Helicobacter pylori infection in patients with Barrett's oesophagus: a prospective immunohistochemical study. *J Clin Pathol* 49: 176-177.

1580. Ricciardone MD, Ozcelik T, Cevher B, Ozdag H, Tuncer M, Gurgey A, Uzunalimoglu O, Cetinkaya H, Tanyeli A, Erken E, Ozturk M (1999). Human MLH1 deficiency predisposes to hematological malignancy and neurofibromatosis type 1. *Cancer Res* 59: 290-293.

1581. Richards FM, McKee SA, Rajpar MH, Cole TR, Evans DG, Jankowski JA, McKeown C, Sanders DS, Maher ER (1999). Germline E-cadherin gene (CDH1) mutations predispose to familial gastric cancer and colorectal cancer. *Hum Mol Genet* 8: 607-610.

1582. Riddell RH, Goldman H, Ransohoff DF, Appelman HD, Fenoglio CM, Haggitt RC, Ahren C, Correa P, Hamilton SR, Morson BC, et a (1983). Dysplasia in inflammatory bowel disease: standardized classification with provisional clinical applications. *Hum Pathol* 14: 931-968.

1583. Rieger-Christ KM, Brierley KL, Reale MA (1997). The DCC protein - neural development and the malignant process. *Front Biosci* 2: 438-448.

1584. Ries LAG, Hankey BF, Miller BA, Hartman AM, Edwards BK (1991). Cancer statistics review 1973-88. In: *NIH Publication No. 91-2789*, National Cancer Institute: Bethesda (MD).

1585. Riikonen P, Tuominen L, Seppa A, Perkkio M (1990). Simultaneous hepatoblastoma in identical male twins. *Cancer* 66: 2429-2431.

1586. Rijken AM, van-Gulik TM, Polak MM, Sturm PD, Gouma DJ, Offerhaus GJ (1998). Diagnostic and prognostic value of incidence of K-ras codon 12 mutations in resected distal bile duct carcinoma. *J Surg Oncol* 68: 187-192.

1587. Riley E, Swift M (1980). A family with Peutz-Jeghers syndrome and bilateral breast cancer. *Cancer* 46: 815-817.

1588. Rindi G (1995). Clinicopathologic aspects of gastric neuroendocrine tumors. *Am J Surg Pathol* 19: S20-S29.

1589. Rindi G, Azzoni C, La-Rosa S, Klersy C, Paolotti D, Rappel S, Stolte M, Capella C, Bordi C, Solcia E (1999). ECL cell tumor and poorly differentiated endocrine carcinoma of the stomach: prognostic evaluation by pathological analysis. *Gastroenterology* 116: 532-542.

1590. Rindi G, Bordi C, Rappel S, La-Rosa S, Stolte M, Solcia E (1996). Gastric carcinoids and neuroendocrine carcinomas: pathogenesis, pathology, and behavior. *World J Surg* 20: 168-172.

1591. Rindi G, Luinetti O, Cornaggia M, Capella C, Solcia E (1993). Three subtypes of gastric argyrophil carcinoid and the gastric neuroendocrine carcinoma: a clinicopathologic study. *Gastroenterology* 104: 994-1006.

1592. Rindi G, Paolotti D, Luinetti O, Wiedenmann B, Solcia E (2000). Vesicular monoamine transporter 2 as a marker of gastric enterochromaffin-like cell tumors. *Virchows Arch* 436: 217-223.

1593. Riopel MA, Klimstra DS, Godellas CV, Blumgart LH, Westra WH (1997). Intrabiliary growth of metastatic colonic adenocarcinoma: a pattern of intrahepatic spread easily confused with primary neoplasia of the biliary tract. *Am J Surg Pathol* 21: 1030-1036.

1594. Risk JM, Field EA, Field JK, Whittaker J, Fryer A, Ellis A, Shaw JM, Friedmann PS, Bishop DT, Bodmer J, et a (1994). Tylosis oesophageal cancer mapped. *Nat Genet* 8: 319-321.

1595. Risk JM, Ruhrberg C, Hennies HC, Mills HS, Di-Colandrea T, Evans KE, Ellis A, Watt FM, Bishop DT, Spurr NK, Stevens HP, Leigh IM, Reis A, Kelsell DP, Field JK (1999). Envoplakin, a possible candidate gene for focal NEPPK/oesophageal cancer (TOC): the integration of genetic and physical maps of the TOC region on 17q25. *Genomics* 59: 234-242.

1596. Rivera JA, Fernandez-del CC, Pins M, Compton CC, Lewandrowski KB, Rattner DW, Warshaw AL (1997). Pancreatic mucinous ductal ectasia and intraductal papillary neoplasms. A single malignant clinicopathologic entity. *Am J Gastroenterol* 91: 2414-2417.

1597. Robbins EG, Franceschi D, Barkin JS (1996). Solitary metastatic tumors to the pancreas: a case report and review of the literature. *Am J Gastroenterol* 91: 2414-2417.

1598. Roberts LJ2, Bloomgarden ZT, Marvey SR, Jr., Rabin D, Oates JA (1983). Histamine from the gastric carcinoid provocation by pentagastrin and inhibition by somatostatin. *Gastroenterology* 84: 272-275.

1599. Roberts PL, Veidenheimer MC, Cassidy S, Silverman ML (1989). Adenocarcinoma arising in an ileostomy. Report of two cases and review of the literature. *Arch Surg* 124: 497-499.

1600. Robertson PL, Muraszko KM, Axtell RA (1997). Hepatoblastoma metastatic to brain: prolonged survival after multiple surgical resections of a solitary brain lesion. *J Pediatr Hematol Oncol* 19: 168-171.

1601. Robey CS, el-Naggar AK, Sahin AA, Bruner JM, Ro JY, Cleary KR (1991). Prognostic factors in esophageal squamous carcinoma. A study of histologic features, blood group expression, and DNA ploidy. *Am J Clin Pathol* 95: 844-849.

1602. Roder JD, Bottcher K, Busch R, Wittekind C, Hermanek P, Siewert JR (1998). Classification of regional lymph node metastasis from gastric carcinoma. German Gastric Cancer Study Group. *Cancer* 82: 621-631.

1603. Roder JD, Busch R, Stein HJ, Fink U, Siewert JR (1994). Ratio of invaded to removed lymph nodes as a predictor of survival in squamous cell carcinoma of the oesophagus. *Br J Surg* 81: 410-413.

1604. Rodriguez BM, Vasen HF, Lynch HT, Watson P, Myrhoj T, Jarvinen HJ, Mecklin JP, Macrae F, St.-John DJ, Bertario L, Fidalgo P, Madlensky L, Rozen P (1998). Characteristics of small bowel carcinoma in hereditary nonpolyposis colorectal carcinoma. International Collaborative Group on HNPCC. *Cancer* 83: 240-244.

1605. Rogers EL, Goldkind SF, Iseri OA, Bustin M, Goldkind L, Hamilton SR, Smith RL (1986). Adenocarcinoma of the lower esophagus. A disease primarily of white men with Barrett's esophagus. *J Clin Gastroenterol* 8: 613-618.

1606. Rogers LF, Lastra MP, Lin KT, Bennett D (1973). Calcifying mucinous adenocarcinoma of the gallbladder. *Am J Gastroenterol* 59: 441-445.

1607. Roggo A, Wood WC, Ottinger LW (1993). Carcinoid tumors of the appendix. *Ann Surg* 217: 385-390.

1608. Roland CF, van-Heerden JA (1989). Nonpancreatic primary tumors with metastasis to the pancreas. *Surg Gynecol Obstet* 168: 345-347.

1609. Rolleston H, McNee JW (1929). Diseases of the Liver, Gall Bladder and Bile Ducts. MacMillan: London.

1610. Romero Y, Cameron AJ, Locke GR, Schaid DJ, Slezak JM, Branch CD, Melton LJ (1997). Familial aggregation of gastroesophageal reflux in patients with Barrett's esophagus and esophageal adenocarcinoma. *Gastroenterology* 113: 1449-1456.

1611. Ronnett BM, Shmookler BM, Diener WM, Sugarbaker PH, Kurman RJ (1997). Immunohistochemical evidence supporting the appendiceal origin of pseudomyxoma peritonei in women. *Int J Gynecol Pathol* 16: 1-9.

1612. Ronnett BM, Zahn CM, Kurman RJ, Kass ME, Sugarbaker PH, Shmookler BM (1995). Disseminated peritoneal adenomucinosis and peritoneal mucinous carcinomatosis. A clinicopathologic analysis of 109 cases with emphasis on distinguishing pathologic features, site of origin, prognosis, and relationship to "pseudomyxoma peritonei". *Am J Surg Pathol* 19: 1390-1408.

1613. Rood JC, Ruiz B, Fontham ETH, et al (1994). Helicobacter pylori-associated gastritis and vitamin C concentrations in the gastric juice. *Nutr Cancer* 22: 65-72.

1614. Rosch T (1995). Endosonographic staging of gastric cancer: a review of literature results. *Gastrointest Endosc Clin N Am* 5: 549-557.

1615. Rose PG, Abdul KF (1997). Isolated appendiceal metastasis in early ovarian carcinoma. *J Surg Oncol* 64: 246-247.

1616. Rosenberg JM, Welch JP (1985). Carcinoid tumors of the colon. A study of 72 patients. *Am J Surg* 149: 775-779.

1617. Rosioru C, Glassman MS, Halata MS, Schwarz SM (1993). Esophagitis and Helicobacter pylori in children: incidence and therapeutic implications. *Am J Gastroenterol* 88: 510-513.

1618. Rosser C (1931). The etiology of anal cancer. *Am J Surg* 328-333.

1619. Rossini FP, Risio M, Pennazio M (1999). Small bowel tumors and polyposis syndromes. *Gastrointest Endosc Clin N Am* 9: 93-114.

1620. Roth A, Kolaric K, Dominis M (1978). Histologic and cytologic liver changes in 120 patients with malignant lymphomas. *Tumori* 64: 45-53.

1621. Roth A, Marti MC (1998). Malignant tumours of the anal canal and anus. In: *Surgery of the Anorectal Diseases*, Marti MC, Givel JC (eds). Springer Verlag: Berlin.

1622. Roth S, Sistonen P, Hemminki A, Salovaara R, Loukola A, Johansson M, Avizienyte E, Cleary KA, Lynch P, Amos C, Kristo P, Mecklin JP, Kellokumpul, Jarvinen H, Aaltonen LA (1999). Smad genes in juvenile polyposis. *Genes Chromosomes Cancer* 26: 54-61.

1623. Roy P, Piard F, Duserre-Guion L, Martin L, Michiels-Marzais D, Faivre J (1998). Prognostic comparison of the pathological classifications of gastric cancer: a population-based study. *Histopathology* 33: 304-310.

1624. Rozenblum E, Schutte M, Goggins M, Hahn SA, Panzer S, Zahurak M, Goodman SN, Sohn TA, Hruban RH, Yeo CJ, Kern SE (1997). Tumor-suppressive pathways in pancreatic carcinoma. *Cancer Res* 57: 1731-1734.

1625. Rubbia-Brandt L, Brundler MA, Kerl K, Negro F, Nador RG, Scherrer A, Kurt AM, Mentha G, Borisch B (1999). Primary heatic diffuse large B-cell lymphoma in a patient with chronic hepatitis C. *Am J Surg Pathol* 23: 1124-1130.

1626. Rubel LR, Ishak KG (1982). Thorotrast-associated cholangiocarcinoma: an epidemiologic and clinicopathologic study. *Cancer* 50: 1408-1415.

1627. Rubinfeld B, Albert I, Porfiri E, Fiol C, Munemitsu S, Polakis P (1996). Binding of GSK3beta to the APC-beta-catenin complex and regulation of complex assembly. *Science* 272: 1023-1026.

1628. Rubio CA, Saito Y, Watanabe M, Koizumi K, Takahama KK, Hirata I, Nakano H, Jaramillo E, Slezak P, Kumagai J, Nakamura K, Yanagisawa A, Kato Y, Kawaguchi M, Miyaoka M, Horimukai H, Taguchi Y, Katayama A, Hirota T, Watanabe X, Masaki T, Muto T (1999). Non-polypoid colorectal neoplasias: a multicentric study. *Anticancer Res* 19. 2361-2364.

1629. Ruck P, Kaiserling E (1992). Extracellular matrix in hepatoblastoma: an immunohistochemical investigation. *Histopathology* 21: 115-126.

1630. Ruck P, Xiao JC, Kaiserling E (1995). Immunoreactivity of sinusoids in hepatoblastoma: an immunohistochemical study using lectin UEA-1 and antibodies against endothelium-associated antigens, including CD34. *Histopathology* 26: 451-455.

1631. Ruck P, Xiao JC, Pietsch T, von-Schweinitz D, Kaiserling E (1997). Hepatic stem-like cells in hepatoblastoma:expression of cytokeratin 7, albumin and antigens detected by OV-1 and OV-6. *Histopathology* 31: 324-329.

1632. Rudolph P, Gloeckner K, Parwaresch R, Harms D, Schmidt D (1998). Immuno-phenotype, proliferation, DNA ploidy, and biological behavior of gastrointestinal stromal tumors: a multivariate clinicopathologic study. *Hum Pathol* 29: 791-800.

1633. Rugge M, Busatto G, Cassaro M, Shiao YH, Russo V, Leandro G, Avellini C, Fabiano A, Sidoni A, Covacci A (1999). Patients younger than 40 years with gastric carcinoma. Helicobacter pylori genotype and associated gastritis phenotype. *Cancer* 85: 2506-2511.

1634. Rugge M, Cassaro M, Farinati F, Di-Mario F (1997). Diagnosis of gastric carcinoma in Japan and western countries. *Lancet* 350: 448.

1635. Rugge M, Cassaro M, Leandro G, Baffa R, Avellini C, Bufo P, Stracca V, Battaglia G, Fabiano A, Guerini A, DiMario F (1996). Helicobacter pylori in promotion of gastric carcinoma. *Dig Dis Sci* 41: 950-955.

1636. Rugge M, Correa P, Dixon MF, Hattori T, Leandro G, Lewin K, Riddell RH, Sipponen P, Watanabe H (2000). Gastric dysplasia: the Padova international classification. *Am J Surg Pathol* 24: 167-176.

1637. Rugge M, Correa P, Dixon MF, Hattori T, Leandro G, Lewin K, Riddell RH, Sipponen P, Watanabe H (2000). Gastric dysplasia: the Padova international classification. *Am J Surg Pathol* 24: 167-176.

1638. Rugge M, Leandro G, Farinati F, Di-Mario F, Sonego F, Cassaro M, Guido M, Ninfo V (1995). Gastric epithelial dysplasia. How clinicopathologic background relates to management. *Cancer* 76: 376-382.

1639. Rugge M, Sonego F, Militello C, Guido M, Ninfo V (1992). Primary carcinoid tumor of the cystic and common bile ducts. *Am J Surg Pathol* 16: 802-807.

1640. Rugge M, Sonego F, Pollice L, Perilongo G, Guido M, Basso G, Ninfo V, Pennelli N, Gambini C, Guglielmi M, Pennelli A, Leandro G, Keeling JW (1998). Hepatoblastoma: DNA nuclear content, proliferative indices, and pathology. *Liver* 18: 128-133.

1641. Ruol A, Merigliano S, Baldan N, Santi S, Petrin GF, Bonavina L, Ancona E, Peracchia A (1997). Prevalence, management and outcome of early adenocarcinoma (pT1) of the esophago-gastric junction. Comparison between early cancer in Barrett's esophagus (type I) and early cancer of the cardia (type II). *Dis Esophagus* 10: 190-195.

1642. Rustin RB, Broughan TA, Hermann RE, Grundfest-Broniatowski SF, Petras RE, Hart WR (1988). Papillary cystic epithelial neoplasms of the pancreas. A clinical study of six cases. *Arch Surg* 121: 1073-1076.

1643. Sachatello CR, Hahn IS, Carrington CB (1974). Juvenile gastrointestinal polyposis in a female infant: report of a case and review of the literature of a recently recognized syndrome. *Surgery* 75: 107-114.

1644. Sahin AM, Foulis AA, Poon FW, Imrie CW (1998). Late focal pancreatic metastasis of renal cell carcinoma. *Dig Surg* 15: 72-74.

1645. Sakamoto M, Hirohashi S (1998). Natural history and prognosis of adenomatous hyperplasia and early hepatocellular carcinoma: multi-institutional analysis of 53 nodules followed up for more than 6 months and 141 patients with single early hepatocellular carcinoma treated by surgical resection or percutaneous ethanol injection. *Jpn J Clin Oncol* 28: 604-608.

1646. Sakamoto M, Hirohashi S, Shimosato Y (1991). Early stages of multistep hepatocarcinogenesis: adenomatous hyperplasia and early hepatocellular carcinoma. *Hum Pathol* 22: 172-178.

1647. Sakamoto M, Hirohashi S, Tsuda H, Shimosato Y, Makuuchi M, Hosoda Y (1989). Multicentric independent development of hepatocellular carcinoma revealed by analysis of hepatitis B virus integration pattern. *Am J Surg Pathol* 13: 1064-1067.

1648. Sakurai S, Fukasawa T, Chong JM, Tanaka A, Fukayama M (1999). Embryonic form of smooth muscle myosin heavy chain (SMemb/MHC-B) in gastrointestinal stromal tumor and interstitial cells of Cajal. *Am J Pathol* 154: 23-28.

1649. Salem P, el-Hashimi L, Anaissie E, Geha S, Habboubi N, Ibrahim N, Khalyl M, Allam C (1987). Primary small intestinal lymphoma in adults. A comparative study of IPSID versus non-IPSID in the Middle East. *Cancer* 59: 1670-1676.

1650. Salmon P, Fenton J, Asselain B, Mathieu G, Girodet J, Durand JC, Decroix Y, Pilleron JP, Rousseau J (1984). Treatment of epidermoid anal canal cancer. *Am J Surg* 147: 43-48.

1651. Salo JA, Kivilaakso EO, Kiviluoto TA, Virtanen IO (1996). Cytokeratin profile suggests metaplastic epithelial transformation in Barrett's oesophagus. *Ann Med* 28: 305-309.

1652. Sameshima Y, Tsunematsu Y, Watanabe S, Tsukamoto T, Kawa hK, Hirata Y, Mizoguchi H, Sugimura T, Terada M, Yokota J (1992). Detection of novel germ-line p53 mutations in diverse-cancer-prone families identified by selecting patients with childhood adrenocortical carcinoma. *J Natl Cancer Inst* 84: 703-707.

1653. Sanchez BF, Garcia MJ, Alonso JD, Acosta J, Carrasco L, Pinero A, Parrilla P (1998). Prognostic factors in primary gastrointestinal non-Hodgkin's lymphoma: a multivariate analysis of 76 cases. *Eur J Surg* 164: 385-392.

1654. Sanders KM (1996). A case for interstitial cells of Cajal as pacemakers and mediators of neurotransmission in the gastrointestinal tract. *Gastroenterology* 111: 492-515.

1655. Sanfey H, Mendelsohn G, Cameron JL Solid and papillary neoplasm of the pancreas. A potentially curable surgical lesion. *Ann Surg* 197: 272-275.

1656. Sano T, Tsujino K, Yoshida K, Nakayama H, Haruma K, Ito H, Nakamura Y, Kajiyama G, Tahara E (1991). Frequent loss of heterozygosity on chromosomes 1q, 5q, and 17p in human gastric carcinomas. *Cancer Res* 51: 2926-2931.

1657. Santoro E, Sacchi M, Scutari F, Carboni F, Graziano F (1997). Primary adenocarcinoma of the duodenum: treatment and survival in 89 patients. *Hepatogastroenterology* 44: 1157-1163.

1658. Santoro IM, Groden J (1997). Alternative splicing of the APC gene and its association with terminal differentiation. *Cancer Res* 57: 488-494.

1659. Sarbia M, Bittinger F, Porschen R, Dutkowski P, Torzewski M, Willers R, Gabbert HE (1996). The prognostic significance of tumour cell proliferation in squamous cell carcinomas of the oesophagus. *Br J Cancer* 74: 1012-1016.

1660. Sarbia M, Bittinger F, Porschen R, Dutkowski P, Willers R, Gabbert HE (1995). Prognostic value of histopathologic parameters of esophageal squamous cell carcinoma. *Cancer* 76: 922-927.

1661. Sarbia M, Porschen R, Borchard F, Horstmann O, Willers R, Gabbert HE (1994). p53 protein expression and prognosis in squamous cell carcinoma of the esophagus. *Cancer* 74: 2218-2223.

1662. Sarbia M, Porschen R, Borchard F, Horstmann O, Willers R, Gabbert HE (1995). Incidence and prognostic significance of vascular and neural invasion in squamous cell carcinomas of the esophagus. *Int J Cancer* 61: 333-336.

1663. Sarbia M, Verreet P, Bittinger F, Dutkowski P, Heep H, Willers R, Gabbert HE (1997). Basaloid squamous cell carcinoma of the esophagus: diagnosis and prognosis. *Cancer* 79: 1871-1878.

1664. Sarlomo RM, el-Rifai W, Lahtinen T, Andersson LC, Miettinen M, Knuutila S (1998). Different patterns of DNA copy number changes in gastrointestinal stromal tumors, leiomyomas, and schwannomas. *Hum Pathol* 29: 476-481.

1665. Sarlomo RM, Kovatich AJ, Barusevicius A, Miettinen M (1998). CD117: a sensitive marker for gastrointestinal stromal tumors that is more specific than CD34. *Mod Pathol* 11: 728-734.

1666. Sarlomo RM, Miettinen M (1995). Gastric schwannoma - a clinicopathological analysis of six cases. *Histopathology* 27: 355-360.

1667. Sarmiento JM, Wolff BG, Burgart LJ, Frizelle FA, Ilstrup DM (1997). Paget's disease of the perianal region - an aggressive disease? *Dis Colon Rectum* 40: 1187-1194.

1668. Sarmiento JM, Wolff BG, Burgart LJ, Frizelle FA, Ilstrup DM (1997). Perianal Bowen's disease: associated tumors, human papillomavirus, surgery, and other controversies. *Dis Colon Rectum* 40: 912-918.

1669. Sasaki M, Nakanuma Y, Ho SB, Kim YS (1998). Cholangiocarcinomas arising in cirrhosis and combined hepatocellular-cholangiocellular carcinomas share apomucin profiles. *Am J Clin Pathol* 109: 302-308.

1670. Sasaki M, Nakanuma Y, Kim YS (1996). Characterization of apomucin expression in intrahepatic cholangiocarcinomas and their precursor lesions: an immunohistochemical study. *Hepatology* 24: 1074-1078.

1671. Sasaki M, Nakanuma Y, Shimizu K, Izumi R (1995). Pathological and immunohistochemical findings in a case of mucinous cholangiocarcinoma. *Pathol Int* 45: 781-786.

1672. Sasaki S, Masaki T, Umetani N, Futakawa N, Ando H, Muto T (1998). Characteristics in primary signet-ring cell carcinoma of the colorectum, from clinicopathological observations. *Jpn J Clin Oncol* 28: 202-206.

1673. Satarug S, Haswell-Elkins MR, Sithithaworn P, Bartsch H, Ohshima H, Tsuda M, Mairiang P, Mairiang E, Yongvanit P, Esumi H, Elkins DB (1998). Relationships between the synthesis of N-nitrosodimethylamine and immune responses to chronic infection with the carcinogenic parasite, Opisthorchis viverrini, in men. *Carcinogenesis* 19: 485-491.

1674. Satoh H, Iyama A, Hidaka K, Nakashiro H, Harada S, Hisatsugu T (1991). Metastatic carcinoma of the gallbladder from renal cancer presenting as intraluminal polypoid mass. *Dig Dis Sci* 36: 520-523.

1675. Satoh K, Ohtani H, Shimosegawa T, Koizumi M, Sawai T, Toyota T (1994). Infrequent stromal expression of gelatinase A and intact basement membrane in intraductal neoplasms of the pancreas. *Gastroenterology* 107: 1488-1495.

1676. Satoh K, Sasano H, Shimosegawa T, Koizumi M, Yamazaki T, Mochizuki F, Kobayashi N, Okano T, Toyota T, Sawai T (1993). An immunohistochemical study of the c-erbB-2 oncogene product in intraductal mucin-hypersecreting neoplasms and in ductal cell carcinomas of the pancreas. *Cancer* 72: 51-56.

1677. Savio A, Franzin G, Wotherspoon AC, Zamboni G, Negrini R, Buffoli F, Diss TC, Pan L, Isaacson PG (1996). Diagnosis and posttreatment follow-up of Helicobacter pylori-positive gastric lymphoma of mucosa-associated lymphoid tissue: histology, polymerase chain reaction, or both? *Blood* 87: 1255-1260.

1678. Saw EC, Yu GS, Wagner G, Heng Y (1997). Synchronous primary neuroendocrine carcinoma and adenocarcinoma in Barrett's esophagus. *J Clin Gastroenterol* 24: 116-119.

1679. Scates DK, Spigelman AD, Phillips RK, Venitt S (1992). DNA adducts detected by 32P-postlabelling, in the intestine of rats given bile from patients with familial adenomatous polyposis and from unaffected controls. *Carcinogenesis* 13: 731-735.

1680. Scerpella EG, Villareal AA, Casanova PF, Moreno JN (1996). Primary lymphoma of the liver in AIDS. Report of one new case and review of the literature. *J Clin Gastroenterol* 22: 51-53.

1681. Schafer DF, Sorrell MF (1999). Hepatocellular carcinoma. *Lancet* 353: 1253-1257.

1681A. Schaldenbrand JD, Appelman HD (1984). Solitary solid stromal gastrointestinal tumors in von Recklinghausen's disease with minimal smooth muscle differentiation. *Hum Pathol* 15: 229-232.

1682. Schlemper RJ, Dawsey SM, Itabashi M, Iwashita A, Kato Y, Koike M, Lewin KL, Riddell RH, Shimoda T, Sipponen P, Stolte M, Watanabe H (2000). Differences in diagnostic criteria for esophageal squamous cell carcinoma between Japanese and Western pathologists. *Cancer* 88: 996-1006.

1683. Schlemper RJ, Itabashi M, Kato Y, Lewin KJ, Riddell RH, Shimoda T, Sipponen P, Stolte M, Watanabe H, Takahashi H, Fujita R (1997). Differences in diagnostic criteria for gastric carcinoma between Japanese and western pathologists. *Lancet* 349: 1725-1729.

1684. Schlosnagle DC, Cambell WG, Jr. (1981). The papillary and solid neoplasm of the pancreas: a report of two cases with electron microscopy, one containing neurosecretory granules. *Cancer* 47: 2603-2610.

1685. Schmidt HG, Riddel RH, Walther B, Skinner DB, Riemann JF (1985). Dysplasia in Barrett's esophagus. *J Cancer Res Clin Oncol* 110: 145-152.

1686. Schmutte C, Marinescu RC, Copeland NG, Jenkins NA, Overhauser J, Fishel R (1998). Refined chromosomal localization of the mismatch repair and hereditary nonpolyposis colorectal cancer genes hMSH2 and hMSH6. *Cancer Res* 58: 5023-5026.

1687. Schneider A, Stolte M (1993). Differential diagnosis of adenomas and dysplastic lesions in patients with ulcerative colitis. *Z Gastroenterol* 31: 653-656.

1688. Schneider BG, Pulitzer DR, Brown RD, Prihoda TJ, Bostwick DG, Saldivar V, Rodriguez MH, Gutierrez DM, O'Connell P (1995). Allelic imbalance in gastric cancer: an affected site on chromosome arm 3p. *Genes Chromosomes Cancer* 13: 263-271.

1689. Scholefield JH, Johnson J, Hitchcock A, Kocjan G, Smith PA, Ferryman S, Byass P (1998). Guidelines for anal cytology - to make cytological diagnosis and follow up much more reliable. *Cytopathology* 9: 15-22.

1690. Scholefield JH, Thornton JH, Cuzick J, Northover JM (1990). Anal cancer and marital status. *Br J Cancer* 62: 286-288.

1691. Schrager CA, Schneider D, Gruener AC, Tsou HC, Peacocke M (1998). Clinical and pathological features of breast disease in Cowden's syndrome: an underrecognized syndrome with an increased risk of breast cancer. *Hum Pathol* 29: 47-53.

1692. Schraut WH, Wang CH, Dawson PJ, Block GE (1983). Depth of invasion, location, and size of cancer of the anus dictate operative treatment. *Cancer* 51: 1291-1296.

1693. Schreiner SA, Gorman B, Stephens DH (1998). Chemotherapy-related hepatotoxicity causing imaging findings resembling cirrhosis. *Mayo Clin Proc* 73: 780-783.

1694. Schron DS, Mendelsohn G (1984). Pancreatic carcinoma with duct, endocrine, and acinar differentiation. A histologic, immunocytochemical, and ultrastructural study. *Cancer* 54: 1766-1770.

1695. Schulz W, Hagen C, Hort W (1985). The distribution of liver metastases from colonic cancer. A quantitative postmortem study. *Virchows Arch A Pathol Anat Histopathol* 406: 279-284.

1696. Schussler MH, Skoudy A, Ramaekers F, Real FX (1992). Intermediate filaments as differentiation markers of normal pancreas and pancreas cancer. *Am J Pathol* 140: 559-568.

1697. Schutte M, da-Costa LT, Hahn SA, Moskaluk C, Hoque AT, Rozenblum E, Weinstein CL, Bittner M, Meltzer PS, Trent JM, et a (1995). Identification by representational difference analysis of a homozygous deletion in pancreatic carcinoma that lies within the BRCA2 region. *Proc Natl Acad Sci U S A* 92: 5950-5954.

1698. Schutte M, Hruban RH, Geradts J, Maynard R, Hilgers W, Rabindran SK, Moskaluk CA, Hahn SA, Schwarte W, I, Schmiegel W, Baylin SB, Kern SE, Herman JG (1997). Abrogation of the Rb/p16 tumor-suppressive pathway in virtually all pancreatic carcinomas. *Cancer Res* 57: 3126-3130.

1699. Schwartz S, Yamamoto H, Navarro M, Maestro M, Reventos J, Perucho M (1999). Frameshift mutations at mononucleotide repeats in caspase-5 and other target genes in endometrial and gastrointestinal cancer of the microsatellite mutator phenotype. *Cancer Res* 59: 2995-3002.

1700. Schwarz RE, Klimstra DS, Turnbull AD (1998). Metastatic breast cancer masquerading as gastrointestinal primary. *Am J Gastroenterol* 93: 111-114.

1701. Sclafani LM, Reuter VE, Coit DG, Brennan MF (1991). The malignant nature of the papillary and cystic neoplasm of the pancreas. *Cancer* 68: 153-158.

1702. Scott NA, Bear-RW J, Weiland LH, Cha SS, Lieber MM (1989). Carcinoma of the anal canal and flow cytometric DNA analysis. *Br J Cancer* 60: 56-58.

1703. Scott RJ, Taeschner W, Heinimann K, Muller H, Dobbie Z, Morgenthaler S, Hoffmann F, Peteri B, Meyer UA (1997). Association of extracolonic manifestations of familial adenomatous polyposis with acetylation phenotype in a large FAP kindred. *Eur J Hum Genet* 5: 43-49.

1704. Segal Y, Peissel B, Renieri A, de-Marchi M, Ballabio A, Pei Y, Zhou J (1999). LINE-1 elements at the sites of molecular rearrangements in Alport syndrome-diffuse leiomyomatosis. *Am J Hum Genet* 64: 62-69.

1705. Seidman JD, Elsayed AM, Sobin LH, Tavassoli FA (1993). Association of mucinous tumors of the ovary and appendix. A clinicopathologic study of 25 cases. *Am J Surg Pathol* 17: 22-34.

1706. Seifert E, Schulte F, Stolte M (1992). Adenoma and carcinoma of the duodenum and papilla of Vater: a clinicopathologic study. *Am J Gastroenterol* 87: 37-42.

1707. Seki M, Tsuchiya E, Hori M, Nakagawa K, Ohta H, Ueno M, Takahashi T, Ohashi K, Ishikawa Y, Yanagisawa A (1998). Pancreatic metastasis from a lung cancer. Preoperative diagnosis and management. *Int J Pancreato* 24: 55-59.

1708. Selby DM, Stocker JT, Waclawiw MA, Hitchcock CL, Ishak KG (1994). Infantile hemangioendothelioma of the liver. *Hepatology* 20: 39-45.

1709. Sellner F (1990). Investigations on the significance of the adenoma-carcinoma sequence in the small bowel. *Cancer* 66: 702-715.

1710. Seo IS, Azzarelli B, Warner TF, Goheen MP, Senteney GE (1984). Multiple visceral and cutaneous granular cell tumors. Ultrastructural and immunocytochemical evidence of Schwann cell origin. *Cancer* 53: 2104-2110.

1711. Sequens R (1997). Cancer in the anal canal (transitional zone) after restorative proctocolectomy with stapled ileal pouch-anal anastomosis. *Int J Colorect Dis* 12: 254-255.

1712. Seremetis MG, Lyons WS, deGuzman VC, Peabody-JW J (1976). Leiomyomata of the esophagus. An analysis of 838 cases. *Cancer* 38: 2166-2177.

1713. Seruca R, Santos NR, David L, Constancia M, Barroca H, Carneiro F, Seixas M, Peltomaki P, Lothe R, Sobrinho SM (1995). Sporadic gastric carcinomas with microsatellite instability display a particular clinicopathologic profile. *Int J Cancer* 64: 32-36.

1714. Sessa F, Bonato M, Frigerio B, Capella C, Solcia E, Prat M, Bara J, Samloff IM (1990). Ductal cancers of the pancreas frequently express markers of gastrointestinal epithelial cells. *Gastroenterology* 98: 1655-1665.

1715. Severson RK, Schenk M, Gurney JG, Weiss LK, Demers RY (1996). Increasing incidence of adenocarcinomas and carcinoid tumors of the small intestine in adults. *Cancer Epidemiol Biomarkers Prev* 5: 81-84.

1716. Seymour AB, Hruban RH, Redston M, Caldas C, Powell SM, Kinzler KW, Yeo CJ, Kern SE (1994). Allelotype of pancreatic adenocarcinoma. *Cancer Res* 54: 2761-2764.

1717. Shafford EA, Pritchard J (1993). Extreme thrombocytosis as a diagnostic clue to hepatoblastoma. *Arch Dis Child* 69: 171.

1718. Shah SM, Smart DF, Texter-EC J, Morris WD (1977). Metastatic melanoma of the stomach: the endoscopic and roentgenographic findings and review of the literature. *South Med J* 70: 379-381.

1719. Shank B, Cohen AM, Kelser D (1993). Cancer in the anal canal. In: *Cancer: Principles and Practice of Oncology*. DeVita VT Jr, Hellman S, Rosenberg SA (eds), 4th ed. Lippincott: Philadelphia, PA.

1720. Sharma P, Morales TG, Bhattacharya A, Garewal HS, Sampliner RE (1997). Dysplasia in short-segment Barrett's esophagus: a prospective 3-year follow-up. *Am J Gastroenterol* 92: 2012-2016.

1721. Sharma P, Morales TG, Sampliner RE (1998). Short segment Barrett's esophagus - the need for standardization of the definition and of endoscopic criteria. *Am J Gastroenterol* 93: 1033-1036.

1722. Sharma P, Weston AP, Morales T, Topalovski M, Mayo MS, Sampliner RE (2000). Relative risk of dysplasia for patients with intestinal metaplasia in the distal oesophagus and in the gastric cardia. *Gut* 46: 9-13.

1723. Shashidharan M, Smyrk T, Lin KM, Ternent CA, Thorson AG, Blatchford GJ, Christensen MA, Lynch HT (1999). Histologic comparison of hereditary nonpolyposis colorectal cancer associated with MSH2 and MLH1 and colorectal cancer from the general population. *Dis Colon Rectum* 42: 722-726.

1724. Shaw PA, Pringle JH (1992). The demonstration of a subset of carcinoid tumours of the appendix by in situ hybridization using synthetic probes to proglucagon mRNA. *J Pathol* 167: 375-380.

1725. Shek TW, Ng IO, Chan KW (1993). Inflammatory pseudotumor of the liver. Report of four cases and review of the literature. *Am J Surg Pathol* 17: 231-238.

1726. Shekitka KM, Sobin LH (1994). Ganglioneuromas of the gastrointestinal tract. Relation to Von Recklinghausen disease and other multiple tumor syndromes. *Am J Surg Pathol* 18: 250-257.

1727. Shelton AA, Lehman RE, Schrock TR, Welton ML (1996). Retrospective review of colorectalcancer in ulcerative colitis at a tertiary center. *Archives of Surgery* 131: 806-810.

1728. Shelton NA, Bussey HJR, Jass JR (1987). Epithelial misplacement in Peutz-Jeghers polyps. A diagnostic pitfall. *Am J Surg Pathol* 11: 743-749.

1729. Shepherd NA (1993). Inverted hyperplastic polyposis of the colon. *J Clin Pathol* 46: 56-60.

1730. Shepherd NA (1995). Pouchitis and neoplasia in the pelvic ileal reservoir. *Gastroenterology* 109: 1381-1383.

1731. Shepherd NA, Blackshaw AJ, Hall PA, Bostad L, Coates PJ, Lowe DG, Levison DA, Morson BC, Stansfeld AG (1987). Malignant lymphoma with eosinophilia of the gastrointestinal tract. *Histopathology* 11: 115-130.

1732. Shepherd NA, Hall PA (1990). Epithelial-mesenchymal interactions can influence the phenotype of carcinoma metastases in the mucosa of the intestine. *J Pathol* 160: 103-109.

1733. Shepherd NA, Hall PA, Coates PJ, Levison DA (1988). Primary malignant lymphoma of the colon and rectum. A histopathological and immunohistochemical analysis of 45 cases with clinicopathological correlations. *Histopathology* 12: 235-252.

1734. Shepherd NA, Scholefield JH, Love SB, England J, Northover JM (1990). Prognostic factors in anal squamous carcinoma: a multivariate analysis of clinical, pathological and flow cytometric parameters in 235 cases. *Histopathology* 16: 545-555.

1735. Shepherd T, Tolbert D, Benedetti J, MacDonald J, Stemmerman G, Wiest J, DeVoe GW, Miller MA (2000). Alterations in exon 4 of the p53 gene in gastric cancer. *Gastroenterology*

1736. Sherman SP, Li CY, Carney JA (1979). Microproliferation of enterochromaffin cells and the origin of carcinoid tumors of the ileum: a light microscopic and immunocytochemical study. *Arch Pathol Lab Med* 103: 639-641.

1737. Sheyn I, Noffsinger AE, Heffelfinger S, Davis B, Miller MA, Fenoglio PC (1997). Amplification and expression of the cyclin D1 gene in anal and esophageal squamous cell carcinomas. *Hum Pathol* 28: 270-276.

1738. Shiao YH, Bovo D, Guido M, Capella C, Cassaro M, Busatto G, Russo V, Sidoni A, Parenti AR, Rugge M (1999). Microsatellite instability and/or loss of heterozygosity in young gastric cancer patients in Italy. *Int J Cancer* 82: 59-62.

1739. Shiao YH, Bovo D, Guido M, Capella C, Cassaro M, Busatto G, Russo V, Sidoni A, Parenti AR, Rugge M (1999). Microsatellite instability and/or loss of heterozygosity in young gastric cancer patients in Italy. *Cancer* 82: 59-62.

1740. Shields HM, Zwas F, Antonioli DA, Doos WG, Kim S, Spechler SJ (1993). Detection by scanning electron microscopy of a distinctive esophageal surface cell at the junction of squamous and Barrett's epithelium. *Dig Dis Sci* 38: 97-108.

1741. Shimada HM, Fukayama M, Hayashi Y, Ushijima T, Suzuki M, Hishima T, Funata N, Koike M, Watanabe T (1997). Primary gastric T-cell lymphoma with and without human T-lymphotropic virus type 1. *Cancer* 80: 292-303.

1742. Shimamatsu K, Wanless IR (1997). Role of ischemia in causing apoptosis, atrophy, and nodular hyperplasia in human liver. *Hepatology* 26: 343-350.

1743. Shimaya K, Shiozaki H, Inoue M, Tahara H, Monden T, Shimano T, Mori T (1993). Significance of p53 expression as a prognostic factor in oesophageal squamous cell carcinoma. *Virchows Arch A Pathol Anat Histopathol* 422: 271-276.

1744. Shimizu M, Itoh H, Okumura S, Hashimoto K, Hanioka K, Ohyanagi H, Yamamoto M, Kuroda Y, Tanaka T, Saitoh Y (1989). Papillary hyperplasia of the pancreas. *Hum Pathol* 20: 806-807.

1745. Shimodaira H, Filosi N, Shibata H, Suzuki T, Radice P, Kanamaru R, Friend SH, Kolodner RD, Ishioka C (1998). Functional analysis of human MLH1 mutations in Saccharomyces cerevisiae. *Nat Genet* 19: 384-389.

1746. Shimoyama Y, Gotoh M, Ino Y, Sakamoto M, Kato K, Hirohashi S (1991). Characterization of high-molecular-mass forms of basic fibroblast growth factor produced by hepatocellular carcinoma cells: possible involvement of basic fibroblast growth factor in hepatocarcinogenesis. *Jpn J Cancer Res* 82: 1263-1270.

1747. Shinagawa T, Tadokoro M, Maeyama S, Maeda C, Yamaguchi S, Morohoshi T, Ishikawa E (1995). Alpha fetoprotein-producing acinar cell carcinoma of the pancreas showing multiple lines of differentiation. *Virchows Arch* 426: 419-423.

1748. Shinozaki H, Ozawa S, Ando N, Tsuruta H, Terada M, Ueda M, Kitajima M (1996). Cyclin D1 amplification as a new predictive classification for squamous cell carcinoma of the esophagus, adding gene information. *Clin Cancer Res* 2: 1155-1161.

1749. Shirai Y, Wakai T, Ohtani T, Sakai Y, Tsukada K, Hatakeyama K (1996). Colorectal carcinoma metastases to the liver. Does primary tumor location affect its lobar distribution? *Cancer* 77: 2213-2216.

1750. Shiu MH, Farr GH, Papachristou DN, Hajdu SI (1982). Myosarcomas of the stomach: natural history, prognostic factors and management. *Cancer* 49: 177-187.

1751. Sho M, Nakajima Y, Kanehiro H, Hisanaga M, Nishio M, Nagao M, Ikeda N, Kanokogi H, Yamada T, Nakano H (1998). Pattern of recurrence after resection for intraductal papillary mucinous tumors of the pancreas. *World J Surg* 22: 874-878.

1752. Shorten SD, Hart WR, Petras RE (1986). Microcystic adenomas (serous cystadenomas) of pancreas. A clinicopathologic investigation of eight cases with immunohistochemical and ultrastructural studies. *Am J Surg Pathol* 10: 365-372.

1753. Shtutman M, Zhurinsky J, Simcha I, Albanese C, D'Amico M, Pestell R, Ben-Ze'ev A (1999). The cyclin D1 gene is a target of the beta-catenin/LEF-1 pathway. *Proc Natl Acad Sci U S A* 96: 5522-5527.

1754. Siegal A, Swartz A (1986). Malignant carcinoid of oesophagus. *Histopathology* 10: 761-765.

1755. Siersema PD, ten-Kate FJ, Mulder PG, Wilson JH (1992). Hepatocellular carcinoma in porphyria cutanea tarda: frequency and factors related to its occurrence. *Liver* 12: 56-61.

1756. Siewert JR, Stein HJ (1998). Classification of adenocarcinoma of the oesophagogastric junction. *Br J Surg* 85: 1457-1459.

1757. Sigel JE, Petras RE, Lashner BA, Fazio VW, Goldblum JR (1999). Intestinal adenocarcinoma in Crohn's disease: a report of 30 cases with a focus on coexisting dysplasia. *Am J Surg Pathol* 23: 651-655.

1758. Silverman JF, Holbrook CT, Pories WJ, Kodroff MB, Joshi VV (1990). Fine needle aspiration cytology of pancreatoblastoma with immunocytochemical and ultrastructural studies. *Acta Cytol* 34: 632-640.

1759. Simon D, Knowles BB, Weith A (1991). Abnormalities of chromosome 1 and loss of heterozygosity on 1p in primary hepatomas. *Oncogene* 6: 765-770.

1760. Simpson EL, Dalinka MK (1985). Association of hypertrophic osteoarthropathy with gastrointestinal polyposis. *AJR Am J Roentgenol* 144: 983-984.

1761. Sin IC, Ling ET, Prentice RS (1980). Burkitt's lymphoma of the appendix: report of two cases. *Hum Pathol* 11: 465-470.

1762. Sircar K, Hewlett BR, Huizinga JD, Chorneyko K, Berezin I, Riddell RH (1999). Interstitial cells of Cajal as precursors of gastrointestinal stromal tumors. *Am J Surg Pathol* 23: 377-389.

1763. Sitzmann JV, Coleman J, Pitt HA, Zerhouni E, Fishman E, Kaufman SL, Order S, Grochow LB, Cameron JL (1990). Preoperative assessment of malignant hepatic tumors. *Am J Surg* 159: 137-142.

1764. Sjoblom SM (1988). Clinical presentation and prognosis of gastrointestinal carcinoid tumours. *Scand J Gastroenterol* 23: 779-787.

1765. Slater G, Greenstein A, Aufses-AH J (1984). Anal carcinoma in patients with Crohn's disease. *Ann Surg* 199: 348-350.

1766. Slattery ML, Potter JD, Samowitz W, Schaffer D, Leppert M (1999). Methylenetetrahydrofolate reductase, diet, and risk of colon cancer. *Cancer Epidemiol Biomarkers Prev* 8: 513-518.

1767. Smiley D, Goldberg RI, Phillips RS, Barkin JS (1988). Anal metastasis from colorectal carcinoma. *Am J Gastroenterol* 83: 460-462.

1768. Smith DP, Spicer J, Smith A, Swift S, Ashworth A (1999). The mouse Peutz-Jeghers syndrome gene LKB1 encodes a nuclear protein kinase. *Hum Mol Genet* 8: 1479-1485.

1769. Smith JW, Kemeny N, Caldwell C, Banner P, Sigurdson E, Huvos A (1992). Pseudomyxoma peritonei of appendiceal origin. The Memorial Sloan-Kettering Cancer Center experience. *Cancer* 70: 396-401.

1770. Smith RR, Hamilton SR, Boitnott JK, Rogers EL (1984). The spectrum of carcinoma arising in Barrett's esophagus. A clinicopathologic study of 26 patients. *Am J Surg Pathol* 8: 563-573.

1771. Soares TF, Queiroz DM, Mendes EN, Rocha GF, Oliveira AMR, Cabral MM, de Oliveira CA (1998). The interrelationship between Helicobacter pylori vacuolating cytotoxin and gastric carcinoma. *Am J Gastroenterol* 93: 1841-1847.

1772. Sobesky R, Duclos VJ, Prat F, Pelletier G, Encaoua R, Boige V, Fritsch J, Castera L, Bedossa P, Buffet C (1997). Acute pancreatitis revealing diffuse infiltration of the pancreas by melanoma. *Pancreas* 15: 213-215.

1773. Sobin LH (1985). Inverted hyperplastic polyps of the colon. *Am J Surg Pathol* 9: 265-272.

1774. Sobin LH (1991). WHO: Histological Typing of Tumours of the Gallbladder and Extrahepatic Bile Ducts. 2nd ed, Springer-Verlag: Berlin.

1775. Soga J, Tazawa K (1971). Pathologic analysis of carcinoids. Histologic reevaluation of 62 cases. *Cancer* 28: 990-998.

1776. Soini Y, Welsh JA, Ishak KG, Bennett WP (1995). p53 mutations in primary hepatic angiosarcomas not associated with vinyl chloride exposure. *Carcinogenesis* 16: 2879-2881.

1777. Solcia E, Bordi C, Creutzfeldt W, Dayal Y, Dayan AD, Falkmer S, Grimelius L, Havu N (1988). Histopathological classification of nonantral gastric endocrine growths in man. *Digestion* 41: 185-200.

1778. Solcia E, Capella C, Buffa R, Usellini L, Frigerio B, Fontana P (1979). Endocrine cells of the gastrointestinal tract and related tumors. *Pathobiol Annu* 9: 163-204.

1779. Solcia E, Capella C, Fiocca R, Rindi G, Rosai J (1990). Gastric argyrophil carcinoidosis in patients with Zollinger-Ellison syndrome due to type 1 multiple endocrine neoplasia. A newly recognized association. *Am J Surg Pathol* 14: 503-513.

1780. Solcia E, Capella C, Fiocca R, Sessa F, La-Rosa S, Rindi G (1998). Disorders of the endocrine system. In: *Pathology of the gastrointestinal tract*, Ming SC, Goldman H (eds), 2nd ed. Williams&Wilkins: Baltimore.

1781. Solcia E, Capella C, Kloppel G (1997). Tumours of the Pancreas. AFIP: Washington, D.C.

1782. Solcia E, Capella C, Sessa F, Rindi G, Cornaggia M, Riva C, Villani L (1986). Gastric carcinoids and related endocrine growths. *Digestion* 35 Suppl 1: 3-22.

1783. Solcia E, Fiocca R, Rindi G, Villani L, Cornaggia M, Capella C (1992). The pathology of the gastrointestinal endocrine system. *Endocrinol Metab Clin North Am* 22: 795-821.

1784. Solcia E, Kloppel G, Sobin LH (2000). WHO: Histological Typing of Endocrine Tumours. Springer: Berlin - New York.

1785. Solcia E, Rindi G, Fiocca R, Villani L, Buffa R, Ambrosiani L, Capella C (1992). Distinct patterns of chronic gastritis associated with carcinoid and cancer and their role in tumorigenesis. *Yale J Biol Med* 65: 793-804.

1786. Sommers SC, Meissner WA (1954). Unusual carcinomas of the pancreas. *Arch Pathol* 58: 101-111.

1787. Songsivilai S, Dharakul T, Kanistanon D (1996). Hepatitis C virus genotypes in patients with hepatocellular carcinoma and cholangiocarcinoma in Thailand. *Trans R Soc Trop Med Hyg* 90: 505-507.

1788. Songun I, van d, V, Arends JW, Blok P, Grond AJ, Offerhaus GJ, Hermans J, Van-Krieken JH (1999). Classification of gastric carcinoma using the Goseki system provides prognostic information additional to TNM staging. *Cancer* 85: 2114-2118.

1789. Sons HU, Borchard F (1984). Esophageal cancer. Autopsy findings in 171 cases. *Arch Pathol Lab Med* 108: 983-988.

1790. Sons HU, Borchard F (1986). Cancer of the distal esophagus and cardia. Incidence, tumorous infiltration, and metastatic spread. *Ann Surg* 203: 188-195.

1791. Soule JC, Potet F, Mignon FC, Julien M, Bader JP (1976). [Zollinger-Ellison syndrome due to a gastric gastrinoma]. *Arch Fr Mal App Dig* 65: 215-225.

1792. Southern JF, Warshaw AL, Lewandrowski KB (1996). DNA ploidy analysis of mucinous cystic tumors of the pancreas. Correlation of aneuploidy with malignancy and poor prognosis. *Cancer* 77: 58-62.

1793. Souza RF, Appel R, Yin J, Wang S, Smolinski KN, Abraham JM, Zou TT, Shi YQ, Lei J, Cottrell J, Cymes K, Biden K, Simms L, Leggett B, Lynch PM, Frazier M, Powell SM, Harpaz N, Sugimura H, Young J, Meltzer SJ (1996). Microsatellite instability in the insulin-like growth factor II receptor gene in gastrointestinal tumours. *Nat Genet* 14: 255-257.

1794. Soweid AM, Zachary PE, Jr. (1996). Mucosa-associated lymphoid tissue lymphoma of the oesophagus. *Lancet* 348: 268-268.

1795. Soyer P, Bluemke DA, Hruban RH, Sitzmann JV, Fishman EK (1994). Hepatic metastases from colorectal cancer: detection and false-positive findings with helical CT during arterial portography. *Radiology* 193: 71-74.

1796. Soyer P, Levesque M, Elias D, Zeitoun G, Roche A (1992). Detection of liver metastases from colorectal cancer: comparison of intraoperative US and CT during arterial portography. *Radiology* 183: 541-544.

1797. Spechler SJ (1999). The role of gastric carditis in metaplasia and neoplasia at the gastroesophageal junction. *Gastroenterology* 117: 218-228.

1798. Spechler SJ, Goyal RK (1986). Barrett's esophagus. *N Engl J Med* 315: 362-371.

1799. Spechler SJ, Goyal RK (1996). The columnar-lined esophagus, intestinal metaplasia, and Norman Barrett. *Gastroenterology* 110: 614-621.

1800. Spechler SJ, Zeroogian JM, Antonioli DA, Wang HH, Goyal RK (1994). Prevalence of metaplasia at the gastro-oesophageal junction. *Lancet* 344: 1533-1536.

1801. Spence RW, Burns CC (1975). ACTH-secreting 'apudoma' of gallbladder. *Gut* 16: 473-476.

1802. Spencer J, Cerf BN, Jarry A, Brousse N, Guy GD, Krajewski AS, Isaacson PG (1988). Enteropathy-associated T cell lymphoma (malignant histiocytosis of the intestine) is recognized by a monoclonal antibody (HML-1) that defines a membrane molecule on human mucosal lymphocytes. *Am J Pathol* 132: 1-5.

1803. Spencer J, Diss TC, Isaacson PG (1989). Primary B cell gastric lymphoma. A genotypic analysis. *Am J Pathol* 135: 557-564.

1804. Sperti C, Pasquali C, Pedrazzoli S, Guolo P, Liessi G (1997). Expression of mucin-like carcinoma-associated antigen in the cyst fluid differentiates mucinous from nonmucinous pancreatic cysts. *Am J Gastroenterol* 92: 672-675.

1805. Spigelman AD, Crofton SC, Venitt S, Phillips RK (1990). Mutagenicity of bile and duodenal adenomas in familial adenomatous polyposis. *Br J Surg* 77: 878-881.

1806. Spigelman AD, Farmer KC, James M, Richman PI, Phillips RK (1991). Tumours of the liver, bile ducts, pancreas and duodenum in a single patient with familial adenomatous polyposis. *Br J Surg* 78: 979-980.

1807. Spigelman AD, Murday V, Phillips RK (1989). Cancer and Peutz-Jeghers syndrome. *Gut* 30: 1588-1590.

1808. Spigelman AD, Talbot IC, Penna C, Nugent KP, Phillips RK, Costello C, DeCosse JJ (1994). Evidence for adenoma-carcinoma sequence in the duodenum of patients with familial adenomatous polyposis. The Leeds Castle Polyposis Group (Upper Gastrointestinal Committee). *J Clin Pathol* 47: 709-710.

1809. Spigelman AD, Williams CB, Talbot IC, Domizio P, Phillips RK (1989). Upper gastrointestinal cancer in patients with familial adenomatous polyposis. *Lancet* 2: 783-785.

1810. Spirio L, Olschwang S, Groden J, Robertson M, Samowitz W, Joslyn G, Gelbert L, Thliveris A, Carlson M, Otterud B (1993). Alleles of the APC gene: an attenuated form of familial polyposis. *Cell* 75: 951-957.

1811. Spirio LN, Samowitz W, Robertson J, Robertson M, Burt RW, Leppert M, White R (1998). Alleles of APC modulate the frequency and classes of mutations that lead to colon polyps. *Nat Genet* 20: 385-388.

1812. Sreekantaiah C, Ladanyi M, Rodriguez E, Chaganti RS (1994). Chromosomal aberrations in soft tissue tumors. Relevance to diagnosis, classification, and molecular mechanisms. *Am J Pathol* 144: 1121-1134.

1813. St Martin MC, Chejfec G (1999). Barrett esophagus-associated small cell carcinoma. *Arch Pathol Lab Med* 123: 1123.

1814. Stambolic V, Suzuki A, de-la-Pompa JL, Brothers GM, Mirtsos C, Sasaki T, Ruland J, Penninger JM, Siderovski DP, Mak TW (1998). Negative regulation of PKB/Akt-dependent cell survival by the tumor suppressor PTEN. *Cell* 95: 29-39.

1815. Stamm B, Burger H, Hollinger A (1987). Acinar cell cystadenocarcinoma of the pancreas. *Cancer* 60: 2542-2547.

1816. Stamm B, Hedinger CE, Saremaslani P (1986). Duodenal and ampullary carcinoid tumors. A report of 12 cases with pathological characteristics, polypeptide content and relation to the MEN I syndrome and von Recklinghausen's disease (neurofibromatosis). *Virchows Arch A Pathol Anat Histopathol* 408: 475-489.

1817. Stangl R, Altendorf HA, Charnley RM, Scheele J (1994). Factors influencing the natural history of colorectal liver metastases. *Lancet* 343: 1405-1410.

1818. Stanley MW, Cherwitz D, Hagen K, Snover DC (1986). Neuromas of the appendix. A light-microscopic, immunohistochemical and electron-microscopic study of 20 cases. *Am J Surg Pathol* 10: 801-815.

1819. Starink TM, van d, V, Arwert F, de-Waal LP, de-Lange GG, Gille JJ, Eriksson AW (1986). The Cowden syndrome: a clinical and genetic study in 21 patients. *Clin Genet* 29: 222-233.

1820. Steck PA, Pershouse MA, Jasser SA, Yung WK, Lin H, Ligon AH, Langford LA, Baumgard ML, Hattier T, Davis T, Frye C, Hu R, Swedlund B, Teng DH, Tavtigian SV (1997). Identification of a candidate tumour suppressor gene, MMAC1, at chromosome 10q23.3 that is mutated in multiple advanced cancers. *Nat Genet* 15: 356-362.

1821. Steele G, Bleday R, Mayer RJ, Lindblad A, Petrelli N, Weaver D (1991). A prospective evaluation of hepatic resection for colorectal carcinoma metastases to the liver: Gastrointestinal Tumor Study Group Protocol 6584. *J Clin Oncol* 9: 1105-1112.

1822. Stein A, Sova Y, Almalah I, Lurie A (1996). The appendix as a metastatic target for male urogenital tumours. *Br J Urol* 78: 647-648.

1823. Stein HJ, Barlow AP, DeMeester TR, Hinder RA (1992). Complications of gastroesophageal reflux disease. Role of the lower esophageal sphincter, esophageal acid and acid/alkaline exposure, and duodenogastric reflux. *Ann Surg* 216: 35-43.

1824. Stein HJ, Hoeft S, DeMeester TR (1993). Functional foregut abnormalities in Barrett's esophagus. *J Thorac Cardiovasc Surg* 105: 107-111.

1825. Stein HJ, Kauer WK, Feussner H, Siewert JR (1998). Bile reflux in benign and malignant Barrett's esophagus: effect of medical acid suppression and nissen fundoplication. *J Gastrointest Surg* 2: 333-341.

1826. Stein HJ, Panel of Experts (1996). Esophageal cancer: screening and surveillanc. Results of a consensus conference. *Dis Esophagus* 9, Suppl 1: 3-19.

1827. Stein HJ, Siewert JR (1993). Barret's esophagus: pathogenesis, epidemiology, functional abnormalities, malignant degeneration and surgical management. *Dysphagia* 8: 276-288.

1828. Steiner PE, Higginson J (1959). Cholangiocellular carcinoma of the liver. *Cancer* 12: 753-759.

1829. Stemmermann GN (1994). Intestinal metaplasia of the stomach. A status report. *Cancer* 74: 556-564.

1830. Stemmermann GN, Goodman MT, Nomura AM (1992). Adenocarcinoma of the proximal small intestine. A marker for familial and multicentric cancer? *Cancer* 70: 2766-2771.

1831. Stemper TJ, Kent TH, Summers RW (1975). Juvenile polyposis and gastrointestinal carcinoma. A study of a kindred. *Ann Intern Med* 83: 639-646.

1832. Stephens M, Williams GT, Jasani B, Williams ED (1987). Synchronous duodenal neuroendocrine tumours in von Recklinghausen's disease - a case report of co-existing gangliocytic paraganglioma and somatostatin-rich glandular carcinoid. *Histopathology* 11: 1331-1340.

1833. Stephenson CA, Kletzel M, Seibert JJ, Glasier CM (1990). Pancreatoblastoma: MR appearance. *J Comput Assist Tomogr* 14: 492-493.

1834. Stevens HP, Kelsell DP, Bryant SP, Bishop DT, Spurr NK, Weissenbach J, Marger D, Marger RS, Leigh IM (1996). Linkage of an American pedigree with palmoplantar keratoderma and malignancy (palmoplantar ectodermal dysplasia type III) to 17q24. Literature survey and proposed updated classification of the keratodermas. *Arch Dermatol* 132: 640-651.

1835. Stewenius J, et al (1995). Incidence of colorectal cancer and all cause mortality in non-selected patients with ulcerative colitis and indeterminate colitis in Malmo, Sweden. *Int J Colorectal Dis* 10: 117-122.

1836. Stinner B, Kisker O, Zielke A, Rothmund M (1996). Surgical management for carcinoid tumors of small bowel, appendix, colon, and rectum. *World J Surg* 20: 183-188.

1837. Stocker JT (1998). An approach to handling pediatric liver tumors. *Am J Clin Pathol* 109: S67-S72.

1838. Stocker JT, Conran R (1997). Hepatoblastoma. In: *Liver Cancer*, Okuda K, Tabor E (eds), Churchill Livingstone: New York.

1839. Stocker JT, Conran R, Selby D (1998). Tumor and Pseudotumors of the Liver. In: *Pathology of Solid Tumors in Children*, Stocker J, Askin F (eds), Chapman & Hall: London.

1840. Stocker JT, Ishak KG (1978). Undifferentiated (embryonal) sarcoma of the liver: report of 31 cases. *Cancer* 42: 336-348.

1841. Stocker JT, Ishak KG (1983). Mesenchymal hamartoma of the liver: report of 30 cases and review of the literature. *Pediatr Pathol* 1: 245-267.

1842. Stolte M, Kroher G, Meining A, Morgner A, Bayerdorffer E, Bethke B (1997). A comparison of Helicobacter pylori and H. heilmannii gastritis. A matched control study involving 404 patients. *Scand J Gastroenterol* 32: 28-33.

1843. Stolte M, Sticht T, Eidt S, Ebert D, Finkenzeller G (1994). Frequency, location, and age and sex distribution of various types of gastric polyp. *Endoscopy* 26: 659-665.

1844. Stommer P, Kraus J, Stolte M, Giedl J (1991). Solid and cystic pancreatic tumors. Clinical, histochemical, and electron microscopic features in ten cases. *Cancer* 67: 1635-1641.

1845. Strodel WE, Talpos G, Eckhauser F, Thompson N (1983). Surgical therapy for small-bowel carcinoid tumors. *Arch Surg* 118: 391-397.

1846. Stromeyer FW, Ishak KG, Gerber MA, Mathew T (1980). Ground-glass cells in hepatocellular carcinoma. *Am J Clin Pathol* 74: 254-258.

1847. Stubbe Teglbjaerg P, Vetner M (2000). Gastric carcinoma I. The reproducibility of a histogenetic classification proposed by Masson, Rember and Mulligan. *Acta Pathol Microbiol Scand* 85: 519-527.

1848. Sturm PD, Baas IO, Clement MJ, Nakeeb A, Johan G, Offerhaus A, Hruban RH, Pitt HA (1998). Alterations of the p53 tumor-suppressor gene and K-ras oncogene in perihilar cholangiocarcinomas from a high-incidence area. *Int J Cancer* 78: 695-698.

1849. Su CH, Shyr YM, Lui WY, P'Eng FK (1997). Hepatolithiasis associated with cholangiocarcinoma. *Br J Surg* 84: 969-973.

1850. Su GH, Hilgers W, Shekher MC, Tang DJ, Yeo CJ, Hruban RH, Kern SE (1998). Alterations in pancreatic, biliary, and breast carcinomas support MKK4 as a genetically targeted tumor suppressor gene. *Cancer Res* 58: 2339-2342.

1851. Su GH, Hruban RH, Bansal RK, Bova GS, Tang DJ, Shekher MC, Westerman AM, Entius MM, Goggins M, Yeo CJ, Kern SE (1999). Germline and somatic mutations of the STK11/LKB1 Peutz-Jeghers gene in pancreatic and biliary cancer. *Am J Pathol* 154: 1835-1840.

1852. Su JY, Erikson E, Maller JL (1996). Cloning and characterization of a novel serine/threonine protein kinase expressed in early Xenopus embryos. *J Biol Chem* 271: 14430-14437.

1853. Suduca P (1994). [Malignant epidermoid tumors of the anus. Etiopathogenesis and clinical aspects]. *Ann Gastroenterol Hepatol Paris* 30: 189-191.

1854. Sugarbaker PH (1994). Pseudomyxoma peritonei. A cancer whose biology is characterized by a redistribution phenomenon. *Ann Surg* 219: 109-111.

1855. Sugarbaker TA, Chang D, Koslowe P, Sugarbaker PH (1996). Patterns of spread of recurrent intraabdominal sarcoma. *Cancer Treat Res* 82: 65-77.

1856. Sugaya Y, Sugaya H, Kuronuma Y, Hisauchi T, Harada T (1989). A case of gallbladder carcinoma producing both alphafetoprotein (AFP) and carcinoembryonic antigen (CEA). *Gastroenterol Jpn* 24: 325-331.

1857. Sugihara S, Kojiro M (1987). Pathology of cholangiocarcinoma. In: *Neoplasms of the Liver*, Okuda K, Ishak KG (eds), Springer-Verlag: Tokyo.

1858. Sugimachi K, Matsuura H, Kai H, Kanematsu T, Inokuchi K, Jingu K (1986). Prognostic factors of esophageal carcinoma: univariate and multivariate analyses. *J Surg Oncol* 31: 108-112.

1859. Sugitani S, Sakamoto M, Ichida T, Genda T, Asakura H, Hirohashi S (1998). Hyperplastic foci reflect the risk of multicentric development of human hepatocellular carcinoma. *J Hepatol* 28: 1045-1053.

1860. Sugiyama M, Atomi Y (1999). Extrapancreatic neoplasms occur with unusual frequency in patients with intraductal papillary mucinous tumors of the pancreas. *Am J Gastroenterol* 94: 470-473.

1861. Sugo H, Takamori S, Kojima K, Beppu T, Futagawa S (1999). The significance of p53 mutations as an indicator of the biological behavior of recurrent hepatocellular carcinomas. *Surg Today* 29(9): 849-855.

1862. Sun K, Zhang X, Zhang D, Huang G, Wang L (1996). Prognostic significance of lymph node metastasis in surgical resection of esophageal cancer. *Chin Med J Engl* 109: 89-92.

1863. Sun L, Hui AM, Kanai Y, Sakamoto M, Hirohashi S (1997). Increased DNA methyltransferase expression is associated with an early stage of human hepatocarcinogenesis. *Jpn J Cancer Res* 88: 1165-1170.

1864. Sun Z, Lu P, Gail MH, Pee D, Zhang Q, Ming L, Wang J, Wu Y, Liu G, Zhu Y (1999). Increased risk of hepatocellular carcinoma in male hepatitis B surface antigen carriers with chronic hepatitis who have detectable urinary aflatoxin metabolite M1. *Hepatology* 30: 379-383.

1865. Sunlder F, Eriksson B, Grimelius L, Hakanson R, Lonroth H, Lundell L (1992). Histamine in gastric carcinoid tumors: immunocytochemical evidence. *Endocr Pathol* 3: 23-27.

1866. Suster S (1996). Gastrointestinal stromal tumors. *Semin Diagn Pathol* 13: 297-313.

1867. Suster S, Huszar M, Herczeg E, Bubis JJ (1987). Adenosquamous carcinoma of the gallbladder with spindle cell features. A light microscopic and immunocytochemical study of a case. *Histopathology* 11: 209-214.

1868. Suzuki A, de-la-Pompa JL, Stambolic V, Elia AJ, Sasaki T, del BB, I, Ho A, Wakeham A, Itie A, Khoo W, Fukumoto M, Mak TW (1998). High cancer susceptibility and embryonic lethality associated with mutation of the PTEN tumor suppressor gene in mice. *Curr Biol* 8: 1169-1178.

1869. Suzuki K, Hayashi N, Miyamoto Y, Yamamoto M, Ohkawa K, Ito Y, Sasaki Y, Yamaguchi Y, Nakase H, Noda K, Enomoto N, Arai K, Yamada Y, Yoshihara H, Tujimura T, Kawano K, Yoshikawa K, Kamada T (1996). Expression of vascular permeability factor/vascular endothelial growth factor in human hepatocellular carcinoma. *Cancer Res* 56: 3004-3009.

1870. Swanson PE, Dykoski D, Wick MR, Snover DC (1986). Primary duodenal smallcell neuroendocrine carcinoma with production of vasoactive intestinal polypeptide. *Arch Pathol Lab Med* 110: 317-320.

1871. Szych C, Staebler A, Connolly DC, Wu R, Cho KR, Ronnett BM (1999). Molecular genetic evidence supporting the clonality and appendiceal origin of Pseudomyxoma peritonei in women. *Am J Pathol* 154: 1849-1855.

1872. Taal BG, den-Hartog-Jager FC, Steinmetz R, Peterse H (1992). The spectrum of gastrointestinal metastases of breast carcinoma: I. Stomach. *Gastrointest Endosc* 38: 130-135.

1873. Tachibana M, Kinugasa S, Dhar DK, Tabara H, Masunaga R, Kotoh T, Kubota H, Nagasue N (1999). Prognostic factors in T1 and T2 squamous cell carcinoma of the thoracic esophagus. *Arch Surg* 134: 50-54.

1874. Tachibana M, Yoshimura H, Kinugasa S, Hashimoto N, Dhar DK, Abe S, Monden N, Nagasue N (1999). Clinicopathological features of superficial squamous cell carcinoma of the esophagus. *Am J Surg* 174: 49-53.

1875. Tada M, Ohashi M, Shiratori Y, Okudaira T, Komatsu Y, Kawabe T, Yoshida H, Machinami R, Kishi K, Omata M (1996). Analysis of K-ras gene mutation in hyperplastic duct cells of the pancreas without pancreatic disease. *Gastroenterology* 110: 227-231.

1876. Tada M, Omata M, Kawai S, Saisho H, Ohto M, Saiki RK, Sninsky JJ (1993). Detection of ras gene mutations in pancreatic juice and peripheral blood of patients with pancreatic adenocarcinoma. *Cancer Res* 53: 2472-2474.

1877. Tada M, Omata M, Ohto M (1991). Ras gene mutations in intraductal papillary neoplasms of the pancreas. Analysis in five cases. *Cancer* 67: 634-637.

1878. Tada M, Omata M, Ohto M (1992). High incidence of ras gene mutation in intrahepatic cholangiocarcinoma. *Cancer* 69: 1115-1118.

1879. Tahara E, Semba S, Tahara H (1996). Molecular biological observations in gastric cancer. *Semin Oncol* 23: 307-315.

1880. Takada M, Yamamoto M, Saitoh Y (1994). The significance of CD44 in human pancreatic cancer: II. The role of CD44 in human pancreatic adenocarcinoma invasion. *Pancreas* 9: 753-757.

1881. Takahashi H, Shikata N, Senzaki H, Shintaku M, Tsubura A (1995). Immunohistochemical staining patterns of keratins in normal oesophageal epithelium and carcinoma of the oesophagus. *Histopathology* 26: 45-50.

1882. Takayama T, Makuuchi M, Hirohashi S, Sakamoto M, Okazaki N, Takayasu K, Kosuge T, Motoo Y, Yamazaki S, Hasegawa H (1990). Malignant transformation of adenomatous hyperplasia to hepatocellular carcinoma. *Lancet* 336: 1150-1153.

1883. Takayasu K, Wakao F, Moriyama N, Muramatsu Y, Sakamoto M, Hirohashi S, Makuuchi M, Kosuge T, Takayama T, Yamazaki S (1993). Response of early-stage hepatocellular carcinoma and borderline lesions to therapeutic arterial embolization. *AJR Am J Roentgenol* 160: 301-306.

1884. Takeda S, Nakao A, Ichihara T, Suzuki Y, Nonami T, Harada A, Koshikawa T, Takagi H (1991). Serum concentration and immunohistochemical localization of SPan-1 antigen in pancreatic cancer. A comparison with CA19-9 antigen. *Hepatogastroenterology* 38: 143-148.

1885. Takei K, Watanabe H, Itoi T, Saitoh T (1996). p53 and Ki-67 immunoreactivity and nuclear morphometry of 'carcinoma in adenoma' and adenoma of the gallbladder. *Pathol Int* 46: 908-917.

1886. Takeuchi H, Ozawa S, Ando N, Shih CH, Koyanagi K, Ueda M, Kitajima M (1997). Altered p16/MTS1/CDKN2 and cyclin D1/PRAD-1 gene expression is associated with the prognosis of squamous cell carcinoma of the esophagus. *Clin Cancer Res* 3: 2229-2236.

1887. Takubo K, Nakamura K, Sawabe M, Arai T, Esaki Y, Miyashita M, Mafune K, Tanaka Y, Sasajima K (1999). Primary undifferentiated small cell carcinoma of the esophagus. *Hum Pathol* 30: 216-221.

1888. Talbot IC, Neoptolemos JP, Shaw DE, Carr LD (1988). The histopathology and staging of carcinoma of the ampulla of Vater. *Histopathology* 12: 155-165.

1889. Talley NJ, Cameron AJ, Shorter RG, Zinsmeister AR, Phillips SF (1988). Campylobacter pylori and Barrett's esophagus. *Mayo Clin Proc* 63: 1176-1180.

1890. Tam PC, Siu KF, Cheung HC, Ma L, Wong J (1987). Local recurrences after subtotal esophagectomy for squamous cell carcinoma. *Ann Surg* 205: 189-194.

1891. Tamura G, Ogasawara S, Nishizuka S, Sakata K, Maesawa C, Suzuki Y, Terashima M, Saito K, Satodate R (1996). Two distinct regions of deletion on the long arm of chromosome 5 in differentiated adenocarcinomas of the stomach. *Cancer Res* 56: 612-615.

1892. Tamura M, Gu J, Matsumoto K, Aota S, Parsons R, Yamada KM (1998). Inhibition of cell migration, spreading, and focal adhesions by tumor suppressor PTEN. *Science* 280: 1614-1617.

1893. Tanaka H, Hiyama T, Okubo Y, Kitada A, Fujimoto I (1994). Primary liver cancer incidence-rates related to hepatitis-C virus infection: a correlational study in Osaka, Japan. *Cancer Causes Control* 5: 61-65.

1894. Tanaka M, Nakashima O, Wada Y, Kage M, Kojiro M (1996). Pathomorphological study of Kupffer cells in hepatocellular carcinoma and hyperplastic nodular lesions in the liver. *Hepatology* 24: 807-812.

1895. Tanaka Y, Ijiri R, Yamanaka S, Kato K, Nishihira H, Nishi T, Misugi K (1998). Pancreatoblastoma: optically clear nuclei in squamoid corpuscles are rich in biotin. *Mod Pathol* 11: 945-949.

1896. Tang LH, Modlin IM, Lawton GP, Kidd M, Chinery R (1996). The role of transforming growth factor alpha in the enterochromaffin-like cell tumor autonomy in an African rodent mastomys. *Gastroenterology* 111: 1212-1223.

1897. Tang WY, Elnatan J, Lee YS, Goh HS, Smith DR (1999). c-Ki-ras mutations in colorectal adenocarcinomas from a country with a rapidly changing colorectal cancer incidence. *Br J Cancer* 81: 237-241.

1898. Tanimura A, Yamamoto H, Shibata H, Sano E (1979). Carcinoma in heterotopic gastric pancreas. *Acta Pathol Jpn* 29: 251-257.

1899. Tanimura M, Matsui I, Abe J, Ikeda H, Kobayashi N, Ohira M, Yokoyama M, Kaneko M (1998). Increased risk of hepatoblastoma among immature children with a lower birth weight. *Cancer Res* 58: 3032-3035.

1900. Tantachamrun T, Borvonsombat S, Theetranont C (1979). Gardner's syndrome associated with adenomatous polyp of gall bladder: report of a case. *J Med Assoc Thai* 62: 441-447.

1901. Tanum G, Holm R (1996). Anal carcinoma: a clinical approach to p53 and RB gene proteins. *Oncology* 53: 369-373.

1902. Tarao K, Hoshino H, Shimizu A, Ohkawa S, Nakamura Y, Harada M, Ito Y, Tamai S, Akaike M, Sugimasa Y, et al (1994). Role of increased DNA synthesis activity of hepatocytes in multicentric hepatocarcinogenesis in residual liver of hepatectomized cirrhotic patients with hepatocellular carcinoma. *Jpn J Cancer Res* 85: 1040-1044.

1903. Tatsuta M, Iishi H, Okuda S, Taniguchi H (1985). Early adenocarcinoma of the gastric cardia. *Oncology* 42: 232-235.

1904. Taxy JB, Battifora H (1988). Angiosarcoma of the gastrointestinal tract. A report of three cases. *Cancer* 62: 210-216.

1905. Taylor BA, Williams GT, Hughes LE, Rhodes J (1989). The histology of skin tags in Crohn's disease: an aid to confirmation of the diagnosis. *Int J Colorectal Dis* 4: 197-199.

1906. Taylor RS, Foster GR, Arora S, Hargreaves S, Thomas HC (1997). Increase in primary liver cancer in the UK, 1979-94. *Lancet* 350: 1142-1143.

1907. Teh M, Wee A, Raju GC (1994). An immunohistochemical study of p53 protein in gallbladder and extrahepatic bile duct/ampullary carcinomas. *Cancer* 74: 1542-1545.

1908. Temellini F, Bavosi M, Lamarra M, Quagliarini P, Giuliani F (1989). Pancreatic metastasis 25 years after nephrectomy for renal cancer. *Tumori* 75: 503-504.

1909. Templeton AC (1973). Tumours in a Tropical Country. Springer-Verlag: Berlin.

1910. Tenti P, Aguzzi A, Riva C, Usellini L, Zappatore R, Bara J, Samloff IM, Solcia E (1992). Ovarian mucinous tumors frequently express markers of gastric, intestinal, and pancreatobiliary epithelial cells. *Cancer* 69: 2131-2142.

1911. Tenti P, Romagnoli S, Pellegata NS, Zappatore R, Giunta P, Ranzani GN, Carnevali L (1994). Primary retroperitoneal mucinous cystoadenocarcinomas: an immunohistochemical and molecular study. *Virchows Arch* 424: 53-57.

1912. Terada T, Ashida K, Endo K, Horie S, Maeta H, Matsunaga Y, Takashima K, Ohta T, Kitamura Y (1998). c-erbB-2 protein is expressed in hepatolithiasis and cholangiocarcinoma. *Histopathology* 33: 325-331.

1913. Terada T, Makimoto K, Terayama N, Suzuki Y, Nakanuma Y (1996). Alpha-smooth muscle actin-positive stromal cells in cholangiocarcinomas, hepatocellular carcinomas and metastatic liver carcinomas. *J Hepatol* 24: 706-712.

1914. Terada T, Nakanuma Y (1990). Pathological observations of intrahepatic peribiliary glands in 1,000 consecutive autopsy livers. II. A possible source of cholangiocarcinoma. *Hepatology* 12: 92-97.

1915. Terada T, Nakanuma Y, Ohta T, Nagakawa T (1992). Histological features and interphase nucleolar organizer regions in hyperplastic, dysplastic and neoplastic epithelium of intrahepatic bile ducts in hepatolithiasis. *Histopathology* 21: 233-240.

1916. Terada T, Ohta T, Kitamura Y, Ashida K, Matsunaga Y (1998). Cell proliferative activity in intraductal papillary-mucinous neoplasms and invasive ductal adenocarcinomas of the pancreas: an immunohistochemical study. *Arch Pathol Lab Med* 122: 42-46.

1917. Terada T, Ohta T, Nakanuma Y (1996). Expression of oncogene products, anti-oncogene products and oncofetal antigens in intraductal papillary-mucinous neoplasm of the pancreas. *Histopathology* 29: 355-361.

1918. Terada T, Ohta T, Sasaki M, Nakanuma Y, Kim YS (1996). Expression of MUC apomucins in normal pancreas and pancreatic tumours. *J Pathol* 180: 160-165.

1919. Terayama N, Terada T, Nakanuma Y (1996). A morphometric and immunohistochemical study on angiogenesis of human metastatic carcinomas of the liver. *Hepatology* 24: 816-819.

1920. Terhune PG, Heffess CS, Longnecker DS (1994). Only wild-type c-Ki-ras codons 12, 13, and 61 in human pancreatic acinar cell carcinomas. *Mol Carcinog* 10: 110-114.

1921. Terhune PG, Memoli VA, Longnecker DS (1998). Evaluation of p53 mutation in pancreatic acinar cell carcinomas of humans and transgenic mice. *Pancreas* 16: 6-12.

1922. Tetsu O, McCormick F (1999). Beta-catenin regulates expression of cyclin D1 in colon carcinoma cells. *Nature* 398: 422-426.

1923. Thakker RV, Bouloux P, Wooding C, Chotai K, Broad PM, Spurr NK, Besser GM, O'Riordan JL (1989). Association of parathyroid tumors in multiple endocrine neoplasia type 1 with loss of alleles on chromosome 11. *N Engl J Med* 321: 218-224.

1924. Thibodeau SN, Bren G, Schaid D (1993). Microsatellite instability in cancer of the proximal colon. *Science* 260: 816-819.

1924A. Thibodeau SN, French AJ, Cunningham JM, Tester D, Burgart LJ, Roche PC, Mc Donnell SK, Schaid DJ, Vockley CW, Michels VV, Farr-GH J, O'Connell MJ (1998). Microsatellite instability in colorectal cancer: different mutator phenotypes and the principal involvement of hMLH1. *Cancer Res* 58: 1713-1718.

1924B. Thibodeau SN, French AJ, Roche PC, Cunningham JM, Tester DJ, Lindor NM, Moslein G, Baker SM, Liskay RM, Burgart LJ, Honchel R, Halling KC (1996). Altered expression of hMSH2 and hMLH1 in tumors with microsatellite instability and genetic alterations in mismatch repair genes. *Cancer Res* 56: 4836-4840.

1925. Thieblemont C, Bastion Y, Berger F, Rieux C, Salles G, Dumontet C, Felman P, Coiffier B (1997). Mucosa-associated lymphoid tissue gastrointestinal and nongastrointestinal lymphoma behavior: analysis of 108 patients. *J Clin Oncol* 15: 1624-1630.

1926. Thiede C, Morgner A, Alpen B, Wundisch T, Herrmann J, Ritter M, Ehninger G, Stolte M, Bayerdorffer E, Neubauer A (1997). What role does Helicobacter pylori eradication play in gastric MALT and gastric MALT lymphoma? *Gastroenterology* 113: S61-S64.

1927. Thirlby RC, Kasper CS, Jones RC (1984). Metastatic carcinoid tumor of the appendix. Report of a case and review of the literature. *Dis Colon Rectum* 27: 42-46.

1928. Thomas RM, Sobin LH (1995). Gastrointestinal cancer. *Cancer* 75: 154-170.

1929. Thompson FM, Warren BF, Mortensen NJ (1998). A new look at the anal transitional zone with reference to restorative protocolectomy and the columnar cuff. *Br J Surg* 85: 1517-1521.

1930. Thompson GB, Pemberton JH, Morris S, Bustamante MA, Delong B, Carpenter HA, Wright AJ (1989). Kaposi's sarcoma of the colon in a young HIV-negative man with chronic ulcerative colitis. Report of a case. *Dis Colon Rectum* 32: 73-76.

1931. Thompson GB, van-Heerden JA, Martin-JK J, Schutt AJ, Ilstrup DM, Carney JA (1985). Carcinoid tumors of the gastrointestinal tract: presentation, management, and prognosis. *Surgery* 98: 1054-1063.

1932. Thompson LD, Becker RC, Przygodzki RM, Adair CF, Heffess CS (1999). Mucinous cystic neoplasm (mucinous cystadenocarcinoma of low-grade malignant potential) of the pancreas: a clinicopathologic study of 130 cases. *Am J Surg Pathol* 23: 1-16.

1933. Thorban S, Roder JD, Nekarda H, Funk A, Siewert JR, Pantel K (1996). Immunocytochemical detection of disseminated tumor cells in the bone marrow of patients with esophageal carcinoma. *J Natl Cancer Inst* 88: 1222-1227.

1934. Thorlacius S, Olafsdottir G, Tryggvadottir L, Neuhausen S, Jonasson JG, Tavtigian SV, Tulinius H, Ogmundsdottir HM, Eyfjord JE (1996). A single BRCA2 mutation in male and female breast cancer families from Iceland with varied cancer phenotypes. *Nat Genet* 13: 117-119.

1935. Tio TL (1998). Diagnosis and staging of esophageal carcinoma by endoscopic ultrasonography. *Endoscopy* 30 Suppl 1: 1982.

1936. Toft NJ, Arends MJ (1998). DNA mismatch repair and colorectal cancer. *J Pathol* 185: 123-129.

1937. Tolbert DM, Noffsinger AE, Miller MA, DeVoe GW, Stemmermann GN, Macdonald JS, Fenoglio PC (1999). p53 immunoreactivity and single-strand conformational polymorphism analysis often fail to predict p53 mutational status. *Mod Pathol* 12: 54-60.

1938. Toliat MR, Berger W, Ropers HH, Neuhaus P, Wiedenmann B (1997). Mutations in the MEN I gene in sporadic neuroendocrine tumours of gastroenteropancreatic system. *Lancet* 350: 1223-.

1939. Tomaszewska R, Okon K, Nowak K, Stachura J (1998). HER-2/Neu expression as a progression marker in pancreatic intraepithelial neoplasia. *Pol J Pathol* 49: 83-92.

1940. Tomimatsu M, Ishiguro N, Taniai M, Okuda H, Saito A, Obata H, Yamamoto M, Takasaki K, Nakano M (1993). Hepatitis C virus antibody in patients with primary liver cancer (hepatocellular carcinoma, cholangiocarcinoma, and combined hepatocellular-cholangiocarcinoma) in Japan. *Cancer* 72: 683-688.

1941. Tomita T, Bhatia P, Gourley W (1981). Mucin producing islet cell adenoma. *Hum Pathol* 12: 850-853.

1942. Tomizawa M, Kondo F, Kondo Y (1995). Growth patterns and interstitial invasion of small hepatocellular carcinoma. *Pathol Int* 45: 352-358.

1943. Tomori H, Nagahama M, Miyazato H, Shiraishi M, Muto Y, Toda T (1999). Mucosa-associated lymphoid tissue (MALT) of the gallbladder: a clinicopathological correlation. *Int Surg* 84: 144-150.

1944. Torlakovic E, Snover DC (1996). Serrated adenomatous polyposis in humans. *Gastroenterology* 110: 748-755.

1945. Torres C, Turner JR, Wang HH, Richards W, Sugarbaker D, Shahsafaei A, Odze RD (1999). Pathologic prognostic factors in Barrett's associated adenocarcinoma: a follow-up study of 96 patients. *Cancer* 85: 520-528.

1946. Tortola S, Marcuello E, Gonzalez I, Reyes G, Arribas R, Aiza G, Sancho FJ, Peinado MA, Capella G (1999). p53 and K-ras gene mutations correlate with tumor aggressiveness but are not of routine prognostic value in colorectal cancer. *J Clin Oncol* 17: 1375-1381.

1947. Torzewski M, Sarbia M, Verreet P, Dutkowski P, Heep H, Willers R, Gabbert HE (1997). Prognostic significance of urokinase-type plasminogen activator expression in squamous cell carcinomas of the esophagus. *Clin Cancer Res* 3: 2263-2268.

1948. Tosi P, Filipe MI, Luzi P, Miracco C, Santopietro R, Lio R, Sforza V, Barbini P (1993). Gastric intestinal metaplasia type III cases are classified as low-grade dysplasia on the basis of morphometry. *J Pathol* 169: 73-78.

1949. Toyooka M, Konishi M, Kikuchi YR, Iwama T, Miyaki M (1995). Somatic mutations of the adenomatous polyposis coli gene in gastroduodenal tumors from patients with familial adenomatous polyposis. *Cancer Res* 55: 3165-3170.

1950. Toyota M, Ahuja N, Ohe TM, Herman JG, Baylin SB, Issa JP (1999). CpG island methylator phenotype in colorectal cancer. *Proc Natl Acad Sci U S A* 96: 8681-8686.

1951. Tracey KJ, O'Brien MJ, Williams LF, Kilbaner M, George PK, Saravis CA, Zamcheck N (1984). Signet ring carcinoma of the pancreas, a rare variant with very high CEA values. Immunohistologic comparison with adenocarcinoma. *Dig Dis Sci* 29: 573-576.

1952. Trau H, Schewach-Millet M, Fisher BK, Tsur H (1982). Peutz-Jeghers syndrome and bilateral breast carcinoma. *Breast* 50: 788-792.

1953. Traverso LW, Peralta EA, Ryan-JA J, Kozarek RA (1998). Intraductal neoplasms of the pancreas. *Am J Surg* 175: 426-432.

1954. Travis WD, Linnoila RI, Tsokos MG, Hitchcock CL, Cutler GB, Nieman L, Chrousos G, Pass H, Doppman J (1991). Neuroendocrine tumors of the lung with proposed criteria for large cell neuroendocrine carcinoma. An ultrastructural, immunohistochemical, and flow cytometric study of 35 cases. *Am J Surg Pathol* 15: 529-553.

1955. Trede M, Schwall G, Saeger HD (1990). Survival after pancreatoduodenectomy. 118 consecutive resections without an operative mortality. *Ann Surg* 211: 447-458.

1956. Trentino P, Rapacchietta S, Silvestri F, Marzullo A, Fantini A (1997). Esophageal metastasis from clear cell carcinoma of the kidney. *Am J Gastroenterol* 92: 1381-1382.

1957. Trier JS (1985). Morphology of the columnar cell-lined (Barrett's) esophagus. In: *Barrett's Esophagus: Pathophysiology, Diagnosis, and Management*, Spechler SJ, Goyal RK (eds), Elsevier Science: New York.

1958. Troisi RJ, Freedman AN, Devesa SS (1999). Incidence of colorectal carcinoma in the U.S.: an update of trends by gender, race, age, subsite, and stage, 1975-1994. *Cancer* 85: 1670-1676.

1959. Trudgill NJ, Kapur KC, Riley SA (1999). Familial clustering of reflux symptoms. *Am J Gastroenterol* 94: 1172-1178.

1960. Trudgill NJ, Suvarna SK, Kapur KC, Riley SA (1997). Intestinal metaplasia at the squamocolumnar junction in patients attending for diagnostic gastroscopy. *Gut* 41: 585-589.

1961. Tsang WY, Chan JK, Lee KC, Leung AK, Fu YT (1991). Basaloid-squamous carcinoma of the upper aerodigestive tract and so-called adenoid cystic carcinoma of the oesophagus: the same tumour type? *Histopathology* 19: 35-46.

1962. Tschang TP, Garza GR, Kissane JM (1977). Pleomorphic carcinoma of the pancreas: an analysis of 15 cases. *Cancer* 39: 2114-2126.

1963. Tsioulias G, Muto T, Kubota Y, Masaki T, Suzuki K, Akasu T, Morioka Y (1991). DNA ploidy pattern in rectal carcinoid tumors. *Dis Colon Rectum* 34: 31-36.

1964. Tsou HC, Teng DH, Ping XL, Brancolini V, Davis T, Hu R, Xie XX, Gruener AC, Schrager CA, Christiano AM, Eng C, Steck P, Ott J, Tavtigian SV, Peacocke M (1997). The role of MMAC1 mutations in early-onset breast cancer: causative in association with Cowden syndrome and excluded in BRCA1-negative cases. *Am J Hum Genet* 61: 1036-1043.

1965. Tsuboniwa N, Miki T, Kuroda M, Maeda O, Saiki S, Kinouchi T, Usami M, Kotake T (1996). Primary adenocarcinoma in an ileal conduit. *Int J Urol* 3: 64-66.

1966. Tsuchiya R, Noda T, Harada N, Miyamoto T, Tomioka T, Yamamoto K, Yamaguchi T, Izawa K, Tsunoda T, Yoshino R, et a (1986). Collective review of small carcinomas of the pancreas. *Ann Surg* 203: 77-81.

1967. Tsuda H, Hirohashi S, Shimosato Y, Ino Y, Yoshida T, Terada M (1989). Low incidence of point mutation of c-Ki-ras and N-ras oncogenes in human hepatocellular carcinoma. *Jpn J Cancer Res* 80: 196-199.

1968. Tsuda H, Hirohashi S, Shimosato Y, Terada M, Hasegawa H (1988). Clonal origin of atypical adenomatous hyperplasia of the liver and clonal identity with hepatocellular carcinoma. *Gastroenterology* 95: 1664-1666.

1969. Tsuda H, Satarug S, Bhudhisawasdi V, Kihana T, Sugimura T, Hirohashi S (1992). Cholangiocarcinomas in Japanese and Thai patients: difference in etiology and incidence of point mutation of the c-Ki-ras proto-oncogene. *Mol Carcinog* 6: 266-269.

1970. Tsuda H, Zhang WD, Shimosato Y, Yokota J, Terada M, Sugimura T, Miyamura T, Hirohashi S (1990). Allele loss on chromosome 16 associated with progression of human hepatocellular carcinoma. *Proc Natl Acad Sci U S A* 87: 6791-6794.

1971. Tsui WM, Colombari R, Portmann BC, Bonetti F, Thung SN, Ferrell LD, Nakanuma Y, Snover DC, Bioulac SP, Dhillon AP (1999). Hepatic angiomyolipoma: a clinicopathologic study of 30 cases and delineation of unusual morphologic variants. *Am J Surg Pathol* 23: 34-48.

1972. Tsui WM, Loo KT, Chow LT, Tse CC (1993). Biliary adenofibroma. A heretofore unrecognized benign biliary tumor of the liver. *Am J Surg Pathol* 17: 186-192.

1973. Tsukuma H, Tanaka H (1996). Descriptive epidemiology of hepatitis C virus related liver cancer in Japan. In: *Hepatitis Type C*, Hayashi N, Kiyosawa K (eds), Igaku-shoin: Tokyo.

1974. Tsunoda A, Shibusawa M, Kawamura M, Marumori T, Kusano M, Ohta H (1997). Colorectal cancer after pelvic irradiation: case reports. *Anticancer Res* 17/1B: 729-732.

1975. Tsunoda T, Eto T, Tsunfune T, Tokunaga S, Ishii T, Motojima K, Matsumoto T, Segawa T, Ura K, Fukui H (1991). Solid and cystic tumor of the pancreas in an adult male. *Acta Pathol Jpn* 41: 763-770.

1976. Tsunoda T, Ura K, Eto T, Matsumoto T, Tsuchiya R (1991). UICC and Japanese stage classifications for carcinoma of the pancreas. *Int J Pancreatol* 8: 205-214.

1977. Tuchmann-Duplessis H (1968). Embryologie. Travaux pratiques et enseignement dirige. Masson: Paris.

1978. Tucker JA, Shelburne JD, Benning TL, Yacoub L, Federman M (1994). Filamentous inclusions in acinar cell carcinoma of the pancreas. *Ultrastruct Pathol* 18: 279-286.

1979. Turcot J, Despres JP, St Pierre F (1959). Malignant tumors of the central nervous system associated with familial polyposis of the colon: report of two cases. *Dis Colon Rectum* 2: 465-468.

1980. Tworek JA, Appelman HD, Singleton TP, Greenson JK (1997). Stromal tumors of the jejunum and ileum. *Mod Pathol* 10: 200-209.

1981. Uchino S, Tsuda H, Noguchi M, Yokota J, Terada M, Saito T, Kobayashi M, Sugimura T, Hirohashi S (1992). Frequent loss of heterozygosity at the DCC locus in gastric cancer. *Cancer Res* 52: 3099-3102.

1982. Ueki Y, Naito T, Oohashi T, Sugimoto M, Seki T, Yoshioka H, Sado Y, Sato H, Sawai T, Sasaki F, Matsuoka M, Fukuda S, Ninomiya Y (1998). Topoisomerase I and II consensus sequences in a 17-kb deletion junction of the COL4A5 and COL4A6 genes and immunohistochemical analysis of esophageal leiomyomatosis associated with Alport syndrome. *Am J Hum Genet* 62: 253-261.

1983. Uetsuji S, Yamamura M, Yamamichi K, Okuda Y, Takada H, Hioki K (1992). Absence of colorectal cancer metastasis to the cirrhotic liver. *Am J Surg* 164: 176-177.

1984. Ueyama K, Sowa M, Kamino K, Kato Y, Satake K (1982). Gastric carcinoma in young adults in Japan. *Anticancer Res* 2: 283-286.

1985. Ulich T, Cheng L, Lewin KJ (1982). Acinar-endocrine cell tumor of the pancreas. Report of a pancreatic tumor containing both zymogen and neuroendocrine granules. *Cancer* 50: 2099-2105.

1986. Umeyama K, Sowa M, Kamino K, Kato Y, Satake K (1982). A clinicopathologic and immunohistochemical study of gastrointestinal stromal tumors. *Cancer* 69: 947-955.

1987. Urbanski SJ, Marcon N, Kossakowska AE, Burce WR (1984). Mixed hyperplastic adenomatous polyps - and underdiagnosed entity. *Am J Surg Pathol* 8: 551-556.

1988. Utsunomita J, Miki Y, Kuroki T, Iwama T (1990). Phenotypic expressions of Japanese patients with familial adenomatous polyposis. In: *Familial Adenomatous Polyposis*, Herrera L (ed), Alan R. Liss, Inc.: New York.

1989. Uttaravichien T, Bhudhisawasdi V, Pairojkul C (1996). Bile duct cancer and the liver fluke: pathology, presentation and surgical management. *Asian J Surg* 19: 267-270.

1990. Uttaravichien T, Bhudhisawasdi V, Pairojkul C, Pugkhem A (1999). Intrahepatic cholangiocarcinoma in Thailand. *J Hepatobiliary Pancreat Surg* 6: 128-135.

1991. van-de-Rijn M, Hendrickson MR, Rouse RV (1994). CD34 expression by gastrointestinal tract stromal tumors. *Hum Pathol* 25: 766-771.

1992. Van-Krieken JH, Medeiros LJ, Pals ST, Raffeld M, Kluin PM (1992). Diffuse aggressive B-cell lymphomas of the gastrointestinal tract. An immunophenotypic and gene rearrangement analysis of 22 cases. *Am J Clin Pathol* 97: 170-178.

1993. van-Leeuwen DJ, Reeders JW (1999). Primary sclerosing cholangitis and cholangiocarcinoma as a diagnostic and therapeutic dilemma. *Ann Oncol* 10: 89-93.

1994. van-Lieshout EM, Roelofs HM, Dekker S, Mulder CJ, Wobbes T, Jansen JB, Peters WH (1999). Polymorphic expression of the glutathione S-transferase P1 gene and its susceptibility to Barrett's esophagus and esophageal carcinoma. *Cancer Res* 59: 586-589.

1995. van-Sandick JW, van-Lanschot JJ, Kuiken BW, Tytgat GN, Offerhaus GJ, Obertop H (1998). Impact of endoscopic biopsy surveillance of Barrett's oesophagus on pathological stage and clinical outcome of Barrett's carcinoma. *Gut* 43: 216-222.

1996. van-Spronsen FJ, Thomasse Y, Smit GP, Leonard JV, Clayton PT, Fidler V, Berger R, Heymans HS (1994). Hereditary tyrosinemia type I: a new clinical classification with difference in prognosis on dietary treatment. *Hepatology* 20: 1187-1191.

1997. Van-Tornout JM, Buckley JD, Quinn JJ, Feusner JH, Krailo MD, King DR, Hammond GD, Ortega JA (1997). Timing and magnitude of decline in alpha-fetoprotein levels in treated children with unresectable or metastatic hepatoblastoma are predictors of outcome: a report from the Children's Cancer Group. *J Clin Oncol* 15: 1190-1197.

1998. van den Berg W, Tascilar M, Offerhaus G, Albores-Saavedra J, Wenig B, Hruban R, Gabrielson E (1999). Pancreatic mucinous cystic neoplasms with sarcomatous stroma: molecular evidence for monoclonal origin with subsequent divergence of the epithelial and sarcomatous components. *Mod Pathol* 13: 86-91.

1999. Vandendriessche L, Bonhomme A, Breysem L, Smet MH, Uyttebroeck A, Brock P, Baert AL (1996). Mesenchymal hamartoma: radiological differentiation from other possible liver tumors in childhood. *J Belge Radiol* 79: 74-75.

2000. Vardaman C, Albores SJ (1995). Clear cell carcinoma of the gallbladder and extrahepatic bile ducts. *Am J Surg Pathol* 19: 91-99.

2001. Varley JM, McGown G, Thorncroft M, Tricker KJ, Teare MD, Santibanez KM, Martin J, Birch JM, Evans DG (1995). An extended Li-Fraumeni kindred with gastric carcinoma and a codon 175 mutation in TP53. *J Med Genet* 32: 942-945.

2002. Vartio T, Nickels J, Hockerstedt K, Scheinin TM (1980). Rhabdomyosarcoma of the oesophagus. Light and electron microscopic study of a rare tumor. *Virchows Arch Pathol Anat* 386: 357-361.

2003. Vasen HF, Mecklin JP, Khan PM, Lynch HT (1991). The International Collaborative Group on Hereditary Non-Polyposis Colorectal Cancer (ICG-HNPCC). *Dis Colon Rectum* 34: 424-425.

2004. Vasen HF, Watson P, Mecklin JP, Lynch HT (1999). New clinical criteria for hereditary nonpolyposis colorectal cancer (HNPCC, Lynch syndrome) proposed by the International Collaborative group on HNPCC. *Gastroenterology* 116: 1453-1456.

2005. Vasen HF, Wijnen JT, Menko FH, Kleibeuker JH, Taal BG, Griffioen G, Nagengast FM, Meijers HE, Bertario L, Varesco L, Bisgaard ML, Mohr J, Fodde R, Khan PM (1996). Cancer risk in families with hereditary nonpolyposis colorectal cancer diagnosed by mutation analysis. *Gastroenterology* 110: 1020-1027.

2006. Vatanasapt V, Kosuwon W, Pengsaa P (1993). Unit cost analysis in a university hospital: an example from Srinagarind Hospital, Khon Kaen. *J Med Assoc Thai* 76: 647-653.

2007. Vatanasapt V, Martin N, Sriplung H, Chindavijak K, Sontipong S, Sriamporn H, Parkin DM, Ferlay J (1995). Cancer incidence in Thailand, 1988-1991. *Cancer Epidemiol Biomarkers Prev* 4: 475-483.

2008. Vatanasapt V, Sripa B, Sithithaworn P, Mairiang P (1999). Liver flukes and liver cancer. *Cancer Surv* 33: 313-343.

2009. Vatanasapt V, Tangvoraphonkchai V, Titapant V, Pipitgool V, Viriyapap D, Sriamporn S (1990). A high incidence of liver cancer in Khon Kaen Province, Thailand. *Southeast Asian J Trop Med Public Health* 21: 489-494.

2010. Vermeulen PB, van der Eynden GG, Huget P, Goovaerts G, Weyler J, Lardon F, van Marck E, Hubens G, Dirix LY (1999). Prospective study of intratumoral microvessel density, p53 expression and survival in colorectal cancer. *Br J Cancer* 79: 316-322.

2011. Veyrieres M, Baillet P, Hay JM, Fingerhut A, Bouillot JL, Julien M (1997). Factors influencing long-term survival in 100 cases of small intestine primary adenocarcinoma. *Am J Surg* 173: 237-239.

2012. Vicari JJ, Peek RM, Falk GW, Goldblum JR, Easley KA, Schnell J, Perez PG, Halter SA, Rice TW, Blaser MJ, Richter JE (1998). The seroprevalence of cagA-positive Helicobacter pylori strains in the spectrum of gastroesophageal reflux disease. *Gastroenterology* 115: 50-57.

2013. Vieth M, Grunewald M, Niemeyer C, Stolte M (1998). Adenocarcinoma in an ileal pouch after prior proctocolectomy for carcinoma in a patient with ulcerative colitis. *Virchows Arch* 433: 281-284.

2014. Vijeyasingam R, Darnton SJ, Jenner K, Allen CA, Billingham C, Matthews HR (1994). Expression of p53 protein in oesophageal carcinoma: clinicopathological correlation and prognostic significance. *Br J Surg* 81:1623-1626.

2015. Villanueva RP, Nguyen-Ho P, Nguyen GK (1994). Needle aspiration cytology of acinar-cell carcinoma of the pancreas: report of a case with diagnostic pitfalls and unusual ultrastructural findings. *Diagn Cytopathol*10:362-364.

2016. Vinik AI, McLeod MK, Fig LM, Shapiro B, Lloyd RV, Cho K (1989). Clinical features, diagnosis, and localization of carcinoid tumors and their management. *Gastroenterol Clin North Am* 18:865-896.

2017. Visvanathan R, Thambidorai CR, Myint H (1992). Do dysplastic and adenomatous changes in large bowel hamartomas predispose to malignancy? A report of two cases. *Ann Acad Med (Singapore)* 21: 830-832.

2018. Vogelstein B, Fearon ER, Hamilton SR, Kern SE, Preisinger AC, Leppert M, Nakamura Y, White R, Smits AM, Bos JL (1988). Genetic alterations during colorectal-tumor development. *N Engl J Med* 319: 525-532.

2019. Vogelstein B, Fearon ER, Kern SE, Hamilton SR, Preisinger AC, Nakamura Y, White R (1989). Allelotype of colorectal carcinomas. *Science* 244:207-211.

2020. von-Brevern M, Hollstein MC, Risk JM, Garde J, Bennett WP, Harris CC, Muehlbauer KR, Field JK (1998). Loss of heterozygosity in sporadic oesophageal tumors in the tylosis (non-tylosis) (TOC) gene region of chromosome 17q. *Oncogene* 17: 2101-2105.

2021. von-Herbay A, Sieg B, Otto HF (1990). Solid-cystic tumour of the pancreas. An endocrine neoplasm? *Virchows Arch A Pathol Anat Histopathol* 416: 535-538.

2022. von-Schweinitz D, Hecker H, Schmidt-von AG, Harms D (1997). Prognostic factors and staging systems in childhood hepatoblastoma. *Int J Cancer* 74: 593-599.

2023. von-Schweinitz D, Schmidt D, Fuchs J, Welte K, Pietsch T (1995). Extramedullary hematopoiesis and intratumoral production of cytokines in childhood hepatoblastoma. *Pediatr Res* 38: 555-563.

2024. von-Schweinitz D, Wischmeyer P, Leuschner I, Schmidt D, Wittekind C, Harms D, Mildenberger H (1994). Clinicopathological criteria with prognostic relevance in hepatoblastoma. *Eur J Cancer* 30A: 1052-1058.

2025. Vortmeyer AO, Kingma DW, Fenton RG, Curti BD, Jaffe ES, Duray PH (1998). Hepatobiliary lymphoepithelioma-like carcinoma associated with Epstein-Barr virus. *Am J Clin Pathol* 109: 90-95.

2026. Vortmeyer AO, Lubensky IA, Fogt F, Linehan WM, Khettry U, Zhuang Z (1997). Allelic deletion and mutation of the von Hippel-Lindau (VHL) tumor suppressor gene in pancreatic microcystic adenomas. *Am J Pathol*151:951-956.

2027. Vossen S, Goretzki PE, Goebel U, Willnow U (1998). Therapeutic management of rare malignant pancreatic tumors in children. *World J Surg* 22: 879-882.

2028. Voutilainen M, Farkkila M, Juhola M, P, Kaiserling E (1998). Incidence and pattern of liver involvement in haematological malignancies. *Pathol Res Pract* 194: 781-789.

2029. Vuitch F, Battifora H, Albores-Saavedra J (1993). Demonstration of steroid hormone receptors in pancreatobiliary mucinous cystic neoplasms. *Lab Invest*68:114A.

2030. Wada A, Ishiguro S, Tateishi R, Ishikawa O, Matsui Y (1983). Specialized columnar epithelium of the esophagogastric junction: prevalence and associations. The Central Finland Endoscopy Study Group. *Am J Gastroenterol*94: 913-918.

2031. Wada I, Kanada H, Nomura K, Kato YMR, Kitagawa T (1999). Failure to detect genetic alteration of the mannose-6-phosphate/insulin-like growth factor 2 receptor (M6P/IGF2R) gene in hepatocellular carcinoma in Japan. *Hepatology*29: 1718-1721.

2032. Wada K, Asoh T, Imamura T, Tanaka N, Yamaguchi K, Tanaka M (1998). Rectal carcinoid tumor associated with the Peutz-Jeghers syndrome. *J Gastroenterol* 33: 743-746.

2033. Wade DS, Herrera L, Castillo NB, Petrelli NJ (1989). Metastases to the lymph nodes in epidermoid carcinoma of the anal canal studied by a clearing technique. *Surg Gynecol Obstet*169: 238-242.

2034. Waetjen LE, Grimes DA (1996). Oral contraceptives and primary liver cancer: temporal trends in three countries. *Obstet Gynecol*88: 945-949.

2035. Wagner JS, Adson MA, van-Heerden JA, Adson MH, Ilstrup DM (1984). The natural history of hepatic metastases from colorectal cancer. *Ann Surg* 199: 502-508.

2036. Wain SL, Kier R, Vollmer RT, Bossen EH (1986). Basaloid-squamous carcinoma of the tongue, hypopharynx, and larynx: report of 10 cases. *Hum Pathol* 17: 1158-1166.

2037. Walker JH (1978). Giant papilloma of the thoracic esophagus. *AJR Am J Roentgenol*131: 519-520.

2038. Walker P, Dvorak AM (1986). Gastrointestinal autonomic nerve (GAN) tumor. Ultrastructural evidence for a newly recognized entity. *Arch Pathol Lab Med* 110: 309-316.

2039. Wallrapp C, Muller PF, Solinas TS, Lichter P, Friess H, Buchler M, Fink T, Adler G, Gress TM (1997). Characterization of a high copy number amplification at 6q24 in pancreatic cancer identifies c-myb as a candidate oncogene. *Cancer Res* 57: 3135-3139.

2040. Walsh MM, Hytiroglou P, Thung SN, Fiel MI, Siegel D, Emre S, Ishak KG (1998). Epithelioid hemangioendothelioma of the liver mimicking Budd-Chiari syndrome. *Arch Pathol Lab Med* 122: 846-848.

2041. Walsh N, Qizilbash A, Banerjee R, Waugh GA (1987). Biliary neoplasia in Gardner's syndrome. *Arch Pathol Lab Med* 111: 76-77.

2042. Walz-Mattmuller R, Horny HP, Ruck P, Kaiserling E (1998). Incidence and pattern of liver involvement in haematological malignancies. *Pathol Res Pract* 194: 781-789.

2043. Wanebo HJ, Rao B, Pinsky CM, Hoffman RG, Stearns M, Schwartz MK, Oettgen HF (1978). Preoperative carcinoembryonic antigen level as a prognostic indicator in colorectal cancer. *N Engl J Med*299: 448-451.

2044. Wang DG, Johnston CF, Anderson N, Sloan JM, Buchanan KD (1995). Overexpression of the tumour suppressor gene p53 is not implicated in neuroendocrine tumour carcinogenesis. *J Pathol* 175: 397-401.

2045. Wang HH, Antonioli DA, Goldman H (1986). Comparative features of esophageal and gastric adenocarcinomas: recent changes in type and frequency. *Hum Pathol*17: 482-487.

2046. Wang HP, Rogler CE (1988). Deletions in human chromosome arms 11p and 13q in primary hepatocellular carcinomas. *Cytogenet Cell Genet*48: 72-78.

2047. Wang NP (1995). Coordinate expression of cytokeratin 7 and 20 defined unique subsets of carcinoma. *Appl Immunohistochem*3: 99-107.

2048. Wang Q, Lasset C, Desseigne F, Frappaz D, Bergeron C, Navarro C, Ruano E, Puisieux A (1999). Neurofibromatosis and early onset of cancers in hMLH1-deficient children. *Cancer Res* 59: 294-297.

2049. Wang W, Gu G, Hu M (1996). [Expression and significance of hepatitis B virus genes in human primary intrahepatic cholangiocarcinoma and its surrounding tissue]. *Chung Hua Chung Liu Tsa Chih* 18: 127-130.

2050. Wang XW, Forrester K, Yeh H, Feitelson MA, Gu JR, Harris CC (1994). Hepatitis B virus X protein inhibits p53 sequence-specific DNA binding, transcriptional activity, and association with transcription factor ERCC3. *Proc Natl Acad Sci U S A*91: 2230-2234.

2051. Wang XW, Gibson MK, Vermeulen W, Yeh H, Forrester K, Sturzbecher HW, Hoeijmakers JH, Harris CC (1995). Abrogation of p53-induced apoptosis by the hepatitis B virus X gene. *Cancer Res* 55: 6012-6016.

2052. Wang ZJ, Ellis I, Zauber P, Iwama T, Marchese C, Talbot I, Xue WH, Yan ZY, Tomlinson I (1999). Allelic imbalance at the LKB1 (STK11) locus in tumors from patients with Peutz-Jeghers' syndrome provides evidence for a hamartoma(-adenoma)-carcinoma sequence. *J Pathol*188: 9-13.

2053. Wanless IR (1990). Micronodular transformation (nodular regenerative hyperplasia) of the liver: a report of 64 cases among 2,500 autopsies and a new classification of benign hepatocellular nodules. *Hepatology*11: 787-797.

2054. Wanless IR (2000). Epithelioid hemangioendothelioma, multiple focal nodular hyperplasias, and cavernous hemangiomas of the liver. *Arch Pathol Lab Med* 124: 1105-1107.

2055. Wanless IR, Albrecht S, Bilbao J, Frei JV, Heathcote EJ, Roberts EA, Chiasson D (1989). Multiple focal nodular hyperplasia of the liver associated with vascular malformations of various organs and neoplasia of the brain: a new syndrome. *Mod Pathol*2: 456-462.

2056. Wanless IR, Lentz JS, Roberts EA (1985). Partial nodular transformation of liver in an adult with persistent ductus venosus. Review with hypothesis on pathogenesis. *Arch Pathol Lab Med* 109: 427-432.

2057. Warfel KA, Faught PR, Hull MT (1988). Pancreatic cystadenoma in an infant: ultrastructural study. *Pediatr Pathol* 8: 559-565.

2058. Warfel KA, Hull MT (1992). Hepatoblastomas: an ultrastructural and immunohistochemical study. *Ultrastruct Pathol* 16: 451-461.

2059. Warkel RL, Cooper PH, Helwig EB (1978). Adenocarcinoid, a mucin-producing carcinoid tumor of the appendix: a study of 39 cases. *Cancer*42: 2781-2793.

2060. Warshaw AL, Compton CC, Lewandrowski K, Cardenosa G, Mueller PR (1990). Cystic tumors of the pancreas. New clinical, radiologic, and pathologic observations in 67 patients. *Ann Surg* 212: 432-443.

2061. Warshaw AL, Fernandez-del CC (1992). Pancreatic carcinoma. *N Engl J Med*326: 455-465.

2062. Wasan HS, Park HS, Liu KC, Mandir NK, Winnett A, Sasieni P, Bodmer WF, Goodlad RA, Wright NA (1998). APC in the regulation of intestinal crypt fission. *J Pathol*185: 246-255.

2063. Watanabe H, Enjoji M, Imai T (1976). Gastric carcinoma with lymphoid stroma. Its morphologic characteristics and prognostic correlations. *Cancer*38: 232-243.

2064. Watanabe H, Enjoji M, Yao T, Iida M, Ohsato K (1978). Accompanying gastroenteric lesions in familial adenomatosis coli. *Acta Pathol Jpn* 27: 823-839.

2065. Watanabe H, Enjoji M, Yao T, Ohsato K (1978). Gastric lesions in familial adenomatosis coli. *Hum Pathol*9: 269-283.

2066. Watanabe H, Jass JR, Sobin LH (1990). WHO: Histological Typing of Oesophageal and Gastric Tumours. Springer-Verlag: Berlin.

2067. Watanabe M, Asaka M, Tanaka J, Kurosawa M, Kasai M, Miyazaki T (1994). Point mutation of K-ras gene codon 12 in biliary tract tumors. *Gastroenterology*107: 1147-1153.

2068. Watanabe S, Okita K, Harada T, Kodama T, Numa Y, Takemoto T, Takahashi T (1983). Morphologic studies of the liver cell dysplasia. *Cancer*51: 2197-2205.

2069. Watanabe T, Tada M, Nagai H, Sasaki S, Nakao M (1998). Helicobacter pylori infection induces gastric cancer in mongolian gerbils. *Gastroenterology* 115: 642-648.

2070. Watson KJ, Shulkes A, Smallwood RA, Douglas MC, Hurley R, Kalnins R, Moran L (1985). Watery diarrhea-hypokalemia-achlorhydria syndrome and carcinoma of the esophagus. *Gastroenterology* 88: 798-803.

2071. Watson P, Lynch HT (1993). Extracolonic cancer in hereditary nonpolyposis colorectal cancer. *Cancer* 71: 677-685.

2072. Watts JL, Morton DG, Bestman J, Kemphues KJ (2000). The C.elegans par-4 gene encodes a putative serine-threonine kinase required for establishing embryonic asymetry. *Development* 127: 1467-1475.

2073. Webb JN (1977). Acinar cell neoplasms of the exocrine pancreas. *J Clin Pathol* 30: 103-112.

2074. Webber EM, Fraser RB, Resch L, Giacomantonio M (1997). Perianal ependymoma presenting in the neonatal period. *Pediatr Pathol Lab Med* 17: 283-291.

2075. Weber HC, Marsh DJ, Lubensky IA, Lin AY, Eng C (1998). Germline PTEN/MMAC1/TEP1 mutations and association with gastrointestinal manifestations in Cowden disease. *Gastroenterology* 114S: G2902-

2076. Weber HC, Venzon DJ, Lin JT, Fishbein VA, Orbuch M, Strader DB, Gibril F, Metz DC, Fraker DL, Norton JA, et a (1995). Determinants of metastatic rate and survival in patients with Zollinger-Ellison syndrome: a prospective long-term study. *Gastroenterology* 108: 1637-1649.

2077. Weckstrom P, Hedrum A, Makridis C, Akerstrom G, Rastad G, Scheibenplug L, Utilen M, Juhlin C, Wilander E (1996). Midgut carcinoids and solid carcinomas of the intestine: differences in the endocrine markers and p53 mutations. *Endocr Pathol* 7: 273-279.

2078. Wee A, Ludwig J, Coffey-RJ J, LaRusso NF, Wiesner RH (1985). Hepatobiliary carcinoma associated with primary sclerosing cholangitis and chronic ulcerative colitis. *Hum Pathol* 16: 719-726.

2079. Weger AR, Falkmer UG, Schwab G, Glaser K, Kemmler G, Bodner E, Auer GU, Mikuz G (1990). Nuclear DNA distribution pattern of the parenchymal cells in adenocarcinomas of the pancreas and in chronic pancreatitis. A study of archival specimens using both image and flow cytometry. *Gastroenterology* 99: 237-242.

2080. Weiderpass E, Partanen T, Kaaks R, Vainio H, Porta M, Kauppinen T, Ojajarvi A, Boffetta P, Malats N (1998). Occurrence, trends and environment etiology of pancreatic cancer. *Scand J Work Environ Health* 24: 165-174.

2081. Weidner N, Flanders DJ, Mitros FA (1984). Mucosal ganglioneuromatosis associated with multiple colonic polyps. *Am J Surg Pathol* 8: 779-786.

2082. Weinberg AG, Finegold MJ (1983). Primary hepatic tumors of childhood. *Hum Pathol* 14: 512-537.

2083. Weinstein S, Scottolini AG, Loo SY, Caldwell PC, Bhagavan NV (1985). Ataxia telangiectasia with hepatocellular carcinoma in a 15-year-old girl and studies of her kindred. *Arch Pathol Lab Med* 109: 1000-1004.

2084. Weisenburger DD, Armitage JO (1996). Mantle cell lymphoma - an entity comes of age. *Blood* 87: 4483-4494.

2085. Weiss L, Harlos JP, Torhorst J, Gunthard B, Hartveit F, Svendsen E, Huang WL, Grundmann E, Eder M, Zwicknagl M, et a (1988). Metastatic patterns of renal carcinoma: an analysis of 687 necropsies. *J Cancer Res Clin Oncol* 114: 605-612.

2086. Weiss SW (1994). Histological Typing of Soft Tissue Tumours. WHO International Histological Classification of Tumours. 2nd ed, Springer-Verlag: Berlin Heidelberg New York.

2087. Wellmann KF (1962). Anal duct carcinoma. Case reports. Adenocarcinoma of the anal duct origin. *Can J Surg* 5: 311-318.

2088. Wenig BM, Albores-Saavedra J, Buetow PC, Heffess CS (1997). Pancreatic mucinous cystic neoplasm with sarcomatous stroma: a report of three cases. *Am J Surg Pathol* 21: 70-80.

2089. Wenig BM, Heffess CS, Adair CF (1997). Atlas of Endocrine Pathology. WB Saunders: Philadelphia.

2090. Werdmuller BF, Loffeld RJ (1997). Helicobacter pylori infection has no role in the pathogenesis of reflux esophagitis. *Dig Dis Sci* 42: 103-105.

2091. Werner M, Mueller J, Walch A, Hofler H (1999). The molecular pathology of Barret's esophagus. *Histol Histopathol* 14: 553-559.

2092. Werness BA, Levine AJ, Howley PM (1990). Association of human papillomavirus types 16 and 18 E6 proteins with p53. *Science* 248: 76-79.

2093. Westerman AM, Entius MM, de Baar E, Boor PP, Koole R, van Velthuysen ML, Offerhaus GJ, Lindhout D, de Rooij FW, Wilson JH (1999). Peutz-Jeghers syndrome: 78-year follow-up of the original family. *Lancet* 353: 1211-1215.

2094. Weston AP, Campbell DR, Hassanein RS, Cherian R, Dixon A, McGregor DH (1997). Prospective, multivariate evaluation of CLOtest performance. *Am J Gastroenterol* 92: 1310-1315.

2095. Westra WH, Sturm P, Drillenburg P, Choti MA, Klimstra DS, Albores SJ, Montag A, Offerhaus GJ, Hruban RH (1998). K-ras oncogene mutations in osteoclast-like giant cell tumors of the pancreas and liver: genetic evidence to support origin from the duct epithelium. *Am J Surg Pathol* 22: 1247-1254.

2096. Wheeler DA, Edmondson HA (1985). Cystadenoma with mesenchymal stroma (CMS) in the liver and bile ducts. A clinicopathologic study of 17 cases, 4 with malignant change. *Cancer* 56: 1434-1445.

2097. Whelan AJ, Bartsch D, Goodfellow PJ (1995). Brief report: a familial syndrome of pancreatic cancer and melanoma with a mutation in the CDKN2 tumor-suppressor gene. *N Engl J Med* 333: 975-977.

2098. Whitcomb DC, Gorry MC, Preston RA, Furey W, Sossenheimer MJ, Ulrich CD, Martin SP, Gates-LK J, Amann ST, Toskes PP, Liddle R, McGrath K, Uomo G, Post JC, Ehrlich GD (1996). Hereditary pancreatitis is caused by a mutation in the cationic trypsinogen gene. *Nat Genet* 14: 141-145.

2099. Whitman M (1998). Smads and early developmental signaling by the TGFbeta superfamily. *Genes Dev* 12: 2445-2462.

2100. Whittaker MA, Carr NJ, Midwinter MJ, Badham DP, Higgins B (1999). Acinar morphology in colorectal cancer is associated with survival but is not an independent prognostic variable. *Histopathology* 35: 45.

2101. Wienert V, Albrecht O, Gahlen W (1978). [Results of incidence analyses in external hemorrhoids]. *Hautarzt* 29: 536-540.

2102. Wijnen J, de Leeuw W, Vasen H, van der KH, Moller P, Stormorken A, Meijers-Heijboer H, Lindhout D, Menko F, Vossen S, Moslein G, Tops C, Brocker-Vriends A, Wu Y, Hofstra R, Sijmons R, Cornelisse C, Morreau H, Fodde R (1999). Familial endometrial cancer in female carriers of MSH6 germline mutations. *Nat Genet* 23: 142-144.

2103. Wijnen J, Khan PM, Vasen H, van-der-Klift H, Mulder A, van LC, I, Bakker B, Losekoot M, Moller P, Fodde R (1997). Hereditary nonpolyposis colorectal cancer families not complying with the Amsterdam criteria show extremely low frequency of mismatch-repair-gene mutations. *Am J Hum Genet* 61: 329-335.

2104. Wilentz RE, Geradts J, Maynard R, Offerhaus GJ, Kang M, Goggins M, Yeo CJ, Kern SE, Hruban RH (1998). Inactivation of the p16 (INK4A) tumor-suppressor gene in pancreatic duct lesions: loss of intranuclear expression. *Cancer Res* 58: 4740-4744.

2105. Wilentz RE, Iacobuzio-Donahue CA, Argani P, McCarthy DM, Parsons JL, Yeo CJ, Kern SE, Hruban RH (2000). Loss of expression of Dpc4 in pancreatic intraepithelial neoplasia: evidence that DPC4 inactivation occurs late in neoplastic progression. *Cancer Res* 60: 2002-2006.

2106. Wiley TE, McCarthy M, Breidi L, Layden TJ (1998). Impact of alcohol on the histological and clinical progression of hepatitis C infection. *Hepatology* 28: 805-809.

2107. Willert K, Shibamoto S, Nusse R (1999). Wnt-induced dephosphorylation of axin releases beta-catenin from the axin complex. *Genes Dev* 13: 1768-1773.

2108. Willett CG, Lewandrowski K, Warshaw AL, Efird J, Compton CC (1993). Resection margins in carcinoma of the head of the pancreas. Implications for radiation therapy. *Ann Surg* 217: 144-148.

2109. Williams AO, Prince DL (1975). Intestinal polyps in the Nigerian African. *J Clin Pathol* 28: 367-371.

2110. Williams GR, du BC, Roche WR (1992). Benign epithelial neoplasms of the appendix: classification and clinical associations. *Histopathology* 21: 447-451.

2111. Williams GR, Talbot IC (1994). Anal carcinoma - a histological review. *Histopathology* 25: 507-516.

2112. Williams GR, Talbot IC, Leigh IM (1997). Keratin expression in anal carcinoma: an immunohistochemical study. *Histopathology* 30: 443-450.

2113. Williams GR, Talbot IC, Northover JM, Leigh IM (1995). Keratin expression in the normal anal canal. *Histopathology* 26: 39-44.

2114. Williams GT, Arthur JF, Bussey HJ, Morson BC (1980). Metaplastic polyps and polyposis of the colorectum. *Histopathology* 4: 155-170.

2115. Williams RA, Whitehead R (1986). Non-carcinoid epithelial tumours of the appendix - a proposed classification. *Pathology* 18: 50-53.

2116. Willis TG, Jadayel DM, Du MQ, Peng H, Perry AR, Abdul RM, Price H, Karran L, Majekodunmi O, Wlodarska I, Pan L, Crook T, Hamoudi R, Isaacson PG, Dyer MJ (1999). Bcl10 is involved in t(1;14)(p22;q32) of MALT B cell lymphoma and mutated in multiple tumor types. *Cell* 96: 35-45.

2117. Willnow U, Willberg B, Schwamborn D, Korholz D, Gobel U (1996). Pancreatoblastoma in children. Case report and review of the literature. *Eur J Pediatr Surg* 6: 369-372.

2118. Wilson DM, Pitts WC, Hintz RL, Rosenfeld RG (1986). Testicular tumours with Peutz-Jeghers syndrome. *Cancer* 57: 2238-2240.

2119. Wilson MB, Adams DB, Garen PD, Gansler TS (1992). Aspiration cytologic, ultrastructural, and DNA cytometric findings of solid and papillary tumor of the pancreas. *Cancer* 69: 2235-2243.

2120. Wilson TM, Ewel A, Duguid JR, Eble JN, Lescoe MK, Fishel R, Kelley MR (1995). Differential cellular expression of the human MSH2 repair enzyme in small and large intestine. *Cancer Res* 55: 5146-5150.

2121. Winawer SJ, Fletcher RH, Miller L, Godlee F, Stolar MH, Mulrow CD, Woolf SH, Glick SN, Ganiats TG, Bond JH, Rosen L, Zapka JG, Olsen SJ, Giardiello FM, Sisk JE, Van-Antwerp R, Brown DC, Marciniak DA, Mayer RJ (1997). Colorectal cancer screening: clinical guidelines and rationale. *Gastroenterology* 112: 594-642.

2122. Winawer SJ, Zauber AG, Ho MN, O'Brien MJ, Gottlieb LS, Sternberg SS, Waye JD, Schapiro M, Bond JH, Panish JF, et a (1993). Prevention of colorectal cancer by colonoscopic polypectomy. The National Polyp Study Workgroup. *N Engl J Med* 329: 1977-1981.

2123. Wise L, Pizzimbono C, Dehner LP (1976). Periampullary cancer. A clinicopathologic study of sixty-two patients. *Am J Surg* 131: 141-148.

2124. Wistuba II, Albores-Saavedra J (1999). Genetic abnormalities involved in the pathogenesis of gallbladder carcinoma. *J Hepatobiliary Pancreat Surg* 6: 237-244.

2125. Wistuba II, Gazdar AF, Roa I, Albores SJ (1996). p53 protein overexpression in gallbladder carcinoma and its precursor lesions: an immunohistochemical study. *Hum Pathol* 27: 360-365.

2126. Wistuba II, Miquel JF, Gazdar AF, Albores SJ (1999). Gallbladder adenomas have molecular abnormalities different from those present in gallbladder carcinomas. *Hum Pathol* 30: 21-25.

2127. Wistuba II, Sugio K, Hung J, Kishimoto Y, Virmani AK, Roa I, Albores SJ, Gazdar AF (1995). Allele-specific mutations involved in the pathogenesis of endemic gallbladder carcinoma in Chile. *Cancer Res* 55: 2511-2515.

2127A. Witteman BJ, Janssens AR, Terpstra JL, Eulderink F, Welvaart K, Lamers CB (1991). Villous tumours of the duodenum. Presentation of five cases. *Hepatogastroenterology* 38: 550-553.

2128. Wogan GN (1999). Aflatoxin as a human carcinogen. *Hepatology* 30: 573-575.

2129. Wolf C, Friedl P, Obrist P, Ensinger C, Gritsch W (1999). Metastasis to the appendix: sonographic appearance and review of the literature. *J Ultrasound Med* 18: 23-25.

2130. Wolf C, Isaacson E (1953). An analysis of 5 stomach cancer families in the state of Utah. *Cancer* 14: 1005.

2131. Wong AY, Rahilly MA, Adams W, Lee CS (1998). Mucinous anal gland carcinoma with perianal Pagetoid spread. *Pathology* 30: 1-3.

2132. Wotherspoon AC, Diss TC, Pan L, Singh N, Whelan J, Isaacson PG (1996). Low grade gastric B-cell lymphoma of mucosa associated lymphoid tissue in immunocompromised patients. *Histopathology* 28: 129-134.

2133. Wotherspoon AC, Doglioni C, Diss TC, Pan L, Moschini A, de-Boni M, Isaacson PG (1993). Regression of primary low-grade B-cell gastric lymphoma of mucosa-associated lymphoid tissue type after eradication of Helicobacter pylori. *Lancet* 342: 575-577.

2134. Wotherspoon AC, Finn TM, Isaacson PG (1995). Trisomy 3 in low-grade B-cell lymphomas of mucosa-associated lymphoid tissue. *Blood* 85: 2000-2004.

2135. Wotherspoon AC, Ortiz HC, Falzon MR, Isaacson PG (1991). Helicobacter pylori-associated gastritis and primary B-cell gastric lymphoma. *Lancet* 338: 1175-1176.

2136. Wotherspoon AC, Pan LX, Diss TC, Isaacson PG (1990). A genotypic study of low grade B-cell lymphomas, including lymphomas of mucosa associated lymphoid tissue (MALT). *J Pathol* 162: 135-140.

2137. Wotherspoon AC, Pan LX, Diss TC, Isaacson PG (1992). Cytogenetic study of B-cell lymphoma of mucosa-associated lymphoid tissue. *Cancer Genet Cytogenet* 58: 35-38.

2138. Wotherspoon AC, Soosay GN, Diss TC, Isaacson PG (1990). Low-grade primary B-cell lymphoma of the lung. An immunohistochemical, molecular and cytogenetic study of a single case. *Am J Clin Pathol* 94: 655-660.

2139. Wouters K, Ectors N, van Steenbergen W, Aerts R, Driessen A, van Hoe L, Geboes K (1998). A pancreatic mucinous cystadenoma in a man with mesenchymal stroma, expressing oestrogen and progesterone receptors. *Virchows Arch* 432: 187-189.

2140. Wrba F, Chott A, Schratter M, Ludvik B, Krisch K, Holzner JH (1988). Fine-needle puncture cytology of a solid cystic tumor of the pancreas. *Pathologe* 9: 340-344.

2141. Wright DH (1995). The major complications of coeliac disease. *Baillieres Clin Gastroenterol* 9: 351-369.

2142. Wright DH, Jones DB, Clark H, Mead GM, Hodges E, Howell WM (1991). Is adult-onset coeliac disease due to a low-grade lymphoma of intraepithelial T lymphocytes? *Lancet* 337: 1373-1374.

2143. Wu CM, Hruban RH, Fishman EK (1998). Breast carcinoma metastatic to the esophagus. CT findings with pathologic correlation. *Clin Imaging* 22: 343-345.

2144. Wu TT, Kornacki S, Rashid A, Yardley JH, Hamilton SR (1998). Dysplasia and dysregulation of proliferation in foveolar and surface epithelia of fundic gland polyps from patients with familial adenomatous polyposis. *Am J Surg Pathol* 22: 293-298.

2145. Wu TT, Rezai B, Rashid A, Luce MC, Cayouette MC, Kim C, Sani N, Mishra L, Moskaluk CA, Yardley JH, Hamilton SR (1997). Genetic alterations and epithelial dysplasia in juvenile polyposis syndrome and sporadic juvenile polyps. *Am J Pathol* 150: 939-947.

2146. Xu WS, Ho FC, Ho J, Chan AC, Srivastava G (1997). Pathogenesis of gastric lymphoma: the enigma in Hong Kong. *Ann Oncol* 8 Suppl 2: 41-44.

2147. Yagihashi S, Sato I, Kaimori M, Matsumoto J, Nagai K (1988). Papillary and cystic tumor of the pancreas. Two cases indistinguishable from islet cell tumor. *Cancer* 61: 1241-1247.

2148. Yamada M, Kozuka S, Yamano K, Nakazawa S, Naitoh Y, Tsukamoto Y (1991). Mucin-producing tumor of the pancreas. *Cancer* 68: 159-168.

2149. Yamada Y, De-Souza AT, Finkelstein S, Jirtle RL (1997). Loss of the gene encoding mannose 6-phosphate/insulin-like growth factor II receptor is an early event in liver carcinogenesis. *Proc Natl Acad Sci U S A* 94: 10351-10355.

2150. Yamaguchi K, Chijiiwa K, Saiki S, Shimizu S, Takashima M, Tanaka M (1997). Carcinoma of the extrahepatic bile duct: mode of spread and its prognostic implications. *Hepatogastroenterology* 44: 1256-1261.

2151. Yamaguchi K, Enjoji M (1987). Cystic neoplasms of the pancreas. *Gastroenterology* 92: 1934-1943.

2152. Yamaguchi K, Enjoji M (1988). Carcinoma of the gallbladder. A clinicopathology of 103 patients and a newly proposed staging. *Cancer* 62: 1425-1432.

2153. Yamaguchi K, Hirakata R, Kitamura K (1989). Papillary cystic neoplasm of the pancreas: radiological and pathological characteristics in 11 cases. *Br J Surg* 77: 1000-1003.

2154. Yamaguchi K, Miyagahara T, Tsuneyoshi M, Enjoji M, Horie A, Nakayama I, Tsuda N, Fujii H, Takahara O (1989). Papillary cystic tumor of the pancreas: an immunohistochemical and ultrastructural study of 14 patients. *Jpn J Clin Oncol* 19: 102-111.

2155. Yamamoto H, Sawai K, Perucho M (1997). Frameshift somatic mutations in gastrointestinal cancer of the microsatellite mutator phenotype. *Cancer Res* 57: 4420-4426.

2156. Yamamoto H, Adachi Y, Itoh F, Iku S, Matsuno K, Kusano M, Arimura Y, Endo T, Hinoda Y, Hosokawa M, Imai K (1999). Association of matrilysin expression with recurrence and poor prognosis in human esophageal squamous cell carcinoma. *Cancer Res* 59: 3313-3316.

2157. Yamamoto M, Nakajo S, Miyoshi N, Nakai S, Tahara E (1989). Endocrine cell carcinoma (carcinoid) of the gallbladder. *Am J Surg Pathol* 13: 292-302.

2158. Yamamoto H, Takahashi I, Iwamoto T, Mandai K, Tahara E (1984). Endocrine cells in extrahepatic bile duct carcinoma. *J Cancer Res Clin Oncol* 108: 331-335.

2159. Yamamoto M, Takasaki K, Nakano M, Saito A (1998). Minute nodular intrahepatic cholangiocarcinoma. *Cancer* 82: 2145-2149.

2160. Yamamoto M, Takasaki K, Yoshikawa T (1999). Lymph node metastasis in intrahepatic cholangiocarcinoma. *Jpn J Clin Oncol* 29: 147-150.

2161. Yamamoto M, Takasaki K, Yoshikawa T, Ueno K, Nakano M (1998). Does gross appearance indicate prognosis in intrahepatic cholangiocarcinoma? *J Surg Oncol* 69: 162-167.

2162. Yamanaka N, Okamoto E, Ando T, Oriyama T, Fujimoto J, Furukawa K, Tanaka T, Tanaka W, Nishigami T (1995). Clinicopathologic spectrum of resected extraductal mass-forming intrahepatic cholangiocarcinoma. *Cancer* 76: 2449-2456.

2163. Yamanaka Y, Friess H, Kobrin MS, Buchler M, Kunz J, Beger HG, Korc M (1993). Overexpression of HER2/neu oncogene in human pancreatic carcinoma. *Hum Pathol* 24: 1127-1134.

2164. Yamao K, Nakazawa S, Fujimoto S, Yamada M, Miichgrub S, Albores-Saavedra J (1994). Intraductal papillary mucinous tumors; non-invasive and invasive. In: *Atlas of Exocrine Pancreatic Tumors*, Pour PM, Konishi Y, Kloppel G, Longnecker DS (eds), Springer-Verlag: Tokyo.

2165. Yamato T, Sasaki M, Hoso M, Sakai J, Ohta H, Watanabe Y, Nakanuma Y (1998). Intrahepatic cholangiocarcinoma arising in congenital hepatic fibrosis: report of an autopsy case. *J Hepatol* 28: 717-722.

2166. Yanagisawa A, Ohtake K, Ohashi K, Hori M, Kitagawa T, Sugano H, Kato Y (1993). Frequent c-Ki-ras oncogene activation in mucous cell hyperplasias of pancreas suffering from chronic inflammation. *Cancer Res* 53: 953-956.

2167. Yang D, Tannenbaum SR, Buchi G, Lee GC (1984). 4-Chloro-6-methoxyindole is the precursor of a potent mutagen (4-chloro-6-methoxy-2-hydroxy-1-nitroso-indolin-3-one oxime) that forms during nitrosation of the fava bean (Vicia faba). *Carcinogenesis* 5: 1219-1224.

2168. Yang K, Ulich T, Cheng T, Cheng L, Lewin KJ (1983). The neuroendocrine products of intestinal carcinoids. An immunoperoxidase study of 35 carcinoid tumors stained for serotonin and eight polypeptide hormones. *Cancer* 51: 1918-1926.

2169. Yasuda H, Takada T, Amano H, Yoshida M (1998). Surgery for mucin-producing pancreatic tumor. *Hepatogastroenterology* 45: 2009-2015.

2170. Yasui H, Hino O, Ohtake K, Machinami R, Kitagawa T (1992). Clonal growth of hepatitis B virus-integrated hepatocytes in cirrhotic liver nodules. *Cancer Res* 52: 6810-6814.

2171. Yeh SH, Chen PJ, Lai MY, Chen DS (1996). Allelic loss on chromosomes 4q and 16q in hepatocellular carcinoma: association with elevated alpha-fetoprotein production. *Gastroenterology* 110: 184-192.

2172. Yeo CJ, Cameron JL, Lillemoe KD, Sitzmann JV, Hruban RH, Goodman SN, Dooley WC, Coleman J, Pitt HA (1995). Pancreaticoduodenectomy for cancer of the head of the pancreas. 201 patients. *Ann Surg* 221: 721-731.

2173. Yeong ML, Wood KP, Scott B, Yun K (1992). Synchronous squamous and glandular neoplasia of the anal canal. *J Clin Pathol* 45: 261-263.

2174. Yim H, Jin YM, Shim C, Park HB (1997). Gastric metastasis of mammary signet ring cell carcinoma - a differential diagnosis with primary gastric signet ring cell carcinoma. *J Korean Med Sci* 12: 256-261.

2175. Yin J, Harpaz N, Tong Y, Huang Y, Laurin J, Greenwald BD, Hontanosas M, Newkirk C, Meltzer SJ (1993). p53 point mutations in dysplastic and cancerous ulcerative colitis lesions. *Gastroenterology* 104: 1633-1639.

2176. Yiikorkala A, Avizienyte E, Tomlinson IP, Tiainen M, Roth S, Loukola A, Hemminki A, Johansson M, Sistonen P, Markie D, Neale K, Phillips R, Zauber P, Twama T, Sampson J, Jarvinen H, Makela TP, Aaltonen LA (1999). Mutations and impaired function of LKB1 in familial and non-familial Peutz-Jeghers syndrome and a sporadic testicular cancer. *Hum Mol Genet* 8: 45-51.

2177. Yokoyama A, Muramatsu T, Ohmori T, Tokoyama T, Okuyama K, Takahashi H, Hasegawa Y, Higuchi S, Maruyama K, Shirakura K, Ishii H (1998). Alcohol-related cancers and aldehyde deshydrogenase-2 in Japanese alcoholics. *Carcinogenesis* 19: 1383-1387.

2178. Yonezawa S, Horinouchi M, Osako M, Kubo M, Takao S, Arimura Y, Nagata K, Tanaka S, Sakoda K, Aikou T, Sato E (1997). MUC2 gene expression is found in noninvasive tumors but not in invasive tumors of the pancreas and liver: its close relationship with prognosis of the patients. *Hum Pathol* 28: 344-352.

2179. Yonezawa S, Sueyoshi K, Nomoto M, Kitamura H, Nagata K, Arimura Y, Tanaka S, Hollingsworth MA, Siddiki B, Kim YS, Sato E (1997). MUC2 gene expression is found in noninvasive tumors but not in invasive tumors of the pancreas and liver: its close relationship with prognosis of the tumor. *Pathol Int* 49: 45-54.

2180. Yoo CC, Levine MS, Furth EE, Salhany KE, Rubesin SE, Laufer I, Herlinger H (1998). Gastric mucosa-associated lymphoid tissue lymphoma: radiographic findings in six patients. *Radiology* 208: 239-243.

2181. Yoshikawa K, Maruyama K (1985). Characteristics of gastric cancer invading to the proper muscle layer - with special reference to mortality and cause of death. *Jpn J Clin Oncol* 15: 499-503.

2182. Yoshimi N, Sugie S, Tanaka T, Aijin W, Bunai Y, Tatematsu A, Okada T, Mori H (1992). A rare case of serous cystadenocarcinoma of the pancreas. *Cancer* 69: 2449-2453.

2183. Yoshinaka H, Shimazu H, Fukumoto T, Baba M (1991). Superficial esophageal carcinoma: a clinicopathological review of 59 cases. *Am J Gastroenterol* 86: 1413-1418.

2184. Younes M, Katikaneni PR, Lechago J (1995). Association between mucosal hyperplasia of the appendix and adenocarcinoma of the colon. *Histopathology* 26: 33-37.

2185. Younes N, Fulton N, Tanaka R, Wayne J, Straus FH, Kaplan EL (1997). The presence of K-12 ras mutations in duodenal adenocarcinomas and the absence of ras mutations in other small bowel adenocarcinomas and carcinoid tumors. *Cancer* 79: 1804-1808.

2186. Young HM, Ciampoli D, Southwell BR, Newgreen DF (1996). Origin of interstitial cells of Cajal in the mouse intestine. *Dev Biol* 180: 97-107.

2187. Young RH, Gilks CB, Scully RE (1991). Mucinous tumors of the appendix associated with mucinous tumors of the ovary and pseudomyxoma peritonei. A clinicopathological analysis of 22 cases supporting an origin in the appendix. *Am J Surg Pathol* 15: 415-429.

2187A. Young RH, Rosenberg AE, Clement PB (1997). Mucin deposits within inguinal hernia sacs: a presenting finding of low-grade mucinous cystic tumors of the appendix. A report of two cases and a review of the literature. *Mod Pathol* 10: 1228-1232.

2188. Young RH, Welch WR, Dickersin R, Scully RE (1982). Ovarian sex cord tumour with annular tubules: review of 74 cases including 27 with Peutz-Jeghers syndrome and four with adenoma malignum of the cervix. *Cancer* 50: 1384-1402.

2189. Youssef EM, Matsuda T, Takada N, Osugi H, Higashino M, Kinoshita H, Watanabe T, Katsura Y, Wanibuchi H, Fukushima S (1995). Prognostic significance of the MIB-1 proliferation index for patients with squamous cell carcinoma of the esophagus. *Cancer* 76: 358-366.

2190. Yu HC, Shetty J (1985). Mucinous cystic neoplasm of the pancreas with high carcinoembryonic antigen. *Arch Pathol Lab Med* 109: 375-377.

2191. Yu Y, Taylor PR, Li JY, Dawsey SM, Wang GQ, Guo WD, Wang W, Liu BQ, Blot WJ, Shen Q, et a (1993). Retrospective cohort study of risk-factors for esophageal cancer in Linxian, People's Republic of China. *Cancer Causes Control* 4: 195-202.

2192. Yustein AS, Harper JC, Petroni GR, Cummings OW, Moskaluk CA, Powell SM (1999). Allelotype of gastric adenocarcinoma. *Cancer Res* 59: 1437-1441.

2193. Z'graggen K, Rivera JA, Compton CC, Pins M, Werner J, Fernandez-del CC, Rattner DW, Lewandrowski KB, Rustgi AK, Warshaw AL (1997). Prevalence of activating K-ras mutations in the evolutionary stages of neoplasia in intraductal papillary mucinous tumors of the pancreas. *Ann Surg* 226: 491-498.

2194. Zamboni G, Bonetti F, Castelli P, Balercia G, Pea M, Martignoni G, Iacono C, Donati LF (1994). Mucinous cystic tumor of the pancreas recurring after 11 years as cystadenocarcinoma with foci of chorio carcinoma and osteoclast-like giant cell tumor. *Surg Pathol* 5: 253-262.

2195. Zamboni G, Bonetti F, Scarpa A, Pelosi G, Doglioni C, Iannucci A, Castelli P, Balercia G, Aldovini D, Bellomi A, Iacono C, Serio G, Mariuzzi GM (1993). Expression of progesterone receptors in solid-cystic tumour of the pancreas: a clinicopathological and immunohistochemical, and ultrastructural study of three cases. *Virchows Arch A Pathol Anat Histopathol* 423: 425-431.

2196. Zamboni G, Franzin G, Bonetti F, Scarpa A, Chilosi M, Colombari R, Menestrina F, Pea M, Iacono C, Serio G, et a (1990). Small-cell neuroendocrine carcinoma of the ampullary region. A clinicopathologic, immunohistochemical, and ultrastructural study of three cases. *Am J Surg Pathol* 14: 703-713.

2197. Zamboni G, Pea M, Martignoni G, Zancanaro C, Faccioli G, Gilioli E, Pederzoli P, Bonetti F (1996). Clear cell "sugar" tumor of the pancreas. A novel member of the family of lesions characterized by the presence of perivascular epithelioid cells. *Am J Surg Pathol* 20: 722-730.

2198. Zamboni G, Scarpa A, Bogina G, Iacono C, Bassi C, Talamini, Sessa F, Capella C, Solcia E, Rickaert F, Mariuzzi GM, Kloppel G (1999). Mucinous cystic tumors of the pancreas: clinicopathological features, prognosis, and relationship to other mucinous cystic tumors. *Am J Surg Pathol* 23: 410-422.

2199. Zanelli M, Casadei R, Santini D, Gallo C, Verdirame F, La-Donna M, Marrano D (1998). Pseudomyxoma peritonei associated with intraductal papillary-mucinous neoplasm of the pancreas. *Pancreas* 17: 100-102.

2200. Zanghieri G, Di-Gregorio C, Sacchetti C, Fante R, Sassatelli R, Cannizzo G, Carriero A, Ponz-de LM (1990). Familial occurrence of gastric cancer in the 2-year experience of a population-based registry. *Cancer* 66: 2047-2051.

2201. Zar N, Holmberg L, Wilandeer E, et al. (1996). Survival in small intestinal adenocarcinoma. *Eur J Cancer* 32A: 2114-2119.

2202. Zerhouni EA, Rutter C, Hamilton SR, Balfe DM, Megibow AJ, Francis IR, Moss AA, Heiken JP, Tempany CM, Aisen AM, Weinreb JC, Gatsonis C, McNeil BJ (1996). CT and MR imaging in the staging of colorectal carcinoma: report of the Radiology Diagnostic Oncology Group II. *Radiology* 200: 443-451.

2203. Zhang WD, Hirohashi S, Tsuda H, Shimosato Y, Yokota J, Terada M, Sugimura T (1990). Frequent loss of heterozygosity on chromosomes 16 and 4 in human hepatocellular carcinoma. *Jpn J Cancer Res* 81: 108-111.

2204. Zhang ZF, Kurtz RC, Marshall JR (1997). Cigarette smoking and esophageal and gastric cardia adenocarcinoma. *J Natl Cancer Inst* 89: 1247-1249.

2205. Zhang ZF, Kurtz RC, Sun M, Karpeh M, Yu GP, Gargon N, Fein JS, Georgopoulos SK, Harlap S (1996). Adenocarcinomas of the esophagus and gastric cardia: medical conditions, tobacco, alcohol, and socioeconomic factors. *Cancer Epidemiol Biomarkers Prev* 5: 761-768.

2206. Zheng W, Sung CJ, Hanna I, DePetris G, Lambert-Messerlian G, Steinhoff M, Lauchlan SC (1997). Alpha and beta subunits of inhibin/activin as sex cord-stromal differentiation markers. *Int J Gynecol Pathol* 16: 263-271.

2207. Zhou H, Fischer HP (1998). Liver carcinoma in PiZ alpha-1-antitripsin deficiency. *Am J Surg Pathol* 22: 742-748.

2208. Zhu L, Kim K, Domenico DR, et al. (1996). Adenocarcinoma of duodenum and ampulla of Vater: clinicopathology study and expression of p53, c-neu, TGF-α, CEA and EMA. *J Surg Oncol* 61: 100-105.

2209. Zinner MJ, Shurbaji MS, Cameron JL (1990). Solid and papillary epithelial neoplasms of the pancreas. *Surgery* 108: 475-480.

2210. Zippel K, Hoksch B, Zieren HU (1997). [A rare stomach tumor - Hodgkin's lymphoma of the stomach]. *Chirurg* 68: 540-542.

2211. Zucca E, Bertoni F, Roggero E, Bosshard G, Cazzaniga G, Pedrinis E, Biondi A, Cavalli F (1998). Molecular analysis of the progression from Helicobacter pylori-associated chronic gastritis to mucosa-associated lymphoid-tissue lymphoma of the stomach. *N Engl J Med* 338: 804-810.

2212. Zuckerberg LR, Ferry JA, Southern JF, Harris NL (1990). Lymphoid infiltrates of the stomach. Evaluation of histologic criteriafor the diagnosis of the low-grade gastric lymphoma on endoscopic biopsy specimens. *Am J Surg Pathol* 14: 1087-1099.

2213. Zwas F, Shields HM, Doos WG, Antonioli DA, Goldman H, Ransil BJ, Spechler SJ (1986). Scanning electron microscopy of Barrett's epithelium and its correlation with light microscopy and mucin stains. *Gastroenterology* 90: 1932-1941.

2214. Zwick A, Munir M, Ryan CK, Gian J, Burt RW, Leppert M, Spirio L, Chey WY (1997). Gastric adenocarcinoma and dysplasia in fundic gland polyps of a patient with attenuated adenomatous polyposis coli. *Gastroenterology* 113: 659-663.

Subject Index